Keech

Monetary Policy in the United States

A Cato Institute Book

Richard H. Timberlake

Monetary Policy in the United States

An Intellectual and Institutional History

The University of Chicago Press

Chicago and London

The University of Chicago Press, Chicago 60637
The University of Chicago Press, Ltd., London

Printed in the United States of America
02 01 00 99 98 97 96 95 94 93   5 4 3 2 1

ISBN (cloth): 0-226-80382-1
ISBN (paper): 0-226-80384-8

Library of Congress Cataloging-in-Publication Data

Timberlake, Richard H.
Monetary policy in the United States : an intellectual and institutional history / Richard H. Timberlake.
p. cm.
"A Cato Institute book."
Includes bibliographical references and index.
ISBN 0-226-80382-1 (cloth).—ISBN 0-226-80384-8 (pbk.)
1. Monetary policy—United States—History. I. Title.
HG501.T59 1993
332.4′973—dc20 92-44937
CIP

♾The paper used in this publication meets the minimum requirements of the American National Standard for Information Sciences—Permanence of Paper for Printed Library Materials, ANSI Z39.48–1984.

Richard H. Timberlake is a retired professor of economics and finance at the University of Georgia. His previous books include *Gold, Greenbacks and the Constitution,* and *Origins of Central Banking in the United States.*

To Hildegard
my *sine qua non*

Contents

Tables

Preface

> The nations with which economic historians are chiefly concerned organize their economic activities under the form of making and spending money. This practice supplies the basic framework for economic theory. Cannot economic history be organized most effectively around the evolution of pecuniary institutions?
>
> If this suggestion merits serious consideration, the first step toward trying it out in practice would be to frame the best account now feasible of the way men came to organize their dealings with one another on the basis of money payments.
>
> Wesley C. Mitchell, "The Role of Money in Economic History," 1953

This book chronicles the economic and political circumstances, events, and ideas that have led to the practice of positive, progressive, discretionary governmental control of the U.S. monetary and banking system. It begins with the constitutional discussions and precepts on money, and traces the evolution of hands-on monetary policies up to the present time.

An earlier, more limited version of the present work, published by the Harvard University Press in 1978, concentrated on the development of monetary laws, institutions, and policies before the coming of the Federal Reserve System. Since no official public or central bank existed in the United States between 1836 and 1914, a span of seventy-eight years, monetary historians had generally slighted the monetary events of this era and had focused primarily on the Banks of the United States and the Federal Reserve System. I therefore concentrated my earlier work on the institutional developments in this somewhat neglected period. This much-expanded edition adds a chapter that treats the economic, political, and judicial aspects of the legal tender issue, which became prominent during and after the Civil War, and another chapter that analyzes the clearinghouse system as a private lender of last resort before 1910. It also adds eleven chapters that cover the various stages of Federal Reserve policies as they have appeared since 1914.

My particular research approach to the study of monetary institutions utilizes congressional debates and official government reports and documents. Economists have not much used this route. However, I found such sources so informative and revealing that I have concentrated my findings in one account to treat both pre–Federal Reserve institutions and the institutional evolution of the Federal Reserve System over the last eighty years.

In extending the scope of my earlier book, I have brushed against the public-choice character of the Federal Reserve System. The incentives that Fed policymakers experience as self-interested maximizers in promoting their own interests and the welfare of the federal government are very similar to the invisible hand in the private sector, but with some notable exceptions: The Federal Reserve System faces no competition in the production of money, and it cannot fail as a cost-recovering enterprise. It also has been and is subject to formidable political pressures. It comes through as a prototypical governmental institution operating under the rule of men rather than the rule of law.

In this new work I have tried to focus my attention and research on fundamental political-economic questions: What is the optimal control machinery for the monetary system? Is it a central bank, a gold standard, or a government treasury department? Or can it be an institutional arrangement operating under the conventional rules that apply to other businesses, and completely divorced from any governmental controls and regulations? Is a free banking system viable regardless of its political improbability? Indeed, experience over the centuries with institutions of human control prompts this contrary question: Can well-intentioned men actually design a system of monetary control superior to what would prevail as a natural development under general rules of law? When the Founding Fathers constructed monetary principles for the U.S. Constitution, they clearly thought and acted in favor of rules—the gold and silver (bimetallic) standard—while excluding discretionary fiat money.

To implement the plan of this book, I have examined facts, events, statements, and ideas as they occurred or were expressed by government officials, academicians, and anyone else who might have been able to influence policy. This evidence cannot speak for itself because I have chosen only the material that seemed to me most important, and also because I have added economic interpretation where it seemed called for. I acknowledge that in doing so I have not exhausted either the rich history of monetary institutions or its range of interpretation. This book is not *the* history of central banking. The bounty of facts, episodes, and circumstances, plus the endless diversity of interpretation, preclude any such effrontery.

The principal theme of my earlier book was that central banks are made, not born. They are products of human design and not results of the spontaneous behavior that produced laws, languages, and systems of weights and measures. This finding is particularly puzzling when one recalls that primitive money did appear spontaneously in similar fashion to languages, laws, and various mechanical devices; but, unlike these other products of mankind's advancement, money has hardly ever been free of monopoly control by the state. The intriguing question is: Why would money, originally a natural development from systems of barter, become so universally and pervasively subject to man-made institutions of control? One might reason that anything that appeared in so many different circumstances and places on its own had best be left alone—that government, having had no hand in the origin of money, could hardly improve upon the quality of private media of exchange by any means, no matter how well intentioned. Yet from the time of the ancient

Greeks to the present, wherever and whenever money has appeared, state intervention, regulation, and monopoly privilege for state-sponsored institutions have not been far behind.

Much of the state's interest in controlling money has been for the obvious purpose of generating seigniorage. On this score the state's interest is clear—be it the coinage debasements of the ancient Romans or the central banks' more sophisticated monetization of government debt in the twentieth century. What is difficult to understand is why popular polity so condones these practices. The simple conclusion is that the popular mind does not understand the monetary machinery and therefore must put its trust in "experts" who presumably have in their hearts the best interests of the general public. It is here that the public-choice question intrudes: Since the policymakers are self-interested mortals, can they behave as altruists on behalf of the people they allegedly serve?

The latter part of this book explores this question in the light of Federal Reserve behavior since 1917. (I pay little attention to the first three years of the Fed's existence, when it was building up its infrastructure and developing norms for policy from the scanty and very general guidelines of the Federal Reserve Act.) My conclusion is: No; policymakers are not altruists. Federal Reserve policies over the decades have been largely a series of politically inspired, government-serving actions that have taxed the private economy. The evidence for some kind of alternative is sketchy but logically convincing. I treat this issue in the concluding chapters.

This book is different from others in its field because it examines monetary institutions from the expressed ideas and thoughts of policymakers as well as from the record of their actions. I offer a conceptual norm for evaluating their performance—maximization of the real quantity of money. The logic of this norm and the Fed's fulfillment of its role as a caretaker of the real money stock since 1960 are evaluated in the last chapters.

I have tried to apply well-established principles of English usage in order to make this account of monetary policy and central banking intelligible to the interested and literate layman as well as to the interested and literate economist. If a person concerned with public affairs cannot understand this chronicle, it can have little effect on the course of public policy. Therefore, I have tried to demystify the supposed enigmas of monetary policies as they have occurred over the decades so that almost anyone reading this book can understand how the present-day monetary system works, and how it got from there to here.

So far as I can determine, no other book currently in print systematically treats the subject of the monetary system as I have tried to do here except for the magnificent treatise by Milton Friedman and Anna J. Schwartz. Their work, however, concentrates more on the performance of monetary variables.

It also begins much later (1867) and ends much earlier (1960) than this account. I hope I have meaningfully supplemented their work as well as added some other perspectives to their monumental analysis.

A few other specialized works on central banking, such as the one by Vera Smith, have appeared in the past. Valuable as is the work by Smith, it is severely dated and limited in scope. Other books on the subject that have appeared recently are somewhat superficial, or take an ideological approach to the subject. I hope that my account comes through as dispassionate and factual. Since it concentrates on men's ideas of monetary control together with some little-known or misinterpreted facts, it should help to clarify the long-enduring mystique of this subject.

Nonetheless, the subject is highly controversial. Many people believe what they want to believe, and are not about to be "confused by the facts." Furthermore, I am realistic enough to understand that some of my interpretations are bound to be challenged, reinterpreted, and supplemented. Over the last thirty-five and more years that I have been doing this kind of research, I have drastically changed some of my own views on the proper norms for optimal monetary policy. Therefore I would not be very surprised if new evidence and new interpretations offer alternatives to some of the conclusions in this volume that now seem so reasonable to me. So be it. In the free world of ideas no governmental authority can vest a privileged few with monopoly powers to reap intellectual seigniorage.

Acknowledgments

An author should first acknowledge those parts of civilization that have been helpful to him, and should second try to advise and disarm critics who might review his book. Very rarely can an author address criticisms, valid or invalid, after his book is in print.

The present work began when I wrote a doctoral dissertation on nineteenth-century Treasury monetary policy. My research focused on the period between 1830 and 1860. As I read the works of scholars, the congressional debates, and other government documents covering this period, I observed that the central-banking concept had been fully understood and appreciated by the time of Andrew Jackson. Therefore, I presumed it must have first appeared even earlier. For a postdoctoral project, I looked back through the congressional debates and reports to see where the central-banking idea had originated and who was responsible for it. Much to my surprise, I could find no trace of its formal initiation. On the contrary, all the evidence pointed to proscription of any kind of conscious, deliberative control of the monetary system. I then decided that the whole subject of central-banking origins, growth, thought, and institutions needed further treatment.

My sources of primary materials for this work were the *Annals of Congress,* the *Register of Debates in Congress,* the *Congressional Globe,* and the *Congressional Record.* These documents compose the serial record of congressional debates since 1789. In addition, I have also examined executive documents, executive replies to congressional inquiries, reports of commissions, annual reports of secretaries of the Treasury, comptrollers of the currency, and other government officials, and almost all the issues of the *Federal Reserve Bulletin.* I also use statistical data, but primarily to emphasize institutional developments.

The central-banking idea is the belief that positive human control over the monetary and banking system can provide a more rational and better-behaved monetary structure. The traditional wisdom admits the central-banking nature of the First and Second Banks of the United States, but presumes a chaotic monetary Dark Ages between the end of the Second Bank (as a quasi-governmental institution) in 1836 and the formation of the Federal Reserve System seventy-eight years later. The probable reason for this hiatus is that some central-banking institutions of the era—for example, the Independent Treasury—did not take the outward and visible form of a bank. They were therefore dismissed as freakish and undesirable accidents even though at some point they reflected the notion of positive control over the monetary system. Ironically enough, many of the central banking institutions that appeared were sanctioned in order to reduce political tampering with the monetary system. But the penchant for human manipulation being what it is, hands-on control of monetary affairs was not to be denied, despite the strictures of the Constitution. Each successive institution developed its own pattern of intervention.

In spite of the appearance of central banks and quasi-central banks, the dominant monetary institution during the period before 1914 was the self-regulating specie standard. Since central-banking institutions had to operate within this formal framework, their scope for action was limited. Only in the twentieth century did specie standards fade away like the Cheshire cat. Discretionary central banks have become the dominant form of monetary control, and not even the "grin" of metallic standards remains. The U.S. government actually forbade the monetary use of gold in 1934. However, the development of free world markets for commodity-gold since the early 1970s has provided some possibility that the metal may return as a commodity-money. This possibility becomes more probable as the world's central banks show little disposition to stabilize the value of their units of account.

Several chapters of this book are drawn from articles I have had published in various professional journals since 1960. Chapter 2 is largely derived from an article that appeared in the *Revue Internationale d'Histoire de la Banque* 2 (1969): 209–25. A less detailed version of chapter 5 appeared in the *Journal of Political Economy* 68 (April 1960): 109–17 (copyright 1960 by the University of Chicago; all rights reserved). Parts of chapter 6 are drawn from an article in the *Southern Economic Journal* 27 (October 1960): 92–103. Chapters 7, 8, and 9 include material that appeared in the *Journal of Economic History* 24 (March 1964): 29–52 and 34 (December 1974): 835–50. Chapter 8 also incorporates research done for an article published in the *Journal of Monetary Economics* 1 (1975): 343–54. Research assistance for chapter 10 was provided by the Durell Foundation, Berryville, Virginia. Chapters 12 and 14 are reprinted by permission from the *Journal of Money, Credit, and Banking* 10 (February 1978): 27–45 and 16 (February 1984): 1–15 (coypright 1978 by the Ohio State University Press; all rights reserved). Part of chapter 13 was first written as an article for the *Quarterly Journal of Economics* 77 (February 1963): 40–54. Most of chapters 17 through 27 have not appeared in other publications. Chapter 22 draws from an article in *Kredit und Kapital,* 9 (Heft 4, 1976). Much of chapter 24 was published as an article in the *American Economic Review* 75 (May 1985): 97–102.

Most of these articles have been reworked extensively and supplemented with additional material before incorporation into this book. The high quality of professional criticism provided by these journal editors and their referees has been of inestimable value to me in synthesizing these parts into a coherent chronicle.

Several critics and contributors deserve special mention. I am especially indebted to the late Earl J. Hamilton and to Milton Friedman, formerly of the University of Chicago, who were instrumental in guiding the initial phase of this work, and who have made additional constructive comments at various times since. I also have had worthwhile suggestions and encouragement over a considerable span of time from the late Clark Warburton, Leland Yeager, Anna J. Schwartz, the late Ross Robertson, Frank W. Fetter, Murray Rothbard, the late Alfred Bornemann, the late Robert R. Dince, Thomas Humphrey, George Selgin, William Beranek, Larry White, and Kevin Dowd. I also have had excellent secretaries who have deciphered my innumerable revisions and corrections. These include workmates Delphine Burton, Jennifer Gunn, Rose Rouse, and Mary Beth Bennett. I would also like to express my appreciation and admiration for the excellent professional production of this book by the staff of the University of Chicago Press, especially to Salena Krug, Karen Peterson, and Claudia Rex. I apologize for anyone I may have overlooked in this lengthy literary odyssey.

Above all, I thank my wife Hildegard for her continuous help and encouragement. To her, I gratefully dedicate this work.

1 The Genesis of Monetary Control and the First Bank of the United States

Whereas it is conceived that the establishment of a bank for the United States, . . . will be very conducive to the successful conducting of the national finances; will tend to give facility to the obtaining of loans, for the use of the Government, . . . and will be productive of considerable advantage to trade and industry in general: Therefore, *Be it enacted,* etc. That a bank of the United States shall be established . . .

Annals of Congress, 25 February 1791

Institutions of Monetary Control

Contemporary societies accept the institutional presence of central banks without understanding what they are and how or where they originated. The layman's understandable ignorance of central banking and the economist's near-universal acceptance prompt the questions: How did central banking come about? What was the origin of this powerful institution? How did central banking, in contrast to commercial banking, evolve? Was central banking simply an offshoot of commercial banking, or were other institutions instrumental in its development? And finally, is the institution in its present form as a monetary control agency of the government really necessary?

Specie standards based on gold and silver were the usual means for officially structuring monetary systems in most countries during the eighteenth and nineteenth centuries. Central banks then appeared as auxiliary institutions to specie standards—as means to make metallic standards function more efficiently. These earlier institutions were private banking corporations with loose and ill-defined relationships to their governments.[1] Whatever they did as institutions, their operations were strictly subordinate to the workings of specie standards. In the twentieth century this position has been reversed. Central banks have become dominant institutions, while metallic standards are hardly more than vestigial and functionless façades.

That the central bank proper has become the recognized agency for controlling the community's stock of money[2] seems to imply that central banks were appointed by executive or legislative decree to carry out this task. Yet if this implication has a grain of truth, it is only a grain. By and large, central banks as recognized official manipulators of the money stock evolved; they grew into their role, rather than being born to it. A stronger argument can be made that they were originally enjoined from discretionary operations to effect changes in the quantity of money or influence the volume of trade or credit, and that they were officially abolished if they showed too much enthusiasm for monetary regulation. The story of how and why their original proscriptions became their ultimate prescriptions constitutes the political economy of central banking.

An institution is not necessarily bound by a particular physical structure. Control of the money supply in the United States is a good example of an institutional function that has been carried out by physical establishments of divergent forms. The gold and silver (specie) monetary standards, the commercial banking system, the First and Second Banks of the United States, the Independent Treasury System, the national banking system, clearinghouse associations, and the Federal Reserve System have all been instrumental in altering the quantity of money at different times and by various means. The one first in force and largely fundamental to the others was the metallic-standard system.

Principles for the Operation of Metallic Standards

A typical metallic-standard system is automatic and self-regulating after a legislature or a constitution establishes the original rules or conditions for its operation. The first rule is that the unit of account be specified in terms of a weight of precious metal, such as gold. Between 1834 and 1934 in the United States, the law specified that a ten-dollar piece—a gold eagle—should contain 232.2 grains of pure gold.[3] The second rule is that the coined metal be legal tender for all debts, public and private. This provision is made operational by the enforcing agencies of the government, that is, by the judicial and penal systems. If governmental money is not legal tender, private parties may refuse it either in payment of debts or in transacting ordinary business. Once the law specifies the precise relationship between a commodity such as gold and the dollars' worth of debt that this quantity of gold will legally pay off, the system is self-regulating. Private coin-smiths or government mints may strike the various coins as the coinage laws define them. Although governments that have adopted gold and silver standards have almost always produced the coins they "regulate," this function is neither necessary nor desirable. In like fashion, just because a government "fixes the standard of weights and measures" does not mean that it must produce scales and yardsticks. All that the government needs to do to ensure the standard it has set is to prevent fraud in currency dealings and to use legitimate privately produced money in its transactions with the private sector.[4]

A nongovernmental gold standard is also possible. In such a system the government would not specify the precise relationship between the quantity of gold and the corresponding number of dollars. It would only proclaim by statute or constitution that gold was the ultimate means of payment, and it would set an example by using gold for its own transactions and by requiring gold in payment of tariffs and taxes. The price of gold relative to other goods and services would be free to fluctuate in markets. Nonetheless, anyone who wished to ensure a gold value for goods bought or sold could do so by means of a sales contract or purchase agreement in which a sum of gold was the agreed-upon means for ultimate satisfaction of the contract.[5]

Other economic conditions are also necessary for the self-regulating gold standard to work smoothly. The money supply has to be responsive to the quantity of monetary gold; prices must be sensitive to changes in the quantity of money; and gold must be allowed to flow freely in or out of the economy in response to private demands. Given a downturn in business activity, for example, prices of goods and services in terms of the unit of account (dollar) fall. Since the money price of gold is fixed by statute, it remains constant. However, the purchasing power of gold—its real value—increases. Fresh supplies of gold for monetization then flow into the monetary system from three sources: (1) Nonmonetary gold—that is, "plate" and ornaments—is monetized. (2) Gold mines produce additional quantities of gold if the economy has a gold-mining industry. (3) Gold from foreign monetary stocks flows in to purchase the now lower-priced domestic goods. Any or all of these gold flows tend to restore prices, incomes, employment, and business activity.

One observer has described the ideal specie (or gold) standard as a system in which the "proportionate increment of [the economy's real] revenue . . . [is] always as great as the proportionate increment of its aggregate quantity of gold."[6] Actual working systems have not usually followed this blueprint. Whether or not the economic prerequisites exist in the real world to the degree necessary, the fact remains that the world's gold mines have not produced a relatively smooth flow of gold. Mining is an extractive industry acutely subject to diminishing returns. Fresh discoveries of gold may buoy up the world's monetary systems for a time, and from time to time, but diminished rates of gold output tend to produce a secular drag on the growth in the quantity of money. Money, prices, and business activity then taper off until another big discovery repeats the process. This pattern might be repeated indefinitely except that gold discoveries may be subject to diminishing returns within the framework of a limited earth.

A second drawback of the gold-standard system is the real cost of using gold as money. Since gold is a valuable commodity as well as a money, banks, businesses, and households that hold it incur foregone capital costs. They therefore constantly seek means for economizing its apparent idleness, for reducing its wear and tear as a currency, and for minimizing the costs of transporting it. Both paper currency and bank deposits are economically cheaper substitutes for gold, and both have been used extensively in response to gold-economizing motives.

Metallic-standard systems, in spite of their operating costs, were trustworthy. A system of rules offered less opportunity for monetary malpractice than any other arrangement. Even so, Roman emperors and medieval monarchs were ingenious at finding means for debasing precious metal currencies in order to provide themselves with seigniorage revenues. Specie standards written into law may have been the best-known means for constraining ambitious despots who were eager to plunder the monetary system, but they were by no means sufficient for the task. A determined monarch could change the law. Only after constitutional principles and the rule of law constrained arbitrary political power could the economization of gold and silver as media of exchange proceed more confidently. Whether this confidence was well founded has reappeared as a troublesome question in the twentieth century.[7]

The first change from a purely metallic monetary system to a mixed-money system was the substitution of paper money for either gold coin or gold bullion, even though gold was still the ultimate redemption medium for the paper. This change, which occurred principally during the eighteenth century, resulted primarily from the development of commercial banking. Banking was a natural offspring of goldsmithing, and banks and bank notes grew together. The growth of banks raised the complementary question of how banks were to fit into the political economy of their era. The Bank of England was incorporated under a charter from the crown in 1694. In the United States, three state governments chartered banks before Congress incorporated the First Bank of the United States in 1791. Thereafter, the activities of the First Bank marked the real beginning of the government's positive monetary control.

The First Bank of the United States: Arguments of Alexander Hamilton

The First Bank, which Congress chartered to begin operations in 1791, was not intended to be a central bank; it was not to control the quantity of money. Nor was it to act as a centralized depository, an office of discount for commercial banks, or a lender of last resort. All these latter-day responsibilities of central banks were originally denied it—not even considered possibilities—for two principal reasons. First, the new Constitution specified that *Congress* should have the power "to coin money and regulate the value thereof." This stipulation presumed a simple, self-adjusting specie standard, and it limited the power of Congress to setting the legal tender value of the monetary metal. No one imagined that a complete currency would consist only of gold and silver. However, the Constitution, by emphasizing the exclusive legal tender properties of the precious metals, took monetary manipulation out of the range of political discretion—or so the Founding Fathers believed. Second, the four banks in existence in 1791 did not need a central bank in any of its manifestations. In fact, each of these banks approached the model of a single isolated banking system. Since transportation was primitive, collection of specie for outstanding notes and checks was both slow and erratic; so notes and checks did not move very far beyond the local financial circle served by a given bank.[8]

Alexander Hamilton, acting in his capacity as the first secretary of the Treasury, described in detail the kind of institution the First Bank of the United States should be.[9] His "Report on a National Bank," delivered to Congress in 1790, reads remarkably like Adam Smith's normative account of the Bank of England published fourteen years earlier in *The Wealth of Nations*. The Bank of England, Smith wrote, "acts, not only as an ordinary bank, but as a great engine of state." Its duties, he continued, included receiving taxes, paying interest on the government debt, circulating temporary currency (monetary debt) of the government, and discounting bills for banks in England and sometimes for banks in Hamburg and Holland. "In those different operations," Smith added somewhat undiplomatically, "its duty to the public may sometimes have obliged it, without any fault of its directors, to overstock the circulation with paper money."[10] Even though the crown had sanctioned the bank, Smith explicitly denied that the sovereign had any power to tamper with the currency by means of the Bank of England or otherwise.[11] The bank's character in his view was purely fiscal and commercial.

Hamilton took his cue from Smith: "It is to be considered that such a bank," he wrote in his report, "is not a mere matter of private property, but a political machine of greatest importance to the State." A public bank would give "facility to the Government in obtaining pecuniary aids," that is, loans. It would aid in sales of public lands; its profits would accrue to the government; and it would eventually provide a uniform paper currency.[12]

Both Smith and Hamilton regarded banks as a means for "augmenting the active or productive capital of a country." The judicious operations of banking, they alleged, converted the "dead stock of gold and silver" into active and productive capital by substituting paper in place of metal. Paper money, being easier to transport, "economized" specie while it made possible the "quickening of circulation."[13] Smith cautioned that commerce and business were less secure when "suspended upon the Daedalian wings of paper money, [than] when they travel about upon the solid ground of gold and silver."[14] Hamilton, too, recognized that banks could furnish "temptations to overtrading," and thereby banish gold and silver from the country. But the force of his objection rested "on their being an engine [*sic*] of paper credit."[15] So long as banks' issues of paper money were "payable upon demand without any condition, and . . . readily paid as soon as presented," the danger of overissue was minimal, Smith wrote in optimistic answer to his own caveat.[16] Hamilton also replied to his own caution on how banking excesses might lead to overtrading. "If the abuses of a beneficial thing are to determine its condemnation," he observed, "there is scarcely a source of public prosperity [welfare] which will not speedily be closed."[17]

Hamilton perceived that another necessary step in the formation of a public or national bank was to minimize the risk of possible abuses. While he did not want the state to participate in the executive direction of the bank, nor "to own the whole or a principal part of the stock, . . . the ordinary rules of prudence require that the Government should possess the means of ascertaining . . . that so delicate a trust is executed with fidelity and care."[18] To this end, he thought, the state should hold some of the stock and be able to check on the bank's affairs at any instant.

The bank Hamilton foresaw was a national or public bank as well as an extra-large bank. It was required, in his view, as an auxiliary to the fiscal operations of the federal state. Unlike the state banks, it would not be subject to the constraints of any one set of state laws. It would have branches in those states where its business was served. It would be able, therefore, to issue a uniform national currency that would greatly facilitate the payments and receipts of the national government. The privately owned, publicly operated bank would also be a commercial bank, subject to the discipline of redeeming its notes in gold and silver on demand. A government-owned bank, while able to furnish a uniform paper currency, would have only its own discretion to limit emissions of currency. This discretion could not always be trusted because of the "temptation of momentary exigencies" that the government might face.[19]

The final and most important function of the public bank was that of sustaining government credit. To this end, government debt would constitute the bulk of its capitalization. Since the new federal government had taken over much of the states' Revolutionary War debts as its own responsibility, it was understandably concerned about the management and repayment of the debt and wished to ensure the possibility of additional flotations if they became necessary. Capital stock of the bank, therefore, would be payable one-fourth in specie and three-fourths in the 6 percent public debt. The specie would serve as reserves; the debt would allow a capital structure "sufficiently large to be the basis of an extensive [note] circulation, and an adequate security for it."[20]

Hamilton recognized that a public bank might take up only a small fraction of the debt. (The First Bank originally held $6.20 million of a total national debt of $75.5 million.) However, even a minor holding could strengthen the total market for the debt so that interest rates could be kept "low." Hamilton gave the "low"-interest issue its obvious due: Interest was a cost to the government, and for the sake of fiscal economy it should be minimized; low interest rates promoted national growth. Finally, existing government debt would be a respectable collateral for the uniform paper currency the bank would issue.[21]

Smith's and Hamilton's writings clarified the case for a paper currency based on specie and redeemable in the same on demand. Indeed, the course of the Bank of England throughout the eighteenth century demonstrated the reconciliation between a paper currency based on specie and the classic specie standard. The issue of exchequer bills by the British government and the issue of notes by the Bank of England were examples of this evolution.[22]

Congressional Debate over the Bill for the First Bank

The bill for chartering the First Bank provoked a controversy in Congress that was concentrated in the House of Representatives. One congressman, James Jackson of Georgia, noted that a geographical line separated those who were for the bank from those who were against it. All representatives to the "eastward" were for it and all to the "southward" were against it, almost without exception.[23] The principal spokesman for the group against the bank was James Madison of Virginia. Madison did not believe that the bank would have an appreciable effect on "raising the value of stock" because the government "stock" that the bank absorbed would be replaced in the market by the bank's stock. Madison cited Smith's *Wealth of Nations* to show that bank paper would "banish the precious metals by substituting another medium to perform their office."[24]

Madison's chief arguments were not economic but political and legal. They focused on the constitutionality of such a bank and the possible conflict between the states' interests and the federal interest. A national bank issuing notes on a national basis "would directly interfere with the rights of the states to prohibit as well as to establish Banks, and [it would also interfere with] the circulation of [state] bank notes."[25] Madison was correct that the states would not be able to prohibit the paper of a national bank; but they could (and did) continue to charter their own banks to issue "local" paper.

The other half of the state/federal argument, given by John Laurence of New York, was that if the law for a national bank interfered with state laws, "the particular interest of a State must give way to the general interest."[26] Not much more can be said on either side of this argument except that each event involving a conflict of interests must be decided on its own merits. In the case of a paper-currency issue, hindsight would support the efficacy in exchanges that results from uniformity in design. However, neither monetary theory nor experiences with the private production of money show that a national bank is a necessary institution for this purpose, nor that private-sector banks in a competitive market environment would fail to produce a virtually uniform currency.

The debates over the First Bank emphasized that a "national" bank by definition would have branches anywhere its directors thought proper. This feature implied that state governments no longer would have jurisdiction over the operational existence of the bank's branches. More than this political argument, a national bank with branches would have a technical economic advantage over a state bank not necessarily free to branch in its own state, and almost never allowed to branch in other states. The national bank would also have the right to operate in a state that had prohibited banking as an enterprise—no matter how misguided such a prohibition. More important, branching was an organizational means for ensuring the safety of note issues. Therefore, a national bank with branches would have multiple statutory advantages in both safety and efficiency over any ordinary state bank.

Madison had additional powerful arguments against the incorporation of a national bank. The right of Congress to establish a bank, he stated, was a logical precedent for Congress to incorporate any other business. Then, in a passage notable for its insight into the kind of expansion central banks and congresses might one day assume, he said, "If . . . Congress, by virtue of the power to borrow, can create the means of lending, and, in pursuance of these means, can incorporate a Bank, they may do any thing whatever creative of like means. . . . If again, Congress by virtue of the power to borrow money, can create the ability to lend, they may, by virtue of the power to levy money [taxes], create the ability to pay it."[27]

The proponents of the bank rested their case on the powers given in the Constitution that enabled Congress to borrow money and to lay and collect taxes. Especially important was the aid the bank would furnish in making quick credit available to the Treasury in time of emergency. "If we have not the power to establish [the bank]," said Fisher Ames of Massachusetts, "our social compact is incomplete, we want the means of self-preservation."[28]

The only monetary power implied by the Constitution is the clause instructing Congress to coin money and regulate its value. "Money" at that time and for a good while afterward was presumed to include only gold and silver coin. Since bank paper was not money, Congress did not have the power to regulate it.[29] Nevertheless, promotion of a uniform paper currency in 1790 did not imply inflation; and several statements in support of this function by the First Bank, including Hamilton's report, were forthcoming. Adam Smith's authority was cited three times in the House debate—twice in favor of bank-issued currency and once against it.

The debates demonstrated a sharp distinction between paper currency issued as an economical substitute for specie, based on specie and convertible into specie, and paper money issued in order to regulate trade. The issue of specie-based currency need be nothing more than the substitution of an economical medium of exchange for one more costly; but the issue of currency to control trade is a true central-banking operation. Some congressmen had cited the power of Congress to regulate trade as an argument for the bank. "But what has this bill to do with trade? Would any plain man suppose that this bill had anything to do with trade?" Madison asked rhetorically.[30] Fisher Ames, an outspoken supporter of the bank, made the same disclaimer. While he was much in favor of the bank's possible utility in furnishing a national currency, "he would not pause to examine" its power to regulate inland bills of exchange and bank paper as the instruments of such trade. Such a power would be "an injury and wrong which [would] violate the right of another."[31]

Supporters promoted the First Bank both as a private commercial bank and as a public (or national) bank, but not as a central bank. It would serve as a fiscal agent to the Treasury; it would issue a uniform national paper currency based on commercial credit; and it would furnish credit to the government, perhaps soaking up long-term government debt as a "permanent" investment. It definitely would not increase or decrease its issues of paper money as a means of stabilizing trade. The bill passed both houses of Congress by two-to-one majorities in 1791 and was incorporated much along the lines of Hamilton's original plan.

The Operational Role of the First Bank

The impression from the scanty evidence on the operations of the First Bank compiled by John Thom Holdsworth is that it used its public position discreetly. The dividends it paid were somewhat more modest than those of competing commercial banks, and the market value of its stock showed at best no appreciation even before its recharter became an issue. Meanwhile, the market values of its competitors' stocks increased considerably. The bank and its branches had over half of total bank-held specie ($5 million of a total of about $10 million) in 1811. This amount gave it a specie reserve that was 37 percent of its outstanding demand obligations and almost 50 percent of its capital and surplus.[32] It might therefore have generated considerably more credit and demand obligations than it actually did.

The First Bank in its public aspect was both a creditor and a debtor of the government, a creditor because it held government debt and a debtor because it held government deposits. Gradually its government deposits became much greater than its government debt. In fact, the government's fiscal operations reduced the outstanding national debt by about 50 percent between 1804 and 1812. The First Bank's holdings of federal debt dropped from $6.20 million to $2.23 million over this same period, and virtually eliminated the function of the bank as a sustainer of government credit.

Holdsworth's final comment was that the bank had been managed with extreme caution—too much so "for its full usefulness to the business community and its returns to the stockholders."[33] At the same time other factors prevented the bank from extending maximum credit. First, its position as a public bank required it to hold a fairly high fraction of specie reserves in anticipation of monetary demands by the government. Second, aggressive lending operations by the bank would have emphasized its enviable position as a receptacle for public deposits and as a beneficiary of special privileges. A growing volume of private-bank competition in the decade 1800–1810 made this factor more important.

The First Bank's relationship to the growing number of commercial banks became invidious despite careful efforts by the bank's managers to restrain its activities. Both the Bank of England and the First Bank had so much private business, observed Bray Hammond, that their "public function was to many persons quite unapparent except as usurpation and privilege."[34]

The First Bank as a Central Bank

The First Bank's relatively high reserve ratio, as well as the sheer dollar volume of its reserves, suggested the possibility of its development as a central bank, albeit with limited powers. It felt constrained from operating purely for profit, and its very size meant that it would have a significant influence on the volume of bank credit. For such an institution to have been in this strategic position and then to have adopted an attitude of "no policy" would have denied the utility of human management and the very human notion that positive intervention could make a good thing work better.

The First Bank's central-banking function became manifest through its currency transactions with other banks. If it felt that credit restraint was called for, it presented the notes of other banks for redemption in specie. If it felt that credit ease was in order, it expanded its own credit availability to businesses and to other banks and generally treated the notes of other banks with "forbearance." It was able to manage such operations because much money went through its offices in fulfillment of its fiscal aids to the government and because it kept a reserve balance large enough to maneuver in this way. It may not have seemed much more than a first among equals to the state banks; but it must have looked much more first than equal when it was able to curtail the credit activities of these banks by acquiring the public deposits they might have had.

The directors of the First Bank soon recognized its emerging role as a regulatory institution. Their "memorial" to the Senate in 1810 arguing for recharter noted that the bank had acted as a central bank, although they did not use the term, and that its actions were beneficial. The bank, they said, had been a "general guardian of commercial credit, and by preventing the balance of trade in the different States from producing a deficiency of money in any, has obviated the mischiefs which would have been thereby produced. It has fostered and protected the banking institutions of the States, and has aided them when unexpectedly pressed."[35]

Another memorial to the Senate from the Philadelphia Chamber of Commerce implied a similar and desirable central-banking result of the First Bank's operations due to the unavoidably "great and constant accumulation of paper of other banks in its vaults." During the banking crisis of 1810, the memorial continued, the bank had "diffused its accommodations to the greatest extent."[36]

Henry Clay in the Senate also recognized the First Bank's central-banking potential, but he believed that such power demanded restraint rather than license. The bank, he argued, had been chartered to assist the Treasury in its fiscal functions and should have done nothing more. "It is mockery," he exclaimed heatedly, "worse than usurpation, to establish [the institution] for a lawful object, and then extend to it other objects which are not lawful. . . . You say to this organization, we cannot authorize you to discount—to emit paper—to regulate commerce, etc. No! Our book has no precedents of that kind. But then we can authorize you to collect the revenue, and, while occupied with that, you may do whatever else you please!"[37]

Clay's statement provides a sharp contrast between the Federalist thought for which he was such an astute spokesman and the Democratic position as expressed by Secretary of the Treasury Albert Gallatin and Senator William Crawford of Georgia.[38] Gallatin advocated the bank's continued existence and urged renewal of its charter for the usual fiscal reasons in 1809, but he had to phrase his brief for the bank's usefulness in sustaining the government's credit in the past tense: "The bank had heretofore been eminently useful in making the advances which . . . were necessary. . . . And a similar disposition has been repeatedly evinced whenever the aspect of public affairs has rendered it proper to ascertain whether new loans might, if wanted, be obtained."[39] Otherwise, it was a good bank. It had kept the public moneys safely, it had transferred government payments efficiently, and it had aided in the collection of the revenues. In 1810, Gallatin noted, the bank had supplied short-term funds to the government, thus avoiding the necessity for an increase in "permanent" debt outstanding.[40]

Unlike Clay, Gallatin at this time showed no recognition of any regulatory monetary powers in the First Bank. He saw only its ancillary and subordinate role to Treasury operations. Later Clay and his party would embrace the central bank as a desirable and utilitarian organization, while the Democrats, on finding that a central bank was loose in the land, would conduct a campaign of extermination.

The First Bank, by reason of an organization that included branches and by reason of its legal relationship to the government, was undoubtedly a more enthusiastic supporter of government credit than the state banks would have been. This factor was emphasized in a letter from Gallatin to Crawford, who was then chairman of the Senate Committee on Finance. The state banks could manage the government's funds, Gallatin said, "without any insuperable difficulty." But the First Bank was generally safer since it was responsible for all the deposits in its separate branches.[41]

Crawford took the case for renewal of the bank's charter to the Senate. He urged Gallatin's authority, even though he knew that Gallatin was unpopular with many senators. He also stressed the bank's aid in the fiscal operations of the government, and he pointed out that the opposition to renewal of the charter came primarily from state legislatures. These bodies wanted the First Bank compromised so that the state banks, in which the states themselves had extensive stock holdings, would profit by the deposit of federal government moneys.[42]

Crawford was correct, but other nonfiscal and nonmonetary factors were also important. The continuing question of the bank's constitutionality and the alleged dominance of British stockholders contributed to the indecisive one-vote margin by which the bill for renewal of the bank's charter was laid on the table "indefinitely"—forever.[43]

2 Treasury Policy, 1811–1820

> The power of the federal Government to institute and regulate [the monetary system] must . . . be deemed . . . an exclusive power.
>
> Secretary of the Treasury A. J. Dallas, *American State Papers Finance*, 4 December 1815

The Conventional View of Monetary Policy, 1811–1820

A persistent fallacy that has marred monetary operations for centuries is the belief that a monetary system requires hands-on human control for its optimum operation. A contemporary version of this notion is that a central bank provides this control, and that without a central bank the monetary system disintegrates into chaos. One popular example for this contention in the United States is the series of financial events that occurred in the period 1811–1820. The year 1811 marked the end of the First Bank of the United States; the interval 1812–1815 included the years of the War of 1812; 1816–1818 saw the Second Bank become operational; the final years of this period, 1818–1820, were marked by a severe crisis or "panic" and subsequent recovery.

The myth that has come to govern analysis of the monetary-fiscal happenings in the United States between 1811 and 1820 is usually told along the following lines. Congress created the First Bank of the United States in 1791 with a charter permitting it to operate for twenty years. This institution early showed its propensities as a central bank, most particularly by controlling the flow of state bank notes that passed through its offices on their way to being redeemed or cleared in specie by the state banks.[1] Unfortunately, shortsighted policy by national leaders in 1810–11 allowed the First Bank to expire just as a national emergency developed. When war actually occurred between England and the United States in June 1812, the federal government did not have the services of a central bank. Consequently, it was forced to conduct fiscal and monetary policies on an ad hoc basis. The extraordinary resource demands of the war caused government expenditures to increase substantially, while ordinary revenues declined. The resulting fiscal deficits put a heavy administrative burden on the Treasury Department.

Having no First Bank to assist it, the Treasury financed its expenditures as best it could through the state banks. The number of state banks mushroomed. Without the central-banking restraint of the First Bank, "the state banks would neither pay specie nor accept each other's notes at par, . . . and hence, the government was forced to receive its revenues in state-bank paper and treasury notes of all degrees of depreciation."[2] Inflation developed from the proliferation of banks and the concurrent expansion of bank credit. After the war ended, the government instituted a new central bank, the Second Bank of the United States. This new bank, in cooperation with the Treasury Department and by skillful technique, was able to induce the state banks to resume specie payments, and it was ultimately able to provide a uniform and sound currency for the economy.[3]

This traditional analysis includes at least the following errors of judgment or omissions of pertinent details:

(1) An almost complete failure to notice or assess the effects of the inflationary issues of treasury notes during the period 1812–1817; (2) a similar lack of attention to the influence that the retirement of these same notes had on the recession of 1819 and on the resumption of specie payments; (3) the incorrect or highly questionable allegation that the presence of a central bank would have prevented either the proliferation of state banks or the inflation; (4) the idea that mere multiplication of banks promotes or causes inflation.

Government Financial Operations during the War of 1812

When the War of 1812 began, just one year after the end of operations by the First Bank, the increase in the federal government's expenditures to wage the war generated a fiscal deficit that Congress attempted to meet by authorizing sales of government securities. However, the loan at advertised interest rates was taken up by the public and banks so slowly that the government resorted to an issue of treasury notes.

Treasury notes had a combination of characteristics. The government issued them as a nonmoney interest-bearing debt, but people and banks could and did use them as currency. The interest rate on them in the case of the 1812 issue was 5⅖ percent per year, and they were redeemable in one year. They were also legal tender for payment of all duties and taxes to the United States until redeemed, and for all government purchases from the private sector.[4] Therefore, they were practically acceptable in all private transactions. Their use as hand-to-hand currency was restricted by the high denominations in which they were issued (few under $100), so most of them became bank reserves. What could be more attractive to a bank than reserve assets that were effectively legal tender and yet returned interest income as a part of the bank's investment portfolio? In addition, because of their high denominations, they were an efficient means for clearing balances among banks.

The federal government authorized the first issue of $5 million in June 1812. The notes were supposed to be redeemable in specie one year after their date of issue, but many of them circulated or were held as bank reserves long after they were due—that is, for some time after interest accruals had stopped. The total issues authorized and the amounts outstanding during the period 1813–1817 are shown in table 2.1.

TABLE 2.1 Authorizations and outstanding issues of treasury notes, 1812–1817

Authorized by act of	Total issued ($ millions)	Cumulative total of issues outstanding ($ millions)	As of or near
June 20, 1812	5.00	2.84	Jan. 1, 1813
Feb. 25, 1813	5.00	4.91	Jan. 1, 1814
Mar. 4, 1814	10.00	8.00[a]	Sept. 30, 1814
Dec. 26, 1814	8.23	10.65	Jan. 1, 1815
Feb. 24, 1815			
($100 notes)	4.42		
(Small notes)	3.39	15.46	Jan. 1, 1816
		8.73	Aug. 1, 1816
		0.64	Sept. 30, 1817

Source: *ASPF* 3, pp. 23, 32, 70, 79, 103, 136, 229.
[a] Approximate value.

Specie in the banking system during this same period amounted to between $5 million and $10 million. Table 2.2 shows specie and the other major assets and liabilities of reporting incorporated banks in the United States, as compiled by J. Van Fenstermaker. While this table covers only part of the banking system, it includes most of the specie-paying (New England) banks. It does not include treasury notes in either the specie or notes columns so far as can be determined. If the specie entries are good approximations to the total specie actually in the banks, the outstanding volumes of treasury notes were 39 percent of total specie and treasury notes (that is, of all bank reserves) by 1813 and 65 percent by 1816. Even with large errors in the available data, treasury notes had to be a significant fraction of total bank reserves, especially for banks outside of New England. This contention is also suggested by John Jay Knox's investigation and his remark, "The banks would give the Government credit for [the notes] and in return the Government could draw gold and silver from the banks."[5]

Secretary of the Treasury G. W. Campbell in his report for 1814 observed that of approximately $8 million of treasury notes in circulation at that time, only about $6 million could be circulated "without embarrassment," if past monetary experience was any guide.[6] Campbell made this judgment on the basis of the amount of bank currency in existence before the issues of treasury notes and on the assumption that the infusion of treasury notes would displace specie of equal value. The economy was indeed embarrassed. All banks except those in New England had suspended specie payments, so "the circulating medium of the country . . . [is] placed upon a new and uncertain footing." Campbell looked to Congress for a solution to this problem, all the while seemingly oblivious to the possibility that the treasury notes were the fundamental cause of the currency "redundancy."[7]

TABLE 2.2 Principal assets, liabilities, and number of reporting incorporated banks in the United States, and total treasury notes outstanding, 1809–1818 (dollar values in millions)

Date[a] (June-Dec.)	Chartered banks	Reporting banks		Loans and discounts ($)	Specie ($)	Total bank notes in circulation ($)	Individual deposits ($)	Total notes and deposits ($)	Treasury notes outstanding ($)
		No.	%						
1809	92	31	34	12.63	1.99	3.80	2.91	6.71	—
1810	102	30	29	14.69	2.49	5.58	4.22	9.80	—
1811	117	30	26	16.22	2.57	5.68	5.27	10.95	—
1812	143	32	22	17.94	5.70	6.32	7.43	13.75	2.84
1813	147	39	27	21.65	7.72	7.23	10.44	17.67	4.91
1814	202	63	31	36.74	9.29	13.69	15.76	29.45	10.65
1815	212	98	46	44.07	5.40	19.91	11.67	31.58	15.46
1816	232	91	39	40.46	4.74	17.22	9.14	26.36	8.73
1817	262	100	38	32.76	4.79	13.31	9.66	22.97	0.64
1818	338	147	44	48.24	5.47	18.07	9.65	27.72	—

Source: J. Van Fenstermaker, *A Statistical Summary of the Commercial Banks Incorporated in the United States prior to 1819* (Kent, Ohio: Bureau of Economics and Business Research, Kent State University, 1965), p. 5.

Note: Van Fenstermaker's statistics on the banking system seem to be as good as are obtainable. However, the number and percentage of *reporting* banks more than tripled between 1812 and 1817, probably because of improvements in communications, growth in the number of banks, and the use of commercial banks as government depositories. Therefore the growth in the values cited, especially in the specie item, is biased upward. Many of the banks included in this table enjoyed specie inflows from other banks in the economy (because of interregional balance-of-payments surpluses) and did not suspend specie payments.

[a] Reports from banks were not available at a point in time, such as June 30 or December 31. For expediency's sake, the time for each year's data had to be an interval, and the six-month period of June to December was chosen by Van Fenstermaker. The column showing treasury notes outstanding (taken from table 2.1) is synchronized with the bank data as closely as possible, discontinuous data and the judgment of the author permitting.

The usual account of the inflation of 1814–1817 stresses as a primary cause the large number of banks that came into existence with the demise of the First Bank. As table 2.2 shows, the annual rate of growth in the number of banks was highly variable after 1811. The rate of growth was negligible in 1812–13, when no public bank existed, and one of the greatest rates of growth occurred during 1817–18, after the Second Bank was in operation. These data suggest that something more than the mere presence of a United States bank must have had a significant effect on the number of state banks.

A more technical criticism of this thesis is that the mere *number* of banks is virtually unrelated to inflation. Claiming that they are is analogous to arguing that the distance a vehicle travels depends on the number of wheels it has rather than on the amount of fuel propelling it. Inflation in all known and measurable cases has resulted from significant increases in the quantity of money. During the period 1814–1817 the issues of treasury notes were the fuel that moved the inflation vehicle. The number of banks was both incidental and irrelevant to the increase in the quantity of money and the inflation that developed. Very probably, the increase in high-powered money extended the scope of the payments system. It encouraged the initiation of banking enterprise where none had existed, and the use of paper treasury notes as reserves facilitated clearing operations at the same time that their issue provoked inflation.

Government officials of the era persistently denied that their policies were responsible for the inflation and corresponding suspension of specie payments by the banking system. Secretary of the Treasury A. J. Dallas, in his report for 1815, noted that the banks south and west of New England had ceased specie payments. "In this act," he declared, "the Government of the United States had no participation." Not only were the state banks responsible for inflation and suspension, but it was with them that "the measures for restoring the national currency of gold and silver must originate." He expressed the hope "that the issue of bank paper [would] soon be reduced to its just share in the circulating medium of the country." The Treasury "from necessity" had been accepting bank paper, but, he warned, "the period approaches, when it will probably become a duty to exact the payment [of government dues] either in Treasury notes, or in gold and silver coin, the lawful money of the United States."[8]

Treasury notes held as bank reserves enabled the banks to increase their own note issues by multiples of the treasury notes. The public then used bank notes as hand-to-hand currency.[9] (See figure 2.1.)

The monetary effects on the economy were just what should have been expected. Prices rose as the quantity of money increased. The market prices of gold and silver as commodities tended to do likewise. But since the mint prices of gold and silver were fixed by statute, their mint values tended to be lower than their market prices. The consequence was that specie moved where

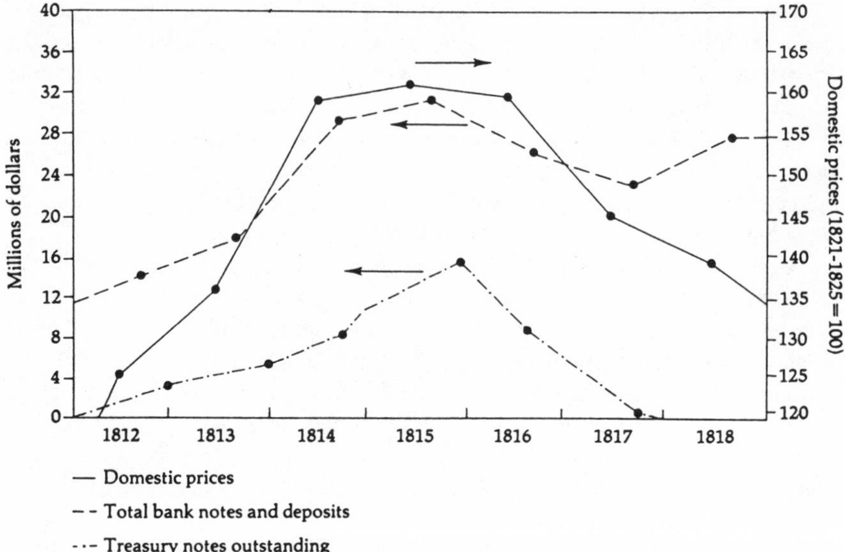

Figure 2.1 Total bank notes and deposits, treasury notes outstanding, and prices, 1812–1818. Domestic commodity prices are from *Historical Statistics,* Series E69, p. 119 (Bezanson). For bank notes and deposits and treasury notes, see table 2.2.

the price-specie flow mechanism directed it, that is, where paper money was not inflated. Besides flowing to foreign countries, much of the specie went to New England. The banks there, as Secretary of the Treasury William H. Crawford later observed, were "fettered by the stipulations of their charters. . . . Their issues of notes have been very limited, and the necessities [*sic*] for a circulating medium have been principally supplied by Treasury notes. . . . Government revenue . . . has been, almost entirely, collected in Treasury notes."[10] Unlike the bank notes of other regions, the bank notes of most New England banks were at par in specie and therefore at a *premium* over treasury notes.

Incorporation of the Second Bank of the United States

By 1816, the Treasury Department kept as many as four accounts with each depository bank: (1) cash, meaning local bank currency; (2) notes issued by other banks and held as a credit to the Treasury, but not at par with local currency; (3) treasury notes that bore interest; and (4) treasury notes that did not bear interest.[11] The Treasury, reported Crawford in 1816, was obliged to accept all bank-note currency. A requisition for coin payments would generate distress in private business and result in general liquidation and bank failures.[12] But resumption had to take place. The questions then were, How would the government promote it, and how could it be carried out so that distress to the private economy was minimized?

Secretary Dallas, Crawford's predecessor, gave the general drift of governmental policy when he declared that the state banks would have to reduce their outstanding amounts of paper money. Then, he added, the "interposition of Government will still be required to secure a successful result."[13] The possible "interposition" Dallas had in mind was the creation of another Bank of the United States that might facilitate resumption by absorbing some of the outstanding national debt in its capital structure.

In his brief for a new United States Bank in 1815, Dallas felt obliged to discuss the government's monetary strategy. Notes of the First Bank, he stated, had been declared receivable by law for all debts due the government. "Treasury notes," he continued, "which have been since issued for the services of the late war, have been endowed with the same quality."[14] Dallas found a defense for issuing treasury notes in the "adequacy" of the "motive" that prompted them. The government's motive had been its incurrence of fiscal deficits, payments for which could be anticipated from future tariff revenues. The war over, fiscal budgets would be balanced and no government "motive" for issuing paper money would remain.[15] A national bank, however, could assume the note-issuing function. Since its notes would be partial legal tender in the same fashion as treasury notes, they would be received uniformly everywhere.

Unfortunately, the irresponsible state banks posed a problem to the stability and soundness of the system. The government had to accept the paper currency that these banks had so capriciously created. To do otherwise, wrote Crawford a year or so later, would "visit the sins of the banks upon the great mass of unoffending citizens."[16] In virtually the same language as Dallas he then declared: "To restore the national currency of gold and silver it is essential that the quantity of bank paper in circulation should be reduced. . . . By reducing the amount of bank paper its value must be proportionably increased."[17]

The national bank could help. Since it would open its doors on a specie-paying basis, it would not need to resume, only to commence. The state banks would have to cooperate by restraining their issues, but such cooperation would be rewarded. "It will be proper to apprise them," Dallas said pointedly, "that, after a specified day, the notes of such banks as have not resumed their payments in the current coin will not be received in payments, either to the Government or to the national bank." At the same time, he suggested some compensation for their cooperation. "It will be peculiarly incumbent upon the national bank, as well as the Treasury," he said, "to conciliate the state banks;

to confide to them, liberally, a participation in the deposits of public revenue, and to encourage them in every reasonable effort to resume the payment of their notes in coin."[18]

Dallas's views were presumably official. The national bank he envisaged would function as an auxiliary of Treasury policy. It would be the shepherd in the field keeping the flock both disciplined and nourished. It would be "responsible" to Congress, but also "independent" of Congress. Dallas explicitly denied the possibility of governmental interference: "Whatever accommodation the Treasury may have occasion to ask from the bank can only be asked under the license of law; and whatever accommodation shall be obtained must be obtained from the voluntary assent of the directors acting under the responsibility of their trust."[19]

Dallas likewise provided an exalted and enlarged role for the proposed bank. "The national bank," he wrote, ". . . ought not to be regarded simply as a commercial bank. It will not operate upon the funds of the stockholders alone, but much more upon the funds of the nation. . . . In fine, it is not an institution created for the purposes of commerce and profit alone, but much more for the purposes of national policy, as an auxiliary in the exercise of some of the highest powers of the Government." Making the notes of the bank legally acceptable for government dues and payments, he continued, is "the means of preserving entire the sovereign authority of Congress relative to the coin and currency of the United States."[20]

Five years earlier David Ricardo had observed a Bank of England operating in the mode anticipated for the Bank of the United States. His perceptive comment on the relationship of a central bank to its government stands as a caution for all time. "It may be questioned," he remarked, "whether a bank lending many millions more to Government than its capital and savings can be called independent of that Government."[21]

The new bank bill went through Congress early in 1816 and was approved by President Madison on 10 April. The first president of the bank was William Jones, a career bureaucrat who had previously held cabinet posts in a temporary capacity. Almost simultaneously Secretary Dallas was succeeded in office by Crawford, a prestigious politician who had been chairman of the Senate Finance Committee, and who would have been president of the United States in 1824 except for a sudden and debilitating illness.

Preparations for the Resumption of Specie Payments

The long series of communications between Crawford and Jones reflected both the order of the monetary decision-making process and the contemporary official concept of the Second Bank. Crawford was clearly the dominant master and Jones the obsequious man in this exchange.

A popular prejudice of the times was that if *all* the banks and the government simply agreed to resume specie payments at the same time, ipso facto resumption would be accomplished. This optimistic belief was based on the correct presumption that all money prices and wages are merely nominal. It was also based on the faulty inference that all prices and wages can be cried up or cried down by popular voice if the voice is unanimous, without regard to the level of the current cost-price structure as determined by an existing stock of money. While unanimity would be impossible to obtain in practice, the real flaw in this reasoning was that many interest-bearing fixed-dollar claims and money wages had been contracted for later payment on the then-current value of money. Any decline in the general price level, therefore, was bound to hurt debtors and residual-income claimants and to enrich creditors. It would also enhance both the value and the utility of the money stock beyond what people wanted them to be. Therefore price level adjustment by decree—or "jawbone price control," as it has been labeled—simply could not and would not take place. It was and is King Canute railing at the waves.

Jones saw the banks in 1817 as being "not only solvent but rich in surplus funds and resources."[22] His implication was that the banks could resume specie payments if only they wished to do so. Secretary Crawford, in contrast, recognized a fundamental interrelationship between the outstanding stock of treasury notes, the "overissues" of state bank notes, and the obstacles these moneys posed to a genuine policy of resumption. To effect resumption, he promised Jones, the government would withhold "from circulation as much of their paper [currency] now in the Treasury . . . as the demands upon the Treasury during the ensuing year will permit. . . . As the sum which it will be in the power of the Government to retain in the Treasury will be considerable, it may present a sufficient inducement [to the state banks] to change their determination not to resume specie payments before the first day of July next [1817]."[23] Since the banks used treasury notes as reserves, the notes were outside money supporting the inflated bank credit. When the notes were withdrawn, bank credit would contract and prices would fall.

Crawford issued a circular to all the depository banks on 20 December 1816. The essence of his memorandum was that the Bank of the United States would commence operations on 1 January 1817, but that the public funds would not be transferred to it if the state banks would agree to resume specie payments on 20 February 1817, in conjunction with the Second Bank's "commencement." If the banks were agreeable, treasury balances with them would be reduced only gradually to pay public dues. The Second Bank, Crawford reassured the state banks, must be "friendly" to them: "The deep interest which the Treasury has in the support of bank credit . . . would . . . be sufficient to protect [the state banks] against an illiberal policy on [the] part [of the Bank of the United States]."[24]

In June 1817, Crawford sent out another circular to all depository banks,

TABLE 2.3 Federal fiscal expenditures and receipts and cash balance position of the Treasury, 1812–1821

Calendar year	Ordinary receipts[a]	Ordinary expenditures[a]	Treasury cash balance (near Jan. 1)		
			Treasury notes	Bank notes	Total
1812	9.80	20.28	—	3.95[b]	3.95
1813	14.34	31.68	—	2.36[b]	2.36
1814	11.18	34.72	—	5.20	5.20
1815	15.73	32.71	—	1.53	1.53
1816	47.69	30.59	6.36	6.75	13.11
1817	33.10	21.84	10.67	11.30	21.97
1818	21.59	19.83	8.81	6.18	14.99
1819	24.60	21.46	—	1.45	1.45
1820	17.88	18.26	—	2.08	2.08
1821	14.57	15.81	—	1.20	1.20

Sources: *Historical Statistics* Series Y-259 and Y-350, pp. 712 and 719, for fiscal receipts and expenditures. *Treasury Reports* for the years indicated, *ASPF* 2 and 3, for cash balances.

Note: Expenditures and receipts in millions of dollars per year; cash balance in millions of dollars.

[a] Does not include debt flotations or reductions.

[b] Near October 1 of year indicated.

urging that all their reserves of treasury notes be canceled against treasury deposits and returned to the Treasury. As late as November 1817, substantial amounts of notes were still outstanding despite Crawford's pleas and reports to the contrary.[25]

Table 2.3 shows the U.S. Treasury's monetary-fiscal flows in this period and its cash balance at the beginning of each year. During the war and up to the beginning of 1815, expenditures outran receipts by two or three to one. Issues of treasury notes made up for some of this deficit. Peacetime conditions dramatically reversed this pattern. As receipts soared past expenditures in 1816, the Treasury accumulated a large balance of bank notes and treasury notes. The treasury notes still in circulation and largely held by banks as reserves were finally returned to the Treasury, and the federal government's balances in depository banks were correspondingly debited.

The retirement of treasury notes was both a necessary and a sufficient condition to force the contraction of bank credit and of bank-note currency. It also provoked a general deflation. Prices started declining in 1818, after having been stable for two years, and fell 30 percent in the next three years.[26]

The new Bank of the United States could do nothing about the existence of treasury notes; the Treasury Department had sole responsibility for their issue and retirement. In an attempt to get state bank agreement on resumption in early 1817, the new bank agreed to accept responsibility to the government for the public deposits held by the state banks, but to refrain from demanding redemption of these deposits until 1 July 1817. The Second Bank also promised to discount $6 million of paper for either individuals or banks before any other balances against state banks were called for.[27]

The letters of William Jones, the president of the bank, to Secretary Crawford reveal Jones's principal tenets: (1) The bank should be operated profitably for its stockholders (including the government). (2) It should set a good example by paying specie on demand for its notes. (3) It would have to make concessions to the state banks to prevent invidious feelings on their part. Jones clearly did not realize that the structure of bank credit and the cost-price framework would have to suffer a general contraction for resumption to be genuine, universal, and permanent. Under his direction the bank acted as if it had the means to indulge the state banks, as the Treasury Department had implied it should. When the Treasury pinched the money supply by wholesale retirements of treasury notes in 1816–17, the bank compensated in part for Treasury austerity by expanding credit in accordance with concessions it had made to the state banks to encourage their resumption of specie payments, apparently without realizing that it could not contradict Treasury policy. It simply did not have the resources necessary to compensate for the Treasury's note retirement operation. On balance the bank absorbed notes of state banks on government account, *agreeing not to demand specie for the notes from the state banks*. It then paid out its own notes convertible into specie.[28] This process could not go on indefinitely, and the inevitable shakedown promised to be painful.

Crawford was the architect of the deflation and of subsequent resumption. He understood what had to be done; he had the power to do it; and he had enough bureaucratic hypocrisy to carry out what was bound to be an austere and unpleasant policy. He somewhat prematurely congratulated himself and the bank for the shaky resumption that was in effect during 1817. The Second Bank had assisted in this process, Crawford told its directors in a letter, despite resistance from the state banks, which felt that "the circulation of their paper is contracted within narrower limits than heretofore." This complaint was natural, he allowed; but the bank had nothing to fear from the state banks so long as it continued to make credit available "to the commercial class which it has amply furnished from the commencement of its operation."[29]

The Recession of 1818–1819

If 1817 was a period of monetary fasting and cleansing, 1818 was penitence. One manifestation of the coming recession was the state banks' hesitation to pay specie when the Bank of the United States requested them to do so. Their reluctance raised the question of whether the bank or the Treasury was responsible for the redeemability of notes received by the depository banks to the credit of the government. Jones complained to Crawford that the bank was paying out specie on demand for its notes, "whilst the banks, our debtors, plead inability, require unreasonable indulgence, or treat our reiterated claims and expostulations with settled indifference."[30] The Treasury, Jones continued in another letter to Crawford, had made "suggestions of forbearance" to the Second Bank on the collections of state bank notes. The bank, however, "is bound to receive and transfer but not collect the public money. A state bank note is nothing more than a bill at sight, payable to the bearer at the place of location; it is not money. Many banks have recently failed; many more will certainly fail." Many "specie banks (so called)," he noted bitterly, were unwilling or unable to liquidate their debts to the bank, or even to prevent their increase. He concluded with a final despairing (and revealing) complaint. The public money was to have been deposited with the bank and its branches. However, the unexpended public money in the offices of the Treasury had not been so deposited. "If these deposits were faithfully made and kept in the Bank and its branches it would have a salutary effect. They are now made to operate directly to the prejudice of this institution."[31]

Well might Jones say so. Not only had the public moneys in the form of treasury notes been withheld and retired, but the policy was contrived, purposeful, and deliberate. The Treasury Department was the acting central bank.

Crawford answered his subordinate with contemptuous brusqueness. On Jones's "intimation that the Government has prepared a crisis by the legitimate employment of the public money in payment of the public debt," he wrote, "comment is considered unnecessary." (He nevertheless commented, albeit briefly.) The interests of the Second Bank and of the state banks had to be weighed against the interests of the community. Treasury notes were part of the public debt. Their retirement was likewise retirement of that debt and was thus in the interest of the community. This advantage had to be balanced against the beneficial effects the Second Bank and banks would experience if the notes were redeposited in banks and used as reserves.[32] With these dicta, he dismissed the case.

Retirement of treasury notes was the equivalent of a contemporary central-bank open-market sale that erases bank reserves. It was the kind of harsh action that had to be taken if resumption was to be accomplished. The alternative was to maintain price level stability at the inflated plateau then current. Bankers who were unable to resume specie payments would have preferred Treasury support of bank credit. In this case, however, the maintenance of the gold-standard system at the prewar parity was considered worth some sacrifices, especially if the sacrifices were borne by banks that had "overtraded" and "speculated" in the first place.

Jones's account of the Second Bank's problems demonstrated the frictions involved in the resumption process. The Treasury used the bank's credit to hide its basic policy of contracting the money supply. This role made the bank the target for complaints by those who were most immediately hurt, namely, banks that issued bank notes and people who used bank notes. The Second Bank's directors were no better able to tolerate this pressure than anyone else. Their practical solution was to accept commercial bank notes that might or might not be the equivalent of specie, for what constituted a specie equivalent was a matter of judgment.

The price level decline of 1818–1820 that resulted in full-scale resumption was accompanied by the usual symptoms of failing banks and business hardships. Crawford may have had the only overall view of what was actually going on. The pressure now on the banks, he stated in his report for 1818, resulted from "the excessive issues of the banks during the suspension of specie payments, and the great exportation of the precious metals to the East Indies during the present year." The banks then found that they were forced "to contract their discounts for the purpose of withdrawing from circulation a large proportion of their notes. This operation, so oppressive to their debtors, but indispensably necessary to the existence of specie payments, must be continued until gold and silver shall form a just proportion of the circulating medium." If the depression became too severe, Crawford hedged, the Treasury might again be forced to issue treasury notes![33]

"Resumption was an achievement and the Secretary's own," Bray Hammond has written. "Central banking policy was more intelligently developed in the Treasury than in the central bank itself."[34] Hammond's appraisal contains both explicit truth and implicit error. Crawford was indeed the "central banker" who promoted deflation and resumption after the treasury note issues of his predecessors had provoked inflation and suspension. But the Second Bank of the United States was several years away from becoming the central bank that it became under the leadership of Nicholas Biddle. In this early era the bank proved to be nothing more than a convenient buffer for the unpalatable but "necessary" policies of the Treasury Department.

Secretary Crawford's Norms for the Monetary System

The dramatic fall in the price level and in business activity prompted a committee in the House of Representatives in March 1819 to ask for a report from Secretary Crawford on the relationship of the Bank of the United States and other banks to the currency. Crawford's reply to this inquiry contains some extraordinary thoughts.

Crawford began by reviewing the means by which resumption had been achieved. He noted that the stock of bank-issued paper money had to be reduced, but he conveniently overlooked the fundamental role that treasury notes had exerted on the supply of bank credit. The war had required money. Banks were suffered to increase their note issues, which in turn caused suspension of specie payments. The suspension had to be tolerated until the end of hostilities. If banks had not been allowed to expand, Crawford argued, even more treasury notes would have been required. That is, the treasury notes in his view were a supplement to bank-note issues rather than the means that enabled the banks to extend credit. He dismissed the fundamental monetary character of the treasury notes and their inflationary consequences with this bit of outrageous taxonomy: "By the term *currency,* the issue of paper [money] by Government, as a financial resource, is excluded."[35]

By this time (1819) most of the treasury notes had been redeemed, canceled, and destroyed, Crawford observed proudly, while a large volume of bank notes were unredeemed and still in existence. (He did not say unredeemable.) In the event, this comparison emphasized the "superiority" of treasury notes to bank notes.[36]

The last section of the congressional inquiry seemed to question the necessity of a specie standard. It asked Crawford to "suggest such measures as, in his opinion, may be expedient to procure a circulating medium, in place of specie, adapted to the exigencies of the country, and within the power of the Government."[37] That such a request could be made at all is indeed surprising in view of the constitutional provisions prohibiting bills of credit and limiting legal tender to gold and silver. Early legislators may have been more experimental and less bound by the Constitution than reputed.

Crawford replied forthrightly that such a question would be only academic "if the power of Congress over the currency [were] not absolutely sovereign. . . . The general prosperity [welfare] will not be advanced," he continued, "by demonstrating that there is no intrinsic obstacle to the substitution of a paper for a metallic currency, if the power to adopt the substitute has been withheld from the Federal Government."[38] In short, Congress's very act of inquiring implied that the constitutional power might be available for the development of a paper-currency system. The primary obstacle to such a system in his opinion was not the lack of a sovereign right, but "the danger of the instability and want of integrity and intelligence of the Government." In addition, the division of powers between federal and state governments would encourage the possibility of "collisions" in jurisdictional controls over the monetary system. Crawford was not opposed to a bank-issued paper currency. In fact, he advocated such a system. In the mode of most "mixed-currency" spokesmen, he recommended that bank paper currency be coordinated with the growth of trade. The quantity of paper money was properly regulated, he felt, by the requirement that the paper money be convertible into specie on demand.[39]

Crawford concluded his testimony to the congressional committee with this statement: "Coinage and the regulation of money have, in all nations, been considered one of the highest acts of sovereignty. It may well be doubted, however, whether a sovereign power over the coinage necessarily gives [the government] the right to establish a paper currency."[40]

Crawford's reiterated assertions of Congress's "sovereignty" over the currency flout the U.S. Constitution's explicit provision proscribing bills of credit. Congress certainly did not have any sovereignty to institute a paper-currency system. Its authority was limited to specifying the legal tender values of gold and silver and, by the principles generally understood for a specie standard, to set these values once and for all. Even more fundamentally, sovereignty in the new United States did not reside in Congress or the government, but with the people. The Constitution was simply a limitation-by-specification of governmental powers.

James Monroe, the president at whose pleasure Crawford served, was one of the Founding Fathers who had hammered these principles into existence. Yet Congress and Crawford as early as 1819 could toy with the notion of a government-issued paper currency. The extraordinary aspect of Crawford's disclaimer is not what he stated—that was valid enough—but what he left unsaid. Nothing in his discussion referred to the proscriptive tenets of the Constitution. His denial would have been much stronger and much more appropriate if he had simply replied that even in the presence of angels the Constitution forbade any issue of paper currency under governmental discretion.

3 Central-Banking Growth of the Second Bank of the United States

That the [Second] bank adds facilities to trade and commerce generally, and, to a certain extent, regulates the course of exchange, will not be questioned: but does that justify Congress in erecting a broker's shop to do what is the business of individual enterprise, and the natural channel of trade itself?

McDuffie Report, House of Representatives, 1830

Origin of the Second Bank as a Public-Commercial Bank

Scholars have almost universally neglected the emergence of many central-banking institutions and concepts, but they have more than made up for this oversight in their specific studies on the Second Bank of the United States. Books and articles on both this institution and its most illustrious president, Nicholas Biddle, abound—to the extent, in fact, that little can be added. The obvious case for research on such a glamorous institution has cast a penumbra around other historical monetary areas worthy of study. The Second Bank, though short-lived, became one of the most notable examples of incipient central banking during the nineteenth century.

Bray Hammond has argued that the function of the early American commercial banking system was to furnish the economy with the credit it "needed" to grow, while the central bank's primary role was to stabilize the banking system. Hammond's general thesis is that the Second Bank, and to some extent the First Bank, was *intended* by its more sophisticated sponsors to stabilize the unrestrained state banking system; that under Nicholas Biddle in the 1820s the Second Bank fulfilled this role; but that its potential usefulness was cut short in the 1830s by the ignorant and acquisitive segment of society led by the Jackson administration. Enlightened central-banking thought and action in the United States, Hammond concludes, were stifled until the organization of the Federal Reserve System in 1913.[1] (W. B. Smith shares this view in his book on the Second Bank.)[2]

Though based on extensive and competent research, none of the books on the Second Bank confirms the thesis that its supporters created this institution in the image of a central bank. Similarly to the First Bank, Congress chartered the Second Bank for the practical purpose of housing the interest-bearing debt that the government incurred in financing the War of 1812. The bank was supposed to be nothing more than a fiscal auxiliary to the Treasury Department. The kind of monetary intervention that a central bank might be a party to was dismissed as either undesirable or unconstitutional.[3] When the Treasury's debt-retirement policy in the early 1820s provided an opportunity for a central-banking operation, the Second Bank was not even considered. Instead, Secretary Crawford recommended that Congress authorize the repurchase of a portion of the public debt at a "fair" price (above the par value) with the fiscal surplus of $8.61 million that had accrued to the government that year. He suggested that the commissioners of the sinking fund be authorized as what is now called an "open-market committee" to carry out the repurchase.[4] The bill to repurchase passed routinely, but the Second Bank was not even mentioned. In his report for 1824, Crawford offhandedly remarked that the bank was a useful instrument for assisting in debt flotations and reductions.[5]

Up to this point Secretary Crawford had been directing all the monetary and fiscal policies of the government. Ill health, however, caused him to forgo further administrative or political activities. At approximately the same time Nicholas Biddle succeeded Langdon Cheves as president of the Second Bank. During the four years that Cheves had been president, the bank had been a part of and a focal point for the monetary contraction that had resulted in resumption of specie payments. Cheves had thought of the bank as "small" and decentralized. He felt that each branch should be largely autonomous and responsible in specie for only its own notes.[6] He was apparently well read in the economic literature of the time; and the principles of the discipline would indeed have deterred him from allowing the Second Bank any regulatory role. He clearly did not regard it as a central bank. Resumption of specie payments had just reaffirmed the primacy of the specie standard, and it—not the Second Bank—was the recognized regulator of the money supply.

Biddle had become a director of the bank in 1819, shortly before Cheves was appointed president. By the time he himself became president in 1823, the Second Bank had been refortified with specie reserves through its public depository role for the government and by the severe reduction of its loans and discounts. Not only was its reserve ratio a high 37 percent, but it had about one-half of total bank-held specie. It was also the exclusive collector and depository of government revenues, and its notes were legal tender for all payments to and by the government. This last provision meant that its notes had the same qualities as the treasury notes issued between 1812 and 1815, as well as those issued in several other periods before 1860. (See table 3.1.)

The Treasury and executive administrations of the war period regarded the issue of treasury notes as a distasteful and temporary emergency measure of questioned constitutionality. Even so, the notes were issued by an agency of the government under congressional authorization, whereas the notes of the Second Bank were issued by a primarily private corporation with virtually no legal constraints on their quantity or duration. Yet observers of the era have hailed the notes of the Second Bank as the basis of a sound and uniform currency, and have disparaged the treasury notes as disreputable and spurious. In both cases outright unconstitutionality was avoided by making the notes legal

TABLE 3.1 Selected assets and liabilities, and reserve ratios of the Second Bank of the United States, 1817–1840 (millions of dollars)

Year	Loans and dis-counts	Notes of state banks held by Second Bank	Specie	Circula-tion[a]	Deposits[b]	Total circula-tion and deposits	Reserve ratios (%)[c]
1817	3.49	0.59	1.72	1.91	11.23	13.14	13.1
1818	41.18	1.84	2.52	8.34	12.28	20.62	12.2
1819	35.77	1.88	2.67	6.56	5.79	12.35	21.5
1820	31.40	1.44	3.39	3.59	6.57	10.16	33.4
1821	30.91	0.68	7.64	4.57	7.89	12.46	61.3
1822	28.06	0.92	4.76	5.58	8.08	13.66	34.9
1823	30.74	0.77	4.43	4.36	7.62	11.98	37.0
1824	33.43	0.71	5.81	4.65	13.70	18.35	31.7
1825	31.81	1.06	6.75	6.07	12.03	18.10	37.3
1826	33.42	1.11	3.96	9.48	11.21	20.69	19.1
1827	30.94	1.07	6.46	8.55	14.32	22.87	31.1
1828	33.68	1.45	6.17	9.86	14.50	24.36	25.3
1829	39.22	1.29	6.10	11.90	17.06	28.96	21.0
1830	40.66	1.47	7.61	12.92	16.05	28.97	26.3
1831	44.03	1.50	10.81	16.25	17.30	33.55	32.2
1832	66.29	2.17	7.04	21.36	22.76	44.12	15.9
1833	61.70	2.29	8.95	17.52	20.35	37.87	23.6
1834	54.91	1.98	10.04	19.21	10.84	30.05	32.9
1835	51.81	1.51	15.71	17.34	11.76	29.10	54.0
1836	59.23	1.74	8.42	23.08	5.06	28.14	29.9
1837	57.39	1.21	2.64	11.45	2.33	13.78	19.1
1838	45.26	0.87	3.77	6.77	2.62	9.39	40.2
1839	41.62	1.79	4.15	5.98	6.78	12.76	32.5
1840	36.84	1.38	1.47	6.70	3.34	10.04	14.6

Source: *Historical Statistics,* Series N, p. 261.
[a] Circulation is the sum of the bank's own notes in circulation.
[b] Deposits are the sum of both private and government deposits.
[c] The reserve ratios given are computed by dividing the sum of circulation and deposits into specie.

tender only for payments to and by the government. But in practice, all private households and businesses would accept without hesitation anything that the government issued and had to accept, and that its creditors had to accept.

Emergence of the Second Bank as a Central Bank

The Second Bank, by virtue of its most-favored position in the financial fabric, could discreetly assume certain central-banking functions. It was a public bank, and it was also a commercial bank. It had financial ties with the state banks, both because of its own commercial nature and because it was *the* government depository. Its only constraint, self-imposed, was maintenance of a reserve ratio slightly greater than that deemed sound for ordinary commercial banks. One would have to be either obtuse or modest in the assumption of power not to recognize and cultivate the central-banking potential of such an institution, even if such power was ultimately subordinate to the discipline of a specie standard. Langdon Cheves was probably not obtuse, but he probably was unassuming. Nicholas Biddle was neither. He soon recognized the bank's forceful position; but the argument that he came to the presidency with such a preconception is untenable.[7] Undoubtedly he cultivated central-banking ideas and policies in the later 1820s, but they were a pragmatic realization of the bank's circumstantial role in the financial structure and not the result of a previously determined central-banking philosophy. Hammond quotes Albert Gallatin's remark in 1831 that the bank "operates as a screw" and "was for that very purpose . . . established";[8] but this role for the bank was wishful thinking and historically inaccurate. Not only was it absent from the charters of the First and Second Banks, but no one even imagined it for them—particularly secretaries of the Treasury, including Gallatin—before about 1828.

The report of the secretary of the Treasury for 1828, however, expresses lengthy approbation over the operations of the Second Bank. The bank and the John Quincy Adams administration were, to use a contemporary expression, in accord; and Richard Rush, Adams's secretary of the Treasury, praised the bank highly. He cited first the bank's utility as a helpmate to the Treasury: "This capacity in the treasury to apply the public funds at the proper moment, in every part of a country of such wide extent has been essentially augmented by the Bank of the United States." It aided in the collection of public moneys, and in so doing,

> it receives the paper of the State banks paid on public account, . . . and, by placing it to the credit of the United States as cash, renders it available wherever the public service may require. By this course, a course not enjoined by its charter, it widens the field of business and its usefulness to the State Banks. [It also secures stability of property to the community] . . . by confining within prudent limits its issue of paper. . . . Sometimes (judiciously varying its course) it enlarges its issues to relieve scarcity, as under the disastrous speculations of 1825.[9]

The state banks had also behaved themselves, thus demonstrating that "a national bank is the instrument alone by which Congress can effectively regulate the currency of the nation."[10]

This report reveals several beliefs that Rush held. First, he saw the Second Bank not only as a public bank and as a commercial bank but also as a central bank. Second, while he thought its policies beneficial to the financial system, he acknowledged that its charter had not included any provisions for regulating the currency. This sequence of ideas is surely ex post facto justification of an institution that seemed to work. But it also indicates that the central-banking concept had emerged—a genesis resulting from the strategic position of the bank in the monetary system and from the entrepreneurship of Nicholas Biddle.

In an unpublished manuscript, Jacob Meerman concluded that Biddle "developed a system of control over the state banks, a system of keeping them within their means," and that this control was his own innovation. Meerman cites Biddle's prediction that if the Second Bank withdrew its control, within three months "there [would] be no general specie payments throughout the union."[11] Time proved this claim false, but it emphasizes the importance Biddle attached to his own central-banking operations.

The alleged necessity for some agency such as the Second Bank to contain state bank credit was part of the myth that state bank credit had expanded capriciously during the War of 1812, an expansion that actually resulted from government issues of treasury notes. As long as the state banks had to obey the requisites of specie convertibility, they could not overexpand to any great extent. Too zealous an extension of credit would lead to exports of specie and in turn to an intense reappraisal of bank portfolios by commercial bank managers. Retrenchment and contraction of loans and discounts would stop the specie losses.

This typical money-market picture suggests some practical questions. First, would the ordinary commercial banker realize soon enough the boundaries of credit expansion he might safely approach in his desire to maximize returns? If not, he would very soon be an ex-banker. Still, why not have a central bank working within the confines of the specie standard to limit commercial bank expansion before specie reserves became too fragile to support the expanding volume of bank credit? Such an arrangement might well be an improvement; but it might also be disastrous if the central banker, whose judgment determined tightness and ease of bank credit, made a mistake.[12] It might also encourage bankers to take unusual risks if they felt certain that the central bank would unreservedly support them. To some extent, these undesirable effects could be avoided by congressional prescription for the central bank; but Congress has ever been reluctant to give such direction, and central bankers have long discouraged it.

The Second Bank under Biddle's presidency, Hammond wrote, undertook policies "with a consciousness of quasi-governmental responsibility and of the need to subordinate profit and private interest to that responsibility." Biddle's primary signal for action was the state of the foreign exchanges. A tendency for the exchanges to fall against the United States saw the bank redeem more state bank notes and deposits for specie, and reduce its own discounts. In addition, the bank would counter the effects of an adverse trade balance by means of its open credits with Baring Brothers, its London correspondent, "allowing banks time to diminish their issues without ruin to their customers."[13]

All these accounts of Biddle's countercyclical policies emphasize again the primacy of the metallic standard in determining the stock of money. Biddle and the Second Bank simply facilitated the process of change by a timely awareness and evaluation of the foreign exchanges. Perhaps they kept the changes less radical than they otherwise might have been, but they could not (and did not try to) thwart the effects of a specie-standard adjustment as central banks came to do in the twentieth century. The analogy of the Second Bank as a balance wheel is faulty; it was more a shock absorber when it operated according to the Biddle blueprint.[14]

The bank was also the fiscal agent for the Treasury, a function consistent with the notion of a public or national bank. Such a duty was legitimate for such a public institution, although one that a mere administrative extension of the Treasury itself could have accommodated.[15] Its fiscal role, however, gave the bank an entrée to monetary policy, as Henry Clay had earlier observed. If the bank was collecting money for the Treasury, it was a depository for the money; and if it was a depository, it had sizable amounts of money in it and flowing through it; and if it had all that money within its reach, it had every opportunity under the "right" kind of leadership to manipulate that stock in ways both good and evil. Under Nicholas Biddle the ways were mostly good, even though limited by meeting specie requirements. But as Clay had concluded with respect to the First Bank, Congress had not delegated to it the power to intervene in the money market whether for good or for evil.

The Second Bank Investigated by a Congressional Committee

With the election of Andrew Jackson as president of the United States in 1828, the bank's continued existence became questionable. Rush's extensive and favorable report on the bank in December 1828 was no doubt inspired by Jackson's election in November.[16] Knowing he was part of a lame-duck administration, Rush wished to offer some favorable testimony for the institution while he still had the chance.

The bank had been in existence for twelve years and therefore had eight years left to operate on its current charter. In his inaugural message in 1829 Jackson gave the first implication of trouble by stating that the question of recharter should be considered soon, since the constitutionality of the bank and its utility in providing a uniform and sound currency were "well questioned by a large portion of our fellow citizens."[17]

The president's charges were referred to congressional committees for investigation and report. The House Committee on Ways and Means, to whom this duty fell, analyzed and discussed at length the issues Jackson had raised. In so doing, it revealed the quality of central banking at that time and the extent to which the central-banking concept had developed.[18]

The particular questions the committee faced were: (1) Has Congress the constitutional power to incorporate such a bank? (2) Is it expedient to establish and maintain such an institution? (3) Is it expedient to establish an alternative national bank, founded on the credit and revenues of the federal government—that is, a government-owned and -operated agency?

The probank majority of the committee, headed by George McDuffie of South Carolina, stated that the constitutionality of the bank was in accordance with the grant of power to Congress "to coin money and regulate the value thereof." The word *coin,* they argued, did not refer only to metallic money, because the term was synonymous at the writing of the Constitution with the word *currency:* "It was then generally believed that bank notes could only be maintained in circulation by being true representatives of the precious metals. The word 'coin,' therefore, must be regarded as a particular term, standing as the representative of a general idea." Congress's power to regulate the value of money, they continued, was in the same clause as its power to specify uniform weights and measures. "The one was designed to ensure a uniform measure of value, as the other was designed to ensure a uniform measure of quantity."[19]

The forty-three or so years that had passed since the Founders had constructed the Constitution may have allowed this interpretation to slip in. However, the "coin money" clause, as the Founding Fathers had used it, did not apply to stabilizing the purchasing-power value of paper money, whether paper money was anticipated or not. It pertained solely to specifying the metallic contents of gold and silver coins. These values were analogous to the system of weights and measures that appeared in the same sentence. Despite the desirability of a unit of money of constant purchasing power, inclusion of the "coin money" clause rested on an even more compelling tenet: prevention of any constitutionally limited sovereign, such as Congress or the Executive, from tampering with the monetary system, whether the sovereign's intentions were for the general good or for personal plunder.

Supporters had found the authorization for the First Bank in the provision allowing Congress to levy and collect taxes, a duty for which the First Bank became an auxiliary. By 1830 the primary function of the Second Bank had shifted to monitoring the banking system and regulating the value of money. The committee felt no embarrassment in this convenient and opportunistic shift of principles for justifying the existence of the bank.

The majority, moreover, had a sophisticated approach to the value of money. They did not say that it was a specified weight of some precious metal; they had already disallowed this too-literal definition by their generic interpretation of the word *coin*. In discussing the inflation of 1815–1817, they stated: "No proposition is better established than that the value of money, whether it consists of specie or paper, is depreciated in exact proportion to the increase in its quantity, in any given state of the demand for it. . . . A rise in the price of commodities [equals] depreciation in the value of money." And money, they concluded in their summary of theory, "is nothing more nor less than the measure by which the relative value of all articles of merchandise is ascertained." John Stuart Mill did not state the case much differently or much better in his *Principles,* published eighteen years later.[20]

The question of a metallic versus a mixed currency was precluded, they argued, "by the existing state of things"—that is, by the fact that the currency was mixed. The practical normative issue was between a paper currency of uniform value and a paper currency subject to a fluctuating value. The Second Bank, they suggested, was admirably equipped to provide the former alternative and had been doing so.[21] In fact, by saving the cost of transporting as much specie as would have been necessary without it, the bank "*has actually furnished a circulating medium more uniform than specie.*"[22]

Neither this committee nor any other defined a uniform currency. Two interpretations are possible. First, the currency could be uniform in size, shape, and value, and redeemable at par "in every part of the Union," meaning redeemable in specie at the mint price at any location. The Second Bank in exchanging its own notes at par tended to promote this kind of uniformity. To the extent that it did, it subsidized the collection and clearing of notes and deposits. Although it may not have charged explicitly for this service, the costs of clearing were real and had to be borne by some part of the bank's operations. Private bill brokers performed this function at an explicit cost and brought Shylock calumnies on themselves. Naturally, public sentiment would favor an institution that did it "without cost," even though the costs were hidden in general expenses.

Second, the currency could be uniform in purchasing power over time, regardless of its exchange value from place to place at any given time. The majority, recognizing the merit of such a characteristic, implied that the bank had been instrumental in furthering it.

This second notion, however, exaggerated the scope of the bank's operations. The bank could have significant short-run effects, but it could not counteract flows of specie for more than a limited time. Its own gold reserves would determine just how long that time would be, and many of the bank's policies had been simply to anticipate specie flows and provide for them as comfortably as possible.

The last part of the majority report raised the issue of control by a central bank. It even used the term *central bank,* but conceived of it as a completely government-owned and -operated institution, in contrast to the hybrid commercial-national bank with branches then under consideration. "A great central bank established at the seat of the Government without branches" would provide a uniform currency, they argued, but "the promise to pay specie for its notes would almost be purely nominal." Their opinion was that the notes would circulate so far from the "seat of the Government" that they would never be redeemed but would continue to be exchanged indefinitely. They did not find such a currency illegal; however, "the notes of a central Government bank . . . would be subject to depreciation from a cause which constitutes a conclusive objection to such an institution. *There would be nothing to limit excessive issues, but the discretion and prudence of the Government or of the direction*." The implication was that government prudence and discretion would be neither prudent nor discreet. Political considerations would rule in locating branches; and patronage powers would promote evil, especially since the central bank would be a bank of discount and deposit, with the government a "great money lender."[23]

The Bank of the United States, by contrast, was a superior organization to the "central Government bank" or to a treasury department because all relations between the bank and the government "are fixed by the law, and nothing is left to arbitrary discretion." It was, primarily, a privately owned company. Even so, "the interest of stockholders . . . is quite a subordinate consideration. The maintenance of a uniform currency, and the facilities afforded for collection, transferring, and disbursing the public revenue, are the great and paramount objects to be accomplished by such an institution."[24]

The Second Bank's charter from the federal government gave it license to act as a commercial bank and to assist in the fiscal affairs of the government. In these respects "nothing was left to arbitrary discretion." But the maintenance of a sound and uniform currency, however defined, was not prescribed by any statute and, to the extent that it was practicable under a specie standard, was left very much to the discretion of the bank's executive. The majority of the committee had spelled out some of the characteristics that describe a central bank and had argued convincingly that the Second Bank fit the mold. They had only *alleged* that the law chartering the bank had provided a pattern for such powers. They now had to recommend that the new charter fit the structure that had emerged. Intuitively they sensed this disparity—this lack of congruity between the role the bank had been born to and the regulatory function it had assumed. Their conclusions were accordingly subdued. They did not recommend centralized discretionary control over the money market, the exchanges, the commercial banking system, or any other areas peculiar and unique to central banking. They saw the bank furnishing a uniform paper currency and assisting the Treasury; but these tasks were incidental to the principal central-banking function of regulating the money supply and could have been performed by a number of institutions. Probably McDuffie and the other members of the majority sensed that a bank bill embodying too many overt central-banking features would have no chance of getting past Jackson, nor of getting the two-thirds vote in Congress necessary to override a presidential veto.

The minority portion of the same committee consisted of two members, Mark Alexander of Virginia and Naithan Gaiter of Kentucky. They faced the central-banking operations of the Second Bank and objected. The bank, they said, "cannot be necessary . . . to regulate trade and commerce, which if left to individual enterprise, will regulate itself without such agency, under the rules which have been prescribed by law."[25] The minority did not allow the majority opinion on the constitutional license for the bank to slip by without comment. The bank, they argued, could not have been formed under the clause that gave Congress power to coin money and regulate its value because this provision applied to metallic money. Even if the states were authorized to establish banks that subsequently issued unsound currency, "it does not follow," they argued," that you have the right to control them, by substituting the same currency [of a Bank of the United States], which is liable to the same consequences. . . . It is not the *paper currency* which Congress is entrusted with the power of regulating."[26]

The minority also correctly criticized the inconsistency between the two constitutional points on which proponents had based their arguments for the First and Second Banks. They cited Henry Clay's caustic statement on the constitutional rationale for the bank in 1811: "This vagrant power to erect a bank . . . has at length been located by the gentleman from Georgia [Mr. Crawford] on that provision to lay and collect taxes."[27] This accurate criticism again emphasizes that the central-banking function was not included in the original charters of the two banks. The convenient shift to "coin money and regulate the value thereof" from "lay and collect taxes" was ex post facto acknowledgment that monetary regulation had not been born but had been made.

Many of their other arguments had merit. They denied that the Second Bank had been instrumental in restoring the currency to specie convertibility after the War of 1812. The secretary of the Treasury had been instructed at the time by both houses of Congress not to receive any notes except those of specie-paying banks. And it was the Treasury, they continued, that brought about the desired result before the Second Bank was in operation. The secretary, by accepting convertible notes and refusing inconvertible ones, "could prove as salutary a check against excessive issues as any supposed agency of the bank, and is the only rightful control which the Government should exercise over such local institutions of the States." Only the limited legal tender status given to the notes of the Bank of the United States, they correctly pointed out, gave the notes their nearly universal acceptability.[28]

The Second Inquiry by a Congressional Committee

As the bill to recharter the Second Bank became current in early 1832, yet another committee was formed to respond to Jackson's later allegation that the bank had violated provisions of its charter. This time antibank forces had a majority on the seven-man committee. Its chairman was Augustin Clayton of

Georgia. George McDuffie, chairman of the former committee, was a member of the probank minority, as was John Quincy Adams. The committee was formed in the middle of March 1832 and was supposed to report its findings by the end of April, six weeks later.[29]

The antibank majority report is notable for its damnation by allegation and innuendo. It criticized the open-market sales of government securities conducted by the bank in 1825, but only on the grounds that the government might better have realized the profits itself. More significant, in the committee's opinion, was the bank's action in the business depression that developed in late 1831. At the same time that the bank let its specie be drained off, it increased its note and deposit obligations. The majority of the committee criticized this true central-banking operation on the grounds that the additional issues of notes caused specie to flow out of the country to Europe, "and but for a decline in the price of specie in Europe, it would still continue to be exported. . . . No measure can be invented to restore a sound currency," the majority concluded, "but a withdrawal of a large portion of notes in circulation, by the Bank, which will compel other banks to do the same."[30] They recognized that the bank was ultimately unable to stop specie outflows and that its note issues actually provoked such outflows. The committee prescribed that the bank contract its loans and notes so that its specie balance would accumulate. They did not indicate whether they realized the hardship this policy would impose on the economy.

The probank minority of the investigating committee excused the Second Bank's open-market sales in 1825 as a defensive measure that protected the reserves of the bank. They argued further that the bank in protecting itself from "the extraordinary pressure upon the money market . . . averted from this country the calamity of a general failure of the banks."[31] This argument again suggests a public bank rather than a central bank. The bank sold its securities in order to protect itself; as a central bank it would have bought securities to enhance the reserves of the other banks, thus parlaying its excess specie reserves as effectively as possible among the satellite banks. The bank's policy in 1825, except for its correct anticipation of a shift in the balance of payments, hardly rates as a central-banking operation as that term is generally understood today.

The minority report also pointed out that the bank's discounts had remained stable from 1829 to 1831, so the unfavorable balance of trade that developed had its causes in the internal economies of European export countries. The bank had subsequently extended its discounts "to relieve the community from the temporary pressure to which it was thus exposed."[32] Clearly the bank did act as a central bank at this point, and its balance sheet substantiates such an inference (see table 3.2). Not only did it expand loans, notes, and deposits while reserves fell, but it practiced forbearance in presenting notes of other banks for redemption.

TABLE 3.2 Principal items in the balance sheet of the Bank of the United States (millions of dollars)

Date	Specie	Notes of other banks	Loans	Circulation (notes out)	Deposit
Sept. 1, 1831	11.55	2.08	35.81	22.40	15.88
April 1, 1832	6.80	2.84	42.12	23.72	17.06

Source: U.S. Congress, 22d Cong., 1st sess., Reports of Committees, House Report No. 460, pp. 330–31.

The minority upbraided the majority's inconsistency for complaining that the bank was too ready to grant discounts and at the same time too stingy in extending credit. "The very complaint urged by [the majority] of the committee against the bank is, that it has been too liberal in its discounts; . . . and yet it is here set down as a subject of lamentation, that the bank is not able to *extend* this relief still further!"[33]

The bank clearly acted like a central bank in 1831. The majority of the investigating committee at times saw it as such and at other times thought of it as nothing more than a corporation receiving unwarranted favors. In either case it condemned the bank, and the impression from the report is that the decision to find the bank guilty was prejudged.

The minority report was much more sophisticated and incisive, not to say objective. Similar to the McDuffie report of two years earlier, it emphasized the regulatory and benevolent power of the bank in guiding the monetary system. Despite its more objective investigation of the facts and its considerate analysis of testimony, it was in the predicament of having to support the central-banking activities of the bank by referring to "provisions" of the charter that were not there. The probank report continually alleged that they were there, just as Nicholas Biddle had done in his testimony. They had to admit as well that the bank had power; and power was hard to defend, especially when it was not circumscribed by rules. "Power for good," wrote John Quincy Adams in his part of the report, "is power for evil, even in the hands of Omnipotence." In discussing bank policy when overtrading took place, he remarked that "it was difficult to determine" the means and ends of policy; and "the soundest discretion may come to different results in different men." Put these judgments together, and the neophytic central bank and its director come out as potentially authoritarian and despotic. Never mind that the policies of the despot were benevolent; with such unbridled power, probabilities were not certainties that benevolent results would continue. Coincidentally, and as if to confirm the worst possible fears of the bank's enemies, Biddle blandly stated, "There are very few banks which might not have been destroyed by an exertion of the [Second] bank."[34] He meant only that the bank had been supportive, but his antagonists heard only "destroyed."

Biddle's Case before the Congressional Investigating Committee

Biddle had his opportunity to defend the bank when the majority of the committee presented him with a volume of complicated and detailed questions meant to embarrass him by their implications and ambiguities. The questions were conceived by Churchill C. Cambreleng of New York, a leading Jacksonian and antibank man, and they amounted to a comprehensive examination on central-bank policy. Since the majority had already indicted Biddle, they did not wait for his answers but turned in their report. They concluded meanly that Biddle had "not been able, from the press of his other indispensable duties, to answer" their questions.[35] The probank minority, however, delayed its report long enough to allow Biddle to respond.

Biddle's answers to Cambreleng's questions were sophisticated and polished, but by no means internally consistent. He underplayed the extent of bank policy—for example, its action during 1831–32. The attitude of the bank then, he said, was "to deal with the utmost gentleness to the commercial community, . . . to stand quietly by, and assist, if necessary, the operations of nature, and the laws of trade, which can always correct their own transient excesses."[36]

This passage suggests deference and restraint. In the next paragraph, however, the tone of Biddle's remarks implies an exertion of power, a power legally vested in the bank. In assuming the role of a central bank, he said, "the bank deemed itself only acting as it was designed to act by the Congress which created it, and [only] placing itself in its true national attitude to the Government and the country."[37] Like others before and since who have argued that Congress provided the two Banks of the United States with such powers, Biddle cited no evidence to show that the allegation was well founded.

The bank in Biddle's opinion was in little danger of overissuing paper currency. The issue of new currency was beneficial if the "trade and business of the country require it"; and "if they do not require it, the evil will soon correct itself, because [the new money] will be converted into coin." While discussing the demand for and supply of money, he repeated that he saw "no connection whatever between the bank and the demand for money, except that the bank has supplied the demand. . . . Now, if there was a demand for money, and the bank had the means for supplying it, why should it not? The object of its creation was precisely that. . . . It seems a singular objection to a bank, that, finding a demand for money, and having the means of supplying it, it did supply it."[38]

Whatever Biddle and the probank supporters claimed, the bank was not created to supply money as a *policy* matter; if anything, it was created to maintain the market for government securities. Especially revealing in this passage is the use of "a" in front of "bank." A commercial bank might well furnish money "when there was a demand for it"; a central bank might do just the reverse in order to moderate a developing boom in business activity. The commercial bank/central bank roles that the bank had come to play were again muddled, and the hybrid nature of the institution was underscored.

Biddle's answers to the questioned relationship between the United States Bank and the state banks were ambiguous. Does not an increase in Bank of the United States notes increase local currency? was one question. No, he answered. Circulation of the bank "supersedes, in many cases, the local circulation, as it was designed to do, and no inference can be drawn" on what the net effects might be.[39]

This question and the frank answer to it could not make many friends for the bank. The antibank forces had already shown that the bank was not so designed. And if bank currency superseded local currency, was not the bank a potential engine of inflation and with unbounded powers? Was it not squeezing out the local banks? The antibank faction clearly thought so.

"Does not a national bank . . . excite overtrading among local banks as well as among merchants?" was another question. "Not necessarily," answered Biddle. "Its natural tendency would be to control them, and thus prevent, rather than excite excessive issues." His general theme was to cast the bank as a stern but gentle shepherd: The Bank of the United States did not "encroach on [the state banks'] freedom." It only kept them strictly responsible for their issues. It was "the enemy of none, but the common friend of all."[40]

Jackson's Veto of the Recharter Bill

The House passed the bill to recharter the Second Bank in the early summer of 1832 by a vote of 107 to 85, and the Senate by 28 to 20. Jackson vetoed the bill on 11 July and returned it to the Senate with his objections.

His arguments for vetoing the bill hinged on three factors: First, the unrestrained power of the bank: "The President of the Bank," his veto message read, "has told us that most of the State banks exist by its forbearance."[41] Second, the bank's constitutionality with respect to the "necessary and proper" power of Congress in carrying out governmental functions: "The public debt . . . has been nearly paid off." Therefore the greater capital of the Second Bank (as compared to the First Bank) was not *necessary.* It could exist only "for private purposes [profits]," in which case governmental sponsorship was improper. Third, a denial that Congress had the right to delegate its powers: "It is maintained by some that the bank is a means of executing the constitutional power 'to coin money and regulate the value thereof.'" But the mint was the institution that coined money, and "Congress . . . passed laws to regulate the value thereof." In any event, this power could not be delegated; "it was conferred to be exercised by [Congress], and not to be transferred to a corporation."[42] This state of things, Jackson decided, was unconstitutional and not to be prolonged. On this case he registered his veto.

In all fairness it is not a bad case; indeed, it is a very good one. The bank had extended its powers without license; it did not operate within Congress's original design; and its activities were not sanctioned by congressional statute. It may have operated benignly in the past, but it would not necessarily do so in the future. Its only constraint was the necessity of converting its demand obligations into specie when requested to do so—the same limitation any other bank faced. While an ultimate obligation, such a constraint still permitted variable amounts of discretionary monetary policy that could have extended the scope of the bank's operations to the point where it usurped the functions of the gold standard.

4 Decline of the Second Bank and Rise of the Treasury

When you give power to a Secretary of the Treasury (we know of what stuff they are made of) [*sic*] to transfer at pleasure the deposits of the revenue to such banks as may court his favor, you are adding to the President of the United States, whose creature he is, and that by the legislation of this House, a most tremendous and gigantic power.

William F. Gordon, House of Representatives, 10 February 1835

Political Conflict over the Second Bank of the United States

One of the major issues in the 1832 election between the federalist Whig Henry Clay and the agrarian Democrat Andrew Jackson was the rechartering of the Second Bank of the United States. Jackson's victory was considered a vote of confidence on his veto of the bank bill. Other evidence suggests that this conclusion is unwarranted. Several issues besides rechartering were of major importance—internal improvements of roads and canals and the tariff, to mention just two. Jackson's personal charm and his glamorous military career also enhanced his power to get votes. Finally, if the bank issue had been at the root of Jackson's victory, the complexion of Congress would have changed to suit the same consensus. But Congress did not change appreciably; the majorities in favor of the Second Bank in 1832 remained majorities in the next session.

During the early years of the campaign against the bank, Jackson's secretary of the Treasury, Louis McLane, joined with a few other administration confidants in tactful but unsuccessful attempts to persuade Jackson that a national bank would be desirable.[1] After his election and second inauguration Jackson and his antibank lieutenants felt that some overt act of hostility to the bank was called for. The tactic they chose was to remove the government's deposits from the Second Bank and its branches. Secretary McLane, within whose office any such action had to originate, resisted. Jackson thereupon shuffled his cabinet, switching McLane to secretary of state and bringing in a relatively unknown newcomer, William J. Duane, as secretary of the Treasury. Duane was neither a legislator nor a jurist. His only previous experience in public office had been in the Pennsylvania House of Representatives; but he was known to be antibank, and he had an aura of respectability that Jackson may have needed to give a less buccaneering tone to his administration.[2]

Duane proved to be opposed to all banks, not just the Bank of the United States. He refused to order the removal of the deposits when given this directive by Jackson, because he felt that the government's deposits were safer in the Second Bank than in state banks of questionable status.[3] He was summarily dismissed for his obstinacy. Jackson then appointed Roger B. Taney as secretary in September 1833, and had him affix his signature to a predated order for the removal of the deposits.[4]

Taney defended this action in a letter to the House of Representatives. According to the charter of the Second Bank, he wrote, the public deposits were to be kept in the Second Bank "unless otherwise directed by the Secretary." He noted that Secretary of the Treasury Crawford had mentioned this same provision in a letter to the president of the Mechanics' Bank of New York in 1817. In that letter Crawford had stated that the secretary "will always be disposed to support the credit of the State banks, and will invariably direct transfers from the deposits of the public money in aid of their legitimate exertions to maintain their credit."[5]

When Congress resumed after this incident, an unprecedented uproar began. The Whigs were especially critical. They held that the secretary's duty to report to Congress, particularly when a movement of the public funds was involved, implied that Congress could judge and even overrule such action.[6] The removal of the deposits had not only denied this control to Congress, but had seemingly opened up unlimited discretionary power for the use of the executive branch in the future. Senator Samuel Southard voiced the sentiment of the majority when he noted that the secretary might decide at his pleasure which state banks should be depositories, when transfers from bank to bank should take place, and what security, if any, should be required of the banks. "All this he may do for causes entirely unconnected with the business of the Treasury, and in no way concerning the public interest. . . . This state of things is prescribed by his discretion. And the man who presumes thus to act tells Congress that his acts are under the control of the President. . . . If there has been a larger or more dangerous stretch of executive power and influence, I have not discovered it."[7]

Most of the critics of Jacksonian policy, and they were a majority in Congress, wanted the Second Bank to continue because it had been acting as a central bank as well as a fiscal agent to the government. At issue were the powers that Jackson and his close advisers had seemingly usurped for the executive branch. The Treasury Department was the focal point of this conflict.

Henry Clay, Jackson's presidential opponent, was the major spokesman for the Whig view. Clay, who had been so outraged and critical of discretionary policy on the part of the First Bank when its charter was up for renewal in 1810, had by this time recanted. As early as 1816 he had dismissed his earlier objections. "War," he had noted, "could not be carried on without the aid of banks." The attempt had resulted in a huge debt and a ruined Treasury.[8] By the 1830s Clay was a key supporter of the Second Bank and made recharter of the bank a major issue in his presidential campaigns.

Clay argued that the duties of the secretary of the Treasury were "altogether financial and administrative. He [the secretary] has no legislative powers; and Congress neither has nor could delegate any to him." Clay did not explain how Congress could delegate such powers to a private, commercial, national bank—the Second Bank of the United States. The report of the Committee on Finance, chaired at this time by Daniel Webster, was equally critical. "It is no part of his [the secretary's] duty," the report stated, "either to contract or expand the circulation of bank paper." A more tolerant view came from Representative Horace Binney, a close friend of Biddle's and an enthusiastic supporter of the Second Bank. Although he held no brief for policy activism in the Treasury Department, he observed: "The direction which is to govern the Secretary is left, by the terms of the act [creating the office], to be settled according to the character of the function to be exercised."[9]

The Jacksonians tried to give the impression that their actions and arguments were simply reflections of a great "popular" movement, but this movement was not mirrored in Congress. Clay's resolutions that Jackson had acted unconstitutionally in removing Duane and that Taney's reasons for the removal of the deposits were unsatisfactory and insufficient passed by an overwhelming majority in the Senate, while similar resolutions lost in the House by only a small margin. Nor did the general public express much antibank sentiment. Countless memorials to Congress from all over the country overwhelmingly "prayed" for the restoration of the deposits and recharter of the Second Bank.[10]

Taney, Senator Thomas Hart Benton, and the other doctrinaire Jacksonians had been quick to condemn the monetary policy activities of the Second Bank, but they soon learned that the fiscal policies of the Treasury could not take place in a monetary vacuum. At first the Jacksonians had argued that the state banks were just as much a menace to the economy as the Second Bank. But the routine fiscal cash flows through the Treasury Department forced the administration to accept and use these banks.

Secretary Taney rationalized toleration of the state banks by arguing that their abolition would seriously interfere with states' rights. He also claimed that banks of credit were relatively innocuous, and that only the suppression of state bank notes was necessary.[11] He did not explain how commercial banks might generate credit without issuing notes.

Taney's official statements showed that he was willing to use his office to promote policy strategies. In his letter to Congress on the removal of the deposits, he said that the safety of the deposits was only "a part of the considerations by which his [the secretary's] judgment must be guided. The general interest and convenience of the people must [also] regulate his conduct." Similarly, his letter of instruction to the state banks selected as depositories urged the banks to be generous with their credit to importers: "The deposits of the public money will enable you to afford increased facilities to commerce, and to extend your accommodation to individuals," he wrote. "And as the duties [tariffs] which are payable to the Government arise from the business and enterprise of the merchants engaged in foreign trade, it is but reasonable that they should be preferred, in the additional accommodation which the public deposits will enable your institution to give."[12]

Devaluation of the Gold Dollar (1834)

The recession developing in the economy in the spring of 1834 was another problem for the Jacksonians. Fortunately for them, one measure could be quickly legislated that had the approval of unbiased authorities and the support of many antiadministration congressmen. It was also compatible with the principle of hard money. This measure was devaluation of the gold dollar, known in the statutes as the Gold Coin Act.

On 15 April 1834, Taney wrote a letter to James Polk, chairman of the House Committee on Ways and Means, in which he gave current administration views toward devaluation: "The first step towards a sound condition of the currency," he wrote, "is to reform the coinage of gold. . . . As this general paper currency [notes of the Bank of the United States] is gradually retiring from circulation the gold should be prepared to take its place." Benton made several speeches to the same effect in the Senate and added that devaluation would end the necessity for *any* paper money. He further noted that four previous secretaries of the Treasury (Gallatin, Dallas, Crawford, and Ingham) had recommended "correction of the error" in fixing the bimetallic ratio at 15 to 1.[13]

Gold at this time was undervalued at the U.S. mint relative to silver. France and other continental countries had ratios of 15.5 to 1, while England was on a monometallic gold standard after 1816. Fixing the U.S. mint ratio at 16 to 1, therefore, would slightly overvalue gold at the mint and undervalue silver. (The current market rate was estimated at 15.625 to 1.) By enhancing the mint value of gold, the new act would consequently align U.S. trade policy most closely with that of England.

The anti-Jackson contingent in Congress had every incentive to go along with the proposal for gold-dollar devaluation. The Whigs were as aware as the Democrats of the developing business recession and had to forget (remember!) politics long enough to pass an antideflationary measure. No one in Congress who approved of increasing the gold-silver value from 15-to–1 to 16-to–1 would have accomplished the change by increasing the silver content of the silver dollar.[14] The measure passed 145 to 36 in the House and 35 to 7 in the Senate. It devalued the gold dollar by 6.6 percent.

From 1 October 1833 to 1 November 1835, net imports of specie to the United States were $27 million.[15] Secretary Taney estimated that $8 million of this amount came in between January and May of 1834.[16] In response to the continuing increase in the stock of specie, the stock of money (currency plus bank deposits) increased by approximately 42 percent between 1834 and 1837, while the price level rose a corresponding 36 percent.[17]

Federal Regulation of the Deposit Banks

Just about the time the Gold Coin Act passed, the Senate refused to confirm Taney's nomination as secretary of the Treasury, thus registering formal disapproval of Jackson's tactic in removing the deposits. In Taney's place, Jackson nominated Levi Woodbury, who was duly confirmed. Woodbury, who had been attorney general, was one of the few cabinet members to have approved the removal of the deposits the previous year. He remained in the office of secretary of the Treasury through Van Buren's administration, then returned to the Senate, and finally became a justice of the Supreme Court.

By the time Woodbury took office only a few doctrinaire hard-money men still talked of a completely metallic currency and abolition of the state banking system. The public deposits were not hard money, and their placement in the state banks required the discretion of the secretary of the Treasury. The power and responsibility of this operation raised misgivings in Congress. John Robertson in the House inquired incredulously: "Who is to conduct all this complex machinery [of deposit banks]. A Secretary of the Treasury: the incumbent of an office filled once in four years; perhaps . . . four times in one year. This officer [is] to become . . . the head of what might be called the confederated banks of North America?"[18] Senator Southard then observed that if the administration did not exterminate the state banks but used them, "either the Government must itself become responsible for these banks, or the banks themselves must become responsible for each other."[19]

All parties agreed that legislation was needed to regulate the deposit banks; and in the session of Congress that opened in December of 1834, the bill appeared that would prescribe rules for their continuing role as government depositories. This bill was especially interesting because it incorporated for the first time in the banking history of the United States a minimum legal reserve requirement against all demand liabilities. Daniel Webster inserted the measure as an amendment. It directed deposit banks to hold at least 20 percent of all deposits and notes in specie. Benton called for even tighter requirements by amending the ratio to 25 percent. His amendment lost by a vote of only 17 to 19, while Webster's original amendment carried 27 to 6. In the House, Horace Binney made the same amendment (20 percent) to the bill as it came out of committee. The House carried the measure by a vote of 109 to 99.[20]

The reserve requirement bill, whether ill-advised as proper commercial bank policy or not, was a sophisticated measure. It was a product of knowledgeable Whig leaders and hard-money Democrats and reflected the general antipathy of Congress to discretionary executive control. Reserve requirements on the deposit banks at this time would have tended to restrain their credit expansion and would have moderated the inflation that took place within the next three years. It also would have enabled the deposit banks to administer the federal government's surplus distribution to the states a few years later with much less disruption to the monetary system than what actually occurred.

A week after the reserve requirement measure had passed both houses, it was brought up for reconsideration in the House of Representatives on the motion of James Polk. He argued that the deposit banks would have to be specie-paying in any case and that the specie reserve requirement therefore was superfluous. Clearing the notes of country banks took so long, he continued, that no bank could meet the requirement if an inordinate demand were put upon it as a transaction agency of the government—as would happen, for instance, in the sales of public lands. He implied that the requirement was a political effort, passed only as a means of sabotaging the new deposit bank system and forcing the revival of a national bank.[21]

Polk succeeded in getting the bill buried for the remainder of the session, but in 1836 it came up again in the Senate with the provisions for the distribution of the government's fiscal surplus tacked on at the end. After much debate—confused and confusing because two bills were now combined into one—Calhoun moved to strike the reserve requirement, arguing that it would operate "oppressively." Many others echoed his sentiments, including Webster, who said that he did not think the provision was of much value and that he had proposed it only to keep specie in the country.[22]

After the Senate agreed to delete the reserve requirement, Senator Silas Wright of New York offered the substitute that finally became section 8 of the distribution bill. It stated that each of the selected depository banks must "keep in its vaults such an amount of specie as shall be required by the Secretary of the Treasury, and shall be in his opinion, necessary to render the said bank a safe depository of the public moneys."[23]

Only Benton resisted. He objected both to the absence of a specific reserve requirement and the discretion left the secretary of the Treasury. Some of the deposit banks were "far in arrear," he observed, and "as a whole, they are far behind the point of specie responsibility at which the Bank of the United States stood at the time of the removal of the deposits."[24]

The action on the specie reserve requirement is strong evidence that Congress was functionally unable to prescribe or to conduct monetary policy. Having initiated legislation for the express purpose of limiting the discretion of the secretary of the Treasury in monetary affairs, Congress terminated action with a bill that made de jure the exact powers it had originally intended to limit! Such a performance argues that the legislature could handle monetary policy only in broad terms and that details of policy had to be left to an administrative agency. The final alternative—letting invisible but powerful market forces regulate monetary necessities—never seemed to get a hearing.

Secretary Woodbury's Policy toward the Deposit Banks

Woodbury's only reference to his new discretionary powers over the specie reserves of the selected depository banks was that measures (unspecified) had been adopted "and recommendations urged, that the specie in the vaults of the selected state banks should be still more increased in comparison with their [note] issues and deposits."[25] In his report for 1836 he said vaguely that the state banks had been selected "according to the discretion of this Department" because they were "regulated in a manner considered most secure to the Treasury and convenient to the community."[26] Notwithstanding his official confidence, the deposit banks were practically unregulated, did not even face state restrictions, and would soon show that the public deposits were not "safe"—that is, redeemable in specie on demand.

Although Woodbury did very little to control the reserves of the deposit banks, he was aware that bank paper was increasing substantially and that bank credit was expanding more rapidly than the large importations of specie. The ratio of specie to paper money had "improved" from one-third to one-half between 1833 and 1835, he said, but had "much deteriorated in the last year and a half [to the end of 1835]. . . . The currency may be considered as too redundant [*sic*], and in an unnatural and inflated condition." Such redundancy, he held, was a result of "numerous incorporations of new banks, without suitable legal restrictions, in many states, on either the amount of discounts or of the paper issued, in proportion to the specie on hand." He recommended that the states repress issues of small notes and restrict paper issues of banks to three times their holdings of specie; but he gave no indication that he could exercise exactly this control over the deposit banks if he chose to do so.[27]

At the same time that he was urging state laws requiring specie reserves against outstanding notes, Woodbury held that the economy needed more specie because specie was a "substitute" for paper. He also saw paper money advantageously "economizing" specie.[28] Obviously he was reasoning tautologically. If the economy "needed" more specie to drive out paper, but then "needed" more paper to economize the use of specie, the result would have been continuous inflation.

Woodbury expressed the narrow but proper view that the power of Congress to coin money and regulate its value "is a power evidently referring to specie and not to paper, as the latter is not coined, nor its value regulated by law." By way of contrast, John C. Calhoun had earlier stated: "Whatever the Government receives and treats as money, is money; and if it be money, then they have under the Constitution the right to regulate it."[29]

Such an interpretation of Congress's monetary power is astonishing, and even more so coming from Calhoun. Nothing in the Constitution states that any governmental relationship to money—either paying it out or taking it in—implies a power of the government to regulate it. The Constitution states that Congress has only the power to regulate the legal tender values of gold and silver, and that no government—state government explicitly, and federal government implicitly—may print paper money. If the government were tendered money, say bank notes that appeared to be unsound, it could refuse them and demand specie just as could any private business. However, the government's right to refuse unsound money did not imply a right to regulate the monetary system. Calhoun's step to a positive regulatory role for Congress and the Second Bank, no matter how well intentioned, was unwarranted; but it was also one that would gain popularity and respectability decade by decade from this point on.

5 The Specie Circular and the Distribution of the Surplus

[The suspension] was the effect of necessity with the deposit banks, exhausted by vain efforts to meet the quarterly deliveries of the forty millions to be deposited with the States.

Thomas Hart Benton, *Thirty Years View*

The Effects of the Specie Circular on Public Land Sales

Congress passed the Act to Regulate the Deposits of Public Money on 23 June 1836 after prolonged debate. The first dozen sections of the act defined the terms on which the deposit ("pet") banks might hold the fiscal balance due the Treasury of the United States,[1] and the last three sections ordered the distribution of the surplus fiscal balances in these banks. The cash balance of the government was already on deposit in the eighty-odd depository banks as a credit to the Treasury; the new statute simply prescribed how these balances should be transferred to the credit of the state governments.[2]

Daniel Webster voiced the majority sentiment of contemporary legislators: "[The public money] is hoarded. It is withdrawn . . . and with great inconvenience and injury to the general business of the country."[3] But his observation contained only specious truth. Far from being locked up and withdrawn, the public money had been deposited in the chosen deposit banks and subjected to the multiplying effect of fractional reserve bank-credit expansion. "Depositing" the money with the states could have had the liberating effect implied by Webster only if the federal government had held a balance of hard cash outside of the banking system.[4]

The bill finally passed both houses of Congress with large majorities and went to Jackson for his signature. Senator Thomas Hart Benton, a presidential intimate and adviser on monetary and banking policies, reported that the president signed the bill "with a repugnance of feeling," primarily because he realized that the popularity of such a measure might facilitate the election of Van Buren in the fall of that year.[5]

Even though he felt compelled to sign a bill he did not want in order to help elect a successor he did want, Jackson found a neutralizing executive order for which he could take personal responsibility, thereby causing no detriment to Van Buren. This order was the Specie Circular. The secretary of the Treasury issued it to the collectors and disbursers of the public money on 11 July 1836, less than three weeks after passage of the Act to Regulate the Deposits of Public Money and, more significant, two weeks after Congress had adjourned. It declared that between 15 August and 15 December 1836, conventional media—i.e., bank notes and deposits—would still be acceptable for purchases of public lands, but only for parcels of 320 acres or less. After 15 December 1836, all purchases of public lands would have to be made with specie.

Secretary of the Treasury Levi Woodbury signed the order, but initiative for the action came from Senator Benton, who had sponsored a very similar bill in the session just ended. He had been the only senator to favor the bill, so congressional dissatisfaction with the measure was abundantly clear.[6]

The Specie Circular was surely intended to operate as a deflationary device to prevent distribution of the surplus, first by reducing the volume of spending on public lands, and second by tending to reduce the amount of treasury balances available for distribution.[7] Simple analysis shows, however, that this dramatic political flourish had negligible economic results.

Sales of public lands during 1836 yielded $25 million, or about one-half of total government receipts (see table 5.1). Even if the Specie Circular had had the absolute effect of reducing sales of public lands to zero, the result on the general economy would have been infinitesimal. Aggregate spending in the economy at the time was about $1,000 million per year.[8] If no public land had been sold between 11 July and the end of 1836, total spending would have declined by a maximum of 1 percent. Since the amount spent on public lands did not fall to zero, the reduction in spending due to the Specie Circular was at most a fraction of 1 percent. People who had only state bank notes and were thus unable to buy land might still have bought other goods and services currently produced. Taken alone, a policy that tended to make the public lands unavailable would have had slightly inflationary effects and would have opposed the principal thrust of Jacksonian policy at that time.[9] Finally, in almost all sections of the country, state bank notes were redeemable in specie on demand for ten months following the issuance of the Specie Circular. General economic effects could hardly have resulted from an alleged cause that included such a lag.

Whether the Specie Circular decelerated total spending and whether it affected the size and location of the federal government's balances are distinct questions. In fact, the deposit balance to the credit of the Treasury in the deposit banks *increased* from $37.28 million to $45.06 million between 1 June 1836 and 1 November 1836, while the specie in these banks increased from $10.45 million to $15.52 million.[10] Secretary Woodbury's report for 1836 stated that weekly selections of new depository banks had been necessary because revenues had "increased over our expenditures so constantly and in such large amounts."[11] The damping effect of the Specie Circular on government receipts, therefore, was also negligible.

The lack of any recurrence of large-scale purchases of public lands after Congress repealed the Specie Circular in the middle of 1838 also attests to the impotence of the measure. Sales of public lands resumed their average level

TABLE 5.1 Land sales in the United States by quarters, 1836–1838 (calendar years, millions of dollars)

Year	Quarter: First	Second	Third	Fourth	Total[a]
1836	6.05	8.42[b]	5.86[b,c]	4.83[c]	25.16
1837	3.40	1.90[d]	0.35	1.13	6.78
1838[e]	0.50	0.50[f]	0.70	2.20	3.90

Source: *Treasury Reports, 1836–1838.*
[a] Total land revenues for 1835 were $14.26 million.
[b] For the second and third quarters of 1836, data were provided by Professor Harry Scheiber.
[c] Specie Circular was issued July 11, 1836, and became effective December 16, 1836.
[d] Banking system suspended specie payments.
[e] Data for 1838 taken from W. B. Smith and Arthur Cole, *Fluctuations in American Business, 1790–1860* (Cambridge, Mass.: Harvard University Press, 1935), p. 712.
[f] Specie payments resumed and Specie Circular repealed.

of $2 million to $3 million per year even though the economy experienced a substantial recovery during fiscal 1838–39.

The changes that occurred in the real prices paid for land readily explain the land boom of the middle 1830s. The nominal price of land was fixed by statute at $1.25 per acre. When the general price level increased, the real price of land declined proportionally and land became a profitable investment for households and firms. Then, as the extensive margin of good land was pushed back—as better land was picked over and acquired—the remaining land was not so economically desirable even at the lower real price, and sales resumed their normal volume. This pattern of behavior is economically rational and does not depend on the existence or nonexistence of a Specie Circular.

Even though the federal government made available much new land (including much supermarginal land) for sale through 1837, it was able to sell unusual amounts only when the real price fell in 1835 and 1836. By 1836 the real price was 25 percent less than in 1834. (See table 5.2.) These data demonstrate the high elasticity of demand for land.

Events Leading to the Surplus Distribution

Although the Specie Circular was of no consequence, the same cannot be said for the distribution of the surplus under the provisions of the Deposit Bank Act. Most descriptions and analyses of the distribution and the consequent panic of 1837 draw heavily from the first documentation on the subject, *The History of the Surplus Revenue of 1837,* by Edward G. Bourne. According to the usual treatment, the orders of the federal government for distributing the surplus among the states caused a flow of funds in opposition to the normal course of trade. Specie allegedly flowed westward to further the sales of pub-

TABLE 5.2 Sales and prices of public lands, 1833–1837

Year	New land offered (millions of acres)	Land sold (millions of acres)	Receipts from land (millions of dollars)	Nominal price per acre ($)	Real price per acre ($)[a]
1833	6.615	3.856	4.972	1.29	1.36
1834	13.057	4.658	6.100	1.31	1.46
1835	13.767	12.564	16.000	1.27	1.27
1836	0.509	20.071	25.168	1.25	1.10
1837	—	4.805	6.127[b]	1.28	1.11

Source: U.S. Congress, 25th Cong., 2d sess., *Sen. Doc. No. 85*, p. 3.

[a] Computed using Warren and Pearson's series for WPI, 1789–1890 (1910–1914 = 100), *Historical Statistics*, p. 115.

[b] To September 30.

lic lands in accordance with the Specie Circular, but was needed in the East in order to provide for the surplus distribution.[12] All the accounts treat the distribution as if an actual transfer of specie caused the general economic collapse of the times. None examined the actual flow of funds to see whether the quantity of specie moved was significant, nor did any investigator include the possibility of bank-credit contraction in general as a primary cause of the panic. The argument developed here is that plenty of specie was available in any section of the country to satisfy the distribution of funds in that section; that the relatively small amount of specie actually withdrawn from the deposit banks initiated a crucial bank-credit contraction; and that the collapse of bank credit was primarily responsible for the panic of 1837.

Many influential men inside and outside government recognized that the distribution involved more than a transfer of specie. Secretary Woodbury reported in December of 1836 that "the utmost care had been exercised . . . to prevent any unnecessary derangement or pressure in the money market, by affording reasonable time for all those transfers [of treasury balances] to be effected."[13] In another part of the same report he registered a less confident attitude: "The embarrassments incident to the transfers of such large sums of money, . . . and the consequent temporary withdrawal of considerable portions of it from immediate use, are embarrassments inseparable from the provisions and faithful execution of the law in its present form."[14] Woodbury sensed that the banking system might lose specie to the various state treasuries when the surplus was distributed; so his "embarrassment" (his key word) was probably well advised.

Many others also registered apprehension. Nicholas Biddle declared that banks had tolerated each other's notes in payments due the government, "and now that government has let loose upon them a demand for specie to the whole amount of these notes."[15]

Henry A. Wise of Virginia, one of the most articulate critics of the government's financial policies, said in the House of Representatives before passage of the Deposit Bank Act that "to touch the surplus would be to lose it in the ruins of the deposit banks." He felt that the surplus would not be distributed, but he reckoned without his more determined colleagues.[16] Senator Benton observed afterward that "the first installment [was] delivered the first of January, in specie or its equivalent; the second in April, also in valid money." But for the third installment, "the federal government could only do as others did, and pay out depreciated paper." The government, he alleged, was "taken by surprise in the deprivation of its revenues."[17]

Woodbury, who had already shown some misgivings, added after the event: "It is not to be expected that several of [the banks] would be able to pay over at once, and in specie, the whole of the large amount then in their possession."[18] If the probability of the payments had been in doubt, Woodbury's failure to impose defensive reserve requirements on the deposit banks when deposits were building up in the latter half of 1836 constituted a major fault in his administration of the Treasury Department.

The Effect of the Surplus Distribution on the Banking System

Previous analyses based on the statistics of the distribution have not sharply distinguished between government deposits in the banks and the specie reserves available to pay such deposits. As tables 5.3 and 5.4 show, the deposit banks had specie reserves of only $15.52 million against government deposits alone of $45.06 million. The specie reserves of the whole banking system, being only $40.02 million, could not have satisfied the government's potential specie demand; and obviously the government would not and did not demand specie for the bulk of the funds it distributed. The data of the distribution suggest that about $5 million of specie was put into transit, and other evidence supports this estimate.

Table 5.5 groups the states into North and East, West, and South, and shows the amounts on deposit in these regions, the amounts due them as a

TABLE 5.3 Specie reserves and demand liabilities of all banks (millions of dollars), and reserve ratios (percent)

Item	Jan. 1, 1836	Jan. 1, 1837	July 1, 1837	Change from Jan. 1, 1836, to July 1, 1837
Specie	40.02	38.71	30.03	− 9.99
Circulation	140.30	151.31	117.76	−22.54
Deposits	115.10	129.66	93.76	−21.34
Total liabilities	255.40	280.97	211.52	−43.88
Reserve ratio	15.67	13.78	14.20	—

Sources: *Treasury Report to Special Session*, 1837, p. 61, and *Treasury Report*, 1837, p. 39.

TABLE 5.4 Specie reserves and demand liabilities of deposit banks (millions of dollars) and reserve ratios (percent)

Item	Nov. 1, 1836	May 1, 1837	Aug. 15, 1837	Change from Nov. 1, 1836, to Aug. 15, 1837
Specie	15.52	13.33	10.53	− 4.94
Circulation	41.48	37.62	32.63	− 8.85
U.S. Treasury	45.06	26.86	12.94	−32.12
Private deposits	26.57	30.78	29.49	+ 2.92
Total liabilities	113.11	95.26	75.15	−38.05
Reserve ratio	13.72	13.99	14.01	—

Sources: *Treasury Report to Special Session,* 1837, p. 61; and *Treasury Report,* 1837, p. 39.

result of the distributional statute, and treasury balances available for satisfying the distribution requirement. If the regional definition is accepted, and assuming that each region took care of itself insofar as it was able, only the South would have required funds from other regions. The Northeast had $8.57 million of government deposits in "surplus" states with which to pay off $1.58 million to "deficit" states; the West had $10.32 million with which to pay off $0.72 million. Even the South required only $1.90 million more than was at the disposition of the Treasury in that region for the distribution, and the total amount that had to be transferred from all surplus states to all deficit states in any case was only $5.58 million.[19]

Such a statistical breakdown denies the East-West funds-in-transit hypothesis. The deposits in both regions were many times the amount necessary for satisfying the demands of those regions. The critical factor was the amount of specie reserves that had been stretched thin in the support of bank credit.

General Bank-Credit Contraction, Suspension, and the Panic of 1837

The analysis that follows rests on the assumption that the Treasury would transfer no specie to a state or even within a state unless the amount due from the distribution was greater than the amount of treasury deposits in the banks of that state. Such an assumption is reasonable and proper. State treasuries, to which the U.S. Treasury sent checks drawn against the deposit banks, would very likely deposit the checks in banks they used for the same purpose. In many cases both state and federal governments would use the same bank. Or if a state government did not employ a depository bank within its boundaries against which the federal government had drawn a check, chances were good that the state government would henceforth keep an account in that bank in

TABLE 5.5 Statistics of Treasury balances in state banks and distributional shares due each state and each region (thousands of dollars)

State	Due from distribution in three installments (1)	Treasury deposits with banks as of Dec. 19, 1836 (2)	Deficit (−) or surplus (+) (2) − (1)
East and North			
Maine	956	508	− 448
New Hampshire	669	632	− 37
Vermont	669	162	− 507
Massachusetts	1,338	2.386	+1,048
Rhode Island	382	350	− 32
Connecticut	765	741	− 24
New York	4,015	11,536	+7,521
New Jersey	765	534	− 231
Pennsylvania	2,868	2,685	− 183
Delaware	287	170	− 117
Totals	12,714	19,704	6,990
South			
Maryland	956	1,225	+ 269
Virginia	2,199	1,239	− 960
North Carolina	1,434	661	− 773
South Carolina	1,051	937	− 114
Georgia	1,051	559	− 492
Alabama	669	1,408	+ 739
Tennessee	1,434	492	− 942
Kentucky	14,34	1,803	+ 369
Totals	10,228	8,324	−1,904
West			
Mississippi	382	1.791	+1,409
Louisiana	478	4,382	+3,904
Ohio	2,077	3,131	+1,054
Indiana	860	2,136	+1,276
Illinois	478	46	− 432
Missouri	382	1,881	+1,499
Arkansas	287	0	− 287
Michigan	287	1,462	+1,175
Totals	5,231	14,819	9,598
Total	28,173	42,857	net 14,684

Source: E. G. Bourne, *The History of the Surplus Revenue of 1837* (New York, 1885), p. 142, with corrections to the arithmetic in the original.

order not to embarrass the bank by a sudden withdrawal of the bank's specie reserves.

A state government that received a check drawn against an out-of-state bank would not be so charitable, especially if the bank was in a distant state. In addition, any state that had no banks, or refrained from using banks as a matter of principle, would likely withdraw the money from the federal depository bank and deposit it as a balance in the state treasury until the legislature distributed the money sometime in the future. Only when state governments withdrew the specie might the depository banks find their liquidity positions precarious, since they held only fractional specie reserves against their notes and deposits.

The absolute loss of $4.94 million of specie from the deposit banks (table 5.4) during the distribution is significant because it is between the $1.90 million the South required on net balance and the $5.58 million estimated as the maximum interstate transfer necessary for carrying out the provisions of the distribution. The specie loss triggered a corresponding contraction of bank credit that was seven times as great. The rest of the banking system also lost specie and correspondingly contracted; but the nondepository banks lost less in absolute terms, even though they held a greater total of specie. Their credit also contracted less than the credit of depository banks relative to the specie reserves lost.

The *Letters on State Deposits* in the National Archives provide the details on the transfer of bank reserves during the three installments of the distribution.[20] Secretary Woodbury sent these letters to the state bank depositories just after 1 November 1836, apprising them of the amounts that would be drawn against the government's accounts. Starting in January 1837, Woodbury sent other letters with warrants for these amounts to the state treasuries. No records exist showing in what form the states cleared the warrants they had against the depository banks; but each state received checks from the Treasury drawn against banks in that state insofar as such coordination was possible. The residual, that part drawn in favor of states *not* from banks in those states and presumably paid in specie, was transferred as indicated in table 5.6. These values show that of more than $18 million distributed to the states in the first *two* installments, only $2.29 million required an interstate transfer.

The New York City depository banks were the ones drawn against most heavily for the whole distribution. These banks saw their treasury deposits fall by $9.90 million between November 1836 and August 1837. At the same time they lost only $2.39 million in specie, which was over half the total amount lost from all depository banks.[21] The fact that this loss was only one-fourth the decrease in their treasury deposits implies that three-fourths of New York City banks' payments to the states were made either in their own notes or in deposit accounts credited to the different states.

Woodbury's reports, both before and after the distribution, suggest the

TABLE 5.6 Interstate transfers ordered by Treasury for first *two* installments of the surplus

Transfer	Amount (millions of dollars)
From Massachusetts (all Boston banks and payable to Maine and New Hampshire)	0.395
From New York (almost all New York City banks and payable to Vermont, New Jersey, North Carolina, Connecticut, and Virginia)	1.431
From Mississippi (from Natchez banks to Arkansas)	0.115
From Indiana (State Bank of Indiana and branches to Illinois and Missouri)	0.351
Total	$2.292

Source: National Archives and Records Service, Record Group no. 56, *Letters on State Deposits,* June 27, 1836, to Sept. 11, 1837 (Washington, D.C.).

same pattern of specie losses and bank-credit transfers. In December 1836 he foresaw the "trouble and embarrassment" of sudden transfers of money in January but anticipated that these effects could be minimized "by combining . . . the transfers ordered by Congress to be soon made from banks having an excess [of treasury deposits] with transfer of that excess to other banks in the States where it was to be paid—and in which last-described banks and States a deficiency existed."[22]

An interesting case that developed during the distribution again demonstrates the validity of the intrastate deposit-distribution hypothesis. Woodbury issued warrants for first installment payments of $225,000 against the Agricultural Bank of Mississippi at Natchez as part of the allotments going to Tennessee and Arkansas. The state government of Tennessee demanded payment in specie, but the Agricultural Bank refused to honor the drafts: It would not or could not pay specie. Woodbury then shifted the payments due Tennessee and Arkansas to banks in Louisville, Cincinnati, New York, and New Orleans and issued warrants for $225,000 against the Agricultural Bank of Natchez for the second and third installments to the state of Mississippi—*because* this bank had not honored the specie request from Tennessee. Obviously, the Mississippi draft did not require specie in order to clear.[23]

Secretary Levi Woodbury's Financial Policy

The financial crisis of 1837 induced President Van Buren to call a special session of Congress in September of that year. In his report to that session Woodbury again confirmed that specie movement had been minimal. "A considerable portion of the money since [the beginning of the suspension]," he admitted, "as well as formerly, paid by the banks on transfers and drafts [for the distribution] has not been demanded nor paid in specie."[24]

The most logical conclusion on the substance of the distribution is that the depository banks and the state treasuries cooperated in great part, but that in cases of interstate demands (particularly against New York banks) the state treasuries required specie and thereby provoked the bank-credit contraction that initiated the crisis of 1837. Once the state treasuries had divested themselves of these funds (one year later), the banks could resume specie payments.[25]

Secretary Woodbury had the deposits in the depository banks as judiciously placed as possible for the expedient transfer of deposits to the state governments. However, his responsibilities under the Deposit Bank Act required more of him. Since he had been given the authority to regulate the reserves in the deposit banks almost six months before the distribution began, he could have specified a specie requirement that would have forced the depository banks to hold extra reserves in anticipation of the distribution. If he had assumed an excess of only $5 million, a reasonable assumption in view of the insights he and others had shown into the forthcoming increased demand for specie, a 20 percent specie reserve requirement would have buffered the depository banks' specie loss from the distribution. The depository banks would have had to restrain note and deposit liabilities to about $77 million instead of letting them expand to $113 million as they did (see table 5.4). Since treasury deposits in the banks increased by $8 million and specie reserves by over $5 million between 1 June and 1 November 1836, increased reserve requirements would have adequately restricted bank-credit expansion and thereby forestalled the subsequent contraction. As the titles to the deposits were transferred to the states, the requirements could have been eased accordingly.

Any such imposition on the banking system at this time would have resulted in protests from the banks and from some legislators.[26] Playing it safe, as Woodbury did, by following the letter of the distribution law absolved him of any responsibility for the collapse that followed. He recognized that the bank failures were serious but reported with "pleasure" that most of the deposit banks had reduced circulation and discounts.[27] In an earlier year he had piously denied that treasury deposits had been moved from one section of the country to another for any but fiscal reasons. At the time he had said that any transfers he had made had tended "to obviate rather than create any pressure in the money market."[28]

The conclusions here are criticisms—substantive and methodological—of what actually happened and of the reasoning usually applied to what actually happened.

First, the Specie Circular was dramatic but inconsequential.

Second, the effect of the distribution was appreciable almost entirely because a small portion of it was a quasi-increase in the demand for specie by the state governments, a demand that had to be fulfilled by an internal specie drain from key metropolitan commercial banks. Since the commercial banking system operated on a fractional reserve basis, a decline of the banks' specie holdings forced a manifold contraction of their demand liabilities, the medium used by the general public for conducting almost all of its purchases and sales.

Third, a nominal but courageous Treasury policy for increased reserve ratios in the deposit banks during the predistribution period would have largely neutralized any specie losses the banks subsequently suffered.

The Effects of Imports and Exports of Specie on the Banking Crisis

The preceding analysis and conclusions deny that the Specie Circular had any fundamental economic effects. Political it may have been; economic it was not.[29]

The distribution of the surplus, on the other hand, had pervasive effects on the banking system and the economy. It distributed titles to bank deposits from United States Treasury offices to state treasuries. It thus transferred discretion over this money to twenty-six state governments. This windfall—a nineteenth-century version of revenue-sharing—required time for its ultimate disbursement. Once the state legislatures had the money, they had to go through the process of administering its disposition. In addition, some state governments demanded redemption of their claims in specie from the federal government's depository banks. The states' small but significant demand for specie from depository banks then provoked a fractional reserve bank-credit contraction of substantial proportions during the first half of 1837.

This view is relatively short-run. It ignores external specie movements for the period under consideration. Redemption of bank obligations in specie meant an increase in the private sector's ratio of specie to bank-created money,[30] while the contraction of bank credit tended to increase the specie-deposit ratio. These two ratio changes occurred during the year in which Congress passed the Distribution Act and in which the banks suspended specie payments and contracted credit.

A study by Peter Temin that focuses more on international specie flows argues persuasively that the "bank war" did not initiate the bank-credit expansion and inflation of 1834–1837. Temin attributes the boom at this time directly to voluminous specie inflows, which he claims were primarily a result of capital exports from England to the United States. This capital flow allowed the United States to keep its specie (silver) in the face of a trade deficit rather than lose it through trade to the Orient. The inflation of the period, Temin concludes, was specie-inspired from this source.[31]

The increases in the specie-currency and specie-deposit ratios in 1837 subsequently caused the money stock to decline. Specie inflows continued but at a rate only half as great as the average for the preceding three years.[32] The rate of increase in specie (that is, in what is now called the monetary base) declined considerably as the two money-determining deposit ratios increased. These changes had predictable effects. The banks' attempts to stay solvent resulted in suspension of specie payments, and they also restricted loans to reduce their demand obligations.

Temin argues that the distribution, "while it posed a burden for the banking system, and while it created much trouble after the suspension of payments, did not cause the suspension."[33] Temin attributes the primary cause of the suspension to the actions of the Bank of England in the summer of 1836, when it raised its discount rate to attract specie and imposed other credit restrictions. These policies had repercussions in the United States on interest rates, on the price of foreign exchange, and eventually on the price of cotton.[34]

A comprehensive table on specie flows for the period appears in Hepburn's *History of Currency* and is summarized here in table 5.7. Temin, apparently unaware that Hepburn had previously compiled these data, re-created them from House Documents on Commerce and Navigation.[35] He also added im-

TABLE 5.7 Net specie flows to (+) or from (−) the United States, 1832–1843, (calendar year, millions of dollars)

Year	Net gold	Net silver	Net domestic coin	Net total
1832	0.1	1.6	−1.4	+0.3
1833	0.1	4.8	−0.4	+4.5
1834	3.5	12.7	−0.4	+15.8
1835	1.7	5.7	−0.7	+6.7
1836	6.9	2.5	−0.3	+9.1
1837	0.5	5.3	−1.3	+4.5
1838	11.0	3.8	−0.5	+14.3
1839	−1.7	0.4	−1.9	−3.2
1840	1.8	1.1	−2.2	+0.7
1841	0.5	−2.7	−2.7	−4.9
1842	−0.3	0.8	−1.2	−0.7
1843	17.1	4.2	−0.1	+21.2

Source: A. Barton Hepburn, *A History of Currency in the United States* (New York: Macmillan Company, 1924), p. 69.

portant details on where the gold and silver came from or went to as it was imported into or exported from the United States. In any event, his figures on net imports and exports are very close to Hepburn's.

Over the six-year period 1833–1838, net silver imports totaled almost $35 million, and net gold imports were approximately $24 million. In no year were there net exports of either metal.

These data leave little doubt that the inflation of the mid–1830s was specie-dominated. Temin's very useful table 3.2 of wholesale prices shows that from April 1834 to November 1836 (two and one-half years) prices rose 35 percent, or approximately 12 percent per annum.[36] The specie inflow therefore started at the same time as the gold-dollar devaluation that Congress debated in mid–1834, and which became law in August of that year.

The gold-dollar devaluation was 6.6 percent. It stimulated net gold imports of $3.5 million in 1834. This amount does not sound very significant; but gold imports in both 1832 and 1833 were almost nothing, and the increase was more than 7 percent of total bank holdings of specie at that time. (See table 5.3.) Furthermore, gold imports continued very high in 1836 and 1838. During the following four years, 1839 through 1842, $8 million of specie went out of the United States, leading to the recession and trough in business activity in 1842.

Since all these events—the gold-dollar devaluation, the issuance of the Specie Circular, the specie inflows, the distribution, the capital inflows from England, and the action by the Bank of England—were closely bunched, assigning primacy of cause and effect is difficult. The fact remains, however, that in the first half of 1837 the banking system lost considerable specie at the same time that specie inflows to the United States were still substantial. Furthermore, specie held by people and state governments outside the banks increased at the expense of bank-held specie. Even if the state governments had simply transferred their claims on the distribution from the federal government's depositories to the institutions they used for the same purposes, the ratio of specie to bank obligations would have increased. The specie-losing banks would have had to contract, and only after a lag would the specie-receiving banks have been able to expand commensurately. Add to this lag the fact that some state governments kept the specie in their own state treasuries until it was distributed within these states, and much of the decline in bank-held specie is explained. The initiating factor could have been the Bank of England's policy in the latter half of 1836; but without the distribution of the surplus as a major aggravating factor, the bank panic and suspension would probably have been nothing more than a gentle decline to the new equilibrium that appeared by mid–1838.

In summary, Temin's account and my earlier analysis agree on two points: the Specie Circular had virtually no economic effects, and the inflation of the era was specie-inspired. In addition, I attribute major importance to the gold-dollar devaluation, to the disequilibrating effect of the distribution on the reserves of the banking system, and to the subsequent bank-credit contraction. Temin largely spurns these last three factors. He argues that the primary causes of specie flows were Bank of England policy, the opium trade with the Orient, and changes affecting the international cotton market.

6 The Independent Treasury System before the Civil War

You propose to enable . . . the Secretary of the Treasury . . . to purchase said stocks at their "market value." . . . Why to purchase it at the market value, you make your Treasury Department a broker! And I shall move that "market value" be stricken out, and "par value" be substituted. . . . There is no reason why this engine of corruption should be placed in the hands of any party, or any officer in any department of the Government.

W. F. Giles, House of Representatives, 21 January 1847

Political Development of the Independent Treasury

Historians have debated whether recovery after the panic of 1837 was genuine or merely a stage in a longer decline to the trough of 1843. Events of 1838 and contemporary opinion on the state of that economy confirm that no downward *trend* was evident at the time. Most states permitted banks a year of grace, either by custom or by law, in which to reestablish specie payments after a suspension; and by May 1838 specie payments were again general and genuine. Specie imports of $14 million to the United States between September 1837 and September 1838 considerably helped resumption and recovery.[1] Congress repealed the unpopular Specie Circular by overwhelming majorities in both houses on 29 May 1838. This action had little effect—it was more of an afterthought—as banks had resumed specie payments several weeks earlier.

In his Treasury report of December 1838, secretary of the Treasury Levi Woodbury exuded optimism over the state of business. The banking system had more specie reserves than it had ever had before, but it had refrained from expanding notes and deposits to their inflated volume of a few years earlier.[2]

During 1839 the prospects for continuing prosperity, which had seemed so bright at the beginning of the year, dimmed. The constant specie imports of the preceding six years gave way to a specie export of $3 million to help finance a trade deficit of $39 million for the year. Prices, which had held steady from the middle of 1837, started to decline about the middle of 1839 and continued falling until 1843, when they reached a trough 30 percent below their 1837–1839 level.[3] Recovery was a mirror image of recession, although business activity did not really become buoyant until after the gold discoveries of 1848–1850. (See table 6.1 for the behavior of money stocks, specie, and prices during this period.)

The institution most prominent in the development of monetary policies during the later thirties and early forties, and for a long time afterward, was

TABLE 6.1 Stock of money, prices, and specie flows, 1833–1860 (all values except prices in millions of dollars)

Year	Beginning-of-year state bank notes and deposits[a]		Specie in banks	Prices (1913 = 100)	Export (−) or import (+) of specie
					(Oct. 1–Sept. 30)
1833	170		25	56	+ 4.5
1834	190		26	57	+15.6
1835	204		44	60	+ 6.7
1836	278		40	68	+ 9.1
1837	288	160[b]	38	72	+ 4.5
1838	201	158	35	71	+13.2
1839	225	176	45	71	− 3.1
1840	183	159	33	60	+ 0.4
1841	172	139	35	60	− 5.0
1842	146	144	28	55	− 0.7
					(Oct. 1–June 30)
1843	115	128	34	51	+20.8
					(July 1–June 30)
1843–44	160	137	50	52	+ 0.4
1845	178	165	44	54	− 4.5
1846	178		44	54	− 0.1
1847	203		42	58	+22.2
1848	198		35	58	− 9.5
1849	232		46	54	+ 1.3
1850	206		44	51	− 2.9
1851	241		45	54	−24.0
1852	284		49	60	−37.1
1853	298			60	−23.3
1854	292		47	64	−34.4
1855	393		59	64	−52.6
1856	377		54	67	−41.5
1857	409		59	68	−56.6
1858	445		58	70	−33.3
1859	341		74	69	−56.5
1860	453		105	63	−58.0
1861	461		84	61	+16.5

Sources: Most of the data in this table for bank notes, deposits, and specie were taken from *Historical Statistics of the United States* (1789–1945) (Washington, D.C.: Department of Commerce, 1949). These values are probably fairly accurate for years after 1845. For years before 1845, the figures compiled by George Macesich, "Monetary Disturbances from 1834–45" (Ph.D. diss., University of Chicago, 1958), are superior.

The price index and the import and export of specie were also taken from *Historical Statistics*. The price index was compiled originally by the Federal Reserve Bank of New York and drew from work done by Alvin H. Hansen.

Note: Due to a change in statistical measurement in 1843, the values for specie import and export begin a quarter of a year before the year indicated, while the other values are as of January 1. After 1843 the specie values lead the other values by six months.

[a] Where there is only one figure for "notes" and "deposits," that figure is from the *Historical Statistics* series.

[b] This column (1837–1845) is from Macesich's data, from "Monetary Disturbances from 1834–45."

the Independent Treasury System. Its emergence was pragmatic and circumstantial; but it initiated many of the monetary policies that became prominent in the twentieth century, including open-market operations in government securities. Advocates and detractors of this system debated most of the controversial issues still current in contemporary policy-making.

Sentiment favoring such a system appeared in Congress as early as 1834, when William F. Gordon of Virginia, an anti-Jackson Democrat, offered the plan. He opposed the increase in power of the executive branch under Jackson and wished "to make those who received the revenue the agents for its custody . . . and also for its disbursement."[4] An independent treasury as Gordon and others envisaged it would replace the "pet bank" system, thereby eliminating the executive prerogative of appointing any private banks as depositories for treasury balances. Ultimately, the Independent Treasury would also become a policy arm of the executive. At this time, however, legislators viewed it as a means of keeping the banking system free of the Treasury's fiscal influence.

Gordon's proposal lost by a vote of 33 to 161 in spite of the support it received from hard-money Democrats such as Senator Thomas Hart Benton and William M. Gouge, an influential Treasury official.[5] In 1835 R. T. Gamble of Georgia made the same proposal, but Congress also rejected his resolution. Congressional sentiment leaned toward a trial for the state bank depository system.

When the state depository banks suspended specie payments in 1837, the doctrinaire group of hard-money men favoring an independent treasury was joined by a second force of disillusioned "pet bank" supporters. This alliance was able to pass the Independent Treasury Act in 1840, and to pass it again in 1846 after the Whigs had made one more attempt to reinstitute a national bank in 1841.[6]

The Independent Treasury in practice did not begin operations precisely upon enactment of a statute; it developed gradually as a result of the difficulty the state bank depository system experienced in conducting the monetary affairs for the government during the later 1830s. When the state bank depositories were paying specie, their notes, specie, and treasury notes were by law all payable and receivable in government transactions. When the state banks were not paying specie, only treasury notes and specie were legally acceptable for transactions with the government. Banks that did not pay specie on demand could not qualify as government depositories. Therefore, while the state bank depository system was operating properly, no immediate depository problems or monetary crises called for a change in that system; and when the state bank system defaulted, the government was practically operating on an independent treasury basis anyway. Only after approximately ten years of this makeshift arrangement did a majority of Congress and a Democratic administration establish the Independent Treasury de jure.

A bill to create an independent treasury again appeared in the special session of Congress in 1837 but was postponed. It came up again in 1838 and was passed in the Senate but rejected in the House. It was introduced yet again in 1840 and passed by decisive margins. Debate over the bill in the House was extensive and became heated. When it finally passed, Caleb Cushing of Massachusetts, an outspoken Whig, moved that the title be changed to "An act to enable the public money to be drawn from the Treasury without appropriations made by law." His reference was to the discretionary power of the secretary, granted by the tenth section of the act, to transfer money from one depository to another. As soon as Cushing had made his motion, "a disordered debate was renewed with tenfold fury, and some members made use of some very hard words, accompanied by violent gesticulation."[7] Lawmakers seem to have taken their responsibilities very seriously in those days.

Whig Attempts to Reincorporate a National Bank

The Whig victory in the general elections of 1840 changed the whole political picture. The Whigs now had their chance to incorporate another national, quasi-central bank. They contended that such an institution might somehow be able to reverse the downward course of business activity. Accordingly, President Harrison scheduled a special session of Congress for the summer of 1841. However, the new president died before he could assume any presidential duties, and Vice President John Tyler took office. Tyler had been a U.S. senator from Virginia when Jackson was president, and the recently appointed secretary of the Treasury, Thomas Ewing of Ohio, had held similar office.

With their majorities in Congress, the Whigs easily repealed the Independent Treasury Act. They next turned their attention to the creation of a fiscal bank, their new name for a third bank of the United States. Henry Clay, the leader in the Senate, asked for a report from the secretary of the Treasury on the feasibility of incorporating a national bank, a report that would presumably include all the qualities that would make a bank bill acceptable to President Tyler.[8] Ewing and the rest of the cabinet had been appointed by Harrison, not Tyler, but no one felt that any incompatibility existed between Tyler and his cabinet; so Congress received Ewing's report as one that essentially met the standards and objectives of the president.

This report stated, among other things, that the fiscal bank should be "so selected or framed as to exert a salutary influence over the business and currency of the country. . . . The active business of the country . . . [is] intimately connected with and dependent upon the financial arrangements of the General Government. If they be wise and beneficient [*sic*], they indirectly, but efficiently, promote those great interests of the people; if constant and uniform in their action, they give to those interests confidence and stability."[9] This statement emphasized three aspects of the Whig monetary program: first, a clear acceptance of a policy-making national bank; second, the liaison of this bank with the federal government's fiscal affairs; and third, an active use of monetary policy to promote general economic stability.[10]

The bill for the Fiscal Bank that Congress reported out called for a reserve requirement of at least 33 percent specie to bills (paper currency) in circulation, and it limited deposits to 175 percent of capital, or to a total of primary deposits plus $20 million.[11] The bill passed by a narrow margin in the Senate, but by a much larger majority in the House, and went to the president on 7 August 1841.

Even though Ewing had worked very hard to get out a bill that, according to Benton, would "avoid the President's objections, and save his consistency—a point upon which he was exceedingly sensitive," Tyler vetoed the bill, much to the surprise of everyone both for and against it.[12] Not suspecting any deviousness, supporters of the bill in the House then revived a dormant currency bill, dressed it up as a "Fiscal Corporation" bill, and rushed it through Congress. The Whig sponsors of the bill made every conciliatory gesture to the president in framing this second bill, but again Tyler vetoed the measure, and the Whigs could not muster nearly enough votes to override his veto.[13]

Senator Benton gave what seems to be the most valid interpretation of Tyler's unseemly actions. According to Benton, a political splinter of the Whig party approached Tyler early in the special session with the idea of forming a third party that would be anti-Clay, anti–national bank, and pro–state's rights. It hoped to draw enough support from the Whigs and Democrats to form a new political majority. By enlisting Tyler as its leader, the new movement would have some initial momentum and prestige. Tyler apparently accepted the scheme.[14]

The orthodox Whigs went to great lengths to conciliate the splinter group, as they did not know that the new party would not allow *any* bank bill to get through. Tyler's ostensible compromise on the Fiscal Corporation bill after the defeat of the Fiscal Bank bill was deceitful. He had to give the appearance of support, but he hoped that enough negative votes would be negotiated in Congress to defeat the bill before it reached him. When the bill passed both houses of Congress, Tyler had to veto it because his veto was, according to Senator Benton, "the edifice of the new party, and the democratic baptismal regeneration of Mr. Tyler himself."[15]

All of Tyler's cabinet except Webster resigned.[16] In his letter of resignation Ewing pointed out that Tyler had asked him to be the agent and negotiator for the bill and that the bill had been "framed and fashioned according to your own suggestions." The veto message, he continued, "attacks in an especial manner the very provisions which were inserted at your request."[17]

Ewing's indictment emphasized Tyler's hypocrisy. Far from promoting the conditions for a viable third party, Tyler's actions only resulted in his repudiation and condemnation by the Whig party. This schism proved crippling to any further Whig legislation—and the first regular session of Congress in Tyler's presidential term was yet to meet! Benton summed up the situation in characteristic hyperbole: "To the Whigs, it was a galling and mortifying desertion, and ruinous besides. A national bank was their life—the vital principle—without which they could not live as a party—the power which was to give them power. . . . To lose it, was to lose the fruits of the election, with the prospect of losing the party itself."[18]

During the next four years, the Tyler administration had to operate as a lame duck; only a handful of Virginians stayed with it. The remainder of the Whigs simply repudiated Tyler and his supporters, so no cooperative program between the party and the administration was possible. Nevertheless, the administration still had to carry out routine operations, and Tyler duly appointed a new cabinet with Walter Forward of Pennsylvania as secretary of the Treasury. Forward had been a member of Congress from 1822 to 1825 and had played an important role in the original formation of the Whig party. As a reward for his services in the campaign of 1840, he had been appointed first comptroller of the currency. He then accepted the secretaryship when Ewing resigned.

Tyler, perhaps in some spirit of reconciliation, suggested yet another fiscal-banking organization in his message to Congress in late 1841, and the Senate Committee on Finance dutifully asked the secretary of the Treasury to submit the draft of a bill for a "Board of Exchequer."

Secretary Forward in his reply to the Senate went even further than had his predecessors in arguing for a policy-making institution. He noted that the question to be considered was whether the "Government shall attempt to supply a sound paper medium for payments to the Treasury, and for the general uses of the people . . . [and whether] it shall attempt to benefit the general business of the community."[19] He argued that the government had the *duty* of furnishing a paper money with a countercyclical bias. A board of exchequer would further such a duty, because it "would furnish [treasury] notes for disbursement and receive them for taxes. With these means, and, by faithful and skillful management, though it might be embarrassed by the prostration of other institutions around it, it would still retain its own credit; and that credit would be a fructifying and vivifying germe [*sic*], amid general blight and barrenness."[20]

Forward's report suggested that the Board would have to exercise some control over the banking system in order to control the stock of money advantageously: "Whenever a bank makes a loan, or a discount, by the issue of its bills, it adds so much to the circulating medium of the country. To such a system there must be some check." He confessed that he was "to some degree uncertain" on just how note issues by the Board should be limited. Nevertheless, he argued, the notes would convert "the most austere . . . duty of the Government, the collection of taxes, into the very means of sustaining the industry . . . by whom taxes are paid."[21]

Although the plan for a board of exchequer showed sophistication in the development of purposive monetary policy, it never came up for consideration in Congress. Benton reported that in the House of Representatives "it died a natural death on the calendar on which it was placed. In the Senate the fate of the measure was still more compendiously decided." The Committee on Finance, "deeming [the bill] unworthy of consideration, through its chairman, Mr. Evans of Maine, prayed to be discharged from the consideration of it, and were so discharged accordingly."[22]

Tyler mentioned the plan again in his message to Congress the following year, but nothing more was done about it. The Whigs in Congress were too disillusioned by Tyler's inconsistencies and political machinations to consider anything except routine legislation. The Democrats subsequently obtained control of Congress in the elections of 1842, thereby ruling out adoption of any Whig financial program.

Treasury Note Issues between 1812 and 1860

Historians have largely neglected these Whig attempts to promote a central-banking institution during their short-lived political dominance during 1840–1842, and they have also paid little attention to the treasury note issues made by both Whig and Democratic administrations. These notes were usually reserved for "emergencies," for example, the War of 1812. For the twenty years following the formation of the Second Bank no fiscal emergencies had occurred, so Congress had had no occasion to authorize issues of notes.

After the distribution of the surplus in 1837, however, the government's primary source of income—tariff revenues—had become significantly smaller due to revised tariff schedules and a decline in trade. Sales of public lands had also fallen off sharply from their peak in 1836. Fiscal deficits again appeared, but they were seen as temporary; so Congress resorted to the expedient of authorizing temporary treasury notes to finance them. These notes had slightly different characteristics from one issue to the next. Usually they were not reissuable, and they drew interest for only one year. But they were a legal tender for all payments due to and from the government, and many of the issues were suitable as bank reserves.

The policy implications of such notes surfaced in the debates over their issue. Henry Clay argued that the measure authorizing the notes in 1837 would turn the government into a bank "with Mr. Woodbury [the current secretary] as the great cashier."[23] In a debate over a similar bill in 1840 Daniel Webster alleged that Woodbury had been depositing the notes in the state banks still used as depositories and checking against the accounts thus created.[24] A deposit implied that the banks and Treasury were willing to treat the notes as primary reserves on which the banks could expand credit. Had the notes been sold in the securities market, the banks would have purchased them as income-earning assets in competition with other financial instruments. In this latter case they would have been conducive to an expansion of credit only if the banking system had acquired them with "excess" reserves.[25] Since the public could deposit the notes in banks, prohibition of similar action by the Treasury was unreasonable no matter how the banks subsequently treated the notes. Nonetheless, Webster's protest stimulated a special inquiry from the Senate to Woodbury asking "whether Treasury notes, bearing interest, have been deposited in banks for the purpose of raising a credit to be drawn against by the Treasury Department."[26]

Woodbury rather evaded the question. The notes, he replied obliquely, had been utilized as a fiscal expedient since 1837. When they could be sold to the banks for specie, the interest rate paid on them was 5 to 6 percent. Otherwise the notes were issued as currency at infinitesimal rates of interest.[27] He pointed out that the Treasury Department had discretion over the rates at which it issued the notes, and that the Treasury had changed the rates from time to time "so as to accommodate the state of the money market and the condition of the currency, as well as to sustain the public credit."[28] He then gave statistics for the issues made during the three years 1837–1839. Of $19.57 million issued, $7.78 million had been either sold or issued to banks as interest-earning assets and $11.79 million had been issued as currency.[29] Interestingly enough, $7.44 million (almost 49 percent) of the three-year total was issued in the second quarter of 1838 just before the resumption of specie payments in May of that year.

Woodbury made available to Congress some correspondence he had had with a Treasury agent in New York in April and May of 1838. The agent, John Barney, wrote that he could not get specie for the notes in New York, but that he was sure he could get $5 million from the Bank of France. Obtaining the specie from abroad, he thought, would "prevent the whole ten millions [of securities] being brought into market here, to absorb all the floating capital [specie], and increase distress." Then on 20 May 1838, Barney wrote that since the new treasury note act would probably pass Congress that day, "there is a constant demand for six percent Treasury notes in exchange for specie, at par."[30] All the notes were subsequently deposited in banks on "special deposit" at 6 percent.

In what regard the banks held the treasury notes and how many of the notes not bearing interest they held as reserves are questions difficult to answer precisely. In an exchange with John Brockenbrough, president of the Bank of Virginia, that took place in early 1839, Woodbury reported that he had offered Brockenbrough some of the current listing of treasury notes at 6 percent with redemption anticipated in about six months. Brockenbrough had replied that his bank could not accept the offer unless the notes could be used if necessary "to meet the reflux of our circulation"—that is, unless the notes could be used as bank reserves. Woodbury said that they could not be so used and would have to be held to maturity, thus indicating that *he* would not sanction deposit of the notes.[31] Woodbury's opinion had no force of law, or even custom, behind it, and the banks did not face legal reserve requirements. So the only question was whether the general public would accept the notes as redemption media for state bank notes and deposits. Since the notes were legal tender for government dues and were generally treated as money, their reserve function was practically established. Of course, the notes issued at nominal interest rates (0.01 percent) served as bank reserves and as hand-to-hand currency without question.

In 1841 several opinions by Whig leaders in the House of Representatives over subsequent treasury note bills focused the Treasury's monetary position even more sharply. Daniel D. Barnard of New York objected that under the treasury note act proposed for that year "paper may be issued designed to become, and which would become, a common medium of payment and circulation between the Government and its creditors and debtors, and, as far as it would go, a common money medium in circulation in the community."[32]

John C. Calhoun, a leader in congressional monetary thought, favored treasury note authorizations as he felt "that the elements of a true and stable currency . . . would be found to consist partly of gold and silver, and of paper, resting not on the credit and authority of banks, but of the Government itself."[33]

Calhoun's reasoning, no matter how practical it sounds, does not fit the norms of the Constitution as the Founding Fathers constructed that document. The Constitution explicitly forbids state government issues of paper money, and gives Congress the power only to fix the mint values of gold and silver. Surely Calhoun, a believer in the rule of law, knew and understood these principles. What compulsion had him abandon them in arguing the case for treasury notes? One can only guess. Perhaps he felt the treasury notes were so limited in quantity and duration that they posed no real violation of constitutional rules. Or he felt that the government in accepting bank-issued currency had the right to regulate it, even if the Constitution was silent on the subject. However, as noted herein (chapter 3), officials in the Treasury Department could always "regulate" bank currency by presenting it to the issuing banks for redemption in specie. Indeed, anyone—Treasury official or private individual—could apply this test at any time. It was sufficient by itself for establishing limits to bank-note expansion and ensuring the specie equivalence of the notes.

Even the Whigs found treasury notes to be a useful expedient after their unsuccessful attempts to establish a fiscal bank in 1841. Walter Forward, secretary of the Treasury, wrote a special message to the House Committee on Ways and Means in January 1842 asking for a substantial treasury note issue. A few years later John Spencer of New York, Forward's successor, issued a relatively small amount of treasury notes that were convertible into specie at either treasury depository in New York City. That the notes were redeemable on demand, and not after some intervening time period, confirmed that they were not issued in anticipation of tax payments but were issued as paper currency. The House Committee on Ways and Means condemned Spencer's action on the obvious grounds that the Treasury had no need to issue notes if specie was available, and that such an issue could only be regarded as an unconstitutional emission of paper money.[34] The committee's opinion was strictly constitutional and entirely correct.

Countercyclical Treasury Policy

The issue of treasury notes to cover government deficits gave the Independent Treasury some monetary initiative similar to that exercised by a central bank. Given (1) an international specie standard, (2) a fairly fixed volume of government expenditures, (3) tariff revenues that were highly elastic with respect to domestic national income, and (4) government revenues that were an appreciable fraction of domestic national income, certain built-in stabilizers would come into play. If, for example, the internal price level declined, a favorable balance of trade would arise that would lead to a specie inflow. Long-term credits granted by the creditor country would—and frequently did—reduce the specie movement (for example, in 1839–1841). In addition, the decline in the internal price level with the proportionally greater decline in tariff revenues would result in a fiscal deficit to the government. If the government issued treasury notes to meet the deficit, the economy's money stock would increase. The combined effects of a specie inflow and an issue of treasury notes to finance a fiscal deficit argue that buoyancy in business would most likely appear when a low absolute volume of imports occurred simultaneously with a large surplus in the balance of payments and a large federal deficit. The reverse of these conditions would be similarly constraining.

The time series in table 6.2 tend to support this general argument. Gold imports were over $13 million in 1838, for example, while treasury note issues were almost $5 million net for the whole year. Since the total stock of bank-held specie was $35 million, these liquidity inputs were large enough to cause the short-lived but well-defined prosperity of 1838–39.

The Independent Treasury's unique monetary-fiscal footing practically guaranteed that it would assume some policy-making features, especially when it used treasury notes to finance fiscal deficits. Several congressmen showed awareness of this possible role in 1847 when they debated the treasury

TABLE 6.2 Governmental expenditures, receipts, cash balances, and changes, 1832–1861 (millions of dollars)

Year	Total expenditures excluding payments on debt	Total receipts from customs, lands, and miscellaneous	Jan. 1 Treasury notes		Jan. 1 Long-term debt		Treasury cash balance	
			Out	Change	Out	Change	Jan. 1	Change over year
1832	34.36	31.87	—		—		4.50	− 2.49
1833	24.26	33.95	—		—		2.01	+ 9.69
1834	24.60	21.79	—		—		11.70	− 2.81
1835	17.57	35.43	—		—		8.89	+17.86
1836	30.87	50.83	—		—		26.75	+19.59
1837	33.81	18.03	—	+ 2.99	1.50		46.34	−37.27
1838	31.42	19.37	2.99	+ 4.76	1.50		5.09	− 0.09
1839	25.00	30.40	7.75	− 6.67	1.50		5.00	− 3.26
1840	22.35	16.99	1.08	+ 1.60	1.50		1.74	− 0.58
1841	26.39	15.95	2.68	+ 4.80	1.50	+ 3.17	1.16	− 1.16
1842	23.92	19.61	7.48	+ 2.71	4.67	+ 4.13	—	—
1843 (first half) (Jan 1–July 1)	11.56	8.07	10.19	+ 0.34	8.80	+13.54	0.04	+10.39
1843–44	21.84	27.50	10.53	− 8.17	22.34	− 0.06	10.43	− 2.57
1844–45	22.84	29.77	2.36	− 1.47	22.28	− 5.66	7.86	− 0.20
1845–46	27.66	29.50	0.89	− 0.24	16.62	+ 0.13	7.66	+ 1.47
1846–47	57.79	26.35	0.65	+14.99	16.75	+ 9.02	9.13	− 7.43
1847–48	45.21	35.43	15.64	− 0.82	25.77	+ 9.05	1.70	− 1.55
1848–49	44.75	31.07	14.82	−11.09	34.82	+26.80	0.15	+ 2.03
1849–50	40.06	43.38	3.73	− 2.95	61.62	+ 4.05	2.18	+ 4.42
1850–51	47.48	52.31	0.78	—	65.67	− 3.11	6.60	+ 4.31
1851–52	43.73	49.73	—	—	62.56	+ 2.57	10.91	+ 3.72
1852–53	47.22	61.34	—	—	65.13	+ 2.21	14.63	+ 7.31
1853–54	54.35	73.55	—	—	67.34	−20.10	21.94	− 1.80
1854–55	59.55	65.00	—	—	47.24	− 6.67	20.14	− 1.21
1855–56	62.51	73.92	—	—	40.57	− 6.61	18.93	+ 0.97
1856–57	66.92	68.63	—	—	33.96	− 4.90	19.90	− 2.19
1857–58	74.05	46.55	—	+19.75	29.06	− 3.90	17.71	−11.31
1858–59	68.98	53.40	19.75	− 5.03	25.16	+18.54	6.40	− 2.06
1859–60	63.03	55.97	14.72	+ 4.97	43.70	+ 1.38	4.34	− 0.71
1860–61	66.44	41.34	19.69	+ 0.35	45.08	+23.36	3.63	− 1.37
			20.04		68.44		2.26	

Source: The data in this table were derived from the *Treasury Reports* for the years shown.

Note: Total expenditures includes interest payments on the national debt, but not debt repurchases. Total receipts does not include "receipts" from issues of treasury notes or long-term debt. The values for notes and debt are contained in columns further to the right, as are year-to-year changes in these values. The same procedure is followed for the Treasury's cash balance.

This table cannot be taken too literally, not only because of the variable accounting practices followed by different secretaries, but also because of events such as the Texan Indemnity issue, which unilaterally increased the outstanding debt of the federal government in 1850–1852 by $10 million. At the same time this issue of debt had no offsetting "deficit" to fulfill, and other debt was being retired at the same time by ordinary repurchase. Thus at times the values in this table will not appear to be consistent or complete. They are generally correct and give a useful fiscal-monetary picture of the federal government's role in the period covered.

note measure that was designed to cover the fiscal deficit due to expenditures on the Mexican War. W. S. Miller, a representative from New York, expressed typical Whig sentiment when he said that the new treasury notes would offset to some extent a principal evil of the Independent Treasury System—the evil of tying up specie. But sooner or later, he thought, the Treasury would provoke mischief, "and at that moment the Secretary of the Treasury will hold in his hands the destinies of the trading community." Proponents of the Independent Treasury, he said, "disturb the commercial world by a pretended adoption of a government currency exclusively metallic, and the actual issue of mere government paper."[35] Other opinions were in agreement with Miller's. This opposition was mainly from the Whigs and a few hard-money Democrats. Thomas Hart Benton, for example, continually asserted that the power to emit treasury notes made the Treasury a bank of issue.[36]

When the last pre–Civil War spate of notes was issued between 1857 and 1860, opinions about them seemed much less cautious than those expressed ten and twenty years earlier. Senator R. M. T. Hunter, chairman of the Committee on Finance, believed that the forthcoming issue of notes in late 1857 "would relieve the community more . . . than any other mode in which we can borrow money." He also observed that by serving as bank reserves the notes would help the banks resume specie payments: "We offer incidentally to the merchant and to the banks a great advantage in Treasury paper of this sort, which is equivalent to specie."[37]

Senator John Crittenden of Kentucky was even more explicit than Senator Hunter. "One of the circumstances which invite, at this time, to the issue of a paper currency by the Government," he said, "is the ease and alleviation it may give to the commercial and pecuniary distresses and wants of the country." Senator John Bell replied that he did not think the treasury notes would furnish much relief, but he would favor such an issue if it would help. He did not deny the monetary character of the notes.[38]

Secretary of the Treasury Howell Cobb, although he favored an issue of treasury notes during the crisis of 1857, claimed that he did so primarily for fiscal reasons. He doubted the constitutional power of the government to provide relief as such.[39]

James A. Dixon, a Whig senator from Connecticut, took exception to Cobb's negative attitude. He saw the issue of treasury notes as consistent with and complementary to subtreasury policy, although it was a policy he and other Whigs felt they could improve upon. "We were told," he said, "that the sub-Treasury was to prevent all contraction or expansion; . . . that it was to save the banks, or at least, to save the Government. The Secretary of the Treasury . . . only offers to us a bankrupt law for the banks [and] . . . this issue of paper money."[40] In company with other Whigs, Dixon felt that a national bank was the best medium for conducting monetary policy. Bell seconded Dixon in a speech that concluded: "If the Government has no power to regulate the currency, it fails in one of its great purposes."[41] Bell's statement echoed Calhoun's identical opinion in the debate over recharter of the Second Bank.

The Whigs were in a more secure position when arguing for control over the currency than were the Democrats. They wanted regulation of the currency by a quasi-central bank and openly avowed this principle. The Democrats, on the other hand, constantly had to arbitrate a schism. Many of them opposed central-banking control over the monetary system; and to some, such as Thomas Hart Benton and other sound-money men, hostility to central banking was consistent with antipathy to all banks and unremitting advocacy of a completely metallic currency. The less-than-hard-money Democrats developed a compromise policy somewhere between a governmentally sponsored national bank and a purely metallic coin-currency. Their pragmatic approach must have succeeded since their policies were generally the ones adopted during this period. Part of this development is seen in their views toward issues of treasury notes; the other major policy action was their initiation of treasury open-market operations.

The Whigs, being descendants of the banking school of monetary thought, argued that a national bank was desirable to prevent the extreme variations in prices and business activity that sometimes occurred under metallic standards. They recognized that economic adjustments within the economy had to take place, but they felt that a national bank could provide monetary relief at critical times.

Treasury Open-Market Operations

The sound-money men were responsible for creating the Independent Treasury in 1846, but they had a lot of support from disillusioned state bank supporters. Both these groups wanted a separation of all banks from the state. However, the institution they created as independent eventually assumed more central-banking potential than any of the Whig schemes they had so virtuously crushed. Its central-banking function developed as a practical result of its fiscal position and because of the innovative skill of some of its executives.

The Independent Treasury had hardly started operations when policy developments suggested that the divorce of the state from the banks had not necessarily released the banks from the state. The words and the actions of key Treasury officials under the new system reflected an emergence of policies not designed in the original scheme.

Robert J. Walker was the first secretary of the Independent Treasury. An independent treasury was a major goal of President James Polk, Walker's chief, but Walker was its most vociferous, energetic, and capable supporter.[42] Under the Independent Treasury, Walker claimed, specie would "neither expand nor contract beyond the legitimate business of the country." If left to the caprices of the banking system, specie would be "made the basis, as often heretofore, of bank paper expansions, and if so, ruinous revulsions would not fail to ensue."[43] The Independent Treasury, he continued, would give "stability to all [manufacturers'] operations, and insure them, to a great extent, against those fluctuations, expansions, and contractions of the currency so prejudicial to their interests. . . . Stability, in both the tariff and the currency, is what the manufacturer should most desire. Stability [again] is what the manufacturer should most desire, and especially that that question should be taken out of politics by a just and permanent settlement."[44]

Walker could not have foreseen all the policy measures that he and successive secretaries might promote, and his implication that the Independent Treasury would buttress a hard-money policy was hardly more than window dressing.[45] He nevertheless regarded the Independent Treasury as a policy-making institution. Even so, his subsequent activities implied a degree of control over the monetary system that this institution could not sustain so early in its career.

During the Mexican War the Independent Treasury under Walker operated unexceptionably. Its monetary policies were limited, but it transferred specie for military purposes without even rippling the money market while it floated three major loans to finance the war.

Congress included in the second of these war loans the incongruous limitation that the securities had to be sold *at par or above,* but could only be repurchased, when a fiscal surplus was available, *at par or below.* Both Polk and Walker felt that such a provision prevented the administration from undertaking desirable policies for retiring the debt. Therefore, at the end of the war they asked Congress for authorization to repurchase outstanding government debt "at the market rate above or below par."[46]

Walker's repeated entreaties on this issue did not settle comfortably on Julius Rockwell, a Whiggish Whig from Massachusetts. Rockwell felt that government repurchases at the time would inflate the prices of the securities, embarrass the incoming (Zachary Taylor) administration, and give too much discretionary power to the secretary of the Treasury.[47]

Rockwell criticized Walker for what may have been one of the first policy-loaded, open-market operations in government securities that a central monetary agency of the United States ever conducted. Walker had repurchased $800,000 of the loan of 1847 at a time when the market price of the securities was well above par. He had contrived this apparently illegal feat by buying the securities at par and agreeing to resell them to those who made them available, again at the par value, thus effectively granting a loan using the securities as collateral. According to Rockwell, specie had accumulated in the subtreasury in New York, and "the Secretary was urged to this unauthorized proceeding by many gentlemen of great respectability in business, as well as by those dealing largely in stocks, with the view of relieving the pressure upon the money market in New York, and indirectly other parts of the country."[48]

Walker's procedure anticipated central-bank repurchase agreements, a common twentieth-century device. While the volume of his operations was small, he clearly intended to influence the economy by a contrived monetary operation. Rockwell's criticisms confirmed such intentions and also indicated that the condition of the money market was a concern of Treasury policy.

Walker verified the intentions of his money-market activities by declaring that the Independent Treasury would check "not the issues, but the over-issues [of banks], and [would] mitigate if not prevent those revulsions which are sure to ensue when the business of the banks, and as a consequence that of the country, is unduly extended."[49] Such an overt expression of banking policy, together with the open-market operations he modeled, suggests that Walker would have developed the Independent Treasury into a thoroughgoing policy agency. It also suggests that the independence of this institution was destined to be one-way.

Even though the Whigs generally won in the elections of 1848, thus ending Walker's tenure as secretary, they made no serious attempt to overthrow the Independent Treasury or to incorporate another national bank. The Whig secretaries had no particular affinity or zeal for the system fathered by the Democrats, so they showed no imaginative insights or developments in monetary policy at this time.[50] The Whig secretary of the Treasury continued to ask Congress for authorization to repurchase the outstanding debt at the market price. And because a sizable specie balance had accumulated in the subtreasury offices by early 1853, Congress finally repealed the provision of the Loan Act of 1847, which had prohibited such repurchases at prices above par. Although this action turned out to be momentous, it was so inconsequential at the time that it was not even recorded in the *Congressional Globe* but was buried in the Appropriations Act.[51]

Since the bulk of government income came from tariff revenues, a source decidedly sensitive to changes in the flow of national money income, total government receipts increased appreciably after 1850 following the gold discoveries in California and Australia. Expenditures tended to increase much less rapidly. The resulting fiscal surpluses led to a gold balance in the Treasury by late 1852 that was an appreciable fraction of the total stock of specie and other reserves held by the banks. The gold balance in the Treasury was $14 million, bank reserves were $45 million, and notes and deposits were slightly less than $300 million. Thus a $10 million transfer of specie, say, from the Treasury to the banks would permit the outstanding stock of bank notes and deposits to increase by more than 20 percent.

The new secretary of the Treasury under President Franklin Pierce was James Guthrie, an industrialist and banker from Louisville, Kentucky. Though Guthrie had not held public office before his appointment, he was prominent in state politics and in railroad and banking enterprises. He later became a United States senator.[52]

Guthrie noted in his annual report for 1853 that his predecessor, Thomas Corwin, had made a few private arrangements for debt repurchases at the beginning of the year, but he himself felt that a continuation of such cryptic methods might lead "to a misapplication of the public funds, and to favoritism. [Therefore,] public notice was at once given that the $5 million of the loan of 1843 would be redeemed at the treasury on July 1, 1853." Other portions were also repurchased in New York and Philadelphia until 1 July. Then, Guthrie reported,

> the amount still continuing to accumulate in the Treasury, apprehensions were entertained that a contraction of discounts by the city banks of New York would result, . . . and combining with the fact of the large amount in the Treasury, might have an injurious influence on financial and commercial operations. With a view, therefore, to give public assurance that money would not be permitted to accumulate in the Treasury, . . . a public offer was made on the 30th of July to redeem . . . the sum of $5 million of the loans of 1847 and 1848, at a premium of 21%, and interest from the 1st of July, 1853, on the principal. And on the 22nd of August another public offer was made for $2 million.[53]

As a result of these actions, the Treasury repurchased $20.1 million of the debt during 1853–54 at an average premium of 15 percent and effectively replaced income-earning assets held mostly by the banks with high-powered specie. The magnitude of the premium paid indicates that these transactions were no mean fiscal dabble.

Guthrie's silver-purchase policy accentuated his intentions. The surplus, he said, had become a cause for alarm in commercial and financial circles, and to relieve this situation advances were made to the mint "for the purchase of silver for the new coinage, and to enable the mint to pay promptly and in advance of coinage for gold bullion."[54]

The New York money market had shown some signs of stringency in the fall of 1853. In 1854 a more serious situation developed. As a result of a decline in the value of railroad securities, banks in Ohio, Indiana, and Illinois suspended specie payments in the spring. At the same time call rates went to 8 percent and good short paper to 12 percent in the New York money market.[55] Indexes of prices, the data on the stock of money, and Guthrie's report for 1854 confirm the supposition that the economy was on the verge of a bank panic. Total bank notes, deposits, and bank-held specie declined approximately 5 percent during the year. Guthrie remarked on the "pressure in the money market [and] disorder in money matters . . . [from] the failure of many of these . . . banks, and the curtailment of the circulation and discounts of others—which in the last six months must have reached forty or fifty millions of dollars."[56] His debt repurchases continued at a rate of $5 million to $7 million per year. And in December 1855 he was able to report that the stock of money, so reduced in the latter half of 1854, had "more than recovered."[57]

Guthrie continued to advocate hard money. He felt that the use of banks as depositories of treasury balances would cause specie to leave the country. Bank paper (less-good money) would drive out specie (better money). He reasoned from this axiom that the federal and state governments could "increase the specie in the country to any amount that is desirable . . . by creating an effective demand for specie," that is, by permitting only specie in the collections and disbursements of local governments.[58] He hardly imagined that the country would be able "to dispense with banks of issue, and their attendant evils, and have the gold and silver contemplated by the constitution,"[59] as he alleged. He was nonetheless one of the first influential government officials to recommend a prohibitive tax on bank notes.[60]

That Guthrie's policies evolved as a pragmatic result of the events occurring while he was in office is suggested by a letter from A. T. Burnley to Guthrie in July 1854. Burnley, an obscure lobbyist of some sort, had asked Judge George Bibb, a Whig predecessor of Guthrie's in the secretaryship and a fellow Kentuckian, for some definition of the implied and discretionary powers inherent in the office of secretary. Bibb cited a Supreme Court judgment (McDaniels case VII Peters 14) which stated that a cabinet officer was often compelled to exercise discretion in the execution of the duties and responsibilities of his office. "Numberless things," the opinion concluded, "must be done that can be neither anticipated nor defined."[61]

After several years of open-market operations during which the Treasury repurchased $38 million of a total of $63 million of outstanding government securities, Guthrie gave a seasoned account of Treasury policy. Uncertainties in economic life due to wars, political strife, and other phenomena, he said,

> destroy confidence and with it credit, inducing the hoarding of the precious metals, the withdrawal of deposits, the return of bank notes for redemption, the consequent stagnation of commerce, in all its channels and operations, the reduction of prices and wages, with inability to purchase and pay, bank suspensions and general insolvency. . . . The independent treasury, when over-trading takes place, gradually fills its vaults, withdraws the deposits, and pressing the banks, the merchants and the dealers, exercises that temperate and timely control, which serves to secure the fortunes of individuals, and preserve the general prosperity.
>
> The independent treasury, however, may exercise a fatal control over the currency, the banks and the trade of the country . . . whenever the revenue shall greatly exceed the expenditure. . . . [Without the repurchases of debt since 4 March 1853], the accumulated sum would have acted fatally on the banks and on trade.[62]

Although Guthrie's exposition seems to overemphasize the downswing of business activity, it describes well the balancing effect that he thought the Independent Treasury could have on the private economy. He regarded the restrictive policies of the Treasury as largely automatic. Specie would accumulate in its vaults as a result of "overtrading," but more specie in the Treasury would leave less in the banks and thus retard their expansion. Too much restraint by the Treasury, however, would result in a "fatal control." In the recent past Treasury repurchases of government debt had forestalled this latter effect. His case for Treasury policy developed circumstantially from the expansion of business activity due to the gold boom.

In March 1857 President James Buchanan appointed Howell Cobb of Georgia, a longtime congressman and a former Speaker of the House, to be his secretary of the Treasury. When the financial panic developed in the autumn of that year, Cobb continued the open-market operations that Walker and Guthrie had initiated. He reported that "the large sums from the Treasury . . . [afforded] relief to the commercial and other interests of the country."[63]

But the Treasury's specie balance had been used too prodigally, not only in purchasing securities in the open market but also in financing the fiscal deficit of 1857. When the balance reached the minimal value thought necessary for routine transactions (about $6 million), Cobb seemed to lose confidence in what he was doing. He defensively backpedaled, completely denying any governmental responsibility for restoring monetary or business equilibrium. He sermonized in his report with a hand-washing statement that was in marked contrast to what Walker and Guthrie had declared: "There are many persons who seem to think that it is the duty of the government to provide relief in all cases of trouble and distress. . . . And their necessities, not their judgments, force them to the conclusion that the government not only can, but ought to relieve them." He then prescribed the orthodox and austere alternative of "liquidation and settlement as the surest mode for the restoration of the equilibrium." Whereas Walker and Guthrie had been incisive and positive, Cobb was hesitant and unconvincing. He recommended the issue of treasury notes, not for any countercyclical purposes, but because he felt that the government's deficit would be temporary and should therefore be met by temporary means.[64]

Congress authorized notes as well as longer-term debt in 1857 and in the following three years to provide for the recurring fiscal deficits. The economy recovered quickly from the panic; the only improvidence felt was in the flow of revenues to the Treasury itself. In this situation Treasury policy was primarily fiscal.

Summary of Central-Banking Development before 1860

The central-banking performances of the pre–Civil War Independent Treasury and of the other institutions that attempted monetary policies during the nineteenth century were perhaps less important than the ideas that they both reflected and fostered. No one spelled out explicitly the functions of a central bank vis-à-vis the private economy. The early Bank of England and the Banks of the United States were not created as central banks, nor dared they recognize themselves as such. The Bank of England in fact became famous for declaring what it could *not* do in the area of monetary policy, and at times led as precarious an existence as the Second Bank of the United States. It was perhaps tolerated because of its self-effacing character and its self-styled commercial emphasis as "just another bank." By contrast, the Second Bank of the United States was denationalized because of its more purposive attitude toward monetary policy.

Other factors retarded the development of policy-making institutions. The states, for example, were properly jealous and fearful of encroachment by the federal government. Since a central bank would necessarily be a federal bank and would maintain and operate state branches from a distant center, proponents of states' rights found opposition to a national (central) bank almost mandatory.[65]

The institution of metallic standards also deterred central-banking development. Although the Whigs thought they could marry the principles of metallic-standard self-regulation to central-bank manipulation of the financial structure, long-run adherence to a policy of metallic standards was inconsistent with customary central-bank policies. Even a central bank with bountiful gold reserves could not permanently retard an external gold drain without allowing prices to fall. Ultimately, the price-specie flow mechanism would have to dominate—barring the unlikely event of currency devaluation.

The policies that the Independent Treasury carried out became strikingly similar in purpose to those of the national bank institution it replaced. They developed through force of circumstances, and, while sporadic and opportunistic, were a logical emergence. When would an independent treasury not adopt a policy-making role? Evaluated in the full sweep of history, the Independent Treasury may well appear in retrospect as the optimal monetary-fiscal institution within the basic framework of a gold standard. It was indeed unique, for it had all the necessary features for coordinating the government's monetary and fiscal affairs. With the dualistic structure of national banking that the Whigs subsequently developed, or such as the United States ultimately obtained in the Federal Reserve System, powers and responsibilities were destined to overlap and duplicate because of the impossibility of rationalizing precisely and permanently the bounds of authority for each of the agencies.

7 Civil War Inflation and Postwar Monetary Policies

No human intelligence can fix the amount of currency that is really needed. . . . So long as the volume of currency depends upon legislative enactment, uncertainty and instability will pervade all financial operations.

Hiland R. Hulburd, 1869

If we cannot [get free coinage of silver] I am in favor of issuing paper money enough to stuff down the bondholders until they are sick.

Richard P. Bland, 1878

Civil War Effects on the Currency System

The banking and monetary system on the eve of the Civil War had enjoyed fifteen years of relative stability, a condition often aspired to by secretaries of the Treasury during that era. Strangely enough, historians and analysts have not given the era a good press. Hepburn, for example, saw the currency system as "far from satisfactory." There was, he said, "no central place of redemption, hence most notes were at a discount, varying with the distance from the bank of issue. It was estimated that there were 7000 kinds and denominations of notes, and fully 4000 spurious or altered varieties were reported."[1]

The appearance of wildcat banks supposedly was symptomatic of these "chaotic" banking conditions. Yet neither Hepburn nor other historians have offered much hard evidence to support such a dismal picture. In fact, a recent study by Hugh Rockoff reliably indicates that by 1860 note holders' losses from all "free" banks, including wildcats, were less than what they would have lost in that year from a 2 percent inflation. Rockoff also points out that the thousands of "spurious and altered varieties" of notes reported by Hepburn were a *cumulative* total over decades. The bank-note reporters and counterfeit detectors continued to list such notes on the contingency that batches of worthless notes from broken banks would be circulated long after the books of the issuing banks had been closed.[2] At the base of the disorganized monetary system was seen a bumbling, destabilizing Independent Treasury that not only had no control over the banking system and the note issues of the banks, but also tied up specie and disturbed the money market because of its unsynchronized fiscal receipts and expenditures.[3]

The records for the period 1845–1860 imply an economic tranquillity that contradicts this critical view of the Treasury and the monetary system. Growth in bank credit and the stock of money was as orderly as it had been or would be in any other period in the financial history of the United States. The Independent Treasury behaved creditably. It effectively prevented pressures from developing in the money markets and in the economy by its monetary-fiscal stabilizing actions. Its separation from the banking system allowed it to exert an influence it might not otherwise have had, and the banking system seemed no worse for its independence. Only the panic of 1857 rippled the surface, and even this event was short-lived and relatively harmless.

The Civil War put an end to these idyllic conditions. Its real demands on the economies of both North and South were long-run and pervasive, as were its institutional effects on the banking and monetary systems.

The development of hostilities in 1861 provoked major economic and financial questions for both North and South. The principal monetary question was where to get the money to prosecute the war successfully. The three time-worn methods of answering this question included (1) taxing a larger part of the national product, (2) borrowing by issues of interest-bearing fixed-dollar claims (government securities) redeemable sometime in the future, and (3) simply printing money. Each of these means had its recommendations and its failings.[4]

Taxes were principally tariffs. Since the international trade that gave rise to tariff revenues was seriously impaired during a war, revenues from this source were more likely to decrease than increase. Government expenditures ultimately increased tenfold, and the tariff system just could not provide for such a load even in the beginning. Internal taxes were a second possibility. The government did impose an income tax and other domestic taxes, but these programs were ponderous to get into operation and slow to yield revenues.[5]

Bond sales were a natural and legitimate alternative. Congress could quickly authorize their issue; and for the long-run conduct of the war, sales of government securities raised the bulk of the increased revenues.

The third method of diverting resources to the government was the printing of fiat money. Most of the paper money printed in the North consisted of the famous United States notes, more popularly known as greenbacks or legal tenders. The only precedent for the issue of this currency was the frequent issue of treasury notes during the previous fifty years. A large fraction of these notes had looked like currency and had been treated as such—to a limited extent as hand-to-hand currency and to a large extent as bank reserves. However, Congress had confined the issues of treasury notes to amounts between $3 million and $20 million. Most of the time the notes had been issued for only one year and were not reissuable, although they frequently stayed out for an extra year or two. Most of them also were interest-bearing, and all of them were only legal tender for payments due to and from the government.

The new issues of greenbacks were unprecedented in that they were full legal tender for all debts public and private, in seeming violation of constitutional prohibition of "bills of credit." In addition, the quantities issued were massive compared to the earlier issues of treasury notes. The greenbacks were considered temporary and were supposed to be redeemed sometime (two years) after the end of hostilities, but they became a permanent government-issue currency. They also were reissuable when they came back into the Treasury as payments of taxes and tariffs. The common feature of the United States notes of the 1860s and the earlier treasury notes was that both looked like currency and bank reserves and were used as such.

The stock of money in general circulation in 1860 was on the order of $500 million, composed of roughly equal amounts of currency and bank deposits. Virtually all of this money was bank-issued. When the issues of United States notes began to appear, prices began to rise. Embedded in the general price level was the market price of gold, which fluctuated in a narrow range around the mint price in accordance with the operations of the gold standard. The issues of new currency gave the commercial banking system additional reserves, which the commercial banks used to extend credit and issue more bank currency. As the price level responded, people anticipated that the market price of gold would rise significantly above the mint price. Business firms that were engaged in international trade demanded gold for their greenbacks. Gold was also demanded for bank notes. Then the gold was either hoarded in anticipation of still higher prices or shipped abroad to settle foreign accounts. These drains forced the government and then the banks to suspend specie payments on 30 December 1861.

Suspension of gold payments did not mean the end of the monetary system. Prices, including the price of gold, rose as people tried to get rid of unwanted money balances. Obviously they could not get rid of them; all they could do was bid down the value of each money unit until the total stock of money was held with no further change in prices. By the time the war ended in 1865 the price level was about double its 1860 value, while the market price of gold peaked at 258 percent of its prewar value in July 1864.

The National Bank Act

The secession of southern states was also a secession of southern congressmen from the federal Congress. Since these men were all Democrats, their absence left the Whig-Republicans as a congressional majority, a position they had not enjoyed since 1840. They could now bring out of mothballs some of their more treasured projects, one of which was a national bank, and feel fairly certain of favorable legislative action.

The National Bank Act (or National Currency Act, as it was formally labeled) passed in 1863 as a war measure, but the national banking system did not really become an established institution until after 1865. While the act had its roots in Whig banking philosophy, the system that finally emerged was a multibank organization and not a monolithic bank of the United States with branches. The system nevertheless embodied the principle of a reserve-holding core of banks in the central reserve cities, or redemption centers, as well as a satellite system of "country" banks in all the smaller communities.

All banks in the national system had to be chartered by the federal government—specifically by the office of the comptroller of the currency in the Treasury Department. Membership in the system was permissive, but to some degree exclusive. Banks were not forced to join, but some banks could not meet the requirements. However, the system-wide regulations, which all banks had to adhere to, promised a degree of assurance to reasonably sound banks that other national banks would also be sound.[6]

The act specified reserve requirements for all the banks in the system: 25 percent for banks in reserve cities, and 15 percent for all others (country banks). Note issues of national banks were to be uniform in design and had to be accepted by all other national banks at par. Participating banks had to hold government bonds as collateral for their notes,[7] and each bank also had to hold government securities equal in value to at least one-third of its capital.

Joining the national system meant that a bank could become a Treasury depository, and also that it could advertise its existence by printing its name on its notes. Nonetheless, many state banks found that the costs of joining the new system exceeded the benefits; and, of course, until the war ended, southern banks could not join. To make participation more "attractive," Congress in 1865 amended the original act so that non-national banks had to pay a 10 percent prohibitory tax on their note issues. This provision had two results. First, many more banks became national banks; and second, banks that still did not want to be coerced avoided the tax by using demand deposits exclusively to finance loans and investments. Thus, the use of demand deposits was greatly accelerated and state bank-note issues became a thing of the past. Like the prewar treasury notes and the notes of the Banks of the United States, the national bank notes were legal tender for payments due to and from the federal government, except for customs payments to the Treasury and interest payments on the national debt by the Treasury.

The national banking system did not become fully operational until after the war's end. But by 1867 the economy had two major paper currencies roughly equal in volume: government-issued legal tender currency composed of United States notes, demand notes, and 3 percent certificates, and national bank notes. The National Bank Act limited note issues to $300 million. The note authorizations were at the discretion of the secretary of the Treasury, who was directed by law to allocate half the notes on the basis of "representative population and the remainder . . . [on the basis of] existing banking capital, resources, and business."

The presence of inconvertible paper currencies meant that federal government policy now ruled the monetary system, and would continue to do so until the resumption of specie payments. Politicians were not accustomed to making decisions for the monetary system and were ill suited to the task. Nevertheless, through the years after the war ended, the stock of paper money was reduced and resumption did occur at the prewar parity of gold and the dollar. So something worked. The question is, was that something devious bureaucratic hypocrisy, fortunate happenstance due to external factors, lucky blundering into the desired results, or some combination of all three?

Alternative Possible Policies after the Civil War

In the fourteen-year interval between 1865 and resumption, political, social, and economic forces clashed and compromised over the base on which the monetary system should rest. The traditionalists wanted gold, while the opportunists wanted silver or a fiat paper money. No public opinion group of any significance argued for a market-determined money. All of the conflict was over which government policy would have priority. The struggle that took place among the proponents for the various systems is instructive even if the question of hypocrisy, happenstance, or luck is left unsettled.

Resumption of gold payments was the long-run policy to which all parties paid lip service at the end of hostilities in 1865. But progress toward resumption proved to be anything but simple and straightforward. The struggle to achieve it took place under the following conditions or circumstances: (1) Congressional opinion was *not* sharply polarized into gold-standard resumptionists and paper-money inflationists. (2) The price-level discipline necessary to effect resumption was hedged by numerous compromises that allowed monetary expansion in some sectors of the financial system to counteract constriction in other parts. (3) The Treasury Department, with little more than a congressional prescription to do good (resume), undertook certain central-banking functions to obtain the desired end. (4) The strategic political position that the free-silver movement managed to establish, even though little silver currency came into circulation before 1879, exerted significant leverage on resumption policy. (See chapter 8.)

The seventeen-year suspension period of specie payments (1862–1879) has provided data for much monetary analysis. For example, James Kindahl has described the price level path that the preresumption economy had to take for specie payments to be reestablished. Kindahl's statistical analysis is both competent and enlightening, but he refers only superficially to the ideological struggles of the period. Like most other observers, he argues that monetary policy was largely negative and that no serious movement could be observed in favor of alternatives to a return to the prewar parity of the gold dollar.[8]

Congressional debates give a very different impression. The problem in 1865 was obvious enough. Issues of government currency after 1860 had tripled the stock of money, while the price level had approximately doubled during the same period. The market price of gold had fallen by this time from its 1864 high to about 150 percent of its prewar parity value, so it was still 50 percent higher than the mint price. Such circumstances permitted several courses for monetary policy. The most obvious combinations of ends and means were as follows.

1. Contract the paper-money stock so that general prices and the market price of gold would also fall. When the market price of gold reached the mint price, resumption would occur.
2. The same decline in the price level could be realized by freezing the stock of government currency and letting the increase in production—natural growth—produce a gradual decline in prices until the market price of gold was again within reach of the mint price.
3. The mint values of gold and silver could be increased by a statutory decrease in the gold and silver contents of the two metallic dollars legally defined. In other words, Congress could legislate a simple devaluation that would raise the mint values of the gold and silver dollars to their postwar market values.
4. The specie standard could be completely abandoned in favor of the inconvertible paper-money standard then current. This program, adopted in force by the Greenbackers, implied de facto gold and silver demonetization. It differed from de jure devaluation in that the precise amount of dollar depreciation would not be stipulated by law but would be left to market forces.
5. Another (nonpolicy) alternative was to hope for an increase in the output of monetary metals. Their relative prices might then fall enough within the framework of the inflated price level to reduce or eliminate the premium on them.

The Policy of Currency Contraction

The first policy undertaken after the war was an austere contraction of the money stock. Congress proclaimed it by resolution in December 1865, and Hugh McCulloch, secretary of the Treasury in the Johnson administration, enthusiastically carried it out. Tax revenues abounded in the peacetime climate of trade under a wartime tax framework. At the same time government expenditures declined significantly, leaving fiscal surpluses in the form of cash balances, which included United States notes and gold coin. The Treasury duly retired and destroyed the United States notes that were in excess of its fiscal needs. Other notes that remained outstanding were funded—that is, exchanged for long-term interest-bearing bonds.

But people very soon found out that price levels come down much more painfully than they go up. Congress, reflecting popular pressure from constituents, subjected McCulloch's "immediate and persistent contraction of the currency" to an intensive reappraisal on account of those "who had incurred pecuniary obligations in the expanded currency."[9] In April 1866, just four or five months after the beginning of the contraction policy it had blessed, Congress limited the contraction of greenbacks to $10 million in the succeeding six months and to $4 million per month thereafter.

Contraction even at this new rate was harsh medicine. As table 7.1 shows, private-sector holdings of government currency declined at a rate of 15 percent per year from 1865 to 1868. The reinclusion of southern population and production imposed an additional burden on the remaining money stock. During the three years of the contraction period (1865–1868), the price level fell at least 8 percent per year.[10] James M. Blaine, in his *Twenty Years of Congress,* reported public sentiment of the times: "The great host of debtors who did not wish their obligations to be made more onerous, and the great host of creditors who did not desire that their debtors should be embarrassed and possibly rendered unable to liquidate, united on the practical side of the question and aroused public opinion against the course of the Treasury Department. In the end, outside of banking and financial centers, there was a strong and persistent demand for the repeal of the Contraction Act."[11]

McCulloch's use of his discretionary powers found no favor even among members of his own party in Congress. Senator William B. Allison of Iowa

TABLE 7.1 Stock of money and components, 1860–1868 (millions of dollars)

							Wholesale prices (1910–1914 = 100)	
Year	Deposits national banks	Deposits non-national banks[a]	National bank notes	Non-national bank notes	Government currency	Total[b]	Warren and Pearson	Kindahl
1860		310		207	21	538	93	86
1861		319		202	16	537	89	89
1862		357		184	139	680	104	98
1863	10	494		239	433	1176	133	118
1864	147	233	31	179	612	1202	193	148
1865	614	75	146	143	646	1624	185	200
1866	695	64	276	20	524	1579	174	172
1867	685	58	287	5	476	1511	162	172
1868	745	53	294	3	394	1489	158	158

Source: *Historical Statistics,* pp. 624–30, 648–49. Price indexes are Warren and Pearson's from *Historical Statistics,* p. 115, and from James Kindahl, "Economic Factors in Specie Resumption," *Journal of Political Economy* (1961): 36.

[a] The last four or five values in this column certainly understate the total volume of non-national bank deposits.

[b] The total stock of money given here is at best a rough approximation to reality. The total amounts in the hands of the public cannot be found simply by adding the various components because some of the components served as a reserve base for the others. Government currency, for example, was held as a reserve by national banks, against which these same banks issued national bank notes. National bank notes, in turn, were held as reserves by non-national banks, against which non-national banks created deposits. The whole problem is made more complex by the division of the Union during 1861–1865. In addition, deposit values include interbank deposits. If interbank deposits are excluded, as they should be for proper measurement, changes in the net money stock would closely approximate changes in prices. (See Friedman and Schwartz, *Monetary History,* p. 704.)

claimed that McCulloch had not retired any of the greenbacks in the first four or five months of 1867. However, Allison complained, "when it was necessary to use a large amount of money in the western states for the forwarding of the crops [in September and October of 1867], the Secretary of the Treasury then reduced the greenback circulation $16 million in two months; . . . so that when Congress came together in December 1867, they withdrew from the Secretary of the Treasury the power which they believed he had abused." Senator John Sherman affirmed Allison's interpretation: "I do not differ from the Senator from Iowa."[12]

In February 1868, Congress enacted a measure that prohibited the secretary of the Treasury from making "any [further] reduction of the currency by retiring or canceling United States notes." From this time on, the moderate conservative policy of "growing up to the money stock" (the second alternative) was followed officially. Unofficially, procrastination became the norm; and after a few years many congressmen were paying only lip service to the resumption ideal.

Ulysses S. Grant was elected president in 1868 following the general disaffection of the Republican party with Andrew Johnson. Grant replaced Secretary of the Treasury McCulloch, who had been a supporter of Johnson, with George S. Boutwell of Massachusetts. Boutwell had been a member of Congress in the House of Representatives before his appointment to the Treasury and was asked to serve in the cabinet as a result of his anti-Johnson activity in the House. He later became a U.S. senator from Massachusetts.[13]

Treasury Gold Policy

Boutwell had been secretary only about six months when the notorious Black Friday incident occurred on 24 September 1869. This drama was an attempt to "corner" gold by the famous speculators James Fisk and Jay Gould. Prices of all goods and services, including gold, had been falling as a result of the Treasury's contraction policy. Fisk and Gould felt that they could artificially escalate the price of gold to their advantage if they could be sure of a temporary do-nothing policy by the Treasury. They undertook aggressive gold-buying policies in the summer of 1869. At the same time they propagandized Grant and Boutwell with the admonition that gold sales by the Treasury Department would adversely affect the impending movement of the crops. By means of adroit financial maneuvers they finally effected a temporary corner in gold, although the Treasury Department quickly broke their scheme with a sale of $4 million in New York's "gold room."[14]

The notoriety accompanying the Black Friday incident led to a congressional investigation in the course of which several congressmen and Treasury officials advanced norms for Treasury policy. The majority report of the investigating committee recognized that "for all purposes of internal trade, gold is not money, but an article of merchandise; but for all purposes of foreign commerce it is our only currency." Common opinion was that Treasury accumulations or disbursements of gold could somewhat affect both foreign and domestic commerce. The rationale of this view went as follows. If the Treasury sold gold in the open market and held on balance the currency it received in exchange, the greenback price of gold would fall. Traders would export gold and import goods and services. Domestic prices would fall and the movement of the crops, especially, would be threatened. If the Treasury subsequently spent the dollar proceeds from the gold sales by, say, purchasing government securities in financial markets, only the price of gold would be lower than initially and movement of the crops would not be impeded. This view was essentially correct if the Treasury gold balance was the result of a fiscal surplus.

Boutwell's statements before the Garfield committee reflected this argument. To prevent a decline in business after the sale of gold during September 1869, he had ordered an immediate purchase of bonds in the open market. His decision to sell the gold, he said, was "not for the purpose of forcing down the price of gold, . . . but because we thought the business of the country was in danger."[15]

The minority of the investigating committee addressed themselves to the question of "disasters" in general. "It is impossible," they said, "to prevent large amounts of gold from accumulating in the Treasury." They cited McCulloch's policy of countering "speculative combinations," but they alleged critically (and incorrectly) that Boutwell was indifferent to the course of the money market. At the same time they complained of the "aggrandizement of power in the federal government . . . which affects at its will all the values of the country."[16]

The minority here expressed a common contradiction in popular norms for policy. While blaming the secretary for not properly overseeing the state of the money market, they criticized the central government's centralized discretionary control. They concluded with this indefinite prescription: "The amount of coin . . . kept in the Treasury in reserve as a preparation for unforeseen emergencies, and to give steadiness to the convertible value of the legal tender issues, must depend upon contingencies that cannot be anticipated."[17]

This ambivalence emphasized the need for a specific congressional policy. The amount of cash the Treasury should keep, what the Treasury should be permitted and prescribed to do with it, what long-run currency policy should be—all these questions Congress should have answered by resolution or statute. Even when resumption was accomplished, some of these issues would still be unsettled.

Governmental Policies in Allocating National Bank Notes

Congress did nothing at this time to clarify Treasury policy. It did try to do something about the currency. The act preventing further contraction in 1868 had frozen greenbacks at $356 million, and national bank notes were still fixed at $300 million. Also outstanding were about $45 million of the Treasury's 3 percent certificates, which were in large denominations and used exclusively as bank reserves. Congress directed its attention in early 1870 to retiring these certificates and extending the permissible issues of national bank notes.

The secretary of the Treasury was supposed to have allocated half of the national bank notes on the basis of "representative population," and the other half with "due regard to existing banking capital, resources, and business of each State."[18] Although the secretary made most of the apportionment after the end of the war, the South and West did not get allotments of national banks or national bank notes anywhere near their pro rata share. By 1868, with the quotas almost complete, national banks in southern states had only 4 percent of the banks and 3 percent of the total notes.[19]

The reason for this misallocation, in apparent disregard of the apportionment provision in the act, is to be found in a section of the Internal Revenue Act of 1864, which stated that existing state banks had preference in converting to national banks over newly organizing banks. The National Bank Act itself implied as much. The comptroller of the currency and the secretary of the Treasury also acted on the presumption that the primary intent of Congress in framing the National Bank Act was to nationalize the existing system.[20] This principle necessarily conflicted with the principle of apportionment.

The Civil War had seriously disrupted banking in the South. Between 1850 and 1860, deposits of southern and western banks had grown at roughly the same rates as those of all banks in the country. But between 1860 and 1870, bank deposits in these regions declined 34 and 26 percent respectively, while all bank deposits increased 149 percent. Part of this disparity very likely is statistical error due to incomplete data compilations. Some of it also resulted from regional antipathy to banks, especially to banks organized under "the money power of the north"; and some of the apparent deficiency was due to general populist mistrust of banks and bankers. Lower population densities in southern and western states also contributed to fewer banking facilities. Even in the decade of the 1870s, southern bank deposits grew only 8 percent compared to growth in the national average of 27 percent.[21]

Secretary McCulloch had expressed in his report for 1865 the idea that the national bank notes would simply substitute for retired state bank notes. He felt, he said, that it was his "duty to discourage, in many instances, the organization of new banks" in order to keep the stock of money under control and on the rigorous path to resumption.[22] McCulloch was well aware that the South and the West were not getting their proportionate shares when the national bank notes were allocated. However, he disagreed with the comptroller of the currency, Hiland R. Hulburd, who favored further issues of notes beyond the original $300 million on the condition that United States notes would be retired simultaneously. McCulloch agreed with Hulburd that the issue of notes could be left unconstrained by quotas once specie resumption was accomplished.[23]

The unfulfilled provision in the National Bank Act calling for rationing half the notes in strict proportion to "representative population," together with retirement of United States notes and the accompanying hardships of the contraction policy, led to some serious reconsiderations of currency policy in Congress. Two related issues appeared in addition to the question of the sheer quantity of money: elasticity of the currency and per capita distribution. Greenbacks were touted as a government debt issued without interest charges, so they had the advantage of saving the government interest expense. It was a short step for Greenbackers to recommend that *all* remaining interest-bearing bonds should also be converted into greenbacks. The conservative, Republican, "banking school" spokesmen, however, favored the extension of national banks and national bank-note issues because of their greater potential as an elastic medium. United States notes, Comptroller Hulburd stated in 1867, are "an iron currency in [their] utter want of elasticity so essential in a circulating medium."[24]

Elasticity of the currency was understood to be a change in the quantity of currency outstanding that would accommodate seasonal changes in the output of goods, particularly agricultural commodities. The idea of per capita currency came from the "representative population" phrase in the National Bank Act, and it became a ubiquitous point of congressional discussion. The population figures, which were supposed to be the basis of national bank-note apportionment, were revised as a matter of course by the census of 1870. Bills for new apportionments and reapportionments were duly introduced and discussed during the Forty-first Congress.[25]

Arguments for more money per capita to correct the obvious malproportion in the South were made in conjunction with the idea of retiring the 3 percent treasury certificates. Since these certificates were "lawful money" as bank reserves and amounted to about $45 million, the bill that went through Congress was a kind of monetary omnibus. It looked to the retirement of the $45 million in 3 percents and the apportionment of an additional $45 million in national bank notes to fill the glaring inequities in the distribution of existing notes.

The absolute deficiencies in the South and West amounted to over $94 million, and considerable sentiment was expressed in the House of Representatives for adding this amount to the original apportionment. The Senate, however, insisted on limiting the increase to the value of the 3 percent certificates about to be retired ($45 million) and on making the new issues of notes contingent on the actual retirement of the 3 percents.[26]

Opinion in both houses was favorable to a compromise through a conference committee so that the currency would at least be redistributed, if not increased. However, some congressmen expressed misgivings about the bill's ability even to maintain the currency. Ebon C. Ingersoll of Illinois thought the bill would provoke a net contraction. The bill, he said, "proposes to increase the present national bank circulation . . . by $45,000,000. It then proposes to withdraw the $45 million [of 3 percents] that are now held . . . by the banks as a reserve under existing law. . . . I hold that this proposition involves a positive contraction."[27]

To this valid insight James Garfield replied that retiring the $45 million of 3 percents would not be a contraction because these certificates could not be used as currency, but were "only" reserves in the banks. This feature, of course, was what made the certificates high-powered money. They provided a base for multiple issues of national bank notes and deposits that the nonbank public could use for transactions and the non-national banks could use as reserves for creation of even more deposits. Garfield noted that national banks held $55 million in reserves in excess of legal requirements. Therefore, he reasoned, the retirement of the 3 percents would only reduce "surplus" reserves. He believed that national banks would use part of the "surplus" reserves to increase loans and deposits by enough to offset the reduction in hand-to-hand greenbacks that the national banks would need as reserves in lieu of the retired 3 percents.[28] Because national banks held "surplus" reserves, Garfield held, retirement of the 3 percents could and would leave the money stock unchanged. His "could" was correct, but his "would" was problematic.

Confusion arising from the retirement of one kind of money while granting permissive increases in another is evident in the debates. Benjamin Butler of Massachusetts reported that one banker had told him that the bill would produce an expansion of the currency, while another banker had insisted it would cause a contraction.

"Now," he asked Garfield, "if such able and experienced men cannot tell what this bill is, why should we vote for it? [Laughter]."

Garfield answered: "If so, you had better not vote for it." And Butler allowed that indeed he would not.[29]

To stay alive the bill had to go before a conference committee composed of four members, two from the House and two from the Senate. It was reported back to the House, but was rejected and went to another conference. In the second conference the anticipated increase of $45 million in national bank notes was seen to necessitate about $9 million of United States notes as national bank reserves for the additional issue of national bank notes.[30] This adjustment would take $9 million of greenbacks out of hand-to-hand circulation, even while permitting the desired increase in national bank notes, and the stock of money would consequently contract by $9 million. Therefore, to keep the money supply constant—the compromise desideratum—another $9 million had to be added to the $45 million of allowable national bank notes, making a total of $54 million. The compromise bill was agreed to and became law on 12 July 1870.

The act also provided that $25 million of the new total of $354 million could be reapportioned, but only after the supplementary $54 million had been used up. Even then the comptroller of the currency would be required to give one year's notice to the banks that had an excess. Yet another delay would result from the provision that the apportionment values be calculated as soon as practicable after the census of 1870, which meant that at least an additional six months would elapse before any kind of reapportionment would or could occur. The general provisions for note issues were as follows:

1. The secretary of the Treasury could apportion an additional $54 million of national bank notes to banks in states that had a deficiency from the original issue. National banks still had to apply for the right to issue the notes, and they still had to deposit "approved" U.S. government securities with the treasurer of the United States in order to obtain physical possession of the notes from the comptroller of the currency.
2. About 80 percent of the new notes were to go to the South and the West; but banks in these regions had this priority only if they applied for their quotas within one year after the act was passed.
3. The secretary of the Treasury was "to redeem and cancel" the 3 percent certificates in amounts equal to the national bank notes so authorized and issued. To enforce the retirement of the certificates, interest payments on them and their "lawful money" (bank reserve) function were to cease.
4. After the additional notes were all distributed, the comptroller of the currency could reapportion $25 million upon application by national banks in the still-deficient states. The $25 million were to come first from banks having the largest amounts of notes outstanding.[31]

Table 7.2 compares bank-note circulation in 1862 and 1873. It also shows the growth (+ or −) in note circulation, the amount each region was due by the law of 1870, and the remaining excess or deficiency. Eastern states were relatively well endowed with bank notes, while the South and the West were deficient. Notes in the Midwest show a high rate of growth, but these states were due even more than they had. Since national banks did not form in the South and the West as anticipated, the secretary had allocated their quotas of notes to new and existing banks in other sections.[32]

The time series in table 7.3 show the major monetary variables in the national banking system between 1870 and 1879. To deflate the intrasystem credit structure, total currency and deposits and total reserves (columns 1 and

TABLE 7.2 Bank-note circulation in 1862 and 1873, with rates of increase and authorized amounts according to the apportionment provisions (all but changes in millions of dollars)

Region	Circulation 1862	Circulation 1873	Change (%)	Authorized apportionment, 1870	Excess (+) or deficiency (−)
East	65.62	110.49	+ 69	39.80	+70.69
Middle	82.37	124.61	+ 52	115.19	+ 9.42
South and West[a]	71.10	38.16	− 47	89.25	−51.09
Midwest	19.68	78.79	+295	100.21	−21.42

Source: *Report of the Comptroller,* 1873, pp. 71, 75.
[a] Does not include Mississippi, Arkansas, or Texas.

4) are reduced by the deposit reserves ("Due from redemption agents") in reserve city national banks. The residuals (columns 3 and 5) give the net currency and net deposits for which the national banking system was responsible to both the nonbank public and the nonnational banks, and the *net* reserves available to support these obligations. Column 6 is the comptroller's calculation of required national bank reserves. Columns 7 and 8 show the ratios of total reserves as defined to comparable totals of notes and deposits.

The retirement of the $45 million of 3 percents that occurred between March 1870 and February 1873 appears in the table as the decline of $28 million in "Basic reserves held" (column 5). "Legal reserves held" (column 4) declined by $8 million to complete the arithmetic. Reserve city national banks and all other national banks continued to increase their balances with New York City banks.[33]

Treasury Monetary Policy in the 1870s

While Congress was simultaneously reducing government issues of basic money and allowing expansion of bank-created currency, the Treasury Department was struggling to establish norms for its own conduct. Secretary Boutwell's experience with the gold crisis, plus opinions expressed in Congress and the uncertainties accompanying a paper-money system, seemed to have impressed upon him the advisability of discretionary action by his department. Since the quantity of national bank notes was fixed by statute just as rigorously as the quantity of greenbacks, he felt that an impartial governing agency—the Treasury—was necessary to provide seasonal elasticity to the money stock. Inactive balances that accrued during the summer, he reasoned, could be used "if necessary, in the purchase of bonds in the autumn, thereby meeting the usual demand for currency at that season of the year." After a specie standard was reestablished, the Treasury's excess of gold receipts over expenditures would permit similar aid to be furnished in coin.[34]

TABLE 7.3 **Selected statistics for all national banks, March 1870 to October 1878 (all but ratios in millions of dollars)**

Date	Total currency and deposits[a] (1)		National bank inter bank balances[b] (2)	Net currency and deposits (3) = (1) − (2)	Legal reserves held (4)	Basic reserves held (5) = (4) − (2)	Legal required reserves (6)	Ratio of legal reserves to currency and deposits (7) = (4) ÷ (1) (%)	Ratio of basic reserves to net currency and deposits (8) = (5) ÷ (3) (%)
Mar. 24, 1870	850	(278)	73	777	236	163	172	27.8	21.0
Oct. 8, 1870	813	(279)	66	747	204	138	163	25.4	18.5
Mar. 18, 1871	891	(289)	84	807	234	150	180	26.3	18.6
Oct. 2, 1871	952	(301)	87	865	233	146	181	24.5	16.9
Feb. 27, 1872	952	(306)	90	862	228	138	190	23.9	16.0
Oct. 3, 1872	947	(318)	81	866	209	128	186	22.1	14.8
Feb. 28, 1873[c]	999	(320)	93	906	228	135	196	22.8	14.9
Sept. 12, 1873	1003	(323)	93	910	225	132	198	22.4	14.5
Oct. 13, 1873[d]	927	(321)	54	873	182	128	188	19.6	14.7
Feb. 27, 1874	1025	(320)	101	924	274[e]	173[e]	205	26.7	18.7
Oct. 2, 1874	713[f]	(315)	84	629[f]	244	160	149	34.2	25.4
Mar. 1, 1875	722	(306)	90	632	238	148	150	33.0	23.4

Oct. 1, 1875	731	(300)	86	645	234	148	152	32.0	22.9
Mar. 10,1876	722	(289)	99	623	251	152	150	34.8	24.4
Oct. 2, 1876	708	(276)	88	620	237	149	148	33.5	24.0
Apr. 14, 1877	697	(277)	85	612	231	146	145	33.1	23.9
Oct. 1, 1877	670	(276)	73	597	211	138	138	31.5	23.1
Mar. 15, 1878	672	(285)	86	586	240	154	139	35.7	26.3
Oct. 1, 1878[g]	678	(285)	85	593	228	143	141	33.6	23.1

Source: Columns 1, 4, 6, and 8 were obtained from *Reports of the Comptroller of the Currency,* 1870–1878. Columns 2, 3, 5, and 7 were derived from these data.

[a] Notes outstanding are shown separately in parentheses.

[b] Inter–national bank balances were labeled, "Due from redemption (or reserve) agents." Reserve agents were national banks in reserve cities and New York City. So these balances, while classified as a part of the reserve balances of national banks to which they were due, were also demand liabilities of the national banks that acted as reserve agents and were no more to be considered reserves for the total national banking system than were national bank notes issued by one national bank and held by another. Deleting them from total currency and deposit issues of national banks (column 3) leaves notes and deposits in possession of the nonbank public. Likewise, deleting them from legal reserves (column 5) leaves the basic high-powered money reserves of the total national banking system.

[c] Almost all 3 percent certificates were retired by this date.

[d] This date marked the low spot for bank-held reserves during the panic of 1873.

[e] By this date United States notes outstanding had been increased to $382 million from $356 million.

[f] From this time on, national bank notes were de facto obligations of the Treasury Department (through the 5 percent redemption fund), so only deposits are included in the obligations of national banks requiring reserves. National bank notes outstanding are shown in parentheses.

[g] United States notes were frozen forever at $346.7 million on May 31, 1878.

Boutwell extended these observations to venture a fundamental doctrine for Treasury policy. "Where but in the Treasury Department," he asked rhetorically, "can the power for increasing and decreasing the currency be reposed? I form the conclusion that the circulation of the banks should be fixed and limited, and that the power to change the volume of paper in circulation, within limits established by law, should remain in the Treasury Department."[35]

Boutwell had earlier initiated the policy of counterseasonal bond buying. The Treasury constantly purchased bonds as required by the sinking fund law, and also in excess of that requirement if it had fiscal surpluses. However, the rate of bond purchases was left to the secretary's discretion. During 1870 one-fifth of the total for the year was made in the eight weeks between 8 September and 27 October. In 1871 almost one-third of the year's total was purchased during a four-week period.[36] The amount of bonds purchased in the autumn was usually between $15 million and $20 million. Since the volume of legal tenders in all national banks was about $100 million, the Treasury purchases contributed a significant seasonal adjustment to national bank reserves.

Whatever his opinions on resumption when he took office, Boutwell's tenure as secretary witnessed little progress toward this goal. The economy enjoyed a vigorous growth; business and banking suffered no crises; and the price level stayed relatively stable. Indeed, rapid progress toward resumption could occur only if the price level fell, and most of Boutwell's actions with respect to monetary policy were taken to counter falling prices.

Yet another Treasury initiative occurred in the fall of 1872. At a time when Boutwell was absent from the department, Assistant Secretary Richardson issued about $5 million of United States notes from what he and Boutwell euphemistically and presumptuously labeled "the reserve." The object of the issue, Boutwell reported later, "was the relief of the business of the country, then suffering from the large demand for currency employed in moving the crops from the South and West. The condition of affairs then existing in the country seems to me to have warranted the issue upon grounds of public policy."[37] Richardson's action and Boutwell's approbation induced another congressional controversy that showed the sharp cleavage of opinion between strict constructionism and liberal pragmatism in the conduct of Treasury policy. It also emphasized the passive acquiescence of Congress to any monetary policy that would maintain a semblance of the status quo.

The "reserve," the kernel of the controversy, was the $44 million of United States notes that made up the difference between the *maximum* amount ($400 million) Congress had authorized during the Civil War and the *minimum* level ($356 million) at which Congress had frozen the greenbacks in 1868. The strict constructionists, who constituted a majority of the Senate Committee on Finance chaired by Senator John Sherman of Ohio, held that the minimum of 1868 was also a maximum, that Congress would have declared otherwise if it had intended otherwise, and that reissue of any of the $44 million difference violated the whole policy of contraction—a policy, they alleged, that was still in force. The reissue powers granted in the original legal tender acts, they argued, were under different *res gestae*. Their conclusion was correspondingly conservative and constitutional: "In all questions of . . . the extent of power conferred by law in matters which affect the public credit or public securities, a reasonable doubt as to a grant of power should be held to exclude it."[38]

Boutwell based the authority for the Treasury's action on the wording of the legal tender acts, on the precedent set by McCulloch before the act of 1868, on the fact that the act of 1868 did not stipulate a maximum, and on formal opinions in the Treasury Department and in the Department of the Attorney General. Before 4 March 1869, he said, large sums of notes were held in the office of the treasurer "as a surplus-fund . . . for the purpose of meeting any sudden drain upon the Treasury, and that practice has ever since been continued."[39]

The minority of the Senate committee supported Boutwell, declaring that the legal tender acts and the act of 1868 fixing the minimum did not conflict and that "Congress intended to leave the amount of cash balance an open question subject to the decision of the Secretary of the Treasury, in accordance with the 'exigencies of the public service.'" They concluded with a permissive statement very much in contrast to that of the majority: "Where no direct conflict between two different measures of legislation is apparent but the legislative power is silent upon any given question connected with those measures, it may become necessary for the executive power to supply the omission."[40]

In fact, Congress had not intended either to grant discretion to the secretary in the use of the "reserve" or to deny it. The issue had simply been overlooked. The committee was trying to impute law to a vacuum. Congress could have promptly settled the issue with a simple act specifying its norms for policy, but it left the issue unresolved. Undoubtedly it was a case of "leave it alone and maybe nothing will happen." Nevertheless, in doing nothing Congress by implication sanctioned the secretary's discretion over the greenback "reserve" of $44 million.

Progress toward resumption during Grant's first administration (1869–1872) was minimal. Prices did not fall appreciably between 1870 and 1873, so the premium of 12 to 14 percent on gold remained. In retrospect a simple devaluation of the gold dollar by the amount of the existing market premium around 1872 would have been well advised. A modest devaluation would have alleviated the anxiety and uncertainty accompanying the ideological conflict over proper monetary policy during the ensuing six years. But it did not happen. It was as if the mint price of gold was written in Heaven.

Since gold resumption was forestalled by the traditional ethic against devaluation, government issues of fiat paper money remained as the monetary base of the system. These currencies were fixed by laws. But the laws could be changed, as everyone knew, and they were changed to fit social and political norms and interests.

The Treasury department that administered the paper money inevitably would assume some degree of discretion over its disposition. George Boutwell, Grant's secretary of the Treasury, had a penchant for assuming authority. His official reports reflected this characteristic, as did his subsequent speeches in the U.S. Senate.

Treasury policies under Boutwell separated the operational Treasury of the day even further from the ideal of nonintervention with the monetary system that the Independent Treasury was supposed to further. By early 1873, the Supreme Court had also validated the greenbacks (see chapter 10), Congress seemed satisfied with the monetary status quo, the silver movement had not yet been charged up, business activity was moderately good, and no international disequilibria had occurred. So the monetary environment seemed tranquil. The five years just ahead, however, proved to be as turbulent in monetary affairs as virtually any similar period in history.

Civil War Financial Policy in the South

Almost all analyses of Civil War finance concentrate on the fiscal-monetary experience of the North. Important and revealing as is this case, the similar experience of the South is just as instructive. Only in recent years have economists examined the southern example in analytical detail.

The first such study was done over thirty years ago by Eugene Lerner as a doctoral dissertation.[41] Lerner opened much new material, and his work is valuable in many regards, especially with respect to prices and wages. However, his analysis of the growth in the Confederate money supply and of the relationship of the money supply to prices is marred by some understandable errors in accounting the money stock, and by a too-general view of the South's institutional arrangements in financing the war. The monetary-fiscal section of Lerner's work was subsequently reappraised and modified by John M. Godfrey.[42]

Godfrey's study significantly revised Lerner's estimates on the growth in the Confederate money stock and therefore on the relationship between money and prices. Most of the errors Godfrey found, both in Lerner's work and in some earlier studies by historians, resulted from insufficient attention to details of accounting and aggregation. (This kind of oversight does not detract from the scholarship of Lerner and the others. It only demonstrates that the monetary analysis itself was worth more intensive investigation than was devoted to it.) Godfrey found that the issues of notes by the Confederate government, while accounting for over 90 percent of the increase in the total stock of Confederate money, had been overestimated by 20 to 30 percent because observers had not taken proper account of certain refunding operations.[43]

Bank-issued money was another item subject to error. Especially important was the accounting of bank-held cash and interbank deposits. When these items were correctly accounted, bank-note and deposit expansion contributed only about 6 percent to the total growth of the Confederate money stock. State currency issues then contributed approximately another 3 percent.[44]

Godfrey's new estimates, when aggregated, show that the Confederate money stock fell between January 1860 and January 1861. It then rose to about twenty-two times its 1861 value by February 1864, fell *by one-third in the next two months* due to a currency reform, and then rose by about 20 percent to January 1865, when data became unavailable.[45]

Increases in Confederate prices were highly correlated with growth of the money stock until the currency reform of February 1864. At this point, prices increased enormously as people tried to get rid of their money in order to escape the burden of the reform, which was a two-for-three exchange of new notes for old. Declines in real output associated with the trauma of defeat aggravated the price picture, with the result that prices doubled during 1864 even though the money stock was 23 percent lower in January 1865 than it had been in February 1864.[46]

The major differences between federal and Confederate financing of the Civil War were in the role banks played and in the fiscal practice of government debt issues. Confederate banks, which had less than 20 percent of the capacity of their northern counterparts, contributed only 6 percent to total monetary growth in the South, while northern banks were responsible for perhaps 75 percent of monetary growth in the North (see table 7.1). Confederate bond issues provided only 21 percent of total government "means" in the Confederacy, while they contributed 65 percent to the total revenues of the northern government's operations.[47] Whether these contrasts of fiscal and monetary policy made any differences in the real sector is a moot question. What they demonstrate is that financial policies in "emergencies" can be diverse.

8 The Panic of 1873 and Resumption

> Gold and Silver! They are the legal tender of Commerce and the Constitution . . . the legal tender of God Almighty, who has made it precious!
>
> Samuel Cox, House of Representatives, 7 June 1870

Monetary Conditions Presaging the Panic of 1873

Boutwell resigned his cabinet position early in 1873 to take a seat as U.S. senator from Massachusetts. His assistant secretary, William Richardson, was then appointed secretary. Richardson had worked very closely with Boutwell. He was a personal friend and had been appointed assistant secretary on Boutwell's urging.[1]

The Treasury's cash balance again increased during the fiscal year 1872–73 (see table 8.1) as practically no open-market purchases of securities were made. "Anticipating the usual autumn stringency," Richardson had the Treasury sell gold in the summer of 1873 and accumulate about $14 million of currency "with the view of using the same . . . in the purchase of bonds for the sinking fund . . . during the autumn and winter."[2]

National banks had increased their issues of notes by $44 million—just about the same amount as the retired 3 percent certificates. Their legal reserves had increased by $21 million, but their basic reserves had fallen by $6 million during this same time (October 1870 to September 1873; see table 7.3). Reserve ratios of national banks had also fallen (see table 8.2), and banks in many states showed deficient legal reserves through the first half of 1873.[3]

In his last annual report Secretary Boutwell had warned: "There is practically no reserve to meet the increased demand for money due occasionally to extraordinary events at home or abroad, and arising periodically with the incoming of the harvest."[4] Boutwell proved to be a prophet in his own time. By September of 1873 the New York banks had insufficient reserves to meet the seasonal demands of the autumn, and on September 8 the big panic began. As table 8.3 shows, greenback reserves declined dramatically—from $34 million on 6 September to just over $5 million by 18 October. The extraordinary demand for cash in New York was a demand for both specie and United States notes. Note and specie reserves of national banks in New York fell by $35.4 million, or by almost 66 percent, in four weeks, while deposits declined by $50 million, or 28 percent, at the same time. At this point the overall reserve ratio for the entire national banking system was down to 19.6 percent,

TABLE 8.1 Current assets and liabilities of the Treasury (millions of dollars as of June 30)

Year	Total cash balance	Coin and coin items	Other lawful money	Currency liabilities outstanding[c]	Ratio of cash balance to current liabilities (%)
1868	131	n.a.	n.a.	444	29.5
1869	159	114[a]	45[b]	392	40.5
1870	150	113[a]	37[b]	398	37.6
1871	113	99[a]	14[b]	398	28.3
1872	108	90[a]	18	399	27.0
1873	132	88	44	402	32.5
1874	156	79	77	429	36.4

Source: *Reports of the Treasurer,* 1868–1875.

[a] Labeled "gold and silver" instead of "coin and coin items."

[b] Cited as "currency" in other parts of the reports, these items presumably consisted of national bank notes and United States notes on hand, but excluded the "reserve."

[c] United States notes and fractional currency.

TABLE 8.2 Ratio of reserves to liabilities on selected dates for national banks in states, redemption cities, and New York City (percent)

	Oct. 5, 1868	Oct. 9, 1869	Oct. 8, 1870	Oct. 2, 1871	Oct. 3, 1872	July 13, 1873[a]	Sept. 12, 1873	Dec. 26, 1873	Oct. 2, 1874
States	22.9	20.5	20.9	21.2	19.2	20.6	20.6	20.8	19.1
Redemption cities	31.6	31.5	29.4	28.7	25.9	28.0	25.2	26.9	25.9
New York City	32.6	34.7	28.5	26.7	24.4	30.1	23.4	29.7	29.7

Source: *Reports of the Comptroller of the Currency,* 1869–1874.

[a] Not seasonally adjusted. Values for July would naturally be much higher than those for October.

and the basic ratio was 14.7 percent (table 7.3). These data reflect the decline in high-powered money (the 3 percents) and the permissive increase of national bank notes outstanding. The decline of $4 million in basic reserves between 12 September and 13 October 1873 was accompanied by a decrease of $76 million in national bank notes and deposits.

Treasury Policy during the Panic of 1873

Secretary Richardson made a pretense of initiating a Treasury policy. He began well enough by buying bonds for the sinking fund with the $14 million he had obtained from gold sales in the summer. After a few days he ordered the purchases stopped because "it became evident that the amount offering [*sic*] for purchase was increasing to an extent beyond the power of the Treasury to accept." He had not, he stated righteously,

TABLE 8.3 Average weekly liabilities and reserves of national banks in New York City for September and October 1873

	Liabilities (millions of dollars)			Reserves			
Week ending	Circulation	Deposits	Total	Specie	Legal tenders	Total	Ratio of total reserves to total liabilities (%)
Sept. 6	27.3	183	210	19.90	34.00	53.9	25.7
Sept. 13	26.4	178	204	17.70	32.50	50.2	24.6
Sept. 20	27.4	169	196	16.10	30.10	46.2	23.6
Sept. 27	27.3	150	177	11.50	17.90	29.3	16.5
Oct. 4	27.4	132	159	9.24	9.25	18.5	11.6
Oct. 11	27.4	132	159	10.50	8.05	18.6	11.6
Oct. 18	27.4	130	157	11.70	5.18	16.8	10.7
Oct. 25	27.4	126	153	11.40	7.19	18.6	12.2
Dec. 26	27.0[a]	169[a]	196	19.70	24.50	44.2	29.7

Source: *Report of Comptroller of the Currency,* 1874, p.170.
[a] Approximate.

used any part of the forty-four millions of United States notes, generally known as the reserve. . . . [General panic conditions] could not be avoided by any amount of currency which might be added to the circulation already existing. Confidence was to be entirely restored only by the slow and cautious process of gaining better knowledge of true values . . . and by conducting business on a firmer basis, with less inflation [*sic*] and more regard to real soundness and intrinsic values.[5]

Many interested business groups suggested proposals for getting United States notes into circulation. Richardson rejected them all because, he said, the Treasury's business did not include dealing in gold or foreign exchange, Congress had not authorized prepayment of the outstanding debt, and the issue of notes from the reserve "for the sole purpose of affecting [the money] market . . . ought not to be the business of the Treasury Department." Since the legal authority of the secretary's discretion over disposition of the reserve was still not clear, Richardson recommended that Congress answer the question "by a distinct enactment."[6]

Richardson's responses reflect a strict adherence to the letter of the law. He was a constitutionalist who did not trust his own judgment in making critical policy decisions.

Congress procrastinated, waiting for something to happen. And, sure enough, something did happen: Fiscal receipts underran fiscal expenditures in November and December of 1873, so that the secretary, for budgetary reasons, was forced to reissue $26 million of the $44 million "reserve." This action relieved the crisis. Comptroller of the currency John J. Knox reported that resumption of currency payments—United States notes for national bank notes—occurred 1 November 1873.[7]

Political Attitudes toward Resumption

Congress had many monetary problems to consider during the session that convened in early 1874: the panic that had just passed, the inelasticity of paper money, the stubborn refusal of national bank notes to apportion themselves "equitably" throughout the country, the relative volumes of national bank notes and United States notes that should be in existence, the Treasury's discretionary control over the currency, and the difficulty of resuming specie payments. John Sherman, assuming the role of cameral critic, indicted his Senate colleagues for favoring the goal of resumption in their speeches while hedging on this principle by promoting devious increases in the money supply. United States notes, fractional currency, and national bank notes had all increased in the past four years, he pointed out, and the premium on gold remained. He gently chastised Boutwell for his part in expanding the money supply and ended by saying that the correct quantity of money was the amount that could be maintained within the framework of a specie standard.[8]

Boutwell answered Sherman by observing that commercial countries were subject to a perverse elasticity in their bank-issued currencies. Relief might then occur either by suspension of specie payments and the issue of additional bank notes or by central-bank intervention to make more credit available. Suspension and the resulting commercial chaos, he thought, were primitive and obsolete; central-banking methods were a contemporary improvement. But relief from the effects of bank panics, he said, had never been attained even in England "without the personal intervention of men possessing power." The use of the "reserve" in four of the last five years was

> in its effect . . . substantially what is done by the Government of Great Britain through the Bank of England. The Secretary furnished temporary relief, not . . . by loans, because the Government of the United States is not engaged in making loans, but by adding to the circulation of the country, diminishing its value, . . . and changing the relations of debtor and creditor. Clothed with authority by law, . . . the Secretary could not sit silent and inactive while ruin was blasting the prospects of many and creating the most serious apprehensions in all parts of the country. It was a great responsibility; but it is a responsibility which must be taken by men who are clothed with the authority.[9]

Further decreases in the price level, Boutwell felt, were uncalled for. "We have no right morally," he argued, "to change the relations of [debtors and creditors]." Government bonds had long since appreciated to par in gold (due to demands for them from national banks) even though United States notes still circulated at a 12 percent discount to gold. The creditor class could therefore have made up losses on the depreciated dollars of the Civil War years "by investing the moneys received in securities of the Government." In short, depreciation losses on paper money had long since been capitalized. Resumption, he suggested, would occur by means of "natural progress . . . in the uses to which currency can be applied." He cited England in 1822 as an example of an economy that grew up to an inflated money stock.[10]

This attitude toward resumption was typical of many conservatives in the Grant administrations. Resumption was always favored, but as a policy that would be implemented sometime in the future by means left unspecified. Some opposition Democrats tried to make political capital of conservative procrastination by arguing vociferously for resumption. Their resumption, however, was always in gold *and* silver coin.[11]

If the Grant administrations had a monetary policy between 1868 and 1874, it was one of ad hoc means for maintaining the existing stock of money in the economy without allowing increases in the outstanding liquid obligations of the federal government. National bank-note policy had been the principal vehicle for effecting these tenuous and unspecified ends, but increases in the circulation of national bank notes had not been accompanied by the more equitable distribution of national bank notes anticipated in the original national bank act.

The cheap money–greenback movement was largely a reaction to this maldistribution. It exerted continuous pressure on the national banking system after 1867—to such an extent, in fact, that the national banking system "suffered a precarious existence for the next ten years with strong probabilities of its abandonment."[12]

Senator John Gordon of Georgia, in a speech in early 1874, emphasized the antipathy of southern and western regions to resumption. "The evil [of the recent panic]," Gordon argued, "is found . . . in the rigidity of volume, the non-elasticity and therefore insufficiency of the currency." He saw money flowing to New York, where it encouraged speculation and then could not be available for crop-moving. After making a comparison of money per capita between the United States and France, England, and Germany, he cited Henry Thornton on the buoyant business effects that resulted from an issue of exchequer bills, which were the British equivalent of United States treasury notes. He advocated low interest rates to encourage production in the South and argued that increases in the money supply would obtain this end. He pointedly objected to any policy that allowed falling prices, because "the people of the South and West are debtors; . . . their obligations were formed . . . when gold was at 110 to 150; and now to force them to pay in a currency equal to gold would be simply to increase their debts by the amount of 10 to 50 percent. . . . Cheap money is the one thing needed for the agricultural and productive interests of this county. . . . Cheap interest is what we want."[13]

In the House of Representatives John Bright of Tennessee also commented on the inequities of national bank-note apportionment and what he regarded as a general insufficiency of the currency. He denied that the currency was superabundant just because of the gold premium, and he closed his speech with an acidic attack on the inhumanity of the movement toward resumption: "To an aristocracy, existing on the annual interest of a national debt, the people are only of value in proportion to their docility and power of patiently bleeding golden blood under the tax-gatherer's thumbscrews."[14]

John Scott, a senator from Pennsylvania, expressed an opposing opinion. "I have no idea," he said, "that we can gratify what seems to be the desire of very many in the land; that is, start a volume of paper currency running past every man's door like the streams that carry him water, so that he can go out with his dipper in hand and take just what he requires to slake his monetary thirst and make him easy and comfortable in his business."[15]

The Act Providing for the Free Issue of National Bank Notes

The discussion in Congress reflected the resentment over the government's inability to ration currency in a manner that would satisfy anyone, let alone everyone. In such a situation grudging compromise was inevitable. The act of 20 June 1874 and the Resumption Act of 14 January 1875 shared this feature.

The act of 20 June 1874 froze greenbacks again, this time at $382 million. By this measure Congress allowed to stand the increase of $26 million that Secretary Richardson had issued in late 1873, but it also denied thereafter any concept or use of a "reserve" at the discretion of the secretary of the Treasury. The act also limited the responsibility for redemption of national bank notes to the Treasurer of the United States in Washington, although in practice the subtreasuries also redeemed notes when called upon to do so. To redeem its notes each national bank had to keep a redemption fund with the Treasury that amounted to 5 percent of notes outstanding. Since the redemption fund also served as part of the required reserves against deposits, this provision sharply reduced national banks' *required* reserves, and dramatically increased their reserve-deposit ratios. In effect, they no longer had to keep a reserve against their issues of notes. The increase of $26 million in greenbacks also contributed to the change in national bank reserve positions between October 1873 and October 1874. (See table 7.3.)

The last provision of the act of 1874 allowed a national bank to retire its own notes by depositing equal amounts of greenbacks with the comptroller of the currency. The comptroller would then pay out the greenbacks to retire the bank's notes and return the collateral securities to the issuing bank. This provision did not affect total greenbacks outstanding; the maximum issue was still $382 million. But it allowed a national bank to decide how much of its own notes it wished to circulate within the constraint of a maximum issue of $354 million for all national banks.

Political Factors in Passing the Resumption Act

The act of 20 June 1874 was an act of monetary ease and temperance. It allowed the first legal increase in high-powered United States notes in over six years. The elections that followed in the fall of 1874 witnessed the first overthrow of Republican majorities in Congress since the Civil War. Party leaders felt that their election setbacks resulted from soft monetary policies and their procrastination over resumption.[16] They resolved to get a resumption bill through Congress in the lame-duck session of 1874–75 before they lost control over legislation to the incoming Democratic majorities. However, they had to be sure they did not do too much, for while resumption was desirable, contraction was not. So any resumption bill, in order to pass, had to be phrased in terms that implied no contraction of the currency. The result of this effort was the Resumption Act of 14 January 1875.[17]

The Resumption Act may appear to be nothing more than a pious determination to do the right thing at the right time. However, it resolved the national bank-note currency problem by abolishing completely the government-imposed limitation on national bank notes. It also proved to be a means for reducing the outstanding volume of United States notes through an interpretative provision that allowed secretaries of the Treasury to effect a modest contraction of these notes over the next three years.

The administration of national bank-note apportionment was beset with complications.[18] The Resumption Act ended these problems by cutting the Gordian knot. It stated that any national banking association could increase circulating notes without limit: "The provisions of law for the withdrawal and redistribution of national bank currency among the several states and territories are hereby repealed."[19]

Tied to the provision for the unrestricted issue of national bank notes was the one that provided some real impetus toward resumption. It specified that

> whenever, and so often, as circulating notes shall be issued to any such [national] banking association . . . it shall be the duty of the Secretary of the Treasury to redeem the legal tender United States notes in excess only of $300 million to the amount of 80 percent of the sum of national bank notes so issued . . . and to continue such redemption . . . until there shall be outstanding the sum of $300 million of such legal tender United States notes and no more. . . . And to enable the Secretary of the Treasury to prepare and provide for redemptions in this act authorized or required, he is authorized to use any surplus revenues . . . in the Treasury not otherwise appropriated, and to issue, sell, and dispose of, at not less than par, in coin, either of the descriptions of bonds of the United States described in the Act of Congress approved July 14, 1870, entitled, "An Act to authorize the refunding of the national debt."[20]

The author of the resumption bill, the guiding hand for its passage, and later the administrator of its successful implementation was Senator John Sherman. He was chairman of the Senate Committee on Finance during the

Forty-third Congress and became secretary of the Treasury under Rutherford B. Hayes in March 1877.

Sherman prepared the resumption bill for passage by caucusing with Republican leaders in Congress before the bill's appearance in the Senate.[21] To get concurrence of the still-existing Republican majorities, Sherman had to use the utmost tact in framing the bill so that it gave no implication of contraction, for contraction had become political anathema. Sherman claimed that the bill would allow national bank notes to expand or contract henceforth only "in case the business of the community demands it." The secretary of the Treasury would retire United States notes equivalent to 80 percent of any additional national bank notes issued, in recognition of the fact that 20 percent in United States notes was the average reserve ratio required against national bank demand obligations. Hence the reduction of United States notes from $382 million to $300 million was supposed to be matched by an increase in national bank notes of $100 million, which would be possible if the national banks were able to attract reserves of $20 million of the remaining United States notes from their use as hand-to-hand currency. "This provision of the bill," Sherman stated blandly, "neither provides for a contraction or expansion of the currency, but leaves the amount [outstanding] to be regulated by the business wants of the community."[22]

The ensuing debate on the bill revealed some interesting congressional sentiments about monetary policy. Carl Schurz of Missouri, a hard-shelled resumptionist, asked Sherman pointedly whether the United States notes that the Treasury would redeem could then be reissued in the same fashion as the $26 million reserve that had been reissued by the Treasury Department in 1873. Sherman replied that he would leave the word *redeem* to be interpreted by future Congresses when greenbacks were down to the target of $300 million. "Practical men dealing with practical affairs," he said, "cannot introduce into this bill a controversy which will prevent that unity that is necessary to carry out the good that is contained in this bill."[23]

Sherman's refusal to make the bill specify unqualified destruction of the United States notes prompted many senators to condemn the bill as inflationary. John Stevenson of Kentucky had perhaps the best characterization of it. "The bill," he said, "is a species of Janus-faced legislation. . . . [It is a measure] upon which expansionists and contractionists could temporarily unite." Both groups, he said, could think that they had triumphed.[24]

The real force in the bill was the hidden contraction in high-powered money (United States notes) that it permitted and encouraged. Whenever national bank notes were issued by the comptroller of the currency, the secretary of the Treasury had to use any fiscal means in his power to redeem United States notes, thereby taking them out of circulation.

This provision made it sound as though the bill would be neutral in its effects on the money supply. However, in practice its effect on the money stock depended on the discretion of the secretary of the Treasury, who administered it. If he had chosen to retire United States notes up to 80 percent of the *net* amount of *new* national bank notes issued, the money supply might have stayed roughly constant.[25] If he had chosen to retire United States notes on the basis of *gross* national bank notes issued, without counting the notes voluntarily retired by the banks themselves as permitted by the act of 20 June 1874, the resulting reduction of greenbacks might have had virtually no relation to the net change in national bank notes.[26] Under the "gross" interpretation, the total currency could increase only if the gross decrease in national bank notes was less than the difference between the gross increase in such notes and the net amount of greenbacks retired.[27] In fact, gross issues of national bank notes over the next three years amounted to about $45 million, permitting the retirement of $36 million in greenbacks. *Net* issues of national bank notes, however, declined by about the same amount ($25 million) as United States notes (column 1 in table 7.3).[28] The outstanding currency, therefore, did not stay constant, with national bank notes reciprocally increasing as United States notes declined. Outstanding quantities of *both* currencies shrank, and prices continued to fall.

How much guile was there in the Resumption Act when it was passed? To what extent was the decrease in United States notes seen as a leverage factor that would decrease the total money supply? Apparently not much. Several senators thought the act would promote inflation. Carl Schurz observed, for example, that to get resumption the proportion of paper to gold would have to decline; "and in this respect," he concluded, "the bill before us is palpably and deplorably inadequate." In addition, an amendment that explicitly proposed contraction of United States notes at the rate of $2 million per month until resumption occurred was defeated in the Senate by a vote of 44 to 6.[29]

Sherman may have had some intuitions about the contraction that would result from the deflation of United States notes. The 80 percent reduction clause, he remarked, "not only leads us toward specie payment, but lessens the volume which we are bound to redeem when the time comes for final redemption." Allen Thurman of Ohio expressed the general sentiment of the Senate: "It is very difficult to find out what is in [the bill]. . . . There is a great deal of omission, but the least possible amount of commission that ever I have seen in a great public measure."[30]

The House of Representatives passed the bill without debate just as it came from the Senate, and it became law on 14 January 1875. Many who voted for it "in principle" undoubtedly assumed or wished that it would never become operational. It called for fractional silver coinage in place of fractional paper money, and it slightly subsidized gold coinage by repealing the coinage charges of $0.002 per $1,000. Finally, the act permitted "free banking" in the sense that national banks could issue as much or as little currency as they wished so long as they obeyed reserve requirements and other national bank regulations.[31] Apportionment problems of national bank notes became a thing of the past.

Treasury Implementation of the Resumption Act

The secretaries of the Treasury who served after passage of the Resumption Act were partisan resumptionists who elected to carry out the "gross" interpretation of the law. When Rutherford B. Hayes became president in 1876, he appointed Sherman secretary of the Treasury. This appointment gave Sherman the opportunity to implement and administer the policy he had authored in the Senate. Since the basic stock of high-powered money was declining slowly but steadily due to the 80 percent provision in the Resumption Act, Sherman could undertake a do-nothing policy and the gold premium would gradually disappear as the general price level fell.

Sherman's opinion on resumption was adamant, but it did not imply that he favored a rigidly metallic monetary system. Far from it. His ideal system called for (1) United States notes, "carefully limited in amount" and "supported by ample reserves of coin in the Treasury," (2) "supplemented by a system of national banks . . . free and open to all, . . . with power to issue circulating notes secured by United States bonds, . . . and redeemable on demand in United States notes or coin," and (3) the limited coinage of silver as a minor currency. The government, he thought, was "a safer custodian of reserves than a multitude of scattered banks"; but banks were better for handling "the ebb and flow of currency caused by varying crops, productions and seasons." Even Sherman's ideal monetary structure had to allow for periods in which it was "impracticable to maintain actual redemption. . . . Every such system," he concluded pragmatically, "must provide for a suspension of specie payments."[32]

The Democratic Congress was not ready to give up so easily. The Resumption Act had been passed in a lame-duck session (Forty-third Congress, second session) just before a legislature much less amenable to resumption convened. Democratic congressmen then introduced bills for repeal of the Resumption Act in the Forty-fourth Congress, but no such bills could get through the Senate, much less past the executive. The elections of 1876 and 1878 likewise resulted in Congresses that were antipathetic to resumption. However, Rutherford B. Hayes, who had become president by a majority of one electoral vote in a bitterly disputed contest, conscientiously supported the resumption ideal. Only a bill to repeal that had better than a two-thirds vote in Congress could get past an executive veto, and no bill had this much support.

The Influence of Silver on the Economics of Resumption

The hostility of Congress and the public to the resumption medicine became intensive during the years 1876–1878. The free-silver/cheap-money movement that appeared in the mid–1870s became a means for populist efforts to thwart resumption. Late in 1876 a joint resolution of Congress formed a silver commission to "do something" for silver. It was composed of three senators (Jones, Bogy, and Boutwell), three representatives (Gibson, Willard, and Bland), and two nonpolitical experts (William Groesbeck of Ohio and Professor Francis Bowen of Massachusetts).[33] The duties of the commission were to inquire into (1) the causes and effects of changes in the relative values of gold and silver; (2) the possibility of restoring the double standard, and the mint values at which it should be restored; (3) the effect of allowing United States notes to exist concurrently with the double standard; and (4) the best means of "providing for facilitating [*sic*] the resumption of specie payments."[34]

The commission subsequently made one majority and two minority reports. The majority, five of the eight members, claimed that a double standard was necessary to prevent chronic crisis and business paralysis. They recommended the restoration of the double standard and the unrestricted coinage of both metals, even though they could not agree on the legal mint value that the law should specify between the metallic currencies. The place for a convertible paper currency in a metallic system, they thought, was uncertain. Great Britain had accomplished a resumption with a mixed-money system, but only after "an unexampled commercial and industrial depression, covering nearly the period of a generation. . . . The Commission," the majority report emphasized, "have been able to arrive at only the one single conclusion that resumption in this country is not practicable under the circumstances, until the laws making gold the sole metallic legal-tender are repealed."[35] This point was reiterated and emphasized in the face of disagreement over the precise monetary ratio that Congress should establish between gold and silver. *The political price of resumption was silver remonetization.* Even the minority report of Boutwell disagreed with the principle of silver remonetization only if it did not occur on an international basis.[36]

The minority report written by Professor Bowen and concurred in by Representative Gibson stressed stability in a standard of value as opposed to mere facility in a medium of exchange. It argued (without much substantiation) that both legal tender paper and silver currency gave rise to undesirable price level fluctuation. "What we dread," the report stated, "is not the *fall,* but the *fluctuation,* in value of the would-be standard, and the feeling of uncertainty thereby produced." It interpreted the price level decline of late 1876 and the corresponding decline in the gold premium on greenbacks as results of decreased issues of national bank notes and United States notes—although it incorrectly contended that the decrease in paper money occurred "spontaneously, and without any aid from legislation."[37]

The minority report concluded that (1) silver was too much subject to depreciation to be a suitable standard of value; (2) the use of legal tender paper was "unjust"; (3) resumption was within reach, due to the "spontaneous" contraction of the paper money at the rate of $3 million per month during the previous two years; (4) Congress should authorize coinage of a fiat (subsidiary) silver dollar of 345.6 grains to replace the fiat greenback dollar; (5) Congress should also authorize devaluation of the gold dollar by about 2.6 percent (from 23.2 grains to 22.6 grains); and (6) *net* contraction of the paper currency should continue.[38]

The minority's advocacy of gold-dollar devaluation was indeed surprising, even though the proposed percentage was small. Jones, Bogey, and Willard of the majority recommended a legal relationship between the two metals of 15.5 to 1 instead of the old relationship of 15.98 to 1. They could have obtained this new relationship either by reducing the silver content of the silver dollar from 412.5 grains to 399.9 grains (0.9 fine) or by increasing the gold content of the gold dollar from 25.8 to 26.6 grains (0.9 fine). These alternatives would have had opposite effects. The former would have encouraged a slight increase in silver currency, the latter a slight reduction in gold coinage. Not unnaturally they recommended the former. They did not imply that easing prices was a desideratum, but their earlier analysis had stressed the evil of falling prices.[39]

Groesbeck and Bland of the majority concurred in recommending the old silver dollar. They disagreed with the rest of the majority that the silver dollar of 412.5 grains was undervalued at the mint, but they felt that reviving the question of relative mint values would impede much of the progress already made toward silver remonetization.[40]

The comprehensive report of the Silver Commission, while it included diverse views on remonetization and on the valuation of both gold and silver, concurred in advocating a cheaper dollar than either of the metallic dollars of 1860. One group was satisfied with the naturally cheaper silver dollar; another group would have devalued even that; while the sound-money group favored a dollar exclusively gold, but one that would be devalued a modest 2.6 percent. Given evidence of such diversity, one can hardly agree with Kindahl's conclusion that "no thought was given to the possibility of resumption through the expedient of devaluation."[41] Even Sherman suggested that "if the financial condition of our country is so grievous that we must at every hazard have a cheaper dollar, . . . it is far better, rather than to adopt the single standard of silver, to boldly reduce the number of grains in the gold dollar, or to abandon and retrace all efforts to make United States notes equal to coin."[42]

The greenback movement itself implied de facto devaluation through inflation and demonetization. Had silver not emerged as a more respectable form of cheap money, the greenback movement might have thwarted resumption until late in the century, when gold became less costly to obtain due to new discoveries in the Yukon and South Africa.

Something for Silver: The Bland-Allison Act

The Bland-Allison Act of February 1878 was the legislative result of the Silver Commission's work. It called for the secretary of the Treasury to purchase monthly between $2 million and $4 million worth of silver at market prices. The bullion was to be coined into dollars of 412.5 grains, but the Treasury Department would issue these dollars only if its other revenues were insufficient for ordinary fiscal payments.

The price of greenbacks in terms of gold gradually approached the prewar parity; the discount by the end of 1877 was only 3 percent. This trend corresponded to changes that had taken place in the money stock since 1874.[43] When the premium on gold seemed certain to reach zero, Congress repealed the 80 percent clause in the Resumption Act and on 31 May 1878 froze the volume of United States notes at $346.7 million. Enough was enough.

Sherman had meanwhile negotiated with bankers and foreign investors in order to accumulate a treasury balance of gold that he presumed would be necessary to cover redemption of paper money. But the gold was not needed; market forces had done their work. Resumption occurred without a tremor on the date set and with virtually no demands for redemption.

Sherman impounded most of the silver coined under the Bland-Allison Act, so silver had little effect on the price level before resumption. His advocacy of a mixed-money system was indeed a compromising position, and it earned him the reputation of being a "shifty Secretary."[44] Nonetheless, resumption would probably not have occurred without his moderate compromises and his devious policy of retiring United States notes via his interpretation of the Resumption Act.

Summary of Post–Civil War Monetary Policies

Resumption of specie payments in 1879 was a remarkable political and economic accomplishment, but it had precedent—in the United States in 1819 and in England in 1822. As a political achievement, it required a disciplined approach to price-level adjustment with corresponding hardships to debtors and with depressive effects on business activity and spending. Paradoxically, it had little effect on total production. That such price-level discipline was obtained several times in constitutional republics during the nineteenth century and once during the early twentieth century following World War I is a tribute to the esteem in which political leaders held the gold standard, and to their wisdom for not chartering omnipotent central banks that would usurp the functions of metallic standards and make paper-money inflations permanent.

The economics of resumption required that prices fall to about the level prevailing before the greenback inflation.[45] Such an adjustment could have resulted from various combinations of (1) reduction in the stock of money, (2) growth in output, and (3) reduction in the rate of use of money. The first of these methods could take any one or a combination of three variants:

(a) reduction of high-powered money, (b) reduction in the deposit-reserve ratio, and (c) reduction in the deposit-currency ratio.

In the immediate postwar period approved policy was the wholesale destruction of high-powered money, harsh medicine even for Victorians. Starting in 1868, accepted policy changed to one of holding the stock of currency (and presumably of all money) constant, with the expectation that growth in output would promote a gentle decline in the price level. This method had the clear consensus of the political center, and nothing could get through Congress that would have openly violated it.[46]

The Resumption Act, on the face of it, left this policy norm undisturbed. However, its wording was imprecise enough to allow the secretary of the Treasury to promote a limited contraction of United States notes. All three secretaries between 1875 and 1879 favored resumption, so they interpreted the Resumption Act in a way that permitted them to reduce outstanding greenbacks.[47]

Milton Friedman and Anna J. Schwartz have presented an accurate and detailed account of monetary developments in this period. They contend that the decline in high-powered money in the last few years before resumption was "an accomplishment of omission, as it were, not of commission. . . . The decline . . . owed less . . . to any Treasury action under the influence of the Resumption Act than to the decline in the two deposit ratios, a decline that we have attributed to a rise in bank suspensions."[48] Friedman and Schwartz correctly assess the causes and consequences of changes in the two deposit ratios, and they heed the decline in high-powered money. They themselves, however, commit a "sin" of omission in not recognizing the monetary effect that was contrived by Treasury interpretation of the Resumption Act. Contrary to what they argue, at least one political factor was of some importance.

What would have happened if the Resumption Act had not been passed? Without a Resumption Act, Rutherford B. Hayes might not have been elected in 1876. Samuel Tilden, the Democratic candidate, might then have signed a bill that would have increased the greenbacks to such an extent that resumption would have become impossible. However, if the policy of constancy in the high-powered money stock had continued unabated, resumption would probably have occurred anyway within a year or two of when it did in 1879. Growth in output, so long as it was not inhibited by too restrictive a monetary policy, would ultimately have lowered money prices by the necessary amount.

9 Controversy over Currency Denominations

> The possession of a few copper cents [in 1862] meant that the owner could ride [the street car] rather than walk. . . . It meant that he could buy a postage stamp without an altercation with the clerk, or a cigar without receiving in change a handful of the dealer's own manufactured currency.
>
> Neil Carothers, *Fractional Money,* 1930

Arguments over the Issue of Small-Denominational Paper Money

Nineteenth-century discussions of currency theory and policy almost always included arguments over the undesirability of small notes in the monetary spectrum, and the states often backed up the rhetorical admonitions with proscriptive laws.[1] Contemporary monetary historians have largely neglected this controversy, or dismissed it as inconsequential.[2] Inattention to an issue that demanded so much energy and resources provokes a sense of uneasiness—a feeling that the present is overlooking an important dilemma or frustration of the past.

Money-users could satisfy their demand for small-denominational money in about five different ways. Gold was one possibility, but it was not a good solution because any gold piece smaller than $5 was too small to be used handily. Silver was one traditional means for providing for lower denominations. However, full-bodied silver coins in the United States were undervalued at the mint from 1834 until 1873, meaning that their values in the market as commodities were greater than their monetary values at the mint. So for fifty years—until silver became cheap enough for general monetary use in the early 1880s—fractional silver currency did not fulfill the demand for small denominations except for coins so worn, clipped, and abraded that their commodity value had fallen to or below their monetary value.

A third possibility was governmental or private coinage of copper, nickel, and silver alloys into token and fractional subsidiary currency. Coins of Spanish origin fulfilled some of the demand for fractional currency, and some Spanish coins were designated as legal tender by the U.S. Congress. However, fractional coin production before 1834 was insufficient, inefficient, uncertain, and beset with political complications. "The coinage of quarters, dimes, and half-dimes, as contrasted with the half-dollar," Neil Carothers reported, "was negligible from 1792 to 1834. . . . The total number of [these denominations] coined before 1830 was less than one piece for each person in the country in that year."[3]

The fourth candidate was commercial bank notes. Small-denomination bank notes, however, suffered for decades from both sound-money proponents and demagogic politicians who could conveniently blame the notes for the occasional banking crisis of the era. Although the sound-money propaganda might not have been completely effective, state laws prohibiting the issue of small bank notes—usually those under $5—had substantial consequences.

The fifth possibility was bank deposits. Deposit banking, however, was still in its infancy; and deposits were a less popular medium in rural and frontier areas such as the South and the West, where transactions were for small amounts, and where the bank population necessary to oversee deposit clearings was thin.[4]

The usual classification of "small" notes in the United States ordinarily included denominations of paper currency for $5 or less issued by banks, corporations, states, or individuals. However, the specification of "small" was in part a function of the price level. If prices rose substantially during an inflation, a nominally valued "larger" note would become smaller in real terms, and small notes then came to include the issues of, say, $10 notes in addition to all those of $5 and less.

The popular argument condemning small notes held that, under an operational metallic standard, banks preferred to issue notes in small denominations in order to minimize the "reflux of their circulation." Small notes, bankers learned from experience, were more likely to continue circulating in a given local area than an equal value of larger notes. Not only were they more useful as hand-to-hand currency, but if ordinary business purposes led an individual or a firm to demand specie for bank notes, a few of the larger denominations cost less in time and trouble to convert to specie than a mass of small notes. Both suppliers of small notes (banks) and demanders of the notes (households and businesses) regarded them as useful and desirable media for daily transactions, especially when fractional coins were in short supply. For this reason they were less likely to come back for redemption in specie.[5]

An inflation of government-issued paper currency within the framework of a mixed-currency system generally caused the disappearance of metallic coin because of the inflated nominal market value of the metal in the coin. Banks would then issue paper notes in the smaller denominations to replace the fugitive coin. This association between inflation and the appearance of small notes "proved" to many observers that the small notes "drove specie out of hand-to-hand circulation, and frequently out of the country as well . . . [thus causing] suspension of specie payments."[6] In fact, inflation resulted from the sheer quantity of the government issues. The burgeoning volume of small bank notes was only possible because of the government paper currency that the banks now held as reserves. The appearance of small denominations was a symptom. It reflected the common need for a transaction medium to handle nominal purchases and sales formerly handled by coin—coin that had gone into "the arts" to take advantage of the inflated market price of monetary metal. Nonetheless, the simultaneous disappearance of specie and appearance of small notes endowed the notes with a mischievous influence.[7]

Small-Note Issues in England and the United States before 1820

Several classical economists joined the chorus in condemning small notes. For example, Adam Smith in *The Wealth of Nations* observed that the minimum bank-note denomination in London was £10. The ordinary customer could use a bank note of this size only to a limited extent before he had to change it into fractional coin. Smith advocated a minimum denomination of £15 as a means of securing the circulation of gold and silver. He proposed this restriction even though he recognized it as "a manifest violation of that natural liberty which it is the proper business of law, not to infringe, but to support." He thought that the right to issue notes of any denomination would endanger the soundness of the currency; so restricting the issue of small notes was like building fire walls to prevent the spread of fire.[8] Henry Thornton, writing in 1802, also charged that the issue of small notes payable to bearer caused "a great and permanent diminution in our circulating coin" and increased the danger of inconvertibility between bank paper and coin.[9]

The views of these economists were typical for their time and, indeed, for the whole era in which a mixed currency was the norm. Banking policies followed these learned prescriptions. The Bank of England, for example, issued no notes under £20 before 1759, when it introduced £15 and £10 notes.[10] During the restriction period when specie redemption of notes was forbidden by law, the bank was permitted to issue notes as low as £1 and £2, thus demonstrating the need for small notes to fill the void of the missing coin. As resumption of specie payments became anticipated after 1816, the bank reduced its issues of the £1 and £2 notes from a peak of £9.3 million in 1814 to £900,000 in 1822, or from 30 percent of its total note circulation to 5 percent.[11] After 1826 English law limited the bank's lowest denomination to £5.[12]

Monetary events in the United States during and after the War of 1812 offer another good example of the small-note problem. The United States Treasury issued large amounts of interest-bearing treasury notes between 1812 and 1815. Of the some $35 million issued, only the final $3.39 million included denominations under $20.[13] The larger denominations, which included about 90 percent of the total value of all issues, were much more desirable as reserves for commercial banks than they were as hand-to-hand currency for the general public. On the basis of these new reserves the banks expanded their loans, deposits, and currency ("circulation") in any and all denominations that the nonbank public needed and demanded. Inflation and suspension followed. All specie, including fractional silver coins, went out of circulation, so the banks had to supply small notes. In his review of this period A. Barton Hepburn claimed that the banks purposely foisted small notes on the public: "In order to increase the volume [of notes] as much as possible, . . . a mass of small denominations, some as low as six cents, were issued. . . . Suspension of coin payments *naturally* followed."[14] The issue of small notes by the banks, Hepburn argued, caused suspension and inflation. In fact, the issue of treasury notes that gave the banks fresh reserves fueled the inflation and thereby initiated the subsequent demonetization of metallic money. The issue of small notes was just an ex post facto symptom.[15]

Before the Civil War, New York and Pennsylvania led the states in prohibiting notes under $5. A dozen other states followed their example, "one of the objects," Hepburn noted, "being to enforce the use of silver and gold in the small transactions of daily barter."[16] The ubiquitous laws against small-note issues were hard to police, but they had significant if not lasting effects on the denominational texture of the monetary system.[17]

This prejudice against small notes was basically contradictory. If small notes were in demand for transaction purposes, they would be used extensively in place of barter and remain in circulation. They could not simultaneously be demanded for monetary purposes and cause embarrassment by being turned in for specie.[18]

Private Issues of Small Notes before and after the Civil War

Gold and silver coins might have defused the small-note controversy if public policy had been more sophisticated and if the discoveries of precious metals had been more regular. In the early part of the century most of the coins in use were Spanish. By 1820 the United States mint had coined less than one piece below a half dollar for each person in the country, and the value per person of the coins in circulation was less than $0.25.[19] This situation was not improved by the Coinage Act of 1834—a law "inspired by crassly partisan motives." It fixed the gold-silver mint ratio too high at the same time that it devalued the gold dollar. It therefore led gradually but inevitably to the cessation of silver coinage and the disappearance of silver currency.[20]

The discoveries of gold in the western United States and in Australia in the late 1840s reduced the real price of gold and correspondingly aggravated the demonetization of silver and the export of silver coins to Europe. The coinage laws of 1834 and 1853 provided for a tiny gold dollar and a subsidiary silver three-cent piece. These two very small coins, together with underweight and worn Spanish coins, were all that were available for ordinary transactions until 1857. The coinage law of 1857, while deficient and imperfect in some respects, effectively complemented the existing coinage system with coins adequate for large and small transactions.[21] No sooner had the coinage reached this satisfactory condition than the monetary events of the Civil War threw it into a new disequilibrium.

The greenback issues of 1861–1865 had the classic, predictable effect of provoking a paper-money inflation. The Treasury issued the new notes in massive amounts and in no denominations below $5. Market prices of the monetary metals rapidly appreciated along with all other prices. By 1862 what had been coin currencies became commodities. Prices rose so quickly that metallic currency disappeared almost overnight, leaving a paralyzing vacuum in the lower denominations. Neil Carothers's account states: "The country found itself, in the midst of a war boom, virtually without a currency between the 1 cent piece and the $5 note."[22] Private businesses and municipalities tried to fill the vacuum by issuing notes, tickets, and due bills, and the government carried out its ill-conceived expedient of a postage-stamp currency. It also passed the National Bank Act in 1863, which allowed national banks to issue $50 million, of a total of $300 million, in denominations under $5 (but only until resumption of specie payments, when the $5 lower limit would again apply).[23]

Several Treasury reports of the early 1870s emphasized the lack of small notes and fractional currency. Also noted were the questionable means used to relieve the shortage. An amendment in 1865 to the National Bank Act had prohibited *banking* corporations from issuing paper currency without paying the prohibitive 10 percent tax, but it had not specified any restrictions on issues of notes by nonbanks. In 1872 the comptroller of the currency, John Jay Knox, titled a section of his annual report "Shinplasters." Under this heading, he criticized notes issued by the state of Alabama, which were payable and receivable for all state debts:

> Savings-banks, railroad, municipal, and other corporations in the States of Florida, Georgia and other Southern States have followed the example of the State of Alabama, and have issued, and are still issuing, a large amount of similar circulation, some in the form of receipts and certificates, and others in the form of railroad tickets, but all issued in the form and similitude of bank notes, and intended to circulate as money. There is no law in existence to prevent the circulation and no legislative provision for the enforcement of the constitutional provision [against bills of credit] of such issues.[24]

Knox pointed out the same practice in 1873 by the Central Railroad and Banking Company of Georgia. "I am informed that these issues are redeemed by the railroad company," he said, "and that . . . arrangements are being made by manufacturing companies and corporations to issue similar devices."[25] The problem was not confined to the South, Knox emphasized. Mining corporations around Lake Superior, and Zion's Commercial Cooperative Institution of Salt Lake City, also issued such notes.[26]

A group of private merchants and bankers of Columbia, South Carolina, petitioned Congress in December 1873 (after the bank panic), protesting similar action. Numerous corporations issued currency that "are *fac similies* [*sic*] of national bank notes," their memorial stated, "forcing that currency upon their employees." On the notes issued by the South Carolina Railroad Company, the petition continued, "the word 'dollars' does not appear." To escape the prohibitive tax on state bank notes, companies lithographed notes "Good for the fare of one passage ____ miles." The memorial cited other examples of questionable paper currency, including notes issued by a building and loan association and by the city of Columbia itself. It concluded by entreating Congress to "bridle this wild delirium which has seized upon these breakers and evaders of the law."[27]

The treasurer of the United States, an official who usually did not report on current monetary conditions, wrote in 1874 that he had had "personal experience and observation" of unauthorized paper money in the South. Issues of local currency, particularly fractional currency, he said, were "put upon everybody [as] change, and unless used in the place of issue are worthless to the holder."[28]

These protests emphasized the dearth of currency generally and of lower denominations in particular, especially in the South and West. The arithmetic of the denominational problem is simple. Only two combinations of the usual denominations make three dollars' worth of currency—a one-dollar and a two-dollar bill or three one-dollar bills. Since one- and two-dollar bills were scarce, especially in the South, the difficulty of making change for the more usual five-dollar bill is readily apparent. Under such circumstances the sheer economic necessity for issues of scrip and trade credit made virtually any merchant a merchant-banker. His customers would readily accept a trade credit for, say, a ten-dollar bill at his general store because they could see that he had a store full of goods, and that they as his creditors could demand these goods as liquidation of the trade-credit balance. These commercial currencies were the spontaneous evolution of an economic good in the presence of a manifest scarcity. Making the notes payable to bearer rather than a bookkeeping credit to the order of a single person was simply a cheaper way of handling this kind of exchange, especially for an institution, such as a municipality, that handled numerous small transactions.

Despite widespread use of "unauthorized paper money," not many observers of the era recognized its utility or had the temerity to contradict those who condemned it. One of the few who did was Charles Moran. He argued outspokenly for free banking and for unconstrained issues of small notes.[29] He correctly stated that the fears and prejudices against the issue of small notes were due to the fallacious theories of English and American bullionists, "who attributing monetary panics and commercial crises to over-issues of bank notes, have always urged legislative restrictions to the issues of bank notes so as to force coin into circulation contrary to the self-interest and desires of the people."[30]

Resumption of specie payments in 1879, the extensive recoinage of silver for smaller denominations during the 1880s, and the rapid development of checkbook banking alleviated most denominational problems. After 1886 the general scarcity of small-denominational currency abated, and the problem faded away.

The Effect of Denominational Shortages on the Measured Velocity of Money

Strange as it may seem, the denominational composition of the currency during the nineteenth century may have had a significant bearing on the decline in the measured velocity of money so prominent for that period. Computations of the income velocity of money over the century indicate a decline from about six per year in the early part of the century to a value of about three per year or less around 1900. Velocity values then stabilize until 1929, fall substantially during the Great Depression and World War II, then climb again during the seventies and eighties, when inflation became pervasive.[31]

Several economists have tried to develop testable hypotheses that would explain the steadily declining velocity of money during the nineteenth century. One hypothesis is that declining velocity results from the effect of secular increases in real income on desired money balances.[32] According to this view money is a superior good having an income elasticity of demand greater than one. As real incomes increase over time, people build up real balances, causing the velocity of money to decline. This theory does not, however, reconcile the apparent secular decline in velocity during the nineteenth century with no apparent *secular* change during the first three quarters of the twentieth century.[33]

A more likely source of bias in velocity measurement stems from the compilation of the data used to measure velocity. Two time series are necessary, money income and the stock of money. To obtain current income values for some past period, the observer must estimate the real volume of goods and services produced, and he then must record the market prices at which the transactions for the goods and services cleared. He must also get an accurate measure of the stock of money for the time during which the transactions occurred. If no money exists other than what is officially accounted, and if money is used for all transactions, the estimates of money income and the stock of money can give reasonably accurate measures of the velocity of money from one time period to another. These velocity values provide a tolerable index of money-using behavior. However, if a significant portion of real income is bartered but still accounted as money income, and if a significant amount of money used to transact real product is not counted or is unaccountable, the velocity quotient obtained by dividing "money income" with the measured stock of money will be greater than the real velocity. It will imply that accounted money is being exchanged much more frequently than is really the case. If, over time, a higher and higher proportion of formerly bartered real product is exchanged for accounted money while money-holding habits remain constant, the *computed* value of monetary velocity will gradually decline. This "decline" is really the elimination of a bias—a computational artifact; money-holding habits would not have changed.[34]

Clark Warburton found from his investigation on this question that national income estimates for the nineteenth century were not sufficiently reliable or well constituted to show how large a proportion of the national product was sold in markets and how much was produced by farm and village families for their own use.[35] Whatever the actual proportions, the amount bartered was significant, but declined secularly as the proportion of nonpecuniary income to total income also declined. These facts are themselves sufficient to account for a substantial bias in measured velocity.[36]

The downward bias in accounted velocity during the nineteenth century is compatible with the supposition that currency in use suffered from serious denominational shortcomings during many decades of the century. Denominational hindrances encouraged swaps, barter, payment in kind, and the use of unaccounted and unaccountable moneys to a much greater degree than has been acknowledged or can be measured. As denominational constraints lessened late in the century, the cost of bringing more and more product and income into the circuit of monetary transactions also lessened. Then, with the virtual disappearance of denominational impediments late in the century and the reduction of barter to a relatively small fraction of income, the decided downward "trend" in velocity ceased.

The task of estimating the extent of barter and the use of unaccounted substitute moneys is even more difficult than measuring velocity accurately. However, the relatively reliable time series on currency denominations in the period following the Civil War allow for some inferences on monetary behavior. From 1865 to 1868 the decline in the money stock caused a general deflation. The period from 1868 to 1879 was a time of fasting and cleansing in preparation for resumption of specie payments, and was a period marked by sharp monetary controversy and uncertainty. The eleven or twelve years after resumption (1880–1891), while not free of controversy, witnessed a reduction of the unsettling pressures from government intervention on monetary behavior.

Table 9.1 summarizes denominational data for United States currency between 1868 and 1891. It includes all currency denominations from $1 to $50, but excepts gold coin.[37] In the first period, 1868–1879, the total dollar value

TABLE 9.1 Number of pieces of standard currency denominations in the United States, wholesale prices, and average denominations, 1868–1891

	(millions of pieces)										
End of fiscal year (June 30)	$1 (1)	$2 (2)	$5 (3)	$10 (4)	$20 (5)	$50 (6)	Total (7)	Total (millions of dollars) (8)	Average money denomination ($) (9)	Prices (1910–1914 = 100) (10)	Average real denomination ($) (11)
1868	22.3	10.9	35.2	16.1	5.37	0.85	90.7	530.4	5.85	158	3.70
1869	23.0	12.3	34.8	16.2	5.90	0.71	92.9	537.0	5.78	151	3.83
1870	26.2	16.7	37.0	18.4	6.64	0.97	105.9	609.6	5.76	135	4.27
1871	27.8	15.6	34.7	16.5	5.93	0.82	101.4	557.2	5.50	130	4.23
1872	31.1	16.1	35.3	17.1	6.18	0.87	106.7	578.2	5.42	136	3.99
1873	31.8	15.8	35.0	17.3	6.32	0.91	107.1	583.9	5.45	133	4.10
1874	31.0	15.9	36.3	17.1	6.62	1.03	108.0	598.8	5.54	126	4.40
1875	29.4	14.4	31.1	17.1	6.66	1.13	99.8	574.5	5.76	118	4.88
1876	31.3	14.7	28.7	16.6	6.55	1.18	99.0	559.8	5.66	110	5.15
1877	29.0	13.3	28.6	16.3	6.40	1.17	94.8	547.5	5.78	106	5.45
1878	25.9	11.9	29.7	17.0	6.57	0.98	92.1	548.3	5.95	91	6.54
1879	29.9	10.5	30.0	17.1	6.56	0.94	95.0	550.0	5.79	90	6.43
1880	42.3	11.1	33.2	19.1	7.46	0.96	114.1	618.1	5.42	100	5.42
1881	53.0	11.7	33.9	21.7	8.49	1.00	129.8	682.3	5.26	103	5.11
1882	58.6	12.6	33.0	27.4	8.79	1.02	136.4	698.8	5.12	108	4.74
1883	63.7	13.0	32.9	23.0	9.53	1.22	143.4	735.2	5.13	101	5.08
1884	67.0	12.6	32.6	23.0	10.0	1.23	146.4	746.5	5.10	93	5.48
1885	63.9	12.8	31.5	22.1	9.76	1.26	141.3	725.9	5.14	85	6.05
1886	70.5	9.2	33.8	21.8	9.25	1.19	145.7	720.9	4.95	82	6.04
1887	78.7	9.1	36.2	22.6	9.56	1.03	157.2	746.8	4.75	85	5.59
1888	87.8	11.9	41.0	24.8	10.1	1.02	176.6	816.8	4.63	86	5.38
1889	86.3	11.9	40.6	24.2	9.53	0.96	173.5	794.1	4.58	81	5.65
1890	90.9	12.8	42.4	26.1	9.76	0.88	182.8	829.0	4.54	82	5.54
1891	94.0	13.0	45.1	27.2	10.3	0.85	190.5	865.5	4.54	81	5.60

Sources: Currency data taken from *Report of the Treasurer* for 1892, and *Report of Comptroller* for 1878. Price index taken from *Historical Statistics,* wholesale prices in the United States, 1749 to 1890 and 1890 to 1951, Series E1 and E13, pp. 115 and 117. Currency includes United States notes, treasury notes, gold and silver certificates, certificates of deposit, and national bank notes outstanding at the close of each fiscal year. Values are not adjusted for either bank or government holdings.

of the currency, although distinctly variable from year to year, stayed roughly constant over the whole period, while prices fell by 43 percent.[38] In the second period, 1879–1891, the dollar value of all currency increased by 58 percent, a significant departure from the low growth of the first period. However, prices still fell by 10 percent.[39]

The quantities of listed denominations together with a reliable price index provide two useful measures of monetary behavior. The denominational distribution provides a weighted index of the average annual money denominations people held, and these values adjusted by means of a price index show the annual real denominations that people held. The average money denomination is obtained by dividing the annual total money value of the currency by the number of notes in existence. The average real denomination is the average money denomination divided by the wholesale price index. Table 9.2 summarizes the most important series in table 9.1 and presents corresponding rates of growth from period to period.

The average money denomination fell slightly in the first period, but the average real denomination increased by 74 percent, due largely to the fall in prices. In the second period the situation was reversed. The average money denomination fell by over 20 percent, while the average real denomination declined about 13 percent. This entire decline (and more) came in the first year after resumption. In that one year the average real denomination declined 16 percent, due primarily to the rapid growth of one-dollar bills in the three years following passage of the Bland-Allison Act and resumption (1878–1881).

The difference in growth in the number of pieces of currency in the two periods is significant. Over the earlier period the number of notes outstanding grew only trivially, despite serious deficiencies in fractional currency and normal increases in money income and real product. In the later period the number of notes increased over 100 percent, or at a rate of about 6 percent per year, reflecting an extraordinary increase in the use of money.

These results, together with the different growth rates in the total dollar value of the currency in the two periods, suggest that the significant increase

TABLE 9.2 Total denominations (by dollars and pieces), average money and real denominations, and corresponding rates of growth, 1868–1879 and 1879–1891

Year	Total ($ millions)	Growth (%)	Total pieces (millions)	Growth (%)	Average money denomination ($)	Growth (%)	Average real denomination	Growth (%)
1868	530	—	90.7	—	5.85	—	3.70	—
1879	550	3.8	95.0	4.8	5.79	− 1.0	6.43	74.0
1891	866	57.5	191.0	101.0	4.54	−20.5	5.60	−12.8

in lower denominations in the second period permitted a much greater absorption of money. No doubt part of this phenomenon was due to the growth of real output in the economy; but much of it must have resulted from the extension of monetary transactions into markets that had more recently been limited to barter or to the use of unaccounted moneys.[40] This behavior is compatible with the apparent decline in velocity and is further supported by the 58 percent growth in the total dollar value of the currency between 1879 and 1891.

The succession of governmental policies that failed to provide adequate denominational proportions of currency in the United States is not commendable. Even less laudable was the overwhelming support of intellectual opinion for such hindrances. The results of these restrictions and prejudices, imposed by custom and law through much of the nineteenth century, was counterproductive. Barter, scrip, trade credit, and other unaccounted moneys tended to compensate for the undesirable effects of lower-denominational scarcities.[41] The significant use of these substitutes biased measurements in the velocity of money until denominational constraints abated in the 1880s. The distinct differences in both monetary and real denominations between that decade and the preceding one lend substantial support to this contention.

10 The Political Origin and Judicial Sanction of the Greenbacks

> Hence, the power of saying what shall be money, at what rate money shall be taken, and what it shall be worth, has, in all civilized countries . . . been deemed one of the badges and attributes of sovereignty, and assigned to the central and supreme authority of the state, as that which may indeed be perverted or abused, but which, yet abused or not, must be exercised uniformly, and according to some common rule, in order to be of utility to all.
>
> Judge J. Hare, cited in Alva R. Hunt, *A Treatise on the Law of Tender,* 1903

> The erroneous belief that it is a duty of the state to regulate the value of money is the parent of all the vicious monetary legislation in the world; born of an old superstition that a mysterious power of sovereignty imparted to coin an added value, it has obstructed the growth of money at every stage of advancement. . . . Bimetallism, monometallism, fiat money, and the notion that the supplying of money is a function of government, are all the logical outcome of the false premise that the state can impart value to money.
>
> William Brough, *The Natural Law of Money,* 1896

Legislative Evolution of the Greenbacks in 1861–1862

Congress first authorized legal tender United States notes (greenbacks) in February 1862, and additional issues in July 1862 and January 1863. In 1869–1870 the Supreme Court found the notes unconstitutional, but reversed itself in 1871 and declared that the notes issued during the Civil War were constitutional. In 1884 the Court ruled that the notes were also legal tender in time of peace.

The events that led to the greenback issues, then the political arguments and the constitutional interpretations that sanctioned the notes, marked a momentous change in monetary practices and policies in the United States. On several occasions prior to 1860, Congress had authorized the U.S. Treasury to issue treasury notes. (See chapter 6.) These notes were usually issued in small quantities and large denominations for only one year, were interest-bearing, not reissuable, and, most important, were a tender only for federal government dues and payments. By way of contrast, the United States notes of the Civil War era were issued in massive quantities, were not interest-bearing, became indefinitely reissuable, and were legal tender for all debts public *and private,* made both *before and after* the dates at which the acts became law (table 10.1). Even though both forms of notes served as hand-to-hand currency and as bank reserves, United States notes clearly differed in kind and not just in degree from the earlier treasury notes.

Wesley C. Mitchell, in his comprehensive monograph *A History of the*

TABLE 10.1 Characteristics of federal government note issues, 1812–1861 and 1862–1865

Treasury notes, 1812–1861	United States notes, 1862–1865
1. Legal tender only for government dues and payments.	1. Fully legal tender for all debts public and private, ex post and ex ante.
2. Interest-bearing (for the most part).	2. Non-interest-bearing.
3. Issued for one year, after which time interest payments ceased.	3. Issued for indefinite period—in practice, forever.
4. Not reissuable when received at Treasury.	4. Reissuable when received at Treasury.
5. Issued in limited quantities, average amount outstanding $5 million to $10 million.	5. Issued in massive quantities, $400 million in circulation in 1865, plus $50 million other legal tender currency.
6. Large denominations.	6. All denominations.

Greenbacks, examined critically the initiation of the legal tender measures in Congress, and especially the arguments that furthered their passage.[1] Mitchell drew his account from Representative Elbridge G. Spaulding's *History of the Legal Tender Paper Money.*[2] Spaulding was the principal architect of the first legal tender act and of the two subsequent acts.

The first legal tender bill came into existence as a provision in the first national bank bill. In late 1861 as the fiscal necessities of the Treasury burgeoned, Salmon P. Chase suggested in his report to Congress the possibility and desirability of a government-sponsored currency. Chase bemeaned state bank notes for being of questionable constitutionality and for representing "loans without interest from the people to the banks." He suggested that the "advantages of this loan be transferred . . . from the banks, representing only the stockholders, to the Government representing the aggregate interests of the whole people."[3]

Spaulding repeated Chase's pejorative remarks about banking practices as an introduction to a bill he was sponsoring that would collect the state-chartered banks into a national system for issuing national bank notes. His bill also provided for a Treasury issue of United States notes redeemable in coin on demand. Both these note systems would be governmentally monitored, regulated, and controlled. The government would ensure itself a monopoly of note issue by taxing state bank notes out of existence.[4]

Spaulding then wrote Chase a letter asking him to draw up a bank bill that would incorporate the features they both found so desirable. But Chase reciprocated, delegating Spaulding, who was chairman of the Subcommittee on Ways and Means in the House of Representatives, to make up the bill for him. Upon reflection, Spaulding came to the conclusion that a bank bill would take too long to get through Congress to be of much help in meeting current government payments. So he "drafted a legal tender Treasury note section to be added to the bank bill, hoping, . . . that [notes] might be made available . . . while the bank bill was [being] put into operation."[5]

Upon still more "mature" reflection, Spaulding concluded that such a comprehensive bill would take too long. The state banks had just suspended specie payments (due largely to U.S. Treasury fiscal policies—although Spaulding did not admit or refer to this fact). He therefore "changed the legal tender section, intended originally to accompany the bank bill, into a separate bill, . . . and on his own motion introduced it into the House by unanimous consent on the 30th of December 1861." The bill was almost rejected by the Committee on Ways and Means; but one congressman on the committee, who opposed it, voted for it just so it could get before the full House for debate.[6]

Spaulding's original and all-important argument for the bill was its "necessity." "The bill before us," he declared, "is a war measure of *necessity,* and not of choice." Yet on the next page, and in the same speech, he stated: "We have the alternative [that is, the choice], either to go into the [securities] market and sell our bonds for what they will command, or to pass this bill, or to find some better mode . . . to raise means to carry on the war."[7]

When bankers who met with House and Senate committees at the Treasury Department spelled out two alternatives to legal tender paper money—"a policy of vigorous taxation and selling [government] bonds at their market value"—Spaulding replied that "selling bonds below par was more objectionable than issuing paper money. . . . Thus," noted Mitchell, "the argument for the legal-tender bill was shifted from the ground of necessity to that of expediency."[8]

The subsequent debates in the House and Senate emphasized congressional aversion to selling government securities below par. Of course, "below par" meant below some governmentally stipulated par value and par rate of interest. If the bonds sold at a discount in the market, this fact simply meant that investors in the market differed from Congress and the Treasury on the appropriate risk-adjusted yield.

In spite of their antibank and not-below-par prejudices, many congressmen were apprehensive over the clear-cut unconstitutionality of the legal tender measure. To counter this fear, Spaulding and other supporters of the bill hit upon the "necessary and proper" clause in the Constitution that Chief Justice Marshall had invoked so notoriously in *McCulloch* v. *Maryland*. "The degree of [a law's] necessity," Spaulding claimed, thereby giving a future Supreme Court comfortable words with which to fashion a pragmatic decision, "is a question of *legislative discretion,* not of judicial cognizance."[9]

Congress's power "to borrow money" also entered the debate here. The Constitution gives Congress the express power "to *borrow* money, on the credit of the United States," meaning the fiscal power to authorize the selling of securities for money that will then be used to buy goods and services for appropriate use by government agencies. Senators Howard and Sherman argued that the express power to borrow money implied the power to make treasury notes a legal tender. But Senator Collamer countered with the conclusive argument that "where there is an express power to do a thing [borrow money], there can be no implied power to do the same thing [create money]."[10]

This denial has even more to support it. The Constitution was silent on certain issues, and such points allow reasonable debate. But when the Framers specified precise powers for Congress or the executive or the Supreme Court, they arrived at the principles they expounded after lengthy and exhaustive debate. They surely did not intend to leave the scope of such powers to be decided by future legislative and judicial pragmatists.

The legal tender bill worked its way through Congress by a process of reluctant acceptance. The House Ways and Means Committee was evenly divided on it, but allowed it to go out of committee to the full House. That body, however, treated the issue as if the committee had recommended it.[11]

Chase was just as responsible for getting the bill through Congress as were the bill's congressional sponsors. As Congress debated and almost stalled on the bill, the Committee on Ways and Means asked Chase "to communicate . . . his opinion as to the propriety and necessity of [the bill's] immediate passage by Congress." Chase replied that it was impossible at that time (late January 1862) "to procure sufficient *coin* for disbursements; and it has, therefore, become indispensably necessary that we should resort to the issue of United States notes." Since some people would not accept the notes if they were payment only for government dues, he argued, everyone should be forced to accept them to prevent "discrimination."[12] Needless to say, if the notes were made full legal tender, the Treasury would not need to disburse *any* coin.

Secretary Chase was ill fitted for the Treasury post.[13] His antibank prejudice was patent. When banker groups recommended that Chase use the banks for governmental deposits and transactions, and that he leave specie in the banks when the banks made loans to the government, he absolutely refused.[14] By a simple amendment to the Independent Treasury Act of 1846, the Treasury could have enlisted the suspended banks as government depositories and avoided many of the ensuing fiscal difficulties. Not only Chase, but Spaulding and other congressmen objected to this readily available remedy.[15]

Barrett pointed out that in early 1862 people could deposit various government issues already authorized, such as demand notes, in Treasury and subtreasury offices for 5 percent certificates of deposit. This system was so popular that Congress wanted to raise the limits on the CDs from $25 million to $100 million or more. Unfortunately, the rate of interest the government paid on the CDs was at the discretion of the secretary of the Treasury. When Chase observed the popularity of the CDs, he reduced the rate to 4 percent (!) and "attempted, unsuccessfully, to force holders of loanable funds to convert to 5–20 bonds." According to Barrett, if the Treasury had treated the demand notes, which were not full legal tender, as an allowable monetary reserve for banks, it could have floated loans that "would have net the government more than the entire amount of legal tender notes authorized by the [three legal tender] acts."[16]

Chase's fiscal "strategy" virtually guaranteed failure and, ultimately, recourse to fiat paper money. He first sold bonds to the banks for "coin," then locked up the coin in the Treasury. The banks thereupon suspended specie payments because the Treasury now had the gold that had been their reserves. The Treasury then stopped redeeming its notes because Chase wanted to keep the gold in the Treasury. Because banks could no longer furnish any more coin for the bonds they bought but had to resort to irredeemable bank notes, Chase assailed bank-issued currency and advocated its replacement with irredeemable, fully legal tender, government-issued paper money. Chase's final letter to Congress on the matter stated: "The legal tender clause is a necessity, . . . and I support it earnestly."[17]

Economists Barrett and Mitchell, and Simon Newcomb the astronomer and political economist, found the legal tender provision unnecessary for several reasons. Taxation had not even been tried, in spite of the sentiment that the general public was "ready" to be taxed. Second, the 6 percent bonds that the Treasury was marketing remained nearly at par value as late as the summer of 1862, six months after the oratorical hyperbole in Congress.[18] Congress debated the legal tender bill for six weeks after the "pressing necessity" argument first appeared and before the act was passed. Even then, several other financial devices, including the demand notes, continued to tide the government over this period. Only a few greenbacks appeared prior to May 1862.[19]

Many congressmen tried to wash their hands of the legal tender taint by promising themselves and their colleagues that the bill would provide legal tender only for the duration of the war. Spaulding was one of them. The provision was clearly constitutional as a war measure, he wrote in 1868 to Hugh McCulloch, who was secretary of the Treasury at the time. "I am equally clear that as a peace measure it is unconstitutional. No one would now think of passing a legal tender act making the promises of the Government . . . a legal tender in payment of 'all debts public and private.' Such a law [in time of peace] could not be sustained for one moment."[20]

The Question of the Greenbacks' Constitutionality

When the war finally ended, $400 million of greenbacks and more than $50 million of other legal tender currency, primarily demand notes, were in circulation. Chase resigned as secretary of the Treasury in 1864, and following an interim appointment, Lincoln in March 1865 appointed Hugh McCulloch to the post. McCulloch was a professional banker of note from Indiana.

Because government expenditures declined precipitously while tax revenues continued unabated, fiscal surpluses appeared in Treasury receipts. Using these surplus balances, McCulloch began a policy of greenback retirement. Congress at first supported his policy with a resounding resolution in December 1865. By April 1866, however, Congress was having second thoughts on the matter. It limited cancellation and retirement of the notes to $10 million in the ensuing six months and $4 million per month thereafter. Finally, in February 1868 Congress suspended altogether any further retirement of the greenbacks (see chapter 7). Since the amount outstanding at the time of the "freeze" was $356 million, the experience seemed to suggest that any reduction of the outstanding legal tenders in excess of 11 percent of the existing stock was not politically feasible. Congressmen who had once supported the legal tender acts as temporary and reversible were now retired, dead, or defeated, or for "practical" purposes had changed their minds.

The legal tender provision was also getting its day in court, both in state courts and in the Supreme Court. Irwin Unger reported that the constitutionality of the legal tender provision came before state courts some sixteen times between 1863 and 1870. The decisions of the courts reflected a pronounced political bias: Of the seventy state court justices who ruled on the cases, all but one Republican judge upheld the legal tender clause, while every Democratic judge except two pronounced the clause unconstitutional.[21]

If this result seems anomalous in view of later Democratic penchants for easy money, it is because traditional Democratic policy at that time still had the Jacksonian momentum of hard money running through it. Republicans, on the other hand, not only had a "national" bank principle in their heritage, but were also in command of the political machinery in both the Congress and the presidency.

Andrew Johnson, Lincoln's successor, retained Hugh McCulloch as secretary of the Treasury. But Ulysses S. Grant, upon becoming president in 1868, appointed George Boutwell, a former governor of Massachusetts and a prominent congressman, to the Treasury post. Whereas McCulloch had favored continuous retirement of the greenbacks and an early resumption of specie payments, both Boutwell and Grant were pragmatists. Boutwell, a radical Republican, was very much opposed to McCulloch's policy of greenback retirement. He favored a policy of maintaining the monetary status quo and allowing natural growth in real output gradually to reduce the price level to the point at which prewar parity between gold and the dollar would allow the gold standard to become operational. (See chapter 7.)

While Congress and the president were Republican, five of the eight Supreme Court justices were Democrats. This label also applied (at times) to the Chief Justice, who was none other than Salmon P. Chase. Even though he had been secretary of the Treasury under Lincoln and a Lincoln appointee to the Court, Chase aspired to the presidency as a Democrat. In fact, Chase in everyone's book "seemed to change his politics to suit his ambitions."[22]

The first legal tender case to reach the Supreme Court was *Hepburn* v. *Griswold*. The decision dealt only with the constitutionality of the legal tender acts as applied to debts incurred before 25 February 1862, the date the first legal tender act was signed into law. By a 5 to 3 vote the Court denied the constitutionality of the act for debts contracted before the law was passed, but left moot the question of its constitutionality for debts contracted after passage.[23] The majority decision argued thus: (1) The power to bestow legal tender quality on the notes was not incident to the coinage power; that is, issuing the notes did not require that they be made legal tender in the mode of gold and silver coins. They were not coined, but printed and issued as paper currency. (2) The war power requiring large expenditures of money no more required the issue of the notes than any other governmental power to spend money. In so deciding the Court observed that some treasury notes had circulated that were not full legal tender. Yet the treasury notes had not passed at a discount relative to the full legal tender issues. Therefore, the greenbacks would have served the government's purposes just as well if they had been made a tender only for payments to the government in the mode of the former treasury notes. (3) Because the legal tender feature impaired the obligation of contracts, it violated constitutional proscription against "bills of credit" (Article I, Section 10, 1) and the Fifth Amendment: "Nor shall any person be deprived of life, liberty, or property without due process of law."[24]

The Court decided the case in 1869 but delayed announcing the decision until early 1870. By the time the decision was made public, one justice (Grier) who had voted with the majority had retired. Therefore, the final decision was accounted as 4 to 3.

The *Hepburn* decision caused no appreciable uneasiness in financial circles. "Businessmen," Unger wrote, "received the decision with surprising calm." Few pre–1862 debts were still outstanding. Long-term private obligations totaled only $350 million. The price of gold did not react either way.[25]

Nonetheless, the Grant administration and the Republican Congress were deeply disturbed. They felt that the Court ruling threatened to destabilize the monetary status quo. It seemed as well to be a contrived Democratic attempt to repudiate the Republican party's war policies. So Grant appointed two new justices to the Court whose opinions on legal tender were well known from their decisions in state court cases.[26] The erstwhile minority on this question thereupon became a majority. On a motion from the Attorney General for further argument on the constitutionality of legal tender cases still undecided, the Court in 1871, in the cases of *Knox* v. *Lee* and *Parker* v. *Davis,* reconsidered and subsequently reversed its previous position by holding that U.S. notes were legal tender for debts contracted both before and after 25 February 1862.[27]

The five-to-four majority of the Court that now sanctioned government issues of legal tender notes based its decision on essentially the same arguments that had appeared in Congress nine years earlier. The Court cases and decisions, as Unger observed, "had become miniature political contests. . . . Republican jurists felt compelled to defend a major item of Republican wartime legislation; Democratic opposition reflected the party's traditional hostility to paper money and expanded federal functions—biases the judges did not abandon as readily as did the party's active politicians."[28]

Justice Strong, one of Grant's new appointees, wrote the majority opinion. He based the decision on the "expediency of voiding the legal tender currency." Since passage of the acts, all debts had been contracted "on the understanding that they might be discharged in legal tenders." If the notes were now found invalid as legal tender, "The government would become the instrument of the grossest injustice; all debtors [would be] loaded with an obligation it was never contemplated they should assume."[29]

Unger in retrospect of ninety-five years sympathized with this decision, but it is palpably invalid on several counts. First, the Supreme Court is not supposed to adjudicate on the basis of "expediency." Justice and expediency are not synonymous. Second, even if the majority felt compelled to be expedient, it could have distinguished easily between pre–1862 debts and post–1862 debts and thereby satisfied the criteria of both expediency and justice. All the Court had to do was to reaffirm the *Hepburn* decision of 1870, and apply the principle implied by the very existence of a contract: that a debt is payable in whatever the contract stipulates, or in whatever is legal tender at the time the contract is drawn. In neglecting this constitutional implication, the Court itself became an "instrument of the grossest injustice." Its decision denied the whole reason for the existence of contracts—that is, their ability to reduce uncertainty by describing and defining ahead of time the means for satisfying the contract when it becomes due. If a contract is payable in whatever is legal tender at the time of payment, it loses its very reason for existence. It fails to protect the creditor who was a party to it, and, at worst, becomes an instrument of expropriation.

Besides the new majority of the Court, several congressmen and Treasury officials treated this issue at one time or another. Boutwell, for example, stated emphatically that "every contract . . . is to be performed in the currency of the country *at the time the contract is liquidated*. The power to decide the quantity and quality of that currency is an essential incident of sovereignty."[30]

Some congressmen addressed the issue at the time of the first legal tender debate. Roscoe Conkling of New York, for example, protested the legal tender clause as unconstitutional for what it would do to the real value of a contractual credit.[31] Simon Newcomb also raised the same objection,[32] as did Hugh McCulloch, Boutwell's predecessor in the Treasury.[33] Boutwell, however, was a "party man," as the title to his book testifies. He reiterated in a few pages all the arguments that his fellows had made in the congressional debates: that the legal tender clause was "necessary and proper," and that resumption of specie redemption for the notes in 1879 negated the impropriety of their full legal tender quality.[34]

"Necessary and proper," as the Supreme Court interpreted it, could have been used to support *any* policy. Hepburn, in his review of the cases, correctly reasoned: If Congress had the power claimed by the Supreme Court majority, it could have issued fiat paper notes unceasingly and paid off its bonded indebtedness with them no matter how much the notes depreciated. "Why then," Hepburn asked, "should the government continue paying interest on the bonds when the principal might be paid in a day?"[35]

The Court added yet another interpretation to its *Knox* decision—one that Spaulding had included in his indefatigable campaign for the notes: that the decision of their issue was "political" and not "judicial," that the decision depended on *Congress's* estimate of the urgency of the express power it chose to exercise as "necessary and proper," and that Congress's decision was not subject to judicial review.[36] Yet the Court paradoxically did review the case. (If it believed its own ruling, it should have said so right away and left the rest of its arguments unrecorded.) It is not, however, a proper subordinate decision, as the majority's behavior in presenting other arguments makes plain. When the "necessary" actions that Congress legislates prove, as in the legal tender debates, to be nothing more than economic misinterpretations and political prejudices, the case for judicial, or perhaps economic, review is even more compelling.

In the third legal tender case, *Juilliard* v. *Greenman,* argued in 1884, the Court held that Congress's legal tender power was constitutional in time of peace as well as war. This reactionary decision reached into the dustbin of history and came up with the sixteenth-century notion of the state's prerogative of sovereignty as the excuse for declaring the greenbacks valid. "Congress, as the legislature of a sovereign nation," the Juilliard decision went,

> being expressly empowered by the constitution to . . . borrow money on the credit of the United States and to coin money and regulate the value thereof . . . and being clearly [!] authorized as incidental to the exercise of those great powers to emit bills of credit, . . . and to provide a national currency for the whole people . . . , and the power to make the notes of the government a legal tender in payment of private debts being one of the powers belonging to other civilized [?] nations, and not expressly withheld from Congress by the constitution, we are irresistibly impelled to the conclusion that the impressing upon the Treasury notes of the United States the quality of being a legal tender in payment of private debts is an appropriate means, . . . consistent with the letter and spirit of the constitution, and therefore . . . "necessary and proper" for carrying into execution the [foregoing] powers vested by this constitution in the *government* of the United States.[37]

In a few words, the reasoning in the decision went along the following lines: (1) The federal government through the Congress has the right to *borrow* "money." (2) It has, therefore, the right to *issue* paper money ("circulating notes") for the money borrowed. This argument is a semantic misapplication. *Borrow* and *issue* are two different words with distinct meanings that both the Framers and all Supreme Court justices could easily comprehend. (3) Congress also has the power to coin metallic currency and declare the value thereof. (4) Because Congress has both the power to issue "circulating notes," which are currency (1 and 2), and the power to impress gold or silver coin as legal tender (3), Justice Gray concluded, "under the two powers, taken together, Congress is authorized to establish a national currency, either in coin, or in paper, and to make that currency lawful money for all purposes."[38]

The legal construction of "taking the two powers together" appeared in several juridical briefs in support of the Juilliard decision.[39] If one "puts together" the two money clauses, the result is: "The Congress shall have power to coin [paper] money on the credit of the United States and regulate the value thereof." Clearly, this "power" is an absurd distortion of what the Framers thought, said, and wrote. No man who attended the Constitutional Convention in 1787 would have endorsed this construction, or even tolerated it as arguable.[40]

In retrospect, Hugh McCulloch commented that the *Juilliard* decision "covered the whole ground of controversy between those who [thought] that Congress possessed no power not expressly granted by the Constitution, . . . and those who [thought] that all power not absolutely prohibited, belonged to Congress, to be exercised whenever a majority of both branches and the President should consider the exercise of it necessary or expedient." McCulloch's final observation was that the decision "relieves Congress from what have heretofore been considered well defined restrictions, and clothes a republican government with imperial power."[41]

Practical Judicial Alternatives to the Supreme Court's Sanction of the Greenbacks

The monetary system in the middle 1880s, at the time of the third legal tender decision, was not teetering on the brink of instability. Resumption of specie payments had been an unqualified success; the stock of U.S. notes was frozen, this time permanently at $346.7 million, which was slightly less than 3 percent below the freeze value of 1868; and the silver question seemed reasonably well settled through passage of the Bland-Allison Act of 1878. The gold standard was also working smoothly and in no immediate danger of any internal or external disequilibria. Given these auspices, what might the Supreme Court have ruled in 1884 to maintain both the integrity of the Constitution and the ongoing monetary and economic equilibrium?

First, the Court could have declared the greenbacks unconstitutional as a forced tender for private debts, but constitutional as tender for all payments due the government. Congress could then have enacted a law ordering the Treasury to convert all the greenbacks into the older form of treasury notes before reissuing them. The treasury notes would have been simply another form of *limited* legal tender government currency, similar to national bank notes and silver currency, and kept at par with the gold dollar by the Treasury's $100 million–plus gold balance. Such a currency policy would have had no more effect on the economy than the successful resumption of specie payments five years earlier. Anyone who did not want the notes could have redeemed them for gold at any Treasury office.

By ruling in this manner, the Court would also have avoided sanctioning any "ex post facto Law or Law impairing the obligation of Contracts" [Article 1, Section 10] by affirming that contracts drawn prior to the legal tender acts were payable in the medium stipulated by the contract, as the first legal tender decision had ruled, and that contracts not specifying the means of payment were payable in whatever was current money when the contract was made.[42] Since most of the contracts in force at the time of the legal tender decisions had been made after the legal tender acts were passed, payments in depreciated paper currency would have resulted in no grave injustices or financial hardships. In any event, the terms in every contract should have determined each case and thereby minimized real injustices due to inflation.[43]

Juridical Review of the Legal Tender Decisions

Juridical analysts may have honestly felt that the federal government had the sovereign power over the monetary system that their brethren on the Supreme Court had adjudicated. They may also have thought that such a power was no longer dangerous in view of the fact that the legal tender notes were frozen, the gold standard was operational, and the "guidance of human wisdom" was a feature of the age. In any case, legal scholars appeared in print to rationalize intellectually the latter two legal tender decisions.

Among the more eminent of these was an article by James Bradley Thayer in the *Harvard Law Review* in 1877.[44] Thayer based his approval of the Supreme Court's rulings on Congress's powers to "borrow money on the credit of the United States," to "coin" money, and to "regulate" commerce. He "put together" the two money clauses. He wore out "necessary and proper." He did not distinguish between government "bills of credit" that were legal tender only for payments to and from the government, and the full legal tender "bills of credit" that were legal tender for all private contracts. He claimed that only the states were prohibited from making anything except gold or silver a tender in payment of debt. He played with the meanings of the words *money* and *regulate,* and concluded that the Framers had given Congress a sovereign power to furnish a legal tender paper currency, similar in extent to the "power which had frequently been exercised by those legislative bodies [Parliament?] with which the framers of the instrument were most familiar, . . . [and that] is included in that complete control over money and the currency which is given to Congress." Thayer argued that the "break-down" of the banking system—by which he meant the Chase Treasury–generated suspension of specie payments—made the issue of government paper money "necessary," and that such currency had to be full legal tender to provide the office of a medium of exchange. "Necessary and proper" meant, among other things, "natural and suitable," "reasonably well," "better," "useful," "appropriate," and, citing Marshall's opinion in *McCulloch,* "most eligible." Thayer, too, justified the issue of notes as a means of "borrowing money," when in fact all economists recognize such issues of fiat paper money notes as a seigniorage tax.[45] Since Congress already had the power to tax directly by straightforward fiscal methods, it could not have been given the power to tax by subterfuge.

Another legal apologist for the Court's decisions was Alva R. Hunt, who wrote a comprehensive treatise on the legal aspects of money in courts of law. Hunt argued that "the power to issue money and declare the extent to which it shall be current is, from the necessity of having a stable and uniform standard, an attribute of sovereignty. A power assumed very early in the history of civilized governments." Hunt cited William Blackstone, the renowned English jurist, to the effect that giving money "authority" and making it "current" were a part of the "King's prerogative."[46]

This opinion seems to contradict the colonists' rationale for separating from England and establishing a constitutional republic in the first place. Surely the Framers were not looking back to the sovereign kings of England for guidance! Rather much to the contrary.

Furthermore, to entrust a sovereign to provide a stable and uniform standard provides a temptation no sovereign has ever resisted. For such a duty also implies a power to debase the currency and tax by unlimited seigniorage. True, every piece of governmental paper currency is identical to every other piece, but the real value of the typical sovereign's currency is anything but uniform and stable over time. The same desirable uniformity would appear and did appear in privately issued currency, including coins, in the few cases where such currency was allowed. Even inferentially one should be no more surprised at uniformity in monetary media than at uniformity in dozens of other conventional items routinely produced and used in everyday life—e.g., containers, books, pens, chair and table heights, playing cards, and building bricks—in short, in any usage where uniformity reduces costs.[47]

Hunt also blessed the clearing of debts with whatever is legal tender at the time of payment.[48] When taken to its extreme, as in the case of a hyperinflation, this dictum as much as says that the government by its "sovereign prerogative" over the currency may dilute the real value of a debt to nothing, or promote it to infinity.

Hunt cited numerous cases on the legal tender question from state court decisions between 1864 and 1867. Virtually all of them allowed greenbacks to serve as surrogates for gold without any reference to the real values of the debts contracted. One case stated that only by virtue of law were either gold coins or greenbacks a legal tender. Therefore, both *had* to be "exactly equivalent for the purpose of payment." The premium on gold at this time (1866), Hunt noted, was a value "men voluntarily choose to give for [it]." Therefore, he concluded, the gold premium could have no bearing on the legality of the case.[49]

Hunt argued that in the *Hepburn* decision the Supreme Court "made its comparison between the wrong things. It compared the declared or nominal value of legal tender notes with the market value of the bullion in a coined dollar. The declared value the government controls, while the value of bullion is controlled by the law of supply and demand. If declared values had been compared (and it seems absurd to compare equals)," Hunt concluded, "it would have been found that . . . $1,400 in 1857 was equivalent to $1,400 in 1868 [!]"[50] With economic sophistication of this magnitude making decisions in courts of law, it is difficult to understand how the government could ever be bothered with a national debt or with any other economic problems. It could simply legislate all of them out of existence.

Economic and Political Review of the Supreme Court Decisions

And what of economists and political scientists? How did they regard the legal tender decisions, and how did they react to the view that federal sovereignty over the monetary system was absolute?

The economists who first reviewed congressional arguments over the greenbacks, Wesley Mitchell and Don Barrett, could find no economic necessity compelling their issue as full legal tender. Indeed, both gave cogent arguments for not issuing them. McCulloch and Hepburn, who were both bankers and appointed Treasury officials at different times, also were opposed to the legalization of the notes and their currency for ex ante debts.

An even earlier economist, Adam Smith, discoursed at length on the proper role of the sovereign in his monumental work on economics and polity, *The Wealth of Nations*. Smith devoted two full chapters to the functions of the sovereign and the legitimate means he had for obtaining the revenues due him.

The sovereign had three principal functions, according to Smith: "First the duty of protecting the society from the violence and invasion of other independent societies; secondly, . . . the duty of establishing an exact administration of justice; and, thirdly, the duty of erecting and maintaining certain public works and . . . institutions, which it can never be for the interest of any individual or small number of individuals, to erect and maintain." Such works consisted of good roads, bridges, canals, and harbors.[51]

The sovereign would get revenues primarily by imposing various kinds of taxes, by obtaining rents from public lands, and by operating post offices. In time of war the sovereign's immediate need for resources was an excuse only to borrow in lieu of taxes, and not any reason at all to tamper with the currency. Devaluations and debasements of the currency cause "a general and most pernicious subversion of the fortunes of private people; enriching . . . the idle and profuse debtor at the expense of the industrious and frugal creditor." Depreciation of the currency, Smith concluded, was a "treacherous fraud."[52] In 168 pages of text Adam Smith found no license for the sovereign either to debase or devalue the coin, or to issue legal tender paper money. The sovereign had prerogatives and rights, but none with respect to issuing currency.

In another section, in which he discussed the gold and silver contents of guineas and shillings, Smith observed that the government's role was only that of "reforming" the coin—the housekeeping function of adjusting marginally the mint values of gold and silver. Just two years earlier (1774), such a "reformation" of the English coin had occurred by which gold became the standard money metal, while silver was invested with legal tender quality only for small-sum transactions.[53] This action had included no reduction of the metallic content of the coinage.[54] Indeed, the gold value of the pound at the English mint was essentially constant from 1665 to 1914.[55]

Smith admittedly was not a political theorist. Nonetheless, he was a competent scholar of his time, an authority on jurisprudence as well as political economy. His exegesis therefore reflected current norms for what was regarded as acceptable practice in the sovereign's management of the state.

The alleged "prerogative of the sovereign over the coinage" had been anything but an unlimited power since the time of Elizabeth. In no sense was it the absolute power implied by the U.S. Supreme Court's decisions. It was in fact nothing more than a license to make minor adjustments in the mint values of gold and silver that would keep both metals active in the currency system. The technological development of paper currency and paper checks obscured for later observers just how important marginal mint-price adjustments had been for the continued presence of both gold and silver coins in the payments system. These occasional and fractional changes gave latter-day nineteenth-century jurists the false notion, or perhaps only the false excuse, that the state could do anything it wanted to the mint values of gold and silver.

A political scientist, S. P. Breckenridge, in 1903 traced the entire evolution of legal tender through the ages. Her monograph was an outgrowth of a seminar class in political economy presided over by J. Lawrence Laughlin, a prominent economist of the time at the University of Chicago. In her survey Breckenridge treated the evolution of the legal tender quality from the time of the Plantagenets in England to the legal tender acts and court cases in the United States. Her conclusion on the greenback decisions was that

> the private individual, the creditor, was by a compulsory act of government, through the agency of the courts . . . , forced to share with the government, or bear for it, the cost of the conflict then being waged. By an extraordinary departure from both legislative and judicial precedents, an act as tyrannical as any act of Henry VIII in [his] dealing with coins, found legislative and executive support and judicial sanction. It was fitting that the law based on the doctrine of the prerogative prevailing in the time of the Tudors [the Case of the Mixt Monies] should be invoked to sustain such legislation.[56]

Review and Analysis of the Money Clauses in the Constitution

Up until the time of the Civil War, almost no one had seriously considered interpreting the money clauses in the Constitution in any light except that of prohibiting state and federal issues of currency on the basis of discretionary authority. "To coin money" meant to provide the technical facilities for minting coins. "Regulate the value thereof" meant only to specify a weight of fine gold or silver as equal to a number of the units of account, which were dollars. "Regulate," while it may have been a questionable choice for the proper verb, did not mean "determine the supply of money," either of precious metal money or of paper. Indeed, the very act of adopting a specie standard precluded even the possibility that "regulate the value" meant anything more profound than simply "specify the weight." The specie standard by its very nature is self-regulating, as all the Framers knew or sensed. Clearly, a self-regulating system is incompatible with any kind of policy-inspired manipulation. The only regulation implied by "regulate" was the small-scale kind of housekeeping change in the specifications of the units of account that would keep both precious metals current as money. This problem was inherent and chronic in the management of bimetallic standards.[57]

The Civil War witnessed an unhealthy shift in political divisions that not many observers have stressed. All the southern congressmen, who were primarily Democrats and opposed to national banks and paper money, left the Federal Congress to become a part of the Confederate Congress. This exodus left the remaining Federal Congress overwhelmingly influenced by Whig Republicans, who could bring out of mothballs all of their pet schemes for a national bank and paper money with assurance of favorable results. By way of contrast, the Confederate government, in four years of war against an adversary with five times its real resources, found no "necessity" to issue full legal tender notes. Rather, its notes took the form of the usual treasury notes of the pre–1860 type—legal tender only for payments due to and receivable from the Confederate government.

Had the monetary ideological makeup of Congress stayed constant after 1860, full legal tender U.S. notes would never have appeared. Even so, most congressmen reluctantly granted their existence under only highly qualified conditions. Those with this mind-set were to express in retrospect what might be called "counterfactual regret": "I would never have voted for the legal tender bill if I had known that the notes would become a permanent part of the circulation." Some thought of them only as an interim measure until the war ended. Others voted for them thinking that a future Supreme Court would declare them unconstitutional, or that some future executive administration would take the heat for their retirement. Still others presumed naively that the Treasury would be able to redeem them for coin as they were issued, and as Chase had at first implied. Nevertheless, both the reasoning available at the time and future economic analysis proved beyond any question that the full legal tender quality of the notes—for all debts public and private, ex post and ex ante—was decidedly unnecessary.

The inflation of 1862–1865 and the corresponding decline in the real value of fixed dollar claims had repercussions that were bound to be tested in the courts. Supreme Court justices used the same arguments that the politicians had used in the congressional debates. They worked over the words of the Constitution and, by means of semantic legerdemain, twisted many of its meanings completely around. Indeed, little else could have been expected, for the justices who made up the Court majority were, first and foremost, federal politicians vindicating Republican party policies. Who could expect that a Supreme Court—an ongoing political institution composed of self-interested mortals—would swear fealty to a Constitution that offered no quid pro quo when real political prizes were at stake right now?

The Court's most questionable decision was to grant the legitimacy of the greenbacks on the grounds that the power to issue the notes was the cumulative sum of Congress's other express powers, including the power to regulate interstate commerce. If this argument is valid, it means that Congress is omnipotent, and that a Constitution is a useless pretense. Such a document, however, could not have included the means for its own negation. Otherwise, it would have had no reason for existence in the first place.

One may wonder, in reviewing the history of the legal tender cases, just where we went wrong. Where was the Achilles' heel in polity that allowed the legislature, executive, and judiciary the opportunity to breach the rule of law in the first place?

The Constitution's charge to Congress—to "coin money, regulate the value thereof, . . . and fix the standard of weights and measures"—seems to be unexceptionable. Allowing Congress to fix the standard of weights and measures has resulted in no inflation of yardsticks or standard weights, but the same cannot be said for monetary values. The money clause, unfortunately, allowed Congress to coin the money that it was also supposed to regulate. The Framers no doubt thought they had rigorously circumscribed the coinage power by specifying coinage of only gold and silver. Once the executive and

Congress had contrived an interpretation of the Constitution that allowed the U.S. Treasury to produce irredeemable paper money, and the Supreme Court had legitimized it by means of the twisted arguments that no constitutional founder could have anticipated or would have accepted, the monetary system was forever after in jeopardy.

Without the coinage power, Congresses would have had no means to debase the coinage and to monopolize currency production in their ongoing quest for seigniorage. Likewise, Supreme Courts would have had no opportunity or incentive to validate Congress's transgressions of its constitutional limits. As William Brough stated the case: "Clearly there is no need of making coin a legal tender at any specified weight. If governments would confine their legislation to fixing by enactment the fineness of the precious metal and the number of grains that shall constitute each piece of a given name, they may safely leave the maintenance of coinage, . . . and the value of the pieces to be regulated [to] individual interest and action."[58]

11 The Golden Cloud with the Silver Lining

Mr. President, if gold does go out of this country by reason of a constant increase in its value, I say let it go, and God speed the day when it starts.

John P. Jones, Senate, 29 July 1886

Currencies in Circulation after the Civil War

The official resumption of specie payments at the prewar parity on 1 January 1879 was thoroughgoing and final. However, the monetary structure of the economy by the time of resumption was appreciably different from what it had been before the Civil War. Even though the monetary system of 1860 had included metallic and paper currencies and bank deposits subject to check, none of the paper money in use had been legal tender issues of the federal government. Beginning in 1862, and continuing indefinitely after 1879, fully legal tender United States notes were a permanent paper currency. To ensure the convertibility of this fixed quantity of paper into gold after resumption, the Treasury accumulated gold coin and bullion as a redemption reserve for the notes. The law did not specify the amount of this reserve, but the actual amount on hand in the Treasury was $135 million in 1878. Then it gradually increased to as much as $324 million in 1888 before starting a steady decline to the low value of $45 million in January 1895.[1]

National bank notes had also become an official obligation of the Treasury because of the government securities that banks had to pledge as collateral in order to issue notes, and more positively because of the 5 percent gold redemption fund that national banks had to keep with the United States Treasury.[2] So after resumption the Treasury's gold balance acted as a redemption fund for two paper currencies, United States notes and national bank notes.[3]

These two paper currencies did not remain the only fiat currencies. The Bland-Allison Act in 1878 provided for the limited coinage of silver, and the Treasury issued various kinds and amounts of silver currency. Despite its metallic substance, the silver coin was also fiat.[4] By the provisions of the Bland-Allison Act the Treasury had to buy not less than $2 million and not more than $4 million worth of silver per month at market prices, and coin the silver into silver dollars of 412½ grains each .900 fine (that is, with 371¼ grains of pure silver). The silver dollars were legal tender for all debts public and private "except where otherwise stipulated in the contract." Although the law allowed for discretion in silver purchases by the secretary of the Treasury, no secretary of the period bought more than the minimum amount of $2 million per month.

The Treasury Department did not have to circulate the coined silver as long as tax revenues were sufficient to cover the cost of the silver purchases. If, for example, the government realized a fiscal surplus of $24 million per year or more before the required purchases of silver, the Treasury could store all of the purchased silver. If the fiscal surplus was between zero and $24 million or if the budget was in deficit, all the coined silver would have to be spent into circulation or else the Treasury would have to issue some amount of silver currency and float new government securities.[5]

These conditions allowed the secretary of the Treasury a certain amount of discretion. Instead of financing a deficit fiscal program with disbursements of silver coin, he could request Congress to authorize additional sales of government securities and by this means pay the deficit and store the coin. Then again, even if a fiscal surplus of $24 million or greater occurred, the Treasury could spend the silver coin into circulation by means of open-market purchases of government securities. Thus the silver-purchase program was just as inflationary or noninflationary as Congress and the secretary of the Treasury wanted, and as fiscal conditions permitted.

That a monetary metal was being purchased, coined, and to a limited extent put into circulation at a mint value significantly greater than the metal's market value has obscured some of the unique features of this operation. F. W. Taussig pointed out that the Bland-Allison Act was the first deliberate policy intended to provide for a regular and periodic injection of currency into the monetary system.[6] No matter that it was silver, even though silver had charisma and silver-state politicians to recommend it. Second, the connection between the purchases of silver and the fiscal necessities of the Treasury induced the secretary of the Treasury to assume some limited authority over monetary policy. Third, the silver coinage need not have been inflationary nor a future threat to the gold standard. As the market price of silver fell, Congress could have increased the silver content of the silver dollar in approximately the same proportion as the fall in its real price. Thus appropriate and timely attention to the mint value of silver could have prevented both the threat of silver inflation and the outflow of gold.[7]

Not much of the purchased silver went into circulation until the latter half of 1880, so a sizable silver balance accumulated in the Treasury. From 1880 to 1886 the Treasury circulated slightly less than the amount currently purchased. Between 1886 and 1891 all the old balance and all current purchases were circulated; and by 1892 all the silver coin and bullion left in the Treasury served as reserves for the paper silver certificates that Congress had authorized the Treasury to issue. (See figure 11.1.)

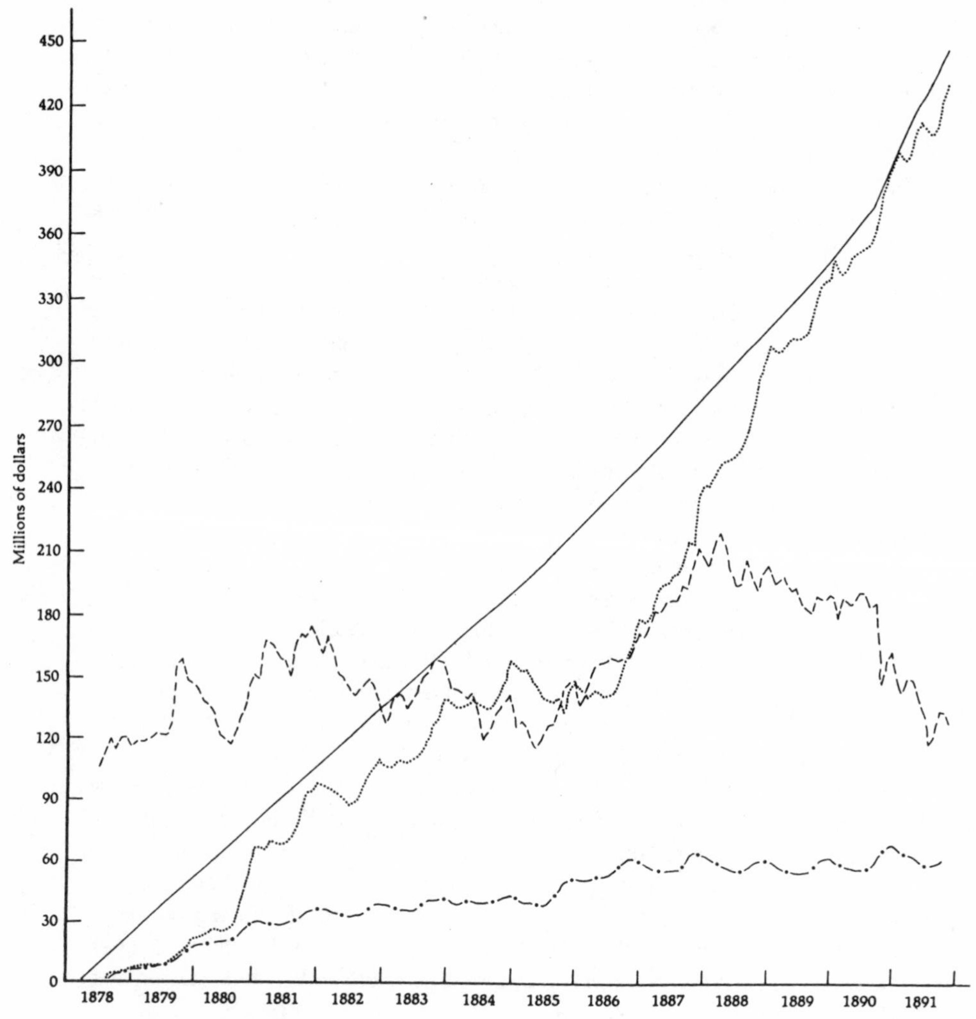

— Total silver currency authorized (silver dollars coined, 1878-90; treasury notes, 1890-91)

······ Total silver currency in circulation (coined silver dollars, silver certificates, and treasury notes of 1890)

-•- Coined silver dollars in circulation

-- Net gold held by the Treasury

Figure 11.1 Components of silver currency and gold in circulation and in the United States Treasury, 1878–1891. From F. W. Taussig, *The Silver Situation in the United States* (New York, 1893), backpiece.

Treasury Currency Policy

The flexibility that the Treasury Department had in circulating silver was analogous to the discretion that it had had at times with respect to greenbacks during the reconstruction period. The Bland-Allison Act allowed the Treasury even more discretion than the greenback acts, although the rate of silver monetization was much less spectacular than the rate of greenback issue during the war.

The Treasury thus had some of the features of a central bank. The secretary following Sherman, Charles J. Folger, said in 1881 that his policy was to keep a gold reserve of about 40 percent against outstanding United States notes in addition to the balance maintained for all ordinary expenditures. "The Government," he stated, "by the issue of its notes, payable on demand, . . . is in a position analogous to that of banking, and should therefore act upon principles found to be sound and safe in that business."[8] In his report for 1882 Folger observed that the government fiscal policy of retiring outstanding debt worked against a monetary policy that would maintain national bank-note circulation. National bank notes required the collateral of government securities; so the net retirement of debt meant also a net decline in national bank notes outstanding. He suggested that national banks be permitted to issue notes up to 90 percent of the *market* value of the bonds, since prices of the bonds were constantly above par in the market, and that other bonds be permitted the circulation privilege.[9]

The balance that appeared in the Treasury in the early 1880s included much of the silver purchased under the stipulations of the Bland-Allison Act as well as gold coin and bullion, some greenbacks and national bank notes, some fractional currency, and Treasury deposits in national banks. Against these reserve assets were outstanding gold and silver certificates, greenbacks, some amount of national bank notes, and some percentage of silver coin. (See table 11.1.)

The Treasury had adopted the custom, which had the implied authorization of Congress, of keeping at least $100 million of gold against the $346 million of outstanding greenbacks, a reserve of about 29 percent. It held additional gold—about $10 million—as part of the 5 percent redemption fund for outstanding national bank notes. National bank notes were also secured by deposit of United States bonds in the Treasury and by the providential reserves held by the national banks themselves. The amount of Treasury gold held as a reserve against silver coin was the difference between the mint (or monetary) and market (or commodity) value of the silver currency circulating in the economy. Table 11.1 shows the dollar volume of the *net* values of the Treasury's precious metal assets, its paper-currency obligations, and the reserve ratios between these two aggregates for the years 1880–1900.

The business boom between 1879 and 1882 effectively silenced the mone-

TABLE 11.1 Gold and silver coin and bullion in the United States Treasury, treasury paper currency in circulation, and ratios of gold and silver to currency and gold to currency, 1880–1900 (all but ratios in millions of dollars)

Year	Gold coin and bullion in Treasury	Silver coin and bullion in Treasury[a]		Total gold and silver in Treasury	Notes in circulation[b]	Gold, silver, and currency certificates in circulation[c]	Total currency obligations in circulation	Ratio of Treasury gold and silver to total currency obligations (%)	Ratio of treasury gold to total currency obligations (%)
1880	139	(73)	64	204	659	31	690	30	20
1881	168	(92)	80	249	670	61	731	34	23
1882	159	(106)	93	252	669	82	751	34	21
1883	198	(142)	123	321	660	143	803	40	25
1884	216	(170)	146	362	634	195	829	44	26
1885	247	(194)	163	410	610	244	854	48	29
1886	245	(211)	168	413	609	195	804	51	30
1887	285	(245)	186	471	595	249	844	56	34
1888	320	(278)	205	525	546	337	883	59	36
1889	315	(312)	225	540	515	402	917	59	34
1890	311	(345)	258	569	516	443	959	59	32
1891	267	(397)	327	594	541	462	1003	59	27
1892	259	(446)	324	583	587	487	1074	54	24
1893	189	(489)	319	508	642	437	1079	47	18
1894	145	(510)	288	434	610	450	1060	41	14
1895	126	(508)	286	412	574	425	999	41	13
1896	155	(511)	297	451	554	420	974	46	16
1897	186	(515)	267	454	570	465	1035	44	18
1898	236	(511)	259	495	612	453	1065	46	22
1899	311	(504)	261	572	643	487	1130	51	28
1900	435	(503)	268	703	695	622	1317	53	33

Sources: *Reports of the Treasurer,* 1895–1901.
Note: Annual averages of end-of-month figures.
[a] Figures in parentheses are monetary values of silver balances. The adjoining figures are the market bullion values of silver at the current market price of silver.
[b] Notes include United States notes, national bank notes, and treasury notes of 1890.
[c] Currency certificates were large-denomination notes used as bank reserves.

tary radicals in Congress. Virtually no monetary issues, let alone controversies, appear in the *Congressional Record* for this period. Still, Secretary Folger had to heed monetary affairs because of the Treasury's cash-balance position. "There is no advisable and lawful mode of disbursing an existing excess of assets," he remarked, "but that of payment of the public debt."[10] This method of relieving the Treasury of cash was somewhat cumbersome because it involved a three-month statutory lag between the call for the debt and its purchase by the Treasury, so it could have aggravated any lack of synchronization between receipts and expenditures. Since the outstanding debt was also at a high premium in the market, Folger felt that he needed express authority to purchase it, even though Congress had already sanctioned Treasury purchases of government securities by a general resolution. Folger argued that "reference to the debates in Congress . . . shows that the motive for adoption of [the resolution] was, that the Treasury Department might at any time break a tightness in the money market by putting out money idle in its vaults."[11]

A banking crisis, a sort of capstone to the mild recession of the time, occurred in the New York money market in the spring of 1884. Large exports of gold to Europe in March and April dramatically reduced reserves of New York City national banks. Price declines on the New York Stock Exchange at the same time placed severe liquidity pressures on "speculators," some of whom had close connections or official positions in a few of the banks. A number of banks suspended during the first week in May. On 14 May 1884, upon the suspension of the Metropolitan National Bank, the New York Clearing House Association (NYCHA) met and authorized what had become their standard strategy in a panic—the issue of clearinghouse loan certificates. The NYCHA subsequently issued over $20 million to solvent but illiquid national bank members. "The steps taken," O. M. W. Sprague reported, "were immediate and effective. During the following week the panic entirely subsided." Most of the certificates were redeemed by 1 July.[12] The Treasury Department did nothing unusual to alleviate the situation; the budget continued in surplus and the Treasury's cash balance burgeoned.

The recession, although not severe, seemed to hang on. Daniel Manning, who succeeded Folger as secretary of the Treasury, commented on the "continuing depression universal in varying degrees over the world."[13] He objected to the purchases of silver because they added to the cash balance in the Treasury. Getting rid of this surplus, he said, would "diminish and finally dissipate the objectionable and invidious influence of the Treasury upon the money market and the business of the country." The Treasury balance would have been used to purchase government securities, he added, except that the market prices of the securities were "too high" at this time. He concluded his views with a normative and strictly constructionist interpretation of Treasury policy. The Treasury's "proper business as a fisc," he wrote, "is to receive the people's revenue from taxes in good money which it has coined for them, and to expend that money as Congress bids, *keeping no surplus* at all beyond what insures punctual payments. A Treasury surplus is standing proof of bad finance—of bad laws, if such have made it necessary."[14]

Manning's reference to the Treasury's surplus was a judgment that embraced not only Treasury debt policy, but also silver policy, fiscal policy, and national bank-note policy. If taxes were reduced, the balance would lessen. It would also decline if the Treasury purchased government debt. But outstanding government debt was collateral security for national bank notes, so a reduction of the debt would also reduce outstanding national bank notes. At the same time, since a significant portion of the Treasury's balance was silver, purchase of the debt would put more silver into circulation.

Congressional Disputes over Silver Policy

Congressional leaders recognized this matrix of monetary combinations, particularly during the recession. In late 1884 the Senate debated a resolution against the suspension of silver coinage. Most of the sentiment against silver came from the North and East and was generally Republican, although it crossed party lines. Prosilver opinions were strongest in the South and West and were usually Democratic and agrarian.

The arguments advanced in favor of the resolution, that is, in favor of silver, were exemplified by the remarks of Nathaniel Hill of Colorado. (Needless to say, representation from Colorado was strongly prosilver.) The trade depression, Hill said, argued against any reduction of silver coinage. In fact, he stated, the Bland-Allison Act was passed because of popular belief that the quantity of gold was inadequate. "There is no inflation of the currency, and it is contraction rather than inflation which is now threatened," he concluded.[15]

John Sherman, back in the Senate after his tenure in the Treasury, answered Hill at length. The expected increase in the commodity value of silver by the act of 1878, he said, had not occurred. At current market prices the silver dollar would have to contain 470 or 480 grains of silver (from 412½) to achieve a bullion value equal to the gold dollar. If this change were not made, he warned, the monetary system might revert to a silver basis. Such a regression, he continued somewhat chauvinistically, would "separate us from the great, powerful, Christian, intelligent, and civilized nations of the world in our financial operations." His own norm for policy would be to stop silver purchases and, "by means of a law five lines long," recoin every silver dollar so that it would weigh 480 grains.[16]

John Williams of Kentucky responded to Sherman with what might be called the "silver paranoid" view. "What is there," he asked, "to prevent the bankers and moneyed men of the world, in other words, the gold-bugs, from

. . . requiring still more silver to be put into the dollar? We believe the fixed purpose of the men who advocate a monometallic system to be to discredit silver altogether and drive it out of the coinage of the world."[17]

Sherman replied as though he were talking to an errant child: "I wish I could cure my friend from Kentucky," he said indulgently, "of the idea that the bankers, or businessmen, or moneyed men of the world have the power to do what he supposes." The values of gold and silver, he explained at some length, were determined in markets. "Market values are mysterious qualities made up by a combination of circumstances, no man can tell how or when. . . . The market value of gold and silver will seek its level, . . . and the money kings are as weak as King Canute in resisting the tide."[18]

William B. Allison of Iowa, coauthor of the Bland-Allison Act of 1878, replied in turn to Sherman that monetary demands and sanctions had a lot to do with "market" value. If the mints of European countries were opened to the free coinage of silver, he claimed, parity between the 25.8-grain gold dollar (.900 fine) and the 412½-grain silver dollar would be restored. But if the United States alone embarked on the free coinage of silver, even though the silver dollar was raised to 480 grains, all the European silver would come to the United States mints and force the United States to a silver standard. The result to foreign countries would be a reduction of their money supplies. Allison held that the governments of these countries would not favor such a result, and therefore any attempt to reach international agreement on an increased silver content of the various silver coins would fail.[19]

Allison was probably correct about international agreement over silver; at least none was ever found. Even if he had been right about a 480-grain silver dollar, *some* weight of silver in a silver dollar would have achieved parity with the gold dollar.

The remainder of this debate centered on the question of why silver coins would not circulate. One faction argued that the Treasury refused to pay them out; the sound-money advocates contended that people simply refused to hold and use them. The evidence suggests that the sound-money men were correct. Some volume of coined dollars, perhaps $50 or $60 million at that time, would stay in circulation for ordinary coin-currency purposes, but any attempt by the Treasury to issue more coin resulted in redemption of silver at the banks and subtreasury offices for other kinds of circulating media. If the silver was in the form of silver certificates, that is, just another paper money, people used it to the same extent that they used other paper currency.

Congress amended silver-currency policy in 1886 in a way that took account of this pattern of currency demand by giving Secretary Manning authority to issue paper silver certificates of $1, $2, and $5, and to stop issues of greenbacks under $5. By 1890 the outstanding volume of silver certificates under $5 was $175 million out of a total of $293 million, while coined silver dollars in circulation remained under $60 million.[20]

Congressional Controversy over the Proper Size of the Treasury's Cash Balance

Attention in the first session of the Forty-ninth Congress (1885–86) shifted from silver policy, which seemed to be in political equilibrium for the time being, to the Treasury's cash balance and how to disburse it. Several events coincided in bringing this issue into focus. First, the money was there in considerable amounts. Second, only part of this sizable balance was used in ordinary Treasury operations. Third, business activity had not rebounded completely from the recession of 1884. And finally, several secretaries of the Treasury had requested guidance on its disposition.

On 13 July 1886, William Morrison, a representative from Illinois and chairman of the Committee on Ways and Means, introduced a joint resolution calling for the Treasury to disburse all the "surplus or balance in the Treasury . . . over $100,000,000 [at a maximum rate of $10 million a month] . . . to the payment of the interest-bearing indebtedness of the United States." Morrison argued that spending the Treasury cash balance would "tend to make money cheaper, increase the means of exchange, . . . help in the transaction of business," and retard government spending. He noted that the average gold balance in the Treasury since resumption had been $150 million, yet almost no United States notes had been redeemed. Also unused was the 5 percent redemption fund for national bank notes, which amounted to about $10½ million of the Treasury's balance. In addition, both national bank notes and United States notes were protected by United States government securities that could act as a redemption medium if necessary.[21] Therefore, the Treasury balance, Morrison concluded, was largely supercargo.

Most of the prosilver forces, who were primarily southern or western and agrarian, favored the resolution. The gold-standard people were quick to point out that the Democratic Cleveland administration opposed the resolution. Frank Hiscock, an antisilver Republican from New York, cited a letter from Secretary Manning in which Manning had stated rather mildly that reduction of the surplus in the face of current fiscal uncertainties would not be "prudent."[22]

Hiscock was supported by another New Yorker, Abram Hewitt, an antisilver Democrat. Hewitt objected in particular to the discretionary power in the Treasury "to make money easy or to make it tight at its pleasure." The Treasury, he stated, "has now become a great bank, it is a bank of issue, a bank of deposit; it is a member of the [New York] clearing house. It could not disregard if it would the condition of the money market." He felt that if the quantity of paper money fell, Congress would authorize the further issue of silver certificates until the bullion value of silver in the Treasury was only 35 to 40 percent of outstanding certificates. The Supreme Court's decisions upholding the constitutionality of United States notes, he thought, permitted such an unprincipled increase in paper money.[23]

The prosilver forces, who were also advocates for paper money, did not on that account wish to give discretion over the issue of paper currency to the secretary of the Treasury. A. J. Warner of Ohio cited British experience and policy in dealing with a mixed currency and concluded with these revealing words: "In adopting a paper circulation we must unavoidably depend for a maintenance of its due value upon the adoption of a strict and judicious rule for the regulation of its amount." Warner made the obvious point that use of the Treasury balance to repurchase outstanding debt would save the government interest expenditures. Why should a balance of over $200 million, he asked, be kept in the Treasury? "I can understand," he concluded, "how an idolatrous superstition could gather millions of talents in a heathen temple to purchase the favors of the gods; but why should we hoard $228 millions in the Treasury of the United States? Is it to purchase the favor of Wall Street and the banks? If so it is altogether too dear a price."[24]

Lewis Payson of Illinois was another who spoke in favor of the resolution. He addressed himself at one point to the constitutionality of the greenbacks. He observed that President Cleveland, among others, had questioned the Supreme Court decisions that had upheld their constitutionality. "What can make them believe it?" he asked rhetorically, referring to the constitutional issue that he thought was an open-and-shut case. "Not [even] one raised from the dead!" The Cleveland administration, he thought, would not abide by the resolution even if it passed. "What is needed now, sir," he stated, "is a recognition on the part of the executive officers of the Government that they are not above the law, but subordinate to the will of the people expressed in these Halls in a constitutional manner."[25]

Republicans tried to make political capital of the fact that the resolution revealed a rift between the Democratically controlled House of Representatives and the Democratic administration.[26] The secretary of the Treasury already had the authority "to apply the surplus money in the Treasury not otherwise appropriated, or so much thereof as he may consider proper, to the purchase or redemption of the United States bonds." William McKinley argued that with this authorization already on the statute books the proposed resolution was a vote of "no confidence" in the administration. The Democratically controlled Congresses from 1875 to 1885 had never attempted such a rebuff to the Republican executives who had been in office. Furthermore, McKinley stated, "I would want that discretion [of the secretary of the Treasury] continued, . . . and if [it] is to be taken away from yours [the Democratic secretary] without qualification or condition, it must be your act, not mine."[27]

Nelson Dingley of Maine supported McKinley's position. The resolution, he said, was the "first attempt . . . in the history of this Government to determine by a legislative resolution what should be the working balance of the Treasury. . . . No cast-iron rule can be laid down on a matter of this kind." Since the Treasury's working balance was an administrative and not a legislative matter, he said, Congress should not interfere.[28]

The issue was not just administrative. It would have been administrative only if the amount involved were trivial, and trivial it was not.[29] Nor was this instance the first of its kind. Exactly fifty years earlier Congress had directed the Treasury to "deposit" its surplus with the states on the basis of each state's representation in Congress.

The House rejected all amendments to the resolution and it passed on 14 July 1886 by a vote of 207 to 67.[30] The political division over the resolution involved not only the disposition of the surplus but also the role of the secretary in disbursing it. The prosilver, cheaper-money faction wanted currency put into circulation by means of laws over which Congress had precise control, and with no discretion of any consequence at the executive level. The gold-standard forces, on the other hand, were willing to allow the secretary of the Treasury to retain discretionary powers, but they were opposed to all currency legislation that would make such discretionary powers substantive. In sum, one side wanted power to alter the currency at will, but wanted this power constrained by legislative rules. The other side was willing to give discretionary power to the secretary, but it was a power to do almost nothing.

The Morrison resolution, as it was called, came up for debate in the Senate a few weeks after it passed the House. One of the first to speak on the issue was James Beck of Kentucky, who was prosilver and in favor of the resolution. Beck made an excellent presentation of the political utility that the resolution could be expected to yield. At the same time he countered the contention of McKinley and others that the resolution was evidence of a conflict between the Democrats in Congress and the Democratic administration. This resolution, he said, would give the secretary of the Treasury a specific law for his guidance and thus relieve him of a large responsibility. Congress was supposed to have this power, and the secretary was only to be "vested with such discretion as we see fit to give him." The secretary of the Treasury, unlike the other cabinet officers who reported to the president, was supposed to report directly to Congress: "We with the Secretary of the Treasury manage the purse; the President and the other Secretaries control the sword."[31]

Some of the prosilver senators, as well as some representatives, opposed the resolution because they felt that the contingency reserve of $100 million in gold that the Treasury would still keep was unnecessarily large. Henry Teller of Colorado suggested that the economy was experiencing a current scarcity of money and the Treasury was locking up money in the face of it.[32]

One of Teller's silver-state colleagues, John P. Jones of Nevada, presented a detailed account of the demand for money. This variable, he lectured correctly, was "equal to the sum of the demands for all other things and was intimately connected to the quantity of money." Therefore "the regulation of the volume and value of money is one of the highest functions of sovereignty and should under no circumstances be surrendered [to national banks]." Jones would have tied the growth in the economy's stock of money to the growth in population. He was sanguine over the maintenance of gold convertibility. If all the gold were squeezed out of the monetary system by issues of silver, he said, it would "leave the country free to adopt a system of money whose volume and value will be regulated, not as the value of gold is now regulated, by the edicts of blind chance, but by the guidance of human wisdom."[33]

Much of the discussion in the Senate centered on the amount of cash the Treasury ought to have on hand before it repurchased debt. John Sherman of Ohio, now president pro tem of the Senate, distinguished three cash reserves: (1) the amount kept for redemption of United States notes, (2) a working balance for ordinary Treasury payments, and (3) the accumulation needed to purchase bonds when the decision had been made to redeem them. He thought that $140 million was approximately the right amount for ordinary purposes before bonds should be purchased. He compared the Bank of England reserve, which he estimated varied between 41 and 54 percent of Bank of England notes, to the 29 percent that the $100 million gold balance provided against outstanding United States notes.[34] Silver currency also required a gold reserve. "It is maintained at par with gold just like your paper money," he stated correctly, "because it is redeemed, it is received, it is used by the Government in exchange for gold. . . . The very fact that the silver dollar is safely stored in the Treasury is the best protection to the value of silver."[35]

The Senate modified the resolution in ways that made its version more conservative than the one passed by the House. First, it added a $20 million supplementary balance, under the discretion of the secretary of the Treasury, to the $100 million already in the resolution. Second, it inserted a contingency amendment allowing the president to stop bond repurchases under conditions of "extraordinary emergency." Third, it inserted four amendments to dispose of the so-called trade dollars.[36]

Samuel Maxey of Texas voiced the opinions of several senators when he contended that the effect of the contingency amendment would be to allow an "emergency" to be declared and bond purchases halted if the purchases required a disbursement of Treasury silver. Issues of silver coin so sought-after by many congressmen could then be prevented by executive fiat. In spite of such objections, the resolution passed by a vote of 42 to 20.[37]

The two versions of the resolution required a conference committee to iron out the differences. Three members from each house of Congress were appointed.[38] The committee agreed that the secretary of the Treasury was a more logical and more appropriate officer than the president to declare a suspension of debt repurchases due to an extraordinary emergency.[39] This amendment to

TABLE 11.2 Values for currencies in circulation, excluding gold coin, and absolute changes between March and September, 1880–1900 (millions of dollars)

Year (end of month)	Silver dollars and fractional silver coin	△	United States notes[a]	△	National bank notes	△	Silver certificates and notes of 1890[b]
1880 March	75		323		340		6
Sept.	77	2	320	−3	340	0	12
1881 March	83	6	325	5	343	3	39
Sept.	86	3	320	−5	354	11	53
1882 March	87	1	318	−2	356	2	59
Sept.	87	0	315	−3	355	−1	63
1883 March	90	3	317	2	355	0	71
Sept.	93	3	309	−8	347	−8	79
1884 March	87	−3	301	−8	336	−11	96
Sept.	86	−1	310	9	324	−12	96
1885 March	84	−2	300	−10	314	−10	113
Sept.	97	13	296	−4	310	−4	94
1886 March	98	1	304	8	312	2	90
Sept.	108	10	302	−2	301	−11	95
1887 March	105	−3	318	16	284	−17	132
Sept.	111	6	323	5	270	−14	154
1888 March	110	−1	314	−9	255	−15	192
Sept.	110	0	293	−21	238	−17	219
1889 March	108	−2	307	14	218	−20	251
Sept.	110	2	310	3	200	−18	277
1890 March	112	2	322	22	186	−14	291
Sept.	118	6	334	2	177	−9	316
1891 March	120	2	334	0	168	−9	344
Sept.	120	0	327	−7	166	−2	379
1892 March	121	1	324	−3	169	3	404
Sept.	125	4	323	−1	165	−4	434
1893 March	126	1	317	−6	172	7	452
Sept.	123	−3	332	15	201	29	474
1894 March	113	−10	291	−41	197	−4	470
Sept.	113	0	267	−24	203	6	452
1895 March	114	1	257	−10	203	0	445
Sept.	117	3	240	−17	207	1	437
1896 March	118	1	232	−8	214	7	441
Sept.	117	−1	250	18	221	7	443
1897 March	115	−2	249	−1	222	1	454
Sept.	118	3	252	3	226	4	465
1898 March	123	5	267	15	222	−4	488
Sept.	127	4	292	25	232	10	490
1899 March	134	7	311	19	240	8	493
Sept.	143	9	315	4	240	0	490
1900 March	143	0	323	8	267	27	488
Sept.	151	8	325	2	319	52	488

△	Treasury notes of 1890	Gold certificates	△	Currency certificates[a]	△	Total currency in circulation	△	Percent △
		8		8		760		
6		8	0	10	2	767	7	1
27		6	−2	7	−3	803	36	5
14		5	−1	8	1	826	23	3
6		5	0	11	3	836	10	1
4		5	0	11	0	836	00	0
8		43	38	9	−2	885	49	6
8		55	12	12	3	895	10	1
17		69	14	15	3	904	9	1
0		87	18	16	1	919	15	2
17		116	29	26	10	953	34	4
−19		118	2	23	−3	938	−15	−2
−4		91	−27	12	−11	907	−31	−3
5		85	−6	8	−3	899	−8	−1
37		94	9	7	−1	940	41	5
22		98	4	7	0	963	23	2
38		92	−6	9	2	972	9	1
27		135	43	13	4	1008	36	4
32		129	−6	14	1	1027	19	2
26		117	−12	15	1	1029	2	0
14		135	18	8	−7	1064	35	3
25	7	158	23	7	−1	1110	46	4
28	34	144	−14	11	4	1121	11	1
35	57	113	−31	18	7	1123	2	0
25	78	154	41	30	12	1202	79	7
30	107	121	−33	17	−13	1185	−17	−1
18	129	112	−9	17	0	1196	11	1
22	149	80	−32	8	−9	1218	22	2
−4	141	70	−10	53	45	1194	−24	−2
−18	121	65	−5	56	3	1156	−38	−3
−7	121	49	−16	37	−19	1105	−51	−5
−8	107	51	2	64	27	1116	11	1
4	104	43	−8	34	−30	1082	−34	−3
2	89	39	−4	34	0	1104	22	2
11	90	37	−2	74	40	1151	47	4
11	90	37	0	53	−21	1151	0	0
23	100	36	−1	38	−15	1174	23	2
2	97	35	−1	18	−20	1194	20	2
3	94	33	−2	22	4	1233	39	3
−3	90	99	66	16	−6	1303	70	6
−2	85	174	75	14	−2	1409	106	8
0	68	209	35	2	−12	1494	85	6

Sources: *Reports of the Treasurer,* 1895 and 1901.

[a] Currency certificates were large denominations ($5,000 and $10,000) of United States notes. This total, including holdings by the Treasury, was supposed to be fixed at $346.68 million.

[b] This column includes only silver certificates until 1890, at which point it includes treasury notes of 1890. The next column presents treasury notes of 1890 as a datum.

the bill, together with allowance for a contingency balance of $20 million, emphasized the strategic position that the secretary of the Treasury would occupy.

J. B. Weaver of Iowa, who favored cheaper money through an easy currency policy, was therefore against the conference committee's version of the resolution. The secretary, he said, would be the sole judge of an emergency, so the resolution in this form was no improvement over the present arrangement. "Congress," he complained, "is called upon to abdicate and give over its discretion to the Secretary of the Treasury."[40]

Abram Hewitt of New York, the hard-money Democrat, argued that secretarial discretion was necessary because "the Treasury has in effect become a bank of issue and the place of final redemption for the currency of the country." He felt that this discretion would be necessary as long as the government had United States notes outstanding and a supervisory role over the national banks. Other representatives objected to the Treasury's "emergency" discretion on constitutional principles and because it violated the spirit of the Independent Treasury Act, which was supposed to keep the Treasury detached from the banks and the private economy. Still others objected because they felt that the secretary would use this power as a means of avoiding silver disbursements.[41]

Those legislators who favored discretion were, anomalously enough, the Republican conservative easterners, who for all their conservatism reflected some authoritarian notions. They considered secretarial discretion over the Treasury's gold balance necessary because of the gold's function as a reserve to outstanding issues of government currency. They also thought that the reserve balance would have to be used at the "moment when the money markets of the country become unsettled and panicky."[42]

The report of the conference committee was finally adopted 120 to 63 in the House and by a simple voice vote in the Senate. Many of the cheap-money populists voted against it.

Deposit of Treasury Balances in National Banks

Secretary Fairchild accepted the Morrison resolution as a mandate for policy and retired all of the 3 percent certificates during calendar 1886 and 1887.[43] Since the 3 percents were authorized collateral for the issue of national bank notes, the quantity of national bank notes in circulation declined significantly.[44] (See table 11.2.) Nonetheless, total deposits in national banks increased from $1,117 million in October 1885 to $1,275 million in October 1887, an increase of $158 million, or about 6 percent per year.[45]

The Treasury surplus at the end of 1887 was still $55 million over the required $120 million, despite retirement of the 3 percents.[46] The remainder of the outstanding government debt was subject to market forces and continued to bear a high premium. All the secretaries of the period commented on this fact and hesitated to purchase more of the marketable debt than was required by the provisions of the sinking fund law—1 percent annually of total debt outstanding. Secretary Fairchild continued this conservatism, if it can be called such, even though Congress had provided for purchases of the debt at the discretion of the secretary in the Appropriation Act of 1881, and by the Morrison resolution in 1886. In lieu of debt retirement, Fairchild formulated a new policy—one that was to have widespread repercussions during the next twenty years: deposit of Treasury balances in national banks.

This policy, which appeared to violate both the letter and the spirit of the Independent Treasury Act, was belatedly authorized during the Civil War. At that time it was nothing more than an administrative expedient given the Treasury in order to make the business of the Treasury more efficient. It was not supposed to be a grant of power for policy purposes. Fairchild in his report for 1887 claimed that the policy, "as a means of keeping the circulating media available for business purposes . . . is very limited under present laws and ought not to be used except in exceptional circumstances such as have existed of late and because there is no better thing to do."[47]

Depositing the Treasury's balance in banks was potentially much more volatile than the simple open-market purchases of outstanding debt for which Congress had twice granted authority. To excuse the deposit policy on the grounds that "there is no better thing to do" implied gross administrative ignorance or some sort of deviousness for political purposes. Further in his report for 1887, Fairchild defended the deposit policy on the grounds that the money would be "at once returned to the channels of business through Government payments, [so] no shock would be caused by such withdrawal." If Congress thought the purchase of bonds with the surplus was a better policy, he stated defensively, "specific authority should be given to the Secretary of the Treasury to do so."[48]

This statement is hard to treat charitably in view of the two laws that Congress had already enacted. Nevertheless, Fairchild spurned further security purchases and in early 1887 began a systematic policy of depositing Treasury balances in selected national banks. These deposits had so far been on the order of $11 million to $13 million with little variation. By April 1888 the amount was just short of $62 million, or about five times the customary balance.[49] (See table 11.3.)

Not only was this volume of Treasury deposits unusual, but the method used was highly questionable. Government deposits in national banks required a pledge of government securities by national banks just as did the issue of bank notes. On his own authority in October 1887 Fairchild determined that national banks depositing 4½ percent bonds might carry the face amount of government deposits on their books, and those carrying 4 percent

TABLE 11.3 Treasury deposits in national banks, 1880–1900 (millions of dollars)

Year	Month	Deposit	Year	Month	Deposit
1880	March	11	1895	March	15
1887	March	19		Sept.	15
	Sept.	25	1896	March	27
1888	March	61		Sept.	17
	Sept.	57	1897	March	17
1889	March	48		Sept.	17
	Sept.	48		Dec.	49
1890	March	32	1898	March	31
	Sept.	31		Sept.	81
1891	March	30		Dec.	95
	Sept.	21	1899	March	89
1892	March	18		Sept.	83
	Sept.	15	1900	March	111
1893	March	15		Sept.	97
	Sept.	16	1901	March	98
1894	March	15		Sept.	109
	Sept.	15			

Sources: *Treasury Reports*, 1895 and 1901.

bonds might carry 110 percent of the face amount of the bonds. Since national banks could issue notes only up to 90 percent of the par value of the bonds, and since the notes required a 5 percent redemption reserve as well, the banks were easily induced to accept the deposit of public moneys.[50] To do so, they had to reduce outstanding issues of national bank notes still further, since bonds held as collateral for government deposits could not also be pledged as collateral for national bank-note currency.

When Congress became aware of Secretary Fairchild's policy, another debt-purchase bill was introduced in the House of Representatives on 29 February 1888. It called for the secretary "to apply the surplus money now in the Treasury, and such surplus money as may hereafter be in the Treasury, and not otherwise appropriated, or so much thereof as he may consider proper, to the purchase or redemption of United States bonds."[51] This new bill followed almost verbatim the clause in the Appropriation Act of 1881 that had already authorized such purchases. William McKinley pointed out this similarity. He criticized the Cleveland administration for dubbing this authorization "suspicious" and noted that the act of 1881, including the debt-purchase provision, had passed by unanimous votes in both houses of Congress. McKinley contended that the Cleveland administration had an ulterior motive in not purchasing the debt. The administration, he said, wanted the cash balance in the Treasury to accumulate in order to cause business hardship that would in turn furnish support for its tariff-reduction policy.[52]

Many Democrats in Congress continued to criticize the Cleveland administration's unorthodox monetary policy. J. B. Weaver of Iowa had a telling argument. "The Secretary of the Treasury," he said, "has serious doubts about his authority . . . to purchase bonds with the money. It is a little singular that some doubt did not arise in his mind as to his power to deposit this amount of money in the national banks." The money had been taxed from the people by the government, deposited in the national banks without interest, he charged, and then "loaned back by the banks to the poor wretches from whom it was extorted." Weaver cited the list of 298 banks in which the Treasury had deposited its balance. Many of these banks, he observed, included directors and large stockholders who in the past had been highly placed officers in the Treasury Department. Finally, he predicted, any attempt to remove the government's deposits would cause serious embarrassment: "The banks, sir, are the masters of the situation, and not the Secretary."[53]

A case was made in support of the administration, but it was not very solid. W. C. P. Breckenridge of Kentucky argued correctly (but irrelevantly) that after the 3 percents were retired, none of the outstanding debt was callable at the option of the government. He recognized that the remaining debt could be acquired on *market* terms. But, he alleged, the money would then accumulate in the larger cities, where it would cause a "glut" and be subject to delays "before it could be returned to the places from which it had been drawn and where it was needed." Depositing the money in national banks, he claimed, scattered it around expediently.[54]

The new debt-purchase bill passed the House of Representatives on 29 February 1888, without a division, as a routine housekeeping matter. It then went to the Senate and passed there on 5 April 1888. A conference committee was appointed in the Senate to compromise the differences that the two houses had incorporated in their versions of the bill, and the bill itself was returned to the House Committee on Ways and Means for modification. But it was never heard from again.[55] The Cleveland administration, which had been procrastinating on the cash-balance issue, accepted the congressional votes on the bill as a mandate for policy and subsequently began systematic purchases of securities by means of a circular issued 17 April 1888. In his report for 1888 Secretary Fairchild stated somewhat pharisaically that "no bonds were bought until there had been an expression of opinion by resolutions in both Houses of Congress, that it was lawful and proper to invest the surplus in bonds at the premium necessary to obtain them."[56] He did not refer to the fact that the same authorization had been made seven years earlier.

Cleveland's defeat in the election of 1888 resulted in part from the relatively tight money policy his administration had followed. Democratic sentiment in Congress was much looser. Debates in both houses also reflected much dissatisfaction with his financial and other policies, such as pension grants.

Benjamin Harrison's secretary of the Treasury, William Windom, in his report for 1889 expressed his disapproval of the deposit policy in the strongest terms. He favored reduction of Treasury balances to their former levels "at the earliest day practicable," but he thought the withdrawal of the balances would be difficult and dangerous because "business is adjusted to the increased supply." The deposit policy, he charged, was contrary to the spirit of the Independent Treasury Act and "necessarily involves favoritism of the most objectionable character. . . . The Secretary of the Treasury . . . may, if so disposed, expand or contract the currency at will, and in the interest of certain favorites whom he may select."[57] Shades of the "pet bank" system!

During the year ending 31 October 1889, the Treasury purchased $99 million worth of bonds; and while it continued to pay a market premium for the securities, the premium lessened. Windom had "advised" (warned) the banks to sell their securities back to the Treasury at "liberal rates" in order to avoid any diminution of their shares of available reserves.[58] The tightness in the money market and the recession in Europe had similar influences on the dispositions of the banks.

Summary of Monetary Events in the 1880s

The decade of the 1880s started out auspiciously. The federal government had disengaged itself from discretionary control over the monetary system late in the previous decade by two separate acts. First, it had fixed forever the total stock of greenbacks, and second, it had succeeded in resuming specie payments. These acts promised to reduce significantly the possibility of governmental mischief on the monetary system. The international gold standard and free markets appeared to be in the ascendancy, and the business boom of the early 1880s emphasized the golden aura of the times.

But the boom turned into a recession, and the fiscal pattern of the period resulted in an accumulating government surplus. A prosperous government side by side with a depressed economy begged for a change in policy that would benefit the private sector. It took no fiscal-monetary expert to understand that a disbursement of government moneys could have the desired effect.

The accumulation of a federal fiscal surplus meant that the Treasury would impound the silver moneys that were a part of the surplus. It also brought chagrin to the friends of silver, who had expected the circulation of significant amounts of silver after the passage of the Bland-Allison Act.

The executive branch of the government continued throughout the period to be ruled by presidents and secretaries of the Treasury who were antipathetic toward easy money in all its guises, while the legislative branch was composed largely of Congresses that favored significant relaxation in the monetary system. Thus policy during the decade, while not overtly controversial, had much dissent and dissatisfaction running through it.

Disbursement of the government's balances and the thorough circulation of accumulated silver certificates by means of open-market purchases of government securities closed the decade. At the same time, the silver bloc was mounting an effective program to increase the circulation of this particular fiat money.

12 The Fall of Silver

> It seems to me that the matter [of the quantity of money] should be referred to statisticians to ascertain the amount necessary, and then we could have some regular rule about reaching the object desired and not be subject to the action of speculators who would devise plans whereby the people would suffer every time.
>
> William P. Stewart, Senate, 8 January 1891

The Political Fortunes of the Silver Movement to 1890

Economists, historians, and political scientists have devoted much attention to the monetary events and policies of the post–Civil War era in the United States. They have treated at length the gold-standard system, the occasional lapses into paper money, and the emergence of silver as a major monetary metal. The silver story always seems to reach a climax and conclusion around 1896 with the first Bryan campaign—as though the fortunes of Bryan and the free-silver movement peaked simultaneously, then declined, unable to meet the political challenge of conservative Republicanism.[1] Horace White gave perhaps the clearest statement of this conventional view in his book *Money and Banking,* first published in 1910. The concerted attempt to restore free silver in the 1880s, he wrote, "culminate[d] in the famous campaign of Bryan in 1896. . . . The long depression beginning in 1893 gave impetus to the movement, and Bryan took advantage of the widespread discontent in his campaign for the presidency in 1896. Had it not been for the increased production of gold . . . which started the price level upward in 1897, it is barely possible that . . . Bryan might have been successful in 1900."[2] This synchronous view of the economic and political fortunes of the free-silver movement misrepresents what actually happened. Its shortcomings become manifest when the succession of events involving silver is summarized without embellishment.

Significant amounts of silver were coined before 1842 and in the 1850s. But silver first appeared as a possible vehicle of monetary policy in the mid–1870s, largely because its costs of production fell sharply at that time. By 1878 it had supplanted greenbacks as *the* means for promoting cheaper-money policies. In that year Congress passed the Bland-Allison Act, which required the Treasury to buy between $2 million and $4 million of silver a month at the fixed price of $1.29 per ounce to be coined into standard silver dollars.[3] Throughout the 1880s most leading members of the Democratic party as well as a significant number of Republicans from the western silver-producing states continued their agitation for a free-silver law. The agrarian debtor groups of the rural South and Midwest sensed correctly that falling prices increased the real burden of their debts, while the silver Republicans of the West wanted political support for one of their major commodities. Finally, much sentiment came from groups opposed to national banking and the issue of national bank notes. Many opponents of national banking were also agrarian debtors. Only the opposition of several presidents to the free coinage of silver thwarted repeated attempts to enact such legislation.

Despite the antisilver administration of Benjamin Harrison, silver proponents won a major battle with the passage of the Treasury Note Act in July 1890. Democratic majorities then swept congressional and presidential offices in 1892, and a permanent silver policy seemed assured. For the first time since 1856 and the administration of James Buchanan, Democrats had won the presidency and had majorities in both houses of Congress. Yet in just a few years politicians representing free silver had lost most of their political capital, and in 1900 Congress declared gold the sole legal tender monetary metal. From this time on, silver remained in the monetary system only as a subsidiary currency.

Nothing in this sequence of events suggests the particular set of circumstances that led to termination of silver monetization. Why did this political-economic force—the free-silver movement—suddenly lose its legislative momentum at just the time (1893–1896) when a cheaper-money doctrine and policy would have seemed most logical and most likely to succeed due to Democratic majorities in Congress and a Democratic administration in the White House? In 1896 the free-silver Populist-Democrat Bryan lost to the conservative-orthodox-Republican McKinley by a larger popular majority than had appeared since 1872. Surely this outcome contradicts the argument that correlates Democratic political success with economic hardship and a doctrine of easy money.

How and why this pattern of events emerged is an intriguing question. Silver's birth and life have been dealt with before, but its crucifixion and death, long neglected, surely occurred before Bryan's Cross-of-Gold speech and campaign in 1896. The result of the subsequent election was anticlimactic to the legislation enacted during the early months of the second Cleveland administration in 1893. The real beginning of the story is the point at which the silver movement achieved its greatest success—the passage of the Treasury Note Act of 1890, usually referred to as the Sherman Silver Purchase Act.

The Treasury Note Act of 1890

Benjamin Harrison defeated Grover Cleveland in 1888 in a very close election.[4] Without a promise to "do something" for silver, Harrison would not have been elected. The issue was not only doing something *for* silver, but also doing something *with* silver *for* everyone who wanted more currency in the monetary system.

Harrison's secretary of the Treasury, William Windom, prepared the administration's silver proposal for congressional consideration. Windom's plan, given in his report for 1889, called for the issue of treasury notes "against deposits of silver bullion at the market price of silver when deposited."[5] This plan anticipated the issue of treasury notes equal in dollar value to the market price of the deposited silver. The market price of the silver would be calculated by the secretary of the Treasury. The silver would still be monetized at the historic value of 371.25 grains of pure silver per dollar, but the given monthly expenditure of $2 million to $4 million would no longer be in force. Furthermore, the secretary would have the right to suspend purchases temporarily and sell silver in the open market.[6]

Both houses of Congress proposed silver bills in the Fifty-first Congress. The original Senate bill would have followed the Windom proposal, but purchase at the market price was unacceptable to a large number of prosilver western Republicans because such a plan did not provide government subsidies to silver producers. Edward Wolcott of Colorado remarked that westerners had given "handsome majorities for the Republican ticket." But, he said, "if the Windom recommendation, approved by the President, could have been announced before the election, it is my humble opinion that not a single state west of the Missouri River would have given a Republican majority."[7]

Several more speeches in the Senate argued the merits and demerits of silver as a currency. John Mitchell of Oregon made the proposal that was to become law. He suggested the purchase of silver at a limited rate, say 4.5 million ounces a month, in place of free and unlimited coinage—a proposal that could not get past the House.[8]

The Senate, despite the opposition to free coinage in the House, approved a free-silver measure by a vote of 42 to 25.[9] The House rejected the Senate's free-silver provision, 152 to 135. A conference committee made up of three members from the House and three from the Senate then worked out a compromise bill. The chairman of the committee was Republican John Sherman of Ohio, who would steer the committee's recommendations to a conservative middle ground and by his successful intermediation endow the bill with his name.

The conference committee report incorporated Mitchell's proposal for the monthly purchase of 4.5 million ounces of silver at the market price, but the price was not to exceed one dollar for 371.25 grains—the traditional Treasury purchase price for monetary silver. Treasury notes issued in payment of the purchased silver would be redeemable in coin on demand and would be legal tender except "where otherwise stipulated in the contract."[10]

Sherman explained the compromise at length to his Senate colleagues. The first order of business, he stated, was to get a bill that would be acceptable to silver proponents while denying free coinage. The silver purchase agreed to was the lower limit that the Senate would accept and the upper limit the House would tolerate.[11]

One free-silver Republican-turned-Populist, Preston Plumb of Kansas, stated that the advantage of free coinage was that it would "release the money supply from the arbitrary control or suggestion of control of anybody. It leaves it subject only to the operation of natural forces."[12] The "anybody" Plumb referred to was the secretary of the Treasury. His statement attests again to the self-regulatory character of a metallic-standard currency. It also provides an interesting contrast to an earlier statement by Senator Jones of Nevada (also a free-silver Republican) on the benefits that would result in monetary affairs from the "guidance of human wisdom." Jones had implied that Congress should supply the wisdom. Plumb only objected to such wisdom when it was supplied by the secretary of the Treasury.

The bill of the conference committee passed the Senate 39 to 26 along strictly party lines. It then went to the House and passed there by a vote of 122 to 90, again along party lines, and President Harrison signed it into law on 14 July 1890.[13]

Monetization of silver under the Sherman Act did not expand the currency stock appreciably because of the simultaneous outflow of gold and corresponding decline in gold certificates. The monetization of silver in fact stimulated the outflow of gold—a classic example of price-specie-flow. National bank notes, which had been declining steadily for ten years, reached a trough in the early 1890s. Nonetheless, the total stock of currency grew slowly until September 1893. During the next two and a half years—until March 1896—it declined 12½ percent (table 11.2). Total commercial bank deposits plus currency peaked in late 1892, seesawed downward until mid–1896, and did not regain their 1892 value until mid–1897.[14]

The persistence of United States policy in maintaining gold convertibility in the face of falling prices in terms of gold throughout the trading world explains the changes in the growth rates of currency and money. Much of this general price decline reflected the world's increased demand for monetary gold. Between 1867 and 1895 most European countries and India abandoned some form of bimetallism for the single gold standard. The possibility that United States policy might fail to maintain gold convertibility and be forced to accept a silver standard added to the instability of the United States position, and capital outflows aggravated the problem.[15] Ordinarily, when the United States realized large merchandise export balances, gold inflows would have in part reciprocated. "Instead," wrote Comptroller of the Currency Hepburn in 1892, "they sent us our securities [for redemption]."[16]

The decline in world prices and the increased real value of gold reflected the classical adjustment of national money stocks and domestic price levels that had to occur if a gold standard was to endure. However, no one could foresee how far prices would have to fall before they stabilized; no one could predict when and at what price level world production of gold would again match world demand for gold so that growth in national money stocks of the gold-standard countries might again approximate growth in real output. Nor could anyone predict the role silver might play without jeopardizing the gold standard. If the U.S. government monetized too much silver, external equilibrium between prices in the United States and prices in the rest of the trading world could not occur. The anticipation of this possibility made the adjustment even more difficult.

The Schism on Silver Policy between Congress and the Executive

The national elections of 1892 seemed to be an unequivocal victory for the cheaper-money free-silver forces. Democratic candidates for both houses of Congress and the Democratic executive nominee, Grover Cleveland, scored impressive victories. Under such auspices, congressional legislation favorable to the Democratic agenda would have seemed assured.

Political victory, however, obscured a divisive issue between Cleveland and the Democratic Congress—the monetization of silver. The Congresses and administrations of the previous eighteen years had kept this problem a sectional rather than a party issue. Western Republicans, for example, were adamantly for free silver, while eastern Republicans, as well as eastern Democrats, were against it. The ascendance of Democratic majorities in both houses of Congress took the issue out of Republican hands, where it had been successfully compromised, and allowed it to become an item of controversy within the Democratic party.[17] Cleveland's generally unfavorable attitude toward silver was well known. What was not certain was how far he would go in opposition to his own party in order to further his penchant for sound money.

This uncertainty was dispelled in the early summer of 1893 when Cleveland called a special session of Congress. Business recession was by this time apparent to everyone. External gold drains and an accumulation of silver in the Treasury exposed the proximate cause of the problem. In his message of instruction to the special session the president noted that business distress was "principally chargeable to Congressional legislation touching the purchase and coinage of silver." The operation of the Silver Purchase Act, he continued,

> leads in the direction of the entire substitution of silver for gold in the Government Treasury, and . . . the payment of all Government obligations in depreciated silver. . . . [Should this trend continue] we could no longer claim a place among nations of the first class, nor could our Government provide for the use of the people the best and safest money. . . . The Government cannot make its fiat equiv-

> alent to intrinsic value, nor keep inferior money on a parity with superior money. [The attempt] has resulted in such a lack of confidence at home in the stability of currency values that capital refuses its aid to new enterprises. . . . [Therefore,] I earnestly recommend the repeal of [the act of 1890], and that other legislative action may put beyond all doubt . . . the intention and the ability of the Government to fulfill its pecuniary obligations in money universally recognized by all civilized countries.[18]

Cleveland's charge to Congress reflected anything but a free-silver philosophy. The only feature that distinguished him from his Republican counterparts was his equally positive attitude toward tariff reduction. On monetary policy he was more a gold-standard advocate than his Republican predecessors.

Congressional Controversy over the Mint Price of Silver

The division in the Democratic party surfaced when the bill to repeal the entire silver-purchase clause in the Sherman Act came up in the House on 11 August 1893. William Wilson of West Virginia, a "Cleveland Democrat," was the spokesman for the bill. The free-silver forces, led as usual by Richard P. Bland of Missouri, immediately added amendments calling for the free coinage of silver at 16-to-1 and then for ascending ratios of silver-to-gold up to 20-to-1. If these amendments failed—presumably, each successive ratio would command greater and greater support—the last amendment called for reinstatement of the Bland-Allison Act.[19]

These ratios reflected different statutory mint values of silver to gold. All the ratios were to be achieved by holding constant the mint price of pure gold at one dollar for 23.22 grains, while lowering the mint price of silver successively from one dollar for 371.25 grains (16-to-1) to one dollar for 464.4 grains (20-to-1).[20] The amendments gave legislators a multiple choice of policy options: (a) 16-to-1, (b) 17-to-1, (c) 18-to-1, (d) 19-to-1, (e) 20-to-1, and (f) revert to Bland-Allison Act with limited coinage of $2 million to $4 million of silver a month. The higher the ratio—that is, the lower the mint price of silver—the smaller would be the governmental monetary demand for silver, the less silver would be monetized, and the less likely the chance that silver monetization would jeopardize the ability of the United States Treasury to maintain gold convertibility for other currencies. The market price of silver at this time had gone up to 28-to-1, or about one dollar for 650 grains, but for the previous dozen years it had averaged very near the price that would have implied the 20-to-1 ratio.

Those favoring repeal argued that international agreement on bimetallism was necessary before a two-standard system could succeed. John Pendleton of West Virginia was one of many who made this argument. He had intended, he said, to vote for free coinage of silver at the mint price that would have resulted in the 20-to-1 ratio; but the more he studied the question, the more he believed the same troubles would occur at 20-to-1 that had occurred under limited coinage at 16-to-1. He would agree to a ratio, he said, only in concert with three or four of the leading commercial nations. Otherwise the market value of one of the two metals would constantly diverge from par. Pendleton recommended an issue of $500 million in "good old greenbacks" based on a reserve of $100 million in gold to be obtained from Treasury bond sales. He foresaw no calls for redemption of these notes because "our faith is pledged. The creditor is satisfied with the promise."[21]

Josiah Patterson, a Tennessee Democrat, also discussed the ratio. He pointed out that even a three- or four-cent divergence from par was enough to drive the dearer of the two metals (gold in this case) out of circulation. Even the 20-to-1 ratio would therefore not be large enough in the face of the current market ratio of 28-to-1.[22] "Why advance in the direction of the commercial ratio," he asked, "without going all the way?" A colleague then asked, "At what ratio are you willing to allow silver to be coined freely?" Patterson replied that in view of uncertainties and lack of international agreement, "I am not prepared to vote for any ratio you might name. [Great applause.]" He desired, he said, the free and unlimited coinage of silver, but only under international agreement.[23]

Much was made of the monetary planks in the political platforms of all three parties before the elections of 1892. The Democratic platform had argued for the free coinage of both metals under "such safeguards of legislation as will keep the metals at a parity." The Cleveland Democrats first rejected all ratios between the metals, then stated hypocritically that they would vote for free coinage when "proper safeguards" had been assured.[24] Of course, *some* ratio would have provided a proper safeguard, so rejection of all ratios was in effect rejection of any proper safeguard.

Charles Hooker of Mississippi correctly suggested that a change in the ratio would adjust for any change in the relative market prices of gold and silver. "There may have been a change in the relative measuring values of the two metals," he said. "But that change, whatever it may be, can be corrected by a change in the ratio of coinage from the present 16-to-1 to, say, 19- or even 20-to-1. It does not justify the total abolition of silver as a standard monetary metal."[25]

Prestige was another debating point with those opposed to free silver. Cleveland's speech to the special session had emphasized this argument, and Patterson parroted Cleveland. To allow a monometallic silver standard that would certainly result from free coinage, he said, would align United States policy, "not with the enlightened nations of Christendom, but side by side with China, with the republic of Mexico, with the republics of Central and South America, and every other semicivilized country on the globe."[26]

Charles Grosvenor, a Republican from Ohio, graphically described the relative positions of the Cleveland administration on silver and tariff policy. The McKinley Tariff Act and the Sherman Silver Purchase Act were Republican measures, he said, and were like the two goats Aaron had as offerings. The McKinley Tariff Act would be a sacrifice to the Lord. But the Sherman Act would be a scapegoat for the business collapse and would be sent into the wilderness with the sins of the Democrats whispered in its ear. This way the president and his cabinet could "disenthrall [themselves] from their allegiance to free silver." The people had been taught, Grosvenor concluded, that the Sherman Act was the root of all evil.[27]

Many free-silver congressmen saw the antisilver effort as a conspiracy of English moneyed interests who wished to appreciate the real value of the dollar at the expense of debtors in the United States. This notion was picturesquely presented in a speech by William Bowers, a Republican from California. "The nation wants more money," said Bowers, "and the head physician [Cleveland] sends us an English prescription telling us that the remedy for scarcity of money is to destroy half of what we have. [Laughter.]"[28]

Most of the prosilver congressmen explicitly specified a proportionality between the quantity of money and prices.[29] Others presented extensive statistics on general prices, using Soetbeer's index of commodities, and compared the movement of the general price level with changes in the price of silver over the previous twenty years.[30] The gold price of silver had stayed within 4 percent of the gold prices of all commodities over this period, implying that a silver standard would have been compatible with stability in the general price level. Only one commodity, noted Joseph Sibley of Pennsylvania, had appreciated significantly with respect to silver. That commodity was gold. "Why do you say that silver has gone down," he asked his opponents, "and . . . is debased? Why do you not say that gold has . . . been deified? . . . You do not want an honest dollar. . . . You want a scarce dollar." The dishonest dollar, he concluded, was the "150-cent" gold dollar.[31]

Sibley's data on the relative prices of gold, silver, and all other commodities were accurate. The only way that the "price" of gold could rise or fall under an operational gold-standard system was by a general fall or rise in the market prices of all other commodities and services. A general decline in all prices was in fact occurring, but the relative value of silver to all commodities had stayed almost constant. This fact seems to argue that the gold dollar should have been devalued so that a smaller quantity of gold would have had a given monetary value. Such a measure would have arrested the downward trend in the general price level. Even if the gold standard were to continue on the same terms, some low-enough mint price for silver would have neutralized silver's displacement of gold. Usually, too, monetization of a metal would add enough to the metal's overall demand to raise its value appreciably. So silver did not have to be devalued to the 28-to-1 ratio in order to limit its threat to gold convertibility.

Political Pressures from the Cleveland Administration

The economics of the situation were relatively clear, the politics even more so. Cleveland would certainly have vetoed *any* silver-purchase bill. J. Rogers Hollingsworth in *The Whirligig of Politics* stated: "On the issue of silver repeal, . . . Cleveland assumed that he could lead his party without modifying his views, for the patronage at his disposal would provide the requisite power for repeal."[32] His self-assurance and willfulness in getting his way with Congress were noted time and again, not only in Congress but also in contemporary news accounts. John McLaurin of South Carolina quoted an editorial from the *Boston Traveller* of 14 August 1893 that said in part: "He [Cleveland] had issued instructions to all his cabinet officers that there shall be no more appointments made upon the recommendations of men in Congress about whose vote upon the silver problem there is any doubt. He has gone even further, and has directed that there shall be extended no official courtesy whatever to anyone in Congress until it is known how his vote is to be cast on the silver question."[33]

Cleveland had appointed John G. Carlisle of Kentucky, a former member of the House of Representatives, to be secretary of the Treasury. In Congress Carlisle had been a champion of free silver and had made an oft-quoted speech on the subject in 1878. As a cabinet officer, however, he changed his views. His "eloquent tongue," said McLaurin, "is silenced by a Cabinet office."[34] In sharp contrast to the prosilver sentiments expressed by congressional members of his own party, Secretary Carlisle was of the opinion that "the amount of money in the country is greater than is required for the transaction of the business of the people at this time. . . . Money does not create business, but business creates a demand for money, and until there is such a revival of industry and trade as to require the use of the circulating medium now outstanding, it would be hazardous to arbitrarily increase the volume by law."[35] With this argument the secretary fashioned a monetary theory that fit the politics of repeal.

The repeal bill came to a vote in the House on 28 August 1893. The amendment for free coinage at 16-to-1 failed 125 to 226; at 17-to-1, 101 to 241; at 18-to-1, 103 to 240; at 19-to-1, 104 to 238; and at 20-to-1, 122 to 222. Restoration of the Bland-Allison Act failed 136 to 213, and the repeal bill passed without amendments 239 to 108. Achievement of any kind of silver-purchase act in the House would have required a "swing" of about forty votes—an astonishing number given the large Democratic majority and the depressed economy.[36] The vote also emphasized the importance legislators attached to a viable gold standard.

Filibuster in the Senate

The repeal bill took only a few weeks to get through the House of Representatives. The rapidity with which the administration achieved its wishes without compromising its major tenet raised well-founded alarms in the prosilver wing of the Senate. When the Senate Committee on Finance reported out the House version of the bill to the full Senate, debate on it developed into a filibuster.[37]

The Senate Committee on Finance did not change the House version except to tack on a pointless conscience-salving amendment. They took this clause from the Democratic platform fashioned at the Chicago convention the year before in anticipation of the general elections of 1892. It stated that United States policy would be "to coin both gold and silver into money of equal intrinsic and exchangeable value, such equality to be secured through international agreement, or by such safeguards of legislation as will insure the maintenance of the parity in value of the coins of the two metals, and the equal power of every dollar at all times in the markets and in the payment of debts."[38] This kind of political claptrap had been intended to effect a compromise between the two wings of the Democratic party. The free-silverites could believe that it implied bimetallism, while the antisilver element could use it as a pretext for opposing silver monetization. In fact it had several interpretations. The "parity in value of the two metals" could mean parity at 16-to-1, parity at 20-to-1, parity at 24-to-1, or parity at any other ratio. The "equal power of every dollar at all times in the markets and in the payment of debts" did not specify a benchmark. Did it mean that all dollars were to be kept equal to the gold dollar in purchasing power, or to the silver dollar? Or were all dollars to be kept at a constant purchasing power over time? The amendment begged these questions and offered no decisive plank on the monetary issue for general party support.

The House experience with the repeal bill had shown that a change in the ratio—the simple solution to the problem—was not popular. Many free-silverites felt that it compromised principle too far, and that acceptance of a change in the ratio implied the operational, practical failure of a double standard.[39]

A standard money metal that could not maintain its value relative to the other metal in a bimetallic-standard system either would displace the other metal or would require constant devaluation of its mint price. That silver should substitute completely for gold was unthinkable. Yet devaluation of silver was also resisted because it seemed an admission that the value of silver was too unstable to justify its continued use as one of the standard metals. Antisilver forces, of course, would not consider any adjustment in the mint prices of the two metals because they wanted silver demonetized unconditionally.

During the filibuster Senator John P. Jones of Nevada demonstrated the intensity of purpose with which the silver bloc resisted repeal of the silver-purchase clause. His speeches fill almost one hundred pages in the *Congressional Record* and draw on the entire collection of treatises on monetary economics in the Library of Congress.[40] He dwelt at length on the proportionality of the quantity of money and prices and on the automatic functioning of metallic standards. The *level* of prices, he said, was unimportant. "The objection [of free-silverites] is . . . to *the persistence of the lowering process*—the constant and unending fall—which renders it impossible for industry and commerce to find a steady level from which prosperity might begin."[41]

The *New York Times* as early as 3 September predicted how the Senate would divide when the final vote on the bill was tallied. It reported that the faction giving the most trouble was the little group of Republicans from the silver-producing states. "They will oppose any change in the ratio, and they will oppose repeal, and they will oppose it as long as they dare to filibuster. The Democrats can not afford to filibuster. The 'guerrillas' can afford anything, for they have little to lose."[42]

True, not enough of the Democrats could afford to filibuster. "The [Cleveland] Administration," accused Edward Wolcott of Colorado, one of the "guerrillas," "with its petty spoils and patronage, has been able to make . . . many converts [from free silver]." The platform of the Democratic party had "declared in favor of free silver, but the platform meant no more to [President Cleveland] than the wind that blows."[43]

William Stewart of Nevada, another guerrilla, discussed at length the use of patronage as a "club" to persuade wavering Democratic senators to support repeal. Stewart cited an open letter written to Cleveland by T. V. Powderly of Scranton, Pennsylvania. "It has been openly proclaimed," Powderly's letter charged,

> that the Congressman or Senator of Democratic faith who would not act with the Administration in opposition to the expressed sentiments of the platform on which you and they were elected would be ignored in the distribution of patronage. No denial has ever come from your lips; no friend of yours has ever ventured to contradict the statement to which I allude.
>
> On the contrary, those nearest to you . . . have taken the ground that Federal patronage would be made the club to beat back the tide of popular sentiment.[44]

Cleveland and his congressional supporters did not try to excuse the means that justified their ends. They argued only that the developing depression was due to the adverse effects of the Sherman Act. Repeal of the purchasing clause, they alleged, would act as a "faith cure" and restore confidence.

This argument was one that no logic could either deny or confirm. Confidence could have been used just as easily in support of silver policy as it was used against it. It received its due from William Hatch of Missouri. He cited a facetious bill to restore confidence proposed by an editorial writer for the *Washington Post*.

> Be it enacted [editorialized the *Post*], by the Senate and the House of Representatives of the United States in Congress assembled: SECTION 1. That confidence in the financial condition of all business affairs throughout the domain of the Republic is hereby declared to be fully restored. [Laughter.] And all persons are commanded to forthwith conduct their financial and commercial transactions in conformity with this enactment.[45]

Democratic Attempts to Promote a Compromise Bill

As Senate discussion of the bill carried on through September into October, Democrats realized that their inability to agree was damaging party prestige and destroying party unity. Senator Arthur Gorman of Maryland had tried for several weeks to effect a compromise, but Cleveland was openly contemptuous of Gorman and his supporters.[46]

On 4 October the *Cincinnati Enquirer* interviewed Senator Sherman on the stalemate. Its reporter first asked Sherman if he thought the act that bore his name would be repealed. "I do not," Sherman replied. He predicted that the Democrats would arrange a compromise, such as reduction of the monthly purchase to 2.5 million ounces, and the president would have to agree or "he will destroy his party."[47]

On 17 October Sherman made a crucial speech in which he claimed that Senate Democrats had to pass something or give up. If they could not agree on a measure, he charged, "the people of the United States will take them at their word. . . . If they do not agree with the President, let them say so, and formulate their opinions into an act." Otherwise, he said, they must retire, and "we will do the best we can with our silver friends who belong to us, who are blood of our blood and bone of our bone. But yours [addressing the Democrats] is the proper duty. . . . You have the supreme honor of being able to settle this question now, and you ought to do it."[48]

The forty-four Senate Democrats, realizing the validity of Sherman's charge, caucused and came to an agreement that was signed by twenty-one free-silver and sixteen administration Democrats, and was opposed by six others.[49] This attempt failed, reported James Pugh of Alabama, when Cleveland "interposed his objections and demanded unconditional repeal at all hazards.

. . . I am satisfied," Pugh concluded, "that all effort at compromise has failed solely on account of President Cleveland and his Secretary of the Treasury. Their will has been as potential and has served the same purpose as the cloture rule."[50]

The administration was able to preserve its principles intact and refuse the compromise only because it could count on the support of twenty-six Republicans in addition to the twenty or twenty-two Democrats it had bludgeoned into submission. The prosilver forces, said Francis Cockrell of Missouri, had given up more than they wished in the caucus that had initiated the aborted compromise, and now they found Sherman and his "Administration Republicans" arrayed against them.

> Then it was that the incandescent light of nonpartisanism, of the Republican, mugwump-Democratic coalition was cast athwart our pathway, and the Democratic Administration was revealed in all its nonpartisan perfection, with its unconditional repeal banners still in the hands of Republicans and Mug-wumps and Democrats. . . . What does this prove when a Democratic President and Secretary of the Treasury refuse to agree with six-sevenths of the Democratic Senators . . . upon a compromise measure, and prefer to leave the Administration banner in the hands of Republicans and Democrats jointly to placing it in the hands of Democrats only?[51]

What it proved had already been proven. What it forebode was an end to any cooperation between congressional rank and file and the Cleveland administration. Tariff reductions, for example, were doomed by the wounds resulting from the silver conflict.

The battle by this time was over. Voting on amendments began on 27 October 1893. William Peffer of Kansas offered an amendment restoring the coinage law of 1837—effectively a free-silver amendment—which lost, 28 to 39. Stewart then did a man-by-man analysis of the Peffer amendment and compared it with the vote taken on a straight free-coinage bill the year before. He found that eight senators had reversed themselves. Had opinions stayed the same, the Peffer amendment would have passed, 36 to 31.[52]

James Berry of Arkansas offered another amendment that would have revived the Bland-Allison Act. The Senate rejected this option 37 to 33. With this close a division, a three-vote swing would have carried the amendment.[53]

Senator Stewart proposed the only amendment that dealt with the ratio. It called for a reduction of 25 percent in the gold content of the gold dollar, with the silver content of the silver dollar remaining constant. The gold dollar would have gone from 23.22 grains to 18.56 grains of pure gold. This devaluation would have adjusted the mint price of gold upward in recognition of the increased real value of gold relative to all other commodities, including silver. It would therefore have changed the ratio of value between gold and silver from 16-to-1 to 20-to-1, not by reducing the mint price of silver, but by increasing the mint price of gold. It was a logical proposal in view of the constancy in value between silver and other commodities, and as a response to the appreciated real value of gold. It was rejected without even a call for the yeas and nays.[54]

As the final vote approached, with no concessions, no compromises, and no probabilities for any remedial legislation to ease the monetary situation, Donald Cameron of Pennsylvania observed: "The majority of this Chamber seems determined to act without thinking, for fear that if it stops to think it will not act."[55] George Vest of Missouri, after remarking that repeal meant contraction, charged, "This is the first instance in the history of the human race when men of Anglo-Saxon lineage have been punished because they discovered too much of the precious metals."[56]

The bill passed 43 to 32, then went back to the House for concurrence on the meaningless amendment taken from the Democratic platform of the year before. Bland's motion to recommit the bill for further study lost 109 to 176. The bill then passed 194 to 94 and was signed by President Cleveland the same day.[57]

Principles of Polity Revealed by the Repeal of the Silver-Purchase Clause

Scholars have paid only perfunctory attention to the repeal of the silver-purchase clause, primarily because the product of the five months' debate in Congress seemed to be nothing more than deletion of a single simple section of law.[58] However, the Repeal Act of 1893, much more than the Bryan-McKinley campaign and election of 1896, marked the end of silver as a major monetary metal and its decline to the status of a subsidiary currency. By the end of 1893 mankind had already been crucified on a cross of gold through the concerted actions of a Democratic administration and a Democratic Congress. Why should anyone then have believed that a Democratic victory in 1896 would be any more likely to promote a cheap silver money than it had in 1892? Bryan was beaten before he started by the political infection within the Democratic party that the special session of 1893 had fomented.

The debates over repeal proved that political power in the executive branch even at this time was formidable enough to counteract what would otherwise have been continuation of a silver-purchase policy. Whereas the Republican party had successfully compromised the silver issue within itself to avoid alienating the silver wing from the far West, the Democrats engaged in an internecine conflict that ruined their chances of political success for the next eighteen or twenty years. The antisilver Republicans—Sherman, Allison, Aldrich, Morrill, and the rest—can hardly be blamed for helping the Democrats to conclude their fratricide.

The debates revealed much about political concepts of monetary policy. First was the notion that money could be managed; and in the minds of many congressmen was the belief that money *should* be managed. Some congressmen expressed the more sophisticated principle that some rule should make the stock of money grow at the same rate as population and trade—by which, of course, they meant real output. Silver was their vehicle for this kind of monetary management. It was cheap, but not too cheap. It was respectable in a way that greenbacks were not. It was substantial and had an appealing ring. It was a precious metal. Its quantitative growth was self-regulating and subject to natural forces. It also had the virtue of being suitable for lower-denominational usage.

The so-called bimetallic standard could hardly ever be bimetallic in practice. It required that defined quantities of both metals be legal tender for clearing debts written in terms of the unit of account. However, changes in demand and supply for each metal ordinarily tended to change the relative market price. Since the relative mint price was fixed, the only relief for the disparity between mint and market prices was for the government to make a marginal change in the mint price of one or the other metal, or to let the problem work itself out through market actions.

The tendency for the cheaper metal to go to the mint at such times did not ordinarily mean that the dearer metal would disappear entirely from circulation. Market values change gently and incrementally. So even as the cheaper metal began to dominate the coinage, much of the dearer metal would remain in circulation because the costs of removing it from the coinage system exceeded the profits arbitrageurs could realize from their well-publicized swaps.[59] Because the cheaper metal tended to displace the dearer metal—the effect known as Gresham's Law—Alfred Marshall suggested that bimetallism should be labeled "alternative metallism."[60]

This pattern of possible change was not necessarily undesirable. The precious metal industry is extractive and very much subject to diminishing returns in a given state of the art. Therefore, real values of the monetary metals tended to rise over time; and since mint prices were fixed, such a rise was equivalent to a decline in all other money prices. Use of a bimetallic standard, by shifting the burden of monetization to the relatively cheaper metal, moderated the fall in prices.

The increased world demand for gold to implement monometallic gold standards in the period 1870–1895 resulted in an "artificial" premium on gold and made silver seem "too cheap" to be a standard. Fiduciary silver currency could fill the role of a fractional currency, the conventional wisdom had it; but it had to be a knave and not a king. Gold had to be *the* standard.[61]

The conventional wisdom in this case, as in many another, turned out to be wrong. Just as gold had become cheaper in the 1850s, so silver became cheaper after 1875. It could just as easily have shared the monetary function with gold, except that one country after another between 1870 and 1900 demonetized it as a standard money metal. Silver went begging and declined significantly in value relative to gold—all of which proved, not any great volatility in the value of silver, but only the significant impact that standardization had on the value of the money metal chosen as the standard.[62]

Advocates for a viable silver standard in the United States saw silver as a means for tempering the chronic decline in prices. However, the agitation for free silver, in the presence of a gold standard that would endure, actually had the reverse of the intended effect. The anticipated rise in the price of gold relative to silver and to all other moneys, which would have been a consequence of the free coinage of silver, generated a capital outflow. Holders of any fixed-dollar claims payable in dollars tried to get rid of them before the quasi-devaluation of the gold dollar occurred. This behavior further reduced the level of prices in the United States that would have been consistent with external equilibrium. As Friedman and Schwartz point out: "Paradoxically, therefore, the monetary damage done by silver agitation [by causing adverse capital movements] . . . kept the money stock from rising as much as it otherwise would have, rather than producing too rapid an increase in the money stock."[63] Under an operational gold standard the U.S. price level had to assume a value compatible with the price levels of other countries, and the money stock of the United States had to be a quantity that would produce such a price level. Silver was simply one of the moneys that could respond appropriately to this constraint.

If silver had become the monometallic standard under the conditions that existed in the 1890s, the price of gold would have risen above its mint price. The price level in the United States then would not have fallen as much as it did, and perhaps not at all. The monetary demand for the standard monetary metal adds significantly to the nonmonetary demand and, in the case of silver, would probably have prevented any inflation.[64] The very fact that the gold price of silver had remained almost constant relative to the gold prices of all other commodities during the time silver was monetized on a limited basis argues that with full silver monetization the silver prices of all commodities might have declined.

Neither monometallic extreme was necessary. Sometime in the 1880s, Congress could have raised the mint value of gold (devaluation of the gold dollar) and lowered the mint value of silver (appreciation of the silver dollar). Such a compromise would have had some minor repercussions on foreign trade, but would have ended the controversy and long-lasting uncertainty over silver.[65]

Any metallic or bimetallic standard was bound to be affected by changes in the production of metals, as well as changes in the demands for them, that would on occasion require such official adjustments in their mint values.[66] Since the production of both metals occurred at lower real costs after 1897, lower mint costs for both metals might have again become an issue some years later. However, mild inflations under metallic standards never provoked much political agitation for change. Both political and popular sentiment always seemed ready to tolerate gradually increasing prices as long as business remained brisk.

13 Monetary Policy in the Golden Era

The Treasury has always been the bloody angle of criticism of an administration.

Leslie M. Shaw, Secretary of the Treasury, 1906

Most of the practices and projects of the late Secretary [of the Treasury] gave new impetus to the disintegration of that peculiar feature of American finance, the independent treasury system.

A. Piatt Andrew, 1907

Treasury Policy under Secretary Gage: The Gold Standard Act

Most price indexes show a minor peak during 1892. The struggle over the currency during the next year, the uncertainty it produced, and the elimination of silver as a major currency by the mid–1890s, subsequently produced a fall in prices of about 10 percent to the business-cycle trough of 1896–97.[1] The falling price level associated with the controversy over silver and the increased demand for monetary gold stimulated gold exploration both in the United States and abroad. As a result, world gold production almost doubled between 1893 and 1897.

The gold boom came none too soon for the advocates of the single gold standard because controversy over the proper standard was still keen in some quarters. To a sizable fraction of the general public, however, the question of the standard was too abstract and too remote an issue to be of much significance. The popular mind could not identify this issue with the current state of business. By the time of the elections in 1896, repeal was three years old. A new Democratic administration and Democratic Congress could hardly be expected to change radically what the previous coalition had passed after lengthy deliberation; and even if free silver were still a realistic possibility, its net benefit as a public policy remained uncertain. In the end, the "full dinner pail" of the Republicans defeated the "free silver" of the Democrats by a margin of 53 to 47, and both houses of Congress also returned Republican majorities.[2]

The focus of monetary activity after the election shifted from Congress to the executive administration. The new president, William McKinley, felt obliged to reward dissident Democrats, who had rejected the free-silver doctrine and openly voted Republican, with a cabinet office. On this account he appointed Lyman J. Gage, a banker and a Cleveland Democrat from Chicago, as secretary of the Treasury.[3]

John Carlisle, Gage's predecessor under Cleveland, had objected vigorously to the use of the Treasury Department as a supplier of paper money.

"The issue and redemption of circulating notes," he wrote in his last report, "is not a proper function of the Treasury Department, or of any other department of the Government. . . . [This function] ought to be regulated entirely by the business interests of the people and by the laws of trade and the principles which control honest commercial intercourse." All government-issued paper currency, he contended, should be permanently retired.[4]

Gage's first report, in 1897, echoed Carlisle's opinions on the dangers of governmental fiat currencies. The presence of silver moneys subject to gold redemption, he stated, required "the financial wisdom, foresight, and courage of Congress" for safe and proper operation of the monetary system. He urged the creation of a division of issue and redemption, separate from the Treasury Department, that would hold significant stocks of all the major government currencies, as well as the Treasury's gold reserves, so that currency parities with gold would be maintained.[5]

To fill the vacuum that would otherwise arise from taking these currencies out of general circulation, Gage recommended enlargement of the national banking system and additional issues of national bank notes. He wanted an amendment to the National Bank Act to permit issues of the new notes. National banks would deposit government currencies in this new issue and redemption division, and they would be permitted to issue new notes to the extent of 25 percent of their deposited reserves. Their notes would be "unsecured by any direct pledge of security but issued against the [commercial] assets of the bank[s]." The notes outstanding would be taxed at the rate of 2 percent per annum.[6]

The purpose of this scheme was not only to reduce government involvement, but also to provide the monetary system with seasonal elasticity—an ideal that was becoming more and more popular. The current supply of government-issued money was necessarily rigid, but bank-issued currency was "subject to increase at the point where needed, and the needs of the community unite with the motive of the banker in supplying those wants as they find expression."[7]

In his report for 1899 Gage discussed what he considered the two most important monetary issues—the question of the standard and the adaptation of the currency system to the requirements of expanding trade and industry. Although gold was the de facto standard, monetary stability, the main desideratum of policy, could not be achieved unless gold was made the exclusive standard. "Stability in [bank-issued] currency," he wrote, "should be safely guarded, [but] . . . *flexibility*—the power of needful expansion—must also be provided." As an example of inelasticity in the system, he cited the case of the New York City banks during the preceding autumn. The country banks' call for $23 million of currency to move the crops had resulted in a decline of $84 million of deposits in New York, and "havoc was wrought in the regular ongoing of our commercial life." This state of affairs, he concluded, suggested a need for the national bank reform, recommended in his earlier report, that would make the supply of bank notes responsive to the needs of trade.[8]

Gage's recommendations were similar to those of the Monetary Commission of 1898. Supporters introduced the "Bill Embodying the Commission's Proposals" in the House of Representatives in January 1898, and many of its provisions finally emerged in the Currency Act of 14 March 1900. This act, sometimes known as the Gold Standard Act, fixed gold as *the* standard legal tender monetary metal. Gage, by occupation a midwestern banker, felt quite comfortable with the conservative, banking-school doctrine of the Indianapolis group.[9]

The Currency Act liberalized the issue of national bank notes, so no stringency appeared in the money market that year when crops were harvested. But Gage pointed out in his report of 1900 that "there is under our present system no assurance whatever that the volume of bank currency will be continuously responsive to the country's needs. . . . The supply of currency is related most largely . . . to the price of Government bonds in the market." This relationship, he argued, divorced the supply of money from the needs of trade and commerce, because "there is no discernible relation whatever" between these needs and the prices of government securities.[10]

The greatly increased gold production and the lagged effect of this gold on the monetary systems of the world decisively changed the Treasury's strategic financial position vis-à-vis the rest of the economy. Between 1894 and 1899 the government's budget was constantly in deficit. But in the fiscal year 1899–1900 the budget swung into surplus and was to stay that way for most of the time up to World War I. In addition to the $150 million gold reserve stipulated by the Currency Act of 1900, the Treasury held additional gold balances of more than $90 million, plus another $230 million of gold against which it had issued gold certificates. The Treasury also had almost $100 million to its account in 444 national bank depositories, and it was adding new depositories at a rapid rate.[11]

The accumulation of balances in the Treasury created the same situation that had occurred during the gold boom just fifty years earlier: If the gold was in the Treasury, it was not out in markets nourishing trade and commerce. To get the gold out of the Treasury, the secretary had to spend it. Gage spent some of it by anticipating interest payments that were coming due on outstanding debt. He timed debt prepayments to coincide with crop-moving in the fall of the year. In addition, he had the Treasury purchase $19 million of the bonds due in 1904 and 1907 at an average premium to the holders of 12 percent (or 112 percent of par), plus another $23 million of 2 percent bonds that were redeemable at the option of the government.[12]

Purchase of government securities in the open market was a logical means of reducing Treasury balances, and many secretaries carried out such operations. The decision to buy had to be combined with the decision of when and how much to buy. Congress might have made these decisions for the secretary, but legislative awareness of financial conditions significantly lagged the events themselves. So most congressmen were willing to let the technical experts in the Treasury handle the details as long as no adverse political repercussions developed.

The figures for foreign trade demonstrate the magnitude of the changes in commerce. In the four years 1898–1901, Gage reported, the total trade *balance* was a $2,354 million surplus, an average of almost $600 million per year. (The aggregate net surplus for the preceding 108 years had been $357 million.) The Treasury's cash balance increased commensurately and was disbursed again during 1901 to purchase outstanding government securities.[13]

In his last report in 1901, Gage discussed at length the imperfections he had observed in the banking and monetary system. Individual banks, he wrote, "stand isolated and apart . . . with no tie of mutuality between them. There is no . . . method of legal association for common protection or defense in periods of adversity and depression." Banks, he noted, essentially manufacture or create the medium of exchange in common use. He listed three "causes" for the expansion of bank credit: "a rise in prices of commodities and securities; an increase in the *volume* of these things; [and] an enlarged activity in the sale and transfer of goods and securities."[14]

Gage appeared here to have mistaken symptoms for causes. His next remarks confirm that he was discussing expansion of bank credit within the framework of a given volume of reserves. Ultimately "the diminishing ratio of cash reserves puts a strain on the expanding movement [of business] and impedes further development in that direction." Prosperity follows. But this state of affairs is invariably upset by a host of possible random events. The banking system would then face the prospect of a crisis; so bank credit "is withdrawn at the very moment when support is most needful."[15]

The solution Gage advocated was the incorporation of a central bank. He disapproved of "a large central bank with branches" because of its lack of general political acceptability. Instead he supported a federated institution. "Can not the principle of federation be applied," he asked, "under which the banks as individual units, preserving their independence of action in local relationship, may yet be united in a great central institution?"[16] His statement exhibits remarkable prescience considering the fact that the passage of the Federal Reserve Act incorporating a federated central-banking system along these very lines was still twelve years in the future.

The Independent Treasury Becomes a Central Bank under Secretary Shaw

When Theodore Roosevelt became president after the assassination of William McKinley, he appointed Leslie M. Shaw secretary of the Treasury. Shaw was from Iowa and, similar to his predecessor Gage, was a banker with orthodox and conservative views on finance. His principal political experience had been to champion the gold standard against the attacks of William Jennings Bryan.[17]

Nothing about Shaw's previous professional life could have suggested the policies he was to innovate or appreciably extend during his tenure as secretary. Before he retired early in 1907, he had added the following policies to the Treasury's agenda:

1. Strategic transfers of Treasury deposits from the subtreasuries to the national banks, thereby reintroducing the policy of Secretary Fairchild that Congress had found so objectionable.
2. Acceptance of security other than government bonds as collateral for government deposits in national banks, thus freeing the government bonds for use as national bank-note collateral.
3. Abolition of the enforcement of the reserve requirement against national bank holdings of government deposit balances.
4. Allowance of the interest-free use of government gold holdings to gold importers as soon as the gold was purchased abroad and until it was delivered in the United States.

The first policy listed—deposit of the Treasury's gold reserves in national banks in order to meet the seasonal demand for bank credit—was the one Shaw used most vigorously. It also turned out to be the most controversial. The Treasury for most of this period was in the position of a central bank with varying amounts of free gold reserves that it could spend into the private sector by various means. It had outstanding currency obligations of about $1,000 million, two-thirds of which was silver currency; the remaining one-third was United States notes. Against these obligations the law required it to keep $150 million of gold reserves. In addition, it had about $100 million of excess gold and other cash items in subtreasury offices. It transferred this high-powered money from subtreasury offices to the national banks in season, thereby increasing the banks' primary reserves so that they could expand bank credit.[18]

Shaw reinterpreted the laws governing the outlays of federal moneys in ways that would legitimize his policies. An article in the Constitution states: "No money shall be drawn from the Treasury but in consequence of appropriations made by law." Before 1903 the Treasury could deposit internal revenue receipts in national bank depositories as they accumulated, but it had to hold customs receipts (about 40 percent of total revenues) in its own offices.[19] Shaw claimed that the depository banks were offices of the Treasury. Movement of funds into or out of the banks, from or to the subtreasuries, was not money drawn *from* the Treasury, but a transfer of the money *in* the Treasury from one "apartment of the Treasury" to the other. He also reasoned that if the bank depositories were part of the Treasury and held legal collateral in the form of government securities against their public deposits, the Treasury had no need to require them also to hold reserves against these deposits. He thereupon announced that this provision of the law would not be enforced (policy 3).

The National Bank Act required national banks to pledge United States bonds as collateral against issues of national bank notes and to hold "United States bonds and otherwise" against deposits of government money. Government deposits in the banks, therefore, increased the demand for the given stock of government securities, raised security prices, and tended to diminish national bank-note circulation. Bank credit could then expand only at the expense of bank-issued currency. "We have to bear in mind," Shaw pointed out, "that [national] bank notes are not available for reserve in national banks, but are as good as [lawful] money in all other banking institutions."[20]

Shaw pragmatically interpreted "*and* otherwise" in the depository provision to imply "*or* otherwise." With this alteration he was able to extend collateral privileges on Treasury deposits to state and municipal bonds up to 75 percent of their face value, on the condition that the federal government bonds thereby released be made the basis of an immediate circulation of national bank notes (policy 2).[21]

Policy 4, undertaken in 1906, was a one-time action. It called for delivery of gold from the Treasury to gold importers before they received gold contracted for shipment from abroad. In effect it subsidized the interest costs of gold in transit, thus decreasing by a few cents the gold-import point. Its effect was to provide a small quasi-devaluation of the gold dollar.

Shaw used two signals for undertaking monetary action: Short-term rates of interest in the money market, and the volume of surplus reserves that the national banks held during the summer. He noted that the call loan rate was perhaps only 1 percent in midsummer but might reach 25 percent in November. "Such extremes," he wrote, "can and should be rendered impossible."[22] His concern with short-term interest rates did not imply that Shaw was an incipient Keynesian. It simply revealed his practical need for an index that would reflect seasonal variations in the demand for money.

During his first year in office, 1902, he used both novel and traditional monetary policies. In an effort to bolster national bank circulation, Shaw ordered the surplus revenues deposited in national banks during the spring. Institutions that maintained their limit of circulation received preference. During the summer months when interest rates were low, no deposits were made.[23]

The New York money market was more stringent than usual in the fall of 1902. Reserve ratios of national banks had fallen below the legal minimum of 25 percent. Shaw thereupon ordered the purchase of government securities in the open market, a policy that had been used frequently during the past fifty years. During the fall of 1902, the Treasury purchased outstanding government debt at 137 percent of par.[24]

The securities that remained commanded a substantial market premium.

Purchasing the debt with gold would have added gold to national bank reserves and permitted credit expansion. At the same time it would have required the retirement of national bank notes and would have altered the currency-money ratio. Shaw expressed the view that "either the Government debt must be perpetuated as a basis for national bank [note] circulation, and additional bonds issued as occasion may require, or some other system must be provided." The other system he recommended was a "circulation based upon general credits, . . . properly safeguarded."[25] He suggested that national banks be permitted to issue a government-guaranteed currency equal to 50 percent of their outstanding bond-secured currency, but subject to a 5 or 6 percent tax until redeemed. Not only did he expect this system to work automatically, he also argued that it would make "10 percent money well-nigh impossible, and the Treasury Department would be saved a most embarrassing responsibility."[26]

The negative elasticity of currency with respect to the volume of trade, and the paucity of government bonds available to secure bank-note circulation, encouraged Shaw to undertake what became his primary means of control: the direct deposit of Treasury balances in national banks. Since cash balances over $150 million in the Treasury's own offices were "excess" as reserves for government-backed currencies, the Treasury could deposit these excess balances in national banks and thereby increase national bank reserves. The banks could then expand credit for moving the crops and for other seasonal needs. In January and February the reserves usually returned to the reserve city banks from their country correspondents. The Treasury would then deposit its revenues in the subtreasuries and demand its balances from the national banks to soak up what had by then become an out-of-season plethora of bank reserves.

In 1903 Shaw had $40 million available in Treasury offices, but he used only $16 million despite a severe contraction in the securities markets. In 1904 he again had the Treasury buy government securities, this time $19.4 million; and in 1905 the need for crop-moving money once more resulted in Treasury monetary operations.[27] The fiscal deficits in 1904 and 1905, which arose principally from construction of the Panama Canal, left Treasury reserves too depleted to be used for policy purposes. Treasury deposits in national banks therefore were transferred only "to the points where seasonal demands were highest." Fiscal requirements necessitated a withdrawal of Treasury credits from the national bank depositories; but since these demands were for immediate payment to other sectors of the economy, Shaw claimed, they were "accomplished without disturbance to business."[28]

In 1906 the gold policy was innovated at the same time that the Treasury had to float $30 million in Panama Canal bonds. To expedite this sale Shaw advertised that any national bank depository purchasing the bonds would have one-third of the money used in the purchase left on its books as a public deposit (the device of compensating balances). He also made sure the banks would have reserves in the fall by withdrawing "$60 million from the channels of trade and locking it up." He dryly observed in retrospect: "Everything seemed serene to everybody [during the summer] except to those who recognize that in this latitude crops mature in the fall. . . . The strain inevitable [*sic*] began to develop. Interior banks called their loans and shipped the proceeds home, but . . . seemed to think it strange that the actual withdrawal of money from financial centers . . . should cause any stringency at these centers."[29] In the third quarter of 1906 the Treasury increased its deposits in national banks from $90.4 million to $134.6 million.[30] The national banks then either expanded credit themselves or shipped the reserves in the form of gold or Treasury currency to their country correspondents, who could expand credit even more than the national banks since they maintained lower reserve ratios.

The significance of the $25 million to $75 million that the Treasury made available as reserves to banks is not overwhelming even when the lower reserve requirement of country banks is included. Specie and legal tender reserves in all banks between 1902 and 1907 varied from $800 million to $1,100 million. (See table 13.1.) The national banks held about two-thirds of this amount, and the non-national banks one-third. The usual Treasury deposit, along with equivalent easy-money policies, permitted about a 10 percent seasonal expansion. This amount was, however, sufficient at that time to provide for the seasonal bulge in agricultural production.

Popular and Professional Criticism of Shaw's Policies

Policies as unorthodox as Shaw's in the era before World War I were certain to find some disfavor. One would hardly expect, however, such universal criticism. Among his most vociferous critics was the *Nation,* a liberal periodical that regarded his actions in the money market as relief for "a ring of powerful Wall Street speculators." Shaw's policies, the *Nation* observed, constituted "meddling by a Government officer in a market where he had no business whatever. . . . What is to hinder some benevolent autocrat of the Treasury hereafter," it asked rhetorically, "from . . . buying stocks in support of the stock market?"[31]

Perhaps even more caustic than the *Nation*'s criticism was that from such academic conservatives as Eugene Patton and J. Lawrence Laughlin of the University of Chicago, A. Piatt Andrew of Harvard, and David Kinley of the University of Illinois. Others, such as O. M. W. Sprague, also of Harvard, made incidental references to Shaw's policies.[32]

Both Patton and Andrew objected to the Independent Treasury System as a policy institution. The problem of revenues in excess of expenditures, Patton

TABLE 13.1 Selected items in balance sheets of all national banks and Treasury balances, 1901–1907 ($ millions)

Year	Month and day	Specie and legal tender in national banks[a]	Private deposits in national banks	Treasury deposits with national banks	Treasury funds in treasury offices[b] (near date)	National bank notes out-standing
1901	Feb. 5	552	2,754	89	52	309
	Apr. 24	550	2,894	90	65	317
	Sept. 30	540	2,938	101	68	324
	Dec. 10	521	2,964	104	60	319
1902	Feb. 25	562	2,983	106	68	314
	Apr. 30	559	3,112	114	70	310
	Sept. 15	508	3,209	117	93[c]	318
	Nov. 17	533	3,153	139	63[d]	337
1903	Feb. 6	571	3,160	141	75	335
	Apr. 9	536	3,168	141	80	335
	Sept. 9	555	3,156	140	89	375
	Nov. 17	520	3,176	153	65[c]	376
1904	Jan. 22	614	3,301	155	70	381
	Mar. 28	617	3,255	152	70	386
	Sept. 6	662	3,458	101	45	411
	Nov. 10	642	3,708	101	41	419
1905	Jan. 11	670	3,613	97	47	424
	Mar. 14	641	3,778	85	54	431
	Aug. 25	666	3,821	52	73	469
	Nov. 9	622	3,990	56	76	486
1906	Jan. 29	668	4,088	55	89	498
	Apr. 6	621	3,978	93	93	506
	Sept. 4	625	4,200	105	105[e]	518
	Nov. 12	635	4,290	129	91[c]	536
1907	Jan. 26	696	4,116	146	95	546
	Mar. 22	656	4,270	141	99	543
	Aug. 22	702	4,319	143	92	552
	Dec. 3	661	4,177	158	26[e]	602

Sources: All data for national bank statistics were taken from *Annual Reports of the Comptroller of the Currency,* 1901–1908. Treasury deposits in national banks were taken from A. P. Andrew, *Statistics for the United States,* Sen. Doc. No. 570, National Monetary Commission (Washington, 1910), pp. 263–65.

[a] Reserves of non-national banks averaged almost exactly half of national bank reserves during this period, and showed little variation from this value.

[b] Does not include $150 million statutory reserve of gold. Total Treasury balances, therefore, include the sums of columns three and four plus $150 million plus other minor items.

[c] Interpolation.

[d] Open-market operation. Bonds of 1925 purchased.

[e] Panama Canal bonds sold.

observed, had never been solved satisfactorily. "But this," he charged, "is an argument for revision of the sub-treasury law, not for granting autocratic power to the secretary of the treasury."[33] Andrew repeated Daniel Webster's sentiments: "The very idea of keeping one's accumulations in carefully guarded idleness pertains to the conditions and habits of the Middle Ages." He deplored the lack of synchronization in government expenditures and receipts, "exaggerated as they are by the absence of a balanced budget."[34]

Patton and Andrew found their most serious criticism of Shaw in his violations of precedent. Andrew pointed out that "deposit of United States bonds *and* otherwise" as collateral for Treasury deposits in national banks clearly meant collateral *in addition* to United States bonds. He admitted that this law had been phrased in 1865 and that it was "doubtless primarily intended to furnish additional inducement for the organization of national banks and the consequent absorption of [government] bonds." He conceded that other secretaries had prepaid interest on the debt, bought securities in the open market, and transferred some deposits to the national banks beyond the $15 million or $20 million usually held in them for fiscal transactive purposes. However, he found the degree of Shaw's actions "incredible" and legal only under a "strained interpretation of the law."[35] One might well ask how precedent could ever be established if all actions were based exclusively on previous experiences. The only innovations that could then occur would be due to pure chance. Nothing would be left to imagination or the creative instinct, and little would be left to reason.[36]

To the charge of "unprecedented" Shaw answered: "It has been the fixed policy of the Treasury Department for more than half a century to anticipate monetary stringencies, and so far as possible prevent panics." Panics, he held, were in the same category as pestilences, except that the former caused more hardship. Even though public disasters might result from the avarice of bankers, he concluded, "the Treasury Department . . . must to the limit of the authority with which it is clothed, and at the risk of personal reputation [*sic*], grant relief and prevent disaster."[37]

His detractors were in the contradictory position of criticizing the subtreasury system for being archaic and contributing to monetary inelasticity at the same time that they were railing against Shaw for overcoming such difficulties. Their monetary theory also rendered their criticisms questionable. Andrew, for example, argued that "during periods of abounding prosperity, . . . when currency is most in demand, our taxes . . . become unusually prolific." The federal money, he complained, is then locked up in the Independent Treasury "at exactly the time when the community in general, and the banks in particular, stand in the greatest need of it." When business is stagnant and idle hoards swell bank reserves, he continued, the Treasury hoards are dumped on the banks, "although obviously these are the periods when such additions are least needed."[38]

Andrew here continued the flawed doctrine of the commodity theory of money and the commercial credit theory of banking: that the supply of real product generates the supply of money and credit by means of a "real bills" banking policy. When used as central-banking doctrine, this theory implies that the quantity of money that a central-banking institution furnishes ought to be geared explicitly to the flow of goods and services in the private sector. An independent treasury, of course, could not provide this kind of synchronization because it did not supply the real financial assets that real private output generated. Rather it dealt in government securities that resulted from excessive government expenditures and fiscal irresponsibility.

The commodity theory of money (without a central bank) has a completeness and thus an appeal not found in other theories of money. For when the growth in money accompanies the growth in real product, as is the case under an operational metallic standard, the demand for and supply of money act simultaneously through market prices for all goods and services and for the monetary metal in ways that determine the "right" quantity of money. If prices of all goods and services fall, the value of the monetary metal, being reciprocal to the prices of real products, increases. The greater resources devoted to producing the monetary metal, and the subsequent increase in the quantity of common money, arrest the fall in the price level. The commodity theory of money made operational by its link to the gold standard provides a general equilibrium in the markets for money and goods.

When this doctrine adopts real bills, in addition to real gold, as a supplemental guide to the creation of money, it loses its validity. Real gold is an effective anchor because its supplies are limited and its money price is fixed under the rules of the gold standard. But real bills may have any money price that bankers or central bankers attach to them, and their supplies are unlimited. Furthermore, bankers' assessments of their soundness are colored by the current state of business. If business is booming, applications for commercial loans look more appealing, and the generation of new credit and money on the basis of these new bills contributes to the boom.

Andrew, as well as most laymen and most congressmen, embraced this doctrine. But Shaw, who was in an official policy position, could anticipate from past experience the seasonal increase in the traffic of real commodities and make provision for it with the proper deposit of Treasury balances. Shaw felt that as long as his operations were seasonal or short-run, and confined to redistributing the existing stock of high-powered money on the basis of historical precedents, Andrew's norm of goods-creating-money could not be seriously violated.

Patton's criticisms also reflected the principles of the commodity theory. He observed that Shaw had asked for power to control the stock of money through the banking system. "To whom should this power be given?" he asked rhetorically. "To an independent irresponsible treasury official, or to the banking institutions of the country, which are in close touch with business conditions? Is not the Treasury *ex natura* in a position where it cannot possibly know the banking needs of the country, since it is not in contact with the world of trade?"[39]

Andrew denied the necessity for governmental control over the money stock. He felt that Shaw's policies would initiate "among the regular and ordinary functions of the American government the paternal practices of the European central banks." Worst of all, Shaw's policies to some degree subsidized banks and correspondingly discouraged prudent banking. If business crises resulted "from over-trading and over-speculative propensities of the community," Andrew wrote, "a stringent market will spontaneously afford the best sort of a remedy by forcing a reduction of bank liabilities." He advocated a laissez-faire approach that would emphasize a "law-regarding policy involving the least possible amount of state interference with business." He concluded with an impassioned appeal for legislative relief from Treasury meddling "and from all the overnight changes of policy with which the country has been afflicted during the last five years."[40]

Shaw recognized that his actions gave the Treasury a central-banking look. He saw the national banks as the branches of this "great government bank." The system, he thought, was "not unlike that of European countries, . . . and if properly operated, can be made to accomplish much of what is contemplated by those who advocate the large central bank."[41]

Any monetary policy conducted within the general framework of a metallic standard could have only form-seasonal effects. The secular increase in the stock of gold was enough during Shaw's tenure to provide general buoyancy in business. Shaw's principal concern was over the seasonal fluctuation in the demand for money and how the supply would adjust to it. "The average amount of money," he said, "is, in my judgment, abundant."[42]

The subsidization of gold imports should have emphasized the ultimate dominance of the gold-standard system in determining the secular path of monetary activity, but Shaw never recognized this force explicitly. Andrew observed the futility of the gold policy. He imputed to Shaw an attempt to counteract the operations of European central bankers who were trying to attract gold from the United States by an "artful diversion." The gold would have come or gone anyway, Andrew concluded, depending on "deeper lying reasons."[43]

Shaw's gold-import policy and his circular to the national banks advising them that reserve requirements would not be enforced against government deposits were measures that could have only a one-time effect. His acceptance of collateral other than government securities for public deposits and his policy of moving gold reserves into and out of the national banks were long-run measures. A drain of gold to other countries through the price-specie flow mechanism would ultimately have limited all these tactics, just as Andrew implied. Despite this potential check, Shaw was moved in 1906 to make the following claim: "If the Secretary of the Treasury were given $100 million to be deposited with the banks or withdrawn as he might deem expedient, and if in addition he were clothed with authority over the reserves of the several banks, with power to contract the national-bank circulation at pleasure, in my judgment no panic as distinguished from industrial stagnation could threaten either the United States or Europe that he could not avert."[44]

Treasury Policy under Cortelyou in 1907

Shaw's statement provided a refreshing positivism. Perhaps one may doubt that any secretary of the Treasury could or should carry out such discretionary policies. But a high-level policymaker who continually deprecates his own power, and who is forever apprehensive about contingencies over which he alleges he has no control, is not attractive.

George Cortelyou, who succeeded Shaw in March 1907, was somewhat of this latter character. He spoke the same words and followed the same policies that had worked so expediently under Shaw; but his measures lacked timing and decisiveness, and his words lacked vigor and conviction. In the first half of 1907 he did not husband enough Treasury deposits in national banks to provide for an adequate seasonal increase in the fall. Then in May and June he allowed the Treasury to redeem $61 million of the bonds of 1907, although another $50 million of the same issue was refinanced. During September and October, he saw to the deposit of $28 million week-by-week in the national banks. When the crisis developed in October, another $35 million was deposited within four days. These actions reduced the Treasury's *excess* balance to $5 million, and in Cortelyou's judgment precluded further action.[45]

By carrying out the refunding operations too early in the summer, Cortelyou depleted the Treasury's reserves so that not enough was available in the fall. Some imagination on his part might have adjusted the timing and method of this ordinary housekeeping operation so that it would have complemented rather than conflicted with seasonal monetary policies.[46]

The failure of Treasury policy to stop the panic of 1907 demonstrated that when the monetary reserve in the central agency was exhausted, the specie-flow gold-standard mechanism became dominant. All institutions then had to run with the wind; none could lean into it.

Congress, after the fact, asked Cortelyou for a report on Treasury policy during the crisis. His response showed that he did not shoulder responsibility lightly. "The present head of the department," he wrote humbly, "has not assumed the obligation [of caretaking the financial condition of the country] willingly and would be glad to be relieved of it at least in part by suitable legislation." The accumulation of currency and specie balances in the Treasury had imposed this unwanted duty on his office. A more desirable monetary framework would "adapt the movement of currency more nearly automatically to the requirements of business . . . and would greatly diminish the sense of responsibility which must weigh heavily upon any occupant of [this] office."[47]

These remarks provided a ready foil for the use of David Kinley, who was perhaps the Treasury's most exhaustive, if not most dramatic, critic. Kinley quoted Cortelyou's confession with approval. "These are wise words," he appended. He then weighed the various arguments for and against the Treasury Department as an agency of monetary policy. While he allowed that Treasury actions had been at times proper and acceptable, he concluded that any good effects the Treasury had had in the money market were due almost entirely to fiscal happenstance. If, however, the secretary took positive measures to offset the ill effects of undesirable fiscal operations on the money market, he was assuming too much power, he was likely to make mistakes, and his interference was arbitrary.[48] Kinley's conclusions permitted no Treasury policy. Like other major critics who were also banking-school proponents, he favored a central bank that would work automatically and passively even in its seasonal operations. The Treasury itself should do nothing more than keep a tidy fiscal house.

Further Arguments on Treasury Policy

Shaw was so sensitive to his critics that he made official references to them in his last report. He was confident that his means were within the framework of the law and that the results of his policies were good. His critics, he observed, "studied to write articles that would surely be read, and neglected to study actual conditions." Such people "attributed the noticeable tension [in the money market] not to increased business, but to the presence of sudden speculation."[49]

How far a cabinet officer can go in policy-making activities can never be determined to everyone's satisfaction. If he limits himself to the letter of the law in the manner Shaw's critics advocated, his failure to take offsetting operations may aggravate undesirable events. Government officials, Shaw observed, are only too glad to avoid responsibility. "The rejection of a proposition never causes trouble," he stated. "Affirmative acts only are investigated and censured. Technical objections are as good as valid ones with the average bureau official."[50]

Laws in a free society are written with a knowledge that public officials will have to interpret them with discretion in two senses, with tact and with common sense. Three questions can then be asked to test whether a policymaker has gone too far: (1) Have the policies been performed in the light of reason to achieve desirable ends? (2) Have the policies had good results? (3) Could a legislative or executive action reverse the policies that the administrator has initiated?

The evidence seems to answer these questions, yes, in Shaw's favor. The very existence of government-issued greenbacks and government-regulated national bank notes in conjunction with an independent treasury argued for seasonal Treasury policies similar to those Shaw administered. While Shaw may have overstepped his authority in trying to fill a policy vacuum, what was needed was not a central bank that would grow into an omnipotent money-creating machine constantly promoting inflation, but a resolution from Congress specifying the limits to Treasury authority and actions. That such a resolution was not forthcoming is more an indictment of Congress than of Shaw.

The late Professor Lloyd W. Mints, far from a liberal interventionist or leftist in any respect, once stated that Shaw was the "only good secretary of the Treasury we have ever had."[51] Many years later the nonliberal, nonleftist economist Milton Friedman remarked with his coauthor Anna J. Schwartz that Shaw's policies may well have been an outward and visible sign of typical "bureaucratic megalomania."[52]

These two views are not necessarily contradictory; even a bureaucratic megalomaniac may be an effective policymaker. However, Shaw's writings do not give the impression of megalomania. Rather, he seemed to realize after taking office that the Treasury Department had a pivotal role to play in ameliorating seasonal hardship in the monetary system. He simply accepted existing laws and institutions as given conditions, and adapted Treasury policies to the circumstances of the times as practically as he could. Ideally, power should neither choke nor addict its possessor. The evidence is that Shaw stayed within the proper tolerances.[53]

Another possibility that none of Shaw's critics ever addressed was the abolition of governmental controls and regulations over national bank currency and national bank credit operations. Government production of legal tender greenbacks was also undesirable for the most efficient operation of the private economy, but this issue had become case-hardened politically and was no longer arguable. Even if the frozen stock of greenbacks was accepted as a given political condition, a policy of liberalizing national bank-note issues by releasing them from their rigid connection to government securities, abolishing legal reserve requirements on national banks, and removing barriers to interstate branching would have given the banking system the resiliency to cope with liquidity panics. Indeed, the financial upheavals that seemed to require Treasury intervention might never have occurred.

14 The Central-Banking Role of Clearinghouse Associations

> Most of this [clearinghouse] currency was illegal, but no one thought of prosecuting or interfering with its issuers. . . . As practically all of it bore the words "payable only through the clearing house," its holders could not demand payment for it in cash. In plain language, it was an inconvertible paper money issued without the sanction of law, . . . yet necessitated by conditions for which our banking laws did not provide. . . . When banks were being run upon and legal money had disappeared in hoards, in default of any legal means of relief it worked effectively and doubtlessly prevented multitudes of bankruptcies which otherwise would have occurred.
>
> A. Piatt Andrew, "Substitutes for Cash in the Panic of 1907," *Quarterly Journal of Economics,* August 1908

Institutional Origin of Clearinghouse Associations

Most professional economists believe that the free market system is the optimal means for allocating resources and distributing products and incomes. However, economists have traditionally made an exception of the production of money. Even the most ardent supporters of private enterprise have viewed the money industry as a special case requiring some amount of government regulation or control even under a gold standard. The waning of gold or silver standards and the emergence of central banks to supply the basic reserves of the world's monetary systems have reinforced the notion that deliberate and positive human control over monetary systems is the only choice. In such a world private-enterprise central banking is simply regarded as fanciful. Indeed, most economists would deny its desirability as well as its feasibility.[1]

Yet in the practical world of the nineteenth century, just such an institution came into existence and flourished. Banks in that era faced the traditional problem of holding enough reserves to protect themselves in an emergency while operating conventionally with minimal reserves to maximize returns as cost-recovering enterprises. Hobbled by the note issue restrictions and reserve requirements that the federal government imposed on them during the Civil War, commercial banks at times had difficulty coping with liquidity problems in financial centers. However, the circumstances of their existence prompted their defense; and the defense they developed in the United States was an extension of the functions of the clearinghouse associations.

The development of clearinghouse associations as quasi-central-banking institutions occurred over a fifty-year span from 1857 to 1907, and came to an end in the post–1907 era with the organization of the Federal Reserve System. Of particular importance is this question: Given that the clearinghouse system had developed some well-defined central-banking functions and included effective checks and balances, why did influential decision-makers in the banking fraternity and the government fashion a formal central bank—the Federal Reserve System—under governmental auspices when they could have refined and modified the clearinghouse system so it would have continued as an effective lender of last resort?

A number of economists, most of whom were professionally active in the early twentieth century, have treated thoroughly the origin and evolution of clearinghouse associations.[2] Their accounts are much in agreement—as they should be, since clearinghouses are no more mysterious or complicated than grocery stores. Instead of each bank establishing a transactional relationship with all other banks, every bank sends two representatives to one place—the clearinghouse—where all debit items are cleared against all credit items.[3] Then the balance is struck, and payment is due in the clearinghouse accounts from debtor banks to creditor banks. Originally, one bank in the association was assigned the "central" administrative role for clearing the other member banks' accounts. Each bank kept part of its specie (and, later, greenback) reserve as a deposit with this bank, which in turn issued clearinghouse certificates of an equivalent amount to be used in the settlement of daily balances. These certificates were in large denominations—$5,000 and $10,000—to expedite the clearing process.[4] At this stage, the issue of clearinghouse certificates was strictly in lieu of conventional bank reserves. The certificates were only a technical expedient for economizing the payments system.

Development of Clearinghouse Loan Certificates

The panic of 1857 stimulated the extension of clearinghouse issues. Reserves in New York banks had declined during August of that year; and when a prominent bank failed, commercial paper rates approached panic levels. At first, the banks wanted to curtail loans—the usual means of meeting an internal currency drain. However, the clearinghouse banks agreed to "increase their loans so that the clearinghouse balances of all of them would be increased proportionately and would cancel each other without reducing the slender stock of specie."[5] That is, the banks agreed to "cry down" their reserve ratios in concert.

The country banks had already drawn down the balances with which the New York City banks customarily cleared the country banks' notes. The city banks responded by refusing to accept the notes as means of payment, whereupon a policy committee of the NYCHA issued a circular suggesting the propriety of including in the clearinghouse settlement accounts the currently irredeemable notes of the country banks. The committee also allowed the NYCHA to issue clearinghouse *loan* certificates against these notes.[6] The creditor city banks had already deposited the country bank notes in the clearinghouse bank acting as the "central" bank (at that time, the Metropolitan Bank). The country banks, which could not redeem their notes immediately, agreed to pay 6 percent interest on these "loans" from their city correspondents, and the city banks used the notes as collateral for the new clearinghouse loan certificates. The notes, as a basis for issues of certificates, thereby became equivalent to specie in the settlement of clearinghouse balances.[7] New York State bonds already served as collateral for the state bank notes even though the notes were redeemable in specie. Therefore, no extra security was needed for the notes when they were made the basis of clearinghouse loan certificates. The city banks in turn were able to furnish more of their own notes to pay depositors and to extend credit to borrowers.[8]

The issue of clearinghouse loan certificates temporarily made the clearinghouse itself a fractional reserve institution: Total issues of certificates and loan certificates—the clearinghouse's demand obligations—substantially exceeded its specie reserves.

As the Panic subsided, the city banks "began again to redeem country-bank notes, sending them home for redemption at the rate of one-fifth of the total each month. The certificates were retired as the collateral bank notes were redeemed. . . . They bore interest at 6 percent and were a safe investment. It finally took a resolution of the Clearing House Association to persuade the holding banks to part with [the last of] them."[9]

Characteristics of Clearinghouse Policy

The precedent established in 1857 became the basis for all the subsequent issues of loan certificates through 1907. In every instance, though, some new wrinkles were added. In November of 1860, when a stringency developed in anticipation of the Civil War, the NYCHA took in New York State bonds, U.S. Treasury notes, and bills receivable as collateral for the issue of loan certificates. The terms for this and future issues were that the maximum value of the loan certificates be limited to 75 percent of the collateral securities' face value. The annual rate a borrower bank paid was 6 percent.[10]

The clearinghouse committee also had the power, according to the agreement, "to equalize the specie [reserve of the member banks] 'by assessments or otherwise,' treating it as a common fund to be used for mutual aid and protection." In addition, any loss caused by the nonpayment of collateral was to be borne among the clearinghouse banks in proportion to their capitals. Margaret Myers's further comment on this action was that "a higher degree of centralization would have been hard to obtain even with the aid of a strong central bank."[11]

The "pooling"-of-reserves provision was not popular. The more conservatively managed banks that had a stronger reserve position than their fellows objected to it as inequitable. They felt that pooling denied them the rewards for their caution. If pooling had become the norm, the "economics of the commons" would have prevailed. No individual bank would have felt any constraint in making demands on the "pool." Pooling could also be evaded by altering what were held as "reserves." National bank notes were not subject to pooling; so many banks accumulated these notes while paying out greenbacks which were subject to pooling.[12]

Pooling was also unnecessary. Clearinghouse loan certificates cost the borrowing banks an annual rate of 6 percent (plus a small administrative charge), and paid 6 percent to the banks that acquired them through the clearing process. By this means, the clearinghouse became the credit intermediary between the banks with stronger reserve positions and those that were deficient in reserves—a situation that anticipated the contemporary federal funds market. This policy provided individual banks an incentive to use reserves they might otherwise have sequestered. It thereby augmented the usable reserves in the system at just those times when the demand for bank credit, as expressed by market interest rates, was greatest. Ideally, the interest rate charged by the clearinghouse association would ration the amount of accommodation sought and provided.[13] By this means, a market device controlled clearinghouse credit in a way that pooling of reserves would seriously have compromised if it had become a part of conventional policy.

Another innovation during the Panic of 1873 was the issue of irredeemable "certified" checks to stretch the reserve base. These checks did not have cash on deposit as the basis for their issue. They were simply a quasi-currency. To prevent anyone from cashing them and thereby reducing bank reserves, the clearinghouse policy committee adopted this resolution: "All checks when certified by any bank shall be first stamped or written 'Payable through the Clearing House.'"[14] This resolution put certified checks on a par with clearinghouse loan certificates. The banks accepted them as settlement media by common consent through their clearinghouse association, but did not have to redeem them with legal tender.

During this era, the New York City banks held a good fraction of the reserves of the interior ("country") banks, and many of them competed for deposits by paying a nominal interest rate to get them. This practice was seen both then and later as reprehensible because it allegedly induced the interest-paying banks to make risky loans and extend their loan portfolios unduly as a means of recovering the costs of their interest payments. An unusual demand for the conversion of deposits into greenbacks or other legal tender supposedly put such a strain on the more radical banks that they restricted or suspended cash payments. When the clearinghouse association issued loan certificates to cope with this situation, observed O. M. W. Sprague, the clearinghouse banks "were converted, to all intents and purposes, into a central bank, which, although without power to issue notes, was in other respects more powerful than a European central bank, because it included virtually all the banking power of the city."[15]

Extension of Clearinghouse Media

In 1873 the policy of the NYCHA spread to many other "reserve" cities that were secondary money centers (Chicago, St. Louis, New Orleans, Baltimore, Washington, etc.), as well as to other cities or towns that were strictly "country" (Dubuque, Knoxville, Concord, Harrisburg, etc.)[16] Minor panics occurred again in 1884 and 1890, and a major one in 1893. Clearinghouses issued certificates in all of them. Indeed, by 1893, the NYCHA anticipated the need for certificates and began issuing them in the summer before any suspensions or restrictions occurred.

Other clearinghouse media made their appearance at this time. A. Barton Hepburn noted from statistics he compiled as comptroller of the currency that $100 million of clearinghouse loan certificates, clearinghouse certificates, certified checks, certificates of deposit, and cashier's checks in all denominations were issued, "all designed to take the place of currency in the hands of the public."[17] Sprague estimated that $300 million in money and money "substitutes" were added to the supply outside the banks. In addition to Hepburn's list, Sprague reported that "in factory towns pay checks became an acceptable part of the circulating medium."[18]

The episode in 1893 witnessed a significant extension of the loan certificates to other bank-issued items of small denomination. Once this practice started it became ubiquitous and led to denominational "depreciation." For example, the Atlanta Clearing House Association and others issued notes in denominations as low as $10. Since anyone could use these notes for small transactions, the banks paid them out over the counter to customers who used them to buy ordinary goods and services. Since the change people received in the form of legitimate currency tended to deplete bank reserves, the clearinghouse associations had to supply certificates in smaller and smaller denominations, finally as low as $.25. In addition, "a considerable amount of clearinghouse certificates were [issued] in the Southeast in cities where no clearinghouses existed"[!].[19]

The Legality of Clearinghouse Issues

Naturally, the widespread issue of lower-denominational currency raised some questions concerning its legality. Several long-standing laws prohibited the private issue of token and subsidiary coin as well as state bank notes. In Hepburn's opinion neither clearinghouse certificates nor clearinghouse loan certificates were subject to the 10 percent tax on state bank notes, but all of the other currencies issued during the stringency of 1893 were. He concluded his review of the event with this revealing comment. "This temporary currency . . . performed so valuable a service . . . in moving the crops and keeping business machinery in motion, that the government, after due deliberation, wisely forebore to prosecute. . . . It is worthy of note," he concluded, "that *no loss* resulted from the use of this *make-shift* currency."[20]

When a government "wisely" decides not to enforce a law, both because violation of the law is universal and also because everyone is better off in the breach, the law itself must be ill-advised. Yet Hepburn did not draw this conclusion. His use of the adjective *makeshift,* furthermore, suggests a spurious character to the issues of currency that the actual train of events did not support.

If the panic of 1893 initiated the extension of "makeshift" currency, the panic of 1907 saw its full flowering. During the latter year, the NYCHA issued some $100 million of clearinghouse loan certificates (see table 14.1), while the Chicago association issued over $39 million worth of currency items, including $7.5 million in clearinghouse checks in denominations of $1, $2, $5, and $10. In Philadelphia, the clearinghouse issued certified checks for wage payments to depositors who opened special payroll accounts. The checks were printed up by the American Bank Note Company. In many other towns, such checks were issued in small denominations and made payable to "bearer." Sometimes, clearinghouses issued blank checks so the banks could put on them the most suitable denominations.[21] A. Piatt Andrew in his famous article cited this episode as "the most extensive and prolonged breakdown of the country's credit mechanism which has occurred since the establishment of the national banking system." He referred to the "ingenious invention of multifarious other substitutes for legal currency during the weeks of hoarding and suspension," thus conveying by editorial implication his disapproval of the developments he chronicled.[22]

Nonetheless, Andrew's account is scholarly and thorough. He reported that many state auditors and comptrollers had written to the banks under their jurisdictions encouraging them to restrict payments of legitimate cash and to pay out the various array of "substitutes" in restricted amounts. This indulgence was only to be permitted "solvent" banks. But, wrote the Indiana state auditor in a postscript to his letter circulated among Indiana banks, "The question of your solvency is to be determined by yourselves upon an examination of your present condition."[23] One can only imagine the soul-searching and painstaking self-study the banks engaged in prior to issuing their quasi-currencies!

Andrew's admittedly incomplete data revealed that in cities over 25,000 population, clearinghouse issues of all kinds totaled $330 million. The issues began in late October 1907, and the last of them was retired by late March

TABLE 14.1 Loan certificate issues and reserves of the New York clearinghouse banks for selected dates

Year	Date of first issue	Aggregate issue ($ millions)	Maximum outstanding ($ millions)	Reserves of NYC national banks
1860	November 23	7.38	6.86	
1861	September 19	22.6	22.0	
1863	November 6	11.5	9.61	
1864	March 7	17.7	16.4	
1873	September 22	26.6	22.4	46.9 (September 12)
1884	May 15	24.9	21.9	70.7 (June 20)
1890	November 12	16.6	15.2	92.5 (October 2)
1893	June 21	41.5	38.3	99.0 (July 12)
1907	October 26	101.0	88.4	181.0 (December 3)

Sources: Sprague (1910, pp. 432–33) and United States Comptroller of the Currency (1893, 1907).

1908. Clearinghouses in at least 71 of 145 cities made such issues. For cities under 25,000 population, Andrew's data are even more fragmentary. He recorded $4.5 million in clearinghouse issues, including some in places such as Willacoochee, Georgia, which had only one bank (!), but he acknowledged that his accounting covered "only a small fraction of what actually existed in the smaller localities."[24] In the largest cities the amounts issued in 1907 were 3½ times the amounts issued in 1893. In all cases the note issues were secured by collateral that had 1⅓ to 2 times the dollar value of the notes.[25]

Some Contemporary Views of Clearinghouse Central Banking

To a banker such as James Cannon, who was intimately involved with clearinghouse operations, the issues were not only defensible but highly recommended. He denied that the loan certificates were a currency. Rather, he defined them as "temporary loans," and cited one comptroller of the currency who had called them "due-bills." In addition, Cannon argued, the courts in Pennsylvania had "decided that [the issues] should not be regarded as money. A tax on them," the court decision read, "would have been 'a serious blow to one of the most effective and ingenious contrivances devised, [and] a direct violation of the spirit of the law.'"[26] Cannon concluded that loan certificates were "one of the finest examples the country has ever seen of the ability of the people when left to themselves to devise impromptu measures for their own relief."[27]

One can wholeheartedly endorse Cannon's conclusion without accepting his denial that the certificates were currency. Clearly, the small-denomination items were media of exchange. They were used for transactions of all kinds by everyone, and they were reissuable when returned to their banks of issue. The clearinghouse loan certificates may not have seemed to be conventional currency because only banks held them. However, since the banks used them just as if they were legal reserves, the loan certificates were a quasi-high-powered money, and even more potent than the small-denomination items.

Horace White agreed with Cannon on the utility of the clearinghouse operations. Nonetheless, White, in contrast to Cannon, recognized that all the issues of 1907 were illegal: "Some were engraved to resemble bank notes or government notes," he stated, "and these were doubly illegal; some were as small as twenty-five cents, and these were trebly illegal."[28]

Fritz Redlich remarked that where the initial clearinghouse loan certificates were "extra-legal," the various issues in 1907 were illegal, and presented "new dangerous problems [unspecified]." Legalization of clearinghouse loan certificates, he claimed, would have been "predicated on the incorporation of clearing houses under a federal law."[29]

Proposals for Legalizing the Clearinghouse System

The widespread issues of clearinghouse currency associated with the panic of 1893 stimulated the only formal proposals for organizing the clearinghouse system on a legitimate basis in the manner suggested by Redlich. Several plans appeared in the middle and late 1890s, the most comprehensive of which was one by Theodore Gilman of New York. Gilman objected to a separate reserve held outside the commercial banking system because it might never be needed. "Therefore," he argued, "it should not be provided by capital withdrawn from productive use. It will cost nothing and will be just as serviceable if it is provided by law as a power which may be used in case of need." To provide this potential for the banking system, Gilman proposed what he termed a "grade of banks higher than our ordinary commercial banks," by which he meant a banking institution that would be one stage above commercial banks and able to furnish accommodation when needed.[30]

His choice for this role was the clearinghouse association incorporated under federal law. A clearinghouse in each state would issue notes in much the same fashion as what was already being done in practice. The notes would have a maximum value of 75 percent of the security collateral on which they were based. They would be guaranteed, first by the bank issuing them, second by the associated clearinghouse banks in their home state, and third by all the clearinghouses that would receive the notes at par. "This protecting structure,"

Gilman claimed, "would rise noiselessly over the heads of the people without the sound of axe or hammer."[31]

Gilman emphasized an additional safeguard in the clearinghouse system beyond the note-collateral guarantee. The clearinghouse loan committees would be "conservative" in granting loans because of their "pecuniary interest as stockholders in banks, which they would endeavor to protect from loss on their contingent liability as guarantors."[32] In short, the private clearinghouse "central bank" would operate prudently because it would face a bottom line. "The kind of currency [the clearinghouses] make for themselves," he observed, "[should be] . . . good [enough] for the public."[33]

Gilman claimed that the clearinghouse notes he envisioned would always be redeemed on demand at any clearinghouse and would therefore circulate at par.[34] He may have oversold his scheme with this pledge. It implied that no restrictions or suspensions would occur in the future. Or he may have meant only that if a note holder were willing to go to the time and trouble of redeeming his note *at the clearinghouse,* he could do so.

Gilman saw the clearinghouse currency as a temporizing device that would promote elasticity in the monetary system. It would allow time for goods and services on which loans were based to be sold, so that the currency would return to the banks as payment for liquidating the loans which gave rise to the original issues of notes. Gilman also felt that the interest charge of 6 percent to banks that took out clearinghouse currency "would act as a check upon their issue, and they would not be taken so much for profit as for protection and necessity."[35]

Ben L. Fairchild (R, N.Y.) introduced a bill in the House of Representatives in January 1896 that embodied Gilman's plan. It was referred to the House Committee on Banking and Currency, but it never appeared again and no popular movement ever developed in support of the scheme.

One Treasury official who pointedly objected to the clearinghouse strategy was Leslie M. Shaw, secretary of the Treasury from 1902 to 1907. The clearinghouse loan certificates, he stated in an address delivered in 1905, are a "plea of guilty to an indictment charging bad management locally or bad legislation nationally."[36] Nonetheless, Shaw's prescription for appropriate policy during a panic logically supported the clearinghouse method. First, he suggested, the supplemental currency issued during a panic should be identical with the legitimate currency that already existed. Second, the relief should be capable of immediate and local application. Finally, he concluded, the additional currency should be retired promptly when "the demand therefore ceases."[37]

In point of fact the clearinghouse issues fit Shaw's criteria reasonably well. Their use as currency was ubiquitous; they were very similar to conventional paper currency; they were issued in a multitude of localities on the perceptions and judgments of thousands of bankers; and the notes never stayed out more than a few months. Nevertheless, Shaw regarded them as undesirable because in his opinion they raised an alarm that something was wrong and thereby caused "hoarding."[38]

The comptroller of the currency, James H. Eckels, in his annual report for 1893 was more sympathetic. He lauded the clearinghouse associations for their actions during the previous summer. "The service rendered by them," he wrote, "was invaluable, . . . and to their timely issuance . . . is due the fact that the year's record of suspensions and failures is not greatly augmented."[39] Eckels denied that the issues were currency; but he had tongue in cheek. "If they had been used as currency," he claimed, "the banks issuing them would have been fined."[40] Since the government did not penalize the banks, the law must not have been violated. This "syllogism" is more reasonably viewed as pragmatic accommodation to events than logical defense of the legality of clearinghouse issues.

The comptroller in 1907, William Ridgely, proved to be more of a legal constructionist than Eckels. He noted that under Section 5192 of the Revised Statutes the clearinghouse certificates in the possession of any bank belonging to the clearinghouse association were lawful money.[41] He begged the question of those issues that households and firms used as media of exchange outside of banks.

Later in his report he discussed the possibility of legalizing the other smaller-denominational clearinghouse issues as an "emergency circulation." He found "merit" in this suggestion, but rejected it as a "half-way measure." The full development of the clearinghouse idea, he argued, "should carry us further . . . to the inevitable and logical conclusion . . . , which is that we should have a national central bank of issue and reserve [acting under governmental authority]." This institution would be "more systematic and efficient," and would have none of the "disadvantages" of the clearinghouse system.[42] Ridgely did not elaborate on these "disadvantages," nor did he specify how or why the government central bank would be "more systematic and efficient." He simply offered unsubstantiated assertions. For example: "If we had had such a [government central] bank in operation in 1907, no such bank panic as we have had would have been possible." Had Ridgely been able to witness the monetary and banking events of 1929–1933, he might have experienced a fair amount of intellectual indigestion. Unaccountably, his next paragraph is a description of how well the clearinghouse system generally operated.[43]

Restriction and Suspension of Cash Payments during a Panic

The most characteristic feature of a panic—depositors' attempts to convert demand deposits into legal tender—often induced banks to restrict cash payments. Restriction took many forms; for example, limitation of cash payments to a nominal amount ($25 to $200) per transaction, or this amount per day or per customer. Payments were often "discretionary" with the banks and therefore negotiable with the banks' managers. The general purpose of restriction was to introduce as much friction as possible into any bank transaction that might have led to an "internal drain" of bank reserves.

Sprague argued that the clearinghouse banks in New York fell into the indulgence of restriction too readily.[44] When their reserve ratios reached 25 percent, these banks had to refrain from making any new loans. However, the law did not prohibit them from paying out reserves even though they were in a reserve-deficit position. Therefore the question was, what force prevented them from using their "required" reserves?

William Dewald has more recently reexamined Sprague's argument and found it valid. The New York banks, Dewald notes, "had made a fetish out of their twenty-five percent reserve ratio and held closely to it. . . . Reserve deficits were small during crises, and New York banks in fact held enormous reserves on every occasion when they suspended payments. It was this policy that Sprague attacked and it was this policy that the legal authorization to issue clearinghouse 'currency' promised to change." Sprague, Dewald notes, recommended that reserve banks be required to maintain payments as long as they held any reserves. This principle had been repeatedly urged as well by the comptroller of the currency.[45]

The conclusion of the Sprague-Dewald argument on the banks' restriction-of-payments policy is that, far from being complementary to the issue of clearinghouse currency, it increased uncertainty and generally upset the payments system. It led to the substitution of less efficient media for conventional money, and extended the period of disequilibrium.[46]

A contrary view on restriction comes from Friedman and Schwartz, and also from Margaret Myers in her earlier study.[47] Given a bank panic, Friedman and Schwartz argue, "the fairly prompt restriction of payments was a therapeutic measure that almost surely kept the contraction from being even more severe and much more protracted than it was. . . . The failure of one (unsound) bank did not set in train a chain reaction. Restriction of payments thus protected the banking system and gave time for the immediate panic to wear off, as well as for additional currency to be made available."[48]

The alternative was for the fractional reserve banking system to experience a "black hole" type of collapse in the face of the increased demand for money with the accompanying declines of prices, wages, income, and business activity.[49]

Friedman and Schwartz correctly focus on instability in the fractional reserve banking system as the primary danger to the monetary system and the economy. Nonetheless, given that clearinghouse issues were already in progress, the *prompt* restriction of payments may have been ill-advised. Why not require the clearinghouse banks to run down their reserves to a very small minimum or even to zero, with graduated rate penalties on their reserve deficiencies? A law that provided explicitly for such flexibility would have countered the reluctance of the banks and, in conjunction with the clearinghouse issues, encouraged the banks to maintain the level of their current portfolios as well as their cash payments. Ultimately, they might have suspended; but before they did, their reserves would have been largely utilized in meeting internal and external demands for liquidity.

The banks did not use their required reserves in a panic because of the reaction they anticipated when the depositing public learned that the affected banks were operating below their legal minima. Reserve requirements had become unbreachable barriers. National banks that trenched on their required reserves not only incurred penalties, they also incited runs from a jittery depositor clientele. Sprague noted that the reserve requirements had become "a sort of fetich [*sic*] to which every maxim of sound banking policy is blindly sacrificed."[50]

An obvious option would have been no reserve requirements at all. Banks would then have kept less contingency reserves than the required reserves they had to maintain under most reserve requirement laws, but they also would have felt free to use their reserves without qualms in order to fulfill their liquidity responsibilities. Paradoxically, legal requirements meant in practice a reduction of usable reserves.

Monetary Reform Legislation

The immediate legislative reaction to the events of 1907 was the Aldrich-Vreeland Act of 1908, which called for the grouping of ten or more national banks into a National Currency Association. The associations anticipated from this act were not to operate as clearinghouses, but were to issue "emergency currency" just the way the clearinghouses had done in the past. The only difference was that the new institutions' currency issues were to be under the administration of the secretary of the Treasury, who had some discretion in allocating the notes to different sections of the country. Banks that issued the currency would have to pay a 5 percent (annual rate) tax on the outstanding amount during the first month, and an additional 1 percent each month thereafter, until the annual rate reached 10 percent.[51]

The Aldrich-Vreeland Act marked a critical turning point in United States policy toward the monetary system. As Redlich observed, the act "turned its back on the clearinghouse loan certificate instead of legalizing it. . . . [The] sub-committee [Report] of the Committee on Banking and Currency declared the power to issue loan certificates dangerous as long as clearinghouse associations were not under government control."[52]

The allegation of "dangerous" flies in the face of the clearinghouse system's actual performance. The most extraordinary fact associated with the several clearinghouse episodes between 1857 and 1907 is that the losses from all the various note issues, spurious and otherwise, *were negligible!* The only loss reported in any of the accounts here considered was $170,000 in Philadelphia in 1890 out of an issue of $9.7 million—1.8 percent of that total.[53] Few economists who analyzed clearinghouse operations even noted in passing this astonishing record, and none used it as an argument for formalizing and continuing the system.

Congressional sentiment continued to reflect the notion that the federal government should control the currency. In a typical statement, Congressman William A. Cullop of Indiana contrasted the proposed Federal Reserve Board with the NYCHA executive committee: "Every fair-minded man," he declared, "would prefer that the control over the currency be vested in seven men [on the Federal Reserve Board] selected from different parts of the country than to have it remain in the hands of the five managers of the New York clearing house. . . . To this self-constituted and unauthorized organization, [the Federal Reserve Act] deals a deadly blow in order to secure for us industrial and commercial freedom."[54] Cullop's absurd hyperbole demonstrated the decided influence populist ideology exerted in monetary affairs.

Résumé of the Clearinghouse Episode

Laws that regulated and restricted the fractional reserve banking industry in the United States during the last third of the nineteenth century had a seriously destabilizing effect on the monetary system. The federal government monopolized the supply of all currency—gold, silver, U.S. notes, national bank notes, and silver certificates. All the different kinds of currency were both high-powered money—bank reserves—and the medium for hand-to-hand transactions of households and business firms. Consequently, when the general public tried to cash demand deposits into currency, they depleted bank reserves and thereby reduced the banks' abilities to extend credit and maintain the existing level of demand deposits. This very common occurrence meant that the overall supply of money could be perversely elastic: An increased demand for money in the form of currency could result in a decreased supply of money in the form of demand deposits. Indeed, the negative effect on the supply of deposits could be much greater than the increased demand for currency and consequent loss of reserves, due to the multiplying effect of a fractional reserve banking system on a given quantity of reserves.

Barred from creating their own currency to meet unusual demands, and rendered less flexible by rigid reserve requirements in adapting to liquidity demands, the banks sought a defense that would protect both them and their depositors. The solution arrived at was clearinghouse creation of temporary currency. During a crisis, the banking industry reinstituted itself as an ad hoc "central bank," and through its clearinghouse associations issued additional high-powered money. Since the laws prohibited private issues of money, clearinghouse currency had to be issued discreetly. But it worked so well that no one had any incentive to prosecute its issuers. It was the private money-producing industry's answer to a pronounced need. It was, as well, constrained by market factors—interest-rate charges on its issue, and the real stake the clearinghouse banks' directors had in seeing to it that the clearinghouse association did not make costly misjudgments on the solvency of client banks. In addition, the gold-standard system fixed the value of the monetary base. Bankers who knew the rules of the gold-standard game realized that clearinghouse issues were only a temporizing device. They knew they had to limit their credit accommodations appropriately when their reserves were threatened.

The issue of clearinghouse currency put the brakes on the development of an unstable bank-credit contraction. It did not prevent the demise of inefficient banks; it only stopped the fractional reserve collapse that might otherwise have occurred.

One may then wonder why this system was rejected. Why was a government central bank superimposed on the banking industry when the clearinghouse system had proven so effective?

The accounts of the times suggest several answers. First, a large portion of the clearinghouse issues by 1907 had become recognizably illegal. Since thousands of banks issued clearinghouse currency anyway in spite of its illegality, the correct conclusion was that the laws prohibiting private initiatives in creating money were ill-conceived. Instead, the realization endowed the clearinghouse currency with a hucksterish quality. Because clearinghouse currency was illegal it was "makeshift" funny money—never mind the logic of the laws restricting bank flexibility and prohibiting clearinghouse issues.

Second, since clearinghouse currency was market-regulated, and because it was created and accepted voluntarily, many contemporary observers did not recognize its utility and integrity. They wanted an "official" government-issued currency similar to national bank notes or greenbacks.

Third, the clearinghouse currency seemed to arise out of nothing. Everyone could understand the principle of a quasi-public central bank standing by with an actual gold reserve that it would apply to financial weak spots when a crisis threatened. But few could understand how a clearinghouse system could create emergency currency without seeming to have an emergency reserve on which to base it. It was altogether too mystifying an operation for common understanding and acceptance. It smacked of Wall Street legerdemain.

Last, the clearinghouse issues were associated with the restriction and suspension of cash payments. Sprague clearly demonstrated that the two actions were not at all necessarily related.[55] Nonetheless, the popular mind was only too willing to apply here the fallacy that correlation implies causation.

Many advocates of a central bank saw the Federal Reserve System as an evolutionary development of the clearinghouse associations. The Federal Reserve alternative, however, was critically different from the clearinghouse system. It introduced a discretionary political element into monetary decision-making and thereby divorced the authority for determining the system's behavior from those who had a self-interest in maintaining its integrity.

Critical Reassessment of the Private Clearinghouse "Central Bank"

Professor Charles Goodhart in a recent work has reopened the question of clearinghouse intervention as a means of ameliorating panics.[56] Goodhart admits that the clearinghouse solution worked in "various crises of the late nineteenth and early twentieth centuries," but he claims that several imperfections flawed the system. Goodhart first raises the possibility of a conflict of interest between solvent banks that need aid in the form of clearinghouse loan certificates, and the loan committee of the clearinghouse association. The committee, Goodhart argues, may be overly cautious or, by refusing assistance to the applying bank, may realize a means of disposing of an unwanted rival.[57]

The ideal central-banking institution, Goodhart charges, must be "above the competitive battle, a noncompetitive, non-profit-maximizing body." He cites the experience of the Bank of England, which was at first a competitor of other private banks, albeit with a governmentally sanctioned monopoly of note issue. Gradually, however, in order to provide panic relief, the Bank of England had to maintain supernormal reserves, thereby forsaking the maximization of profits so that it would be able to supply reserves in a panic. This central-banking model, Goodhart correctly observes, was the one Walter Bagehot prescribed under the financial conditions prevailing in Victorian England.[58]

Goodhart's arguments serve to accentuate several features of the monetary environment in general, and of the central-banking function in particular. Indeed, his caveat on the adequacy of clearinghouse relief to individual banks would be well taken had pooling become the norm. Pooling eroded the incentive of banks with surplus reserves to share their bounty, and faced would-be needy banks with the moral hazard of being less than careful in their lending operations. Once the government central bank is in place, ironically, pooling becomes mandatory, and ultimately, as recent experience has confirmed, the moral hazard problem becomes serious.

Goodhart's government central bank, rather than being an answer to the potential problems he raises, becomes an aggravation. Discrimination in the dispensing of central-bank largess is certainly much greater in the case of a government central bank, where political favoritism and political pressures in support of special interests are the rule, than it is in private institutions that live and die in a competitive environment. If a member bank suspects favoritism and discrimination from the local clearinghouse association, it has the option of joining another association (or "club," to use Goodhart's term). The experience of 1907 revealed that clearinghouse associations could arise as spontaneously as primitive moneys had originally appeared. With such ubiquitous competition for the client banks' allegiance, no real problem of favoritism could endure.

Goodhart seems to ignore completely all the governmental interventions that provoked or aggravated liquidity problems in the first place. Governmental dispensation of monopoly powers over note issue, governmental imposition of legal reserve requirements, governmental prohibition of post notes and option clauses, governmental prohibitions of interstate and (often) intrastate branching—in sum, governmental interference with all the machinery of banking that would have allowed banking to function as a free enterprise, was what made the problem that the clearinghouse institution successfully abated. The governmental "answer" of a noncompetitive, "non-profit-maximizing" central bank,[59] superimposed on an industry already so legally restricted, was bound to aggravate the government-inspired problems. Free-enterprise banking would have minimized most of the banking industry's liquidity problems, and clearinghouse associations, though less needed, would have taken care of the rest.

15 Advent of the Federal Reserve System

> Why should we have an emergency currency? . . . The only emergency is the necessity which party leaders imagine confronts them to "do something," even though it be the wrong thing. What the country needs is not a makeshift legislative deformity, . . . but a careful revision and a wise reformation of the entire banking and currency system of the United States whereby panics may be prevented, or, if not prevented, under which their violence may be diminished and the evils consequent greatly abated.
>
> Carter Glass, House of Representatives, 27 May 1908

The Aldrich-Vreeland Act

One little-noticed development in monetary affairs during the early twentieth century was the inclusion of economists in the arguments over economic policy and in the proposals for new legislative measures, which were invariably called reforms. Many of these economists were highly critical of Shaw's Treasury policies. One of them, J. Lawrence Laughlin, was actively associated with the American Bankers Association, and another, H. Parker Willis, was a special adviser to the chairman of the House Banking and Currency Committee, Carter Glass.[1]

Most of the economists who appeared in print, especially Willis and most of Shaw's critics, favored the gold standard, held a commodity theory of money, and derived from these doctrines a commercial credit theory of banking. The issue that most concerned them, and many legislators and bankers as well, was the apparent seasonal rigidity of the money stock with respect to the needs of business. The institution they proposed for furnishing the desired elasticity was one that would be endowed with sufficient gold reserves to provide liquidity to solvent but needy banks on the basis of good commercial paper. Expansion and contraction of commercial paper in the interest-earning portfolio of the proposed agency would expand and contract the supply of bank reserves as needed.[2]

An important element in this picture was the understanding that the central reserve institution be immune from political influence. The need for this feature became particularly acute following the activist policies of Secretary Shaw. All the schemes for reform included negative reactions to Treasury intervention. J. Lawrence Laughlin, for example, stated, "We must establish some institution wholly free from politics or outside influence—as much respected for character and integrity as the Supreme Court—which shall be able to use government bonds or selected securities, as a basis for the issue of forms of lawful money which could be added to the reserves of the banks. . . . It is doubtful if a great central bank—apart from its political impossibility—would accomplish the desired end."[3]

To most economists a great central bank meant a single government-operated institution with a currency monopoly. Even though the U.S. government for all practical purposes already had such a monopoly over currency, economists objected to a central controlling agency that would be a thinly disguised arm of the Treasury Department. Yet the kind of institution that would be desirable was not entirely clear. Laughlin, for example, had government securities as a basis for currency issues; but most economists, bankers, and legislators favored a central-bank currency based on the loans and discounts generated by the commercial banking system.

In the spring of 1908, the Senate and the House produced fairly similar emergency currency bills under Republican sponsorship. The Senate bill passed 47 to 20, and the House bill 152 to 104. A conference committee then met to compromise the differences. This committee was chaired by Nelson Aldrich from the Senate and Edward Vreeland from the House, so the bill as finally enacted became the Aldrich-Vreeland Act.[4]

The version of the bill agreed to in conference called for the voluntary grouping of ten or more national banks into associations that would act as clearinghouses for the participating banks. They would have approximately the same functions and use the same methods that private clearinghouses had long since established on their own. In an attempt to improve the flexibility of national bank-note currency, the associations could issue currency on approved city, county, and state securities and on commercial paper, which was "to include only [paper] representing actual commercial transactions, . . . not exceeding four months [to maturity]." Commercial paper for up to 75 percent of its face value and local government securities for up to 90 percent of their par value would be the basis for issues of notes. The notes would have the same qualities as national bank notes. They were to be issued "under the direction and control of the Secretary of the Treasury" and were to be assigned to the different sections of the country in proportion to existing banking capital, "except that the Secretary of the Treasury may, in his discretion . . . assign [any] amount not thus applied for to any applying association or associations in States in the same section of the country."[5] The currency outstanding was to be taxed at the rate of 5 percent the first month and 1 percent each month thereafter. Not only did this act acknowledge and accept clearinghouse practices, it also reintroduced the discretion of the secretary of the Treasury, whose presence had only recently been found so undesirable!

Senator Carter Glass opposed the idea of a "patchwork" emergency currency. He cited as an authority on the subject a "great banker of the West," Mr. James B. Forgan of Chicago, who was also president of the American Bankers Association. Testifying before the Banking and Currency Committee, Forgan had stated apoplectically that no conditions could ever warrant "the issue of anything that could bear such an infernal name as 'emergency currency.'" The bill, Glass concluded, "puts the Federal Government in the picayune and incongruous business of discounting commercial paper."[6]

Another congressman, John McHenry of Pennsylvania, dramatized for his colleagues the Wall Street bogeyman. The bill, he said, enables "Wall Street interests" to turn panics on and off at will. The secretary would "become the 'hired man' of Wall Street," and so on. "Shall we close," he concluded, "as a fitting climax to this billion-dollar Republican Congress by crowning our masters, King Morgan and King Rockefeller, the heroes of the last panic, or shall it be King Taft, Wall Street's hired man? [Prolonged applause.]"[7]

Theodore Burton of Ohio, who favored the bill, pointed to its expediency as well as to the necessity for a more comprehensive measure. "The time is coming," he said, "when that general principle [of currency issue commensurate with the volume of business] is going to be adopted," either through a central bank or by other means. The trouble with the emergency currency bill was "that it would tend to perpetuate this present system of rigidity, in which there is no flexibility of the currency."[8]

The bill agreed to in conference passed the House 166 to 140. It then went to the Senate, where it was met by a filibuster headed by Robert LaFollette of Wisconsin. LaFollette's harangue was more a protest than a serious effort to block ultimate passage. Although he spoke for eighteen hours against the bill and issued thirty-six calls for quorums, he said nothing momentous. His main criticism of the bill was its evil effect in allowing railroad bonds to act indirectly as a basis for the issue of currency.[9]

Thomas Gore of Oklahoma, who also opposed the concept of emergency currency, ridiculed such issues as "electroscoot" currency, after an imaginary railway line between New York and San Francisco by which passengers would arrive in San Francisco two hours *before* they embarked in New York. This electroscoot currency, he said, "a carload or two of this 'V and A' panic panacea—will be shipped to San Francisco and will arrive two hours before the panic [initiated in New York] and will prevent the panic."[10]

Gore had some criticism of the distribution of Treasury balances to move the crops in 1908. The secretary, he charged, "deposited $34 million in the 'Southern and Western' State of New York, and . . . 62 cents to the great State [of Missouri]."[11] His criticism demonstrated the invidious feelings that could immediately arise over disposition of government largess at the discretion of a government official. It appeared to Gore that Treasury policy was confined to helping the wealthy and influential eastern region of the country. The balances so deposited might, of course, have done more financial good for Oklahoma and Missouri by being placed in New York than by being deposited in Kansas City or Tulsa, but this possibility could never be apparent to provincial legislators however tolerant they otherwise might be of their wealthier neighbors.

The Senate passed the conference version of the bill 43 to 22, and President Taft signed it the same day.[12]

The National Reserve Association

Two sections of the Aldrich-Vreeland Act described the formal structure of the National Monetary Commission.[13] This commission was cochaired by Senator Aldrich and Representative Vreeland and included fifteen other congressmen plus a special assistant, Professor A. Piatt Andrew of Harvard University. The commission farmed out various research projects in monetary economics, including both empirical and institutional studies, to numerous economists in the United States and Europe. In 1910, the commission published twenty-four volumes, many of lasting value.

The final volume included a summary of norms that Senator Aldrich had drawn from the commission's work. His principles for a central-banking organization included the following:

1. It should *not* copy the central-banking structures of European institutions "without many material modifications."
2. The American institution should mobilize and centralize reserves.
3. The means for maintaining the central bank's reserve should be its rate of discount.
4. In a period of distress the central bank should follow the Bagehot principle of extending credit "liberally to everyone whose solvency and condition entitles him to receive it." At the same time, it should keep its discount rate high enough to encourage a gold inflow.
5. The gold reserve should be used to the extent necessary.
6. The central bank should have a monopoly of note issue, but its discretion should be limited by specific law.
7. Its operations should be free of political influences.[14]

The immediate result of the commission's recommendations in Congress was a proposal for a national reserve association. A bill to incorporate such an institution was introduced in the Senate by Senator Burton in December of 1911, and President Taft recommended it to Congress at the same time. In his discussion of the matter Taft noted that the National Reserve Association (NRA) would eliminate the "troublesome question" of a central bank. The proposed association, he said, "is a logical outgrowth of what is best in our present system, and is, in fact, the fulfillment of that system." Bankers would devise and operate the new association, but it would be subject to some form of governmental supervision.[15]

The president's contention that the National Reserve Association was not a central bank was contradicted in the House by Richard Hobson of Alabama. Hobson cited a "critical analysis by Mr. R. C. Milliken, a monetary expert in the Bond Building of this city." Milliken stated in his report to Hobson that he could find no difference between the NRA and European central banks; nor, he added, "is there any reasonable excuse for not terming [the NRA] a central bank."[16]

Milliken had several objections to the whole scheme. "It teaches the public two fallacies," he argued. First, because it would impose reserve requirements, it implied that "the ratio of a bank's resources to its total demand liabilities should be uniform throughout the year." Second, "it gives undue emphasis to [reserves,] thereby detracting from the more important factor—the convertibility and character of the whole of [a bank's] assets." He argued that the new institution should discount only bills "issued for productive credit arising from real commercial transactions to solvent persons furnishing convertible paper payable at short and fixed periods"—a perfect description of what came to be known as "real bills." He felt that a central bank should be divorced from the banking business in the manner of the Bank of England. The British, he commented, "have no kindergartens for bank presidents as is our Treasury Department."[17]

The NRA bill was discussed just once in Congress—by Representative Vreeland—and his discussion was allowed only as a courtesy. Vreeland claimed that "practically all the bankers of the United States [and] all the political economists . . . in the colleges of the United States" approved the measure. The present banking system, he contended, was analogous to a faulty railroad that would cease operations once every ten years. The dispersion of reserves in the present system was an invitation to disaster. Five or six of the larger New York banks currently acted as a central bank, but their commercial nature—their profit motivation in particular—meant that they could not "afford to carry great reserves of from 40 to 60 percent when business is good, in order to release them when business is bad. . . . We must have an institution to hold our reserves which is not a money-making institution. The idea of profit must be eliminated from its management," he concluded.[18]

Vreeland very clearly posed the dilemma and the conflict that accompanies the creation of a central bank in an economy largely operating on principles of private enterprise and in which a metallic standard regulates the monetary system. If the institution were to keep enough gold reserves to be effective in a crisis, it could not operate in the ordinary sense as a private commercial bank and make normal profits. If it was organized as a hybrid, such as the Bank of England, either its income had to be subsidized by some sort of government bounty or it had to have eleemosynary characteristics. If it was then brought into existence as either a subsidized or a nonprofit institution, the rules governing its operations would have to be carefully drawn. Otherwise, it would find itself in direct conflict with the corrective adjustments forced by the gold standard, or else it would have to operate in violation of sound commercial banking principles.

No one in this era thought of controverting the gold standard as the secular determinant of the money stock. Gold was to be *the* reserve, though it was to be centralized and economized. The NRA, Vreeland observed, would face a 40 percent gold reserve requirement, thus enabling it to create two and one-half times as much bank reserves or notes as the gold it held.[19]

The structure of the NRA was to include a central administrative and advisory bureau in Washington and fifteen regional or district branches. The commercial banks in each local community would also congregate into local associations, which would be linked to the regional branches. The NRA would be a bank of banks, and commercial banks would be its owners and stockholders. It would set its discount rate as a matter of policy each week, and it would discount bona fide commercial paper having no more than twenty-eight days to maturity. A basic cadre of NRA notes would supplant existing national bank notes; the rest of the institution's issues would develop from the discounts of commercial paper for its participants. It would have forty-six directors who would be recruited from the several districts. Included in this corps of directors would be the secretaries of agriculture, commerce, labor, and the Treasury, and the comptroller of the currency, plus a governor appointed by the president of the United States and two deputy governors. The plan was approved by the American Bankers Association.

Its spokesmen denied that it was a central bank. "Do I mean," Vreeland asked rhetorically, "that we should bring to life the central bank of Andrew Jackson's time? No," he answered. "We should . . . adapt [central-bank principles] to American conditions. . . . We must let the bankers run the banking business of the country."[20]

The elections in the fall of 1912 significantly modified the political face of the federal government. The Republican party had held the executive office for fifty-two years, with the exception of the two Cleveland administrations, and Cleveland was in most ways more conservative than the Republican executives. His role in the demise of silver showed that. The rift within the Republican party split the Republican vote so that the Democratic candidate, Woodrow Wilson, won the presidency. In addition, both houses of Congress went Democratic. This change meant that no monetary measure sponsored by the Republican party could pass. Lame-duck president Taft recommended the NRA again in his annual message to Congress late in 1912, but his effort was futile. If nothing else, the name of the National Reserve Association had to be changed, and its sponsors had to be Democrats. This mutation was to take place in the Sixty-third Congress.

Issues in the Formation of the Federal Reserve Act

The Number of Reserve Banks

Carter Glass of Virginia, chairman of the House Committee on Banking and Currency, introduced the bill to create the Federal Reserve System in the late summer of 1913. Glass emphasized the large popular demand for "reform" of the "barbarous" national bank system then in operation. His committee, he said, had received thousands of letters plus resolutions passed by hundreds of commercial bodies calling for change. He cited the two major deficiencies of the present system. First, no reserve was available to the banking system at critical times. Second, currency outstanding was based on "the Nation's debt," that is, on government securities, rather than on something that would reflect the variable needs of business, such as the short-term paper of commercial banks. The previous Republican-sponsored measures, the Aldrich-Vreeland Act and the National Reserve Association, Glass stated, were dismissed by his committee because they had been denounced by both the Democratic and the Progressive party platforms, "while the platform of the Republican Party was silent on the subject." The principal objection to the NRA (the Aldrich scheme) was that it was "saturated with monopolistic tendencies" and faced an "absolute lack of adequate governmental control." It fell short of being a central bank, Glass said, only because it did not provide for the transaction of business with the public.[21]

Strangely enough, any institution that looked like a central bank was politically impossible at this time. A central bank was "monopolistic." It was run by bloodsucking bankers who were given special privileges to soak the poor, keep interest rates up, and conspire with Wall Street speculators to cause panics that were profitable to the speculators and themselves. Glass noted that "great pains were observed and much ingenuity exercised" in the Aldrich bill to avoid the appearance of a central bank.[22]

In lieu of such an unacceptable institution, the Democrats conceived of the Federal Reserve System. Instead of one central bank, the Banking and Currency Committee proposed not less than eight nor more than twelve regional banks. The decision-making process by which this number was derived gives an index of the intellectual construction of the system. First, one central bank located in Washington was unacceptable. Well, if not one bank, then how many? The Republican, conservative, northeastern, pro–national bank answer was three or four. This number simply carried over to the new institution the three central reserve cities so defined for the national bank system—New York, Chicago, and St. Louis—and added one for the West Coast in San Francisco. The Republicans argued that a minimum number was needed to mobilize and centralize reserves most effectively.[23] The more populist (provincial) rural element of the Congress proposed one bank for each state, plus one, perhaps, for the District of Columbia and Alaska, a total of forty-eight or fifty.

The argument that finally carried the most weight in the determination of the right number was provided by John Shafroth of Colorado in the senate debate on the bill. He presented the pragmatic scenario of a banker pressed for funds because of a run developing on his bank. A bank subject to such adversity, said Shafroth, should be within "one night's [train] ride of a reserve bank." The president of the stricken bank "could then gather the 30, 60, and 90 day commercial paper he wanted cashed, take the train for the city where the Federal reserve bank is situate [*sic*], and be able to wire he had cashed sufficient securities to meet the demand of all depositors." Shafroth contrasted this expedient relationship with that of "one central bank located several days' run from many of the interior banks." In addition, he argued, a regional system would preserve the personal relationship between the commercial banker and the Reserve banker.[24]

Twelve sounded like a good nonmonopolistic compromise between three or four and forty-eight or fifty, and Shafroth's scenario expressed very well the reserve-in-emergency nature of what the legislators were looking for. Another practical argument was that twelve Reserve banks would just about have adequate endowment for their capital structuring if all national banks were required to enter the system.[25]

Populist Concept of the Federal Reserve Board

The acceptance of a regional association concept was one thing; who was to control it and what would be the vehicle for its operations were others. The coordinating agency, of course, would be the Federal Reserve Board. Unlike the bankers who would have directed the NRA, the Federal Reserve Board would be nonprofit. "No financial interest," claimed Carter Glass, "can pervert or control [the Board]. It is an altruistic institution, a part of the Government itself, representing the American people, with powers such as no man would dare misuse."[26] One of its powers was to permit or require one Federal Reserve bank to rediscount the paper held by another Federal Reserve bank. In this manner it could mobilize reserves for the whole system if need be. Bankers opposed this provision, reported Glass.

> They were perfectly willing, under the Aldrich scheme, to confide this power to [themselves], operating for gain, but are unwilling to lodge it with the Government of the United States to be used for patriotic purposes under a system devised for the good of the country. . . . It is somewhat analogous to the power exercised for years by the Secretary of the Treasury alone, when, in times of emergency, he has withdrawn the Government deposits at will from banks in one part of the country and transferred them to banks in another part of the county, . . . the difference being that, whereas the transfers have heretofore been made to the great money centers for the purpose of arresting stock-gambling panics, the transfers under this bill, if ever required at all, will be made to promote legitimate commercial transactions.[27]

Glass's brief is significant because it uses the Treasury policies developed under Shaw as a precedent for anticipated Federal Reserve policy. It does not explain how or why the devil in the form of the secretary of the Treasury would be transformed into St. Michael and all the angels when in the form of the Federal Reserve Board.

Glass also invoked the fallacious people-control-it-through-the-government doctrine. The Federal Reserve Board, he said, "is strictly a board of control . . . doing justice to the banks, but fairly and courageously representing the interests of the people. . . . The talk of political control [of the Board] is the expression of a groundless conjecture."[28] Yet he cited no checks and balances that would prevent the abuses he inveighed against. Under the NRA plan national bankers in reserve cities would at least have competed with each other for the reserves of the participating banks.

H. H. Seldomridge of Colorado expressed a similar opinion. "Who dares to advocate," he asked, "that the Government should not exercise a controlling and beneficial influence in regulating the volume and distribution of our currency? The great outstanding merit of this bill is that it places this great power in the hands of the people."[29]

In another exchange between Alben Barkley of Kentucky and William Baltz of Illinois, the relationship between "the people" and the government again appeared.

> MR. BALTZ: If this bill is enacted into law, will it not give the Government control of the finances?
>
> MR. BARKLEY: It will, and the Government ought to have the control.
>
> MR. BALTZ: Who is the Government?
>
> MR. BARKLEY: The Government is the people, and the people act through their authorized agents, the chief of whom is the President of the United States. [Applause on the Democratic side.][30]

Such bland naiveté demonstrated the decided influence that populist doctrine exercised at this time. To defend his point Barkley would have had to show how the people communicated with the president and by what means the president would then control the finances. Any attempt to define and describe such a process immediately reveals its ludicrous character.

One dissenter from this doctrine was John Shafroth of Colorado, who had also given the rationale for locating regional banks "one night's train ride" from every commercial bank. "Our bill," Shafroth declared, speaking of the Glass-Owen bill, "is framed upon the theory that this is a bank of banks for the purpose of preventing runs on banks. . . . We have 25,000 people's banks now. What is the use of turning this into another people's bank? Every national bank in the United States is a people's bank. . . . You do not want to mix a bank of banks with a people's bank."[31]

Frank Mondell of Wyoming also threw some cold water on the people-government fallacy. "The people pretty clearly understand nowadays that control through a Government bureau, by political appointees, is not synonymous with control by the people and for the people," he stated.[32] As if to extend Mondell's arguments, George Norris argued that the Federal Reserve Board, consisting of four persons appointed by the president, plus two cabinet officers and the comptroller of the currency, "is made at once a football of partisan politics. . . . Our banking and financial system [will] be on edge at every presidential campaign."[33]

Glass was anxious to promote the nonpolitical character of the new system even though it was to be people-controlled through the government. "There is no politics in this matter; there can be none," he stated. "[No one] has yet pointed out how any part of this system can be perverted to political uses."[34]

A few months later, when the bill was on its final passage through the Senate, some congressmen were still complaining that it was a political bill. James Lewis of Illinois took the bull by the horns. "What does my distinguished friend expect in a political government?" he asked, addressing his rhetorical question to one of the complainers. "The senator is right. The bill is political, political to the extent that it voices the political ideas of the people of this country, political in that it expresses in legislation the platform of the [Democratic party]. . . . All things must be guided, honorable sir. To some *men* each system must be intrusted."[35]

All sides seemed to believe that some group of mortal beings had to control the banking and monetary system. In practice only two groups could possibly exercise this control—bankers or government authorities—and sentiment was overwhelmingly in favor of a government connection. Bankers could not be trusted, neither their competence nor their integrity, claimed Rufus Hardy of Texas. The very fact that the government deposited its fiscal revenues in banks, he continued, argued for government control.[36] "It is the business of Government," added William E. Borah of Idaho in the Senate, "to provide a sound and sufficient volume of currency and money upon which to do the business of the country."[37]

Hardy minimized the powers of the Federal Reserve Board. "A central bank, so much desired by Wall Street," he said, "[would have] powers for evil which the Board does not have." He then enumerated the powers the Board did not have. It could not loan, earn, own, or borrow one dollar. It could not finance an enterprise. It could not finance a candidate or a campaign.[38] He did not say that the Board could not create money or control the money supply.

The opinion of Frank Mondell of Wyoming was not so sanguine. He warned prophetically that

> the Federal Reserve Board under this bill is an organization of vastly wider power, authority, and control over currency [and] banks . . . than the reserve associations contemplated by the National Monetary Commission. . . . It is of a character which in practical operation would tend to increase and centralize. . . . It will be the most powerful banking institution in all the world. . . . In your frantic efforts to escape the bogey man of a central bank, . . . you have come perilously near establishing in the office of the Comptroller of the Currency, under the Secretary of the Treasury, the most powerful banking institution in the world.[39]

The Federal Reserve's "Scientific" Creation of Money and Credit

To avoid undesirable political control, several congressmen suggested that the reserve system should feature scientific management. This institution, said Everis Hayes of California, should not become "the football of politics. A banking and currency system is a great, complex, scientific, and business proposition." Science in the management of money would be obtained by the Reserve banks' dispassionately discounting commercial paper. "The only limit to a commercial bank's ability to discount," said Charles Korbly of Indiana, "is the limit to good commercial paper. . . . Such paper springs from self-clearing transactions. . . . It is the duty of the banker to discount freely for his customer in a crisis or panic. The only limit . . . is the limit to good commercial paper."[40]

The notion that production of goods creates money is apparent in Korbly's speech. "The possession of reserves in greater or lesser amount does not in the slightest degree increase the ability of the bank to lend," he argued. "It is what is happening to goods and merchandise . . . that causes high discounts. . . . The banker no more deals in money because he handles money," he continued, "than grocers or druggists. . . . A bank deals in debts, . . . notes and bills of exchange." Once a banker knew that the rediscounting privilege would be refused on illiquid paper, he would be anxious to confine his loans to paper that he would have no difficulty rediscounting in time of trouble. "The whole purpose of the Federal Reserve Act," Korbly emphasized, "is to enforce this practice."[41]

The scientific rationale of Federal Reserve policy centered on this "production" theory of money and credit. To get the necessary elasticity in the monetary system, commercial banks would bring their eligible paper to the regional Reserve banks for rediscounting. This paper, if truly eligible, would have arisen from loans that were the basis for the generation or marketing of new goods and services. New products would indirectly create new money. So long as commercial and Reserve banks discounted or rediscounted only eligible paper, any increase in the quantity of credit would match an increase in the quantity of goods and no danger of too much money could arise. The necessity for bankers to extend credit on good loans would likewise prevent too little money in the system.

The only theoretical question that remained was the definition of *eligible*. It meant short-term, but how short? It excluded investment (long-term) loans and certainly speculative loans (those based on stocks bought on margin). But what did it include? Not until late in the debates did congressmen face this question, probably because a definition seemed so intuitively obvious. When its meaning was finally scrutinized, the term seemed to imply the need for a scientific authority that was not presently available in the banking system or Congress, but would spring fully qualified from the Federal Reserve Board after it was appointed. The possibility of such a discovery seemed remote after John Weeks of Massachusetts pointed out that he had "tried to get 12 or 15 banking men" to define *eligible commercial paper,* and not one of them could do it.[42] How the Board would obtain the expertise to handle this matter later was a question no one could answer.

Because of doubt about the definition of *eligible* and the discretion necessarily implied by its interpretation, legislators favoring the Hitchcock bill over the Glass-Owen version wanted to make discounting by the Reserve banks a right rather than a privilege. To prevent "gross discrimination . . . and great favoritism," said Hitchcock in his rebuttal to Owen, every member bank should "as a matter of right . . . have the privilege of discounting eligible paper." This right was to be limited to twice a member bank's capital stock.[43] Knute Nelson of Minnesota expressed a similar view. Nelson believed that eligibility was capable of rigorous definition. If so, there could be no excuse for not discounting all eligible paper, and discounting should be a routine right rather than a privilege granted by the authority of a board. Discretion by the Board and the Reserve banks, Nelson added, was unnecessary and undesirable.[44] The eligibility doctrine, as he conceived it, was intimately tied to the elasticity principle. Only short-term paper generated by the production of real goods and services was eligible and would give elasticity to the system. "Short-time commercial paper, which is liquid and collects itself [provides] a natural system of elasticity," he concluded.[45]

Another senator, Porter McCumber of North Dakota, warned that the currency might be "stretched out three feet and come back only one foot," implying the possibility of chronic inflation. How, he asked, was currency to be contracted after a Reserve bank had expanded it?[46] Robert Owen, the manager of the bill in the Senate, answered. The currency would be expanded by the discounting of bona fide commercial paper. When the bills were liquidated, the currency would be contracted automatically as the Federal Reserve notes went out of circulation. Owen's argument again implied that physical output generated money.[47]

The Federal Reserve Banks as a "Public Utility"; the Board as a "Supreme Court of Finance"

Another principle that legislators wanted to see embodied in law was the Federal Reserve banks as a public utility. Everis Hayes of California said that the new institution would provide "public control over the finances . . . similar to the control that is now exercised over the interstate commerce of the country through the Interstate Commerce Commission. [Applause on the Democratic side.]"[48] Some congressmen extended the idea of public utility and argued that Federal Reserve banks should "give the borrowing public a stable and uniform low rate of interest," in the same way that the ICC established low freight rates.[49]

This norm was clearly at odds with the Bagehot principle, which was invoked as a guide for policy in the new system by Theodore Burton of Ohio. The Bagehot doctrine argued that the central bank should lend freely in a crisis at a high rate of interest in order to stay the panic and to prevent depletion of the central bank's gold reserve.[50] The high-rate-of-interest doctrine implied the traditional wisdom of the time: that the central-bank rate of interest should be kept higher than the market rate.[51] The Federal Reserve Board in Washington, Hitchcock observed, could also order the Federal Reserve banks to raise discount rates in order to "check the excessive inflation of bank credit."[52]

Complementary to the public-utility notion was the idea that the Board could operate as a "supreme court of American finance."[53] The men chosen for the Board, said John Weeks of Massachusetts, should be "as representative and of generally recognized capacity in the business world as are appointees to the Supreme Court in the legal world."[54]

L. C. Dyer of Missouri disputed this idealized view of the new system. In doing so he cited a lengthy report from the St. Louis Clearing House Association of bankers. This report noted that appointees to the Federal Reserve Board would not be like justices on the Supreme Court. Justices were appointed for life and therefore were not subject (supposedly) to political pressures. Justices had been trained specifically for a profession that was compatible with a judgeship, whereas the new board was prohibited from including a stockholder or an officer of any banking institution. Nor would the Federal Reserve System be similar to the ICC, the report stated, because the ICC had no power to divert assets from one railroad company to another in the fashion that one Reserve bank might be commanded to discount the paper of another Reserve bank.[55]

Congressmen seemed to want an objective, scientific, disinterested, nonpolitical organization. They wanted the Treasury Department out of policymaking, even though the secretary would serve both as an ex officio member of the Board and as its chairman![56] And they did not want commercial bankers running the new system, since such a liaison would involve a conflict of interests. Too lenient a discounting policy would amount to nothing more than a special interest subsidy for member banks. "Banks should have no more to do with the issue and control of public currency," said Finley Gray of Indiana, "than an elevator company should have to control the supply and distribution of grain. . . . [Bankers] are not better nor more to be trusted in serving the public welfare as against their own private interests than other men. Bankers should be prohibited from any association at all with the Board."[57] While most congressmen agreed with this view, they believed that appointees to the Board should have had banking experience.[58]

The legislators' requirements and restrictions for staffing the new system underscored the difficulties in moving an organization from market control into a political environment. The only eligible political appointees for the new system would have been a group of vestal virgins. It was a lot easier to imagine goals to which the institution should aspire than it was to fashion politically a machine that would function within constitutional bounds and accomplish everyone's well-understood objectives.

The House passed its bill on 18 September 1913 by a vote of 299 to 68. One of the last issues discussed before passage was the propriety of the clause that stated, "Nothing in this act . . . shall be considered to repeal the parity provisions contained in an act approved March 14, 1900," which referred to the Gold Standard Act of 1900. Necessary or not, it was left in as a precaution to affirm the priority of the gold standard for determining the money supply. The Federal Reserve System was not to serve as a substitute or surrogate for the self-regulating gold standard.[59]

Reserve Requirements for the Federal Reserve Banks and for Member Banks

The House bill went to the Senate, where it was worked over in the Committee on Banking and Currency for several weeks and reported out on 8 October. The manager of the Senate bill was Robert Owen of Oklahoma; the leader of the opposition was Gilbert Hitchcock of Nebraska. Owen was a Democrat and chairman of the committee that reported out the bill. Hitchcock was also a Democrat and a member of the committee but he clustered around himself the conservative Republican contingent that wanted a central bank in the mode of the aborted NRA or Aldrich scheme. The bill that was reported out of committee was printed in three columns: the Glass (House) version, the Owen (Senate majority) version, and the Hitchcock (Senate minority) version.[60]

The early stages of the Senate debate included discussions of the same issues that had been so tediously worked over in the House. One issue largely neglected by the House was the reserve requirement for Federal Reserve banks. Both the Glass and Owen bills called for reserves of 33⅓ percent against all demand obligations—Federal Reserve notes outstanding and member bank reserve-deposit accounts. Hitchcock's group wanted 45 percent against notes and 35 percent against member bank deposits.[61]

With his higher reserve requirements and 100 percent collateral of "good commercial paper," Hitchcock felt secure in arguing again for the right of member banks to discount. "We have given the right to each [member] bank to secure a discount of paper to a certain extent," he stated. "Each reserve bank is a public utility and responding to the natural demands of business." He repeatedly emphasized that the right to discount denied the necessity for any discretion by the Board or Reserve banks. To allow such discretion, he cautioned, "is to provide for possible inflation."[62]

The 45 percent gold reserve against Federal Reserve notes was derived from the statutory requirement that the Treasury maintain a gold reserve of

$150 million against outstanding United States notes, which had been frozen at $346.7 million.[63] These figures imply a ratio of 43.3 percent. The reserve against notes was to be gold, not other "lawful money"—for example, silver. Hitchcock expressed the prevalent feeling on all sides: "We do not think that the Government of the United States in issuing its obligations, its promises to pay, should reserve the right to pay [redeem] their [*sic*] obligations in other obligations."[64]

This same sentiment prevented Federal Reserve notes from becoming legal reserves of member banks. The Owen bill at first incorporated this provision on the grounds that all state banks could use national bank notes as reserves. Senator Burton, however, protested vehemently. National banks and Federal Reserve banks, he pointed out, would be "in the same system," a relationship unlike that between national and state banks. The new federal combination of national banks and Federal Reserve banks would therefore be using its own debts as reserves, a highly inflationary arrangement.[65]

The proscription of Federal Reserve notes as reserves for member banks found more arguments and many more supporters. Already accepted was the provision that one Federal Reserve bank could not pay out the notes of another Federal Reserve bank but had to return them to the bank of issue. Hitchcock made the non-sequitur argument that if a Reserve bank had to return a Federal Reserve note to its source, "it is ten thousand times more important to require the member banks to do so." The use of Federal Reserve notes as reserves, he continued, would encourage the displacement of gold to foreign countries.[66] He could argue this way only by conceiving of Federal Reserve banks as private banking institutions rather than as parts of a central-banking system. If Federal Reserve currency outstanding was that volatile, commercial bank reserve accounts at Federal Reserve banks would be even more so.

Albert Cummins of Iowa made a similar argument in response to a question on the difference between reserve requirements for currency and for demand deposits. A check, Cummins observed, stays in existence only two or three days before redemption, while currency may have a tenure of five years. Therefore (non sequitur again) currency requires a larger reserve.[67] No one challenged Cummins to explain why the checkbook *balance* against which the check was drawn would necessarily be liquidated instead of being transferred to another account.

Several legislators argued that the commercial paper that gave rise to the issue of Federal Reserve notes was the fundamental redeeming medium. The member bank, said John Williams of Mississippi, would get lawful money—gold, greenbacks, or Federal Reserve notes—and pay off its debt to the Federal Reserve bank. So the note lived and died as commercial paper was created and then liquidated.[68]

The possible use of Federal Reserve notes as reserves triggered the question of potential inflation by the new institution. The appearance of this question so late in the debate seems odd, but it was the result of the wide acceptance of the commodity theory of money. "How do checks and bills come into existence?" asked Charles Korbly of Indiana. "They are the offspring of sales."[69]

Once the question of reserve requirements for Federal Reserve banks and the discounting machinery by which Federal Reserve notes would be issued came under detailed scrutiny, some congressmen began to have doubts about the automaticity of the new system. Elihu Root of New York, for example, observed that the Federal Reserve Board faced "no limit whatever upon the quantity of notes that may be issued," and the Reserve banks were similarly unconstrained in their discounting procedures.[70]

Root complemented this criticism with a sophisticated insight into the instability that a central bank could generate during a business boom. He warned against loans made "upon security that is good until the time comes when, through a process of inflation, we reach a situation in which no security is good." Then "the standards which are applied in the exercise of that kind of judgment [for limited discounting] become modified by the optimism of the hour and grow less and less effective in checking the expansion of business."[71]

This statement exposes the instability inherent in real-bills policy. Although Root discussed only the potential magnification of a boom into an inflation, the same argument holds for a downturn and its development into a depression. Once business turns sour—for whatever reasons—all loans begin to look bad.

Another critic in the Senate, Porter McCumber of North Dakota, remarked that only since Root's speech on 13 December, two months after the bill was first debated in the House, had the possibility of Federal Reserve inflation become an issue. "Inflation," he warned, "is not elasticity. . . . A currency whose expansion is not limited by the act of law creating it, but by the will or discretion of a board, will always result in general inflation." Political pressure on the Federal Reserve Board after Reserve banks had expanded notes would prevent contraction, McCumber prophesied; and therefore, he argued, all Federal Reserve notes should be taxed to prevent them from becoming a permanent stock.[72]

The Democratic sponsors of the bill were quick to defend it against the charges of inflation. Owen argued that the Reserve Board could set the discount rate at a level that would discourage borrowing.[73] Furthermore, he said, Federal Reserve notes would not be a fiat currency because they "are secured by commercial bills of a highly qualified class."[74]

John Williams of Mississippi supplemented Owen's arguments. The Board has "no power to initiate, to compel or to consummate any inflation whatsoever. [It has] a power . . . to compel contraction . . . either by raising the interest rate or by refusing its approval to issue of the paper currency by the reserve banks."[75] Williams claimed that the "character" of appointees to the Federal Reserve Board would prevent the fiat issue of paper currency.[76] He thus accepted the vestal virgin concept for the Board.

Although no one doubted that the Federal Reserve Act would pass, many controversial features could have been resolved either way, especially if the Democratic caucus had not been so cohesive. As it was, the Glass-Owen bill commanded only a marginal majority on most points. The "right" to discount, for example, which Benjamin Bristow offered as an amendment in lieu of "privilege," lost only 31 to 37.[77]

The opposition tried to increase the Federal Reserve banks' reserve requirements to 45 percent against notes and 35 percent against deposits of member banks from a flat 33⅓ percent overall. This amendment lost by a narrow margin, 39 to 42.[78] In the conference to reconcile House and Senate versions of the bill, the majority yielded on this point; so the final reserve requirements became 40 percent and 35 percent, respectively.

The bill also included a provision allowing Federal Reserve banks to operate with deficient reserves, but they had to pay a graduated tax on the deficiency. This issue was the subject of much discussion in both houses of Congress, because it was seen as a means for obtaining flexibility in a crisis. In defending this provision, Owen observed that Parliament had permitted the Bank of England a similar indulgence on three occasions during which the bank issued notes in order to stop panics.[79] Without such an escape route, the gold reserve exerted a rigid legal limit on the issue of notes and the expansion of bank credit. With it, the gold reserve could be stretched to provide some flexibility to currency and bank reserve accounts, so it stayed in.

Theodore Burton then moved to strike out the use of Federal Reserve notes as legal reserves for member banks on the grounds that this measure posed the threat of inflation. His amendment lost by another close vote, 37 to 40; a two-vote swing would have carried it.[80] The House-Senate conference later considered this provision and decided in favor of Burton's argument. So the final bill prohibited the use of Federal Reserve notes as eligible reserves for member banks.[81]

Result of the House-Senate Conference on the Federal Reserve Bill

The bill passed in the Senate 54 to 34.[82] It then went back to the House, where the Senate amendments were disagreed to 295 to 59. Both houses agreed on a conference, and conferees were duly appointed.

At first the conferees seemed to face a long negotiation in order to get an acceptable bill. As late as 20 December, Carter Glass stated flatly, "There is no prospect at all of an immediate agreement." However, the conferees worked hard over the ensuing weekend and came up with a conference report on 22 December. The compromise removed the secretary of agriculture from the Board. It also stated that in any conflict of powers between the Board and the Treasury Department, "such powers shall be exercised subject to the supervision and control of the Secretary."[83] Somehow, the secretary of the Treasury could never be excluded from having a major voice in the actual conduct of monetary policy.

The minority against the bill in the Senate complained that they had received little satisfaction in the committee's deliberations; but, as Shafroth observed, irreconcilable differences existed over certain provisions. The Democrats had condemned the whole concept of a central bank, while every Republican member of the committee had announced his support for it. These Republican views could not be tolerated, for the Democrats were not about to create a central bank![84]

One provision often discussed but not included in the final bill was a deposit insurance plan whereby part of the profits of the Reserve banks would be put into a fund to guarantee deposits of member banks. It was thrown out in the conference, reported Carter Glass, because "if bank depositors are to be guaranteed, it should be at the expense of banks not of the United States Government. [Applause.]"[85]

In his benediction on the passage of the bill, Glass recounted the means by which the bill guarded against inflation: "First, by the limited supply of gold; second, by the limited amount of short-time commercial paper; third, by the banking discretion of the individual bank; fourth, by the banking discretion of the regional reserve bank; fifth, by the banking discretion of the Federal Reserve Board."[86] This list of safeguards seems to prove too much as well as to include a lot of discretion. It even implies a bias toward contraction. Nor does it include either scientific objectivity or market forces to determine the system's money supply.

The compromise bill passed the House 298 to 60 and the Senate 43 to 25. Many of the Republicans and other dissenters who had objected to specific provisions voted for the final bill.[87] President Wilson then signed it into law on 23 December 1913.

The Blind Men and the Elephant

What kind of institution did Congress think it had created? What kind of institution did it create? Opinions on the first question were as diverse as the makeup of Congress itself; data bearing on the second question may be obtained only from empirical evidence of the period from 1913 to the present.

One conclusion is certain: The coalition majority that wrote the bill for the new system claimed it was not creating a central bank. Its institution was a system of autonomous regional reserve banks. No matter what was claimed, the Federal Reserve banks compose a central-banking system. Gilbert Hitchcock, not a member of the majority, emphasized that fact in the Senate. "The central bank," he said, "does not consist of a vault. The central bank does not consist of a mass of money. . . . The central bank consists of central control, and that is provided in this bill. The control is central [in the Federal Reserve Board]; and when you get your control centralized you have a central bank."[88]

A second feature of the new institution on which both its sponsors and its opponents agreed was its scope. They did not create the Federal Reserve System to usurp the functions of the gold standard and become an omnipotent central bank. Their intention was only to provide for form-seasonal elasticity in the economy's money supply, and to do so on the basis of bona fide, self-liquidating, short-term commercial loans.[89] In general, most congressmen saw the economy's real product generating appropriate changes in the money supply through this medium. The Federal Reserve System was simply a formalized scheme to expedite this process.

The new institution was also seen as a regulatory public utility. It was to regulate interest rates and to supervise banking. The statutory 6 percent return paid to the commercial member banks, who held stock in the twelve Reserve banks, reflected this idea. This arrangement, however, is contradictory. Since the commercial banks were to receive the dividends, the twelve Reserve banks were analogous to the public utility and the Federal Reserve Board was similar to the regulatory body. But the twelve banks were supposed to be the autonomous regulators as well, and they could not be both the income-earning utility and the regulators of the commercial banking system.

The Reserve banks became the clearinghouse system for their members. Robert Owen confirmed in the Senate that the new system had evolved from the "clearance-house [*sic*] associations of the United States. This bill, for the most part, is merely putting into legal shape that which hitherto has been illegally done."[90] Everis Hayes of California remarked that he would have preferred to see "the present clearing-house associations [enlarged and controlled] under proper governmental regulation so as to embrace all the banks, and intrust to such associations the duty of supplying to the people and business interests the elastic currency which is needed."[91]

The issue of clearinghouse loan certificates and other media during past crises had been the response of private enterprise to an increased demand for high-powered money when some of the real high-powered money was either exported, or hoarded, or rendered unavailable due to legal reserve requirements. The Federal Reserve System was an attempt to put this practice on an official basis and to ensure that the high-powered money was forthcoming by a deliberate and conscious act of policy. Congressmen believed that contrived policy of this sort implied greater certainty than similar results that might be obtained from the profit-seeking actions of commercial bankers.

While policy decisions of a government may be more deliberate than banker or business decisions based on somebody's bread and butter, they are not more certain to be the right decisions. Other factors determine the propriety and correctness of policy: the validity of the theory supporting the policy, political factors that may have nothing to do with the technical correctness of policy, and the self-interest of policymakers. When these factors are taken into account, discretionary policy often loses its advantage over decisions that result from a profit-oriented market system.

Much congressional debate dwelt on the exercise of power in the new system. Those who thought the Reserve Board would be in control, as Hitchcock did, saw the new institution as a central bank. Others, such as Owen and Shafroth, believed that they had created a bank of banks, one in which the Reserve banks (within limits) would be servants of the member banks, while government regulation would be minimal. "Dealing with the amount of money, the paper to be discounted," Shafroth said, "is not a matter in which the Government can be interested." He maintained that the self-interest of bankers would be paramount in a system owned by them, and he argued that bankers should be directors of the Reserve banks but should not be on the Reserve Board.[92]

Some congressmen believed the new system would create the kind of organization that the antitrust laws were supposed to prevent. "This act," said Charles A. Lindbergh, Sr., of Minnesota, "establishes the most gigantic trust on earth, such as the Sherman Antitrust Act would dissolve if Congress did not by this act expressly create what by that act it prohibited."[93] This view contradicted the notion that the new institution would be analogous to a benign Interstate Commerce Commission.

Benjamin Bristow had a criticism similar to Lindbergh's. The bill, he said, "creates a great, top-heavy, organization . . . to provide a flexible currency. A few simple amendments to the Aldrich-Vreeland bill would have accomplished that purpose."[94]

Finally, was creation of the Federal Reserve System the result of a great popular democratic movement? No, answered George McLean of Connecticut. "The present haste to organize the banking system of the country is purely political. There is not one man in ten thousand who cares anything about the subject. . . . There is not one man in ten thousand who knows anything about principles or details of banking, and his ignorance in this regard is as natural and excusable as his ignorance of the Chinese language. If I am not mistaken, the alleged popular demand and need for this bill . . . are born of wishes, earnest, deep, and laudable, but purely political in their nature and of very doubtful fulfillment."[95]

McLean's statement, though true, is not the whole truth. Bankers were willing to accept such an institution, particularly one that would subsidize some of their risks by standing ready to discount their commercial paper; but they wanted such an agency only if they could control it. They did not want a system set up by a hostile Congress that would hamstring their enterprises. Since banking involves technical matters familiar only to bankers, it was natural for bankers to try to take charge of the central bank's operations even though central banking and commercial banking are based on some fundamentally contrary doctrines.[96]

The blind men touched the elephant and each one received a different impression of the animal's physical structure. In the case of the Federal Reserve System, the blind men constructed a machine. Their views of what they had created were as diverse as the impressions of the men who touched the elephant. They did not know what they had done. As Lindbergh concluded when he voted nay on final passage: "Congress is the greatest of humbugs."[97]

16 Summary of Central-Banking Development up to 1914

You set up a National Bank to watch the other banks; but who is to watch the watcher? Where there is but one watchman in a city, albeit the same be a most "grave and ancient watchman," yet does it generally happen, that he betaketh himself soon after twilight to the watch-house, and there most quietly and securely sleepeth out his watch, till his coat be stolen, or the city is set on fire with the candle from his own lanthorn. When it is well burning, and the engines are already at work, he opens his eyes at last, and bawls fire! as lustily as though he had been the first to make the discovery.

Is it not far better to dismiss the watchman, and so to arrange things that it shall be for the interest of the rogues to watch and betray each other's roguery.

Richard Hildreth, *History of Banks,* 1837

Stages of Political Control over the Production of Money

A money-using economy may experience widely different stages of monetary control: (1) No control at all; that is, a policy of complete laissez-faire with respect to money. (2) A metallic standard system in which the government legislates the legal tender value of the unit of account in terms of a precious metal but lets private coin-smiths produce the prescribed coins. (3) The same system, but one in which the government monopolizes the coinage of the monetary metals. (4) A metallic standard system, such as (3), on which is superimposed a central-banking institution that is strictly limited to short-run, seasonal policies. Finally, (5) a central bank standing by itself with complete discretionary control over the supply of money entering the economic system.

In the first stage, anyone can create money. The supply of money, however, would *not* degenerate into a hyperinflation. As long as markets work normally, anyone who offered money would have to be able to verify the real value of his money or he would find no demanders who would accept it. His attempt to print and issue money would be nothing more than a ridiculous charade.

For this reason the first moneys were commodities that had some monetary properties. Precious metals were good candidates to be money, because, when coined, they did not require an act of redemption to secure their value. They thereby avoided the redemption costs of token and ledger-credit moneys. Metallic currency, however, has coinage costs, the costs of transporting it, and depreciation of the coins from wear and tear. In time, institutional developments—banks—so reduced the redemption costs of fiduciary moneys that they became cheap enough to gain widespread use. While gold and silver were the customary media for redemption, anything that was mutually agreeable to both the issuer and the acceptor of the money could have been used.[1]

A monetary system of some sort would surely evolve in almost any kind of economic system for the same reason that round wheels, levers, and inclined planes appear in the industrial system. All these devices greatly reduce the real costs that are incurred without them. Since almost everyone's private interest is better served by a reliable monetary system than by a fraudulent one, the chances are also very high that repudiation and fraud, as well as depression and inflation, would be minimized in a monetary system grounded on private enterprise. Known examples of this kind tried strictly on libertarian terms are rare, although Radford's account of monetary devices used in a prisoner-of-war camp is well known.[2]

Nonetheless, almost no political authorities have permitted the laissez-faire stage of monetary existence to endure for any length of time. Even the most republican governments have begun with the second stage, in which a constitution declares that a certain item shall be legal tender, but provides no active role for government in the production of the designated money. Specification of the legal tender commodity is itself a significant act of government. It means that private persons must accept the monetary item (or items) as payment in satisfaction for outstanding debts. The U.S. Constitution gave Congress the power to establish standard values for monetary metals and to fix the standards of weights and measures.[3] It also gave Congress the power to coin the money it was to "regulate."[4]

Governmental monopoly over the coinage, but with commodity money standards still working more or less freely, constitutes the fourth stage of monetary evolution. In this stage a governmental or quasi-governmental institution issues media of exchange other than the items designated as legal tender. The monetary system becomes mixed. Nineteenth-century systems in the United States and England are good examples of this development. In both countries gold and silver originally provided the monetary base for ordinary bank currency and deposits. During the War of 1812 in the United States, treasury notes, which were a paper currency, first appeared as a temporary, partial legal tender, interest-bearing claim on the federal government. After the Civil War, the greenbacks became a permanent, full legal tender, non-interest-bearing currency.

England's experience was slightly different. The crown issued exchequer bills similar to United States treasury notes; but the Bank of England also issued Bank of England notes that became a much more conventional item in the monetary fabric. These notes were used as currency and as reserves by English commercial banks. The Bank of England thus assumed the characteristics of a central bank somewhat earlier than any of the quasi-central-banking institutions in the United States. Nonetheless, by 1914 the monetary systems of both countries included currency-issuing central banks whose policies, while deliberate and purposeful, were constrained by adherence to the rules of the operational gold standard.

The fifth stage of monetary control appears when governments abandon monetary rules, such as the self-regulating metallic standard, and grant a central-banking institution complete discretion over the management of the monetary system. This stage may include several substages; abandonment of metallic standard rules may be piecemeal. In any case, the ultimate metamorphosis of central banking has little to do with its origins.

Early English Experience with Paper-Money Issues under a Gold Standard

A gold standard does not require a central bank or any other form of governmental intervention. Because such a system is self-regulating, it requires attention only when an excess issue of some kind of governmental paper money has rendered it inoperative. The paper money raises prices and tends to raise the market price of the monetary gold as well. Ultimately, the market price of the gold separates from the mint price and a gold premium appears.

The most notorious and long-tenured departure of the English monetary system from its gold base occurred during the Napoleonic Wars, when bullion payments by the Bank of England were restricted (1797–1821) by an act of Parliament. The paper currency of the bank was not at first unduly overissued; the government adopted the restriction policy in 1797 in anticipation of trouble. Once freed from the discipline of having to convert its notes into specie and having only the real-bills doctrine to govern its actions, even as staid an organization as the Bank of England eventually issued enough paper currency to increase prices substantially.[5]

The displacement of specie with paper money in England after 1797 did not provoke any great theories of policy control for some years. One reason was that the Bank of England did not abuse the largess that Parliament had granted it. Its new powers appeared temporary both to the bank and to government officials—an expedient to be endured (or enjoyed) only for a limited time. But when Parliament extended the tenure of indulgence, the sense of inhibition waned, and so did the anticipation of an early return to specie payments. Contemporary inquiry then turned to fundamental monetary questions. What caused the inflation in the first place? How should an inconvertible paper currency be managed? To these questions Henry Thornton, an exemplary economist of the early nineteenth century, gave enduring answers.[6]

Henry Thornton's Norms for Bank of England Policy

By the time Thornton wrote, the Bank of England was the prototype of hybrid central banks. It carried on a private banking business for profit, and it acted as a bank for the government. Its public feature—its responsibility to make payments for the English government on demand—meant that it had to maintain a sizable coin reserve. It had become, in Thornton's words, "a reservoir of gold to which private banks [could] resort with little difficulty . . . for the supply of their several necessities." But it had no source to which it could turn "for a supply of guineas proportioned to its wants in the same manner."[7] It had become a reserve-holding institution, and this unanticipated role gave it its central-banking potential.

Thornton did not apply the label *central bank* to the Bank of England. He first defined it as a public bank, a public servant, "completely subject to [the public] interest." In another context he noted its commercial character. "The Bank of England," he wrote, "like every other mercantile establishment, carries on its business on such principles as will produce a profit."[8] Its public character, he thought, should expand at a time of alarm or panic into a policy-making role. It should become what is *now* known as a central bank.

A public bank—one that acted as a fiscal agent for the government—could also function as a commercial bank; but a central bank that was also a profit-seeking mercantile corporation would have difficulty. A central bank must expand loans and discounts and extend its accommodations even in the face of declining commercial confidence and business activity, while a commercial bank does just the opposite. The conflict between these two roles was apparent in Thornton's comment about the bank's activities during one of "the late seasons of alarm." By restricting its notes during the panic, Thornton wrote, the bank "aggravated, perhaps, rather than lessened, the demand upon itself for [gold] guineas. . . . It is clear, at least, that it did not . . . succeed by the diminution of its notes in curing the evil which it thus aimed to remedy."[9]

The directors of the Bank of England talked and behaved as though the bank were exclusively commercial and public. When a crisis threatened, they could then justify reductions of their paper-currency liabilities according to established commercial banking tradition.

As a detached and disinterested observer, Thornton could suggest that at such times they should expand rather than contract their outstanding paper currency. That "the paramount duty of the Bank of England [is] to diminish its notes, in some sort of regular proportion to that diminution which it experiences in gold," he advised, "is . . . an idea which is merely theoretic." He admitted the necessity for long-run restriction of notes outstanding to protect the coin reserve. But in the short run, when the panic itself was the immediate problem, he found several reasons for increasing paper-money issues. The first reason was to check the alarm. Since Bank of England notes acted as reserves for the London banks, their maintenance was essential to promote confidence. Once a panic gained headway, the bank's restriction of its notes would lead to a burgeoning demand for gold.[10]

The second reason for maintaining moderate note issues was to prevent a contraction that might hurt production and income more than it would inhibit spending. If output fell more than prices, the crisis would worsen. Lags in the effects of policy would also contribute to this undesirable consequence.[11]

At this stage in his argument Thornton specified important central-banking norms. Gold, he observed, might well flow out of the country due to an unfavorable balance of trade. But the Bank of England for a time and to a certain extent should permit this condition to continue even though the gold leaving the country would be "drawn out of [the bank's] own coffers: and it must, in that case, necessarily increase its loans [and notes] to the same extent to which its gold is diminished."[12] Only a central bank could act this way; a commercial bank would have to do just the opposite, that is, contract its credit and notes in the event of a specie outflow.

Thornton's summary of central-bank doctrine included five principles for Bank of England policy:

1. Limit the total amount of paper issued by credit rationing, or by what could be called the "hard look" loan. (Here it is *this* time; but watch your accounts closely, for there might not be enough to go around next time.)
2. Let the sum of bank notes in circulation "vibrate only within certain limits."
3. Allow a slow and cautious extension of paper currency as the general trade of the kingdom increases.
4. Allow a temporary increase in currency "in the event of any extraordinary alarm or difficulty, as the best means of preventing a great *demand* at home for guineas."
5. However, "lean to the side of diminution, in the case of gold going abroad, and of the general exchanges continuing long unfavorable."[13]

Thornton's extensive prescriptions did something that had not been done up to this time. They answered in some detail the question: What could be the role of a central bank operating within the framework of a specie standard? Any answer except "nothing" had to modify the notion of exclusive control by a self-regulating specie standard. Thornton's principles centered around the desirable results that could result from Bank of England issues of paper money to alleviate short-term stress in financial markets, even though he recognized the traditional wisdom and practical necessity of following the rule of the gold standard in the long run.

Early Experience in the United States with Government Paper Money

The monetary system in the United States was subjected during the War of 1812 to the same kind of paper-money inflation that England experienced throughout the Napoleonic Wars. Governmental issues of paper money in the United States were in the form of treasury notes rather than issues by a public bank; but both English and American notes were tenders for all debts and payments to and from the government. The American experience also covered a shorter period of time; all the paper money was issued between 1812 and 1815, and all of it was retired by 1817. During the contraction that followed the inflation, the economy went through all the usual withdrawal symptoms—falling prices, general liquidation, and unemployment.[14]

Resumption of specie payments in the United States occurred in 1819. Just when it was all but accomplished, Congress sent a resolution to the secretary of the Treasury, William H. Crawford, asking for his opinions on norms for the monetary system. Crawford, like most nineteenth-century policymakers, regarded a mixed currency as a pragmatic necessity. The paper money, he noted, was very much in existence and could only be replaced by "the delivery [from foreign countries] of an equal amount of gold or silver." Such an event was not likely. But if the banks judiciously extended paper money based on specie, a workable mixed-currency system could endure. Government issues of paper money, Crawford argued properly, had to be rejected because he doubted "whether a sovereign power over the coinage necessarily gives the right to establish a paper currency." A reasonable doubt of its constitutionality would mar the most ingenious paper-money system. Specie, he noted, tended to preserve a greater uniformity of value than any other commodity, and was recommended by "the facility with which it returns to that value, whenever, by temporary causes, that uniformity has been interrupted."[15]

Crawford had read Thornton and was well informed on the monetary experience of England. He attributed England's inflation to the "will of nearly four hundred banks . . . when released from all restraint against excessive issues." He dismissed the excessive issues of treasury notes in the United States by means of outrageous taxonomy: "By the term currency," he wrote, meaning *metallic* money, "the issue of paper by Government, as a financial resource, is excluded."[16] In other words, the late issues of treasury notes were not currency and therefore could not have contributed to the inflation just ended! Despite his unwillingness to recognize the fundamental role the Treasury had played in the inflation, Crawford did not make the mistake of casting the new Second Bank of the United States in any kind of regulatory role. A bank-generated inflation had occurred. It had been whipped by an austere fiscal policy. The gold standard was once again operational. And that was that.

Central-Banking Features of the Banks of the United States

Central-banking practices of the First and Second Banks of the United States differed somewhat in detail from the operations of the Bank of England. Whereas the Bank of England regulated the monetary system by extending or contracting accommodation directly to the London bill brokers, the Second Bank of the United States adopted as its primary method of control deliberate regulation over the flow of commercial bank notes that came through its offices. If it wished to retard the progress of loans and investments by the state banks, it presented state bank notes for redemption in specie to the banks that had issued them. If it felt that the pace of business activity was satisfactory, it paid out the state bank notes routinely. If it wanted to speed up financial activity, it encouraged the state banks to go into debt to it. By this last means it actively increased the general stock of money, for its own notes were legal tender for all debts due to and claims on the government and were widely used as bank reserves.[17]

A special feature of Second Bank policy was the means by which it ameliorated the shock of an external gold drain. A change in the exchange rate was its signal for action. When the rate changed, the bank intervened to modify the change by using its own gold, by enlarging its credit with its English correspondents (Baring Brothers), and by tightening accommodations to its customers.[18]

Bray Hammond ably documented the central-banking character of the Second Bank. "The Bank," he wrote, "performed these functions deliberately and avowedly—with a consciousness of quasi-governmental responsibility and of the need to subordinate profit and private interest to that responsibility."[19] Clearly, Hammond's description fits the necessary condition for central banking—that a regulatory function be conducted consciously and purposefully.

The evidence is conclusive that the Bank of England and the Banks of the United States performed as central banks. But to allow this much is not to confirm or admit that a "quasi-governmental responsibility" was vested in either institution. Indeed, ample evidence shows that Congress at the inception of the Banks of the United States specifically discouraged, if it did not outright prohibit, such activity. The First and Second Banks nonetheless became recognizable central banks; and this development inspired Jacob Viner in his analysis of Bank of England policy and Hammond in his treatment of Second Bank policy to make the fundamental error of imputing to both institutions central-banking functions that were not theirs. Both writers seemed to assume that because these institutions initiated certain central-banking activities, some sort of implicit governmental sanction *must* have been granted. Viner, for example, furnished the following judgment: "From about 1800 to about 1860 the Bank of England almost continuously displayed an inexcusable degree of incompetence or unwillingness to fulfill the requirements *which could reasonably be demanded of a central bank*."[20] Hammond, after quoting Viner's passage approvingly, reviewed the sophisticated policies of the Second Bank after 1825 and observed how crude the Jacksonian program was that destroyed the bank. Without elaboration or substantiation he claimed that the Second Bank faced a central-banking responsibility, that Nicholas Biddle, the bank's most famous president, accepted this charge forthrightly, and that this duty "was not stumbled upon as in England. . . . The Bank [was] the one effective means of meeting the federal government's responsibility, under the Constitution, for the circulating medium." That is, if the federal government was going to "regulate" the value of coin, it had to have a central bank as an enabling agency: "The idea that the Federal Bank regulated the monetary supply in accordance with the Constitution's assignment of powers made no appeal to people who did not see that bank credit was part of the monetary supply, or, if they did see, were unwilling to have it regulated."[21]

Hammond's statement and Viner's similar implication about the Bank of England are blatant misinterpretations. The Constitution says nothing about deliberate regulation of the money supply by *any* institution. In fact, it says nothing at all about money, except that Congress shall have the power to "regulate," i.e., specify, the monetary value of the metallic commodity designated to be legal tender coin.

Nor do the charters of the First and the Second Banks of the United States imply or assert any such conscious and deliberate regulation. The constitutional basis on which lawmakers established the First and Second Banks was the provision allowing Congress to lay and collect taxes.[22] The central-banking activities and powers subsequently seen in the policies of these two banks grew out of the public fiscal functions for which Congress chartered them. To allege that the banks were created in the image of the control that they came to assume, when no explicit evidence can be adduced to support such an argument, is an obvious fallacy of *post hoc, ergo propter hoc*.

Frank W. Fetter made a similar observation about the Bank of England. Its central-banking qualities, he wrote, were unbestowed and unanticipated. It was not established in 1694

> to perform "central banking functions." . . . [The] development of the note issues of the Bank of England into an important part of the total currency supply, and the use of their notes and deposits as the form in which other banks held reserves, took place so surely, but so gradually, that by 1797 institutional realities no longer squared with legal provisions or expressed beliefs. The events of 1793 and 1797 had made clear . . . that with a system of fractional reserve banking some agency—either the Bank [of England] or the Government—must assume responsibility in time of crisis.[23]

Though Fetter's statement excuses the presence of the Bank of England as a central bank on the grounds of necessity, it also confirms that neither Parliament nor the Crown deliberately created the bank to be a central bank.

In the "long-run," the Bank of England endured, but the federal government's connection to the Banks of the United States ended when Congress allowed their charters to expire. Hammond conjectured that the Second Bank did not try "to avoid acknowledgement of its principal purposes and *raison d'etre* or pretend that its accomplishments in the public interest were incidental to the conduct of its private business. . . . Perhaps, the Bank of England owed its survival somewhat to its shirking [*sic*] the responsibility and to its reticence, for the interests that wished to annihilate it differed little from their American counterparts."[24]

When Nicholas Biddle realized the antipathy of the Jacksonian forces to regulation, he tried to compromise. But he was too late. The movement against the Second Bank did not distinguish between the regulatory function that the bank had assumed and the ordinary and innocuous commercial and fiscal functions it had been granted. The Jacksonians did not have the sophistication or the incentive to understand this difference, so they simply obliterated the whole institution. The Bank of England, although subjected to many investigations and some of the same hostile sentiment, was more diplomatic. By insisting that it filled the central-banking role gratuitously, it avoided most of the political chastisement that assumption of central-banking norms would have unleashed on it.[25] It is well written: "Whosoever exalteth himself shall be abased; and he that humbleth himself shall be exalted" (Luke 14:1).

Monetary Policies of the Independent Treasury

The formation of the Independent Treasury (IT) system in the United States in 1846 seemed to mark a departure from previous financial frameworks in both the United States and England. The IT was clearly a reaction to and a rejection of the Second Bank/Bank of England type of regulatory control. It called on the Treasury Department to keep its own revenue balances and to use only specie or its own notes for government disbursements. The act was frequently referred to as the "divorce of bank and state."

The Bank of England was similarly constrained. Palmer's Rule of 1832, which required the bank to increase or decrease its issues of paper notes in accordance with external specie movements, was a rejection of discretionary regulatory control. The Act of 1844 (Peel's Act), which separated the bank into the Issue and Banking departments, was another step in the same direction.[26]

The Independent Treasury kept its own cash and made its own payments through subtreasury offices. As long as its expenditures were greater than or equal to its receipts, it could not build up a cash balance with which to nudge the monetary system. During the gold-inspired commercial boom of the 1850s, however, specie balances accumulated in the Treasury and were disbursed by Secretary Guthrie through purchases of government securities in the open market.

Although Guthrie and some of his predecessors carried out significant monetary policies before 1860, very little central-banking doctrine as such accompanied Treasury policies. The specie standard seemed to discourage discretionary monetary experiments. The policies that occurred were primarily circumstantial. They were appropriate at the time in order to disburse residual cash balances that resulted from unforeseen fiscal surpluses.

The real opportunities for central-banking innovation became much more favorable when the federal government suspended specie payments in 1862. The U.S. monetary system then operated on an inconvertible paper standard until 1879. Contraction of the stock of paper money after the Civil War seemed the most straightforward answer to the inflation that the paper money had created. But this diet was too austere for public tolerance, and Congress discontinued it in 1868.

Secretaries of the Treasury during the suspension used the Treasury's balances of gold and greenbacks to influence the monetary system. Even such an avowed contractionist as Secretary McCulloch argued for discretionary manipulation of the Treasury's gold balance to discourage "conspiracies" that might attempt "to bring about fluctuations [in the price of gold] for purely speculative reasons." He also acknowledged the use of the gold as an open-market device "to prevent commercial panics."[27]

Monetary control arose primarily because the paper currency was not redeemable in specie. If common money was not redeemable, the monetary system could not be self-regulating. If it was not self-regulating, someone had to regulate it—Congress ideally, but the Treasury Department practically and realistically.

The abandonment of the contraction policy in 1868 coincided with the appointment of George Boutwell as secretary of the Treasury. Boutwell's administrative experience with the existing irredeemable paper currency prompted him to favor a certain amount of discretionary policy. He saw no reserve in the private economy that could provide seasonal elasticity, a new norm for the monetary system. He concluded that the Treasury Department should have the power to alter the volume of paper currency in circulation in order to take care of this problem.[28]

After his election to the Senate in 1873 Boutwell presented another extensive argument for the Treasury's central-banking powers. He commented on the flow of currency to New York City in the summer and the difficulty of getting it back in the fall. Elasticity of the currency in commercial countries tended to be perverse, he claimed, "without special intervention from the [monetary] authorities." He also discussed in considerable detail the Bank of England's general policy for insuring elasticity. The policy was not automatic but required official intervention.

To several queries about the extent of Treasury responsibility, Boutwell replied that the Treasury should keep the real relationship between debtor and creditor undisturbed, by which he implied the goal of a stable price level. The means of effecting this responsibility, he argued, was Treasury discretion to issue temporarily the $44 million of greenbacks in the "reserve" and to maintain permanently the statutory minimum stock of $356 million.[29]

Despite Boutwell's arguments, Congress resisted all schemes that would have thwarted the progress of the monetary system toward resumption of specie payments. It also rejected any further discretion for the secretary of the Treasury in monetary affairs. So the system functioned until resumption with neither a bank nor a treasury department acting as a central bank.

Resumption occurred on schedule in 1879, but it did not return the U.S. monetary system to its 1860 status. By this time the quantities of United States notes, national bank notes, coined silver, and silver certificates either were already significant or would become so during the next decade. Since the federal government guaranteed redemption of all these currencies in gold, the monetary system remained mixed and subject to Treasury policy in the short run. In the long run the international gold standard was again operational.

In England the same mixture of paper money and gold prevailed. However, the only paper currency of consequence there was Bank of England notes. Therefore, Bank of England policy together with the gold standard ruled the British monetary system.

Bank of England Policy after 1844 and Bagehot's Prescriptions

The most famous treatise on central-banking doctrine to appear in the latter half of the nineteenth century was Walter Bagehot's analysis of Bank of England policies. Bagehot's book, *Lombard Street,*[30] appeared some seventy years after Henry Thornton's *Paper Credit.* It was written when the pound sterling was the kingpin currency of the trading world and in no danger of sustained suspension.

The major governmental policy applicable to the bank at this time was still the Bank Act of 1844, which separated the Bank of England into the Issue and Banking departments. The Issue Department did nothing but regulate the volume of Bank of England notes. The maximum amount it could issue was equal to the sum of its gold bullion holdings plus £15 million in government securities. Since the bank earned interest from the securities, it had every inducement to keep its portfolio close to the maximum. Gold flows then altered the currency in practical accord with the currency principle, which argued that a paper currency should be managed so it would behave as if it were strictly metallic.

The Banking Department was the prototype for all hybrid central banks. It was commercial in its dealings with discount houses and bill brokers; it was a public bank because of its fiscal relationship to the government; and it was at times a central bank in the ad hoc manner typical of that era.[31] Despite the obvious public interest that the bank maintained, as exemplified by its significant policy actions in 1847, 1857, and 1866, its directors never acknowledged its central-banking functions and frequently denied them. Parliamentary committees and government officials also made similar disclaimers. Bagehot observed that these denials strained a reasonable man's credulity, and also hampered policy initiative in times of crisis. The bank might do the right thing and make advances to the money market despite a commercial predisposition to do just the opposite; but under such circumstances it could not carry out its relief policies to their best advantage.[32]

Bagehot documented his criticisms by referring to a controversy between the *Economist* newsweekly and one of the principal directors of the bank, Mr. Thomson Hankey. (Since Bagehot was the editor of the *Economist,* he was simply citing his own arguments.) The article in the *Economist* analyzed the bank's actions during the panic in the spring of 1866. It observed that the bank had used its reserve with commendable discretion when it made advances to the other banks during the panic and that the governor of the bank, Mr. David Salomons, had admitted as much at a recent proprietors' meeting.[33]

Mr. Salomons's remarks indeed implied that the bank had a central-banking facet. While other banks were seeking accommodation, the Bank of England was granting it. "I am not aware that any legitimate application made for assistance to this house was refused," Mr. Salomons stated firmly; "and if accommodation could not be afforded to the full extent which was demanded, no one who offered proper security failed to obtain [some] relief from this house."[34]

Bagehot (via the *Economist*) considered this statement a clear admission of responsibility. The directors of the bank disagreed. Their spokesman for the rebuttal, Mr. Thomson Hankey, offered what might be called the fair-share doctrine of central banking: "I consider it to be the undoubted duty of the Bank of England," he stated, "in the event of a sudden pressure in the Money Market . . . to bear its full share of a drain on its resources." This deposition was not to admit that the bank should retain unemployed cash to meet such an emergency. "The more the conduct of the affairs of the Bank is made to assimilate to the conduct of every other well-managed bank in the United Kingdom," he concluded brusquely, "the better for the Bank, and the better for the community at large."[35]

Hankey's implication that the bank's commercial character gave it its only responsibility—returning a profit to its stockholders—was clearly inconsistent with the bank's actual practices over many decades. His contention that the bank should not admit to a central-banking function was on firmer ground.

If the bank were to advertise the retention of a reserve to meet panics, he argued in a more comprehensive work, knowledge of this fact would presuppose its necessity: The availability of a reserve would encourage laxity and prodigality in the discounting policies of other commercial banks. In the twentieth century the reality of this condition has come to be known as the "moral hazard problem." Another argument against such a policy, he stated, was that it would require someone with discretion to authorize its use and some recognizable signal for taking positive action. His only prescription for policy was that the bank should not lend below the market rate of interest.[36]

Bagehot did not deal directly with these latter points. He only replied that Hankey's disclaimer put the whole question of policy during a crisis in an "unsatisfactory and uncertain condition. . . . Mr. Hankey leaves us in doubt altogether," Bagehot remonstrated, "as to what will be the policy of the Bank of England in the next panic, and as to what amount of aid the public may then expect from it. His words are too vague. No one can tell what a 'fair share' means; still less can we tell what other people at some future time will say it means."[37]

Bagehot then prescribed his explicit rules for central-bank behavior during a panic. First, the gold reserve should be advanced freely and promptly. Second, the advances should be made only at very high rates of interest. The high rates, he felt, would "operate as a heavy fine on unreasonable timidity," and would ration the limited reserves among the most eager demanders in the same way that a high price rations any scarce commodity in a free market. Third, the attitude of the bank should be to make advances, not on "good" securities, but on securities that would be good under normal conditions. To reject bad bills or bad securities would do no harm; this class of securities was small and would be rejected even in prosperous times. "But if securities, really good and usually convertible, are refused by the Bank," he warned, "the alarm will not abate, the other loans made will fail in obtaining their end, and the panic will become worse and worse." Should the bank find its reserves depleted before it stopped the panic, then it would simply have to run before the wind in fashion similar to ordinary commercial banks. "The only safe plan for the Bank," he emphasized, "is the brave plan. . . . This policy may not save the bank; but if it does not, nothing will save it."[38]

Bagehot's prescriptions were at least compatible, and often identical, with Thornton's. Both observed that Bank of England notes, not gold coin or bullion, were the principal reserve currency and the currency that should be supplied in a panic to satisfy an internal drain. Both emphasized the necessity of extending credit early in a panic—in contrast to the normal reaction of commercial banks, which would be to restrict credit. Central-bank issues of paper money, both believed, would temporarily restrain the external gold drains that might occur because of unfavorable expectations.

No official documents record that Bagehot's crusade was a success. But it was. As Fetter concluded, "The Bank, although officially silent, was taking to heart the advice of Bagehot, and the ever increasing importance of deposit banking made it less likely that the special note issue restriction . . . would present any problems."[39]

Pre–Federal Reserve Monetary Developments in the United States

Central-banking doctrine that calls for active intervention by a monetary authority makes little headway in the presence of an automatic, self-regulating specie standard. Consequently, the United States' resumption of specie payments in 1879 retarded the trend toward what Boutwell had expounded as the personal intervention of men possessing power.

Resumption retarded this trend, but the free-silver movement and the government's silver-purchase programs kept it going. After 1878, the federal government monetized silver in limited quantities at a mint price that was at a greater and greater premium over the market price. Silver was also on that account a currency that yielded important seigniorage revenues to the government, and it was therefore in the same class as greenbacks. It was a fiat government issue, kept in circulation by legal tender provisions, and redeemable in gold at the Treasury. Whereas greenbacks were 100 percent fiat, silver was 3 percent to 45 percent fiat. But this difference was inconsequential. If currency is legal tender, it circulates at its monetary value as long as its commodity value is lower.

Throughout the Silver Era (1878–1893) Congress wrote its own monetary policies. Most of these policies attempted to use silver as the vehicle for altering the quantity of money, although one secretary, Charles Fairchild, deliberately deposited Treasury balances in national banks in order to stimulate lending and business activity. Fairchild's action received much censure from Congress as well as from the next secretary, William Windom, who gradually reversed the policy until all the Treasury's balances were again in its own offices.[40]

The use of silver as a policy vehicle finally ended in 1893. When the chips were down and the gold standard seemed threatened by silver-purchase policies, President Cleveland and Congress destandardized silver. Gold formally became the only standard in 1900. The supply of gold increased throughout the commercial world after 1896 due to new discoveries and technological advances in refining gold ore.

The gold boom at the turn of the century had the same effect on U.S. Treasury receipts as the one in the 1850s. The large excess reserves that accumulated in Treasury and subtreasury offices between 1902 and 1906 provoked overt policy actions by Secretary Leslie Shaw. His major policy was the deposit of the Treasury's excess balances in national banks in the fall to encourage a seasonal expansion of the money supply—the same policy that had received so much congressional criticism fifteen years earlier. Treasury balances were then allowed to reaccumulate in Treasury offices during the following winter.

Academicians, politicians, and journalists were almost unanimous in condemning Shaw's policies, even though Shaw argued that he assumed this power only in response to the major monetary problem of the time—lack of seasonal elasticity in the money supply. Shaw had no quarrel with the gold standard; in fact, he was one of its champions. Neither did he try to influence the secular growth in the stock of money. His policy was limited to placing Treasury balances strategically in order to prevent panics and crises arising from temporary technical stringencies in bank-created credit.[41] He proposed a supplemental bank-issued currency capable of immediate and widespread issue. The massive amount of work involved in evaluating the collateral the banks offered for Treasury deposits, he thought, argued for the note-issuing job to be done wholly by the commercial banks. The additional currency would be retired routinely and promptly once "the demand therefore ceases."[42]

The Treasury had managed the greenbacks before resumption. After resumption it kept a discretionary gold balance as a reserve for a fixed quantity of greenbacks and a declining volume of national bank notes. It bought silver to be coined. Through the comptroller of the currency, it administered the national banking system. It managed the sinking fund for bond redemptions. With all these powers, it logically could assume some extraordinary powers, for example, the deposit of Treasury balances in national banks. Thus the Independent Treasury Act of 1846 that was designed to take the Treasury out of policy and politics came full circle sixty years later. By 1906 the Treasury was more a central bank in its deliberate attempts to influence the monetary system than the Second Bank had ever been.

Such intervention and discretion again proved unpopular. But this time Congress could not retreat to an independent treasury system because the Independent Treasury itself was the offending institution. Besides, bank panics and crises of recent decades seemed to demonstrate the need for fundamental reform. So a more sophisticated institution was conceived—the Federal Reserve System.

Creation of the Federal Reserve banks was in part a reaction to the Treasury policies that Shaw had developed. Equally important was the anticipation that the new system would promote form-seasonal elasticity in the money supply—the monetary problem publicized by many economists and politicians, and by Boutwell and Shaw at the policy level—not through the discretion of a government official, but on the initiative of commercial bankers themselves through a supercommercial (Federal Reserve) bank. The emphasis shifted from discretionary policy by a government agency to automatic and self-regulatory policy in the market. Indeed, the early Federal Reserve System, operating on a real-bills principle and on the doctrine of maintaining its discount rate above market rates of interest, was to be a self-regulating appendage to a more fundamental self-regulating system—the operational gold standard.[43]

One can argue that Congress in fashioning the Federal Reserve System was far from single-valued about either the means or the ends of policy. However, congressmen offered no arguments that would have had the new institution usurp the functions of the gold standard. In giving the Federal Reserve only limited powers, Congress did not feel the need to constrain the Fed's policies with explicit rules and goals.

Power was always the issue of central-bank existence, and the consensus of polity during the nineteenth century was a rejection of power for government institutions. Virtually every central-banking institution that emerged during this period had its powers limited either by the act creating it or by implications in the arguments of its founders. Whenever Congress became aware of central-banking discretion, it undertook legislative initiatives to deny such power. Only in the twentieth century have the constitutional restraints on the power of central-banking institutions been abandoned in favor of centralized discretionary authority.

The Formal Emergence of Central Banks as Lenders of Last Resort

Central banking was not primarily the evolution of a sophisticated theory on the management of money. Rather, it was a circumstantial emergence—an "unpredicted appearance of new characteristics in the course of . . . social evolution."[44] The central-banking function appeared because the financial environment in which banking institutions operated favored its development, and because circumstances such as a bank crisis, a depression, or a war thrust these institutions into new roles.

The creation of a Bank of the United States, or for that matter a Bank of England, was no more than governmental chartering of a commercial banking institution that would also act as a banker for the government. Such an institution was first a commercial bank and second a public bank, and that was all so far as its founders were concerned. Its status as the government's bank suggested and encouraged its intervention in monetary affairs. Numerous currencies—diverse currencies issued by many different banks—went through its hands, and the magnitude of its branch operations as the government's depository set it apart from other commercial banks.

In practice the government-sponsored bank made loans to the government, otherwise assisted in fiscal operations, and kept the government's balances. Because government balances were often sizable, the bank also felt some public responsibility to assist ordinary commercial banks at times of crisis, an action that enlarged its public banking function into a central-banking function. Since crises were infrequent and random while public fiscal actions and the necessity for commercial profit were routine and constant, the commercial-public bank functions dominated its activities. The central-banking role was as infrequent, but also as spectacular, as the appearance of a new comet in the night sky.

A bank panic or liquidity crisis immediately thrust the commercial-public institution into prominence because it had the only reserves that could save anyone and everyone. However, the institution's managers usually had little experience with or precedent for undertaking positive and sophisticated policies. In fact, what they had to do to offset panics and restrain crises was contrary to all their commercial banking instincts. As commercial bankers they confined loans, discounts, and advances to paper that promised a very low risk of default. In a bank crisis no such paper is available. The very nature of a crisis turns good paper—that is, short-term, self-liquidating, bona fide loans—into highly questionable "investments." In addition, a nineteenth-century quasi-central-bank had to restrain itself during prosperous periods from lending on all good paper, which would have maximized its earning assets, so that it would have some reserves to parlay among commercial banks when they were threatened by liquidity drains. When a panic occurred, the now-central bank had to lean into the wind, and, as Bagehot prescribed, lend on what might be called subjunctive paper—paper that *would be* good when general business conditions were again normal. Thus, the commercial-public-central bank had to be more conservative than its fellows during a boom, and radical to the point of foolhardiness in a crisis! No wonder the directors of these institutions had such difficulty afterward explaining their operations to governmental investigating committees. Central-banking policies could never be rationalized by recourse to commercial banking principles.

This explanation does not cover the Independent Treasury. It obviously was not a commercial bank by any definition, but it was the government's depository, and it shared at least one feature with institutions such as the Bank of England and the Second Bank of the United States. It kept the financial accounts of the government, and from time to time had a workable reserve of high-powered money. Here was common ground—the existence of a strategic monetary stock that could be used to shore up financial weak spots at critical times. Whereas the commercial-public bank faced the disagreeable prospect of using its uncommitted reserves on questionable paper under unfavorable circumstances, Treasury officials had only to repurchase government securities previously issued that had little or no profit-and-loss characteristics.

The Independent Treasury's strategic position for carrying out countercyclical policies was fairly good even if it did not try to do so—even if it acted only as a good fiscal housekeeper. For when a business downturn developed, receipts to the Treasury would fall off and a fiscal deficit would appear. To cover this deficit the Treasury could either disburse specie balances, accumulated from tax revenues when business had been prosperous, or persuade Congress to authorize an issue of treasury notes. In either case, it added high-powered money to the system. Secretaries of the Treasury might then assume the credit for having taken the initiative to relieve a panic or prevent a crisis; but simple fiscal necessities would have obtained the same response from any pedestrian administrator.

When a gold boom occurred, the increase in business activity resulted in greater Treasury receipts than expenditures. The fiscal surplus then formed a balance in the Treasury that could be used in a subsequent downturn. In fact, no tightfisted Congress of that era would authorize any new government debt while the Treasury still had substantial cash balances.

Such a treasury/central bank was not technically incompatible with a gold standard, nor was a Bank of England or a Second Bank of the United States. All these institutions could operate as central banks, but only within a limited scope and for short periods. Too pervasive or too chronic a depression would deplete the central institution's gold reserves, leaving it impotent, and returning the gold standard to dominance. Prices, wages, incomes, and the stock of ordinary money would decline until the price level and its supporting money stock were again compatible with the operating equilibrium of the gold standard. Falling prices would encourage new discoveries and better exploitation of the precious metals, because falling commodity prices increased the real value of gold. But this solution could not be expected to furnish short-run relief.

The intellectual weakness of the Independent Treasury was its lack of a real-bills connection to the stock of money. Its relationship to the money market was based on government bonds issued because of fiscal necessities as long-term investments rather than as short-term, self-liquidating securities to encourage the production and marketing of real goods. A treasury/central bank was thus toxic to the belief that the production of goods generated money. The organization of the Federal Reserve System in place of the Independent Treasury was the overt manifestation of the ascendancy of the real-bills doctrine to policy-making eminence.

The clearinghouse system, which arose spontaneously as privately managed bankers' associations, was yet another means for treating the instability that developed at times from overextended bank credit and extensive government legal restrictions on banks. It was critically different from the other central-banking institutions on at least three counts: First, it was initially market-inspired as a means of reducing the costs of banking. Second, it was a private response rather than a governmental intervention, and worked through private incentives. Third, it used no previously accumulated reserves, although, if properly endowed with legal powers, it could have encouraged the banks to use their "required" reserves more exhaustively.

Clearinghouses made the existing payments system work more efficiently. Subsequently, they developed a means of containing a bank-credit collapse by restricting the payout of high-powered money—gold and other legal tender—and by issuing their "inferior," but nonetheless transactable, clearinghouse loan certificates.

The new Federal Reserve Act took the ball away from the clearinghouses and put it in the hands of a system of supercommercial Federal Reserve banks. This new system had governmental oversight, but it was touted as privately owned and managed in the image of the clearinghouse system it had replaced. Its original formation provides a vantage point for evaluating its subsequent evolution into an omnipotent institution with complete control over the monetary system.

17 The Real-Bills Era of the Federal Reserve System

> If for any reason—and God grant it may never be so—these boards of control [in the twelve Federal Reserve banks and the Board of Governors] should lack the wisdom and the courage to do their duty, we would still be subject to all the disasters that now befall us, because of the fact that the control is not wisely exercised.
>
> Rep. Charles Korbly, *Congressional Record* 50, 10 September 1913

Institutional Predecessors of the Federal Reserve System

The monetary system of the pre–Federal Reserve era was supposed to lack form-seasonal elasticity, that is, the ability at critical times to convert one form of money into another without causing undue change in the total quantity of money. The role of the gold standard, which was the dominant monetary institution of the time, was to provide a rate of growth in the quantity of base money compatible with the rate of growth in the economy's real output. The gold flow, however, could not be expected to make short-run adjustments for problems that developed fundamentally from the workings of the fractional reserve banking system.

The Federal Reserve System was supposed to provide the payments system with the desired characteristic of monetary elasticity. Conventional accounts then have presumed that the Fed has forthrightly pursued monetary-economic goals in an environment of political independence, even though buffeted at times by adverse circumstances over which it had no control.

This picture of the Fed's institutional beginnings slights several factual elements of the Fed's ancestry and the financial environment into which the new system was cast. Most important of all, it ignores the characteristics the Fed acquired as a political institution.

The pre-Fed monetary and banking system featured four institutions: (1) an operational gold standard providing secular growth in the economy's stock of money; (2) a national banking system, which acted in part as a reserve depository for non-national banks; (3) an "independent" Treasury that occasionally manipulated its fiscal balances to effect changes in the reserves of the banking system; and (4) a private clearinghouse system that was instrumental in extending the media used for payments when the banking system was threatened with critical drains of reserves. Of these institutions, the gold standard and the national banking system were regarded as acceptable but inadequate. The Independent Treasury was seen as having assumed undesirable interventionist characteristics, while the clearinghouse system was viewed as a haphazard and illegal makeshift. The Federal Reserve Act, therefore, was an attempt to combine and channel the powers then exercised by the Treasury and clearinghouses into a formally structured institution that would be at once legitimate, independent, scientific, federated, and efficient.

Congress intended the Federal Reserve System to be a self-regulating adjunct to a self-regulating gold standard. The Fed was to do at short term what the gold standard did secularly, namely, to provide seasonal money commensurate with seasonal productions of commodities. It would also become a system-wide clearing operation for banks; and it would take over the erstwhile clearinghouse function of issuing "emergency" currency in a crisis, and put it on an official, legal basis.

The Role of the Federal Reserve Board of Governors

The original Federal Reserve Act envisioned the cooperation of the twelve Federal Reserve banks, with the Federal Reserve Board as overseer and adjudicator. The plan included Federal Reserve agents, who acted as representatives of the Board at the Federal Reserve banks to which they were "accredited." Their function was to ensure that Reserve banks performed according to law.[1] The Board as early as November 1914 addressed a letter to all of its agents advising them to read the real-bills principle to their respective banks. Lending policy, specified the letter, required the banks to "confine [discounts] to short-term, self-liquidating paper growing out of actual commercial, industrial and agricultural operations, in the restrictive senses of the terms, and . . . particular care [should] be taken not to discount or purchase paper which had been issued primarily for the purpose of providing capital investment for any business."[2] This advice was in explicit accordance with Section 13 of the Federal Reserve Act, which prohibited the Fed banks from "trading in stocks, bonds, or other investment securities, except bonds and notes of the Government of the United States."[3] This exception, noted the report, was elaborated in Section 14 of the Act, in which the Reserve banks were given authority to purchase U.S. government securities "within the limits of prudence, as they might see fit," but only when Reserve bank reserves were not employed for their principal, "legitimate" purposes.[4]

The original authorization allowing Federal Reserve banks to purchase government securities included two constraints: First, it was a power to be used only occasionally in order to ensure that Reserve bank reserves were not unduly sequestered; and second, it was an operation each Reserve bank administration was to carry out solely on its own initiative. It was not to be a system-wide policy undertaken at the discretion of a centrally organized (open market) committee.

The Board in its 1914 report added other norms for Reserve bank operations. A Reserve bank should not be merely an emergency institution, argued the report, "to be resorted to for assistance only in time of abnormal stress. . . . Its duty . . . is not to await emergencies but by anticipation, to do what it can to prevent them." If interest rates—the indicators for policy—get too high, the report continued, it will be the duty of the Reserve Board, "acting through the discount rate and open market powers, to secure a wider diffusion of credit facilities at reasonable rates."[5]

A natural reaction to a careful reading of the passages quoted here is, "Wait a minute!" Was this report outlining a policy for the Reserve *banks* or the Reserve *Board?* In retrospect, the answer seems to be that it starts out with the banks in center court as specified in the Federal Reserve Act. Then, by a subtle shift of substantives, the Board is suddenly in the role of a policymaker—judging whether interest rates are too high, and exercising open-market powers. Clearly, the very existence of a Federal Reserve Board, politically appointed and based in the heartland of political operations, would be conducive to power intrigues and turf battles within the system.

The report, however, specified certain principles for the Reserve banks and granted them certain powers: They were a public trust; they were to be safe and flexible instruments of guidance and control over interest rates and credit conditions; their expertise had to evolve from their experience; they were not merely profit-making concerns, but they should earn their business expenses and a fair profit besides. Finally, "To influence the [financial] market a Reserve Bank must always be in the market."[6]

The original act, however, had seen the Board as no more than a liaison committee between the Reserve banks and Congress. Furthermore, if the Fed banks were always to be "in the market" taking preventive action, what were to be their criteria for such action? What were "reasonable rates"? A lender of last resort would not be constantly "in the market" because, if it were, it would not be able to distinguish random market signals from the results of its own actions. Such a posture also would require an element of discretion that is at odds with the stated intention of Congress in framing the act.

The secretary of the Treasury and the comptroller of the currency were, by reason of their offices, two of the eight Board members, and the secretary was the statutory chairman of the Board. No Board member could also be a banker, but at least two were supposed to be "persons experienced in banking and finance." Furthermore, the member banks were to pay the expenses of the Board.[7]

Finally, the 1914 report noted—citing again *The Federal Reserve Act,* "When any power vested by this act appears to be in conflict with powers of the Secretary of the Treasury, such powers shall be exercised subject to the supervision and control of the Secretary."[8] Since the secretary of the Treasury was also the chairman of the Board, any power exercised by the Reserve banks or Board that even *seemed* to be in conflict with the powers of his office was to be resolved in his favor. Just on the face of it, how could such an institution be labeled "independent"? What secretary of the Treasury would adjudicate a conflict against his own office? Indeed, an aggressive secretary might even initiate conflicts in order to force decisions compatible with his own political interests.

Every Federal Reserve bank had the power to buy and sell notes and bonds of the United States, not exceeding six months to maturity, and "issued in anticipation of collection of taxes or in anticipation of the receipts of assured revenues by any State, county, district, political subdivision, or municipality in the continental United States."[9] Even at this early stage of development, the Board's 1914 report anticipated open-market operations in such securities and spelled out criteria for the Reserve banks to follow. Again the Board gave itself some lateral powers. "The scope of open market operations must rest largely with the purchasing [Reserve] bank, subject to suggestions based upon analyses by the credit department of the Federal Reserve Board," the report stated. Therefore, the Board would have to make regulations governing the amount of any paper to be held by any one Federal Reserve bank and the aggregate amount to be held by all Fed banks. The open-market section, the report concluded, "was designed to give the Federal Reserve Board the necessary economic control of the domestic money market and to preserve a proper equilibrium in international relations."[10]

No interpretative reading of the Federal Reserve Act can support such a claim. The Board was simply reaching for power by taking positions that it presumed would not be challenged seriously by the Reserve banks or by Congress.

The annual report for 1915 continued this kind of journalistic lobbying. "Under ordinary conditions," the report stated, "the power to engage in open market operations will be an important factor in the control of discount rates by the Federal Reserve Banks. [However,] when money rates 'harden,'" the report continued, the Board's policy "will be to encourage the Federal Reserve Banks, through the active purchase of paper and the increase of investments, to release funds, and thereby to steady rates at what it [the Board] conceives to be the normal level."[11]

One of the major arguments in the writing of the Federal Reserve Act was that a system of autonomous regional banks was superior to a single central bank because each Reserve bank would be thoroughly conversant with credit conditions in its own district. Furthermore, its member banks would initiate credit demands. This contact with local financial institutions was in contrast to a Washington-based central-bank administration that would be insensitive to local credit needs. So from what source came the claim of the Board that it was supposed to stabilize rates at the "normal" level? The statement in the report was simply a ploy for assuming more influence.

Federal Reserve Support of Treasury Policy during World War I

The Federal Reserve banks were just about operational when the United States became involved in World War I. Almost immediately, the U.S. Treasury Department asserted its dominance. The discount policy of the Board was to maintain rates "in harmony with the low interest rates borne by the Government loans," stated the Board's annual report for 1917.[12] Even more pointed was a section in the annual report for 1918, headed "DISCOUNT POLICY," which began: "The discount policy of the Board has necessarily been coordinated . . . with Treasury requirements and policies, which in turn have been governed by demands made upon the Treasury for war purposes."[13] Again, in 1918 the annual report admitted that discount rates were based upon rates currently borne by government securities, and "must for the time being continue to be fixed with regard to Treasury requirements." The Board "recognized its duty to cooperate unreservedly with the Government [i.e., the Treasury] to provide funds needed for the war."[14]

The report for 1919 excused the Fed's subservience to the Treasury by asserting that *no* higher rate structure would have been sufficient to persuade the securities market to absorb the Treasury issues: "It was necessary to cooperate with the Treasury in every way," the report claimed, "to facilitate first the sale of Government securities and then their absorption by investors."[15] Throughout the period, the Reserve banks followed their often discussed policy of allowing a slightly lower discount rate to member banks that used government securities as collateral for their loans.[16]

During the last five months of 1919, Federal Reserve notes in circulation increased by more than $400 million, or by about 15 percent, as a result of Reserve bank credit increases on bills discounted and purchased. The report for 1919 excused this expansion as "an incident of the general credit expansion . . . and occasioned by crop-moving and other seasonal needs."[17] At the same time, the report warned that an early and "substantial advance in all discount rates was necessary and should not be long delayed."[18]

The report for 1920 looked back at the year 1919 as one characterized by "an *unprecedented* orgy of extravagance, . . . overextended business, and general demoralization of the agencies of production and distribution. . . . Deflation," the report added, "could not have been long deferred by any artificial means or temporary expedients."[19]

During 1921, Reserve bank loans and Federal Reserve notes outstanding declined continuously, while gold holdings increased. This contraction offset the antecedent three-year expansion. The increase of Federal Reserve currency during the inflationary period, the 1921 report argued, was "the effect of advancing wages and prices and not their cause." Likewise, the reduction of currency in 1921 was induced by falling wages and prices.[20]

The Gold Standard Act and the Real-Bills Doctrine as Criteria for Creating Money

This view—that changes in money are consequences of changes in real product—permeates Federal Reserve literature. It is a part of the real-bills doctrine, and on that ground has been thoroughly dissected and discredited.[21] It is also an element of gold-standard theory, and as part of that theory it is respectably valid. Wherein lies the difference?

The clauses in the Gold Standard Act specified the terms for the monetization of gold. Gold could be converted into dollars on the *fixed* terms written in the statute. Its monetization did not depend on anyone's judgment or discretion, but only on its monetary price relative to all other market prices. Gold's legal tender value—its mint price—became the Big Constant around which orbited the system of market prices. No one ever had to define "eligible" gold for monetization purposes, because all gold of a certain fineness was eligible at the mint price.

For central-bank executives, who were supposed to manage their institutions to accommodate the needs of commerce and trade and who recognized the gold standard as the dominant policy, the real-bills doctrine for extending bank credit seemed a logical and compatible supplement to the gold-standard rule. Its essential feature is that a bank of any sort—commercial or central—in advancing or lending on the basis of security given by the borrower, should only provide credit and create money if the security for the loan is a "real bill." A real bill is a security that has arisen as a result of the actual production or marketing of real goods whose sale is imminent. The implication is that a bank would provide credit only on the basis of additional goods going to market. The new production would thereby initiate the bank's new credit. This means for gearing the production of money to the production of goods and services seems intuitively sensible and responsible. It was very similar to the monetization of gold, which was simply the kingpin commodity of many commodities that could enter the marketplace.[22]

The decisive difference between the monetization of gold and the monetization of goods is that the gold is monetized on *fixed* dollar terms, while the monetization of goods via the real-bills doctrine must depend on the discretion of the bankers or central bankers who pass judgment on the loan applications of borrowers. A banker's acceptance of a loan always includes an implicit estimate of the dollar value of the goods for which credit accommodation is sought. The interest rate charged reflects this value. The loan does not have, and cannot have, "fixed terms" similar to the price of the gold that is monetized, because the prices anticipated for the goods going to market are not certain. If the banker is too sanguine, his monetization of loans on the basis of the goods to be sold would be inflationary; the new money would exceed the dollar value of the goods being marketed. If he is too skeptical, the contrary would be the case. Clearly, the banker's judgment is bound to be colored by the business climate of the day, and likely on that account to be procyclical. By way of contrast, this variable outlook on business conditions could never affect the monetization of gold. Everyone regarded the mint price of gold as a long-term constant that might be changed only rarely and incrementally, and never simply to stimulate business conditions.[23]

The Fed Board's allegiance to the real-bills doctrine as an operating principle appears repeatedly in its annual reports, as well as in less official pronouncements. It is also written into the Federal Reserve Act itself. Section 13 states, "Any Federal Reserve bank may discount notes, drafts, and bills of exchange arising out of actual commercial transactions . . . drawn for agricultural, industrial, or commercial purposes. . . . The Federal Reserve Board [has] the right to determine or define the character of the paper thus eligible for discount."[24]

Because of their faith in this doctrine, Fed spokesmen could argue that their credit operations followed the needs of business. The report for 1922 observed, for example, that a lag was evident between a change in business activity, measured by price level turns, and changes in currency and loans outstanding. In particular, the report asserted, currency outstanding and loans of Federal Reserve banks followed along *after* business activity had set the course. "This sequence of events shows that the Federal Reserve banks, through their loans and currency issues, are responsive to the needs of trade," the report concluded.[25]

Again in 1923, the report claimed that the Federal Reserve banks "do not feel the impact of increased demand for credit until the whole train of antecedent circumstances which has occasioned it is well advanced on its course; that is, until a forward movement of business, no matter from what impulse it is proceeding, has gained momentum." The report continued, "The qualitative tests appropriate in Federal reserve bank credit administration laid down by the [Federal Reserve] act are, therefore, definite and ample."[26] These statements sound conclusive, but the report added a "quantitative" norm for Reserve bank credit extension—that it should be an amount "justified by a commensurate increase in the Nation's aggregate productivity."[27]

In a scholarly and instructive review of Federal Reserve policy in the 1920s, Elmus R. Wicker emphasizes this quantitative aspect of Fed policy. Wicker argues that the quantitative productivity test "provided the board with a workable substitute for the gold reserve ratio as a guide to credit policy in 1922 and 1923," in the period before the gold standard was again internationally operational.[28] Even though a quantitative criterion is not implied directly by a real-bills doctrine, the emphasis on productivity as a guide to central-bank policy when a gold standard is in abeyance is understandably appealing to central bankers looking for a fixture on which to anchor credit policy.

Early Federal Reserve Experience with Open-Market Operations

Open-market operations in government securities would certainly have been "discovered" either by the Federal Reserve banks or the Federal Reserve Board, even if they had not been anticipated by the Federal Reserve Act. This policy first appeared in 1922 as a means of maintaining earning assets at Reserve banks so that the banks could meet their expenses and pay the statutory dividends owed to member banks. Security purchases also "increased the amount of funds in the market and thus indirectly enabled member banks to continue the liquidation of their borrowings [from the boom period, 1918–1921]."[29]

After their first use in 1922, open-market operations became routine. The report for 1923 noted that they were "capable of giving effective support to the discount policy of Federal Reserve Banks without an accompanying change of rates."[30] Creation of the Open Market Investment Committee of Reserve Bank Officers subsequently formalized the new policy. Citing again the Federal Reserve Act, the Board stated that the new committee's operations should "be conducted with primary regard to the accommodation of commerce and business and to the effect of such purchases or sales on the general credit situation." It also presumed that the committee would operate "under the general supervision of the Board in handling open-market operations."[31] The Board's criteria were the same ones it used for governing discount rate policy. Such a generalized directive is uninstructive; it only says that open-market operations should be used to do good things.

Wicker observes that open-market operations had other facets. Several officials in the system—Reserve bank officers and Board members—thought of the purchases in 1924, for example, as a means of building up an inventory of securities to be used (sold) at any time in the future in which speculative inflation or gold inflation became a threat. The fact that the purchases occurred during a minor recession, Wicker argues, was incidental. Federal Reserve priorities were to provide good footing for the international gold standard without allowing imports of gold to generate an inflation in the United States.[32]

Economists of the time critically observed the Fed's sale of securities in 1923 to prevent a price level increase from U.S. imports of gold. In a paper delivered to the American Economic Association in December 1924, John R. Commons charged that the Federal Reserve Board, without sanctions from Congress or the Executive, had stabilized prices well below what they would have been if only the gold standard were functioning. "The resolution of April, 1923 [in which the Board made the decision to sell securities]," he concluded, "probably goes as far as the present law permits."[33]

T. E. Gregory, speaking in the same session as Commons, saw the Fed's policies as inconsistent with the operations of the gold standard. However, he felt that central-bank policies contra the gold standard could have only short-run effects, since the central banks did not own the world's gold supplies.[34]

The initiation of open-market operations in 1922 signaled a new era in the scope of Federal Reserve activities. Bearing in mind that Congress created the Fed as a lender of last resort to the member banks in the mode of the clearinghouse associations, and that Fed banks were to provide form-seasonal elasticity to the monetary system, the diverse reasons given for undertaking open-market operations between 1922 and 1927 reflect a notable expansion of the Fed's functions.

First, securities were purchased in 1922 to provide some income to Fed banks in order to assist them to meet operating costs and pay dividends to their member bank owners.

Second, the Open Market Committee sold off some securities in 1923 in order to lower interest rates and discourage imports of gold, and thereby dampen any gold-inspired inflation.

Third, securities were purchased again in 1924 to build up an inventory for future sales if gold again "threatened" the price structure.

Fourth, securities were purchased in 1927, in order to generate enough spending stimulus in Europe so that U.S. agricultural products would enjoy a healthy demand from abroad.

These operations had little to do with an elastic currency and nothing at all to do with the role of the Fed as a lender of last resort. They suggest that the Fed was becoming a constant force in the financial markets—monitoring and manipulating gold flows, anticipating export market problems, and becoming involved with foreign central banks in the international control of gold movements.[35] Unlike the clearinghouse associations, the Fed was no longer just an "emergency currency" organization. During the 1920s, it programmed its operations so as to keep the stock of high-powered money on a fairly regular path no matter how gold ebbed and flowed.[36]

Another economist, A. C. Whitaker, in a paper prepared in 1929 and read in 1930, was enthralled with the idea of an economic institution that could effectively iron out economic disturbances. "The modern central bank," he wrote, "is something unknown to the philosophy once held, that economic society can be completely served by all hands seeking profit under the stimulus of mere self-interest." The Federal Reserve System's use of open-market operations, Whitaker claimed, was the key to economic utopia. "Despite two great price booms and collapses [1919–1921 and 1929]," he concluded, "the Federal Reserve System is one of the most brilliant successes among our political and economic institutions."[37] Whitaker's unrestrained adulation of the Fed appeared, ironically, when it was in the beginning throes of its greatest failure.

Harold L. Reed, another prominent monetary economist of the time, argued a position somewhat contrary to Whitaker's. "The Board is a committee," he observed, "and is consequently subject to all the unwieldiness of committee organization. It is composed of men who have been trained in different industrial activities and who have resided in different geographical sections. It is confronted by problems that lie at the very core of much that is controversial in scientific circles, and whenever wide differences of opinion exist it is inevitable that slow and tedious diplomacy must be exercised before substantial unanimity of thought can be gained and aggressive action taken." In addition to the Board's bureaucratic character, Reed continued, "there is the strong presumptive argument that it is not wise to grant great power to a machine the control of which is rendered so difficult by the diffusion of authority between different directorial bodies."[38]

Here, Reed put his finger not only on the ponderous ineffectiveness of bureaucratic policy-making, but on the further possibility of conflicting authorities within the system. However, he offered no suggestions for changing the bureaucratic diffusion of power within the system, nor means for coping with the political pressures that even then he saw attempting to influence decision-making.[39] He only suggested that appointees to the Federal Reserve Board be sophisticated in balance-sheet analysis of the monetary system.[40]

The statements of economists of the time reflected the confusion of norms, technical controls, and focus of responsibility for policy that characterized the Federal Reserve System of the twenties. In spite of the potential for future trouble, however, all the indexes of business activity reflected exemplary conditions. Prices were virtually stable through the decade, with only a slight downward trend. Real output increased at a satisfying pace. The government kept the same modest size it had maintained for almost 150 years. It enjoyed budget surpluses and continued to pay off the national debt. Confidence in the economic system was unparalleled, and showed up in the stock market indexes. It was, indeed, a stable period for the Reserve System and one of unexampled prosperity for the economy.

Monetary Aggregates and Monetary Gold, 1917–1934

A picture of the monetary system for this period and the Fed's part in it can be seen in table 17.1. This table shows annual values in both monetary and real terms for changes in the monetary base and the money stock—columns 1, 2, 3, and 4. It also shows nominal values for the Fed's outstanding monetary obligations (5) and for the Fed's gold and other reserve assets (6). Column 7 is the difference between the Fed's total monetary obligations and its supporting assets. It thereby reflects the Fed banks' creation of monetary liabilities over and above the amounts resulting from gold and other reserves. Column 8

TABLE 17.1 Monetary base, M_1, real M_1, Federal Reserve gold reserves and demand liabilities, prices, and year-to-year growth in these series, 1917–1934

Year or period	Monetary base M_B (1)	Money stock M_1 (2)	Real M_1 M_1^* (3)	Change in real M_1 ΔM_1^* (4)	Federal Reserve outstanding monetary liabilities M_F (5)
1917	5.09	16.9	19.8	—	1.85
18	5.89	18.3	18.3	−1.5	3.56
19	6.52	21.4	18.6	0.3	4.78
1920	7.21	23.6	17.7	−0.9	5.25
21	6.55	21.0	17.7	0.0	4.79
22	6.32	21.6	19.4	1.7	4.29
23	6.68	22.7	20.0	0.6	4.24
24	6.85	23.2	20.4	0.4	4.12
25	6.95	25.4	21.8	1.4	4.07
26	7.13	26.1	22.2	0.4	4.05
27	7.24	25.8	22.4	0.2	4.16
28	7.15	25.8	22.6	0.2	4.26
29	7.10	26.2	23.0	0.4	4.25
1930	6.91	25.3	22.8	−0.2	4.21
31	7.30	23.9	23.6	0.8	4.36
32	7.79	20.5	22.6	−1.0	4.92
33	7.94	19.2	22.3	−0.3	5.63
34	9.26	21.1	23.7	1.4	6.68
Net change, 1917–1934	4.17	4.2	3.9	3.9	4.83
Net change, 1917–1930	1.82	8.4	3.0	3.0	2.36
Net change, 1929–1934	2.16	−5.1	0.7	0.7	2.43
Net change, 1928–1933	0.79	−6.6	−0.3	−0.3	1.37

shows year-to-year changes in the Fed's net liabilities; and column 9 is total bill holdings of Fed banks. Column 10 is the index of prices (CPI) based on 1947–49 = 100.

During this period, the Fed banks faced statutory gold reserve requirements—35 percent against member bank deposits and 40 percent against outstanding Federal Reserve notes. The gold and other lawful money in the Fed banks had been deposited there by the commercial member banks and served to fulfill their legal reserve requirements. If the gold reserve had not been in the Fed banks, the member banks would have held it themselves as prudential reserves for their issues of deposits. Therefore, the only part of the monetary base that the Fed banks created of their own volition in this period was the *excess* of their monetary obligations (column 5, "M_F") over the amount of "Gold and Other Reserves" (column 6, "R_F") that they held as assets. Column

Federal Reserve gold and other reserve assets R_F (6)	Net monetary liabilities of Federal Reserve banks M_{FL} (7)	Year-to-year change in Fed Res. net liabilities ΔM_{FL} (8)	Total bills bought and discounted B (9)	Prices (CPI, 1947–49 = 100) (10)
1.22	0.63	—	1.49	54.8
1.91	1.65	1.02	2.42	64.3
2.07	2.71	1.06	2.87	74.0
2.12	3.13	.42	2.12	85.7
2.63	2.16	−.97	1.09	76.4
3.09	1.20	−.96	0.98	71.6
3.17	1.07	−.13	0.89	72.9
3.11	1.01	−.06	0.86	73.1
2.94	1.13	.12	1.02	75.0
2.89	1.16	.03	1.00	75.6
2.91	1.25	.09	1.26	74.2
2.79	1.47	.22	1.29	73.3
2.86	1.39	−.18	0.82	73.3
3.05	1.16	−.23	0.80	71.4
3.12	1.24	.08	0.62	65.0
3.24	1.68	.44	0.25	58.4
3.56	2.07	.39	0.12	55.3
4.60	2.08	.01	0.01	57.2
3.38	1.45	1.45	−1.48	4.4%
1.83	0.53	0.53	−0.69	30.3%
1.74	0.69	0.69	−0.81	−28.2%
0.77	0.60	0.60	−1.17	−32.6%

Sources: Data on monetary base and M_1 are from Friedman and Schwartz, *A Monetary History of the United States, 1867–1960,* tables B-3 and A-1, pp. 801–4 and 709–14, respectively. Federal Reserve banks' balance-sheet data are taken from *Banking and Monetary Statistics,* Board of Governors of the Federal Reserve System (Washington, D.C.: 1943), pp. 330–32. Price index values are from *Historical Statistics of the United States, Colonial Times to 1957,* Dept. of Commerce, Bureau of the Census (Washington, D.C.: 1960), p. 125, Series E-113.

Note: All values are $ billions except prices. Level values are for June 30.

7, "M_{FL}," shows these net values. Their corresponding year-to-year changes are noted in column 8 as "ΔM_{FL}."

Astonishingly enough, the early Fed's only significant expansion of base money came in the first phase of this period, 1917–1920, when the Fed systematically expanded its own net monetary liabilities to 60 percent of its total obligations. This action was not due to any liquidity crisis or bank panic at that time, but was in response to the U.S. Treasury's fiscal demands ("needs," as they are called politically). (See above, p. 258.) When Treasury fiscal problems subsided around 1920, the Fed raised its discount rate and allowed its earning assets to run down. Thus, the Fed's expansion coincided with the economy's post–World War I boom, and its subsequent stringent policy correlated with (and probably contributed to) the sharp recession of 1921. For at least this period, Fed policy was procyclical.[41]

Through the 1920s, the monetary data indicate that the Fed banks undertook no momentous monetary operations. By 1930 their monetary liabilities exceeded their gold holdings by only $1.16 billion, so their net monetary creation was only 28 percent of the total monetary base.

The years of the Great Contraction, 1929–1934, witnessed a growth in total Fed banks' gold and other reserves of $1.74 billion, but a growth in their monetary output of only $0.69 billion. The Fed banks, therefore, acted as net *absorbers* of base money from what that aggregate would have been without their intercession. The commercial banking system would have had $1.05 billion more in reserve assets for its own production of loans and deposits if the Federal Reserve banks had not existed.

The Fed as a Promoter of Monetary Elasticity

The years of the Great Contraction provided an opportunity for the Fed to do what it was created to do—furnish form-seasonal and cyclical elasticity to the monetary system when banking crises were incipient. The monetary data, when broken into specific components, show the extent to which the Fed fulfilled this mission. Table 17.2 summarizes in index form (1925 = 100) nominal and real values for the total stock of all commercial bank deposits plus currency (M_2), and for each component of this total—currency, demand deposits, and time deposits. The data in the table begin in 1925 and continue to 1935 in order to capture the changes that occurred during the contraction of 1929–1933.

The stock market crash in 1929 had two complementary monetary effects: First, it reduced significantly the real value of all nonmonetary wealth; second, it thereby increased the demand for money. Households and businesses wanted more *real* money in order to compensate for their losses in other real wealth.

During the years 1929–1931, the real stock of M_2 increased 2 to 5 percent per year (from 115 to 125) even as the nominal stock declined at about the same rate. The decline in prices of approximately 12 percent was sufficient to convert the decline in the nominal money stock to an increase in the real money stock. From 1931 to 1933 the nominal stock of M_2 declined about 28 percent, while prices fell 19 percent. The real money stock therefore declined 9 percent.

These changes reflect differential lags inherent in the market system. With

TABLE 17.2 Nominal and real components of the money stock, 1925–1935

Year	All commercial bank dep. adj. plus curr. outside banks		Dem. dep. adj.		Curr. outside banks		Time dep.	
	M_2		D_d		C		T_d	
	$	Real	$	Real	$	Real	$	Real
1925	100	100	100	100	100	100	100	100
1926	105	104	103	102	101	100	107	106
1927	108	109	103	104	100	100	114	115
1928	113	115	104	108	101	103	123	125
1929	114	115	105	107	102	103	123	125
1930	113	118	101	106	94	99	125	132
1931	109	125	93	106	102	117	125	144
1932	94	119	73	93	129	165	107	137
1933	85	115	67	92	133	181	94	138
1934	92	119	78	102	131	170	99	129
1935	102	130	95	125	134	171	103	159

Sources: *Banking and Monetary Statistics,* Board of Governors of the Federal Reserve System, 1943, pp. 34, 35, 368. Real values were derived using the BLS Consumer Price Index, 1935–1939 = 100.

or without a central bank, changes in the money supply are usually much more rapid than the rate of change in market prices. Contractual arrangements and the inertia of the status quo in nominal prices inevitably impede the rate of price level response to the changing aggregate demand resulting from variations in the nominal quantity of money. Therefore, it is possible to say that the demand for money was increasing all through the 1929–1933 period, but that the supply of nominal money, being *perversely elastic,* decreased as the increase in the demand for real money manifested itself in the form of falling prices.

The initial increase in the real stock of money was accompanied by two bank crises (in 1930 and 1931) and many bank failures. The liquidity weakness of the banks translated itself into a form-elasticity problem: Because of their questionable redemption into some form of legal tender, demand deposits became an inferior form of money to currency. The subsequent conversion of demand deposits into currency, therefore, was likewise a conversion of bank *reserves* into hand-to-hand currency. But as the banks lost reserves they also had to reduce their production of loans and demand deposits, thereby aggravating the very problem that the antecedent conversion of the demand deposits into currency was supposed to have relieved. The action and reaction of this destabilizing feedback process can be seen in the growth rate for real currency and the decline in real demand deposits between 1931 and 1933. In those two years the real stock of currency grew by 55 percent, while the real stock of demand deposits fell by 15 percent.[42] Even these disparate percentage changes do not depict adequately the monetary disorder, because the quantitative declines of demand deposits were much greater than the increases in currency.

In a conventional economic market, an increase in the demand for a commodity manifests itself by means of an increase in the commodity's relative price. The industry producing the commodity duly responds by obtaining more resources in order to produce more of the commodity. Prior to the formation of the Federal Reserve System, this reaction also occurred in the money-producing industry. Clearinghouse associations issued currency, and many private nonbank companies did likewise. These currencies relieved the liquidity stringency that took the form of a "shortage" in high-powered money, and thereby prevented solvent but illiquid banks from failing.

The Fed banks' directors, however, never addressed either the cyclical-demand-for-total-real-money problem nor the form-elasticity problem. With the Fed banks in charge, the increase in the demand for real money by households and business firms, as manifested by a 28 percent decline in prices, resulted only in a 30 percent *decrease* in the stock of nominal money and, eventually, some reduction in the stock of real money.

Fed banks' discounts and advances to member banks declined significantly between 1929 and 1932 at the same time that their gold reserves increased (table 17.1, columns 6 and 9). The desire to check security market speculation, observed a contemporary economist, was "allowed to dominate policy to the exclusion of practically every other consideration."[43]

The real value of the nominal money stock depends on prices, which in turn depend on the total productivity of the economy and the demand for the services that money renders. The central bank cannot affect the former of these functions—the economy's productivity—but it can very much affect the utility of money indirectly through its policy actions with respect to the quantity of nominal money. If it promotes a too-rapid rate of growth of money, it vitiates the value of each money unit by the consequent rise in prices. As people see the value of their money holdings depreciate, they logically choose to hold (demand) less money by spending some of it. This action, however, does not get rid of the money (where would it go?), but simply speeds up the rate of money flow and thereby increases prices even more. If the central bank retards the rate at which money is created, prices tend to fall and the value of each money unit rises. People seeing the value of their money appreciating tend to spend it less rapidly, thereby making prices fall somewhat more intensively.

This latter behavior occurred in the United States between 1929 and 1933, and was severely aggravated by the policies of the Federal Reserve System. The changes in real money stocks during this period reflected an increase in the demand for real money while the nominal supply under the general custody of the Fed declined. No private market, no matter how bizarre or how exotic the good or service it regulates, ever behaves so perversely.

The Fed's Discount Policy during the Contraction

The Fed's failure to provide an elastic currency in the 1931–1933 period was linked to its discount policy and to its compulsion to pile up gold. In one of his penetrating articles on Fed policy in the 1930s, Clark Warburton showed how the Federal Reserve banks' discount policy virtually prevented any flexibility in their currency issues. In order to provide an elastic currency without letting member bank reserves contract, he noted, Fed banks had to acquire additional assets—bills of exchange, banker's acceptances—and make loans to member banks. However, in the early 1930s the Federal Reserve banks

> virtually stopped rediscounting or otherwise acquiring "eligible" paper. This was not due to lack of eligible paper. . . . Nor was this virtual stoppage . . . due to any forces outside the Federal Reserve System. It was due to . . . strenuous discouragement of continuous discounting by any member bank, "direct pressure" so strong as to amount to virtual prohibition of rediscounting for banks which were making loans for security speculation, and a hard-boiled attitude toward banks in special need of rediscounts because of deposit withdrawals. . . . The Federal Reserve Banks did not hold sufficient eligible paper [to issue the necessary amount of Federal Reserve notes] solely because the Federal Reserve authorities had discouraged discounting almost to the point of prohibition.[44]

The result of the Federal Reserve banks' policy of nondiscounting is seen again in table 17.1, where "Total Bills Bought and Discounted" (column 9) declines steadily from $1.29 billion in 1928 to $0.12 billion in 1933. In effect, this latter date marked the end of the "real bills" era of Fed policy.

The Federal Reserve Banks' Gold Reserve Policy

Federal Reserve gold policy also severely limited any countercyclical action at this time. The Federal Reserve Act stipulated that the Fed banks maintain a minimum gold reserve of 40 percent of Federal Reserve notes issued, and 35 percent of member bank reserves. This requirement was in keeping with the principle that the banking and monetary system operate under the rubric of the gold standard. In addition, gold was required as collateral for the issue of Federal Reserve notes if the collateral value of eligible paper held by the Fed banks was not sufficient to cover the remaining 60 percent of the notes. (If a Fed bank emitted $100 in Federal Reserve notes, but had only $50 worth of eligible commercial paper, it also had to commit $50 in gold as "backing" for the notes. The effective gold reserve requirement against the notes in such a case was not 40 percent but 50 percent.)

Federal Reserve officials, during the years of the Contraction, expressed great concern about the Fed banks' gold holdings. Their statements implied that Fed policies were very much constrained by limited monetary gold stocks, as well as by the alleged scarcity of commercial paper eligible for discount. The fact of the matter is that these "problems" were largely figments of policymakers' imaginations. The Fed banks had plenty of excess gold, and commercial banks were awash with eligible paper. As Warburton noted, "The leading Reserve bank [of New York] became the world's champion gold hoarder instead of meeting a financial crisis in the manner prescribed by the law under which it operated."[45]

The data describing the twelve Fed banks' gold position are shown in table 17.3. The gold reserve ratio, which was around 70 percent during the late 1920s, reflected an attitude of preparedness in case of a sudden internal or external drain. As business and banking problems became critical in 1930 and 1931, gold flowed into the United States and into the Fed banks, reaching a peak value of $3.62 billion in August 1931. The "free" or excess gold over the amount necessary to fulfill the Fed banks' statutory gold reserve requirements also hit a peak of $1.97 billion at the same time.

If the condition of the Fed banks as nonprofit institutions had been of paramount importance, this financial picture would have been very encouraging. But for a central bank to accumulate gold balances on this scale was disastrous—not only to the commercial banking system of the United States, but also to the banking and monetary systems of foreign countries that were also on operational gold standards. Such a restrictive action by a major player in the game forced all the other gold-based monetary systems to contract or to go off the gold standard.[46] The Fed's accumulation of gold occurred in the presence of two banking crises in 1930 and 1931 and the accompanying "internal drain"—the wholesale conversion of bank demand deposits into hand-to-hand currency discussed above.

The Role of Gold in Central-Bank Policy

Walter Bagehot, the renowned English essayist, economist, and Bank of England critic, had specified five rules or principles of policy that a central bank operating within the framework of a gold standard should follow during a banking crisis. (See chapter 16.) His final emphasis was for the central bank to continue lending to the money market until it had exhausted itself of its gold reserves.[47] Most assuredly, the central bank's main concern was not supposed to be its own liquidity, or even its own solvency.

TABLE 17.3 Federal Reserve banks' outstanding monetary obligations, gold reserves both total and excess, and the reserve ratio of gold to total gold obligations, February and August, 1928–1938 (monthly averages of daily figures)

Date (year and month)	Member bank reserves	Federal Reserve note circulation	Gold and other reserves of Federal Reserve banks		Gold reserve ratio (4) ÷ ((1) + (2))
			Excess	Total	(%)
	(1)	(2)	(3)	(4)	(5)
1928 Feb.	2.37	1.60	1.49	2.97	74.0
Aug.	2.27	1.65	1.27	2.75	69.0
1929 Feb.	2.36	1.66	1.32	2.83	69.4
Aug.	2.32	1.83	1.56	3.12	74.2
1930 Feb.	2.31	1.68	1.66	3.16	78.3
Aug.	2.39	1.35	1.71	3.10	81.7
1931 Feb.	2.37	1.47	1.81	3.25	83.4
Aug.	2.35	1.88	1.97	3.62	81.4
1932 Feb.	1.91	2.66	1.38	3.15	67.4
Aug.	2.07	2.85	1.02	2.91	58.2
1933 Feb.	2.29	2.92	1.35	3.36	63.1
Aug.	2.37	3.00	1.71	3.82	68.1
1934 Feb.	2.82	2.96	1.62	3.87	64.4
Aug.	4.05	3.11	2.44	5.20	70.0
1935 Feb.	4.60	3.12	2.80	5.75	72.1
Aug.	5.23	3.33	3.36	6.63	74.8
1936 Feb.	5.81	3.67	4.24	8.02	78.0
Aug.	6.18	4.00	4.57	8.54	79.2
1937 Feb.	6.75	4.17	4.95	9.14	80.3
Aug.	6.70	4.24	4.91	9.15	79.6
1938 Feb.	7.23	4.13	5.20	9.59	80.3
Aug.	8.12	4.15	6.14	11.03	82.4

Source: Board of Governors of Federal Reserve System, *Banking and Monetary Statistics,* table 93, pp. 347–49.

Note: All values in $ billions except reserve ratios.

The unmistakable sign of a central bank battling internal and external drains of gold—gold going out of the banking system into hand-to-hand currency and out of the country into foreign monetary systems—was a significant decline in its own gold holdings. In late 1931 and up to the summer of 1932, this change was evident in the gold reserves of the Fed banks following the policy of open-market operations undertaken at that time. In August of 1932, however, the Fed's expansion ground to a halt when its excess gold reserves were still $1.02 billion, and the ratio of its gold reserves to its outstanding liabilities was more than 58 percent. As they discontinued open-market purchases, the Fed banks also raised discount rates. Once again gold flowed into the United States Treasury, and the revival in business activity was aborted. In

February 1933, with the economy in deep depression and the commercial banking system in shambles, the Fed banks had as much excess gold in their balance sheets as they had had in February 1929!

Basing the case for Federal Reserve failure on the Fed banks' *excess* gold reserves is not sufficiently damning. In the true sense of Walter Bagehot's prescriptions, *all* of the Fed banks' gold was excess. Indeed, the Federal Reserve Act itself declared that the Fed banks, with the approval of the Board of Governors, could suspend gold reserve requirements in an emergency for thirty days and for successive thirty-day periods thereafter—in other words, indefinitely—in order to provide monetary relief to the banking system. This provision is, of course, ultimately sensible: Reserves are there to be used when needed. Their function is not to embellish balance sheets.

Relief from gold constraints was applied for only once. In March of 1933, the Fed Bank of New York sought and obtained from the Federal Reserve Board suspension of its gold reserve requirements for thirty days. However, the Board did so only reluctantly—"because the Reserve Bank would still be obliged to pay out gold and currency to hoarders[!]"[48] The suspension of requirements went into effect on 3 March 1933, but the Fed Bank of New York and most of the Reserve banks closed on 4 March, the next day, so the gesture by this time was futile.[49]

During the year between August 1931 and August 1932, when the Fed was moderately expansive, its excess gold reserve fell by $0.95 billion as its outstanding monetary base obligations—the total of Federal Reserve notes and member bank reserve-deposits—rose by $0.59 billion. At the same time the Fed banks' total gold reserves fell by $0.71 billion. At this rate, the Fed banks could have increased the base items by $2.5 billion to a total of $7.42 billion before they would have lost all of their gold.[50] This amount of base money, even under the desperate conditions of that time, would surely have stopped the public's "hoarding" of gold and prevented the final banking collapse in early 1933.

The Effects of Reserve Requirements on Monetary Adjustment

The Fed banks' hypercautious attitude toward their gold reserves carried over from the same disposition of national banks in earlier crises. During the crisis of 1907, O. M. W. Sprague observed that "undue importance has come to be attached to the maintenance at all times and at all costs of a certain minimum ratio between reserve and deposit liabilities." At the worst point of the panic—23 November 1907—the New York national banks' lawful money reserves were $216 million, which was $54 million less than what they were legally required to hold. "The reserve deficit," Sprague continued, "was apparently regarded by bankers and the public as a sufficient reason for partial suspension. . . . [This ratio] can only be . . . characterized as a sort of fetich [*sic*] to which every maxim of sound banking policy is blindly sacrificed."[51]

The reserves that the national banks stockpiled on a small scale in 1907 (and in earlier panics) the Federal Reserve banks magnified with their Midas-like policy into the disaster of 1931–1933. Strangely enough, most economists of the era did not fault legal reserve requirements as such, or the Fed's inexcusable and exaggerated gold hoarding. Rather they accepted all the legal restrictions operating against monetary adjustment as given conditions. A. Piatt Andrew, for example, concluded that the issue of clearinghouse media in 1893 and 1907, which had proven so effective, was "an anachronism in our time, yet necessitated by conditions for which our banking laws did not provide."[52]

Indeed the laws did not "provide" a solution. The laws were the problem, and they could not be both problem and solution.

Sprague for his part offered a "solution" that became the accepted norm. "Somewhere in the banking system of a country there should be a reserve of lending power in the central money market," he argued.[53] However, Sprague's "solution" was absurd because it disregarded the fact that the reserve was already there in the national banks' vaults. All that was required was a repeal of the arbitrary laws mandating legal reserve requirements and other restrictions, so that the banks could get access to the reserve funds they already held.

The monetary contraction and decline in business activity would not have continued if the Fed banks had followed Bagehot's principles. Getting the gold into financial channels would have satisfied the internal and external demands for gold, blocked the hemorrhaging of bank reserves, and restored the "normal" conditions that everyone wanted. Even in the worst case, with the Federal Reserve banks exhausted of gold, the U.S. monetary system would have been on a Federal Reserve note standard, and exchange rates would have become market determined.

Such a goldless scenario does not imply a monetary disaster. It occurred anyway in the years following 1933, and continues to the present. The demise of the gold-based monetary system would have been more acceptable, however, if it had occurred in the presence of a Roland-type Federal Reserve System bravely fighting a rearguard action to the last ounce of gold, rather than as a pusillanimous capitulation to a false norm. A proper central bank does not fail because it loses all its gold in a banking crisis. It only fails if it does *not*.

18 The Appearance of the Political Federal Reserve System

The outstanding result of this Act is to give to the Federal Reserve Board, a body possessed of enormous powers, which it has left largely in abeyance or transferred to others, still greater and more inclusive authority which it is now asked to use sanely and constructively. . . . Its high aspirations to become "a supreme court of finance" have not been realized, and at critical moments in American banking life, it is not even called into consultation by administrators.

H. Parker Willis, 1934

New Deal Institutions and Banking Legislation

The episode of monetary disorder that began in 1930 and continued through the decade—indeed, throughout the next decade as well—is almost too much for mortal mind to assimilate, let alone explain.[1] The list of controversial policies, new laws passed, unforeseen political developments, and the emerging dominance of political institutions—all present a mind-boggling historical hodgepodge that seems to defy reasoned analysis.

The economic upheaval was enormous. By the time the monetary debacle ended in March 1933, the number of banks in the banking system had been reduced by nearly a third, unemployment was close to 25 percent, real GNP was off 30 percent, the price level had fallen 25 percent, and the mood of the general public was one of desperation and uncertainty. Many people had a favorite scapegoat or an imagined conspirator as the root cause of the disaster; but virtually no one, not even very many economists, found any fault with the real culprit—the central bank. The man in the street did not even know that a central bank existed. If he had known of its presence, he would have had no more ability to assess its operations, or its lack of operations, than he would to understand the technical workings of the telephone or electric utility industries. However, the ordinary householder may safely ignore the intricacies of telephonic communication and electric power generation because the managers of these industries have a compelling interest in their efficient and continuing operations as cost-recovering enterprises. The central bank, on the other hand, is a government monopoly. It has only congressional overseers, most of whom are relatively unschooled in what it can do and how it functions.

The Federal Reserve System, at the time, had a disarming aura of private ownership that seemed to make it less prone to oversight and manipulation by political bodies. The member commercial banks were the stockholders and titular owners of the Fed banks. Each member bank received a statutory 6 percent dividend on its Fed bank stock, but it also had to maintain a zero-interest reserve-deposit account with its district Fed bank. Only the Board of Governors was politically selected. Governors were appointed for staggered fourteen-year terms so that no president could "pack" the Board. Nevertheless, the Fed was not (and is not) private. No part of the Federal Reserve System faced competition from other similar institutions; Fed banks did not pay residual income to stockholders; they faced no risk that they might fail as private enterprises; and no private household or business firm, including banks, had any property rights in the Fed's capital structure.

Even before the final gasp of the banking system in 1933, the Fed's inability or unwillingness to address the banking and monetary problems of the time on any terms had prompted political authorities to turn to other devices. Fed officials encouraged the view that the economy's disequilibrium was a productivity and not a monetary problem, partly because they believed it themselves but also because it diverted criticism from their unwillingness to initiate even the most rudimentary program of monetary relief. Given the private nonpolitical image political pragmatists had of the Federal Reserve System, and given their inability to understand its operations, congressional leaders of the time were more of a mind to circumvent the central bank in favor of developing other agencies and bureaus for carrying out programs that would attack economic hardships directly. The executive branch, headed first by Herbert Hoover and then by Franklin Roosevelt, was of a similar persuasion.

The first "substitute" institution—one that was an obvious surrogate for a floundering Federal Reserve System—was the Reconstruction Finance Corporation (RFC). The act to form the RFC was passed on 22 January 1932, during the administration of President Herbert Hoover. The RFC was a government corporation. It was capitalized with $500 million from general taxpayer revenues, and it operated under the direction of the U.S. Treasury. It could issue its own bonds, debentures, and notes to raise another $1,500 million. Its mission was to lend to banks, other corporations, and government agencies that could not get "help from conventional sources."[2]

The most obvious and conventional of credit sources had been the twelve Federal Reserve banks. They were the touted lenders of last resort, the legalized descendants from the "extra-legal" and illegal clearinghouse associations. However, during the Great Contraction of 1929–1933, the Fed banks had turned out to be lenders of no resort. Congress and the administration, unable to persuade the Federal Reserve authorities to promote an extensive and consistent lending policy either for the banks or for the government, decided to create an even more fundamental lender of last resort. The RFC was that institution.

The RFC took its cue from President Hoover. He recommended an institution "which should extend loans to banks on assets not now eligible for rediscount at the Federal reserve banks."[3] Hoover's secretary of the Treasury, Ogden Mills, further explained the rationale for the RFC in his annual report for

1932. "What the Government did in creating the RFC," he explained, "was to put the credit of the Government itself back of the total credit structure. . . . Take the banks for purposes of illustration." In rescuing banks from failure, the RFC also "helps the manufacturer to keep his small business going."[4] It also makes "the credit facilities of the Federal Reserve System available to member banks, *whose eligible paper has been exhausted,* by permitting them to borrow on *sound* [in contrast to "eligible"] assets."[5]

Just a year earlier, Secretary Mellon had stated that the banks had $3.2 billion of eligible paper and $4.5 billion in U.S. government securities, all of which would serve "as a basis for additional Federal reserve bank accommodation."[6] Clearly, the banks' eligible paper had not been "exhausted." It had simply been reclassified by Federal Reserve Bank Loan Committees, who had reassessed the "eligibility" of the paper in the light of the depressed state of business.

The absurdity of this burgeoning of institutions is immediately apparent. Why should an RFC have been necessary for making loans to needy banks when an elaborate Federal Reserve System had been in place for twenty years to do just that? The RFC, at best, had no net leverage on the monetary system; it could not create monetary base materials. It was similar to a private financial corporation in that it borrowed from the securities market (after its first endowment of taxpayers' money) and then made loans with the proceeds. True, it made loans to banks when the Fed banks were "unable to help." But it could do so because it was allowed to broaden the eligibility concept to include assets that, although not "eligible," were "sound" and "acceptable," thereby violating the original, operational principle that had justified the creation of the Federal Reserve System.[7]

One month after the RFC became law, Congress passed the Glass-Steagall Act (27 February 1932). This act allowed the Fed banks to "compete" with the new RFC by relaxing the type of collateral security required for member bank discounts at Fed banks. It also permitted Fed banks to use government securities as collateral for the issue of Federal Reserve notes, thereby establishing a formal basis for monetization of the government's recurring fiscal deficits, a large fraction of which resulted from the federal government's outlays for the RFC.

The final banking crisis of the era in early 1933 provoked the Emergency Banking Act, which President Roosevelt signed into law on 9 March 1933. It allowed the president to declare a banking "holiday" in order to stop the drain of bank reserves. It also gave the Executive, through the Treasury Department, the power to call in all gold coin and gold certificates owned domestically.[8]

A few months later, on 12 May 1933, Congress passed the Thomas Amendment to the Agricultural Adjustment Act. This "Inflation Bill," as it was dubbed, authorized and even encouraged the Fed banks to buy $3 billion more government securities than the $1.8 billion they already had. With the securities as collateral, they could have issued an equivalent amount of new Federal Reserve notes. In addition, it gave the president the power to reduce the gold content of the gold dollar by as much as 60 percent.[9] Then on 5 June 1933 Congress passed the Gold Reserve Act that abrogated all gold clauses in all contracts, public and private, including those made by the government in the bonds financing the Liberty and Victory loans of 1917–1919.[10]

A few weeks later (16 June) Congress passed the Banking Act of 1933. This act emerged from the second Glass-Steagall *bill,* and is to be distinguished from the Glass-Steagall *Act* noted above. The sponsors of both these acts, Senator Carter Glass of Virginia and Congressman Henry Steagall of Alabama, proposed two bills for regulating commercial banking and the Federal Reserve System. The act that passed from their first bill in 1932 was named the Glass-Steagall Act in their honor. Since their second bill, passed in June 1933, could not be identically labeled, it was titled simply "The Banking Act of 1933." Nevertheless, it too had the Glass-Steagall trademark.

Besides separating commercial banking from investment banking, the Banking Act of 1933 granted additional powers to the Federal Reserve Board and Federal Reserve banks to oversee loans and investments of member banks. The advertised intention of the act was to prevent "speculative" trading in securities, real estate, and commodities from crowding out "legitimate" credit. The act also had several other "antispeculative" provisions, including prohibition of interest on demand deposits and the long-enduring (fifty-year) Fed authority to set ceiling rates of interest on time deposits (Regulation Q).[11] It also introduced federal deposit insurance for banks' demand deposits, thereby emphasizing the failure of Federal Reserve policy to prevent the earlier bank disasters.

The intended effect of the Banking Act of 1933 was to induce banks to invest in U.S. government securities, both by reason of the conditioned need for liquidity the banks felt after the recent liquidity debacle, and also because government regulators wanted to purge private "speculative" securities from the banks' investment portfolios. The provisions in the new act for ceiling rates of interest on time deposits and zero interest rates on demand deposits also tended to make "investments" in commercial bank deposits less attractive than ownership of U.S. government securities. Interest-rate ceilings on bank time deposits, therefore, had the effect of holding down market interest rates on government securities. In case the banks did not "understand," the act pointedly exempted all security issues of the federal government, state governments, municipalities, and government agencies from the "speculative" class of investment securities prohibited to commercial banks.[12]

Such exclusion should have seemed hypocritical in the extreme since this same government just eleven days earlier had passed the act that eliminated from its outstanding debt all clauses that had promised payment in gold. The government's power to tax resource owners and to create money would always ensure that it could pay off claims against itself in nominal dollars; but experience over the ensuing decades demonstrated that it was more than willing to dilute the real value of the claims against itself by means of monetary inflation. Certainty of redemption for nominal claims speaks nothing about real values. Indeed, the gold clauses in the government's contractual debts had been inserted there as insurance against the very kind of repudiation by inflation that subsequently occurred.

Gold and Silver Legislation in the Mid-Thirties

The federal government now had the path cleared for assuming ownership of the country's monetary gold stock. By his authority under the Gold Reserve Act of 1934, President Roosevelt called in all the gold and paid for it at $20.67 per ounce. The "internal drain" of gold thereby became an official transfer of all privately owned gold to the federal government. In the next few weeks the president by his fiat increased the price of gold by 59 percent to $35 per ounce.[13] Since all gold clauses had been nullified, the government did not have to share its seigniorage profits of $2.8 billion from the gold revaluation with private "speculators" and other "malefactors of great wealth." Two billion dollars of this total went into the Exchange Stabilization Fund to be used to peg exchange rates, but it was also available for government security purchases until needed for exchange-rate maneuvering.

Much of the gold over which the federal government took title was already an asset of the twelve Federal Reserve banks, and had been stockpiled "for" them in the Treasury. While it had not been very visible, it had been freely available for the redemption of other moneys.

President Roosevelt rationalized this usurpation of private property rights in gold during one of his notorious fireside chats. "Since there was not enough gold to pay all holders of gold obligations," he noted, "the Government should in the interest of justice allow none to be paid in gold."[14] If this criterion were a valid excuse for such expropriation, it could have been invoked at any prior instant back to the creation of the most despotic of governments. The use of gold as a recognized *fractional* reserve for monetary and banking systems always precluded any immediate liquidation of *all* outstanding debts for gold.

The Silver Purchase Act of 1934 concluded the government's extensive housekeeping revenue-accruing operations. By this act, the Treasury could buy silver at $.50 per ounce or less, and could then issue silver certificates as though the silver was worth $1.29 per ounce—the historic fixed price for silver monetization. During the next two years, the Treasury realized silver seigniorage worth over $300 million.[15]

The Most Important Variable: Federal Government Revenues

All of these acts taken together suggest a pattern of incentives and strategies that is consistent. First, government spokesmen argued that the evil that provoked the Great Contraction and ensuing depression was unchecked speculation. The evidence for this opinion was the dramatic stock market boom. The most pressing "national" need was to rein in speculation by means of the credit moralities of the Federal Reserve System. Unfortunately, in depriving the Speculative Devil of his substance, the Fed also starved the innocent banking institutions it was supposed to nourish, thereby promoting or aggravating several bank crises. The accompanying decline in the economy's national income severely impeded the government's ability to generate tax revenues. In the presence of a Federal Reserve System that had so bungled, government policy was to undertake direct intervention in the financial industry in order to ensure that the inflow of resources for its own operations was secure.

Government expenditures were burgeoning, but the revenue increases foreseen from the Revenue Act of 1932, which raised tax rates to their 1924 levels, did not materialize.[16] Seigniorage from gold and silver expropriation, however, provided at least a one-time bonanza. The government's "profit" of $2.8 billion from the revaluation of the gold was, by one pen-stroke, almost the equivalent of one year's ordinary tax revenues. That same federal government almost a century earlier (1835–1837) had returned its fiscal surplus to the states. The government of 1934, by way of contrast, legislated the seigniorage into existence and kept all of the proceeds for itself.

The second conventional source of government income, especially on account of the cyclical dearth of tax revenues, was the sale of U.S. Treasury (and other government agency) securities. Almost all of the new laws encouraged or stimulated demands for securities from all levels of government and from government agencies. Commercial banks, Fed banks, the RFC, the twelve Federal Home Loan banks, the Exchange Stabilization Fund—all were induced or permitted to purchase federal government securities. That some of these purchases might have helped revive the private sector was largely irrelevant to government activists, although they professed otherwise as part of their political rhetoric. As it was, most of the legislation that established government corporations, such as the RFC, simply bled off resources from the private sector that private institutions might have used more economically.[17]

U.S. Treasury Monetary Policies in the Mid-Thirties

Two elements dominated the monetary picture of the 1930s. One was the role of the gold stock in the monetary system, and how the ownership of gold was changed to make it fit into a political pattern. The other key factor was the part played by the Treasury Department. These two developments were intimately connected.

Gold of a specified weight and fineness became the only legal standard for the monetary system in 1900. Anyone could own or use gold without constraint. However, banks held most of the gold as reserves, while the U.S. Treasury held a sizable amount (at least $150 million by law) as a redemption reserve against outstanding government guaranteed currency—U.S. notes, silver currency, and national bank notes. When the Federal Reserve Act was passed, the member commercial banks deposited most of their gold in the twelve Fed banks, thereby raising deposit-reserve credits in their accounts.

The Treasury had the option of depositing its gold in Fed banks or of keeping it in its own vaults as a reserve for its outstanding currency. In practice, the Treasury deposited only its fiscal revenues in the Fed banks. It stockpiled its own gold, and it also was the custodian for the gold that member banks deposited in the Fed banks. The Treasury then issued gold certificates, which were titles to the gold. The certificates were an "asset" to the Fed banks and a "liability" of the Treasury. Until the Gold Reserve Act of 1934, gold was a viable property for anyone. After the Gold Reserve Act, the Treasury effectively owned and controlled the entire gold stock. Only foreign demands could deplete the Treasury's hoard. The new law prohibited all domestic ownership of monetary gold and transactions in gold.[18]

The development of the Treasury's gold and silver position up to 1942 is seen in table 18.1. Starting with the $150 million of gold required to support its outstanding paper currency before World War I and in addition to its stockpile of silver, the Treasury also became the custodian of the Federal Reserve banks' gold reserves. The gold stock then showed steady increases, with the exception of 1920, up to 1926. It declined by about 11 percent in 1928 due to a positive policy effort by the Federal Reserve System in support of the international gold standard, then increased again until September 1931. Indeed, the value for 1931 was only 2.5 percent less than the greatest value previously recorded—$3,786 million in 1924.

Great Britain's departure from the gold standard in September 1931 signaled the beginning of a worldwide scramble for gold. The Treasury's holdings declined somewhat after this event, reaching a minimum dollar value of $2,959 million in June 1932. Devaluation of the gold dollar by the act of 1934 then increased the dollar value of the Treasury's gold reserves by 59 percent (noted above, p. 278). Subsequently, the political apprehension in Europe, associated with the activities of the Nazi government in Germany, was the most decisive force promoting the flow of gold to the United States. By the time the United States entered World War II, the value of the Treasury's gold stock was more than $22 billion. In physical volume this dollar amount came to well over 19,000 *tons!*

TABLE 18.1 Gold and silver stocks in U.S. Treasury, 1918–1942 (as of June 30)

Year	Gold reserve fund for U.S. notes (1)	Holdings of gold coin and bullion against gold certificates (2)	Gold in Treasury offices (3)	Gold cert. fund for Federal Reserve System (4)	Total gold in Treasury[a] (5)	Total silver bullion and dollars in Treasury (6)
1918	153	1,027	95	1,205	2,480	450
1919	153	736	212	1,416	2,516	255
1920	153	585	250	1,184	2,172	161
1921	153	717	263	1,538	2,670	280
1922	153	695	200	2,109	3,157	376
1923	153	737	189	2,285	3,364	468
1924	153	1,218	154	2,261	3,786	467
1925	154	1,610	175	1,753	3,691	476
1926	154	1,681	162	1,717	3,714	480
1927	155	1,625	159	1,712	3,651	488
1928	156	1,514	158	1,388	3,216	491
1929	156	1,384	176	1,562	3,278	498
1930	156	1,490	51	1,796	3,494	495
1931	156	1,702	62	1,777	3,696	499
1932	156	1,491	76	1,236	2,959	501
1933	156	1,231	76	1,772	3,234	508
1934	156	959	969	3,973	7,856	505
1935	156	788	861	5,510	9,116	823
1936	156	2,916	445	5,291	10,608	1,217
1937	156	2,903	1,438	6,020	12,318	1,341
1938	156	2,894	292	7,820	12,963	1,541
1939	156	2,888	568	10,699	16,110	1,733
1940	156	2,882	196	14,928	19,963	1,851
1941	156	2,878	292	17,497	22,624	1,928
1942	156	2,874	170	17,735	22,736	1,985

Source: *Annual Reports, Secretary of the Treasury, 1918–1942*.
[a] The totals in this column exceed the sums of columns 1, 2, 3, and 4 because some minor items are omitted.

The gold spectacle of the 1930s seems strange in retrospect. Not only did Federal Reserve policymakers overreact to every minor impact on the gold stock, but all of the appreciation in the value of the gold stock enriched only the federal government. Who could look at the growth in the dollar value of the Treasury's gold and silver reserves between 1932 and 1942—668 percent for gold and almost 300 percent for silver—and imagine that the economy of the United States was foundering all that time in a twelve-year depression? The contrast was between a government awash in gold and silver, and a depressed economy denuded of money and operating in the presence of a shell-shocked banking system.

The Banking Act of 1935: The Rule of Men in Policy

The Seventy-fourth Congress, which convened in 1935, considered economic problems paramount, and monetary conditions were chief among the economic issues that demanded treatment. The general consensus of congressional opinion was that the Great Crash and ensuing depression were caused by (not just correlated with) wild speculation and stock gambling encouraged by the "loose" credit policies of the Federal Reserve System.[19] Not only had the Fed been remiss in preventing speculative credit excesses, its vaunted power was undirected and inadequately controlled. Its decision-making, especially, was marked by uncertain lines of authority. To correct these deficiencies, Congress considered a new "reform" bill—the Banking Act of 1935—that was to change drastically the institutional structure and hegemony of the Federal Reserve System.

The appointment of Marriner Eccles as chairman of the Fed Board in 1934 signaled the Roosevelt Administration's intention to revamp the Federal Reserve System. Eccles, who was recommended for the position by Henry Morgenthau, Jr., Roosevelt's secretary of the Treasury, outspokenly favored lots of federal spending and accompanying budget deficits to counteract the depression. He argued forcefully that the Fed ought to "support expansionary fiscal policy through discretionary monetary policy."[20] His posture subjected monetary policy to fiscal dominance and, in effect, transferred the monetary powers of the Fed to the Treasury Department. Both Eccles and Morgenthau wanted a Federal Reserve System that would be supportive of their fiscal designs. Eccles's overt acceptance of this strategy is what recommended him for the chairmanship.

After Eccles became chairman of the Board of Governors, he worked closely with Professor Lauchlin Currie of Harvard, a monetary activist, on a proposal that would reinstitute the Fed so that it could effect "conscious control and [monetary] management" on a continuing basis. The Eccles-Currie plan would also end the intra-institutional jockeying for control between the Board and the Fed banks by making the Board of Governors the dominant element in the system.[21]

Not only was the Board to be dominant in the formation of monetary policy, it was also to be discretionary. Every business experience was different, Eccles and Currie argued, and therefore every cyclical problem required conscious human adaptation. "The objectives of control . . . should be mandatory [for the banking system]," they claimed; "but the management, or the handling of the instruments of control, must be discretionary."[22]

To make the new Fed look apolitical, the secretary allowed himself to be taken off the Board. Since he now had a surrogate for his fiscal policy in the person of the chairman of the Board of Governors, his purposes could as well be served from a position behind the throne. The rule of men thus spread to the Fed. But the men in charge were not the men in the Federal Reserve System. They were the men in the Executive administration; the Fed simply became their monetary handmaiden.

The Eccles-Currie plan was embodied in an administration-backed bill, H.R. 7617, that eventually became the Banking Act of 1935. While going through Congress, this bill also came under the influence of Senator Carter Glass and Representative Henry Steagall. Glass, however, was highly critical of the new bill, while Steagall very much favored it, primarily because it abolished the real-bills criterion for Federal Reserve action. Many member banks, Steagall complained correctly, "went down in ruin because of the arbitrary, inelastic, straitlaced eligibility requirements of the Federal Reserve System, as a result of which solvent banks were unable to get the accommodations to which they were entitled."[23]

The solution Steagall offered was not to abolish the failed Federal Reserve System and go back to a private clearinghouse network. Rather, his proposal was to replace the "wrong people" with the "right people." The wrong people were the bankers who managed the Federal Reserve banks. The proper group to manage the system was the Board of Governors. The pending law would allow the President of the United States to reconstitute the Board and bring "the System with its vast resources into full harmony with the advanced policies of the present [Roosevelt] administration. We all know," he concluded in a classic statement of men versus law, "that it does not matter so much what we write into the law as it does who administers the law." By diverting control of the system from the twelve Federal Reserve banks to the Federal Reserve Board, the credit and monetary policies of the country would be exercised in the name of the "people of the United States."[24]

Carter Glass, the sponsor of the original Federal Reserve Act in 1913 when he had been a member of the House of Representatives, referred to his legislative colleague, Henry Steagall, as the "worst inflationist in the country."[25] Glass's role became that of a conservative anchor against the activism of the administration. He noted that the open-market committee was only supposed to enhance the impact of the discount rate by buying and selling securities. "It is now presumed," he said critically, "to make the open-market committee the supreme power in the determination of the credits of the country. No such thing was intended [by the original Federal Reserve Act], and no such thing should ever be done," he declared, because the Board "does not have a dollar of pecuniary interest in the Reserve funds or the deposits of the Federal Reserve banks or of the member banks."[26]

The debate on the bill emphasized a number of facts and impressions that had emerged from the Fed's first twenty years of operation. A major problem was the dilemma of control. The original act had provided for regional reserve control by the Fed banks with general oversight by the Board. The Fed banks were seen as supercommercial banks vested with a public interest, but a public interest that would operate through the medium of the member banks. Since the banking system was the vehicle, bankers had to be in control because they alone had the expertise to manipulate the system properly. What was good for the banks—namely, credit relief at critical times—was also good for the general public. At the same time, this policy obviously acted as a welfare program for bankers. The Fed banks were supposed to be the commercial banks' lender of last resort, but who was to say that they would not at times also become the banks' lender of first resort, or, worse yet, their lender of no resort, as in 1931–1933?

The check and balance here was supposed to have been the real-bills/eligible paper doctrine. This device, however, had proven demonstrably unworkable because of the procyclical characteristics of commercial loans: When business was good, all discounts were very, very "eligible"; and when business was bad, they were all horrid. Open-market operations were the answer. Not only did they make the discounting function unnecessary, they also could be conducted by an "impartial" body—the Federal Reserve Open Market Committee (FOMC).

This issue provoked a congressional controversy over which elements in the system should have, and which did have, decision-making powers—particularly, the Board or the Fed Bank of New York. The principal debaters were Senator Glass and Senator Elmer Thomas, a populist Democrat from Oklahoma.

"The Federal Reserve Board," said Thomas, "should be the most powerful, the most important, and most respected tribunal in the United States." Unfortunately, he noted, the Board did not control the Federal Reserve System. Rather, "the policy of the 12 banks is controlled and dictated by the Federal Reserve Bank of New York."

Glass denied Thomas's statement as "inaccurate . . . [and] a humiliating confession that the Federal Reserve Board . . . declined to assert its lawful functions. . . . The Board was instituted to see that the Federal Reserve Banks obeyed the law."

Thomas replied: "Heretofore, the Federal Reserve Board has been so circumscribed with limitations that [it] had virtually no effective power."

Glass: "They had all power."[27]

The senators were arguing over details that had never been properly specified. Each had a different view of who ought to control the system, who did control the system, and how the system was supposed to work in the first place. This confusion over the relationship between the Fed's structure and its functions was the logical result of governmental bureaucracy. It is discussed in picturesque detail in Friedman and Schwartz's *Monetary History of the United States*. They particularly emphasize, as did the debates in Congress, that the effectiveness of policy within the framework of the system at that time depended on the force of personality in those men who knew how the monetary system worked. The most knowledgeable man in the system was Benjamin Strong, president of the Fed Bank of New York until his death in 1928.[28] Ironically, this characteristic is just what the original Federal Reserve Act was supposed to avoid.

The cult of the laying on of hands was rampant in the 1930s. Steagall's remark cited above is an example of much governmental opinion of the time. The same idea was belabored by Senator Thomas in his criticism of monetary policy. "Someone, somewhere," he accused, "has been and is regulating the value [of money]; and I should like to inquire under what law is the value of the dollar being regulated?" The Constitution, he noted, granted Congress the power to regulate the value of money, but the dollar had doubled in value from unknown causes between 1920 and 1935. "Someone," he continued, "is regulating the value of our dollar. No one seems to know who is doing it. There is no authority, there is no commission, there is no board, there is no particular individual who has had enjoined upon it or him, by congressional mandate, the duty of regulating the value of the dollar." His prescription was that the Federal Reserve Board be "charged with this responsibility."[29]

Senators Gerald Nye of North Dakota and William Borah of Idaho also wanted to formalize Congress's power to regulate the value of money. They proposed writing into the new bill a section prescribing a stable-price-level policy to be implemented by the Federal Reserve Board. Indeed, Nye wanted the Board's staff to include the Bureau of Labor Statistics so that the Board could "scientifically and accurately determine the rate at which progressive additions to the stock of circulating money . . . must be made in order to maintain an even and stable purchasing power."[30]

Borah was even more explicit in his wish to avoid discretion. He warned against the open-ended nature of the open-market provision. "There is practically no limit there," he charged, "—nothing but the discretion of such men as [Benjamin] Strong and [John] Mitchell." He urged Congress "to fix a definite policy and enact a definite mandate by which these officers . . . are to be controlled."[31] The Senate rejected Nye's and Borah's proposed amendments by a voice vote. While the legislators foresaw an enlarged role for the Fed, the criterion of a price index rule to make policy objective ran counter to the discretionary positivism of the era.

Senator Glass, who had been secretary of the Treasury under President Wilson and the second chairman of the Federal Reserve Board, exhibited a split personality on this relationship. He observed that as secretary of the Treasury he had treated the Board "as a bureau of the Treasury. . . . I dominated the activities of the Board," he stated matter-of-factly, "and I always directed them in the interests of the Treasury, and so did my predecessor, the present Senator from California [Mr. William McAdoo]."[32] Yet in a statement made a few years earlier following passage of the Banking Act of 1933, Glass had argued that the Federal Reserve System was not supposed to be "the footmat of the Treasury. . . . It was never intended," he continued, "that the Federal Reserve banking system should be used as an adjunct of the Treasury Department, and particularly . . . to . . . curtail the capabilities of the Federal Reserve banks to serve the business interests of the country."[33]

As a secretary of the Treasury and ex officio chairman of the Fed Board he had "dominated" the Board. As a senator offering norms for how the system should operate he effectively condemned his own power-oriented behavior. His self-confessed practice of "dominating the Board" confirms that even in the beginning the Fed's much-heralded political independence was nothing more than a public relations ploy to try to make monetary policy look nonpolitical.

The compromise solution for the bill reached by the House-Senate conference committee was to reconstitute the open-market committee in the form it has had ever since, with five Fed bank presidents and the seven members of the Board of Governors. Board members being a majority, the execution of monetary policy became safely lodged in the "representatives of the people." Glass's efforts prevented the newly constituted Board of Governors from having complete control of the system.[34] Nonetheless, the power center shifted decisively from the banks to the Board.

Was the original Federal Reserve System powerful or impotent? In the epigraph to this chapter, H. Parker Willis warns of the Fed Board's "enormous powers" and its "still greater and more inclusive authority." In the same breath he despairs of its prestige: "at critical moments . . . it is not even called into consultation by administrators." So it was technically powerful yet practically ineffective, and politically shunned for its ineffectiveness.

More than variable personalities and the invalid real-bills doctrine for guiding its operations was the uncertain base on which the system was founded. Federal Reserve banks were private; yet they were also public. The banks were at the cutting edge of policy; yet the Fed Board had some jurisdictional authority over the Fed banks. As a purely technical monetary institution, the Fed banks and Board in allegiance with each other could have maintained price level stability within narrow limits, and certainly could have held the Great Contraction and twelve-year depression to a mild two-year recession. As a political institution subject to internal turf battles and pressures from politicians, and with no self-interest in promoting monetary stability, the Fed let its "action" degenerate into inaction. In contrast to the loan committees of the clearinghouse associations, which were managed by the bankers who might have been engulfed in an illiquidity epidemic themselves, the loan committees of the twelve Fed banks became detached and sanguine credit moralists. Inflation was rampant, they opined from on high; so liquidate a bit, you greedy bankers. When the liquidation became unstable, they retreated into their bureaucratic foxholes in disarray. Their behavior emphasized the difference between a market-oriented institution in which self-interest was a vital stabilizing force and a political institution in which self-interest promoted wimpism and a tendency to mumble.

19 The Reserve Requirement Experiment of the Mid-Thirties

> The Secretary of the Treasury, after conferring with the Board of Governors of the Federal Reserve System, announces that he proposes, whenever it is deemed advisable and in the public interest . . . , to take appropriate action [against inflation] . . . by the sale of additional debt obligations, the proceeds of which will be used for the purchase of gold, and by the purchase or redemption of outstanding obligations in case of [deflationary] movements in the reverse direction.
>
> Annual Report of the Secretary of the Treasury, 1936

Effect of Gold Inflows on Bank Reserves after 1935

The original Federal Reserve System had had few political checks and balances. Its supposed political independence, the regional dispersion of Fed banks, the system's limited powers as an adjunct instituton to the presumably dominant gold standard, and its adherence to the real-bills doctrine seemed to make unnecessary explicit limitations on its authority. The Banking Act of 1935 with its greatly expanded powers for the Fed Board and FOMC—powers that far exceeded the Fed's original mission—would have seemed to argue for constraints on its monetary operations, such as the maintenance of a stable price level as recommended by Senators Borah and Nye. Many other specific targets and goals suggest themselves; a stable-price-level rule is just one possibility. The act of 1935, however, had no operational rules or guidelines with respect to either procedures or targets or goals.

This omission is, again, a commentary on the widespread acceptance of the rule of men that dominated the political spirit of the era. If good men were put in charge, the feeling was, they would do good things. Good men were rational men who had consciences. Social problems would yield to their wisdom and their scruples. In addition, the policies of rational men would be quick and positive. The rule of law, by way of contrast, required time; and the voluntary behavior that resulted from rule-of-law incentives was liable to be uncertain and sporadic.

Besides shifting the institutional authority of open-market operations from the Fed banks to the Fed Board, the Banking Act of 1935 gave the Federal Reserve Board effective control of reserve requirements for member banks. Requirements had been statutory at 7, 10, and 13 percent since an amendment in 1917 to the original Federal Reserve Act.[1] With its new authority the Board could increase reserve requirements within a range up to double the original values.[2]

Before the ink had fairly well dried on the Banking Act of 1935, talk in the

Federal Reserve System turned to the use of the newly authorized policy instrument. The inflow of gold from Europe, both because of U.S. gold-dollar devaluation and because of the fearful political developments there, were generating what were regarded at that time as massive increases in the bank reserves portion of the monetary base. These reserves were entered as such in the ledgers of the twelve Federal Reserve banks and balanced equal amounts of demand deposits in commercial member banks.

The U.S. Treasury had to buy the new gold at the fixed price of $35.00 per ounce. The Treasury buried the gold in vaults and issued two items on the basis of the gold; one was a gold certificate, which was an asset specifying title to the gold; the other was a check to pay for the gold. To the seller of gold the check was a receivable. The Treasury's (partial) balance sheet after the transaction was as follows:

Assets	*Liabilities*
Gold certificates (+)	Checks payable (+)

The Treasury then deposited the gold certificates it had just issued in the twelve Federal Reserve banks—as if the certificates were ordinary currency. Indeed, they were a *kind* of currency. The gold certificates were the same size and design as other U.S. currency, but were issued in a one-hundred-thousand-dollar denomination—hardly suitable for use at the local grocery store. After the Treasury deposited its gold certificates with the Fed banks, its balance sheet and that of the twelve Fed banks, combined as if they were a single institution, appeared as in figure 19.1.

Meanwhile, the checks that paid for the gold were receivables in the possession of the gold sellers who deposited the checks in commercial banks. The banks credited the accounts of these depositors, and sent the checks to their Federal Reserve banks for credit to their reserve-deposit accounts. The Fed banks cleared the checks by crediting the member banks' accounts and debiting the Treasury's account. The balance sheets shown in figure 19.2 reflect these transactions. After the (gold) dust settled, the *net* changes in the monetary system were the accounting items shown by the (+) symbols.

The Move to Increase Member Bank Reserve Requirements

Even though the U.S. monetary system was not, strictly speaking, on a gold standard—since private ownership of gold and transactions in gold were prohibited by law—yet another law required the Treasury and Fed to monetize gold on fixed dollar terms in the mode shown here.[3] The result was a burgeoning of the monetary base and bank demand deposits. From 1933 to 1936, the money stock (M_2) grew at annual rates of 9.5, 14.0, and 13.0 percent.[4] At the same time the commercial member banks built up large volumes of excess

Figure 19.1

	Assets	Liabilities
U.S. Treasury	Deposit account with Fed banks (+) Gold certificates (+)(−)	Checks payable (+)
Federal Reserve banks	Gold certificates (+)	Treasury deposit account (+)

Figure 19.2

	Assets	Liabilities
U.S. Treasury	Deposit account with FR banks (+)(−)	Checks payable (+)(−)
Federal Reserve banks	Gold certificates (+)	Treasury deposit accounts (+)(−) Member banks reserve-deposit accounts (+)
Commercial member banks	Treasury checks receivable (+)(−) Reserve accounts at FR banks (+)	Deposits (+)
Households and firms that sold gold to treasury	Gold (−) Checks receivable (+)(−) Deposits in banks (+)	Immaterial

legal reserves. By the end of 1935 their excess reserves were slightly greater than their required reserves. Put another way, they held more than double the amount of legally required reserves as reserve-deposit balances in Fed banks.

This condition prompted a movement within the Fed, initiated by the Fed Bank of New York, to increase the legal reserve requirements of all member banks, an action that was undertaken in three giant steps. First, requirements were raised by 50 percent from 7, 10, and 13 percent to 10½, 15, and 19½ percent in August 1936. This action increased required reserves by $1.5 billion. Requirements were raised again in March 1937 by another 25 percent, and again in May 1937 by the final 25 percent that the act of 1935 allowed. The May increase meant that member banks' required reserves were 100 percent greater (14, 20, and 26 percent) than they had been nine months earlier.

The ostensible economic reason for these massive increases, which were the monetary equivalent of a $3 billion open-market *sale* of government securities, was *fear of inflation!* The economy had just suffered the most disastrous hyperdepression in history. But before all the foreclosures had been properly settled, the monetary authorities were "worried" about a possible *inflation*.

A more believable (political) reason behind the policy was the competition for power between the Fed Board and Fed banks that the Banking Act of 1935 had accentuated. Only the Federal Reserve Board could manipulate reserve requirements. Once requirements were at their upper limits, the Fed's other traditional policies—setting the discount rate and open-market operations—could come center stage again. These latter two policies were products of both the Fed banks and the Fed Board. The Fed banks set discount rates with the approval of the Board, and five Fed bank presidents were still on the FOMC. Therefore, raising reserve requirements to a level where no tolerance was left would bring traditional policies back into play and thereby allow the Fed banks some share in decision-making.[5]

Internal squabbling aside, the policy of raising reserve requirements to prevent inflation also had a great deal of support outside the Fed. A typical view was expressed by B. M. Anderson, a conservative critic of both New Deal policies in general and monetary policy in particular.

The great increase in excess reserves that had occurred, Anderson argued, had had very little effect on interest rates. Therefore, mopping up excess reserves by raising requirements would also have little effect in reverse, and would in no way compromise the limited effectiveness of current monetary policy.[6]

Anderson's arguments reflected the general economic reasoning of the era. Monetary policy could only influence business conditions by its liquidity effect on interest rates. Since rates were already at rock bottom and would remain there without regard to the magnitude of excess bank reserves, the elimination of excess reserves made no difference.[7]

These arguments are, however, basically contradictory. On the one hand, excess reserves did not have the power to restore full employment levels of borrowing, lending, and spending; on the other hand, they gave rise to a "dangerously high potential of credit expansion."[8]

Possible Monetary Effects from Reserve Requirement Increases

Marriner Eccles, in his new role as chairman of the Federal Reserve Board, defended the reserve requirement increases on technical grounds. The banks' new reserves arising from the gold inflows, he said, "could become the basis of a potential expansion of bank credit of such proportions that the Federal Reserve could lose all control or influence over the supply and cost of money."[9] Even though the Board of Governors at this time saw no evidence of any "overexpansion of business activity," Eccles concluded that an increase of at least 50 percent in reserve requirements was desirable. Reserves would then still be sufficient to "provide a more than adequate basis for legitimate credit expansion."[10]

Although no one at the time saw fit to do so, Eccles's judgments on the adequacy of the member banks' reserve base can be subjected to a rather simple empirical analysis. Eccles himself noted correctly that after the first increase in requirements, the potential increase in bank deposits would still be between $15 billion and $20 billion, and would still be $5 billion after the second increase.[11] The question he did not answer, however, was: How much money would a fully employed economy have required, without inflation, if certain reasonable assumptions were made concerning growth in real output and employment?

Table 19.1 collects the monetary data of the period into time series that provide an answer to this question. The first three columns in the table show member bank deposits for particular dates, and both the usable and excess reserves that resulted from the gold inflows. Excess legal reserves register sharp declines between June and December 1936 because of the first increase in reserve requirements, and again between December 1936 and June 1937 after the second and third increases.

The column titled "Potential Increase in Deposits" (column 5) shows how much "Member Bank Deposits" (column 1) would have increased if "Excess Legal Reserves" (column 4) had been used for bank credit and deposit expansion in the same proportion as required reserves were currently being used. When this possible increase in deposits is added to the actual money stock at each point in time, the sums are the maximum quantities of money that could have been generated. They form the column (7) labeled "Potential Money Stock." The next column (8) shows a computed "Full Employment" money stock based on two adjustments to the existing money stock: one, the additional amount that would have been necessary to accommodate the real output of goods and services a fully employed labor force would produce; and two, the additional amount of money that would have been necessary to get the price level back up to the last value it had had (in 1929) before the current cyclical decline began.[12]

Column 9 is the percentage excess (+) or deficiency (−) of money for 1929 price level stability at full employment for the date indicated. It is calculated by dividing the "Full Employment" money stock into the "Potential Money Stock" and subtracting "1." A plus value indicates the potential inflation that could have occurred if the money stocks had been fully expanded to their technical limits, and a negative value indicates the corresponding depressive potential in the system. The last two columns are data on the current levels of unemployment (percent) and prices (1947–49 = 100) from which the "Full Employment" money stocks are calculated.

The "Full Employment" money stock is a conceptual device, derived by using the quantity theory of money as a policy guide. The argument includes

TABLE 19.1 Selected data of all member banks, unemployment, prices, the actual money supply, the potential money supply, and a computed "full employment" money supply, 1935–1942 ($ billions except prices and unemployment)

Date	Member bank deposits (1)	Member bank usable reserves (2)	Member bank required reserves (3)	Member bank excess (legal) reserves (2) − (3) (4)	Potential increase in deposits of member banks (5)	Actual money stock M_2 (6)	Potential money stock (5) + (6) M_P (7)	Full employment money stock M_F (8)	Percent excess (+) or deficiency (−)[a] (9)	Unemployment (percent of labor force) (10)	Prices (1947–49 = 100) [Datum: $P_{1929} = 73.3$] (11)
1935 Jun. 30	27.4	5.39	2.95	2.44	22.7	38.1	60.8	57.7	+ 5.4	20.1	58.7
Dec. 31	28.9	6.28	3.30	2.98	26.1	40.3	66.4	59.2	+12.2	18.5	59.0
1936 Jun. 30	31.3	6.17	3.58	2.59	22.6	43.3	65.9	62.4	+ 5.6	16.9	59.3
Dec. 31	32.2	7.33	5.28	2.05	12.5	45.0	57.5	63.5	− 9.5	15.6	60.3
1937 Jun. 30	37.3	7.38	6.50	0.88	4.4	45.2	49.6	61.5	−19.3	14.3	61.4
Dec. 31	31.7	7.71	6.64	1.07	5.0	44.0	49.0	61.6	−20.5	16.6	60.9
1938 Jun. 30	31.6	8.61	5.85	2.76	14.9	44.1	59.0	64.4	− 8.4	19.0	60.3
Dec. 31	33.6	9.50	6.27	3.23	17.3	46.6	63.9	67.1	− 4.8	18.1	59.9
1942 Jun. 30	49.4	13.06	10.36	2.70	12.9	69.0	81.9	75.2	+ 8.9	4.1	69.7

Sources: Philip Cagan, *Determinants and Effects of Changes in the Stock of Money,1875–1960,* NBER (New York: Columbia University Press, 1965), table F-8, p. 350; Board of Governors of the Federal Reserve System, *Banking and Monetary Statistics* (Washington, 1943), pp. 396–97; Friedman and Schwartz, *Monetary History of the United States, 1867–1960,* table A-1, pp. 714–15.

[a] The values in this column are calculated as: Excess or Deficiency = (MP/MF − 1). A positive value implies an inflationary potential; a negative value a deflationary tendency.

reflation of prices to the 1929 level because creation and circulation of new money into a market system could not be confined to unemployed sectors. As the new money began to stimulate spending, reemployment of unemployed resources and enhanced production might well occur with little price level increase. However, as fewer and fewer resources were left idle, specialized resources in certain areas would command higher wages or prices, and the general price level would rise. When all unemployed—but willingly employable—factors had been reemployed, prices would rise and the dramatic increases in real output would taper down to the secular increases possible in a fully employed economy.

This pattern would not necessarily hold if the nominal cost structure of resources was flexible downward. The evidence is, however, that while prices and wages were flexible downward to a degree, the adjustment necessary at that time had become unacceptable. Many subsequent government policies also were designed to discourage or prevent money price changes in different sectors of the economy. Further evidence for the necessary reflation of the price level is seen in the entry in the table for June 1942: As diminishing unemployment approached 4.1 percent of the labor force, the 1942 price level (69.7) climbed toward its 1929 value (73.3).

Effects of Reserve Requirement Changes

The first reserve requirement increase in August 1936 came at a time when the actual money stock was less than two-thirds of the potential money stock, and much less in dollar value than the money stock had been seven years before in 1929. The degree of inflation possible before the increase—the ratio of the "Potential Money Stock" to the "Full Employment Money Stock"—was only 5.6 percent. After the first increase, the potential money stock became an invisible ceiling that would have limited business activity to about 90 percent of its full employment potential. Even if the banking system had generated all the money possible within the parameters fixed by Federal Reserve policies, and barring downward cost-price adjustments, no inflation could have occurred. Likewise, unemployment was not likely to decline to less than 10 percent of the labor force.

The final reserve requirement increases of March and May 1937 further aggravated the already potentially depressed banking condition and totally discouraged the recovery. After this bumbling and unreasoning overkill of "inflation," improved employment and business conditions were out of the question. The predicted level of economic activity by this time was in the neighborhood of 20 percent below full employment, or a value about four percentage points below what was currently being experienced.

Eccles observed that total bank deposits and currency by November 1936 were at a higher level than they had been in 1929.[13] In fact, M_1 was slightly greater—$30.4 billion compared to $26.7 billion in October 1929, while M_2 was lower—$44.4 billion compared to $46.4 billion.[14] What Eccles did not take into account was the large increase in employable resources that had occurred in the seven years since 1929. He also noted that the velocity of money had fallen. "If [total bank deposits and currency] were utilized at a rate of turnover comparable to pre-depression levels," he stated, "they would be sufficient to sustain a vastly greater rate of business activity."[15] True, but money was *not* so utilized, and would not be. Even if velocity had regained its 1929 buoyancy, a significant increase in the money stock over its 1929 level would still have been needed. Table 19.1 shows that a full-employment U.S. economy would have required at least $63.5 billion in late 1936, when it had only $45.0 billion.

The potential money stock calculation is an upper limit—a maximum technical creation of money. It takes no account of the state of banking and business confidence—variables that had been deeply injured by the debacle of the early thirties. The potential money stock values are therefore much greater than the money stocks that the banks were likely to create. The very existence of such a level of "excess" reserves as appeared in the mid-thirties is witness to the fact that no great bulge of bank-created money would have occurred. Bankers had come to the conclusion that they had to keep their own contingency reserves—that the Fed was an unreliable lender of last resort. Their reserves, they felt, were excess only in legal terms; they were required as a practical matter to cushion liquidity drains.

The magnitude of the reserve requirement changes was unprecedented in any previous policy action, and, indeed, in any policy undertaken thereafter. The most unforgivable feature of the entire episode was the lack of a compensating adjustment after the damage was observed. Federal Reserve policy continued obstinately on course. The official argument was that since reserves were excess and had been so for several years, they were not "needed." Therefore, shifting them from "excess" to "legally required" by raising requirements had no real effect. This opinion was also in line with the official attitude about money: Money did not matter, except and insofar as it supported fiscal policy.[16]

U.S. Treasury Gold Policy

U.S. Treasury policy, strange to say, was as culpable as Fed policy. The devaluation of the dollar and corresponding appreciation of gold had provided the Treasury with a $2 billion dollar "profit." (See chapter 18, table 18.1.) This money was accounted in an Exchange Stabilization Fund to be used to keep foreign exchange rates closely pegged to the dollar. The Treasury thus had a gold "position" and a license for conducting gold policy.

The excess reserve accumulation of the commercial banks became an object of the new Treasury gold policy. A few months after the first mandated increase in reserve requirements, the Treasury moved "to halt the inflationary potentialities" of all incoming gold by "sterilizing" it. Beginning 22 December 1936, gold purchases were placed in an "inactive" account. Instead of issuing gold certificates and depositing them in Fed banks to raise the necessary balance for payment of the gold, the Treasury paid for the gold by selling government securities in financial markets.[17] This way the gold remained stockpiled but unmonetized in the Treasury. In fact, this policy was somewhat deflationary because it brought more government securities into existence to compete for consumers' and investors' dollars without a corresponding increase in conventional money.

The Treasury's gold policy was not independent of the Federal Reserve's restrictive reserve requirement policy. Secretary Morgenthau announced in a press release that he had decided on this policy after conferring with the Board of Governors.[18] By the middle of 1937 "inactive" gold in the Treasury was $1.087 billion.

The development of the recession in 1937, superimposed on the continuing depression, apparently convinced Secretary Morgenthau that the danger of "inflation" was past. In September 1937, he released $300 million of the gold from the inactive account, thereby restarting the machinery of gold monetization. The $300 million increase in the gold certificate account at Fed banks gave rise as before to increases in monetary base items on the liabilities side of the Fed banks' balance sheets.[19] Then on 19 April 1938 Morgenthau announced the discontinuance of the "inactive" account altogether, and the balance of the Treasury's gold was thereafter monetized in the usual manner.

The time span of the Treasury's gold policy was sixteen months—December 1936 to April 1938—while the Fed's reserve requirement policy started in August 1936 and continued through May 1937. Fed policy effectively neutralized the money-creating potential the banking system had acquired from the gold that had already entered the monetary system. Treasury policy cut off new gold at the initial point of monetization, thus preventing any relief from the strictures of the Fed's ill-conceived reserve requirement increases.

Professional Reaction to Treasury and Federal Reserve Policies

The combined Federal Reserve/Treasury gold demonetization program, far from being roundly condemned by the economists of the time, was heartily supported. "Even the extraordinary increases in reserve requirements in

1936–37," wrote G. Griffith Johnson, "would have been insufficient to bring excess reserves to reasonable size if it had not been for the cooperation of the Treasury through the [gold] sterilization program. . . . One may be skeptical of the wisdom with which monetary instruments will be used," he continued, "but the possibility of abuse extends throughout the whole sphere of governmental activity and is a risk which must be assumed under a democratic or any other form of government."[20]

Johnson's observation again emphasized the political norms of the times. Clearly, monetary instruments had not been used with either "wisdom" or scientific analysis. They were simply seat-of-the-pants responses, sometimes politically motivated, by discretionary authorities who faced no responsibilities for the results of their policies. Furthermore, the "risk of abuse" did not need to be "assumed" under a democratic government if that government was responsibly constrained by constitutional covenants and operated under the rule of law.

Under a true gold standard, as specified by the U.S. Constitution, the Treasury would not have had a "gold policy." The gold standard itself would have been *the* gold policy, and would have been self-regulating. The gold, most important, would not have been stockpiled in the Treasury, where its monetary destiny was highly uncertain, but would have been in commercial banks, where it would have served its intended function of securing demand deposits and bank-issued currency under the dynamic constraint of convertibility. Johnson's "democratic form of government" implied only the laying on of majoritarian hands; constitutional principles were nowhere to be found.

Given a central bank of the new genre as a practical surrogate for the gold standard, some kind of quantity-of-money rule still could have preserved constitutional norms by specification of central-bank targets, goals, and procedures. But current polity would have none of it.

Treasury/Federal Reserve action neutralizing the monetary influence of the gold inflow was a primary feature of their joint policy. Their other major interest was fiscal policy. Eccles himself was a fiscalist who believed that programs for government spending to exceed current tax revenues, i.e., fiscal deficits, were the proper answer to business depression. He was not, however, a permanent deficiteer (to coin a word). When depression abated, he was ready to balance, and even overbalance, the budget.[21]

In spite of Eccles's avowed fiscal emphasis, the Fed's government security purchases during the 1930s were anything but prodigal. First, with the large quantities of excess reserves already in the balance sheets of member banks, additional security purchases would only have added to what was regarded as an undesirable and dangerous surplus. On the other hand, the Fed's existing portfolio of security holdings was too meager to soak up reserves by sales of securities in the open market. If the Fed had used this device, its security holdings of around $2.4 billion would have disappeared, and with them all of the means that the Fed banks had for generating income. When the recession of 1937–38 became pronounced, the Fed did not undertake expansionary open-market purchases because such action would have been tantamount to admitting that the reserve requirement increases were a blunder in the first place.[22]

Virtually all economists, no matter whether they thought Fed policies wise or foolish, agreed that Fed policy had to be man-made and coordinated with Treasury policy. The Treasury's gold policy, wrote Johnson, "was an essential instrument for producing desired political aims."[23] Johnson claimed that Congress had given over the Fed's powers of monetary regulation to the Executive because the central bank had proven ineffective. These powers had become more democratic because "they were now exercised by politically responsible officials . . . [and] would eventually be subject to review by the electorate. . . . In large part," Johnson concluded, "the [Federal Reserve] System has served merely as a technical instrument for effecting the Treasury's policies."[24]

Other mainstream economists also commented on the politicization of the Fed. "The Federal Reserve Board," stated Frederick Bradford in a paper read before the American Economics Association, "although ostensibly independent, has . . . come practically under political domination."[25]

Another prominent economist, John H. Williams, thought that the Fed should be at arm's length from the government—that it should be "governmental" without being "political." He applauded the change in policy-making from the diffused Fed banks to the centralized Board of Governors. "How the System will function," he said, "will depend more upon [the system's] personnel, their understanding and judgment, than upon specific legislative provisions."[26]

Jacob Viner also saw the prominence of personalities in the newly revised system. "The relative strength of personalities" rather than "the legal definition of lines of authority" would determine the path of policy. "Harmonization of the two sets of authorities," he said, "must be through exchange of views between agencies which meet as equals rather than by making one agency the mere instrumentality of the other." Later on, his view of "agencies which meet as equals" vanished. The Fed should face no specific mandate for policy, he stated, because it had to adjust its activities to those of the Treasury, which had "credit control [interest rate] powers . . . co-ordinate with [its own], and [is] pursuing objectives which are avowedly extemporized from day to day."[27]

Even ten years after the event, a prominent economist, Kenneth D. Roose, could write a major policy article, "The Recession of 1937–38," and hardly even mention the effects of Federal Reserve/Treasury monetary policies. Roose noted, only incidentally, that the Fed's reserve requirement policy caused prices of short-term government securities to weaken as member banks sold low-interest assets to obtain reserves. This action tended to raise interest rates and dampen business expectations. He offered four other, more important, factors that contributed to the recession: (1) Excessive accumulation of business inventories; (2) failure of consumption expenditures to expand; (3) a slight cessation of government expenditures; and (4) pressure from increased wage costs on prices and business profits.[28] "Most important of all," he emphasized, "was declining profitability of investment, which . . . resulted from increased costs, of which labor costs were the most important."[29] Roose, a conventional Keynesian, never mentioned at all the changes in the quantity of money. "Monetary and credit conditions were extremely 'easy,'" he claimed, thereby reflecting the view that low interest rates were a sign of an easy money policy.[30]

Economists no doubt wished to see their analytical wisdom crystallized into specific policies that would be good for the economy, which is to say that they favored the laying on of hands for monetary policy if the hands belonged to economists. They were also understandably confused by the severity and depth of a depression that would not go away even when powerful men in high positions manipulated billion-dollar programs. Policies of the time seemed to be momentous, but they obviously were not working. Nonetheless, no politicians of the time, and few economists, thought of linking the strong medicine being practiced in the political sector to the adverse results in the economic sector. If the judgments of one group of men had proven ineffective, some other group would have the acumen and the wisdom to set things right.

20 The Disequilibrium Era: 1940–1951

The policy of a central bank at a moment of time reflects the balance of power among individuals and agencies who influence it. . . . [At the present time central banks have shifted] from faith in automatic laws to dependence on human judgment. . . . Instruments of [central bank] policy have been adjusted to the desires of the treasury. . . . Strong governments have had their way.

Karl R. Bopp, *American Economic Review,* 1944

Money Stock Growth during World War II

On the eve of World War II the Consolidated Statement of Condition of the twelve Federal Reserve banks showed a dollar value of gold certificate holdings almost equal to outstanding demand obligations (table 20.1). The value of the gold certificates, for which gold was "on deposit" in the U.S. Treasury, was \$20.49 billion. This amount allegedly was "backing" member bank reserves plus outstanding currency totaling \$20.64 billion. The value of the monetary gold, therefore, was almost equal to the monetary value of the Fed Banks' demand obligations, but was frozen in the Treasury in accordance with federal law.

The money stock (M_1) had grown by \$24 billion in the seven years since 1933. The Fed's outstanding monetary liabilities (monetary base) had increased by slightly more than \$15 billion, while the Fed's gold holdings had increased by \$16.7 billion over the same period. These changes emphasize, first, that Fed policy was largely passive. The gold increase, which was independent of Fed policy as such, was greater than the increase in the Fed's obligations. These data point to the fact that the Fed's other assets for creating money—government securities and discounts for member banks—had actually declined in this interval. Second, the increase in gold and demand obligations was fully two-thirds of the increase in M_1, which implied that the commercial banking system had not produced much money either. The excess reserve position of the commercial banks also attested to this fact. Third, the Fed was in a technical position to increase enormously the quantity of high-powered money. Since the Banking Act of 1935, it was also in a legal position to do so. The large volume of excess reserves already in the member banking system—\$5.35 billion out of a total of \$13.1 billion—added to the possibility of an inflationary expansion in M_1.

By the end of World War II in 1945, both the Fed's obligations (M_F in table 20.2) and M_1 had more than doubled since 1940, and the privately created money stock (M_P in table 20.2) had about tripled. The CPI, however, had

TABLE 20.1 Federal Reserve banks' Consolidated Statement of Condition (major items), December 31, 1941 ($ billions)

	Assets		Liabilities
Government security holdings	2.25	Deposits	
		Member banks	12.45
Bills discounted and advances to member banks	.01	U.S. Treasury	.87
Gold certificate account	20.49	Federal Reserve note circulation	8.19
	22.75		21.51

Source: Board of Governors of the Federal Reserve System, *Banking and Monetary Statistics* (Washington: Government Printing Office, 1942), p. 332.

Note: Totals do not balance because of exclusion of minor items.

increased by only 25 percent. Such a modest increase was due in part to the large base of unutilized resources in the economy from which the wartime expansion had begun. Unemployment had been over 10 percent as late as 1941, indicating that the nominal wage-price level was still too high to permit a market equilibrium. Consequently, much of the great increase in money—about 14 percent per year—was absorbed by increased real product and income.

The growth in the demand for money during the 1930s had been unprecedented in United States experience. Also unprecedented was the four-year decline in the price level from 1929 to 1933 and the absence of much increase thereafter. By 1941 the price level was only up to about 63 (1947–49 = 100), which was still 14 percent below the 1929 value of 73. Since the growth in nominal money during World War II raised measured prices a modest 10 percent, accounted real money growth also increased significantly. Real M_F, M_P, and M_1 in table 20.2 all show substantial increases, and all reached their peaks during 1945–1947. The growth in accounted real values leading to these peaks ended when the wage-price control program began to be dismantled in 1946.

The wage, price, rent, and profit control program during the war was pervasive and rigorous. Some price controls were put into effect by executive order as early as 1941. Most money prices were then rolled back and frozen at their values of 15 March 1942. Finally, on 2 October 1942 Congress passed the Economic Stabilization Act, on the basis of which President Roosevelt promptly created the Office of Economic Stabilization. From this time until mid–1946, when price controls were largely ended, the U.S. economy operated under a system in which about 85 percent of all consumer goods and services were price-fixed by the Office of Price Administration (OPA) and its associated bureaucracy.[1]

The fixing of money prices below their market-clearing values guaranteed "shortages." The "shortages" were real enough in markets; but the word is in quotes because market freedom would have permitted prices to rise so that no

TABLE 20.2 Federal Reserve monetary liabilities (M_F), M_1, private creation of money (M_P), prices (CPI), and nominal and real values with annual changes, 1934–1951

Year	Bank reserves with Fed (R_B) + F.R. notes (C) + Treas. dep. (T_F) M_F (1)	Annual change in M_F ΔM_F (2)	Real annual change in M_F (1935$) ΔM^*_{FD} (3)	Real capital value of M_F (1935$) M^*_{FC} (4)	Annual change in real capital value of M_F ΔM^*_{FC} (5)	Hand-to-hand currency plus private demand deposits adjusted M_1 (6)	Annual percentage change in M_1 $\frac{\Delta M_1}{M_1}$ (7)
1934	$ 6.68	$ —	$ —	$ 6.86	$ —	$21.1	—
35	8.65	1.97	1.97	8.65	1.8	25.7	21.8
36	10.5	1.85	1.83	10.4	1.7	30.2	17.5
37	11.2	0.70	0.67	10.7	0.3	31.1	3.0
38	12.8	1.6	1.56	12.5	1.8	29.7	− 4.7
39	15.7	2.9	2.87	15.5	3.0	33.3	12.1
1940	18.8	3.1	3.04	18.4	2.9	39.7	19.2
41	20.9	2.1	1.96	19.5	1.1	46.3	16.6
42	23.8	2.9	2.44	20.0	0.5	54.1	16.8
43	28.3	4.5	3.57	22.5	2.5	73.5	35.6
44	33.5	5.2	4.06	26.2	3.7	83.9	14.1
45	39.0	5.5	4.20	29.8	3.6	98.1	16.9
46	41.5	2.5	1.76	29.2	−0.6	107.5	9.6
47	42.5	1.0	0.62	26.1	−3.1	112.1	4.3
48	44.7	2.2	1.25	25.5	−0.6	112.0	0.0
49	44.3	−0.4	−0.24	25.5	0.0	111.3	− 0.7
1950	41.4	−2.9	−1.65	23.6	−1.9	114.1	2.5
51	43.7	2.3	1.22	23.1	−0.5	118.6	3.9
Net change	$37.0	$37.0	$31.1	$16.2	$16.2	$97.5	11.1%[a]

shortages would have occurred. In fact, the correct statement is: "The fixing of market prices below their market-clearing values guaranteed a continuous market disequilibrium, the overt manifestations of which were excess supplies of money and excess demands for consumer goods and services." The disequilibrium continued until two years after market controls had ended, and the primary cause of the disequilibrium was the increase in the quantity of money noted above.

The excess supply of money was both a significant increase in the high-powered monetary base and an even greater increase in bank-created money. The commercial banks used the excess reserves they held at the beginning of World War II to buy interest-earning assets. Since private spending on such things as housing and consumer durables was greatly curtailed during the war, much of the expansion in commercial bank assets was in government securi-

Year	Private creation of money ($M_I - M_F$) M_P (8)	Annual change in M_P ΔM_{PD} (9)	Real annual change in M_P (1935$) ΔM^*_{PD} (10)	Real capital value of M_P (1935$) M^*_{PC} (11)	Annual change in real capital value of M_P ΔM^*_{PC} (12)	Prices (CPI, 1947–49 = 100) P (13)	Annual percentage change in prices $\frac{\Delta P}{P}$ (14)
1934	$14.4	$ —	$ —	$14.8	$ —	57.2	—
35	17.1	2.7	2.70	17.1	2.3	58.7	2.6
36	19.7	2.6	2.57	19.5	2.4	59.3	1.0
37	19.9	0.2	0.19	19.0	−0.5	61.4	3.5
38	16.9	−3.0	−2.92	16.5	−2.5	60.3	−1.8
39	17.6	4.5	4.20	23.7	0.9	62.9	−1.5
1940	20.9	3.3	3.23	20.5	3.1	59.9	0.8
41	25.4	4.5	4.20	23.7	3.2	62.9	5.0
42	30.3	4.9	4.13	25.5	1.8	69.7	10.8
43	45.2	14.9	11.82	35.9	10.4	74.0	6.2
44	50.4	5.2	4.06	39.3	3.4	75.2	1.6
45	59.1	8.7	6.64	45.1	5.8	76.9	2.3
46	66.0	6.9	4.86	46.5	1.4	83.4	8.5
47	69.6	3.6	2.21	42.8	−3.7	95.5	14.5
48	67.3	−2.3	−1.31	38.4	−4.4	102.8	7.6
49	67.0	−0.3	0.17	38.6	0.2	101.8	−1.0
1950	72.7	5.7	3.26	41.5	2.9	102.8	1.0
51	74.9	2.2	1.16	39.6	−1.9	111.0	8.0
Net change	$60.5	$60.5	$53.5	$24.8	$24.8	94.1%	4.1%[a]

Sources: Board of Governors of the Federal Reserve System, *Supplement to Banking and Monetary Statistics*, section 9 (Washington, 1965), pp. 5–6. Department of Commerce, *Historical Statistics of the United States* (Washington, 1958), table E-113, p. 125. Friedman and Schwartz, *A Monetary History of the United States*, table A-1, pp. 714–19.

Note: Values at or near midyear and in $ billions, except for prices.

[a] Average for period.

ties. In addition, the Federal Reserve banks bought significant amounts of government securities, mostly short-term Treasury bills. The very act of purchase by the central bank created more monetary base, which became commercial bank reserves and permitted additional commercial bank expansion. By the end of the war, all commercial banks had reduced their excess reserves to almost nothing, and had increased their government security holdings from $20.1 billion in 1941 to $84.1 billion in 1945. The Federal Reserve banks had increased their government security holdings from $2.25 billion to $24.3 billion over the same period.[2]

Treasury/Federal Reserve Interest-Rate Policy

This pattern of expansion occurred largely because of the way the Treasury and the Executive branch of the government handled the financing of the war. The overriding theme of government policy was to finance the war at "relatively stable prices and yields for government securities."[3] Both Federal Reserve and Treasury officials unanimously embraced this political axiom. In practice the Federal Reserve Open Market Committee (FOMC) was the medium by which the policy was carried out. If government security prices began to fall and yield rates to rise correspondingly, the Fed bought securities in the open market to maintain the pattern of prices and rates. These rates were almost minuscule: ⅜ of 1 percent for ninety-day Treasury bills, ⅞ of 1 percent for one-year Treasury certificates, and 2½ percent for the longest-term marketable bonds.[4]

Market interest rates in the wake of the Great Depression were already very low even as late as 1941. In addition, the Fed and Treasury had a normative excuse for maintaining low rates: "Since a tremendous increase in the amount of securities offered by the government could be expected," explained Marriner Eccles, chairman of the Federal Reserve Board, "and, further, since war expenditures and Federal Reserve operations created the money available to banks and other investors for the purchase of these securities, it would have been wrong for the government to pay increasing rates of interest for the use of these funds it helped create."[5]

Eccles's "ethics" are astonishing, to say the least. The government realized the seigniorage from creating the money and spending it into circulation—over $20 billion by Federal Reserve purchases of securities alone—but judged it "wrong" for investors to realize possible market rewards in the form of higher interest rates for buying and holding the securities. As it was, the creation of so much money was destined to generate an inflation that would make these low nominal rates negative real rates by 1948. The ethics of governmental policies that led to such a volume of real losses in the capital values of government securities held by the public can hardly be called "fair."

At the same time that the Treasury and Fed were maintaining low interest rates on government securities at any price (level), the Fed was agonizing over the sales of securities to commercial banks and the consequent creation of bank deposits. Its spokesmen also lamented its forced role of buying up Treasury bills to maintain the rate pattern while the banks acquired the longer-term 2½ percent bonds.[6] If the rates had been freed up, nonbank investors would have been more interested in buying and holding the securities. The result would have been smaller increases in the stock of money and prices.[7]

The Treasury paid lip service to the principle of selling the securities to nonbank investors; but Treasury officials in charge of the war-loan drives had a personal interest in seeing their securities placed so that their quotas of sales would be reached or exceeded. They relied on the expediency of sales to banks or to customers of banks who, in order to buy the government's securities, borrowed from banks at lower interest rates than the securities paid.[8]

The Fed's support of government security prices also dissipated the acute need that commercial banks had had for conventional reserves in excess of legal requirements. Since the government securities could be liquidated at prescribed market values at any time, the securities were, in effect, interest-earning quasi-reserves.

In conjunction with the mass of money created and its upward effect on prices, the economy's real product also increased. Output growth, however, was significantly less than the growth in money. Direct price and wage controls were the political "solution" devised to counter the inflationary impact of the money stock.

The Federal Government's Price-Wage Control Program

On the surface direct price and wage controls appear to have worked. In the prewar period, 1939–1942, the Consumer Price Index (CPI) rose 17.3 percent, before controls were imposed. During the price control period, 1942–1945, measured prices increased by only 10.3 percent; and in the immediate postwar period, 1945–1948, by 33.7 percent. The price regulators took much pride in these numbers.[9]

Critics of the system, however, pointed out that although the index *numbers* were fairly well stabilized, actual prices were not necessarily so well behaved. For one thing, the quality of goods and services suffered significantly. Quality adjustments are one means manufacturers have of producing cheaper goods when legal price ceilings force a reduction in the real prices of goods and services. (Cuffs, for example, disappeared from men's trousers and all clothing was cut more skimpily.) The means by which quality deterioration took place were legion. In fact, it became a form of defensive "entrepreneurship."[10] How much real waste occurred because entrepreneurial energy was used to avoid and evade the controls cannot be seen in any indexes of "costs" or "prices," but it must have been considerable.

Another result of below-market prices was tie-in sales, whereby the purchaser had to buy a combination of goods one of which might have been unsalable otherwise. Also, discounts, loss leaders, and other price cuts commonly used as a means of reducing quoted money prices became a thing of the past.[11] Evasions of controls through "black" markets, in which goods and services were bought and sold at free market prices, also added to the real costs of controls and, as well, detracted from the alleged "benefits" resulting from controls.[12]

If price controls worked, and they certainly had some effect, they added to the disequilibrium conditions affecting money and all goods and services. To correct this condition, the general price level had to rise, which is to say that the "price" of money had to fall. Fixing money wages and prices added to the original disequilibrium of the price level because it froze *relative* prices. Of course, the disequilibrium price level would have necessitated some relative price adjustments as well as a price level change once corrective forces were allowed to work. The fixing of specific money prices simply made ultimate adjustment more difficult and more extensive.

Even if price controls had worked perfectly, no official statement dealt with the questions of how long they would be kept in force and what would be done to prevent inflation when the controls ended. Given that inflation was bound to occur at some juncture (although many people naively presumed that what went up would inevitably and painlessly come down), a constant rate of inflation could hardly have been worse than one that was first suppressed and then allowed to burgeon. The government would have obtained control over the resources it needed in either case.

Professor Hugh Rockoff argues in his excellent treatise on controls (*Drastic Measures,* p. 175 and passim) that effective price controls enabled the government to buy war materials at lower prices, and so allowed it to acquire the resources for the war effort with a minimal increase in the quantity of money. Therefore, he argues, the degree of inflation was smaller than what would have occurred without controls.

Rockoff's conclusion is specious. If the government had not been so insistent on "low" interest rates, and if it had had the gumption to raise taxes significantly, it could have administered the war with virtually no increase in the quantity of money. If people were willing to be price-controlled and otherwise regulated in the critical years of the war, 1942–1945, as Rockoff shows was the case, surely they also would have tolerated higher taxes and higher interest rates. The latter burdens involve less market interference and result in fewer charges of unfair and discriminatory treatment.

The Validity of the Accounted Price Level Data for the War Years

Another fundamental question may be raised: How credible are the price index values that are accounted for the years 1942–1945? Was inflation even suppressed, and if so, to what degree? If these index values are accepted as valid, they imply an astonishing development in real product for the war years. Table 20.3 shows the time series from which this production "miracle" is derived.

The deflation of dollar GNP values by the Consumer Price Index (CPI) results in a peak value of real output per worker in 1944 that is not surpassed until 1954, and even then the difference in per capita real income is insignifi-

TABLE 20.3 Gross National Product in nominal and real terms, prices, civilian labor force, GNP per worker, 1941–1954

Year	GNP in current prices ($ billions)	GNP in 1929 prices ($ billions)	Prices (1929 = 100)	Total civilians employed (millions)	Real GNP per civilian worker (dollars)
1941	126	139	91	50.4	2,758
1944	211	184	115	50.4	3,407
1946	211	167	126	55.3	3,020
1948	259	174	149	59.4	2,929
1952	347	207	168	61.3	3,377
1954	363	213	171	61.2	3,480

Source: Department of Commerce, *Historical Statistics of the United States* (Washington, 1958).

cant. Not until 1950 did the economy's aggregate real GNP reach its 1944 level. (The 1950 value is not shown in the table.)

This calculated increase in productivity is hardly credible. First, the quality of the civilian labor force suffered significantly as twelve million (mostly) men, who were in their high productivity years, were replaced by less productive workers—youths, women, and elderly workers.[13] Of course, total employed workers increased until 1943 as the prewar unemployed were reemployed. The previously unemployed positions may also have been geared to unemployed capital goods as well, which is to say that every reemployed person may have been matched by a reemployed shovel or lathe. So reemployment may have witnessed an increase in total product more or less in proportion to the increase in the labor force. However, real product per worker could not have increased proportionally because the "new" labor force was not as technically productive as the one it replaced, and also because training the new workers was costly and required additional resources. On the positive side, patriotic fervor and a slightly extended work week may have added something to real product per worker.

By 1948 most of the men in the armed forces had been demobilized and had reentered the labor force. In addition, gross private domestic investment for the three years 1946–1948 was $103 billion, while the total for the *ten* preceding years, 1935–1945, was only $97 billion. Even adjusted for the postwar inflation, this much real investment added significantly to the economy's capital stock and to the total productivity of the economy. Thus, the immediate post–World War II economy had a more productive labor force, plus an improved and enlarged capital structure over the one that operated during the war and before. And even though the wartime work week was somewhat longer, overtime work is substantially less efficient and could not have accounted for the "increase" derived from the index numbers. In fact, the use of "overtime" was often only a ploy that enabled employers to evade wage controls in order to increase real wages and keep their workers from looking for other jobs.

The real GNP values for 1941 and 1948 look to be reasonably valid, since market-clearing prices were largely in force at these times. Real GNP per worker increased by 6.2 percent over this interval. If all of this increase was in proportion to the increase in the size of the employed work force, only one-third of the increase would have occurred in the period 1941–1944, and real income per worker in 1944 would have been $2,815. This value times the 54 million-person work force would give a real GNP of $153 billion. Comparing this value with GNP in current prices for 1944 ($211 billion) implies a price index value of 138 for 1944, not 115. In other words, working backward from real productivity data that seem reasonable in order to derive the change in the price level suggests a price level value 20 percent higher than the one recorded by the Bureau of Labor Statistics.

A strong presumption exists that a price index construction at a time when most money prices are controlled by law is very likely to be biased downward, meaning that the index will read lower than it "should." The statistician collecting prices for the index has an impossible job. First, he must ignore "black market" prices, which are illegal and for which he cannot get accurate information anyway. Second, if he could get estimates of such data to incorporate into the index, the very act of doing so would imply that the laws of the land were being broken, and that the bureau in charge of enforcing price controls was ineffective. These kinds of conclusions are not politically acceptable.[14]

The statistician faced with these conditions simply accounts the legal ceiling prices as though they are the ones actually being paid and received. In truth, however, goods and services are being bought and sold on very different terms. Once price controls end, this statistical problem disappears. Higher free market prices become legal and can be accounted with no reservations or biases.

The conclusion here is that the price control program stabilized a *price index* but not *prices*. Nonetheless, such self-deception may have had a favorable psychological impact because everyone wanted to see prices checked and inflation restrained.

Willy-nilly, price controls had the enthusiastic approval of the general public. The war emergency accelerated popular acceptance of the government's growing intervention in the economy. Many people nurtured the common myth that someone, or some clique, or some special interest group—labor unions, bankers, or "big" corporations—ordinarily fixed (fix) prices. Barely tolerable in peacetime, these price-fixers had to be neutralized during the war so they could not feather their nests with "war profits." The concept of free market prices and wages resulting from the spontaneous actions of millions of individuals receded further and further from the pale of human belief. Most people acknowledged the desirability of an "impartial" government agency that would determine "fair" prices by some kind of reasonable estimates of "costs" of production.

Reaction of Professional Economists to the Fed's Wartime Policies

The Fed did nothing to control any prices except government security prices. The chairman of the Federal Reserve Board, Marriner Eccles, recommended all kinds of price, wage, rent, and profit controls, as well as increased personal income taxation and "compulsory universal saving." But the Fed's role, he knew, was limited: "The pattern of war finance had been firmly established by the Treasury; the Federal Reserve merely executed Treasury decisions."[15]

As the end of the war approached, Eccles criticized even more pointedly the low-interest mind-set of the Treasury Department. "Indeed," he claimed some years later, "it was the continued domination of Treasury policy by a Morgenthau staff, with its chronic bias for cheap money in all seasons, that lay at the source of this difficulty [i.e., of the Fed's inability to fight inflation]."[16] Alan Sproul, president of the Federal Reserve Bank of New York, confirmed the picture Eccles presented. The Fed's control over the cost and availability of credit, Sproul complained, "has been substantially relinquished . . . by obligations assumed in support of the government securities market. . . . So far as inflation is concerned, ours is essentially a holding action. . . . We are not the masters in our own house."[17]

Economists had mixed reactions to the new role of the Fed after 1935, to the general program of government security price supports, and to the fixing of wages and prices during World War II. First, they noted that the Fed did not use its newly acquired powers from the Banking Act of 1935 to do anything monetarily momentous. Indeed, almost no economist, except the FDIC economist Clark Warburton, thought that monetary policy amounted to much anyway.[18] Second, they recognized that the Treasury had become the leader in monetary-fiscal affairs. Because of the fiscal deficits during the depression and the much greater deficits associated with the war, fiscal concerns dominated monetary policy. "The Treasury," noted E. C. Simmons in 1940, "is endowed with monetary control weapons which overshadow those of the Reserve authorities [referring to the Treasury's gold sterilization policy]: and what is perhaps more important the day of the politically independent central bank supreme over monetary policy seems to have passed."[19] In Simmons's eyes the central bank *had* been "supreme" in monetary affairs, but even with its new powers its "independence" had been so violated by political expediency that its effectiveness was in practice severely compromised.

John H. Williams, a Harvard economist who had been an associate economist with the Fed Board, stated in 1942 that he was entirely in agreement with Federal Reserve support of the government securities market. "A restrictive monetary policy is not feasible [politically?] or desirable," he said, "so long as the government is the principal borrower and the [commercial] banks must be relied upon to do a large portion of the lending." This state of affairs, he thought, precluded the exercise of monetary restraint by the Reserve System.[20]

Karl Bopp, an economist at the Fed bank of Philadelphia, offered a profound and accurate observation in 1944. "In broadest outline," he observed, "the history of central banks reflects the gradual ascendence and subsequent decline of the doctrine of laissez faire and cognate habits of thought." The "independent" central bank had been compatible with laissez-faire. In the present age, he noted critically, "central banks, while professing absolute faith in the Simon-pure gold standard, followed various practices to insulate national economies from the rigors of the genuine article." The "new" central bank, Bopp observed, did not just set a rate at which it would automatically discount "eligible paper." Its new lending function was discretionary. The wartime peg on Treasury bills was a part of this discretion. In his view this support was desirable.[21] Nonetheless, it was the Treasury's discretion, not the Fed's, that was responsible for the policy.

Bopp's theme that contemporary central banks were institutionally incompatible with both a "simon-pure" gold standard and, more especially, with a doctrine of laissez-faire was both insightful and accurate. It was also a reflection of the popular passion for control over economic variables by human means. He did not raise the question of constitutionality for these perceived changes.

In the discussion that followed Bopp's paper, Lawrence Seltzer reflected a pragmatic view of the Fed's limited power to influence economic activity. The money created by banks during the war, he thought, did not matter; it would merely be hoarded. "It is this feeble control over the activity of the public's money . . . that imposes the most important limitation upon central banking policy," he contended. New bank-created money had little effect on "the spending and investment activity of the public. Monetary power," he concluded, "resides in the Treasury not in the Federal Reserve System [because the banks hold so much of their assets in government securities]; and the monetary effects of a budgetary surplus are called into being by Congress."[22]

Seltzer's reasoning was contradictory. While arguing that monetary policy was ineffective, he also warned that any curtailment of bank reserves would be "dangerous." Declining government security prices that might be brought about by a deflationary central-bank policy, he thought, would be intolerable.

In a similar discussion in 1946, Seltzer made the same contradiction. Central-banking policy to counteract a severe depression, he argued in a paper on monetary policy, "however well designed and skillfully managed, is sometimes helpless and always limited." Natural phenomena that initiate depressions were outside the central bank's control. A few pages later, the "natural phenomena" had become "powerful political forces that are operating to limit the effective power of the Reserve authorities to raise interest rates." A radical rise in rates, Seltzer warned, might be so effective that it would induce Congress and the Executive "to interfere with the powers or personnel of the Reserve System."[23]

The Federal Reserve System in the immediate postwar economy was hardly more than a department of the Treasury that held the government security-reserves of the commercial banks. Just as the war ended, the Treasury used the large cash balance it had on deposit in the Reserve banks to buy back $23 billion of securities it had recently sold, and it continued this open-market policy with the fiscal surpluses it realized during 1946–1948.[24]

Economists' Guidelines for Federal Reserve Policy

The Fed's thralldom to the Treasury prompted both Fed officials and economists to seek other avenues for Fed policy. Selective credit controls and secondary reserve requirements for banks, based on some amount of their government security holdings, were two of the proposals Fed officials suggested.[25]

In an effort to reduce the obvious inefficacies of Treasury-dominated monetary policy, some economists argued for monetary rules. The gold standard had been such a rule. But by now all the gold was in the U.S. Treasury, and the Treasury was the culprit agency that economists wanted to compromise. Another rule was a stable price level to be maintained by simple technical operations already the province of central banks.[26] Federal Reserve officials tenaciously and persistently opposed such a policy.[27]

The Fed's resistance to stabilization of a price level by monetary means would have been more tolerable if the same Fed officials who opposed such a goal had not been so enthusiastic for the wage, price, and other controls during and after the war period. Where a price level stabilization program by monetary means would have been almost costless in both administration and abrasiveness, the direct and indirect costs of the detailed effort during 1941–1948 were significant. Obviously, costs to the economy were not the principal factor in the Fed's promotion of the price-fixing program, and in its stubborn rejection of a price level stabilization policy for itself.

Most economists gave the Fed a positive vote of confidence. The large body of economists in the late 1940s, according to George L. Bach, "still prescribe the standard discretionary authority. That this scheme has worked as well as long as it has," he concluded, "can but amaze most economists."[28]

Bach's satisfaction with the Fed's performance can only be excused by the general ignorance of economists who took as gospel the Fed's view of itself, its powers, and its analysis of monetary conditions. What economists could glean from the Fed's performance during the 1930s was largely based on what the Fed itself said. With the exception of one or two voices crying out in the monetary wilderness, no one had critically assessed the Fed's performance either by institutional-theoretical analysis or by means of empirical evaluation.[29] The Fed's plea that monetary policy was severely limited had only flawed Keynesian doctrine to support it; and the Fed's cant of the 1940s—that political forces constrained monetary policy—was a valid reason for the Fed's inability to control inflation only because the Fed accepted its role as lackey to the Treasury Department.

The Fed was destined to be dominated in such a situation. Policy-making Treasury officials were part of an elected administration. They came in and went out of office with their president. They were, therefore, much more sensitive to the outward and visible signs of current monetary policy than they were to its ultimate inflationary disgrace.

Professor Bach was also a member of the Hoover Commission Task Force on government efficiency. In his capacity as an economist for that group, he observed that in informal meetings between Fed and Treasury officials "the personalities of the various top officials have influenced substantially the nature of the negotiations and the relative strength exerted by the two agencies." In any exchange between a loosely federated Board of Governors and a "single-headed Treasury," the Fed's position was going to be subordinated. "The Treasury is almost invariably the stronger of the two, basically because of its closer ties with the President and his executive officials." Bach's recommendations were, first, that the Open Market Committee be abolished, leaving the Board of Governors as the policy-making body; second, that the Board be a three-man agency; and third, that it serve at the pleasure of the president in the manner of the president's cabinet.[30] Nothing ever came of these recommendations.

Beginning late in 1948 and continuing through much of 1949, the U.S. economy suffered its first postwar recession. Government security prices firmed up, and in the year from December 1948 to December 1949 the Fed sold off $4.4 billion of its U.S. government security holdings. At the same time the money stock (M_2) declined by about 1½ percent.[31]

The Fed's inopportune policy of selling government securities as a recession developed was a result of its continuing commitment to maintain maximum prices and minimum rates on those securities. Treasury policy, for which the Fed was only an instrument, thus turned out to be procyclical no matter which phase of the business cycle was current.

The Treasury's Further Attempts to Subjugate the Fed after 1950

The outbreak of the Korean War converted a stout recovery into an ongoing boom. People remembered only too well the "shortages" of World War II, a mere five years past, and as well the real austerity of the Great Depression. Money stocks suddenly were in excess supply, and goods, especially consumer durables, were in excess demand. This change occurred in the presence of a Fed monetary policy that was holding nominal money stocks almost unchanged. In the two and a half years between January 1948 and June 1950, the M_1 money stock showed no change, while M_2 rose less than 1 percent. The excess demand for goods and services led to a substantial increase in the velocity of money and a significant rise in prices in the latter half of 1950.[32]

The anticipated fiscal demands the federal government would impose because of the Korean War prompted renewed Treasury interest in Federal Reserve support for the government securities market, even though the fiscal budget showed a $2 billion surplus in the second half of 1950. This situation led to what Marriner Eccles labeled "an extraordinary event in the history of relations between the Treasury and Federal Reserve," which was an attempt by the Truman administration to bring direct pressure to bear on Federal Reserve policy by means of a face-to-face confrontation between the Board of Governors and the president himself.[33]

President Harry Truman had chosen not to reappoint Eccles as chairman of the Board of Governors in 1948. Truman made the change for political reasons having to do with Eccles's public criticism of the Treasury's government security policy, but also in keeping with the wishes of the Giannini banking interests in California and their anticipated support of the Democratic party in the elections of 1948. Eccles had considered retiring altogether, but then decided to stay on as a governor until his term expired.[34]

Prior to the Korean War outbreak, the Fed had made some slight adjustments in policy that implied a change in its support pattern of security rates. Without heed to the Fed's position, Secretary of the Treasury John Snyder in January 1951 made public pronouncements through press releases declaring that Fed support of government security prices and rates would be continued as in years past in order to expedite the Treasury's fiscal operations to prosecute the Korean War. In fact, no such support had been agreed to; the administration simply tried to impose a fait accompli on the Fed. It assumed that Fed officials would not dare to embarrass the Treasury and the president by denying that any agreement had been reached. To do so would have been the equivalent of labeling Snyder, Truman, and other administration officials liars—which indeed they were.

Eccles was apparently the one man on the Board who had both the guts and the prestige to challenge the administration. In cooperation with knowledgeable financial journalists from the *Washington Post* and the *New York Times,* Eccles ably countered the administration's press releases with one of his own in which he confirmed that the Fed Board had made no agreements, either express or implied, to support the prices and yields of government securities. He confirmed his contradiction by publishing the minutes of the unprecedented meeting between the Board of Governors and the president from which the Executive had derived the alleged "cooperation."[35]

The Federal Reserve System had been created on the supposition, correct or incorrect, that it would be independent of just such political influence. The publicity over this ongoing conflict of authorities had caught congressional and professional attention as early as 1949, and it brought the government security support policy into the political limelight. This policy then became the object of a congressional investigation by the Subcommittee on Monetary, Credit, and Fiscal Policies of the Joint Committee on the Economic Report (the "Douglas Committee"). The subcommittee made its report in 1950, a full year before the open conflict surfaced between the Fed and the Treasury.

The essence of the Douglas Committee Report was, first, that monetary policy could be effective, and second, that it had more "timely flexibility" than fiscal policy. The report concluded by specifying that in the future both the Fed and the Treasury

> shall be guided primarily by considerations relating to their effects on employment, production purchasing power, and price levels, and such policies shall be consistent with and shall promote the purpose of the Employment Act of 1946; and . . . it is the will of Congress that the primary power and responsibility, and cost of credit in general shall be vested in the duly constituted authorities of the Federal Reserve System, and that Treasury action relative to money, credit, and transactions in the federal debt shall be made consistent with the policies of the Federal Reserve.[36]

The political compulsions of the Treasury Department and the Truman administration, as evidenced by the way they subsequently flouted the Douglas Committee's report in the episode described by Eccles, must have been formidable. However, the adverse publicity generated by the fracas, and the prestige and power of the congressional report, finally resulted in the famous "Accord" between the two agencies—an agreement that in some central-banking circles was hailed as the equivalent of the Magna Charta. Federal Reserve and Treasury officials worked out the details of this document, and made a joint statement swearing fealty to it on 4 March 1951—just as King John did with the barons at Runnymede in 1215. The statement was couched in general terms: "The Treasury and the Federal Reserve System have reached full accord with respect to debt-management and monetary policies to be pursued in furthering their common purpose to assure the successful financing of the Government's requirements and, at the same time, to minimize monetization of the public debt." One provision stated that the Fed would discontinue or reduce purchases of short-term government securities so that "banks would depend upon borrowing at the Federal Reserve [banks] to make needed adjustments to their reserves."[37]

The furor over this episode and the attention devoted to it by two major congressional reports exaggerated the cleavage of opinion, if not the struggle for power, between the two agencies. The Treasury's unseemly and illegitimate dominance of the Fed is beyond dispute. Most Fed officials, however, were already in accord with the Treasury's rate-fixing policy. The bond support program in fact originated partly in the Reserve System. Not until two years after the Accord did any official Federal Reserve documents "explicitly forswear support of government securities as an aim of policy."[38] Indeed, the only outspoken critic of the support program from inside the Fed was Marriner Eccles, who, for one thing, was something of an individualist, and was preparing to retire anyway. (He retired on 14 July 1951, a few months after he publicized the facts in the Fed-Treasury dispute.) He had also been a sacrificial political pawn of the Truman administration. Therefore, he did not "owe anyone anything," and could speak and act as he saw fit.[39] His colleagues, however, were much more obsequious. By way of contrast, no matter who was secretary of the Treasury—Morgenthau, Vinson, or Snyder—the line taken toward the Fed was the same: You do it *our* way.

The drama of the dispute aside, the real reason for the separation of monetary and debt-management powers was the shift in "world" opinion over the efficacy of monetary policy, and the failure of the current cheap-money, low-interest-rate program to achieve acceptable results. The theme born in the 1930s and nurtured in the 1940s that the long-run problem of advanced capitalist countries was economic stagnation and chronic depression was belied by events after the war. Consequently, monetary policy seemed to deserve a place in the sun, which meant bringing it out from under the shadow of the Treasury.[40]

The inflation that began in mid–1950 witnessed a decline in real Federal Reserve demand obligations as well as a similar decline in the real money stock generated in the private sector (see table 20.2). Both real money series had been declining since 1946, when price level increases came out into the open, and continued through 1951. The Fed, however, was now unfettered. Its new freedom meant that it had to devise criteria for monetary policy in the way of goals, targets, and indicators—details that the Banking Act of 1935 had left untreated. It also meant that economists could take a new interest in devising norms for Fed operations. Finally, a new chairman, William McChesney Martin, was appointed to the Board of Governors. All these circumstances promised major changes in the future course of Federal Reserve operations.

21 The Post-Accord Era of the Fed: 1951–1967

> Neither the United States nor any other country is going to allow its monetary policy—i.e., its internal price level and its internal level of employment—to be determined by the "automatic" requirements of an international standard. To permit this would be tantamount to renouncing the responsibility of the Federal Government, recognized by it in the Employment Act of 1946, for maintaining conditions conducive to high-level employment.
>
> Patman Subcommittee Report, 1952

Treasury/Federal Reserve Relationships

The publicity surrounding the Fed-Treasury dispute and its final resolution in the form of the "Accord," plus the congressional reports that appeared during and after the controversy, mark a watershed in the principles governing Federal Reserve policy-making. The two subcommittee reports from the House of Representatives were instrumental in highlighting, first, the long-term dominance of the Treasury Department over monetary policy; second, the political characteristics that the Fed had come to acquire; and third, the waning effect of gold and the gold standard in monetary affairs.

Political acceptance of the Treasury's long-term influence on the monetary system is difficult either to understand or to excuse no matter what criteria are used in judgment. One of the primary reasons for the formation of the Fed was to disengage the Treasury from the role it had assumed for itself when Secretary Shaw deposited gold and other moneys in depository banks to support the short-term securities market. (See chapter 13.) The new Federal Reserve System was supposed to be an agent of Congress and independent of the Executive branch, particularly the Treasury. Somehow or other, though, the bill that was signed into law had both the secretary and the comptroller of the currency as ex officio members of the Board of Governors, with the secretary as chairman of the Board. Furthermore, the Federal Reserve Act specifically stated that "whenever any power vested by this Act in the Board of Governors . . . appears to conflict with the powers of the Secretary of the Treasury, such powers shall be exercised subject to the supervision and control of the Secretary."[1]

Yes, yes, is the reply, but the Board of Governors was not all that important. It was just a committee to oversee the technical integrity of the Reserve banks. The discounting policies of the Reserve banks were the key elements in the system.

True—for a while. However, when the Banking Act of 1935 demoted the

Reserve banks to all but administrative caretakers and made the Board the supreme arbiter of monetary policy, Section 10, Article 6, of the Federal Reserve Act was not reargued or reworded in any way to take into account the shift of institutional power from the Fed bank presidents to the Board. The new act, therefore, had the effect of giving the last word in monetary policy to the secretary of the Treasury, even as it removed him from his ex officio position as the chairman of the Board.

The Federal Reserve System, as originally conceived, also had an operating principle for keeping the Treasury at bay—the real-bills doctrine. Since the Treasury dealt only in government securities, which by everyone's classification were not real bills, Fed bank managers could reject any enjoinders for support from the Treasury. So, at least, the argument went.

The real-bills doctrine, unfortunately, also proved to be a flawed basis for adapting monetary quantities to the volume of real production and the corresponding growth in real money balances because it had to rely on the questionable discretion of human managers. Their judgment was likely to be colored by the optimism or pessimism of the hour. In practice, monetary policy based on the real-bills doctrine became procyclical.

The cant of central-bank apologists then changed: Yes, the real-bills doctrine is the wrong base for policy, they agreed. We need to give our money managers a more effective vehicle and more power. Let them concentrate on open-market operations in government securities. This vehicle, in conjunction with their objective bird's-eye view of the economy, should provide the most rational policy.

Alas! The terrible state of the economy in the 1930s and the administration's efforts to stimulate it with government spending resulted in serious fiscal deficits. Under these circumstances, the Fed had to keep the government securities market "orderly" so that the deficits would not bankrupt the government. And here comes World War II. Now the Fed must really support the government securities market. Indeed, if the Fed had kept interest rates any lower, they would have been zero, and the war would have been financed with "government-security greenbacks."

Finally the war ended; but by this time the economy was supposed to stagnate. So the Fed had to continue its support of governments until the Treasury's alleged fiscal "emergency" was over. (The Treasury's slogan was to proceed with "extreme caution" whenever its hegemony was challenged.) Then came another emergency—the Korean War. The Fed would just have to stay in tow. Marriner Eccles, in reviewing monetary policies during the depression, World War II, and the postwar period, summed them up as follows: "Political expediency rather than a detached appraisal of economic realities tended to dictate government decisions."[2]

So it was that an institution created to promote an elastic currency for the private sector, to accommodate business, and to be a lender of last resort to private commercial member banks, came to accommodate the government by monitoring and maintaining the prices and yield rates of government securities.

The worst of this evolution was what it implied about the state of polity in the United States, and in the world for that matter. One of the essential and long-recognized principles of democratic government has been the functional separation of the purse and the sword: The legislative branch should control the purse; the executive branch should wield the sword. This principle was prominent in the debates over the Second Bank of the United States as well as in other power struggles going back to the Middle Ages. On account of it, the Federal Reserve System was created as an agent of *Congress;* it reports to *Congress*. Indeed, the Treasury also reports to *Congress,* and not to the president in the mode of other cabinet-level departments.

In view of this long tradition, the acquiescence of Congress to Treasury dominance of the Fed and, as well, to the brutish means the Snyder-Truman team used in their attempt to bully the Fed into submission is astonishing. Legislators, administrators, and jurists all should have been aware of the principle of the separation of powers, and especially the separation of the monetary-fiscal power from the military-executive power. Yet virtually nothing was said about this political impropriety until the time of the Douglas Subcommittee, although Marriner Eccles made some remarks in this direction. In retrospect, Eccles wrote, "I regret that the Federal Reserve did not take a more independent position despite Treasury resistance. . . . There was no justification for our continued support of the Treasury's wartime cheap-money policy."[3]

After the Accord, however, the Federal Reserve System adopted what Friedman and Schwartz have labeled "a near-revolutionary change" in emphasis. First, the FOMC began to realize that its control over the money stock—hand-to-hand currency and demand deposits—was a powerful force that was at its disposal through open-market operations. In addition, Fed officials had to abandon the old notion that if they could prevent the nonproductive use of credit the money stock would take care of itself. Clearly, the money stock could not be an object of policy *and* be controlled by the impersonal operation of the gold standard in conjunction with a real-bills principle. The new Fed policy aimed to synchronize money growth with real growth in the economy.[4]

Congressional Subcommittees Review the Federal Reserve's Role

The Patman Subcommittee of 1952, which included four of the same five congressmen who had been on the Douglas Subcommittee a few years earlier, reviewed and confirmed, as would be expected, the arguments on the conduct of monetary affairs that the earlier subcommittee had advanced. The Patman

Subcommittee recognized that the president appointed the Board of Governors. The question then was: To which branch, executive or legislative, was the Board beholden? The subcommittee based its conclusion on judicial decisions as well as opinions of attorneys general and past presidents. Its report cited approvingly the testimony of Lucius Wilmerding, a jurist, whose statement to the subcommittee went as follows:

> When the execution of a law has been committed by Congress to the exclusive jurisdiction of a subordinate department [i.e., in this case, to the Federal Reserve Board] or officer of the Executive, the interference of the President with such execution, either in the form of direction beforehand or revision and reversal afterward, so far from being permitted by the Constitution, would be a usurpation on the part of the President which the subordinate department or officer would not be bound to respect. In such cases the duty of the President to take care that the laws be faithfully executed extends no further than to see that the officers to whom Congress has given an exclusive jurisdiction perform their duties honestly and capably. Congress has committed certain business to the exclusive jurisdiction of that Board [of Governors], and this business it must perform under the responsibility of its trust and not by the direction of the President.[5]

The subcommittee expressed satisfaction with the "hard-to-define" structure of the Federal Reserve System, and it also gave an undeserved compliment to the Fed's long-term performance. The system, the report stated fatuously, "has been a helpful institutional development. Its roots are sunk deeply in the American economy [?] and it has borne good fruit."[6]

The question of the Fed's relationship to the Executive raised the derivative question of the Fed's independence. The subcommittee rejected "the idea that the Federal Reserve System should be independent of the Government." It thought the more appropriate wording, as Allan Sproul had expressed it in a letter to the subcommittee, was not "'independence *from* the Government but independence *within* the Government.' (Emphasis supplied [by the subcommittee].) . . . *There can be no independence from the Government*."[7]

Sproul's argument and the subcommittee's explicit agreement with it reflected a radical departure from the constitutional norm for the government's relationship to the monetary system. It also violated the principles that Congress espoused when it passed the Federal Reserve Act. If the subcommittee had been able to present this argument to the House Banking and Currency Committee in 1913, it would have met with a storm of protest. The gold standard had become the symbol of a monetary system truly independent of government. The original role of the Federal Reserve System was to make the gold standard work more efficiently. It most definitely was not to be a means by which the executive could thwart the adjusting mechanism of the gold standard or carry out politically attractive fiscal policies without heed to gold-standard principles.

The subcommittee reviewed briefly the original idea of Fed independence.

At one time, they noted, "this independence was much greater. The original Federal Reserve Act *appears* to have conceived the individual Federal Reserve banks as important policy-making agencies and the Board of Governors . . . as principally a regulatory agency. . . . The subsequent *trend*," the report continued, "has been toward a somewhat greater degree of independence of the central board from the President but a much diminished autonomy for the individual [Reserve] banks." The report concluded that the "trend" toward Board autonomy "since the adoption of the original Act . . . is, for the most part, merely a reflection of the growth in the importance of monetary policy."[8]

Anyone who ever studied, even superficially, the formation of the Fed as an institution would recognize that the original act did not just "appear" to give the individual Reserve banks autonomy. It was a clear-cut principle of the act's construction. Furthermore, the "trend" the subcommittee observed was no trend. It was bureaucratic encroachment into activities that were no part of the original compact. Often enough, the additional powers that the Fed had assumed for itself, or that Congress had bestowed on it, had ended up in the bailiwick of the Treasury Department.

Since the Treasury had dominated central-bank policy for so long, essentially since 1935, just what the Fed should do on its own now that it was somewhat free of Treasury imperatives was not altogether clear. The Banking Act of 1935 had set up much more powerful machinery for the Fed's operations without specifying toward what ends it should be used. The two congressional subcommittees were apparently aware of this vacuum, so they provided at least an operational principle for the Fed to follow: Carry out policies that will further the Employment Act of 1946. This act stated that "the continuing policy and responsibility of the Federal Government [is] to use all practicable means . . . to promote maximum employment, production, and purchasing power."[9] The two subcommittees also added the goal of stability in the price level, which, they agreed, the employment act implied.[10]

Congressional Subcommittee Views on the Gold Standard: The Debate with Walter Spahr

At the same time that the subcommittees were disentangling the two government institutions and furnishing them with an operational guideline of sorts, they also treated and disposed of a more traditional institution—the gold standard. Indeed, much of the thrust of their reports was to disparage the gold standard as a guiding principle for central-bank operations in order to emphasize their own man-made substitute, the Employment Act of 1946.

By this time economists, businessmen, politicians, and laymen had little or no interest in reinstituting the gold standard. It had been thoroughly vilified by central bankers, politicians, and government administrators in the early

1930s. Nevertheless, in the name of objectivity the two subcommittees had to give gold-standard advocates a day in court.

The man they tolerated as the gambit for this purpose was Professor Emeritus Walter Spahr of New York University, who headed the Economists' National Committee for Monetary Policy. The subcommittee's economic spokesmen were Allan Sproul, president of the Federal Reserve Bank of New York, and Thomas B. McCabe, recently resigned chairman of the Federal Reserve Board, plus, of course, all of the subcommittee's members and staff.

The Douglas Committee's opening statement confirmed that the gold standard as an operational adjusting device was already fatally compromised. "Gold," the report stated, "may be held or dealt with only in accordance with rules prescribed by the Secretary of the Treasury, [who] prohibits the use of gold domestically for monetary [transactions] or hoarding [holding] purposes."[11] Obviously, if the law (in this case the Joint Resolution on the Discontinuance of Gold Payments of 1933, and the Gold Reserve Act of 1934) forbade its use for transactions or that it be held as a real balance until needed, gold could not possibly fulfill the functions of a medium of exchange and store of value. Man-made laws and governmental gold policies, not any monetary inadequacy of gold as such, prevented the use of gold as money.

Spahr, in his brief for the gold standard, used a vivid metaphor. The gold standard, he said, "provides a system of golden wires to every individual with dollars, over which he can send messages of approval or disapproval to the central signal board. When our government took the people's gold and thrust irredeemable promises to pay on them, it cut all the wires to the central signal box. . . . Thus absolute control of the people's gold and public purse passed to their government."[12]

The Douglas Subcommittee reacted negatively to Spahr's arguments. Adherence to the principles enunciated in the Employment Act of 1946, they asserted, would result in a money of relatively constant purchasing power, while restoration of convertibility of common money into gold "would be neither a reliable nor an effective guard against serious inflation. For this purpose there can be no effective substitute for responsible monetary, credit, and fiscal management."[13] The subcommittee's statement not only included the preposterous implication that a gold-standard policy was compatible with an inflation, it also emphasized again the dominance that the rule of men had obtained over the rule of law.

The subcommittee concluded by citing its guru, Thomas B. McCabe, the immediate past chairman of the Fed's Board of Governors. McCabe's principal argument was that "no government should make promises to its citizens and to the world [that it would redeem paper money with gold] which it would not be able to keep if the demand should arise." The government had expanded its monetary obligations to a multiple of six or seven times the value of the current gold stock, McCabe noted. Therefore, a "return to a gold-coin standard . . . would clearly expose the economy to the risk of drastic and undesirable deflation of gold for hoarding, or else the government would have to withdraw its promise of gold convertibility. Conjecture as to the possibility of such a withdrawal would stimulate a speculative demand for gold and might precipitate the event feared."[14]

Where the committee found a possible threat of inflation from a reinstituted gold standard, McCabe found a deflation. However, McCabe's principal argument admits that the "fault" with the gold standard to begin with was the government's violation of the gold standard's rules of the game. It had printed up so much money that its ability to maintain gold redemption for its obligations had become problematic. McCabe's statement is almost a carbon copy of Roosevelt's excuse for his forced abandonment of gold convertibility in 1934. (See chapter 18.) As Spahr had charged, the very act of printing and issuing legal paper money under the rules of a gold standard implied the government's promise to redeem its currency on demand. If the government could not keep this promise, it had no business printing a quantity of paper money that put its promise in doubt.

No wholesale demand for gold redemption would have arisen in 1932 and 1933 to begin with if the government had not sequestered all the gold, and if the Fed banks and Treasury had not been so reluctant to make redemptions. Even if demands for redemption of government-owned gold had drained the Treasury of its hoarded gold—all twenty thousand tons of it—what would it have mattered? The Treasury would have been no worse off since it was not using this gold for monetary purposes anyway. The Fed's power to create money would not have been abridged, given that the Board could set aside the meaningless gold reserve requirement for the Federal Reserve banks. Most important, all the households and businesses who properly wanted gold could have obtained it and been comforted by it. In fact, merely raising the mint price of gold, which was done anyway a few years later, by the appropriate amount would have equilibrated the demand for gold with the government's existing stock.

The Douglas Subcommittee received additional confirmation of its anti-gold mind-set from William McChesney Martin, who was at the time acting secretary of the Treasury. The Treasury Department was strongly opposed to a free market in gold, Martin stated, because it "would create serious risks [unspecified] to our national monetary and banking structure."[15]

A few paragraphs later gold's detrimental effects on the monetary system gave way to another consideration. "The most important use of gold," Martin asserted, "is for the domestic and international monetary functions of the Government, and that gold should not be held by private individuals as a store of wealth." He then repeated his previous warning about the dangers, again unspecified, that would follow from a free market in gold and private ownership of gold.[16]

Martin's statement put gold into the same category as handguns or heavy water. How or why government ownership of gold was benign when private ownership was dangerous, and how gold could enhance the functions of the government if it was not accessible to the general public, Martin left unexplained. No more did he cite evidence of the evils that he alleged would result from private ownership.

The Patman Subcommittee also responded to Spahr's "golden wires" argument a few years later. Their report stated unequivocally: "The Subcommittee rejects the view that the Government of the United States should be controlled by 'a system of golden wires' and [it] reaffirms faith in the ballot box."[17] The contrast the subcommittee heralded here between "golden wires" and "the ballot box" implies again a belief in the rule of men, as determined by votes in the ballot box, and the rule of law, whereby individual decision-making takes place within a framework of agreed-upon rules.

Under a gold standard neither a government nor any other institution has a "golden wire" connection unless it has issued some kind of money that it has promised to redeem in gold. Any such issue is made only on the volition of the bank, business, or government that is willing to undertake the responsibility of redemption. If this responsibility is distasteful or questionable, the money need not and should not be issued.

Spahr retorted appropriately: "If a person has property he has a right . . . to exchange it for something he prefers; and no government or bank can properly take to itself what he prefers and force him to take instead its promise to pay."[18] Money, Spahr argued, is real property. In prohibiting the conversion of common money into gold, the government was illegally exercising its power of eminent domain without compensation, and thus violating the property rights of the people who held the money.

Spahr was on the high ground of the Constitution, which did indeed imply his "golden wires" construction, while the subcommittee was counting the votes from the "ballot box." The former has absolute precedence over the latter as a principle of democratic polity: Constitutions come before ballot boxes. Furthermore, on a practical level, how could any count from a "ballot box" provide a feasible and responsible monetary policy? Majority voting and political discretion can no more operate a monetary system than they can a nuclear power plant. The only rational choices for such a task are (1) markets, or (2) constitutional principles. Since the U.S. Constitution had priority in this matter, the issue had been settled in 1789. The subcommittee simply made a point of not recognizing it. Further on, the subcommittee stated that "a return to the domestic convertibility of gold would be equivalent to a vote of no confidence in the monetary authorities of this country, including both the Treasury and the Federal Reserve System."[19] Indeed it would, and with good reason, if the gold were drawn out of the Treasury through redemptions. However, if current monetary policies inspired public confidence, nothing would happen.

Since the subcommittee had already expressed a preference for the returns from the "ballot box," it might well have inquired whether the voting public did indeed have confidence in the monetary authorities. But how could such a question be answered? The average voter knew nothing of monetary policy or of the machinery of monetary creation, nor had he any means for judging the competence of the men chosen to manage the system.

The Patman Subcommittee cited Allan Sproul, president of the Federal Reserve Bank of New York, as its authority for rejecting "golden wires." "We had embarrassing personal experience with gold coin convertibility as recently as 1933," Sproul reported, "when lines of people finally stormed the Federal Reserve Banks seeking gold, and our whole banking mechanism came to a dead stop. . . . [Monetary] discipline is necessary in these matters but it should be the discipline of competent and responsible men; not the automatic discipline of a harsh and perverse mechanism."[20]

Spahr took pointed issue with Sproul's "competent and responsible men" who were to discipline the people. These men, he countered, were themselves beyond the discipline of the gold standard or any other law. They were the human designers who faced no check and balance. Spahr here put his finger squarely on the reciprocal responsibilities and rights that underlie the governed and the governors in a constitutional republic. He pointed out further that the experience of the past offered "no valid basis on which to rest a supposition that a managed irredeemable currency can smooth out or prevent fluctuations in the price level. The worst fluctuations the world has ever seen have been under irredeemable currencies."[21]

Possibly the Patman report's most inconsistent argument against the gold standard was its recognition that "gold is the most generally accepted medium for settlement of international balances that the world has yet been able to devise. . . . In the domestic field, however, the risks of gold convertibility are high and the advantages questionable."[22]

How could gold be so advantageous for international exchange and so "questionable" for domestic purposes? Were not the risks more pronounced in international markets than they were at home? Did not domestic households and businesses more legitimately deserve gold now buried in the U.S. Treasury's vaults, if they wanted it, than foreign central banks and governments? The subcommittee's remark reflected the notion of some kind of a scarcity of gold if redeemability were restored. It did not seem to recognize that the gold "scarcity" in the 1930s was a result of *government* gold hoarding. The federal government had plenty of gold then, and it had almost as much in 1952. Sproul's previous remark, in which he claimed that people "stormed the Federal Reserve Banks"—hyperbole at least—indicated that domestic money holders wanted to redeem Federal Reserve notes for gold, but were frustrated by the Treasury's insistence that all the gold remain in the U.S. Treasury. (In February of 1933 the Fed banks' gold reserves were still 63 percent of their outstanding monetary obligations; see chapter 17.) If the "competent and responsible men" who ran the Fed at that time had followed Bagehot's doctrine of lending freely on any usually acceptable collateral and had disbursed the gold, they would have greatly relieved the monetary stringency both in the United States and in foreign countries. What was "harsh and perverse" turned out to be the policies of mortal, ignorant government bureaucrats.

All arguments to the contrary, neither subcommittee was going to allow a gold standard to reenter the picture. The Patman Subcommittee cited the earlier report of the Douglas Subcommittee and came to the same conclusion. "We believe," read the earlier statement, "that to restore the free domestic convertibility of money into gold coin or gold bullion at this time would militate against, rather than promote, the purposes of the Employment Act [of 1946], and we recommend that no action be taken in this direction."[23] The Patman Subcommittee added: "This Subcommittee has given further consideration to the advisability of restoring the free domestic convertibility of money into gold coin or bullion and concludes that such a policy would be unwise either at the present time or as an ideal for future action."[24]

Monetary Principles of Senator Paul Douglas

Notwithstanding his general agreement with the report of the Patman Subcommittee, Senator Paul Douglas, who was on both subcommittees, added a separate statement at the end of the later report that took issue with some of its analysis and suggestions for policy. First, Douglas disagreed with the conclusion that changes in the domestic money stock have influence on the price level only in the long run. "The implication [in the report]," he stated, "[is] . . . that monetary policy is unimportant in the short-run. [However], the long-run . . . is made up of short-runs. If it be assumed that monetary policy has *no* effect in each of a series of short-runs, then it can have no effect in the long-run." The only "sensible assumption," he concluded, is that "the probabilities are overwhelmingly in favor of prices moving directly with changes in the money supply, although perhaps, with some occasional time-lag."[25]

Douglas found much fault with policies that had fostered an inflationary expansion of money over the preceding decade. He noted the inflationary expectations that had logically beset the general public when the Korean episode began, and he expressed the opinion that a prompt and determined anti-inflationary policy would have materially dampened the price level increase.

Douglas felt that the Patman Subcommittee too easily accepted the indulgence of an "insulated" market for Treasury sales of government securities, which meant simply that the Federal Reserve System would buy any Treasury securities that went begging. A slight extension of "insulation," he noted, would be a "rigged" market. "We will have the creation of an artificial market by devices resolutely denied to private firms but eagerly adopted, in the future as they have been in the past, by the Government itself. . . . The end result of such a double standard of financial morality," he warned, "is simply the destruction of confidence in the integrity and purposes of Government." In the final analysis, "'insulation' comes to consist merely in the creation of new and additional supplies of money to take the Government's securities off the market."[26]

Douglas regarded "stability of the price level as far more important to the economic and social well being of the country than any artificially maintained stability of the interest rate." The government was better able to compete in the money market because it was the "ultimate taxing power." With the burden of supporting Treasury securities removed, the Fed would be in a stronger position to exercise countercyclical monetary policies.[27]

Douglas offered suggestions for Federal Reserve strategy that were analogous to the principles Walter Bagehot had specified eighty years earlier. The Fed with its present endowment of powers, he declared, must also have a "degree of independence clearly sufficient to prevent its coercion . . . by any private interest or . . . by the Executive Branch of Government." Second, the Fed's monetary responsibilities should be "fixed in law" so that they are clear "to other agencies [i.e., the Treasury], to the public, to Congress, and to itself." Independence for the Fed, Douglas continued, "cannot be discussed in a vacuum, but can only be meaningfully discussed in terms of independence to do what, when and how; and . . . in terms of responsibility for doing what, when and how."[28]

Douglas noted that the subcommittee's suggestions for giving more powers to the Fed could "prove utterly mischievous" if used in the present mode—that is, with the Board of Governors subservient "to the currently ruling Executive and his political purposes."[29] Douglas called for a congressional mandate specifying responsibilities and the general terms of policy. "I would concede the difficulty of writing a mandate," he allowed. "But if it is alleged that the difficulties are so great that they cannot be surmounted, then that contention is tantamount to saying that we do not know what kind of a general monetary policy we desire; and, if we do not know what kind of a monetary policy we want, then we had better simply abolish the instruments of monetary policy, for they are entirely too dangerous to be used for ill-considered purposes."[30]

Douglas called for a clear separation of Treasury and Federal Reserve powers. "The Treasury and the [Federal Reserve] System," he suggested, "will be better neighbors in the long run, the less they invite themselves to play in each others' back yards. The proper principle is 'Good fences make good neighbors.'"[31]

Congress's mandate to the Fed, Douglas thought, should not be detailed, but should emphasize alterations in the quantity of money that would be countercyclical. The mandate should also be legislated into the Federal Reserve

Act, and "should not be inferential, implicit, or interpretive." Interestingly enough, he regarded the Employment Act of 1946, which had been so often the focal point for discussion by both subcommittees, as anachronistic and ambiguous. The present-day Fed, he concluded, "has been quite confused regarding its responsibilities and the fundamental reason for its being. I do not believe that this situation can now be corrected by inference or indirection." Representative Jesse Wolcott of Michigan added his concurrence with "the views expressed by Senator Douglas."[32]

The Fed's Reserve Requirement Policy from 1948 to 1958

Congress did not formally incorporate Senator Douglas's norms for monetary policy into a legislative act. Nevertheless, Fed policy after 1952 took on a decidedly conservative cast. The nominal monetary base including Treasury deposits at Fed banks remained virtually constant for ten years (table 21.1, M_F), which means that the Fed generated no seigniorage for the federal government during that time. Money privately created through the commercial banking system increased by \$20.7 billion in nominal terms, and by \$8.5 billion in real terms during the same period (1952–1962, table 21.1, M_P and Real M_P).

The increase in M1, with a constant monetary base, resulted from the Fed's policy of gradually reducing member bank reserve requirements from the high end to about the middle of the allowable range. Table 21.2 shows the approximate dates at which the Federal Reserve Board reduced reserve requirements for the three classes of member banks from 1 December 1948 to 1 May 1962. The weighted average of all reserve requirements fell from 21.0 to 14.7 percent, or by 30 percent, over this 14-year period.

Given the demand deposits at member banks in 1962, the reduction of reserve requirements since 1948 was the equivalent of a dollar increase in reserves of approximately \$6.67 billion. That is, if reserve requirements had continued at the prevailing high levels of 1948, member bank reserves would have had to have increased by \$6.67 billion to have generated the same amount of private-sector demand deposits; the value of M_F for 1962 in table 21.1 would have had to reach more than \$54 billion. At the same time, the public's holdings of demand deposits relative to currency holdings also increased, which permitted further creation of private money.[33]

Fed policy clearly aimed at getting the applicable reserve requirement ratios near the middle of the allowable ranges, which were 10 to 22 percent for central reserve and reserve city banks, and 7 to 14 percent for country banks. By 1962, the difference in requirements actually in force was only the spread between the 16½ percent for banks in the larger cities and the 12 percent for "country" banks. This much-reduced difference was an attempt to forestall

TABLE 21.1 Federal Reserve monetary liabilities (M_F), M_1, private creation of money (M_P), nominal and real values with annual changes, and prices (CPI), 1951–1966

Year	Bank reserves with Fed (R_B) + F.R. notes (C) + Treas. dep. (T_F) M_F (1)	Annual change in M_F ΔM_F (2)	Real annual change in M_F (1952$) ΔM^*_{FD} (3)	Real capital value of M_F (1952$) M^*_{FC} (4)	Real change in capital value of M_F ΔM^*_{FC} (5)	Hand-to-hand currency + private demand deposits adjusted M_1 (6)	Annual percentage change in M_1 $\left[\frac{\Delta M_1}{M_1}\right]$ (7)
1951	$43.7	$ —	$ —	$45.1	$ —	$118.6	—
52	46.0	2.3	2.30	46.0	0.9	125.0	5.4
53	46.8	0.8	0.79	46.5	0.5	128.5	2.8
54	46.9	0.1	0.10	46.3	−0.2	130.0	1.2
55	46.5	−0.4	−0.40	46.1	−0.2	134.4	3.4
56	46.7	0.2	0.20	45.6	−0.5	136.0	1.2
57	47.0	0.3	0.28	44.4	−1.2	137.0	0.7
58	46.9	−0.1	−0.09	43.1	−1.3	138.4	1.0
59	46.8	−0.1	−0.09	42.7	−1.4	143.4	3.6
1960	46.0	−0.8	−0.72	41.3	−1.4	140.1	−2.6
61	44.6	−1.4	−1.24	39.6	−1.7	143.0	2.1
62	46.5	1.9	1.67	40.8	−1.2	146.2	2.2
63	48.1	1.6	1.39	41.7	0.9	150.4	2.9
64	50.3	2.2	1.88	43.0	1.3	155.6	3.5
65	53.8	3.5	2.95	45.3	2.3	161.7	3.9
66	56.4	2.6	2.13	46.1	0.8	170.5	5.4
Net change	$12.7	$12.7	$11.15	$1.0	$1.0	$51.9	2.4[a]

invidious comparisons by member banks in the larger cities when they looked at their brethren in the "country." General reduction of requirements also reduced the spread of reserve requirements between member and nonmember banks. Finally, the reduction of reserve requirements, as the principal means of Fed policy, precluded any pressure on the Fed to support government security prices at the behest of the Treasury Department. However, the executive (Eisenhower) administration after 1952 showed little if any inclination to put pressure on the Fed's policy decisions.

Fed Banks' Balance-Sheet Changes after 1958

The Fed's relative inactivity in the years between 1948 and 1958 is visible in the Consolidated Statement of Condition of the twelve Federal Reserve banks. Table 21.3 shows the major items in this statement at the end of 1948. By

Year	Stock of private money ($M_1 - M_F$) M_P (8)	Annual change in M_P ΔM_{PD} (9)	Real annual change in M_P (1952$) ΔM^*_{PD} (10)	Real capital value of M_P (1952$) M^*_{PC} (11)	Real annual change in capital value of M_P ΔM^*_{PC} (12)	Prices (CPI 1957–59 = 100) P (13)	Annual percentage change in prices (14)
1951	$74.9	$ —	$ —	$77.2	$ —	89.7	—
52	79.0	4.1	4.10	79.0	1.8	92.5	3.1
53	81.7	2.7	2.68	81.1	2.1	93.2	0.8
54	83.1	1.4	1.38	82.1	1.0	93.6	0.4
55	87.9	4.8	4.76	87.2	5.1	93.3	−0.3
56	89.3	1.4	1.38	87.2	0.0	94.7	1.5
57	90.0	0.7	0.66	85.0	−2.2	98.0	3.5
58	91.5	1.5	1.38	84.1	−0.9	100.7	2.8
59	96.6	5.1	4.65	88.0	3.9	101.5	0.8
1960	94.1	−2.5	−2.25	84.4	−3.6	103.1	2.4
61	98.4	4.3	3.82	87.4	3.0	104.2	1.1
62	99.7	1.3	1.14	87.5	0.1	105.4	1.2
63	102.6	2:6	2.25	88.7	1.2	106.7	1.2
64	105.3	3.0	2.57	90.1	1.4	108.1	1.3
65	107.9	2.6	2.19	90.8	0.7	109.9	1.7
66	114.1	6.2	5.07	93.3	2.5	113.1	2.9
Net change	$39.2	$39.2	$35.7	$16.1	$16.1	26.1%	1.6[a]

Sources: Board of Governors of the Federal Reserve System, *Supplement to Banking and Monetary Statistics,* section 9 (Washington, 1965), pp. 6–8. Milton Friedman and Anna J. Schwartz, *Monetary Statistics of the United States,* NBER (New York: Columbia University Press, 1970), table 1, pp. 40–53. Board of Governors of the Federal Reserve System, *Federal Reserve Bulletin,* Washington, 1950–1970.

Note: Values at or near midyear and in $ billions, except for prices.

[a] Average for period.

the middle of 1958, the Consolidated Statement appeared as detailed in table 21.4.

While the changes in individual items in the statement were small, they were the beginnings of a trend that would go on for the next ten years. The gold certificate account had begun its decline, which was to continue at a rate of about $1 billion per year until 1968. Most of the titles to the lost gold went to foreign central banks and treasury departments to satisfy U.S. balance-of-payments deficits, while much of the bullion gold remained as an "ear-marked" fund in the Fed bank of New York.

The Fed banks still faced a gold reserve requirement of 25 percent against their demand obligations—Federal Reserve notes outstanding and member

TABLE 21.2 Reserve requirements of member banks (percent of deposits)

Approximate effective date	Central reserve city banks	Reserve city banks	Country banks	Time deposits
Dec. 31, 1948	26	22	16	7 1/2
Aug. 18, 1949	23	19	12	5
Sept. 1, 1949	22	18	12	5
Jan. 25, 1951	24	20	14	6
July 9, 1953	22	19	13	6
Aug. 1, 1954	20	18	12	5
Apr. 24, 1958	18	16 1/2	11	5
Dec. 1, 1960	16 1/2[a]	16 1/2[a]	12	5
May 1, 1962	16 1/2	16 1/2	12	5

Source: *Federal Reserve Bulletin,* June 1962, p. 709.

Note: The data in this table show the approximate dates at which the Federal Reserve Board made changes in reserve requirements. Demand deposits subject to reserve requirements are total demand deposits minus cash items in process of collection, and demand balances due from domestic banks.

[a] After July 28, 1959, the classifications of "central reserve" and "reserve city" became a single classification with a ratio maximum of 22 percent.

TABLE 21.3 All Reserve banks, December 1948 ($ billions)

Assets		Liabilities	
Gold certificates	23.0	Federal Reserve notes outstanding	24.2
U.S. government securities	23.3	Member bank reserve-deposit account	20.5
Gold reserve ratio 49 percent			

Source: *Federal Reserve Bulletin,* March 1949.

TABLE 21.4 All Reserve banks, June 1958 ($ billions)

Assets		Liabilities	
Gold certificates	20.8	Federal Reserve notes outstanding	26.7
U.S. government securities	25.4	Member bank reserve-deposit account	18.8
Gold reserve ratio 47 percent			

Source: *Federal Reserve Bulletin,* October 1958

TABLE 21.5 All Reserve banks, January 1967 ($ billions)

Assets		Liabilities	
Gold certificates	12.7	Federal Reserve notes Outstanding	38.1
U.S. government securities	43.5	Member bank reserve-deposit account	18.8
Gold reserve ratio 33 percent			

Source: *Federal Reserve Bulletin,* April 1967.

bank reserve-deposit accounts. As the Fed banks lost gold, the Federal Open Market Committee (FOMC) bought, and thereby monetized, U.S. government securities. The Consolidated Statement for 1967 (table 21.5) shows that Fed bank holdings of securities increased to $43.5 billion from $25.4 billion in 1958.

By this time the gold reserve ratio applied only to Federal Reserve notes outstanding. In 1965 Congress changed the gold reserve law by abolishing the accounted gold reserve requirement against member bank reserve-deposit accounts. On the former basis of calculation, the ratio was down to 22 percent, which was three percentage points below the former legal minimum.

The gold had not "backed" the U.S. money stock in any real sense. How, indeed, could gold "back" the Federal Reserve notes and demand deposits when the firms and households that held the money were not allowed to hold gold or use it for monetary purposes?

The gold continued to serve as a final settlement for balance-of-payments deficits. If a gold standard had truly determined the U.S. money stock, common money in the United States would have stopped growing and would probably have declined to arrest the gold outflow. Rather, the FOMC bought U.S. government securities in order to prevent any such adjustment.

By 1968, the gold reserve against Federal Reserve notes was down to 15.2 percent, so Congress abolished the gold reserve requirement altogether. Why have a "reserve requirement" when no one is allowed to own the "reserve," and the monetary authorities are not bound by it anyway?

Just about any central banker or monetary authority of the 1950s and 1960s routinely paid lip service to the gold standard, and some of them firmly supported "a" gold standard. The "gold standard" that they favored, however, was not the classical type that functioned freely but a paper gold standard that left the supervision and control of monetary variables to Federal Reserve authorities. The "gold standard" of this era had a political feature that recommended it to central-bank executives. Whenever politicians and executive administrations sought easy money or inflationary policies from the central bank, the authorities could point to the central bank's dwindling gold reserves and warn the inflationists of the dire consequences that would follow if the minimum gold reserve ratio were breached. In fact, nothing did happen except that Congress abolished the gold requirements. Nonetheless, for about fifteen years the "gold standard" was a political buffer that Fed spokesmen could use to thwart the monetary irresponsibilities of ambitious legislatures.

Federal Reserve policy in 1962 shifted from alteration of member banks' reserve requirements to gradual increases in the monetary base (M_F in table 21.1). Commercial bank creation of money also grew at a roughly comparable pace, and the price level showed increases in the mid–1960s that were significantly greater than the 1 percent per year average increase recorded for the previous thirteen years. The stage was set for the unprecedented inflation that would prevail for the next twenty-five years.

22 Destabilizing Factors in Federal Reserve Policy, 1967–1980

> An eclectic approach is thus taken by the Federal Reserve, in recognition of the fact that the state of economic knowledge does not justify reliance on any single forecasting technique. . . . In the short run, the rate of change in the observed money supply is quite erratic and cannot be trusted as an indicator of the course of monetary policy. The upsurge of the price level this year hardly represents either the basic trend of prices or the response of prices to previous monetary or fiscal policies—whatever their shortcomings may have been. . . . The severe rate of inflation . . . in 1973 cannot responsibly be attributed to monetary management or to public policies more generally.
>
> Arthur F. Burns, *Federal Reserve Bulletin*, November 1973

Federal Reserve Policy Generates Seigniorage

Federal Reserve means for supplying money to the economy in the early 1960s shifted from reductions in reserve requirements to nominal increases in the monetary base. Through the mid-sixties and for part of the seventies, both dollar and real values of the increases in the base grew larger (ΔM_F, tables 21.1 and 22.1). At the same time, the price level began to increase by more than what could reasonably be attributed to statistical bias.[1] The increases in the price level (P) shrank the value of the dollar so much that the real increases in the base also declined for several years after 1976. ΔM_F, column (2) in table 22.1, and ΔM_F^*, column (4), show these nominal and real changes.

These columns are year-to-year values of realized *seigniorage* that the Federal Reserve Open Market Committee (FOMC) generated on behalf of the federal government by monetizing U.S. government securities. In the era of precious metal coinage, seigniorage was recognized as the "profit" accruing to the authority that coined the money, and was the difference between the material-operational costs of producing the coin and the monetary value of the coin that a government spent into circulation. (Refer to chapters 11 and 12 herein and the discussion of silver coinage between 1878 and 1893.) Since the costs today of paper money and accounted bank reserves are insignificant, almost all of Federal Reserve creation of base money becomes seigniorage revenue for the federal government.

Interactions between Money and Prices: The Real Money Stock

The monetary sovereignty that Congress has assumed for itself is not an absolute power. The base money that the FOMC creates, and that commercial banks use to create more money, necessarily goes into markets—all markets—and affects all money prices. If prices then rise, as they did throughout this period and in most other periods as well, the value of the money unit falls in the same proportion. Only if prices were to remain constant would the dollar increase in M_F or in M_p be a corresponding real increase.

Changes in the stock of money are not the only determinants of prices. The rate at which money is spent and the rate at which goods are produced can have significant effects on the value of the money unit. Nonetheless, in an economic system where a monetary authority creates fiat money, the stock of money is the controllable variable that most notably affects prices as well as the rate at which money is spent. For if base money and common money increase so rapidly that prices begin an upward surge, people economize on their holdings of cash balances by spending their money faster in order to get rid of it. While an individual can quickly divest himself of his currency and bank deposits, all individuals acting in unison cannot. They are destined to hold the existing stock of money; they cannot destroy it any more than they were able to create it in the first place. People can only spend the money, but now they are spending it faster by holding each dollar for a shorter time period. The net effect of their efforts is to force up prices and force down the value of each money unit until everyone is satisfied to hold the existing money stock at the current rate of increase in prices.

The increased velocity of money is a feedback effect of the prior burgeoning increases in the stock of money and prices. The obvious lesson that producers of nominal money learn from this interaction is that, if they create money too rapidly, the real substance of the new (and the old) money will be vitiated by price level increases—possibly to the point where the real value of the nominal increases becomes negative. Indeed, this condition is seen in this period in the real value of M_F^*, which occasionally registered slight trends upward until 1976, but then declined by 1981 to a real value lower than what it had been in 1966. Nonetheless, the Federal Reserve's creation of monetary base over this period generated real seigniorage for the federal government of \$63.7 billion in 1967 dollars (ΔM_F^*). This seigniorage was the "fruit" from the "money tree." Since the real value of the "money tree" declined over the period, some of the "fruit" was actually part of the tree's substance.

Approximately the same phenomenon appeared in the value of the real stock of privately produced money. Real seigniorage to the banking system measured in 1967 dollars amounted to over \$95 billion for the period. But at the same time the real stock of bank-created money declined by almost \$18 billion.

Annual rates of increase in the two most commonly used money stocks, M_1 and M_2, and in the accounted velocities, V_{M1} and V_{M2}, of these money stock measures for this period are shown in table 22.2. In only two years, 1976 and 1979, did the velocity of the M_1 money stock increase more than the

TABLE 22.1 Federal Reserve monetary liabilities (M_F), M_1, private creastion of money (M_P), nominal and real values with annual changes, and prices, 1966–1981

Year	Bank reserves with Fed (R_B) + F.R. notes (C) + Treas. dep. (T_F) M_F (1)	Annual change in M_F ΔM_F (2)	Real annual change in M_F (1967$) ΔM^*_{FD} (3)	Real capital value of M_F (1967$) M^*_{FC} (4)	Annual change in real capital value of M_F ΔM^*_{FC} (5)	Hand-to-hand currency + private demand deposits adjusted M_1 (6)
1966	56.4	—	—	58.0	—	173.3
7	60.2	3.8	3.85	60.2	2.2	178.9
8	64.4	4.2	4.11	61.8	1.6	191.4
9	66.8	2.4	2.24	60.8	−1.0	203.4
1970	70.7	3.9	3.45	60.8	0.0	209.6
1	77.3	6.6	5.51	63.7	2.9	225.9
2	84.5	7.2	5.84	67.4	3.7	239.3
3	88.6	4.1	3.18	66.6	−0.8	259.6
4	98.3	9.7	6.91	66.6	0.0	271.6
5	104.0	5.7	3.69	64.5	−2.1	286.2
6	118.5	14.5	8.74	69.4	4.9	299.6
7	126.1	7.6	4.31	69.4	0.0	322.1
8	134.8	8.7	4.61	69.0	−0.4	349.9
9	138.5	3.7	1.80	63.9	−5.1	377.4
1980	150.9	12.4	5.34	61.0	−2.9	393.8
1	151.3	0.4	0.16	55.8	−5.2	428.7
Net change	94.9	94.9	63.74	−2.2	−2.2	255.4

M_1 money stock itself, and this volatility was clearly a lagged response to prior outsize increases in M_1.

The Fed's Accommodation–Interest-Rate Policy

The data for money and its growth summarized in tables 22.1 and 22.2 suggest that monetary factors were largely responsible for the inflation of the late sixties and early seventies. William McChesney Martin, while he was still chairman of the Board of Governors, admitted in 1965 that the Federal Reserve System had a tolerable degree of control over the monetary stocks. "It is fair to say," he admitted, "that from month to month and year to year the supply of [bank] reserves is determined by the policies of the Federal Open Market Committee [FOMC]."[2] Yet the official Federal Reserve explanation often given for the growth in the money supply implied that the Fed was no more than a passive agent in the process. "The acceleration in money

Year	Annual percentage change in M_1 $\left[\frac{\Delta M_1}{M_1}\right]$ (7)	Stock of privately created money (M_1-M_F) M_P (8)	Annual change in M_P ΔM_P (9)	Real annual change in M_P (1967$) ΔM^*_{PD} (10)	Real capital value of M_P (1967$) ΔM^*_{PC} (11)	Real annual change in capital value of M_P ΔM^*_{PC} (12)	Prices (CPI, 1967 = 100) P (13)	Annual Percent-age change in prices $\left[\frac{\Delta P}{P}\right]$ (14)
1966	—%	116.9	—	—	120.1	—	97.3	—%
7	3.2	118.7	1.8	1.80	118.7	−1.4	100.0	3.7
8	7.0	127.0	8.3	7.97	121.9	3.2	104.2	4.2
9	6.3	136.6	9.6	8.74	124.4	2.5	109.8	5.4
1970	3.1	138.9	2.3	1.98	119.4	−5.0	116.3	5.9
1	7.8	148.6	9.7	8.00	122.5	3.1	121.3	4.3
2	5.9	154.8	6.2	4.95	123.5	1.0	125.3	3.3
3	8.5	171.0	16.2	12.17	128.5	5.0	133.1	6.2
4	4.6	173.3	2.3	1.56	117.3	−11.2	147.7	11.0
5	5.4	182.2	8.9	5.52	113.0	−4.3	161.2	9.1
6	4.7	181.1	−1.1	−0.64	106.1	−6.9	170.7	5.9
7	7.5	196.0	14.9	8.20	107.8	1.7	181.8	6.5
8	8.6	215.1	19.1	9.78	110.1	2.3	195.3	7.4
9	7.9	238.9	23.8	10.99	110.3	0.2	216.6	10.9
1980	4.3	242.9	4.0	1.62	98.1	−12.2	247.6	14.3
1	8.9	277.4	34.5	12.72	102.2	4.1	271.3	9.6
Net change	6.3%[a]	160.5	160.5	95.41	−17.9	−17.9	174.0	7.2%[a]

Sources: *Federal Reserve Bulletins,* 1966 to 1982. Federal Reserve monetary liabilities include Federal Reserve notes, deposits to depository institutions (or member banks), and deposits of U.S. Treasury—general accounts.
Note: Values at or near midyear and in $ billions except for prices.
[a] Average for period.

growth over the past 2 years," stated the article "Bank Credit and Monetary Developments" in 1965, "suggests that expanding transactions needs may now be having a greater influence on the public's demands for cash balances than formerly."[3] The article argued that the Fed's action in 1962 of raising the interest-rate ceiling on time deposits "may" have encouraged a move toward greater spending, which in turn would have increased "transactions needs related to income and output." Then, the higher level of transactions "may help to explain the larger rate of growth of the money stock in those years."[4]

This rationalization stresses the Fed's "accommodation" principle. It implies that the real sector initiates changes in the demand for money that are translated to the Fed through various money-market indicators, especially interest rates. The greater quantities of money demanded are then supplied by the Fed's "accommodation." All of this action "may" take place, but such a

TABLE 22.2 Annual rates of change in money stocks, M_1 and M_2, and in velocities of money, V_{M1} and V_{M2}, 1966–1981 (percent)

Year	M_1	V_{M1}	M_2	V_{M2}
1966	—	—	—	—
7	6.6	1.6	11.1	−2.2
8	7.9	2.0	9.7	0.0
9	3.4	1.1	2.5	0.8
70	6.0	0.2	8.3	0.8
1	6.3	1.1	11.2	−3.4
2	8.7	2.8	11.0	−0.4
3	5.7	3.8	8.5	1.7
4	6.3	1.6	9.4	−1.3
5	4.8	3.4	8.3	0.0
6	3.5	7.5	8.1	3.0
7	6.2	5.2	10.6	0.8
8	9.6	3.6	8.8	4.1
9	4.6	7.0	7.6	7.8
1980	5.9	3.1	—	—
1	9.7	1.7	10.3	1.2
Average annual change	6.35	3.05	8.96	0.92

Source: *Federal Reserve Bulletins*, 1966–1982. Velocities, V_{M1} and V_{M2}, were calculated using M_1 and M_2 values at midyear, and $GNP for the calendar year.

view ignores the fact that the Fed's willingness to supply reserves is a necessary condition for monetary expansion in the first place.

Chairman Martin acknowledged again before the Senate Select Committee on Small Business in 1967 that "We can . . . alter the volume of both total and required reserves, [and] exert considerable influence over the readiness with which the banks will extend credit."[5] But a few days later before the Senate Committee on Finance in support of the investment tax credit, he studiously neglected the causative role of money on the inflation. The economy in 1965–1966, he claimed, was "overstimulated," not by money, but "by rapidly expanding business investment and defense spending. . . . Monetary policy," he excused, "was doing all it could to restrain aggregate demand."[6]

Clearly, monetary policy could not accommodate spending by increasing monetary stocks, and at the same time do "all it could to restrain aggregate demand." Indeed, the vaunted "independence" of the Fed was supposed to provide it with enough insulation from political pressures so that it could carry out unpopular restrictive policies when they were called for.

The Fed's use of interest rates, or "money-market conditions," as both targets and indicators for monetary policy actions was the proximate cause for much policy-generated disequilibrium. Interest rates are mercurial targets because they respond in diverse ways to both real and monetary forces. For example, an increased demand for liquid assets by households, firms, and banks results in higher market rates of interest, a condition that a money-supplying central bank can relieve temporarily by appropriate action. This kind of situation is labeled a liquidity effect. When business activity picks up, more money is needed for transactions purposes, so interest rates reattain their former levels: the transactions or income effect. If a business boom subsequently develops, a rise in interest rates may result from enhanced investment demands that generate the boom: the investment effect. Further increases in the money supply may then aggravate the boom and provoke significant price level increases that raise interest rates still further: the inflation effect. In sum, increases in the money supply that temporarily lower short-term rates frequently have transactions, investment, and (or) inflation effects that subsequently raise interest rates further than a liquidity effect alone would have done if left unattended.

Some of these tendencies appeared in the U.S. economy late in 1967. "The rise in interest rates since mid-year," Chairman Martin reported, "[has] occurred even though the reserves available to the banking system have been expanding rapidly."[7] Again in 1971, the new chairman of the Federal Reserve Board, Arthur Burns, noted in his July report to the Joint Economic Committee: "Interest rates are responding to fears of inflation by moving up again *despite rapid monetary expansion.*"[8] If the Fed had cut back on the rate of monetary growth in the second quarter of 1971 as many of the indicators suggested, Burns added, short-term interest rates perhaps would have risen even more. But "in view of the delicate state of the economic recovery," he argued, "it seemed desirable to prevent the possible adverse effects of sharply higher interest rates on expenditure plans and public psychology."[9] Burns here was in the inconsistent position of arguing, first, that the Fed continued inflationary monetary growth, despite advisory indications to the contrary, in order to hold down interest rates. At the same time he admitted that interest rates rose anyway due to fears of inflation from monetary expansion. So the economy in the end experienced both more inflation and higher interest rates from Fed policies. The inflation effect dominated the other factors.

Another element of interest-rate instability appeared in 1972 and continued through 1973. As the inflation premium appeared in interest rates, a significant gap opened between money-market rates and the Federal Reserve discount rate. The latter rate is a policy rate and usually lags rapidly changing market rates. The gap widened as FOMC policy tightened slightly in late 1972 when banks with liquidity "needs" exerted pressure on the Fed for increased accommodation at the discount window. Member bank borrowings rose from almost nothing in early 1972 to over $1 billion by the year's end.[10] By September 1973, borrowings were over $2 billion, and by mid–1974 they were $3.5 billion.[11]

The use of the discount window, central-bank legend has it, is a privilege and not a right. Furthermore, the ironclad rule for discount policy in early central-banking theory was that the central bank's rate be kept above current market rates.[12] Otherwise, the discounting privilege becomes a subsidy that the commercial banks can be expected to indulge until the reserves of the central bank are depleted. Jacob Viner once observed that if the central-bank rate was low enough, it "might . . . permit or even . . . foster a wild inflation."[13] The reserves of contemporary Federal Reserve banks are not depleted because reserves no longer exist in any meaningful sense. The principal effect of the discount window, in the presence of a positive interest-rate differential between money-market rates and the central-bank discount rate, is to permit commercial banks to escape what would otherwise be a tight money policy. It thereby complicates a straightforward restrictive action.

The Effect of the Treasury's Fiscal "Needs" on Fed Policy

Another factor that provoked higher interest rates was the appearance of sizable federal budget deficits beginning in 1967 and continuing to the present. The greater supply of government securities coming into investment markets tended to lower security prices and raise yields because of the increasing demand by the federal government for investment resources. The FOMC's "Record of Policy Actions" continuously reflected Treasury "needs." Any targets for policy were always qualified by the clause, "to the extent permitted by Treasury financing." For example, in the record of the meeting of 30 April 1968, the policy directive called for "firmer conditions, to the extent permitted by Treasury financing." One member of the committee, Mr. Braddock Hickman, dissented because he thought that the rise in interest rates had been less than necessary to stem inflationary pressures. But "he agreed that the prospective Treasury financing precluded substantial firming of money market conditions before the Committee's next meeting."[14]

Passage of the 10 percent income tax surcharge in 1968 was an attempt to relieve the fiscal pressures on monetary policy, but it had too euphoric an effect on the Federal Reserve's money managers. The FOMC assumed after passage of the surcharge that it could ease monetary policy and assist the Treasury with no adverse side effects on prices. The policy directive for July 1968 stated: "System open-market operations . . . shall be conducted with a view to accommodating the tendency toward somewhat less firm conditions in the money market . . . while taking account of forthcoming Treasury financing."[15] Staff reports to the FOMC in August then conjectured that "overall activity would slow considerably in the months ahead as a result of the new fiscal constraint measures."[16] Again in September 1968, the committee decided that "greater restraint was not considered desirable in view of the outlook for slowing in overall economic activity, although it was noted that firm evidence was lacking thus far on the amount of slowing in prospect."[17] Not until the meeting of 14 January 1969 did the FOMC adopt a policy of firmness.[18] By this time, the money supply had increased over the year past by 7.9 percent.

Chairman Martin, in testimony before the Joint Economic Committee in February 1969, admitted that the Fed had been "overly hasty last summer in expecting an immediate impact from fiscal restraint." Martin blamed the developing inflation on consumer and business spending decisions. "The ebullient [spending] behavior of consumers," he declared, "infected the business community. . . . In this heady atmosphere, cost increases were rapidly passed on in the form of higher prices."[19] He noted that the money supply had accelerated to a 7.5 percent annual rate of increase in the third quarter even though interest rates were rising, but he attributed the increase to "the larger-than-seasonal rundown in U.S. treasury balances at commercial banks during the fall."[20] He did not seem to notice that excessive growth in the monetary base may have had something to do with the "heady atmosphere" in which consumers and businessmen made spending decisions.

The Monetary Aggregates Come into Fed Policy

Monetary policy firmed markedly throughout 1969. The money supply (M_1) increased during the year by about 3 percent—a value that would have looked "high" in 1963, but was "low" relative to recent monetary growth. In early 1970, the firm policy was eased to one of achieving "modest growth in the monetary aggregates, with about equal weight being given to bank credit and the money stock."[21]

The "aggregates," which referred to the various accounted money stocks, now appeared routinely in FOMC directives.[22] However, Mr. Andrew Brimmer, a member of the Board, gave a statement of official Federal Reserve policy before the Joint Economic Committee in mid–1970 in which he disabused all and sundry of the idea that the Fed had any intention of pursuing "fixed target rates of growth in the monetary aggregates on a more or less continuous basis. . . . We do not propose to let adherence to any fixed growth rate of the money supply," he said, "stand in the way of achieving [the objectives of full employment, rapid improvement in productivity, price stability, and balance-of-payments equilibrium]."[23]

Brimmer's statement implied that the Fed could indeed control the aggregates. It also appeared to be a firm commitment to a multifunction posture for Fed policy, and to reject a narrow construction of the Federal Reserve's role and scope. Yet by the implication of a commitment to all the objectives that would be realized by "good" policies, it promised too much. It overstated by implication the results that could be expected from a money-supplying institution, and made the institution vulnerable to political demands that it deliver on the goals it was not "standing in the way of."[24]

Throughout 1970, policy remained "moderate," which is to say that M_1 grew by 6.0 percent and M_2 by 8.3 percent. In the October meeting of the FOMC, however, several members "stressed the desirability of fostering declines in interest rates over coming months in order to encourage needed recovery in residential construction outlays."[25] Then, in the December 1970 meeting, the emphasis shifted to "money-market conditions" from the previous emphasis on the "aggregates," and some members expressed the view that this shift "was desirable on more general grounds, apart from present uncertainties."[26]

The tenor of FOMC meetings continued expansive throughout 1971. One excuse for allowing an admittedly inflationary growth rate in the money supply was "to compensate for the shortfall [in M_1] in the fourth quarter [of 1970]."[27] In the fourth quarter, M_1 had grown at a rate of 1.0 percent, seasonally adjusted, or 4.6 percent, not seasonally adjusted. The issue of whether a seasonally adjusted money supply can be a target or an indicator is debatable. It is also irrelevant. What was important was the growth rate in the money supply over the entire year. More and more, Fed officials used a previous period's "shortfall" as an excuse for promoting an excessive rate of growth in the aggregates over a later period, without reference to the fact that any given "shortfall" was only partial compensation for yet an earlier period's excess.

In a revealing article in the *Federal Reserve Bulletin* for June 1973, Alan R. Holmes, manager of the System Open Market Account at the Federal Reserve Bank of New York, argued that the outsized growth in money during 1972 resulted from the fact that M_1 was an "elusive target." Holmes's brief seemed to change the Brimmer norm of "we will not," cited above, to "we cannot." It implied that the technical operational facilities of the central bank were at times inadequate to cope with the complexities of precise growth rates in the money supply. When the Fed funds rate rose, Holmes noted, "to the upper limit of the Committee's prescribed tolerance range," the Trading Desk at the New York Fed acted to increase RPDs, whereupon M_1 duly increased.[28] Holmes's money stock target, therefore, was "elusive" because it was not exclusive. The irony of Holmes's argument is that the money-market interest rates on which the FOMC put so much emphasis were (and are) the truly elusive targets. Monetary changes can affect them only ephemerally.

Nixon's "New Economic Policy"—Four Thousand Years Old

In August 1971 the Nixon administration initiated the "New Economic Policy," which included among other things implementation of the Economic Stabilization Act (ESA). The wage-price control section of the act reflected the common notion that the Federal Reserve had tried but failed to control inflation.[29]

Official Federal Reserve reaction to the wage-price freeze was positively favorable. The FOMC had already moved to a tighter monetary policy in midyear. During the first half of 1971, it had increased M_1 at an annual rate of 9.8 percent; during the second half it reduced the rate of increase to 2.4 percent.

According to Federal Reserve reasoning, the wage-price freeze reduced the transactions demand for money and thereby retarded the growth in the money supply.[30] By equally logical reasoning, Fed authorities could have argued that the imposition of price and wage controls would provoke evasions of the law, which in turn would have resulted in a greater demand for money and a correspondingly greater supply. Or they could have reasoned that the imposition of controls made tight money unnecessary; so they could use their money-supplying powers as prodigally as they wished to fulfill the political compulsions of Congress and the Executive.

This last option was seen in subsequent policy actions during 1972. Inflation control in the FOMC's policy directive had become a secondary objective in January 1971, but at least it had been secondary. (First place had been given to "sustainable economic growth.") After passage of the ESA in August 1971, the FOMC policy directive had a new order of priorities. It stated that Fed policy aimed to "foster financial conditions (1) consistent with the aims of the new governmental program, (2) including sustainable real economic growth, . . . (3) increased employment, (4) abatement of inflationary pressures, and (5) attainment of reasonable equilibrium in the country's balance of payments."[31] If the new governmental program was to retard inflation, as was frequently stated, the FOMC's number 4 priority should have been number 1, and number 1 as stated was redundant.

Further grist for the inflationary mill was seen in the Treasury's adoption of the "full-employment budget," which called for a budget deficit on the order of $40 billion during 1972. Fed Chairman Burns also accepted this policy with hardly a murmur of protest in his appearance before the Joint Economic Committee in February 1972. Unbalancing the budget by $40 billion, he said, only "gives me some pause."[32] He recognized that growth rates in the monetary aggregates had been unusually high, but he defended expansive monetary policy for its stimulus in overcoming the "sluggish economic growth" of the economy.[33]

"Stimulation" and "Accommodation": A Recipe for Sustained Inflation

The stimulation principle in Federal Reserve policy in conjunction with the accommodation principle was nothing more than a formula for ratcheting inflation. The stimulation principle appeared at times, such as in 1967 and

1970–71, when the economy was recovering from a recession. The FOMC increased the money supply at a greater rate to overcome the residual drag effects of the preceding recession. When spending and real output finally increased, the stimulative policy then appeared to have been overstimulative and inflationary. To retard the money supply and spending sufficiently at this juncture would have been politically unpalatable. So the Fed invoked the accommodation principle by continuing expansive increases in the money supply to provide for "sustainable economic growth" and the increased "transactions needs" for money. Clear-cut examples of this doctrine appeared in 1967–68, and again in 1971–72.[34]

Through 1972, M_1 increased at the unprecedented rate of 8.7 percent. Late in the summer, some sentiment developed in the FOMC to moderate the rate of growth. However, around Labor Day the Fed funds rate began climbing substantially as a higher inflation premium appeared in the interest-rate structure, and the FOMC saw to it that "reserves were supplied more generously"—again, the accommodation principle, and the same kind of policy that had been recognized in the past as self-defeating in the printed statements of Martin, Burns, and other Fed spokesmen.[35]

Policy in 1973 allowed continued growth in the aggregates of about 6 percent. But late in the year the FOMC repeated its policy of "moderate stimulation" in order to "cushion the effects on production and employment growing out of the oil shortage."[36] Abatement of inflation had top priority in the directives, but it was still compromised by the proviso that "money market conditions be maintained."

Federal Reserve Rationalization of Its Inflationary Policies

The reappearance during 1973 of severe price-level inflation coupled with steadily increasing interest rates required further statements of policy from Chairman Burns. In appearances before congressional committees in 1973 and 1974, he claimed that the mistake of too expansive a monetary policy in 1972 "was swamped by [other] special factors." Burns listed a number of these factors, which included: (1) the move to Phase III of the ESA—that is, "voluntary" wage-price controls (Burns claimed that the public regarded Phase III as the general abandonment of controls); (2) the devaluation of the dollar, which had the effect of raising the prices of imported goods;[37] (3) the oil shortage; (4) the business investment boom ("a major force making for economic instability"); (5) wage push; and (6) government fiscal deficits.[38]

Some of these things may have played a part in the continuing price level increases of the period. Most of them, however, were symptoms of the pervasive oversize increases in the monetary base during the three years past that had caused the inflation. Without them, Burns's "special factors" would hardly have rippled the surface. In fact, several of the "special factors" would not have appeared at all without the expansive policies of the Fed.[39]

In a revealing letter to Senator William Proxmire, chairman of the Senate Finance Committee, titled "Money Supply in the Conduct of Monetary Policy," Burns argued that the market economy is inherently unstable and not self-correcting. He lauded "discretionary economic policy," which he claimed had proven "reasonably successful."[40] One of the destabilizing factors he saw in the economy was the velocity of money. Independent changes in this variable, he alleged, "have historically played a large role in economic fluctuations, and they continue to do so."[41]

To support this contention, he cited the changes in M_1 and velocity for 1969–1971, which were years of recession and recovery, in contrast to M_1 velocity in 1972–1973, when the Fed was carrying out its stimulative policy. Yet over the seven-year period 1966–1973, as table 22.2 shows, the rate of change in velocity was less than one-third the rate of change in M_1 and only half as great as the percentage change in prices. For the entire fifteen-year period, percentage changes in M_1 were more than twice as great as the corresponding changes in velocity. A wealth of empirical evidence on the correspondence between changes in money stocks and changes in velocity confirms that money is the dominant and active variable in this relationship, while velocity changes are lagged responses to the prior increases in money.[42]

Burns, being a prominent business-cycle economist, was surely aware of such studies as well as the scientific importance of empirical work in general. However, he never recanted his irresponsible and erroneous assertions on the velocity of money and the "difficulties" of controlling the aggregates. As Milton Friedman noted in his reply to Burns's letter, the technical "difficulties" the Fed experienced in managing money stocks were largely due to formal rulings that the Fed itself initiated. Lagged reserve requirement accounting, for example, was one such rule.[43]

By 1974, the midpoint of this period, Federal Reserve monetary liabilities, M_F, had increased by $42 billion, or by 34 percent, an almost unprecedented increase even for an economy burdened by a "partial" war. In spite of the excess creation of money, Fed policy in the latter half of the period did not become more restrained. The percentage increases for M_1 in table 22.2 from 1974 to 1981 sum up to the same value as the increases from 1966 to 1974.

The velocity of money, however, reacted more vigorously from 1975 on. Inflationary expectations, as revealed by significant increases in interest rates, appeared in 1969, 1973, and especially in 1980–1981, when several nominal short-term rates exceeded 20 percent.

Federal Reserve officials continued to acknowledge that the Fed could control the aggregates, but it was always a qualified admission. Alan Holmes noted in April 1975 that FOMC policy had "sought to implement its goals for the economy by targeting the longer-run growth of the monetary aggregates."

And, he continued, "The use of aggregate targeting has probably contributed to the clarity of monetary policy discussions, but policy making itself has not proved easier." Holmes reached this conclusion because he saw the expectations and other independent behavior of private households, businesses, and financial institutions interacting with monetary policy "to determine the course of the monetary aggregates and the economy."[44]

In an article that appeared in May 1976, Holmes continued this line of reasoning. "The behavior of a particular monetary measure [M_1] cannot substitute," he claimed, "for an appraisal of the economy as a whole in the formulation and implementation of policy instruments. And 1975 seemed to confirm that policy-makers' judgment, based on an extensive range of information, is more effective than invariant rules for guiding the behavior of policy instruments."[45] He referred here to monetarist rules that would have had the Fed undertake a steady-state nominal rate of increase in M_1, M_2, or the monetary base.[46]

Holmes's explanation of Fed policy mirrored in more detail the views of earlier Fed spokesmen. Ten years before, William McChesney Martin had stated that the "growth of bank reserves reflects in part market factors, which in turn depend on the strength of credit demands in the economy." After taking these demand-for-money determinants into account, Martin continued, proper FOMC policies "are not subject to exact scientific determination but . . . remain a matter . . . on which judgments may differ. . . . I am stressing these limits of our knowledge in order to explain why central banking remains an art rather than a science."[47]

These views emphasize again the continued acceptance of the rule of men in monetary policy. To say that central-bank policy is an "art" and subject to interpretative judgments is to deny to it the best scientific analysis. Even someone who "does not know anything about art" knows what he "likes." So any layman's prescriptions for policy, when policy is an "art," are as "good" as policies that central bankers or the most learned economists would prescribe.

Another characteristic of the Fed's official statements on policy that often accompanied the Fed's grudging acceptance of its exclusive control of the aggregates was a hand-washing declaration of the Fed's inability to cope with the "demand factors" in the private economy. These "unpredictable" demands always turned out to be the primary causes for policymakers' failures. The variable velocity of money that Burns irresponsibly imagined, the "unpredictable" expectations of consumers and businessmen, "special factors" such as the oil "shocks," and, later, the contagious insolvencies of megafirms—such as Penn Central, the savings and loans, and Continental Illinois—all were excuses to justify one decision or another of FOMC policy. Even though "special factors" were sometimes momentous, as Milton Friedman noted in his

"Reply" to Senator Proxmire, they were irrelevant to the long-term effects of Fed policy.[48]

Chairman Burns's Valedictory on Fed Monetary Policy

Two later articles by Burns reflected the essence of Federal Reserve posture for the decade.[49] The tenor of Burns's remarks is the same in both articles. He readily admitted that "serious inflation could not proceed without monetary nourishment." He found the sources of inflation, however, in cost-push elements in the economy. Pressure groups were effective in promoting wage and price increases and in lobbying the federal government to legislate all sorts of welfare services and special interest subsidies. "The essence of the unique inflation of our times and the reason central bankers have been ineffective in dealing with it," Burns charged, "can be understood only in terms of those currents of [social] thought and the political environment they have created."[50]

Burns discussed all the roots of Big Government intervention, and how such operations encouraged Big Federal Budgets. Since taxes did not keep pace with ever-growing Big Government Spending, Big Deficits appeared and burgeoned. These factors "impart a strong inflationary bias to the American economy. . . . When the government runs a budget deficit," Burns stated incorrectly, "it pumps more money into the pocketbooks of the people than it withdraws from their pocketbooks. . . . That is the way the inflation . . . first got started and later kept being nourished."[51]

In fact, the government can only "pump more *money*" into people's pocketbooks if the Federal Reserve System buys some of the securities financing the deficit. Then, and only then, can more *money* come into the picture. Otherwise, the government takes or borrows from Peter to pay Paul and the money stock itself is not affected.

Burns noted that "in most countries the central bank is an instrumentality of the executive branch of government." However, the United States, along with a few other countries, he claimed, has an "independent" central bank.[52]

In the next sentence and in the same paragraph, Burns offered a lengthy disclaimer on why the "independence" of the Fed was not enough to stop the inflation. "Viewed in the abstract [*sic*], the Federal Reserve System had the power to abort the inflation at its incipient stage fifteen years ago or at any later point, and it has the power to end it today," Burns admitted unashamedly. "It could have restricted the money supply and created sufficient strains in financial and industrial markets to terminate inflation with little delay. It did not do so because the Federal Reserve was itself caught up in the philosophic and *political* currents that were transforming American life and culture." The Employment Act of 1946, Burns argued, and again he was factually incorrect, "prescribes that it is the continuing policy and responsibility of the Federal Government to . . . utilize all its plans, functions, and resources . . . to promote maximum employment." But the original prescription did not stop here. It added to the goal "maximum employment" the goals "production and purchasing power," which meant maximum growth in real product and a stable purchasing power of the dollar. (See chapter 21.) If the framers of the employment act had had the sophistication to understand what they were legislating, they would have known that their "maximum purchasing power" implied maximizing the real stock of money—either M_F^* or M_I^* in table 22.1.

"Maximum employment" was and is a political shibboleth. Burns, however, argued that, as the primary goal of Fed policy, it "limited [the Fed's] practical scope for restrictive actions. . . . Every time the government moved to enlarge the flow of benefits to the population at large, or to this or that group, the assumption was implicit that monetary policy would somehow *accommodate* the action. . . . If the Federal Reserve then sought to create a monetary environment that fell seriously short of *accommodating* the upward pressures on prices that were being released or reinforced by governmental action, severe difficulties could be quickly produced in the economy."[53] Furthermore, Burns added, if the Fed dug in its heels, it "would be frustrating the will of the Congress—a Congress that was intent on providing additional services to the electorate and on assuring that jobs and incomes were maintained in the short run." And when the Fed did try to "undernourish the inflation, it repeatedly evoked violent criticism from both the Executive Branch and the Congress and therefore had to devote much of its energy to warding off legislation that could destroy any hope of ending inflation."

After a lengthy discussion of the social, political, and circumstantial factors that promoted disequilibria in the economy, Burns concluded that "it is illusory to expect central banks to put an end to an inflation . . . that is continually driven by political forces. . . . The persistent inflation that plagues industrial democracies will not be vanquished—or even substantially curbed—until new currents of thought create a *political* environment in which the difficult adjustments required to end inflation can be undertaken."[54]

Burns's main argument is an egregious contradiction. If the Fed were truly independent, as Burns and countless others before him alleged, it could have squelched immediately the inflation that it initiated in the mid-sixties. As it was, the Fed "accommodated" every insistent political pressure and justified its collaboration by pleading the "maximum employment" clause in the Employment Act of 1946, just as Burns admitted. It is hard to understand how Burns could have exalted the Fed's imaginary independence in one breath, and in the next pled its weakness in the face of the short-run political compulsions of Congress and the Executive.[55] It also raises the question: Why does the Fed go through the exercise of posturing about employment, interest rates, growth, and other real factors when it can do nothing fundamental about them?

The Federal Reserve System can do one thing—it has one exclusive power: It can at will, and with almost no delays, control the nominal quantity of base money. Control of base money is at one remove control of all other forms of money—demand deposits, NOW accounts, Automatic Transfer Services (ATS), travelers' checks, and any other spendable media. While this power is profound, it is not a means to control interest rates, employment, real growth, or any other real variables in the economy. It is only a power that allows the Fed, if it will, to maintain a fairly stable level of prices. This goal is not the be-all and end-all of a stable economic policy, but it is the best that any central-banking institution can aspire to. When the Fed pretends otherwise in its vain attempts to control real factors, it initiates problems that subsequently become concerns for the next episode of policy.

The Fed's quixotic pursuit of real variables raises a second question: Since the real value of the money stock is so important, why do Fed authorities not make their case for a responsible stewardship over this variable? Why do they not simply say: "Our only control is over the quantity of nominal money. By skillful management of this nominal quantity, we can get the real stock of money to grow a few percent per year and thereby provide a modest real return to all people and businesses who own money while we also minimize monetary uncertainty"? If experience were to answer this question, it would probably reply that the Fed's overriding consideration was (and is) to provide unlegislated tax revenue in the form of seigniorage to the federal government. And—oh yes—a modest premium to the bankers and central bankers who operate the machinery. So where was Burns's "anguish"? Were his the tears of a crocodile?

23 Monetarism and the Pseudo-Monetarism of Federal Reserve Policy, 1979–1983

[The monetary authorities] have leaned against the wrong wind in the wrong way, and as a result, they have been a source of uncertainty and instability in the economy. That's why those of us who believe in monetarist theory and who have examined the way policy is implemented generally have concluded that it would be desirable to have a monetary policy that produces steady growth in the quantity of money. . . . In terms of controlling inflation, the evidence has been overwhelming. Monetarist policies, and *only* monetarist policies, have been successful in stemming inflation.

Milton Friedman, *Manhattan Report,* 1984

The Development of Pseudo-Monetarism in FOMC Policy

When Arthur Burns's tenure as chairman of the Federal Reserve Board expired early in 1978, President Jimmy Carter had the opportunity to reappoint him. However, Burns was a Republican and politically unacceptable to the Democratic Carter administration, so Carter appointed G. William Miller. At the time of his appointment, Miller was chairman of Textron, Incorporated. Burns, who was appointed chairman by President Nixon in 1970 and reappointed in 1974, could have stayed on as an ordinary Board member for another six years but chose not to do so. Miller took office on 8 March 1978.[1]

Miller was chairman for only a year and three months. In July 1979, Carter offered him the cabinet post of secretary of the Treasury, and Miller accepted it. As Miller's successor, Carter nominated, and the U.S. Senate approved, Paul Volcker. Volcker had served for many years as vice chairman of the Federal Reserve Board, and also as president of the Fed bank of New York. He took office as chairman on 6 August 1979.[2]

Shortly after Volcker's appointment, the FOMC made its widely heralded revision of policy that was supposed to deemphasize interest rates as targets and to accentuate the growth rates of the monetary aggregates. This shift of emphasis appeared in the "Record of Policy Actions of the Federal Open Market Committee" for 6 October 1979.[3] The immediate cause for FOMC concern was "speculative excess in financial and commodity markets and additional evidence of strong inflationary pressures." At this time, the monetary base had increased over the year past by 7 percent, while the Fed funds rate was 11½ percent and tending to increase.[4] The FOMC's discussion of policy stated that the current situation called for "a shift in the conduct of open market operations to an approach placing emphasis on supplying the volume of bank reserves estimated to be consistent with the desired rates of growth in monetary aggregates, while permitting much greater fluctuations in the federal funds rate than before."

"The principal reason advanced for shifting to an operating procedure aimed at controlling the supply of bank reserves more directly," the policy directive continued in an apologetic vein that should have surprised no one, "was that it would provide greater assurance that the Committee's objectives for monetary growth could be achieved. In the present environment of rapid inflation [which had been 12 percent over the year past], estimates of the relationship among interest rates, monetary growth and economic activity had become less reliable than before, and monetary growth since the first quarter of 1979 *had exceeded the rates expected despite substantial increases in short-term interest rates*."[5]

To translate into everyday English, the committee was simply admitting that its more recent policies had caused both inflation and public expectations of further inflation. It also implied that its traditional method of regulating interest rates by altering the quantity of money going into financial markets did not work when inflation was pervasive enough to encourage expectations of yet more inflation. The FOMC, therefore, decided to abandon interest rates as targets in order to concentrate on a monetary variable it could control—the growth rate of the monetary aggregates. To emphasize the force of its decision, the Board of Governors, who comprised a majority of the FOMC, raised the Fed banks' discount rate from 11 to 12 percent and increased marginal reserve requirements for some elements of bank credit.[6] Before the end of the month, the fed funds rate approached the 15½ percent value that the committee had allowed for it at its 6 October meeting, but the committee did not alter its resolve to concentrate exclusively on the aggregates.[7]

In reviewing this policy change for committees in the House of Representatives on 17 October and 13 November 1979, Chairman Volcker presented the usual arguments that typified the Federal Reserve's continuous effort to excuse itself from the charge that it was the principal agent of inflation. Volcker first claimed that the current "burst in spending . . . seemed to reflect a 'buy now' attitude spurred by an intensification of inflationary expectations." His implication was that the velocity of money had increased capriciously with nothing more than the whims of consumers propelling it. He blamed "the oil price shock" for initiating the inflation. "There was a clear risk," he noted in an exercise of circular reasoning, "that the runup in energy prices would work its way into wages and prices generally, thereby raising the nation's underlying inflation rate and . . . contributing to pressures on oil prices." Surely the "runup in energy prices," if it were the *cause* of the inflation, could not also "contribute to [upward] pressures on oil prices," that is, be the *result* of the inflation. Volcker also commented on the "speculative pressures in commodity markets [and] . . . in foreign exchange markets."[8]

"*If* the relationship between the public's demand for cash balances and short-term market interest rates is relatively stable," Volcker continued, the fed funds rate could be an effective guide to policy. The recent economic instability and inflation had left this relationship uncertain. Therefore, the FOMC had shifted its tactical operations to management of the aggregates. Volcker concluded with a remonstrance against any congressional specifications of growth rates in the monetary aggregates for the FOMC. He doubted that "Congress would want to inject itself into . . . judgments [of monetary policy] filled with technical complexity and doctrinal controversy." Rather, he argued, "these decisions should emerge from a dispassionate, professional, deliberative process and be shielded from partisan pressures. . . . The present arrangement [of congressional oversight]," he claimed, "seems to be working well. The line of responsibility *and* accountability is clear."[9]

Inflation under "Monetarism"

In the six months that followed this momentous declaration of a change in policy, the FOMC increased the monetary base at a rate of 6.2 percent per year—not significantly different from the rate of increase before the change. However, the growth rate in M_1 during this same interval declined to an annual rate of only 2 percent. (M_1 as it is now known was then labeled M_{1B}. All references to M_1 below are to M_{1B}. The earlier M_1 is not used because as an accounted aggregate it did not capture all the monetary elements of the payments system.)

Around the first of May 1979, Fed policy became highly inflationary as the FOMC increased the monetary base at an annual rate of 10 percent. Thereafter M_1 increased at an annual rate of 15 percent, making up in part for its lagged growth in the preceding period. These rates of growth caused the price level to increase almost 13 percent over the year from October 1979 to October 1980.

The data on money growth rates and price level changes for 1980 raise the question of how policy actions that caused such excesses can be reconciled with the new policy emphasis on the aggregates that the FOMC had adopted just a few months earlier. One accurate answer is that the new emphasis was not *exclusively* on the aggregates. In the FOMC meeting of 22 April 1980, for example, the Record of Policy Actions noted that the agreed-upon growth rates in the aggregates of 4½ to 5 percent per year were still under the proviso that the fed funds rate remain in the range of 13 to 20 percent. Member banks by mid-March had borrowed $3.5 billion from Fed banks, where the discount rate was "only" 13 percent. However, all interest rates turned down in early April and fell precipitously until August.[10] The record then showed that most of the FOMC believed that a recession had begun, but that "inflationary attitudes and behavior had [not] been fundamentally altered." The committee noted ironically that if market interest rates continued to fall of their own accord, as had been occurring for a few weeks, some market participants might interpret the decline as an official easing of policy and conclude that more inflation would surely follow![11]

This point of view revealed again the quixotic folly of a policy that pursued nominal rates of interest as targets. In effect, the committee's observation indicated that the time frame for a Fisher effect—the incorporation of inflation rates into the interest-rate structure—had shortened from years to the few weeks or days normally reserved for just a liquidity effect.[12] The committee, however, did not appreciably change its policy directive to the Federal Reserve Bank of New York, and the fed funds rate fell below 13 percent before the next meeting.[13]

The sharp decline in market interest rates from early April to mid-June of 1980 occurred in conjunction with an abrupt but temporary decline in M_1. This seasonal "shortfall" often appeared at income-tax time as taxpayers transferred some of their M_1 deposit balances to the U.S. Treasury's accounts in Federal Reserve banks, and to the Treasury's Tax and Loan accounts in depository commercial banks.[14] (The Treasury's balances are not accounted as a part of M_1, so M_1 would decline when this transaction occurred.)

At their meeting on 9 July 1980, FOMC members exhibited much uncertainty over the state of the economy, the behavior of money, and the most desirable growth rates for the aggregates. They decided to make up for the slower than expected growth in M_1 over the previous six months (about 3.4 percent at annual rates) by increasing the M_1 growth rate to around 8 percent for the remainder of the year. They saw little danger in this expansive shift because real GNP had contracted in the second quarter, and because "the overall rise in prices of goods and services had moderated in recent months."[15]

By the next meeting on 12 August 1980, M_1 was growing faster than planned. However, the members of the FOMC were satisfied to accept the higher rates of growth. They felt that any appreciable lowering of the rate "would require a reduced provision of nonborrowed reserves, provoking a rise in member bank borrowings *and further increases in interest rates* in the near term." The fed funds rate had dropped below 9 percent during July, so the majority of the committee felt few qualms about keeping M_1 growing at 9 percent and M_2 at 12 percent.[16]

The FOMC meeting on 12 September 1980 reflected a marked change in sentiment due to staff reports on economic conditions. The aggregates, M_1 and M_2, were running "well above . . . the objectives established by the Committee for the June-to-September period." Everyone "favored operations over the period ahead directed toward the deceleration in monetary growth needed to promote achievement of the Committee's objectives for the year."[17]

The approach that the committee adopted, however, was "a middle course." The policy directive to the Fed bank of New York noted that the growth rates of the aggregates were at or above their targeted values for the year, and that short-term interest rates had risen considerably since August. So the directive specified no change in target growth rates.[18]

The directive, however, had a majority of only two-thirds—eight members of the twelve on the FOMC. A sizable minority—Messrs. Guffey, Roos, Wallich, and Winn—dissented. They believed that "the excessive monetary growth in recent months and the outlook for inflation . . . incurred too much of a risk that the Committee's objectives for monetary growth in 1980 would be exceeded."[19]

At the FOMC meeting in October, the same signs of excessive monetary expansion were evident. The Record of Policy Actions noted that "required reserves and member bank demands for reserves expanded substantially in relation to the supply of reserves being made available through open market operations. Consequently, member bank borrowings for reserve-adjustment purposes increased sharply [in October]. . . . These developments were associated with additional upward pressures on the federal funds rate and other short-term interest rates."[20] Since the Fed banks' discount rate was a good 150 basis points, or 1½ percentage points, below the fed funds rate, the Federal Reserve, via the discount window, was accommodating the inflation it was supposedly trying to contain through reduced open-market purchases. Though the Board increased the Fed discount rate from 10 percent in September to 13 percent in December, the market-determined fed funds rate increased from 9 to 20 percent over the same period.

Nonetheless, the FOMC balked at any severe tightening on the growth rates of the aggregates. "Given uncertainties in the economic outlook," the Record reads, "the possibility could not be excluded that very ambitious short-run objectives with respect to restraint could generate undesirable instability in both interest rates and the money supply over a somewhat longer period and thus be counter to the Committee's more fundamental goals."[21] Clearly, this kind of statement, hedging as it does on limiting monetary growth and continuing a concern about interest rates, does not reflect a monetarist or even a quasi-monetarist strategy. The committee had declared that its "more fundamental" goal was to contain inflation by targeting nonborrowed reserves. So this disclaimer was so much gobbledygook.

The policy directive from this meeting did call for a reduction in rates of growth in the money stocks, but not enough to compensate for the "overshoot" earlier in the year. Again, the decision for policy action was not unanimous. The same four members who had dissented at the previous meeting also dissented at this one, and for the same reason—more slowing was desirable.[22]

The FOMC Reversal to a Policy of Monetary Stringency

By the time of the next FOMC meeting on 18 November 1980, the national elections had come and gone, a rhetorical conservative had been elected President of the United States, and conservatives had made net gains in Congress. During November and December of 1980 and January of 1981, financial markets, interest rates, and prices showed some of the greatest short-run variations ever recorded. The prime bank loan rate reached 21.5 percent in early January, while the fed funds rate peaked twice, once in mid-December and again in mid-January, at 20 percent. Only five months earlier in August, it had been as low as 8¾ percent. Prices continued to rise at 1 percent per month in December. The money stock, M_1, which had grown at a rate of 15 percent per year for the previous six months, peaked in mid-November; but the momentum from this monetary burgeoning continued into the next year. (See figure 23.1.)

The Record of Policy Actions at the November meeting reflected a feeling that much was going wrong with the holistic economic measures that the committee continued to monitor, and, second, a concern that monetary policy could not cope with what was happening.[23] In such circumstances the committee adopted a very proper defensive policy: It reverted to the fundamental variables over which it had undisputed control—the aggregates. It voted to reduce rates of increase in M_{1A}, M_{1B}, and M_2 for the September-to-December period to 2½, 5, and 7¾ percent respectively, which meant that these variables would have to have zero or negative rates of growth for the remaining six weeks of the year.[24] This decision included the usual proviso that the fed funds rate stay within a certain range—13 to 17 percent at this time. In the following weeks the fed funds rate kept rising, so the FOMC raised the upper limit of the funds rate to 18 percent. The Board of Governors then increased the Fed banks' discount rate to 13 percent and added a surcharge of 2 to 3 percentage points "on frequent borrowings of large [banking] institutions."[25] On 5 December 1980, the FOMC held a telephone conference because the fed funds rate was going beyond 18 percent. Again the committee provided leeway to the manager for Domestic Operations at the Fed bank of New York to operate without regard to the 18 percent funds rate. Yet again on 19 December the procedure was repeated. Each time all the members of the FOMC except for Mrs. Nancy Teeters, the FOMC's ultra-Keynesian, agreed to subordinate the fed funds rate and hew to the fundamental principle of containing the growth rates of the aggregates.[26] At the meeting on 18–19 December 1980, the FOMC continued its tight rein on the aggregates with almost no provision for any intermeeting adjustment because of increases in fed funds rates.[27]

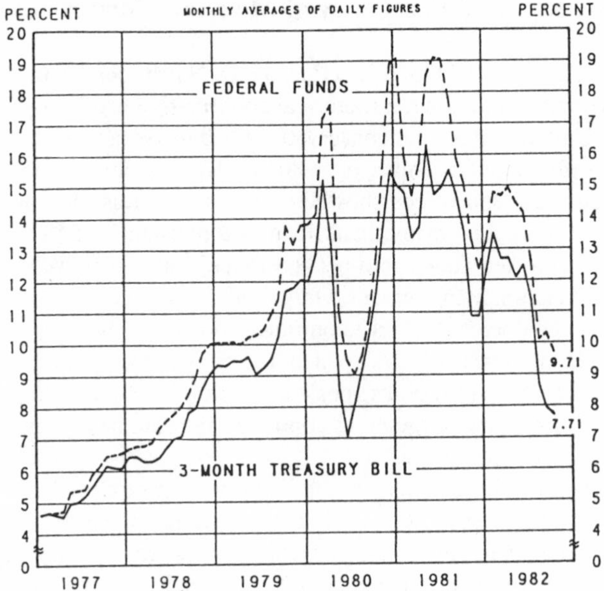

Figure 23.1 Money market interest rates, 1977–1982. Source: Federal Reserve Bank of St. Louis.

Chairman Volcker's Case for Fed Policy

Throughout this period of great financial instability, Chairman Paul Volcker appeared time and again before congressional committees to explain, rationalize, and excuse the Fed's current performance. On 19 November 1980, he claimed that "it should be unambiguously clear that the Federal Reserve has been leaning hard against excessive monetary growth."[28] (At this time the six-month growth rate in M_{1B} was 15 percent.) Volcker complained about the difficulty of promoting a policy of monetary restraint to restore price stability that would not at the same time inhibit investment and dampen productivity. He would welcome, he claimed, informed debate that would show how this basic dilemma could be escaped, and he called for restrictive fiscal policies that would complement an anti-inflationary monetary policy.[29]

The real problem here was the "dilemma" that Volcker saw between a monetary policy that was anti-inflationary and also pro-growth. Monetary policy cannot promote real economic growth beyond a largely useless short run. It is largely useless because whatever real growth results from the monetary stimulus will subsequently be paid for in lower real growth and general recession when the monetary stimulus is stopped.[30] Monetary policy cannot be the factotum that Fed spokesmen forever pretend it is. If it produces a stable and certain monetary environment, it has done all it can. The other horn of the "dilemma"—real growth—is a red herring. It is not a variable that any government policy can promote for any length of time, or even temporarily.

Volcker referred in his testimony to the "New Operating Procedures" that the FOMC had adopted a year earlier (October 1979), which were supposed to emphasize the Fed's single-minded pursuit of monetary objectives.[31] "The point [of these new procedures]," Volcker claimed in the statement following his testimony, "was to underscore, in terms of public perception and debate, the central importance of maintaining control over monetary growth and bank reserves to deal with inflation and to discipline better our internal policymaking with respect to monetary and credit growth, thus enhancing our ability to achieve our objectives."[32]

The remainder of his Statement on the New Procedures, however, constituted a detailed disavowal of any self-imposed adherence to the monetarist principles that media and financial pundits presumed for Fed policy in the months and years that followed. The emphasis on controlling the aggregates by FOMC targeting of nonborrowed bank reserves, Volcker noted, was in lieu of targeting short-term interest rates, particularly the fed funds rate. This shift in emphasis applied only to the targets and not to the goals of FOMC policy. Still in place were all the "concerns" that would thwart a true monetarist policy.

Fed officials always carefully avoided any mention of the monetary base, even though they knew they could control that variable with very little error. Rather, they adopted a wide range of money stocks—M_{1A}, M_{1B}, M_2, and M_3—and a wide range of possible growth rates for these aggregates. So many different accounted money stocks with such wide "target" ranges allowed them almost as much discretion as they pleased, and made their "monetarist" policy just as uncertain as their interest-rate policies had been.

Another loophole in their targeting strategy was the escape route of the discount window, as Chairman G. William Miller implied in his testimony on the Monetary Control Act. (See chapter 24.) When a restrictive FOMC policy checked bank-credit expansion, the banks would make up reserve deficiencies by discounting some of their eligible paper rather than draw down their loans and deposits. The Fed Board seemed to encourage this "safety valve" because it almost always fixed the Fed discount rate lower than the fed funds rate. If the Fed discount rate had been a true "penalty rate," it would usually have been one to three points higher than the fed funds rate.[33] Even though the Fed Board raised the discount rate a full percentage point in February 1980, as Volcker stated, the fed funds rate was still two percentage points higher at that time, and in April was almost seven points higher than the Fed discount rate.

Volcker's rationale reflected a certain model of Fed thinking that destined failure for any quantitative monetary strategy. The FOMC, he told the congressional committee, had recognized "the limitations of using interest rates as a reliable indicator of the thrust of monetary policy." Nonetheless, when money stocks were declining in April and interest rates with them, he argued that the "precipitous drop in interest rates might be misread as a fundamental reversal of policy—a lessening of our resolve to fight inflation. Such a false interpretation could only have undermined the ultimate success of that effort." That is, people would have spent money faster to avoid expected inflation and would thereby have ensured it would happen. Such behavior would have impaired prospects for economic recovery. Therefore, to prevent interest rates from falling too quickly and generating all these hypothetical behaviors of the inflation-minded public, the FOMC saw to a reversal of its restrictive policy toward the aggregates and increased money stocks so that interest rates would not fall so rapidly! Volcker stated elliptically, "A cumulative downward movement that would have reflected eroding confidence was avoided."[34] His argument, summarized, was that the FOMC's anti-inflationary monetary policy *might* have been popularly interpreted as a retreat from an anti-inflationary policy; so the FOMC felt it had to pursue what could only become an inflationary policy in order to counter the inflationary expectations of the anti-inflationary policy. Shades of *Alice in Wonderland!*

Figure 23.1 graphically depicts the Fed's record in smoothing interest rates at the same time that it was promoting inflation and generating a great deal of monetary uncertainty. Of course, it was not the only government agency guilty of exacerbating economic problems by a destabilizing policy. The Department of Energy's "energy policy" caused misallocations, shortages, and queues for petroleum products in 1973–1974 as well as in 1979–1980.

Election Results in 1980 as an Influence on Monetary Policy

The election of Ronald Reagan as President of the United States, and the net additions of conservatives in both houses of Congress, seemed to bode well for a correspondingly conservative monetary policy. Most members of the Federal Reserve Board at the time were Carter appointees. If they aspired to be reappointed when their current tenures ended, they realized, their policy posture had to become convincingly "conservative."

Prior to the presidential election of 1980, Fed policy had been highly stimulative in the face of manifest inflation. This experience, as well as the Fed's performance in earlier presidential elections, inspired observers to rename the FOMC the "Committee to Reelect the President." The Record of Policy Actions of the FOMC never mentioned the retention of the incumbent president as a "goal" of policy. Nonetheless, most of the Reserve Board members in any given election year owed their appointments to the incumbent and had every incentive to "play ball." The Fed's performances just before, during, and just after elections in 1960, 1964, 1968, 1972, 1976, and 1980 seemed to be clear-cut examples of a pattern that was restrictive and then stimulative during the year before the election, and then usually restrictive enough to slow down the inflationary reaction after the election.[35]

This pattern also occurred in 1980, but came too late to help President Carter. Not only did it come too late, but the stimulative phase seemed to settle wholly on prices with little effect on growth of real output. In addition, the roller-coaster behavior of interest rates made matters worse.

After the election, with the incumbent out of the picture, the FOMC put on its black bowler hat and began the almost unprecedented monetary fasting and cleansing outlined earlier. Growth rates for the monetary base, M_1, and M_2 flattened out to near zero, and market interest rates started down.

Chairman Volcker appeared in his accustomed role before congressional committees in early 1981 to discuss the previous year's policies and the Fed's approach to near-term targets and goals.[36] He discussed at length the short-term difficulties the FOMC faced in trying to control the money stocks. He did *not* say that the FOMC could not control the monetary base in the short run, and he did not admit that much of the failure to control the aggregates resulted from problems of the Fed's own making. The self-inflicted procedures or restrictions that contributed to the Fed's awkward performance included: lagged reserve accounting,[37] the indulgence of the discount window for member banks, variable reserve requirements for different accounted segments of the money stocks, the wide ranges for growth in the aggregates, the FOMC's continued emphasis on interest-rate targets, and its unwillingness to target the monetary base.

Volcker blamed the historically high interest-rate volatility in 1980 on "disturbances in the economy itself, to the imposition and removal of credit controls [an ill-conceived program that the Carter administration instituted], to the budgetary [fiscal deficit] situation, and to shifting inflationary expectations."[38] Virtually all of these reasons for interest-rate volatility resulted from Fed policies or some kind of government intervention—either the U.S. Treasury's, or that of a federal credit agency. Volcker spoke forcefully for federal tax cuts and fiscal spending limitations as collateral policy to an anti-inflationary monetary policy. "The new [Reagan] administration," he claimed, "is clearly aware of these realities and has set forth a program of action."[39]

Volcker's proper norms notwithstanding, monetary policy after October 1979 became, if possible, more variable and unsettling than it had been before. Adherence to targets of nonborrowed bank reserves, combined with the procedure of lagged reserve accounting and the other restrictions and procedures referred to above, resulted over the next two years in the greatest volatility in the growth rate of M1 and the widest fluctuations in interest rates ever recorded. Milton Friedman, who analyzed this experience in a *Wall Street Journal* article, suggested that the lip service the FOMC paid to money supply targets was insincere. Most of the members of the FOMC, he charged, were "unreconstructed Keynesians or classical central bankers who regard control of 'credit' or 'credit market conditions' [short-term interest rates] as far more important than steady monetary growth."[40]

Whatever the FOMC claimed, whatever policy it instituted on 6 October 1979, that policy was *not* monetarism. In fact, no one on the Federal Reserve Board or FOMC ever claimed that it was monetarism. The label came from financial market analysts and financial news media journalists who took the word for the deed. Besides the distinctly antimonetarist character of the Federal Reserve Board at the time, no "card-carrying" proponent of monetarism in the economics profession ever acknowledged that FOMC policy in the early 1980s was more than pseudo-monetarist. Furthermore, no avowed monetarist was appointed to the Federal Reserve Board. The astonishing aspect of this near-universal acceptance of the label is that monetarist doctrine and its applied policies are so simple that they can hardly be misunderstood.[41]

Comparison of Fed "Monetarism" with Authentic Monetarism

A truly monetarist policy must first *target* the monetary base. The base, which includes all Federal Reserve note currency and all commercial bank deposits at Federal Reserve banks, is the one monetary aggregate that the Fed can control precisely and immediately, that is, with no "ranges," no lags, and no confusion as to what it includes. The various "Ms"—M_1, M_2, etc.—should be retained only as *indicators*. Since the components of all the Ms require monetary base material for their creation, to control the base is to control the Ms, but not necessarily any one particular M. The growth rates of the Ms, while correlated very highly with the growth rates of the monetary base from year to year, show wide variation from month to month or quarter to quarter. Therefore, a true monetarist policy, contradictory as it sounds, should not concentrate directly on the Ms because they are too variable for short-run policy purposes. Their accounted short-run values, as Volcker noted from time to time, include a lot of "noise." Furthermore, one M may be growing by depleting the substance of another M. A policy that aims at targeting them is hardly more monetarist than one that targets interest rates.

The second criterion for a legitimate monetarist policy is closely related to the first. The policy action that targets the base must be steady, specified in advance, and therefore predictable. If the policy begun in October 1979 had been genuinely monetarist, it would have prescribed a gentle and systematic reduction in the rate of increase in the monetary base until the growth rates of the money stocks, observed as indicators, came down to noninflationary values. This agenda would have achieved some practical goal of price level stability, say plus or minus 2 percent per year, and the value of the money unit

TABLE 23.1 Actual changes in the monetary base and simulated monetarist changes, October 1979 to January 1983 (annual percentage rates of change)

Period	Rates of changes in monetary base	Simulated monetarist rates of change in monetary base		
		Beginning	Ending	Average for Period
Oct. 1979–Apr. 1980	7.8	8.5	7.9	8.2
Apr. 1980–Nov. 1980	10.5	7.9	7.2	7.6
Nov. 1980–Mar. 1981	3.6	7.2	6.8	7.0
Mar. 1981–Nov. 1981	0.5	6.8	6.0	6.4
Nov. 1981–Nov. 1982	8.1	6.0	4.8	5.4
Nov. 1982–July 1983	12.1	4.8	4.0	4.4

Source: *Monetary Trends,* Federal Reserve Bank of St. Louis, September 1983.

would have been essentially stable. The FOMC could then have stopped the systematic reduction in the rate of increase in the base and settled indefinitely on a constant rate of increase that was approximately equal to the historical growth rate of real output. This policy may not have been perfect, but it would have been the best a central bank could achieve.

Table 23.1 compares the actual growth rates in the base for the "monetarist" era of Fed policy with simulated base growth rates as they might have occurred under a monetarist policy.

The growth rate of the base during the year October 1978 to October 1979 was 8.5 percent. Using this value as a starting point, a monetarist policy that reduced the rate of increase in the base by, say, 0.1 percentage point per month, would have yielded the growth rates in the base shown in the right-hand columns of table 23.1. If this policy had continued to March 1983, the rate of increase in the base would have been down to about 4.5 percent. Inflation would have abated and interest rates would have assumed "normal" values.

The policies the Federal Reserve actually fostered saw a rate of increase in the base soaring to 10.5 percent in mid–1980, as the Board put on its reelect-the-president clothes prior to the elections of November 1980. As soon as a conservative was elected, however, the Fed reduced the rate to 3.6 percent, then reduced it again almost to zero. During the next twelve months, the base rate again became highly inflationary, and by early 1983 was almost three times as great as it would have been under true monetarism. No one could look at actual Fed policy toward the base, compare that to what monetarists would have done, and call Fed policy "monetarist."

A third element of Fed practice that denied true monetarism was the host of clumsy institutional arrangements the Fed adopted or accepted (noted above). A true monetarist policy would have scrapped all of these restrictive interventions to the payments system. The FOMC would create monetary base constantly and prescriptively through open-market operations, and do nothing else. Financial markets would then generate conventional moneys in any shape, size, or color that people wanted.

This pattern for policy implies the fourth, and perhaps most important, facet of monetarism—the principle of *minimum agency intervention.* The philosophy underlying monetarism is that free markets for money as well as for ordinary goods and services are a proven institution. Free markets in money include banks free to pay any interest rates they want, other depository institutions likewise, no licenses on the creation of deposits, no restriction or regulation on the exit and entry of banks—in short, a treatment of the commercial money-generating industry similar to what is accorded, say, the electronics industry. Less important than the fact that such a system "delivers the goods," which it most assuredly does, is the certainty that it maximizes individual freedoms.

Federal Reserve policy in the early 1980s was only pseudo-monetarist. All that it proved was that the rate of increase in the monetary base governed the rate of increase in the Ms, which in turn determined price levels and interest rates. Monetarists already had established these truths from the time when they were known as "quantity theorists."

The End of Fed "Monetarism"

Three years after it had begun, Fed "monetarism" ended. In its meeting of 5 October 1982, the FOMC stated that uncertainties stemming from banking deregulation, as a result of the Monetary Control Act of 1980, would "have a substantial impact on the behavior of M_1, but no basis existed for predicting its magnitude. . . . Because of these difficulties, . . . the Committee decided that it would place much less than the usual weight on that aggregate's movements during this period and that it would not set a specific objective for its growth."[42] The committee continued targeting rates of growth for M_2 and M_3, but included the usual provisos about changes in short-term interest rates that might reflect "exceptional liquidity demands."[43]

At its meeting on 8–9 February 1983, the FOMC noted again the wide disparity of growth rates for M_1, M_2, and M_3. For example, M_2 grew at an annual rate of 29 percent in January 1983! This surge was due to "shifts of funds out of non-M_2 assets—such as . . . large denomination CDs—into MMDAs." Financial institutions were marketing new interest-bearing transactable deposits, and households and firms shifted from interest-bearing but less liquid CDs into these new accounts.[44]

The committee again raised its usual but nonfactual alarm that "past cyclical expansions had typically been accompanied by sharp increases in velocity." It "recognized that [due to institutional changes] it could take some time before this newly emerging behavior of M_1 in relation to GNP became clear."[45] The velocity argument, despite its lack of substantiation, allowed the committee to abandon exclusive targeting of the aggregates and to resort to its traditional and comfortable eclectic approach.

The irony of this development was that the so-much-sought-after deregulation of the financial system through the Monetary Control Act of 1980 became the FOMC's excuse for departing from a notably less interventionist monetary policy. In fact, no wide variations in the velocities of the Ms occurred, even though their composition changed. If the FOMC had concentrated its attention solely on stabilizing the rate of increase in the monetary base, it could have avoided any "concern" about the behavior of the Ms. Predictable quantities of money that produce stable prices ensure the stability of monetary velocities.

A *monetarist* policy for a central bank may be "good" or "bad," depending on the result it returns once it is in place, and depending on the central bank's alternative experiences with other policies. The value of any policy is relative. However, no evaluation of a *monetarist* policy for the United States was possible in this era because the money managers of the FOMC not only eschewed monetarist theory, but they continuously used a wide array of nonmonetarist targets and goals to promote their eclectic, pragmatic agenda. Their policies contain only trivial traces of *monetarism*. Consequently, *monetarism* as an official central-bank policy had neither failed nor succeeded. It simply had never been tried.

24 The Monetary Control Act of 1980

> [The Monetary Control Act] is one of the most complex and least understood pieces of legislation that I have ever seen come before a legislative body. It has been referred to as everything from a Christmas tree to a forest primeval, the latter probably being the more appropriate phrase. The monetary control section . . . was never the subject of extensive debate on the Senate floor, . . . and in fact was never even the subject of a final markup [roll-call] in the Senate Banking Committee. The Federal Reserve legislation was written in the conference committee stemming from a House-passed version of the bill which was extremely different from the final product we now have before us.
>
> U.S. Senator Donald Stewart, *Congressional Record,* 27 March 1980

The Legislative Ancestry of the Monetary Control Act

The 1973 court case in Massachusetts that allowed state savings and loan institutions to issue NOW accounts (negotiated orders of withdrawal), which were essentially interest-bearing demand deposits, led almost inevitably to widespread deregulation of the banking and financial industry. Throughout the period from 1974 to 1980, state and federal legislatures relaxed controls and removed restrictions on the freedom of financial institutions to pay interest on demand deposits and undertake other financial services.

The culmination of the deregulatory movement at the federal level was the Depository Institutions Deregulation and Monetary Control Act (DIDMCA) of 1980. Senator William Proxmire, one of its sponsors in the Senate, hailed the act as the "most significant banking legislation since [the passage of the Federal Reserve Act in] 1913."[1] Title I in the bill extended the Federal Reserve's control over reserves to all depository institutions and added some other powers as well. Title II called for the phasing out of all government-imposed interest-rate ceilings, and generally reduced competitive inequities between banks and other financial institutions. The act altogether has eight titles or sections, which deal with truth-in-lending simplification, state usury laws, amendments to the national banking laws, and other matters. The first two titles, however, contain the important substance of the act as well as its contradictory implications: Title I greatly extends the power of the Fed and its regulatory scope at the same time that Title II significantly relaxes restrictions on freedom of economic activity for the rest of the banking and financial system.

Economists and bankers concurred with Senator Proxmire on the importance of the DIDMCA of 1980. They had long recognized the desirability of regulatory simplification, such as homogeneous reserve requirements for banks and abolition of interest-rate ceilings on time deposits, so they applauded the deregulatory aspects of the act. They were remiss, however, in failing to point out the disparate treatment of institutions implied by the two major "titles," and especially the significance of the additional powers that the act gave to the Federal Reserve System.

Debates on the bill in both houses of Congress revealed the procedure and arguments that saw these two dissimilar provisions incorporated into the same law. Fundamental to this result was the testimony of Federal Reserve Board spokesmen whose arguments before congressional committees were instrumental in gaining additional powers for the Fed.

The Monetary Control Act of 1980 began in 1979 in the House of Representatives as the Consumer Checking Equity Act of 1979 (H.R. 3864) and the Monetary Control Act of 1979 (H.R. 7). Also proposed earlier were three different Senate bills: S. 85 would have made membership in the Federal Reserve System mandatory for all depository institutions; S. 353 would have had the Fed banks pay market interest rates on the reserve account balances of commercial member banks; and S. 1347 was another Monetary Control Act. H.R. 7 was the only one of these earlier bills to pass either house before the final bill of 1980. It passed the House of Representatives in 1979, but its counterpart in the Senate, S. 1347, was not debated. All of these earlier bills served as "ancestors" for the bill, H.R. 4986, that finally passed both houses in 1980 and was signed into law by President Carter on 31 March 1980.[2]

The "Problem" of Commercial Bank Membership

Hearings and deliberations on these various House and Senate bills began in early 1979. On 26 February of that year, G. William Miller, who was then chairman of the Fed's Board of Governors, commented at length on both S. 85, the "Proxmire bill," and S. 353, the "Tower bill," before the Senate Committee on Banking, Housing, and Urban Affairs.

The first issue Miller addressed was the attrition of Fed membership. The number of commercial member banks in the Federal Reserve System had been steadily declining for over twenty-five years. Between June 1970 and June 1978, 183 member banks out of about 5,700, or 3.2 percent, left the system. The percentage of member bank deposits to total bank deposits also declined from 81 to 72 percent.[3]

The good reason for member bank resignations was the high interest rates caused by the Fed-fed inflation. Member banks had to keep zero-interest reserve balances with the Fed banks of their districts. In return they were entitled to certain services, such as the clearing of checks and access to the discount window. However, as nominal interest rates rose behind inflation during the 1970s, these zero-return reserve accounts became more burdensome.

In addition, the new freedom that nonbank financial institutions had obtained allowed them to create quasi-demand-deposits and to pay interest on them. This privilege required a similar allowance for commercial banks so that they could stay competitive in the struggle to get and keep depositors.[4]

All Fed officials who testified on the various bills emphasized the "problem" of Fed membership. Their argument was that loss of membership also meant a loss of Federal Reserve control over the banking system. "All the legislative proposals," Paul Volcker stated in his testimony, "need to be judged first of all against the central objective: We need to strengthen our ability to implement monetary policy in a variety of possible circumstances."[5] The bills, H.R. 7 and S. 85, Volcker noted, would reduce reserve requirements and result in a substantial reduction in "reserve balances . . . held in Federal Reserve Banks. These balances," he asserted, "and only these balances, provide the 'fulcrum' for the efficient conduct of monetary policy."[6]

A few months later in the House of Representatives, Henry Reuss of Wisconsin parroted Volcker's argument. "What this bill does," Reuss claimed, "is give the monetary authorities a power they desperately need if they are going to pursue [an anti-inflationary policy]. . . . Unless they have a 'fulcrum,' . . . a reserve base upon which they can conduct their open market policy, they are incapable of regulating the money supply."[7]

The Volcker-Reuss argument is invalid on several grounds. First, it implies that the Fed was "fighting inflation" when, in fact, the Fed was the primary source of inflation. Second, the argument contains an invalid premise—that Federal Reserve monetary control depends critically on member bank reserve accounts in Fed banks. Left out of any such accounting are the banks' holdings of vault cash—Federal Reserve notes—which increased from $7 billion in December 1970 to $17 billion by the end of 1978, and were $30 billion by the end of 1990. These notes when in banks are also legal reserves. The Fed creates them through open-market operations in the same manner that it creates reserve-deposit accounts. Both member and nonmember banks hold them, as do all other financial institutions, while nonbank households and business firms hold them as currency. Substantial amounts are also used as hand-to-hand currency in foreign markets—in places as diverse as Cairo, Istanbul, Delhi, and Moscow.

The Federal Reserve notes and member bank reserve-deposit accounts at Fed banks compose the monetary base, the total of which is under Fed control on a day-by-day basis no matter what the values are of each constituent part. As Fed policies change the base, so both member and nonmember banks must change in varying degrees the components of the conventional money stocks, M_1 and M_2. Furthermore, Fed authorities know accurately the quantity of Federal Reserve notes outstanding, the amount held by member banks, and the total held by all banks. Even if Fed membership were to drop to zero and no financial institutions were legally required to hold reserves, all money-creating institutions would have to hold some kind of providential reserves in the form of these monetary base items to meet liquidity and clearing demands of depositors and depository institutions. Since the Fed manufactures all of the monetary base, which is in turn required for the creation of all common money, Fed control is complete no matter what volume of reserve balances member banks maintain at Fed banks, and no matter how many depository institutions are members of the Federal Reserve System.

The Fed solution to the membership "problem" was to encourage Congress to make reserve requirements mandatory for all depository institutions. H.R. 7, S. 85, and the bill that finally passed both houses of Congress, H.R. 4986, contained this provision. Institutions so affected could still choose to remain nonmembers of the Fed; but after passage of the act they all had to keep zero-interest reserve accounts with Fed banks. In addition, they all became entitled to the "privilege" of discounting at Fed banks.

The Discount Window Anachronism

Fed spokesmen emphasized this perk. Use of the discount window had shrunk, noted Miller in his testimony, due to membership attrition. Nevertheless, he claimed, the window was still "the lender of last resort" to the payments system. "If the proportion of institutions having access to this facility were to decline," he warned, "individual institutions . . . could not . . . cushion temporarily the impacts of restrictive monetary policies. . . . Thus, the Federal Reserve may find that its ability to limit growth in money and credit in order to curb inflation was being unduly impeded because the safety valve provided by the discount window was gradually losing its effective coverage."[8]

Miller's argument is absurd. The Fed's powers to promote, as well as to abate, inflation have nothing to do with the discount window. Furthermore, his remark that the Fed can "limit growth in money and credit in order to curb inflation" implied that Fed policy was effective without direct control over any particular portion of member bank reserve accounts. The thrust of his argument—that the use of the discount window made Fed open-market policies less effective by allowing the member banks an escape route—contradicted his conclusion. His argument was more logically a brief for ending the discount privilege, which had become nothing more than a lollipop for encouraging Fed membership.

No matter; the contemporary Fed has powers far beyond the scope of discount window accommodation. It creates monetary base constantly and positively, not just when an occasional bank needs extra liquidity. To put it baldly, virtually every hour of the day the Fed is acting as a "lender of last resort" by creating notes and reserves via open-market purchases of government securities. In this holistic creation of money, the role of the discount window is negligible. The monetary base at the end of 1989 was $294 billion, while loans to member banks were less than $0.5 billion. As a source of monetary base material, discounts to member banks were therefore one-third of 1 percent of the total.

Not only has discounting become a negligible sideline of Fed policy in the creation of monetary base, but banks have a much broader area in which to market their reserve needs or bounties—the federal funds market. The activity in this market swamps the minor operations of the Fed's discount window. Federal funds and repurchase agreements just for large member banks in late 1990 were over $60 billion, compared to $0.5 billion in Fed bank loans to members.[9]

No essential function in the payments system would be harmed in the slightest by the abolition of the discount window. It is an anachronism. Its only function, besides providing a lower-than-market lending rate to member banks, is to act as a public relations showpiece—a popularly recognized device that suggests to the banks, Congress, the media, and the general public that the Fed is some kind of an insurance agency against financial disaster. The discounting machinery also includes a discount interest rate, which is also a favorite conversation piece for Fed watchers. U.S. congressmen and many financial market gurus keep a close watch on this "leading indicator" and discuss it knowingly. However, it is an inappropriate and misleading signal because real variables in capital and money markets, over which the Fed has no significant or lasting control, determine market interest rates. Furthermore, the publicity that the discount rate gets from the aforementioned groups takes attention away from the only variable the Fed can and does control precisely—the monetary base.

The Mystery of Collateral Provisions for Federal Reserve Notes in Title I

One of the more intriguing sections in Title I of the DIDMCA comes under the subsection labeled "Miscellaneous Amendments." It expands the "eligible collateral" provision for Federal Reserve notes outstanding to include the fully guaranteed obligations of a foreign government or the agency of a foreign government, as well as any other financial assets that the Reserve banks may purchase.[10] The question implied by this provision is: Why would the Fed need additional collateral of such dubious quality for Federal Reserve notes when it could already monetize unlimited quantities of U.S. government securities, the traditional "eligible collateral" for government-sponsored issues of paper money since 1864?

The bill H.R. 7, when first put together in mid–1979, had no provision for any change in collateral allowances. Congressman Ron Paul noted that only in the third version of H.R. 7 did the collateral provision surface for the first time, "but . . . without one word of [formal] testimony from the Fed."[11] Fed leaders had quietly persuaded their congressional allies to work in the amendment at the House-Senate conference committee meetings. Congressman William Stanton of Ohio noted that the amendment was "added to the bill at the last moment without any testimony from the Fed or any other witness."[12] The objections of Paul, Stanton, George Hansen of Idaho, and others succeeded in getting the collateral amendment deleted before the bill passed the House by a vote of 340 to 20.[13]

Fed Chairman Paul Volcker was the principal advocate supporting the amendment before Senator Proxmire's Committee on Banking, Housing, and Urban Affairs in September 1979. The anticipated reductions in reserve requirements for depository institutions in S. 85, Volcker told the committee, "could be technically unworkable because [they] might result in insufficient amounts of . . . eligible financial assets to meet the collateral requirements against notes." The House, Volcker observed, had rejected the extension of collateral provisions in the H.R. 7 bill. To meet these objections, he suggested adding to the present list of "acceptable collaterals assets acquired abroad arising from time to time out of our foreign currency operations." Specifically, he wanted "short-term foreign government securities."[14] In a later statement made on 4 February 1980 to the same committee, Volcker again mentioned the "problem." He volunteered "to supply an appropriate amendment that could be attached to S. 353 or to any bill that would deal with the problem."[15]

When Senator Proxmire presented the bill that was to become the DIDMCA of 1980 to the full Senate, the provision that anticipated reduction of reserve balances at the Fed had suddenly become the "problem" requiring reinclusion of the collateral provision that Volcker had designed. Proxmire's "problem," however, was a result of his programmed misinterpretation of the Fed's procedures for creating money. "A portion of the Federal Reserve's securities portfolio," he "explained" in the Senate debate over the bill, ". . . represent[s] purchases made [by the FOMC] *with reserves deposited by member banks*. Since the Monetary Control Act would release about $15 billion in reserves, a comparable amount of securities would need to be sold. This would reduce the collateral available for Federal Reserve notes." Such a reduction, Proxmire continued, could proceed to the point where the Fed had inadequate collateral for its current volume of notes outstanding. The supplementary collateral provisions in the bill would alleviate this "technical shortage."[16]

Earlier, Proxmire's counterpart in the House, Chalmers P. Wylie of Ohio, who was chairman of the House Banking Committee, had similarly "explained" the Fed–commercial bank relationship to his House colleagues as follows: "The banks hold some of these reserves [created by open-market operations] as vault cash and the rest goes into the Federal Reserve System which it uses for investments—the return from which goes to the Treasury of the United States."[17] With these "explanations" as a basis for discussion, any monetary rationality in the final bill was highly problematic.

Volcker's intense behind-the-scenes lobbying for his amendment deserves more exposure. On 4 March 1980, Volcker sent a letter to Congressman Henry Reuss in Reuss's capacity as chairman of the conference committee that was restructuring H.R. 4986. "Dear Henry," Volcker's letter began,

> The proposals under discussion reducing reserve requirements [for depository institutions] give rise to a *technical* problem regarding collateral against Federal Reserve notes. Put simply, as currency [Federal Reserve notes in circulation] rises and [member bank] reserves [at Fed banks] decline, the Fed might *run out* of collateral, as presently defined (essentially Government securities, discounts [for member banks], and gold certificates) to *back* Federal Reserve notes.
>
> A large part of this collateral problem could be resolved by eliminating the present requirement that notes remaining in the vaults of the Federal Reserve Banks be collateralized. It would also be of assistance if assets arising out of foreign currency operations were added to the list of assets eligible for collateralizing currency. . . . Our operations would be facilitated, and some interest earnings obtained, if the Federal Reserve could invest in short-term foreign government obligations when we acquire foreign currencies as a by-product of our operations.
>
> I am enclosing an amendment that would make these changes and which would effectively solve the problem.[18]

The bill, H.R. 4986, passed the Senate and again went to the House-Senate conference committee for modification. The conference committee was supposed to consider for possible compromise only the substance of the provisions that had previously been debated and passed in both houses. Not included in these provisions was the "Volcker amendment" on extending collateral for Federal Reserve notes to foreign government securities.

The House and Senate had passed H.R. 4986 as the Consumer Checking Account Equity Act on 1 November 1979. Only when the conferees of the two houses met in late March 1980 to iron out differences was the bill combined with H.R. 7 to become the Monetary Control Act of 1980. During the time that the bill was in conference, Volcker sent his "Dear Henry" letter to Reuss, who was a member of the conference committee. Although the "Volcker amendment" was legally ineligible for conference committee consideration, Reuss persuaded the committee to waive the proscriptive rule by unanimous consent so that it could consider Volcker's suggested modification. In spite of a vigorous effort by Congressman Ron Paul of Texas, the conference committee version of what was now the DIDMCA of 1980 passed both houses of Congress by overwhelming majorities on 27 March 1980.[19]

The final bill mandated Federal Reserve administration and control of reserve requirements for all depository institutions—member banks, nonmember banks, savings and loans, and any other institution that carried demand deposits. It also anticipated a general reduction of reserve requirements overall to a uniform value around 12 percent. This reduction implied that bank reserve balances kept at Federal Reserve banks, plus vault cash reserves in the form of coin and Federal Reserve notes, would decline (Fed officials estimated) by about $15 billion. The lower reserve requirements were to be phased in over several years so that depository institutions would experience no immediate hardships or windfalls.

The Impossibility of Inadequate Collateral for Federal Reserve Notes

Even as a technical matter, i.e., without political considerations, the Volcker-Reuss-Proxmire-Wylie explication of Federal Reserve monetary operations is fundamentally wrong. Eligible collateral for Federal Reserve notes is not limited to U.S. government securities. Fed banks can also pledge their holdings of loans, discounts, and advances to member banks, and also their gold certificates, just as Volcker's letter to Reuss had stated. The gold certificates are titles to the Treasury's gold stock. They were (and still are) accounted at a value of $42.22 per ounce even though the market price of gold in 1980 was more than twelve times this value. (The price of gold during the 1980s subsequently fell to a value about ten times the official Treasury price.) Even with this fictitious Treasury "price" for its gold holdings, the Gold Certificate account at Fed banks was sufficient to collateralize Federal Reserve notes without recourse to the purchase of securities issued by foreign governments or agencies of foreign governments.

Every economist and serious student of monetary economics knows that the money-creating process works exactly contrary to the procedure "explained" by Wylie and Proxmire. As the Fed buys U.S. government securities, it perforce creates member bank reserve-deposit accounts or Federal Reserve notes for which the government securities serve as collateral. The Fed can never be short of collateral for monetary base obligations because it must always create exactly the same dollar amount of monetary base as the dollar value of the securities, gold, or member bank discounts that it has purchased.

Regardless of collateral, Federal Reserve notes are "legal tender for all debts, public and private." "Eligible collateral" is at most only a cosmetic restriction that limits the items the Fed is allowed to monetize. It is a leftover from the time fifty to seventy years ago when Federal Reserve notes were not legal tender and the Fed was an entirely different kind of institution. Collateral security is a pointless flourish to the security or acceptance of legal tender currency.

Actual experience since the passage of the DIDMCA demonstrated that no problem would have arisen (as indeed it *could* not) with only conventional collateral available for Fed notes. Even though reserve accounts at Fed banks declined as reserve requirements were phased down toward 12 percent, the Fed's consolidated statement during the period 1981–84 never showed less than an excess of $9 billion in just the conventional collateral of U.S. government securities over the outstanding issues of Federal Reserve notes.[20]

In July 1981, a little over a year after passage of the DIDMCA, Congressman Paul wrote a letter to Chairman Volcker asking for a detailed explanation of what the Fed was doing with its new monetizing powers. Volcker replied to each of Paul's questions at length. He admitted that the Fed had purchased interest-bearing securities of the German and Swiss governments, and it had also bought German marks and Swiss francs from the U.S. Treasury's Exchange Stabilization Fund with newly issued Federal Reserve notes.[21]

Volcker claimed that Section 14 of the Federal Reserve Act permitted Reserve banks to purchase or hold obligations of foreign governments or their agencies. The DIDMCA, Volcker continued, *now* provides for these assets to be used as collateral for Federal Reserve notes. "In addition," Volcker concluded, ". . . the Conference [Committee] Report on H.R. 4986 . . . indicates awareness of the revised collateral provision since it states on page 71 that 'the bill expands the types of Federal Reserve assets that can be used to collateralize Federal Reserve notes.' "[22]

Volcker's statement on congressional "awareness" is a flat misrepresentation of what *any* congressman, except Ron Paul, William Armstrong (in the Senate), and one or two others, either knew or sensed. Volcker further alleged, as he had previously, that the provision was "to enable the Federal Reserve to invest its holdings of non-interest earning foreign currencies in interest bearing obligations."[23]

Not only was such interest income trivial and irrelevant to the Fed's seigniorage powers, but Volcker's documentation of the actual operations in foreign obligations included the purchase of *non-interest-bearing* German marks and Swiss francs with Federal Reserve notes. Instead, the Fed could have purchased the customary interest-bearing U.S. government securities with the Federal Reserve notes it issued, and thereby retired debt on which the U.S. Treasury paid interest.

Chairman Volcker's Financial Connections Suggest a Conflict of Interest

Nothing in Volcker's statements or letters substantiates either the technical or operational necessity for the extended collateral provision. What, then, could have been the real reason for Volcker to have insisted that Congress extend the

Fed's money-creating hegemony if the Fed already had infinite control over the U.S. money supply?

The only answer seems to be that the Fed as an agency of the U.S. government was designing itself to become the international financial arm of the Executive Branch. With this new power it could not create more money than it had before, but it could purchase the outstanding debt of third world governments. Who were the principal creditors of these governments? Several super-sized commercial banks in the United States—Citibank, Chase Manhattan, and others. These banks had made loans at a phenomenal rate to these so-called less developed countries' governments during the 1970s. The banks' managers had believed that loans to governments with sovereign taxing powers were secure. This reasoning proved fallacious. The ability of third world governments to squander the real resources of the loans, and to promote triple-digit inflation at the same time, proved to be unlimited. By 1985, "the proportion of *new* loans devoted to debt service [i.e., to interest payments and administrative costs] will grow to 88 percent, and by 1990 . . . to 95 percent," Mark Hulbert predicted in 1981.[24]

Volcker's professional background has much in it that would support this interpretation. Volcker first became associated with the Federal Reserve Bank of New York in 1949, when he worked as an assistant and then as an economist in the research department. In 1957, he resigned to become a financial economist at the Chase Manhattan Bank. In 1962, he became the director of the Treasury's Office of Financial Analysis, and in 1965 he rejoined Chase Manhattan as vice president of forward planning. At the time of his appointment to chairman of the Board of Governors, he was a member of the board of directors of the Council on Foreign Relations, and he also served on the board of trustees of the Rockefeller Foundation. While he never earned a Ph.D. in economics, he had a master of arts degree in political economy from Harvard and a bachelor of arts degree, summa cum laude, from Princeton.[25]

The circumstances of Volcker's career do not confirm a conflict of interest between his role as the principal architect of U.S. monetary policy and his long-term association with Rockefeller institutions. What is good for the Chase Manhattan Bank is not necessarily bad for the U.S. monetary system. Nevertheless, it is disconcerting to witness an "authoritative" rationale for a national monetary policy that serves the special interests of a large commercial banking institution. If one were to rank all the commodities and securities in the world in the order in which they would serve most appropriately and effectively as collateral for the issue of Federal Reserve note currency, the outstanding debts, *including the unsecured currency issues,* of foreign governments and their agencies would be very near the bottom.

After the DIDMCA of 1980 had been operational for a few years, Charles Partee of the Federal Reserve Board appeared before the House Banking Committee to report on the Fed's use of the new collateral provision. He noted that Fed holdings of foreign currencies "arose as a result of active intervention in foreign exchange markets by the Treasury and the Federal Reserve." In January 1983, such holdings were $5.3 billion, primarily composed of German marks, Swiss francs, and Japanese yen. Partee suggested that the substance of the Monetary Control Act and the responsible policy attitude of Federal Reserve Board members were "ample safeguards to prevent section 105(b)(2) from being used by the Federal Reserve as a basis for assisting [foreign] governments in financial difficulties." Yet in the next paragraph, he admitted that part of the Fed's holdings were Mexican pesos acquired in connection with the Bank of Mexico's drawing on the $325 million swap arrangement with the Federal Reserve. The peso holdings were then "invested" in an interest-bearing account at the Bank of Mexico. "When the swap drawing is unwound," Partee assured the committee, "the pesos will be exchanged with the Mexican central bank for dollars at the same rate of exchange at which they were acquired."[26] However, the income report of the Federal Reserve banks for the year 1983 has the following deduction from current income: "$456 million of unrealized loss on assets denominated in foreign currencies related to revaluation of the assets at market exchange rates."[27]

The "Problem" of Paying Interest on Member Bank Accounts at Fed Banks

The debates and testimony on the DIDMCA emphasized yet a third nonproblem, in addition to the two nonproblems of attrition of commercial bank membership in the Federal Reserve System and the alleged insufficiency of eligible collateral for Federal Reserve notes. The third nonproblem was the anticipated decline in Treasury revenues that would occur if the Fed tried to solve the nonproblem of declining membership by paying interest on the reserve-deposit accounts it held for depository institutions. Payment of interest on these accounts would have complemented the abolition of restrictions on interest payments to private depositors who had demand accounts at the now deregulated depository institutions. It also would have eliminated the real problem these institutions faced in holding zero-interest reserve balances, and would have been an almost certain means for attracting as many new members as the Fed thought desirable. Since the number of members does not determine the Fed's monetary control factor, it would not have affected the Fed's policy powers. However, it would have answered the Fed's arguments with respect to the nonproblem between bank membership and control over the monetary system.

Both G. William Miller and Paul Volcker, on different occasions, commented on this issue. Volcker noted that the costs to the U.S. Treasury of paying interest on reserve balances "would be relatively high—apparently higher than the [Carter] administration or Congress would find tolerable."[28] And Miller several times in his testimony on the deregulation bill commented on how this or that change in Federal Reserve operations or procedures would impinge on revenues to the Treasury.[29]

The "problem" of revenue losses to the Treasury stemmed from the fact that the Fed is the U.S. government's major mint. Every year Fed purchases of U.S. government securities through open-market operations add an equivalent dollar amount of high-powered money to the economy. During calendar year 1989, for example, the Fed bought over $22 billion in U.S. government securities and rebated $21.6 billion of this amount to the U.S. Treasury.[30] The securities are accounted as if they would receive interest returns from the Treasury. Federal Reserve costs are then deducted from this "income," and the balance, which is pure seigniorage, is "rebated" to the Treasury.

In fact, none of this net interest "income" ever gets to the Federal Reserve. The Fed's budget—that part of its government security "income" actually paid from Treasury revenues—appears to the Treasury Department as a net drain on general revenues, and any addition to the Fed's budgetary outlays is seen by the Treasury as an additional cash outflow and cost for servicing the national debt. Therefore, interest payments on the reserve balances of depository institutions in 1980 would not have reduced Federal Reserve "income," but would have increased Federal Reserve costs and reduced the Fed's seigniorage to the Treasury, by an estimated $500 million. These outlays would have gone to the depository institutions that kept reserve accounts at Federal Reserve banks.

Miller noted in 1977 that the estimated aggregate cost of Fed membership to the member banks exceeded $650 million.[31] And Volcker, while he paid lip service to a voluntary system, urged mandatory and universal reserve requirements. "This approach," he said, "is consistent with the position preferred by the Federal Reserve Board for a long time."[32]

Senator Proxmire emphasized the revenue issue when he brought the conference committee's version of H.R. 4986 to the full Senate on 27 March 1980. "The Treasury said it would not approve of any legislation to solve the membership issue costing more than $200 million a year," Proxmire told the Senate. "The Treasury's revenues have been well protected by this legislation."[33]

Provision for interest payments on their reserve-deposit accounts at Fed banks, in all fairness, would simply have offset this real cost to the banks and would have made the banks more competitive with their nonbank rivals. Finally, it would have retained the voluntary character of Fed membership. However, the approach mandating universal reserve requirements was the only one that the Treasury and the Carter administration would accept. They were not about to forgo any of the lucrative seigniorage revenue—in 1979 and

1980, about $16 billion—that the Fed creates for the federal government without legislation or any popular awareness of its existence.

Very few congressmen who voted for the DIDMCA of 1980 realized the additional powers that the act granted the Federal Reserve System in its quest to provide itself with imperial financial control. One who did was George Hansen of Idaho, who claimed that the Fed "has lusted after this bill." The "pin-striped [House] Banking Committee," he charged, "has agreed to nationalize the banking system. We could perhaps go along with this pandering to illicit desires for bureaucratic empire," he continued, "if it were remotely true that it was needed to defeat inflation." However, the Fed already had all the monetary powers it needed to abate inflation, including statutory control over member bank reserves. "In truth," Hansen concluded, "the Fed is not interested in monetary control and only wants more power."[34]

25 The Federal Reserve Approach to Price Level Stability (I)

A few die-hard free-marketeers argue that the virtues of marketplace efficiency so clearly overwhelm the risks of bank failure that deregulation should go all the way to freedom for the banks—including the freedom to fail. [But Paul Volcker and Henry Kaufman have called for] orderly deregulation, so that the emerging financial structure can be carefully designed to meet the nation's basic needs.

Robert A. Bennett, *New York Times,* 19 February 1984

From my perspective, the case for a strong central bank remains compelling. . . . That means retaining . . . a meaningful role in those aspects of regulation, supervision, and services that most closely relate to our monetary policy responsibilities. . . . Pressures to strip away the duties of the central bank are indirectly linked to long-standing challenges to its independence.

Anthony Solomon, Federal Reserve Bank of New York *Occasional Paper,* 26 January 1984

Results of Abolishing Interest-Rate Restrictions

The institutional changes in the financial system that Title II of the DIDMCA initiated in 1980 continued through much of the decade. Depository institutions of all complexions, after almost fifty years of legal prohibition, were now allowed to pay interest on checkbook balances of demand deposits—what are often labeled "transaction accounts" to distinguish them from "savings accounts." The DIDMCA also phased out Regulation Q, a Fed-administered restriction that allowed the Fed Board to put ceiling rates of interest on time deposits. At the same time, many institutions, such as savings banks and savings and loan institutions, formerly restricted from issuing demand deposits, could now make checking services available to their customers. The DIDMCA enlarged and enhanced both the scope of competition in the financial industry and the types of competitive financial practices.

System-wide payment of interest on demand deposits should have had at least two significant monetary effects. It should have increased the ratio of demand deposits to currency that households and firms wished to hold, and it should have increased the general public's holdings of demand deposits relative to short-term financial instruments and other wealth holdings. On balance, demand deposits, and to some extent time deposits due to the ending of Regulation Q, were now a more attractive form in which to hold wealth. After removal of interest-rate restrictions, deposits not only provided the services of money but also paid interest to their owners.

This new liberalization, however, could not affect currency because the federal government still had (and has) a monopoly on all currency issues, and payment of interest on currency is very difficult to manage technically. Ironically, though, a government is just about the only institution that in practice can indirectly contrive a real return on its outstanding currency. To do so, the government's central bank would have to program a monetary policy that resulted in a gradual reduction in the general price level. As the price level fell, currency holders, as well as owners of demand deposit balances, would realize a quasi-interest-return in the form of greater purchasing power for each dollar. Such a policy would channel most of the seigniorage revenue created to the private sector. So a government is the only money supplier technically able in the nature of things to pay a quasi-interest-return on its outstanding currency, and also the only institution that has no incentive to do so.

Interest-Rate Deregulation and the Velocity of Money

Through the first seven years of the decade the behavior of monetary velocity reflected the increased demand for money resulting from interest-rate deregulation. Table 25.1 shows that the growth in the supply of money, ΔM_1, increased during the 1980s at an average annual rate of 7.6 percent compared to 6.4 percent annually from 1966 to 1981. (See table 22.2.) M_1-velocity, VM_1, in the earlier period increased at an annual rate of 3.1 percent. But in the 1980s the annual rate of change was mostly negative through 1987. The velocity growth rate turned positive again in 1988, by which time the interest-rate adjustments from the DIDMCA had largely taken place. The average rates of growth in M_2 and VM_2 were identical to the growth rates of M_1 and VM_1, but were less variable.

The higher deposit-currency ratio should have meant that the Fed's produc-

TABLE 25.1 Annual rates of change in money stocks, M_1 and M_2, and in velocities VM_1 and VM_2, 1981–1990

Year	M_1	VM_1	M_2	VM_2
1981	9.7	1.7	10.3	1.2
1982	5.5	−1.5	9.6	−5.6
1983	13.0	−1.8	10.8	0.0
1984	6.9	3.6	7.5	3.1
1985	8.2	−1.9	8.9	−2.5
1986	12.8	−6.8	8.0	−1.9
1987	12.0	−5.0	6.3	0.0
1988	3.9	4.1	6.2	1.9
1989	−0.7	7.1	2.3	4.3
1990	5.1	1.6	6.0	0.0
Average for period	7.6	0.1	7.6	0.1

Sources: *Federal Reserve Bulletins*, 1980–1990.

tion of monetary base in order to obtain a given stock of M_1 would also decline, which would imply that the "money supply multiplier" would increase. However, depository institutions also increased their holdings of currency as reserves for their issues of demand deposits. The DIDMCA contributed to this result because it brought *all* depository institutions under the control of the Fed. And even though the DIDMCA lowered the Fed's statutory reserve requirement range for its subordinate institutions, the greater number of institutions and their included deposits subject to reserve requirements increased. So total dollar reserves needed to meet reserve requirements also increased. Universal Fed control over the financial sector also had the effect of linking the monetary base more tightly to M_1, since no depository institutions could now escape the Fed's requirements.[1]

Foreign Holdings of Federal Reserve Notes

Another behavioral change appeared in the 1980s—foreigners' absorption of Federal Reserve note currency for use in foreign markets. As the value of the dollar tended to stabilize during the first half of the 1980s, foreign business firms and households increased their demand for Federal Reserve notes for use in their day-to-day transactions. Many third world central banks and government treasuries were at the same time devastating their local economies with hyperinflationary issues of paper currency, so many of the inflation-bedeviled peoples began to use U.S. currency. While the dollar had not stabilized at a zero inflation rate, it was far superior as a store of value to most of the other major currencies around the globe. A few other currencies, such as the Swiss franc, were closer to absolute stability than the dollar, but none had the combination of stability and volumetric availability that the dollar possessed. The volume of international trade that U.S. industries and U.S. financial institutions engaged in during 1985 amounted to $330 billion imports and $214 billion exports, plus $93 billion capital inflows; and transactions for U.S. goods and services constituted approximately 25 percent of total international transactions. Many tourists and travelers in foreign lands, especially in large cities, found that they could make transactions in dollars without first exchanging the dollars into local currencies. Dollars were current to some degree in Cairo, Istanbul, Bogotá, London, Amsterdam, Moscow, and many other cities.

Economic Implications of Foreign Holdings of U.S. Currency

This phenomenon is easily understood; the difficulty lies in measuring it. The Federal Reserve note account on the ledgers of the twelve Federal Reserve banks registers the denominations and quantities of all Federal Reserve notes issued. Some very small amount of currency is lost or destroyed without trace, and this amount is estimated and accounted for. A large volume is held as reserves by all depository institutions, and a significant amount is held by the U.S. Treasury, U.S. post offices, state and local government agencies, and other public agencies and corporations. These amounts can be measured fairly accurately because they appear on the balance sheets of the holder institutions. After deducting these specified amounts from the total notes issued, the Fed's accountants lump the remainder into hand-to-hand currency held by households and business firms in the United States. Thus, "hand-to-hand currency" is a *residual* measure. Fed accounting does not, and cannot, determine what amount of the accounted currency labeled "hand-to-hand" actually remains in the United States and how much drains into foreign markets for use there as currency.

Lack of accountability for the precise whereabouts of Federal Reserve note currency has several implications. If foreigners hold more of the accounted total, U.S. households and firms hold less than the amount residually accounted for the U.S. economy. The actual currency-deposit ratio in the United States, therefore, is less than the accounted data would indicate, and smaller also is the total stock of money that the internal U.S. economy is using to transact its GNP. Thus, the decline in the velocity of the M_1 money stock may be somewhat overstated for the first seven years of the 1980s. It likewise may have increased more than calculated during the latter 1980s. Whatever the bias in the accounting, the trends in velocity nonetheless shifted during the period from 1980 to 1987.

Extensive foreign use of U.S. currency means that to some extent the Federal Reserve System is, willy-nilly, a world central bank. It cannot undertake this function formally and precisely because it cannot measure the amount of currency that foreigners wish to hold. The currency going abroad becomes a part of the "net capital inflow" on the international transactions account. In literally exporting currency, albeit not knowing the quantity exported, the Fed is able to generate more seigniorage for the federal government than would be the case if the Federal Reserve notes were current only in the United States. On net balance, the Federal Reserve notes used in foreign markets represent a fee, payable to the U.S. government, that the Fed has levied for providing a more reliable currency than competing central banks in other countries.

If it wishes to maximize seigniorage, the Fed has some reason to be concerned that the amount of currency issued is not too great. For if the Fed creates so much money that prices rise significantly in the United States and the dollar falls in value, foreigners as well as U.S. holders could reduce their demand for dollars. The dollars abroad would then be repatriated, raising domestic prices further and leading to more reductions in foreign holdings of dollars. The cumulative results of such a flight from the dollar could be both embarrassing and costly. The Fed's proper approach to the potential danger of such a leveraged inflation from a massive repatriation of dollars is to restrain its issues of currency and bank reserves enough so that the dollar maintains its worldly purchasing power.

Chairman Volcker's Eclectic Stance on Monetary Policy

On 6 August 1983, President Ronald Reagan reappointed Paul Volcker chairman of the Federal Reserve Board for a second four-year term. In his message announcing the reappointment, Reagan stated that Volcker "is as dedicated as I am to continuing the fight against inflation. And with him as Chairman of the Fed, I know we'll win that fight."[2]

Just days before his reappointment, Volcker had appeared before Senate and House committees to discuss both the coordination of monetary and fiscal policies and the question of appropriate guides for monetary policy. In his statements before the congressional committees, Volcker emphasized the necessity of eclecticism in the Fed's approach to policy. He had sympathy, he claimed, for a single monetary rule to guide policy. But "changes in technology and government regulations, shifts in the asset preferences of households and businesses, unexpected supply shocks such as food or energy price disturbances, as well as events in foreign economies and financial markets, . . . can alter the relationships between the performance of the economy and the target variables suggested in the various rule proposals."[3]

Volcker's argument was vintage Federal Reserve. Even if the premise—that many shocks and changes buffet the economy—is true, the implication that the Fed must take account of them and do something significant to counteract them is both presumptuous and false.

Volcker agreed that the "relationship between monetary growth and prices or nominal GNP has been long studied, and has demonstrated a certain stability over time. It is a relationship we would ignore at our peril. But it is also true," he hedged, "that, historically, there is considerable variability in the relationship over periods of several quarters."

To confirm this caveat as an excuse for not basing Fed policy on a rule for stabilizing prices or a growth rate in nominal GNP, Volcker pointedly referred to the current change occurring in "velocity." (He put the word *velocity* in quotes, implying, perhaps, its spurious nature or its conceptual imprecision.) He was factually correct. Velocity, as the measured quotient of accounted GNP and the M_1 money stock, was halfway into its five-year slide. "Individuals and businesses," Volcker noted, "apparently desired to hold more money than usual relative to incomes."[4]

Volcker did not refer to the fact that the increase in the demand for money and the downward shift in velocity resulted from the DIDMCA of 1980 that

TABLE 25.2 Federal Reserve monetary liabilities (M_F), M_1, private creation of money (M_P), nominal and real values with annual changes, and prices (CPI), 1981–1990

Year	Bank reserves with Fed (R_B) + F.R. notes (C) + Treas. dep. (T_F) M_F (1)	Annual change in M_F ΔM_{FD} (2)	Real annual change in M_F (1967$) ΔM^*_{FD} (3)	Real capital value of M_F (1967$) M^*_{FC} (4)	Annual change in real capital value of M_{FC} ΔM^*_{FC} (5)	Hand-to-hand currency + private demand deposits adjusted M_1 (6)	Annual percentage change in M_1 $\left[\frac{\Delta M_1}{M_1}\right]$ (7)
1981	$151.3	$—	$—	$55.8	$—	$428.7	—%
1982	158.5	7.2	2.65	54.5	−1.3	452.3	5.5
1983	174.4	15.9	5.33	58.5	4.0	510.9	13.0
1984	184.5	10.1	3.25	59.4	0.9	546.3	6.9
1985	200.7	16.2	5.03	62.3	2.9	591.2	8.2
1986	218.0	17.3	5.28	66.5	4.2	666.6	12.8
1987	248.2	30.2	8.88	73.0	6.5	746.8	12.0
1988	263.3	15.1	4.27	74.4	1.4	776.2	3.9
1989	280.4	17.1	4.60	75.4	1.0	770.7	0.1
1990	289.7	9.3	2.41	74.9	−0.5	809.6	5.1
Net change	138.4	138.4	41.70	19.1	19.1	380.9	7.5%[a]

undid government legal restrictions enacted many decades earlier. Nor did he explain that the shift in money demand also resulted from abatement of the inflationary expectations put into motion by the very same Federal Reserve policies that were now "fighting inflation." If these government-induced disequilibria had not been present in the first place, the velocity of money would have had very little reason to change.

Volcker also emphasized correctly the pressures on the Fed due to Congress's continuing failure to balance the government's fiscal budget. He noted Congress's "focus on the relatively short run." Political pressures, he argued, would make a one-dimensional rule for monetary policy subject to tampering. Volcker concluded, as had all establishment Federal Reservists for decades, that "there is no substitute for a degree of judgment in weighing [diverse] information and determining a course for policy."[5]

First Tendencies toward Price Level Stability

Discretion or not, the enhanced demand for money was bringing down the rate of growth in prices. From mid–1982 to mid–1983, prices rose only 2.6

Year	Stock of private money $(M_1 - M_F)$	Annual change in M_P	Real annual change in M_P (1967$)	Real capital value of M_P (1967$)	Annual change in real capital value of M^*_{PC}	Prices (CPI, 1967 = 100)	Annual percentage change in prices
	M_P	ΔM^*_{PD}	ΔM^*_{PD}	M^*_{PC}	ΔM^*_{PC}	P	$\left[\frac{\Delta P}{P}\right]$
	(8)	(9)	(10)	(11)	(12)	(13)	(14)
1981	277.4	—	—	102.3	—	271.3	—%
1982	293.8	16.4	5.64	101.1	− 1.2	290.6	7.1
1983	336.5	42.7	14.32	112.9	11.8	298.1	2.6
1984	361.8	25.3	8.14	116.5	3.6	310.7	4.2
1985	390.5	28.7	8.91	121.2	4.7	322.3	3.7
1986	448.6	58.1	17.72	136.8	15.6	327.9	1.7
1987	498.6	50.0	14.70	146.6	9.8	340.1	3.7
1988	512.9	14.3	4.04	145.0	− 1.6	353.7	4.0
1989	490.3	−22.6	−6.07	131.8	−13.2	372.1	5.2
1990	519.9	29.6	7.66	134.5	2.7	386.6	3.9
Net change	242.5	242.5	75.16	32.2	32.2	42.5%	4.0%[a]

Source: *Federal Reserve Bulletins*, 1980–1990
Note: Values at or near midyear and in $ billions, except for prices.
[a] Average for period.

percent. While the Fed was increasing M_F by 6 to 12 percent annually during the mid-eighties (see table 25.2), prices rose only 1.5 to 4 percent annually.

Early in 1985, Volcker noted with satisfaction the abatement of inflation to around 4 percent in 1984, and the concomitant growth in real output of 5.5 percent. Nonetheless, he warned, the huge federal budget deficit, and the resulting trade deficit of similar proportion, could not continue indefinitely. The fiscal deficit in particular reflected a fundamental policy disequilibrium that Congress would need to treat. But both deficits required burgeoning issues of debt to satisfy them and were a large reason why real market interest rates in the United States remained well above traditional levels.[6]

Volcker's argument was well taken. Even though institutional changes, rather than Federal Reserve monetary policy, were primarily responsible for the abatement of inflation, monetary policy had at least been restrained enough to harvest the gains that deregulation made possible. As long as federal spending and the federal budget deficit grew at their current pace, however, stability in both the monetary system and the economy was at risk.

In order for the federal government to cover its spending deficit,[7] it must supply its own securities to financial markets. The U.S. Treasury through its agents sells these securities to buyers by making yield rates on them attractive enough to ensure their purchase. To the extent that foreign households and institutions buy U.S. government securities, they must reduce their investment spending that would otherwise finance business expansion, and they also must reduce their purchases of consumer goods from U.S. business firms and farms. Foreign purchases of U.S. government securities "crowd out" sales of privately produced U.S. goods and services, and thereby contribute to the U.S. trade deficit. The federal government fiscal spending deficit is a major *cause* of the U.S. trade deficit. Japanese buyers purchase U.S. government securities rather than U.S. agricultural products because the U.S. Treasury offers its secured debt at attractive prices. This state of world finance kept the international value of the dollar "strong" in the 1980s, in spite of the country's current account deficit in international transactions.[8]

Budget deficit or not, the price level continued to approach a zero growth rate through 1984, 1985, and 1986. A dispassionate observer might have thought that the members of the FOMC, the government's primary agency involved in financial policy, would have hailed the near miss to price level stability in 1986 as a sparkling achievement—one that redounded to the Fed managers' wisdom and skill. The economy had not experienced such a modest increase in prices in twenty years. Furthermore, even transitory success in reaching a stable price level could have initiated a case for a policy of continuing price level stability (within narrow limits). Reaching the goal without any appreciable hardship was a windfall that should have been carefully nurtured. Just as important, everyone can sense that maintaining price level stability once it is achieved is much easier than getting there in the first place.

The disinflation of 1982–1986 was both an unanticipated bonanza and a self-reinforcing phenomenon. No one foresaw the reduction in the velocity of money that would result from the institutional changes that took place. The reinforcing element was the deflationary effect on interest rates that accompanied the general price level disinflation. At the same time that interest rates on both long- and short-term debts were falling—from around 16 to 20 percent down to 8 to 13 percent—interest rates on demand deposits were increasing from zero to around 5 percent. Thus, the differential rate for holding money vis-à-vis other financial securities abruptly closed from both the top and the bottom. The decline in velocity led to a reduction in price level growth rates, which led to dramatically lower interest rates, which led to an even greater demand for money and lower monetary velocity, which led to an enhanced foreign demand for dollars. This series of reinforcing events, nonetheless, was limited; it could not continue forever unless the Fed constantly reduced the rate of increase in money growth, or developed new "institutional" factors that would stimulate U.S. and world demand to hold U.S. dollars.

A couple of lucky breaks also helped make the disinflation painless. The real, and well-advertised, prices of energy and agricultural products fell dramatically. In the case of petroleum products, even their nominal prices fell significantly. By mid–1986, the price of gasoline at the pump was at its lowest point in history, in spite of a five-cents-a-gallon federal tax increase passed in 1982.

Chairman Volcker's Views on Price Level Stability

The Federal Reserve Board's Monetary Policy Report to the Congress in February 1986 recognized the decline in velocity and the related tendency of the price level to stabilize.[9] So also did Chairman Paul Volcker's statement to a congressional committee the same day.[10] Volcker called attention to the relative rise in the international value of the dollar and the abatement of domestic inflation. He noted the factors favorable to continued price level stability, and the amenable political climate signaled by passage of the Gramm-Rudman-Hollings Act for getting the federal spending deficit under control.[11]

Volcker reported that the members of the FOMC and the Fed bank presidents anticipated price level increases of 3 to 4 percent for 1986. The sustainability of the price level performance, Volcker stated, "lies in a combination of prospects for budgetary restraint, the favorable impact of lower oil prices, and improved inflationary expectations."[12] He credited "the sharp decline in energy prices" with helping to ensure "satisfactory price [level] performance" and with "making the job of maintaining progress toward stability much easier."[13]

In furthering the misplaced but popular notion that the decline in energy prices was the cause rather than a symptom of progress toward price level stability, Volcker diverted attention from monetary factors. He did not hail price level stability as a victorious achievement nor swear to defend it to the death. Rather he dwelt on all the extramonetary pressures, such as a continuing deficit fiscal policy, that could lead to the customary posture of Federal Reserve accommodation (although he did not use this word).

Through 1986, the velocity of M_1 continued to fall, as did energy and food prices. In fact, the *general* price level actually fell through February, March, and April of 1986. And while the index of industrial production also declined somewhat throughout 1986, real GNP increased slightly in each quarter, even during the second quarter, when prices were falling.

In July 1986, Volcker cautioned that third world economies such as Mexico's, which depended on oil revenues to cover the interest on debts to United States banks, were having trouble due to the fall in world oil prices. Volcker suggested that "sizable amounts of financing from abroad will be required to support [economic recovery of the Mexican economy]. About half of that financing," he suggested, "can be committed by the IMF, the World Bank, and the Inter-American Development Bank. But Mexico is calling upon commercial banks, with so much already at stake, to play a large role as well."[14]

Boiled down to plain language, Volcker was admitting that the outstanding debt of the Mexican government, which was owed to large commercial banks in the United States such as Chase Manhattan, was "nonperforming": the Mexican government could not pay all of the interest on its debts because of the decline in oil revenues to the state-owned oil companies. Therefore, the IMF, the World Bank, and other international agencies, all of which were largely financed by U.S. taxpayers, would have to make "developmental" loans to the near-bankrupt Mexican government. In addition, the U.S. commercial banks, "with so much already at stake," i.e., who were so heavily involved in lending to the Mexican government that they could not afford to have that government collapse, would need "to play a large role as well."[15] Recall that, as a result of Volcker's urging seven years earlier, these truly "junk bonds" of the Mexican government were now "eligible collateral" under the DIDMCA of 1980 for issues of Federal Reserve notes.

Achievement of near-stability in prices, rather than being a realizable ongoing goal, was to Volcker a fortuitous event unlikely to be sustained. The future course of monetary velocity was uncertain, and would perhaps "take years of experience" to codify. Oil prices could not continue to fall forever, and might well rise again. The large depreciation in the value of the dollar internationally "will bring in its wake an increase in import prices of manufactured goods," which would also add to inflationary pressures. Finally, the constantly increasing costs of housing and services tend "to lend a chronic inflationary bias to the general price level."[16]

All of these forces were present. They could not, however, gainsay a determined policy of price level stability if the central bank stubbornly held the course, as it had in the past in its quixotic pursuit of interest-rate targets. Many *relative* prices can go up or down while monetary policy keeps the price *level* stable. Nonetheless, Volcker's arguments suggest that something besides stable prices was important in Federal Reserve policy norms.

Volcker did not say just what other factor besides price level stability might be a priority of Fed policy. He concluded that experience in 1986 underscored the "impossibility of conducting monetary policy . . . according to one or two simple, preset criteria."[17] The gist of his remarks was, again, that Fed managers had to take many nonmonetary factors into account in conducting policy. The strategic advantage of this traditional stance for Fed policymakers is that it dilutes their responsibility for getting good results. If performance in the monetary sector has many roots, the ability of one institution, such as the Fed, to provide stability is necessarily limited. The institution must also have discretionary powers to deal with the many unforeseen circumstances that may "shock" the monetary system.[18]

Fed Policy in the Presence of Price Level Stability

Throughout 1986, the FOMC continued its policy priorities. It sought monetary conditions that would "foster *reasonable* price stability over time, promote growth in output on a *sustainable* basis, and contribute to an improved pattern of international transactions." It noted at its May meeting that M_1 was growing at an annual rate of 12 to 14 percent, but it evinced no serious concern over this number.[19]

FOMC sentiment did not embrace the idea of continuing efforts toward price level stabilization. Rather, the FOMC prescription for policy continued its multigoal posture. "Against the background of sluggish expansion in economic activity [in the second quarter of 1986] and a subdued rate of inflation, most of the members [of the FOMC] believed that some easing was desirable," stated the Policy Directive.

> Some members commented that further easing could have a favorable impact on interest-sensitive sectors of the economy [i.e., housing], particularly in light of what could be viewed as still relatively high real interest rates. . . . The members took account of an analysis that indicated that appreciably slower growth [in real output] might be expected over the months ahead even if interest rates were to fall somewhat further. . . . All but one member indicated their acceptance of an operational paragraph for the [policy] directive that called for some decrease in the existing degree of reserve pressure [on the banks].[20]

The argument implied that since "reasonable" price stability had been achieved, the FOMC felt it could turn its attention to other worthwhile objectives. Unfortunately, its concern with such matters as low interest rates and real output, over which it has no fundamental control, gave notice that it would compromise its program for achieving unexceptionable price level stability.

Market interest rates reached a trough in late 1986 and early 1987, approximately six to nine months after the declines in the price level that occurred early in March, April, and May of 1986. (See figure 25.1.) Industrial output also picked up, and real GNP, which had not really flagged, continued to grow.

The Fed's Monetary Policy Report to Congress in February 1987 then emphasized this theme: "Monetary expansion, while adequate to support orderly economic growth, needs to be consistent with continuing progress over time in reducing the underlying rate of inflation."[21] The report gave credit to the FOMC "for the anti-inflationary thrust of policies put in place some time ago," but did not refer explicitly to what those policies were.[22] The only truly anti-inflationary policies the Fed had fostered were in the 1981–1982 period. Thereafter, monetary increases as a result of policy decisions were even greater than those of the 1970s. (See table 25.2.)

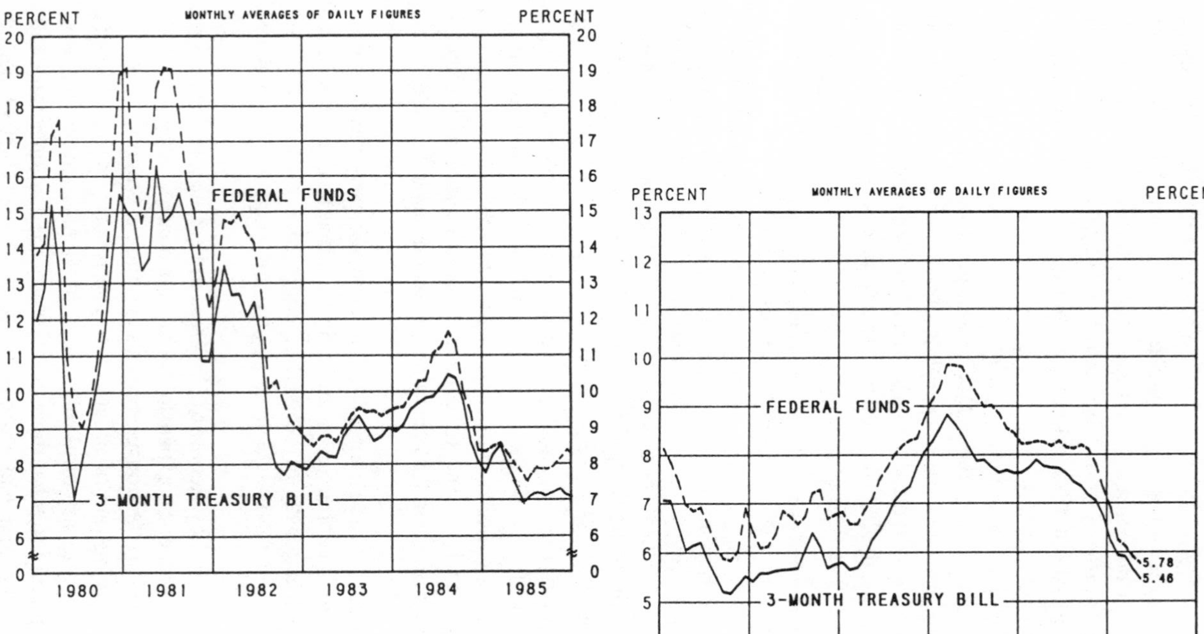

Figure 25.1 Money market interest rates for the decade of the 1980s. Source: Federal Reserve Bank of St. Louis.

The report again stressed declines in certain relative prices, such as energy and agricultural products, and it also noted that "labor cost pressures remained subdued." It contrasted the increase in M_1 with the continuing decline in M_1 velocity. "Last year, M_1 grew in excess of 15 percent," observed the report, "and its velocity . . . declined more than 9 percent, unprecedented during the postwar years."[23]

Neither this report nor any other Federal Reserve discussion of price behavior distinguishes between changes in the general price level and changes in relative prices. In fact, this report repeated the popular fallacy that a change in the relative price of one or another well-publicized commodity—oil, food, housing—causes a change in the general price level. The grain of truth in this notion masks its general error. A sudden drop, say, in the price of oil, and subsequently for final petroleum products to the consumer, might well be unaccompanied by any compensating changes *at that moment* in other product prices. The computed price index would perforce register a decline (or less of an increase) than before. Economic adjustment, however, would not have ended. Total purchasing power in the possession of households and business firms would not have changed. The given lower price of petroleum products would encourage substitution and complementation. Spenders would also realize "income effects": the less of their incomes spent on petro products, the more they could spend on other things. Since the *general* price level is a result of households and businesses spending money on a wide spectrum of goods and services, and since petro products constitute only a small percentage of total expenditures, an unforeseen change in the price of oil can have only a minor and temporary effect on all prices because the total purchasing power of the money stock is only minimally enhanced. Nonetheless, such a fortuitous event provided a useful entrée for initiating the disinflation of 1982–1986 that subsequent monetary policies could have substantiated.

The 1987 Policy Report to the Congress stressed that the declines in relative prices for energy and food probably would not recur. But instead of arguing from this observation that Fed monetary policy would now need to apply the pressure on prices formerly exerted by declining prices for energy and food, the report used the probability of prospective increases in relative prices to excuse itself from responsibility for the price level increases it foresaw in the next period.[24]

Chairman Volcker made his customary appearance before the Joint Economic Committee, just before the Policy Report was released, in order to discuss the FOMC's projected strategy. Volcker, as he had before, mixed up relative prices and the price level. Because "important" prices, especially of imported goods, were again rising, he cautioned, "We cannot reasonably expect so satisfactory a statistical result of [price level moderation] in 1987."[25] Volcker repeated the error in the Policy Report that tied the price level to a highly visible relative price when he argued that "a declining dollar [internationally] . . . generates inflationary pressures."[26]

This notion, which is all too popular with both the economic layman and the politician, mistakes symptom for cause in fashion similar to the glamorous-price argument. *Exchange rates are the prices of foreign moneys in terms of a domestic money.* An increase in the price of a foreign money, given no expected change in its purchasing power in its home country, usually means that the value of the domestic money is deteriorating due to excessive issues in its quantity. The domestic monetary unit buys not only less domestic goods and services, but also less foreign money with which to purchase foreign goods and services. The foreign money is a *commodity* when it is outside of its own political boundaries, and it is subject to all the usual market forces of demand and supply. (It *can* be so stable in value and so familiar that economic agents in foreign markets prefer it to their own unreliable currency.) As a domestic currency unit loses its purchasing power due to an inflation, one could hardly expect it to maintain its value in foreign exchange markets, unless the foreign currency was being inflated just as rapidly.

The Monetary Policy Report to the Congress in mid–1987 continued the tone of previous reports. It restated the FOMC's policy goal of "*reasonable* price stability." It noted again the inflationary effects of increases in prices of imported goods due to the "weakening" of the dollar in foreign markets. It added the "rebound in domestic energy prices that raised the general rate of inflation earlier this year [1987]," plus the potential increase in inflationary expectations, and the possibility of wage-cost increases that would increase prices. It hedged the case for "restraint on inflation" with "continued moderate growth in economic activity." The report stated that the FOMC members expected an inflation rate of 3½ to 4 percent for 1987, and 4 percent for 1988.[27] "Reasonable" price stability precluded any effort directed toward a zero inflation rate. In fact, a zero inflation rate as such was never mentioned in any of the FOMC policy discussions during 1987, or in any prior year.

"Sustainable economic growth," while it may have been a formal target for Fed policy, was a red herring in 1987. Economic growth was already robust, as the Policy Report showed in a number of places.[28] Even if it had been otherwise, monetary policy could have done little to benefit real growth in the short run, and nothing to change it fundamentally in the longer run. Indeed, attempts to offset economic adjustments in the private sector by a stimulative monetary policy can only cause more serious maladjustments that will later require more severe corrections. The experiences of the period 1975–1982 demonstrated this lesson (again).

Price Level Stability: The Road Not Taken

The FOMC's performance in the mid–1980s is an example of a golden opportunity not grasped. As price level stability came within reach in 1985–1986, and while no other economic problems, such as a recession, a stock market sell-off, or an international financial crisis, had appeared, the FOMC could have adjusted monetary growth of the aggregates to a value that would have achieved at least the price level stability of the period from the mid–1950s to the mid–1960s. With interest rates having adjusted to the deregulatory statutes of the DIDMCA of 1980, the declines in the velocities of M_1 and M_2 that had been occurring were likely to be at an end, so policy goals could again have been geared with some confidence to the growth rates in the aggregates themselves. Since real output was growing 2½ to 3 percent annually, a growth rate of, say, 4 percent[29] in either M_1, or M_2, or the monetary base, would have verified the thrust of Fed policy and given market participants confidence that price level stability would be an ongoing achievement.

Why did the FOMC snatch defeat from the jaws of victory? What did it have to gain by allowing price level stability to elude it?

To answer this question, one need only look at table 25.2. Rather than complementing the progress toward price level stability with a policy of sustained monetary constraint, the FOMC in 1984, 1985, and 1986 increased M_F—the sum of its own monetary liabilities—by the largest percentages in at least forty years! In doing so it generated maximum seigniorage for the federal government. In 1986, the nominal increase in M_F was \$30.2 billion, while real seigniorage, M_F^* (in 1967 dollars), was \$8.88 billion.

The alternatives facing Fed policymakers were clear. They could establish a tradition of a stable dollar, and thereby provide inestimable efficiencies for the private sector, and also in the long run for the government, or they could use the fortunate circumstances of the time to generate maximum seigniorage for the government while forsaking price level stability. They followed the latter course, thus demonstrating their self-interest as political rent-seekers. This behavior is very normal in private economic life. But there, competitive forces channel rent-seeking activities into productive results. Political rent-seeking, however, cannot work for the general welfare in a government's central bank where the management has a monopoly on the issue of legal tender money. In the event, the policy of maximizing seigniorage thwarted long-run progress toward a zero rate of inflation.

26 The Federal Reserve Approach to Price Level Stability (II)

The business cycle cannot be repealed, but I believe it can be significantly damped by appropriate policy action. Price stability cannot be dictated by fiat, but governmental decision makers can establish the conditions needed to approach this goal over the next several years.

Alan Greenspan, Chairman of the Federal Reserve Board, 13 July 1988

Federal Reserve Pursuit of Price Level Stability under Chairman Alan Greenspan

In June 1987, Chairman Paul Volcker informed President Reagan of his intention not to be a candidate for another four-year term as chairman of the Federal Reserve Board.[1] To fill the vacancy, Reagan nominated Alan Greenspan, whose appointment was confirmed by the Senate on 3 August. Greenspan was sworn in as chairman on 11 August 1987.[2]

In the weeks that followed the stock market sell-off of 19 October 1987, the FOMC conducted open-market operations that "accommodated substantially enlarged desires for excess reserves and a large increase in required reserves associated with a sharp rise in transactions deposits."[3] Nonetheless, at its meeting on 3 November 1987, the FOMC decided to maintain the same "degree of pressure on reserve positions" that had been in effect for several months.[4]

The FOMC's Monetary Policy Report to the Congress in February 1988 mentioned pressures on prices "that might have led to a significant departure from the longer-run trend toward price [level] stability. In these circumstances," the report stated, "monetary policy was characterized by a tendency toward greater restraint through last October when the stock market fell sharply." The "high rates of capacity utilization and low unemployment . . . suggest the need for added care in maintaining progress toward price stability." And yet a third time, the report emphasized the committee's goals of "sustaining business expansion while maintaining long-run progress toward price [level] stability."[5] Other passages stressed inflation control, while conceding that "no significant change is anticipated in the overall pace of price inflation this year."[6] The rate of inflation from fourth quarter 1985 to fourth quarter 1986 had been 1.1 percent (CPI); from fourth quarter 1986 to fourth quarter 1987, the rate was 4.4 percent, or four times the rate of the previous year.[7]

The factor that generated this shift in the growth of prices is seen in the statistical table, "3. Growth of money and debt," that accompanies the 1988 report. The total growth of M_1 for the five years 1982 through 1986 was 51.8 percent, or 10.4 percent per annum, and growth for M_2 was 47.1 percent, or 9.4 percent per annum.[8] The growth rate of an important aggregate not shown in the table, the monetary base, over which the FOMC has immediate and total control, was 47.1 percent, exactly the same as the rate for M_2. Fed policy statements had constantly deprecated the use of M_1 as a policy target on account of its declining velocity, which allegedly gave uncertainty to its significance as a target. Yet year-in-year-out its growth rate was highly correlated with the growth rate of M_2, and both were very highly correlated with the growth rate of the monetary base, the aggregate that was almost never mentioned in policy reports.

In spite of the lost opportunity to grasp and maintain price level stability in 1986–1987, the FOMC under Chairman Alan Greenspan seemed determined to renew the effort. Through 1988, the FOMC reduced its target ranges for M_2 and M_3. Even more important, general sentiment in the FOMC toward price level policy became significantly more rigorous. At its meeting on 17 May 1988, the FOMC continued its target range of 4 to 8 percent growth in M_2 and M_3. However, two members, W. Lee Hoskins, president of the Cleveland Fed, and Robert T. Parry, president of the San Francisco Fed, dissented. Both favored a greater degree of reserve restraint. An interesting element of Hoskins's disagreement was his contention "that monetary policy should be directed toward a steady reduction of inflation and *not toward meeting short-term business cycle goals*."[9] Hoskins's argument for reducing the inflation rate, in spite of what other economic indicators might be showing, marked a notable departure from standard Fed eclecticism.

For its Monetary Policy Report to the Congress in July 1988, the FOMC again lowered its target ranges for M_2 and M_3 to 3 to 7 percent, and 3½ to 7½ percent, respectively. In addition, the committee discussed the possibility of using the monetary base for its policy strategy.[10] While it decided not to target the base, the very fact that the base came into the discussion was more evidence of a new way of thinking about monetary policy.

In his statement to the Committee on Banking, Housing, and Urban Affairs in July 1988, Chairman Greenspan emphasized for his congressional audience the priority of inflation abatement. He argued that the costs of inflation to the U.S. economy were so serious that "Federal Reserve policy at this juncture might be well advised to err more on the side of restrictiveness rather than of stimulus." The FOMC, Greenspan claimed, had "underscored its intention to encourage progress toward price stability over time by lowering its tentative ranges for [the growth of] money and debt. . . . It is clear to all observers," he continued, "that the monetary [growth] ranges will have to be brought down further in the future if price stability is to be achieved and then maintained." Even though short-run variations in the velocities of M_1 and M_2 might throw off the assumed stable relationship between these aggregates and GNP, "the demonstrated long-run connection of money and prices overshadows the problems of interpreting shorter run swings in money growth."[11]

Greenspan reported that the FOMC had recently begun to track the growth rate of the monetary base; and attached to his statement was an evaluation of the utility of the monetary base in the formation of monetary policy. He registered some doubts about the base because of the large amount of currency in it. The accounted level of currency holdings, he noted—an unbelievable $825 per man, woman, and child living in the United States—"suggests that vast, indeterminate amounts of U.S. currency circulate or are hoarded beyond our borders."[12]

Following the FOMC's Monetary Policy Report to the Congress in February 1989, Greenspan again made his customary appearance before congressional committees to discuss Fed policy for the year.[13] His arguments continued the decisive but unheralded departure from the Fed's traditional eclectic principles to the single-valued quest for price level stability.

Current monetary policy, Greenspan emphasized, was to increase pressure on bank reserves as long as inflation was a threat. The FOMC had reduced growth rates in all the Ms—M_1, M_2, and M_3—through 1987 and 1988, and slower growth would continue through 1989. "The determination to resist any pickup in inflation in 1989 and especially to move over time toward price stability," he stated, "shaped the Committee's decisions with respect to monetary and credit ranges for 1989." Greenspan reported that the members of the FOMC and the Reserve bank presidents anticipated a slight increase in inflation to about 5 percent for 1989. "But let me stress that the current rate of inflation, let alone an increase, is not acceptable, and our policies are designed to reduce inflation in the coming years."[14]

Greenspan seemed to be hedging on his determined anti-inflation posture in the next paragraph when he said, "Maximum sustainable economic growth over time is the Federal Reserve's ultimate objective." But in the next breath he was back to the means of achieving this ultimate objective. "The primary role of monetary policy in the pursuit of this goal," he declared, "is to foster price stability."

> For all practical purposes, price stability means that expected changes in the average price level are small enough and gradual enough that they do not materially enter business and household financial decisions. Price stability contributes to economic efficiency in part by reducing the uncertainties that tend to inhibit investment. Also, it directs resources to productive economic activity that otherwise would tend to be diverted to mitigating the financial effects of inflation. . . . Price stability requires moderate growth in money—at rates below those prevailing in recent years.[15]

Greenspan elaborated further on the relationship between money growth rates and real growth rates. When economic resources were underutilized, he stated, a monetary policy that was expansive could enhance real economic growth. "But when the economy is operating essentially at capacity, monetary policy cannot force demand to expand more rapidly than potential supply without adverse consequences." The attempt would result in increased prices and "in little if any additional output. . . . Monetary policy," he repeated, "is not a useful tool to accomplish [faster growth in real GNP]."[16]

Greenspan referred pointedly to a recent Board of Governors staff study that showed a reliable and consistent empirical relationship between growth rates in M_2 and inflation (as measured by the "implicit GNP deflator").[17] He left no doubt that his actions in support of Fed policy would be based on these very able analyses, which essentially carried on the empirical studies of money and prices pioneered by Friedman, Schwartz, Meiselman, and other monetary economists.

The rather astonishing aspect of Greenspan's exposition was, first, that the principles of the quantity theory of money were now at the forefront of Fed thinking; and second, that the FOMC was quietly but surely modifying its traditional eclectic approach to policy. Instead of going through the customary litany of desirable economic objectives that Fed policy might promote if it were omniscient and omnipotent, Greenspan concluded flatly, "For its part, the Federal Reserve will continue to seek monetary conditions that will reduce inflation."[18] Any monetary economist could only applaud the sensibility of this goal.

Congressional Support for the Fed's Stable Price Level Policy

A congressman who applauded was Representative Stephen Neal of North Carolina, who offered a formal resolution for a Fed goal of price stability in the House of Representatives on 1 August 1989.[19] Neal was a member of the House Banking Committee, and was chairman of that committee's Subcommittee on Domestic Monetary Policy at the time Greenspan discussed the Monetary Policy Report in February. At that meeting, Greenspan had urged Neal to frame the resolution so that price level stability would be realized in a period of time considerably shorter than the five years Neal was proposing.

Neal made a strong case for price level stability, and also for this one specific policy rather than "a wide array of goals and objectives, many of which are in conflict with each other, or are simply beyond the reach of monetary policy. . . . If the Fed is presumed to be, to some degree, coresponsible for helping attain virtually all things economic desired by any administration or Congress, how can it hold out . . . against political pressures to bend policy this way or that, to provide temporary relief for whatever current problems dominate the political landscape? The best defense against these pressures,"

Neal answered, "would be a clear definition of the single objective—zero inflation."[20]

Neal recognized that the Fed had been tightening policy in an effort to reach zero inflation since Greenspan had become chairman. He felt that the goal was so important, however, that he wanted a congressional resolution to formalize the quest, and also to make it the number one objective of Fed policy so that the FOMC would not have to work against political pressures as well as economic conditions to achieve it.

Greenspan supported Neal's resolution in October 1989 when he appeared before Neal's Subcommittee on Domestic Monetary Policy. "The current resolution is laudable," Greenspan stated, "in part because it directs monetary policy toward a single goal, price stability, that monetary policy is uniquely suited to pursue." Greenspan specified the welfare benefits of zero inflation, and especially the fact that "price stability is a precondition to the economy turning in its best possible performance." During the transition period from 4 percent inflation to zero inflation, real output might slow. However, subsequent growth in real output would more than make up for any slowdowns incurred as a result of the necessary monetary discipline.[21]

Greenspan promised that "over the years, monetary policy will be bringing inflation down further, and inflation expectations will adjust downward as well." Nevertheless, he encouraged passage of the resolution. "The mere passage of legislation such as this," he claimed, "could be helpful in reducing [inflationary] expectations more quickly."[22] Not only did he as chairman support the zero-inflation measure, he told the subcommittee, but the other members of the Federal Reserve Board "fully support the thrust of the current resolution."[23]

The resolution, however, died in committee, so no full House vote on it was recorded. One might ask why Congress would not express positive sentiment for a stable dollar. No doubt any congressman would have sworn that he favored just as stable a dollar as anyone else. *But,* if he were to be a part of a formal resolution that required backing a "tight" Fed policy to implement a stable dollar, and if a recession accompanied the operation, the short-run fallout could be politically damaging. Many congressmen also may have doubted the Fed's technical ability to do the job, since so few of them seemed to understand the relationship between the quantity of money and prices. Let the Fed do it, they thought, and also let the Fed suffer any adverse consequences.

A New Norm in the FOMC Policy Directive

Another sign of a change in Fed policy appeared even before Greenspan's statement. The Policy Directive for several years up to early 1988 had stated that the FOMC "seeks monetary and financial conditions that will foster *rea-*

sonable price stability." While price level stability had the highest priority, followed by growth in output and an improved pattern of international transactions, the desired "stability" was always modified by the adjective "reasonable." Since "reasonable" implies a discretionary judgment, it lacks rigor and credibility. Policymakers could argue that a 5 percent inflation constituted "reasonable price stability" compared to, say, 15 or 20 percent.

Something meaningful happened, however, at the FOMC's meeting in March 1988: "Reasonable" came out of the Policy Directive. The 29 March directive stated that the FOMC seeks to "foster price stability over time." Since "reasonable" no longer modified "price stability," the FOMC's clear intention was a *zero inflation rate*.[24]

Fed sentiment for a stable price level policy was not confined to the FOMC. In August 1989, Donald Kohn, director of the Board's Division of Monetary Affairs, in an article on policy targets brushed aside any question of the ultimate target of monetary policy. "I take that target to be price stability," he declared. "Along with others at the Federal Reserve, I believe that the price level is the only variable that over the long run is under the control of the central bank. Moreover, for a variety of reasons having to do with economic efficiencies and with the unsustainability of other inflation goals [i.e., such as a 4 or 5 percent rate of inflation], stability is the only sensible objective for the price level."[25]

Support from Fed Bank Presidents

In the 101st Congress, second session, Representative Neal again brought forward his resolution. He then arranged for four Federal Reserve bank presidents to testify before his Subcommittee on Domestic Monetary Policy in favor of the resolution.

The response of the Fed officials was unexceptionally "enthusiastic." "There is no doubt in my mind," stated E. Gerald Corrigan, president of the New York Fed, "that the primary (but not sole) mission of the central bank should be to promote a noninflationary economic environment. . . . I believe that monetary policy in the United States is capable of achieving that result." Corrigan, however, warned that the disinflation procedure would have costs: "at least some shortfall of actual output relative to potential output over the transition period."[26]

Corrigan's model for noninflationary policy was the 1955–65 period, during which time prices averaged only a 1.4 percent annual increase. Even so, the average rate of productivity growth in the 1955–65 period was markedly greater than productivity growth from 1983 to 1989 (2.6 percent compared to 1.8 percent annually).[27]

Corrigan emphasized that the costs of an inflation, even a mild one, were "ongoing and cumulative." Therefore, "the costs of gradually winding down inflation . . . look far less foreboding [than the costs of living with it]."[28]

W. Lee Hoskins, president of the Cleveland Fed, was the next witness. Hoskins's statement to the subcommittee was if anything even more forceful and extensive than Corrigan's. "While economic growth and the level of employment depend on our resources and the efficiency with which they are used," Hoskins began, "the aggregate price level is determined uniquely by the Federal Reserve. . . . [House Joint Resolution] 409 [Neal's resolution] wisely directs the Federal Reserve to place price stability above other economic goals because price stability is the most important contribution the Federal Reserve can make to achieve full employment and maximum sustainable growth."[29]

Hoskins continued with a professional economist's explanation of how money works in a market economy, and all the ways an economy with too much money suffers from its monetary overdose. "The present value of lost output," he claimed, "from even a very small reduction in the trend of productivity growth would far exceed the adjustment costs associated with the transition to price stability."[30]

Hoskins's arguments on the evils of inflation could profitably be read by any student of economics, and should have been read or heard by every representative and senator in the Congress. "Unfortunately," he lamented, "over the years we have come to believe that we can prolong [business] expansion, or avoid recession, with more inflation. A look at recent history reminds us that there is no trade-off between inflation and recession. . . . With price stability, we would not have recessions induced by inflation and the subsequent need to eliminate it."[31]

The clear advantage of a congressional mandate would be to add credibility to the policy, thus encouraging the anticipation of zero inflation, and thereby reducing the costs of achieving it. "In the long run," Hoskins told the subcommittee, "inflation is the one economic variable for which monetary policy is unambiguously responsible. The zero inflation policy called for in H.J. Res. 409 satisfies the key requirements of sound policy: It is clear, it is verifiable, and it has consistent rules. Unlike other rates of inflation, zero inflation is a policy goal that will be understood by everyone."[32]

It is tempting to cite Hoskins's testimony at greater length, not only because it is so economically sound, but also because it marks such a momentous departure from what seemed to be, until 1987, the ironclad Federal Reserve tradition of multiple goals for policy, multiple concerns about real economic variables over which the Fed had and has no sensible control, and pervasive resistance to any specific mandated rule for policy from Congress, especially one charging the FOMC to maintain a zero inflation rate. Yet here was Hoskins telling a congressional subcommittee to get behind the FOMC and support its price level goal with a formal resolution![33] One wonders what more Congress could have hoped for from its central bank.

Hoskins's witness to anti-inflationary monetary policy seemed so thorough that the last two Fed presidents to testify might simply have said "Me, too" to the subcommittee and sat down. However, both Robert Black of the Richmond Fed and Robert T. Parry of the San Francisco Fed advanced further arguments to support the norm of price stability. Black argued that "inflation may well reaccelerate in the absence of a clear signal to the public that the Congress fully supports the Federal Reserve's commitment to reduce it further. The present members of the FOMC," Black claimed, "are especially strongly committed to fighting inflation." However, the composition of the FOMC "will change, and the [public's] memories of double-digit inflation will gradually fade, but the pressures on the Federal Reserve to make its monetary policy decisions on the basis of short-run considerations . . . will surely persist." This asymmetry, Black argued, was reason enough for a congressional mandate. "Price stability," Black continued, "is really the *only* feasible objective for monetary policy."[34]

Black also countered the argument that since "price stability has always been one of the System's primary objectives, . . . the resolution is not needed [because] it simply instructs the Federal Reserve to seek an objective it is already pursuing." However, surveys indicated that the general public did not believe that the Fed could make much more progress toward reducing inflation. "Confidence in the System's commitment to price stability," Black warned, "suffers because its policy decisions are necessarily influenced by other considerations. Passage of the resolution would send an unambiguous signal to the public and the financial markets that price stability is the overriding goal of the Federal Reserve. . . . A truly clear and unambiguous congressional mandate to eliminate inflation would play a vital role in this process."[35]

Black added a technical note on the feasibility of implementing a zero-inflation strategy. Recent research, he claimed, had established the stability of the growth rate in M_2 since the early 1950s. Consequently, the velocity of M_2 "has not exhibited any trend upward or downward. . . . This constancy in the velocity of M_2 over time," Black argued convincingly, "could bring the trend rate of inflation to zero within a five-year period by gradually lowering the trend rate of growth of M_2 to the longer-run potential rate of growth of real GNP," which, he estimated, was "somewhere in the neighborhood of 2½ to 3 percent a year."[36]

In suggesting this strategy, Black was presenting the model for a monetarist policy explained herein in chapter 23. (Observers had incorrectly claimed a monetarist strategy for Fed policy following the FOMC's ambiguous statement in October 1979 that it would thereafter pay more attention to targeting bank reserves than to targeting interest rates.) While Black's goal was not a rate of growth in the nominal money stock, he would approach the target of price stability by means of a prescribed rate of growth in M_2, the monetary aggregate that historically had registered the most stable velocity.[37]

Robert T. Parry's testimony was explicitly footnoted with references to monetarist literature. He, too, dwelt at length on the real costs of inflation that would be eliminated by "a credible and consistent anti-inflation policy" supported by the Congress. Parry cited research done at the San Francisco and St. Louis Federal Reserve banks showing that the transition costs to zero inflation were much lower than assumed by the layman. Furthermore, he argued, "These costs are transitory only. In the long-run, there is no trade-off between inflation and unemployment. . . . The benefits of price stability, however, would continue indefinitely." The costs would be greatly reduced, he predicted, "as it became apparent that the Federal Reserve, with legislative support, indeed was acting to eliminate inflation."[38]

Parry raised a distinction between "price level stability" and "inflation stability." The former label meant that a price level shock would be countered by means of central-bank policy to restore prices to their targeted level. "Inflation stability" meant that the price level would be allowed "to be permanently affected by a price level shock." Parry preferred the more rigorous policy of price level stability. First, he noted it would be a more credible policy. "Permitting the price level to drift (upward) under a zero-inflation goal inevitably would raise questions in the minds of the public as to whether the Federal Reserve was serious about controlling inflation or instead was losing control of long-run inflation through a series of 'one-time' price-level adjustments."[39]

Parry also treated the always knotty question of the proper means to measure the price level. He preferred, he said, "functional" price level stability—i.e., a pattern of prices such that "businesses and individuals do not need to be concerned about long-run inflation in making their economic decisions."[40] This definition is the same one Greenspan and others used as an operational principle.

This stellar performance by the four Fed bank presidents is at first glance almost unbelievable in view of traditional Fed posture. On second thought, however, it is not so surprising. The men and women who are now in policy-making positions are economists who received their professional training after World War II, during a period that witnessed a twenty-five-year inflation (1965–1990) with a fourfold increase in prices. Even more important, professional emphasis during this time in economics journals, books, classrooms, and conferences has dwelt on the relationship between money and prices. The material that comprised what was labeled the "quantity theory of money," but which was somewhat irrelevant for policy purposes while the economy was on an operational gold standard, came to have a lot more relevance to current conditions when the monetary system was based on a fiat paper standard and was overseen by a discretionary central bank. Now the executives of that central bank were telling their sponsors the truth: The best thing you and we can do for the current monetary system, they were saying, is to fix the value of the money unit. They did not cite the constitutional prescription of Article 1, Section 8—"Congress shall have power . . . to coin money, regulate the value thereof . . . and fix the standard of weights and measures." Their arguments were economic rather than constitutional: A stable value for the monetary unit is optimal. Nonetheless, the Founding Fathers in stipulating that nothing except gold or silver should be legal tender had intuitively realized that by such a principle they maximized the probability of price level stability.

The "Contribution" of the Executive Branch to the Stable Price Level Initiative

At the same time that the Fed had mounted by word and deed the soundest monetary policy of its seventy-five-year history, the Executive Branch of the federal government was in the process of undercutting it. The *Congressional Quarterly* (*CQ*) reported that "administration officials, who have been quietly pressing the Fed in recent months to relax interest rates because they believe an economic slowdown is a greater threat than inflation, oppose Neal's bill. 'I really do not believe it makes sense for Congress to try to micromanage the Federal Reserve,' Michael J. Boskin, chairman of the Council of Economic Advisers, told reporters February 6 [1990]. 'I believe [the Federal Reserve] should stay free of political influence.'"[41]

Boskin's statement is extraordinarily insolent. First of all, the Federal Reserve is both a progeny of Congress and an agent of Congress. Congress is supposed to supply the Fed with goals for policy and has been doing so for decades. Indeed, one of the worst performances of Fed policy came when Congress gave it tremendous power without any norms for policy (1935–1948). The result was that the administration, not Congress, dominated Fed actions. In addition, a price level rule is a far cry from any kind of "micromanagement." The FOMC would continue to "micromanage" the system through its procedures and directives, just as the Fed presidents stated and implied in their testimony. Finally, Congress was not trying to impose its "political influence" on the Fed. Quite the opposite. Fed officials were trying to enlist congressional support to thwart possible political pressure from the very administration that saw fit to criticize the one certain policy the Fed could technically achieve!

Chairman Alan Greenspan appeared before the same subcommittee two weeks later to support again the Neal bill. *CQ* reported that "for Greenspan, the Neal bill would provide a measure of political cover for the Fed's anti-inflationary efforts. Those efforts," *CQ* continued, "have drawn fire from the Reagan and Bush administrations, which have sought a more relaxed monetary policy to lower interest rates in an effort to keep the economy growing. . . . Greenspan rejected the suggestion that the Fed should focus on reducing interest rates rather than on restraining inflation. 'Rather than seek [lower rates] directly, it would be better to seek them through a non-inflationary environment,' he said."[42] Greenspan continued to lobby for a dramatic reduction in the budget deficit, which, he noted correctly, would help "reduce upward pressure on domestic and global interest rates."[43]

What is shaping up with Representative Neal's zero-inflation resolution is a classic confrontation between the Fed and the Executive—similar to what occurred during the Truman administration, but over a different issue. The political incentives for the Executive to intervene with the Fed are powerful. A longtime favorite of many successive administrations is the short-run "quick fix" to stimulate economic activity in time for the next election. Executive pressure for monetary buoyancy appears again and again, in spite of the tremendous weight of professional economic evidence that confirms the "fix" can never endure.

The second, not so obvious, return from a Fed policy that "lowers interest rates" by pumping money into the monetary system is that it generates seigniorage of $15 billion to $20 billion annually for the federal government. This revenue is an unseen and unlegislated tax on the economy. Nonetheless, it is just as real a source of revenue as any other tax. For these reasons any Executive administration wants the central bank to be "pragmatic" and to concentrate on short-run goals, particularly before a national election.

The Neal bill is still in the works. Representative Neal has reintroduced it in the current session of Congress (1991), and is holding hearings on it to muster the needed support to pass it. If it passes, it will go to President Bush, who could veto it. Such an act on his part would be an outrageous (but predictable) intrusion into a sphere of government where the Executive has no business. Indeed, since the bill is a resolution between the Congress and the Fed over a constitutionally specified aspect of policy, it would seem that neither a formal approval nor a veto by the president would be constitutional. (See again Article 1, Section 8.)

The Bush administration's opposition to the stable price level rule adds another element of uncertainty to the long-run efficacy of the concept as an operational principle. Even assuming that the policy could be put in place within the five-year time frame specified in the bill, how could it retain the credibility of the general public in the face of formal opposition from the Executive? At the present time, the Fed chairman, many members of the Board of Governors, and Fed bank presidents "enthusiastically" support the zero-inflation strategy. But Board members and Fed bank presidents come and go. Only by an ironclad commitment on the part of the FOMC and the Congress both to the principle and to its implementation can a stable price rule endure the machinations of presidents looking for pragmatic quick fixes. Otherwise, the principle of zero inflation will suffer the same fate as the Gramm-Rudman-Hollings Act for getting the federal fiscal budget into balance.

The good intentions of the Fed's money managers in this case are laudable and unexceptionable. The real question is whether the current institutional framework will sustain a rule of monetary law to substitute for the rule of men that has dominated Federal Reserve policy for so long.

27 What the Fed Cannot Do; What the Fed Can Do; What the Fed Should Do

From the infinite world of negation, I have selected two limitations of monetary policy to discuss: (1) It cannot peg interest rates for more than very limited periods; (2) It cannot peg the rate of unemployment for more than very limited periods. I select these because the contrary has been or is widely believed, because they correspond to the two main unattainable tasks that are at all likely to be assigned to monetary policy, and because essentially the same theoretical analysis covers both. . . .

The first and most important lesson that history teaches about what monetary policy can do—and it is a lesson of the most profound importance—is that monetary policy can prevent money itself from being a major source of economic disturbance.

Milton Friedman, "The Role of Monetary Policy," 29 December 1967

Federal Reserve Stewardship over the Real Stock of Money

Federal Reserve monetary strategy during the 1950s successfully approximated price level stability by deliberate, timely, and relatively small reductions in bank reserve requirements that allowed banks to expand loans and deposits on the order of 2 to 3 percent a year. Around 1961, the Fed embarked on an open-market policy that for the first time provided bank reserves and currency to the monetary system on a systematic basis. This policy also began to generate significant seigniorage revenue for the federal government. Creation of base money for the monetary system in the twentieth century is a practice that governmental central banks have universally adopted.

When a fiat paper-money standard replaces a gold standard, the central bank becomes the steward of the economy's monetary capital, the real stock of money. If it creates so much base money that it generates an inflation and associated inflationary expectations, it induces households and business firms to reduce the real value of their monetary holdings by bidding up prices and driving down the value of the money unit by more than the increase in the quantity of money. The stock of nominal money grows, but the real stock shrinks. As a government institution that serves the government rather than the private economy, the central bank always has the incentive to go this route and create excess money, especially when the sponsoring government cannot contain its fiscal indulgences. The possibility of obtaining significant amounts of seigniorage tempts both the executive administration and the legislature; and the political incentive to make economic indicators look "good" around election time also encourages the vice of excess money creation.[1]

A central bank that would fulfill its implied stewardship responsibility over the real stock of money must be able to resist political pressures and short-run expedients. It may adopt different goals and targets for its policies, and it may even create some seigniorage revenue for the government while managing the monetary system creditably. Whatever a central bank does with respect to goals and targets, the real measure of its value as a policy-making institution is its performance in shepherding the real stock of money through the slings and arrows of economic "shocks" and political booby traps. If the central bank succeeds in its stewardship function, the real value of the economy's money stock will gradually appreciate. This measure is the surest indicator of sound central-bank policies.

Tables 21.2, 22.1, and 25.2 provide the necessary information for an evaluation of the most recent thirty-year performance of the Federal Reserve's monetary stewardship. These tables include the monetary stocks that both the Federal Reserve System and the private commercial banking system have created (M_F and M_P). Annual changes in these stocks appear as ΔM_F and ΔM_P. The columns M_F^* and M_P^* give the real values of M_F and M_P after adjusting the nominal stocks for changes in the value of the money unit (the inverse value of the change in prices), and the columns ΔM_{FD}^* and ΔM_{PD}^* are the annual real changes in M_F^* and M_P^*. They are analogous to the real dividends that a corporation pays from its earnings. After accounting the dividends, the real changes in the capital stocks ΔM_{FC}^* and ΔM_{pC}^* are analogous to the capital gains (or losses) that could result from corporate capital appreciation or depreciation due to stock "watering" or loss of market favor for the firm's product. The central bank's product is real money; and the capital that generates the product loses market favor when the value of money depreciates or becomes unstable and uncertain. If nominal money stocks increase so rapidly that inflation is anticipated, the real monetary dividends that accrue to the government or to the private sector while the inflation is gathering momentum may be offset by the decreases in the real values of the monetary capital stocks after inflation takes hold.

To see the operational aspects of these changes, consider the values in table 22.1 for 1979. The price level rose 10.9 percent during the year, largely due to the outsize increase of $8.7 billion in M_F during 1978. The real dividend, ΔM_{FD}^*, of money creation that the Fed generated on behalf of the federal government during 1979 was $1.8 billion (in 1967 dollars), while the capital loss on the real capital stock ΔM_{FC}^* to all households and institutions that held M_F was $5.1 billion. Therefore, the net change in M_F^* that year was $ − 3.3 billion. This result for 1979 is an example of "killing the goose that lays the golden eggs," even though the "goose" was not killed in this example but only somewhat debilitated.

Over the period 1951–1966, the value of the M_F^* stock rose $1.0 billion while real dividends were $11.2 billion, for a total gain of $12.2 billion of capital gains and dividends in 1957–1959 prices ($14.2 billion in 1967 prices). Almost all of this gain occurred during the last five years, 1961–1966, of the period. During the prior ten years, 1951–1961, the Fed provided for money creation by lowering reserve requirements of member banks. This policy effectively transferred all of the seigniorage revenues to the private sector. From 1966 to 1981, the real capital value of M_F fell by \$2.2 billion while real dividends were \$63.7 billion, for a net gain of \$61.5 billion in 1967 prices. In the period 1981–1990, the real change in M_F as a capital stock was \$19.1 billion, while real dividends came to \$41.7 billion, for a total gain of \$60.8 billion in 1967 prices.

The privately created real money stock, M_P^*, returned \$35.7 billion in dividend income from 1951 to 1966, and \$16.1 billion of capital gains, for a total increase of \$51.8 billion. In the next period, 1966–1981, the corresponding values for ΔM_P^* were \$95.4 billion and \$ − 17.9 billion for a net increase of \$77.5 billion. The depreciation of real monetary capital in this period indicated that the central bank was less than an adequate monetary steward. In the third period, dividends were \$75.2 billion and money-stock appreciation was \$32.2 billion for a total gain of \$107.4 billion.

Table 27.1 summarizes the data from the tables and derives annual averages for the real monetary returns on the money stocks for both the government and private sectors. The annual averages for real monetary returns show impressive gains between the highly inflationary period, 1967–1981, and the latest period, 1981–1990, when inflation was virtually cut in half. Real seigniorage both to the government and to the private sector increased appreciably in the last period. Real growth in output, for which values are not shown, also increased significantly from the earlier period to the 1980s. If nothing else, these data deny (again) the popular idea that inflation promotes real growth. Inflation detracts from real growth, although it may yield occasional short-run benefits to those doing the inflating, which is why it is so attractive to politicians.

Another measure that may furnish some insights for evaluation of monetary performance is what I label the Real Dollar Ratio (RDR), which is the

TABLE 27.1 Dividend Income from, and Real Appreciation or Depreciation of, Monetary Capital, 1951–1966, 1966–1981, and 1981–1990

	M_F^*				M_P^*			
Period	Dividends	Capital Gains	Total	Annual Average	Dividends	Capital Gains	Total	Annual Average
1951–1966[a]	13.0	1.2	14.2	0.95	41.5	18.7	60.2	4.01
1966–1981	63.7	−2.2	61.5	4.10	95.4	−17.9	77.5	5.17
1981–1990	41.7	19.1	60.8	6.76	75.2	32.2	107.4	11.93

Note: Data in billions of dollars adjusted to 1967 prices.

[a]The values that appear in Table 21.1 were adjusted to real values using 1952 prices, but were readjusted here to 1967 prices. So all the figures for real values in this table are comparable.

percentage change of real dollars to the percentage change in nominal dollars. The RDR for the M_F stock is: $\left[\frac{\Delta M_F^*}{M_F^*}\right] \div \left[\frac{\Delta M_F}{M_F}\right]$; and for the M_P stock, the RDR is: $\left[\frac{\Delta M_P^*}{M_P^*}\right] \div \left[\frac{\Delta M_P}{M_P}\right]$. Table 27.2 gives the RDRs for all three periods, and for both M_F and M_P.

The best hypothetical performance for a Real Dollar Ratio would occur in the presence of a fixed nominal money stock. Continued growth in real output would cause a gradual price level decline and a corresponding increase in the real value of the fixed money stock. Since the nominal stock is assumed to be frozen, the RDR would have a value of "infinity" (something divided by nothing). While such a result by itself is just arithmetic, it suggests the desirability of a plus-value for the RDR. If the central bank kept the rate of growth in nominal money equal to the rate of growth in real output so that prices were constant, RDR would be 1. In the extreme case of a central bank creating hyperinflationary quantities of paper money, the real stock of monetary capital and the RDR would both decline toward zero. In the practical world of existing institutions, 1 is a "good" RDR value that everyone could accept. The central bank could promote a short-run RDR greater than 1 by initiating unanticipated increases in money stocks. However, any long-run value greater than 1 would probably require a falling price level, and would be compatible with Friedman's optimum-quantity-of-money scenario. Contemporary opinion in popular, political, and academic circles may not yet be ready for Friedman's optimum, but his model establishes an ideal for monetary welfare that merits serious consideration.

Until 1961 the Fed was neither increasing M_F nor generating any seigniorage. However, in the ensuing five years—1961–1966—real M_F (M_F^*) increased by 16.4 percent while nominal M_F increased 26.5 percent. For this five-year span, therefore, the RDR for M_F^* was 0.62, and the RDR for M_P^* was 0.42. (These changes are not isolated in table 27.2.)

During the second period, 1966–1981, the Fed increased M_F 6.84 percent per year. Inflation averaged 7.2 percent annually, M_F^* grew \$4.1 billion annually, and the RDR for M_F^* was 0.968. For M_P^*, the RDR was 0.921, up significantly from its value during the first period. Although both real stocks of money M_F^* and M_P^* yielded dividends, their values as stocks fell, reflecting real capital losses. The dividends, therefore, were at the expense of a depreciated monetary capital stock.

The third period data show a distinct parametric shift, due (as argued in chapter 25) to the economy's greater absorption of money resulting from institutional changes, the introduction of interest payments on deposit balances, foreigners' increased demands for U.S. currency, and the abatement of inflation. By 1987, these changes were fairly well completed, and the various measures of velocity looked as though they were back near the tracks they had

TABLE 27.2 Rates of Price Level Change and Ratios of Annual Percentage Changes in Real Dollars to Annual Percentage changes in Nominal Dollars for the Periods 1951–1966, 1966–1981, and 1981–1990

Period	Average percentage rate of change in prices (1)	Average percentage rate of change in nominal dollars (2)		Average percentage rate of change in real dollars (3)		Ratio of percentage change in real dollars to percentage changes in nominal dollars (RDR) (4)		Ratio of dollar changes in real dollars to dollar changes in nominal dollars[a] (5)	
		M_F	M_P	M^*_F	M^*_P	$\left[\frac{\%M^*_F}{\%M_F}\right]$	$\left[\frac{\%M^*_P}{\%M_P}\right]$	$\left[\frac{\Delta M^*_F}{\Delta M_F}\right]$	$\left[\frac{\Delta M^*_P}{\Delta M_P}\right]$
1951–1966	1.7	2.16	2.83	1.71	2.83	0.792	1.00	0.866	0.912
1966–1981	7.2	6.84	6.09	6.62	5.61	0.968	0.921	0.672	0.594
1981–1990	4.0	7.53	7.38	7.31	7.16	0.971	0.970	0.455	0.709

Note: All dollar values in billions. Real values in 1967 dollars.

[a]The values in this column for 1981–1990 are somewhat biased downward because 1967 prices are used to compute the real dollar changes.

This method of evaluating central bank policy is in its formative stages. It has the advantage of showing the economy's response in real money terms to the Fed's actual policies of nominal money changes, but it may need further development.

followed for the previous forty years. (See tables 22.2 and 25.2) During the decade of the 1980s, the real dividend M^*_{FD} that the Fed generated for the government amounted to \$41.7 billion, and the real capital gain ΔM^*_{FC} was \$19.1 billion. The Fed's annual real seigniorage therefore amounted to \$6.76 billion. The RDR for each sector also rose—to 0.971 for M^*_F and 0.970 for M^*_P.

These figures include and summarize a number of both demand and supply effects on real money stocks. They tend to confirm the supposition that restrained monetary management conserves the capital value of the real money stock and maximizes the real dividends that the money stock yields. The Fed was able to increase the monetary base significantly during the third period, and the private sector's money stock also grew vigorously in an environment of reduced inflation. These institutional changes, however, are unlikely to recur. M_1-velocity at the end of the period had reasserted its longtime upward trend.

Academic Treatment of Price Level Stability as a Norm for Fed Policy

The most recent Federal Reserve policy aimed at inflation abatement, and eventually zero inflation, implies a revision of Fed thinking that cannot help but redound favorably upon real money stocks. The Fed's focus, however, is not new. It appeared in serious discussions of monetary policy for the United States over seventy years ago.

The first comprehensive proposal for a stable price level policy was made by Irving Fisher in his book *Stabilizing the Dollar,* published in 1920.[2] Fisher's plan called for adjustments of the gold content of the gold dollar whenever a wholesale price index deviated a few percent from its base value. Fisher would have stabilized the index at its value on 1 January 1921 by increasing the gold content of the dollar when prices tended to rise, and by taking gold out when prices began to fall. The stock of common money—hand-to-hand currency and bank deposits—would then have decreased or increased appropriately in order to alter prices.

The gold base was a cumbersome but necessary vehicle for Fisher's plan because gold was still the official standard of the monetary system. Fisher did not mention the Federal Reserve System until the last paragraph of his "Tentative Draft of an Act to Stabilize the Dollar," and there he saw the Fed only as an auxiliary agency to implement the policy—a part of the "technical details."[3]

Fisher's very subordinate place for the Federal Reserve System was in keeping with the subsidiary role of the Fed. The gold standard was supposed to be the dominant monetary institution, while the Federal Reserve banks were supposed to be only enabling institutions—lenders of last resort, smoothers of seasonal interest rates, and promoters of an "elastic" currency. (See chapter 17.)

Fisher's plan received mixed responses from professional economists, and adamantly negative reactions from Federal Reserve officials. Lloyd W. Mints, a monetary economist at the University of Chicago, took up the same cause thirty years after Fisher's initial proposal. Fisher's arguments for a stable price level, Mints wrote, were both just and desirable. But to these features, Mints added the necessity of a stable price level for the operation of a competitive, market-oriented, enterprise system.[4] He noted that the "desirability of a stable price level is of long standing." His main point, in agreement with Fisher, was that "stability in the level of prices is clearly the one objective susceptible of attainment by monetary measures."[5]

Mints reviewed critically the Federal Reserve System's attitude toward a price level policy. The officials of the Fed, he pointed out, had been the "most effective opponents of price level stabilization. . . . A number of [Fed spokesmen] appeared before the House Committee on Banking and Currency in 1926, giving testimony in opposition to the Strong Bill, which would have directed the Federal Reserve Board to stabilize the price level."[6] Again in the late 1930s, the Board argued that the economy could not achieve maximum output with a monetary policy that fixed the level of prices. Board spokesmen also claimed that controlling the quantity of money was not sufficient to stabilize prices; that the Board's control over the quantity of money was "incomplete"; that stable prices "do not result in lasting prosperity"; and that people were more concerned over a "fair relationship between the prices of what they produce and those which they must buy." Mints ably criticized the arguments of the Fed Board as both specious and unsubstantiated by reference to experience.[7]

By the time Mints proposed his price level policy in the late 1940s, the gold standard was largely a dead letter. Therefore, his suggested method for carrying out the policy was through a central monetary agency that would maintain constancy of a widely based price index by means of open-market operations in government securities. The main advantage of this policy, Mints argued, would "lie in the fact that it corresponds to the most understandable meaning of the concept of monetary stability." The policy would also be simple and verifiable, and expectations of its continued operation would be countercyclical. In the case of an inflationary or a deflationary shock, all economic agents would expect the monetary authority to alter money stocks in the direction counter to the effects of the shock.[8]

When the operational gold standard was the basis of the monetary system, any discussion of stabilizing a price level by a governmental policy was almost inappropriate. The gold standard was *the* policy. And even though experience with the gold standard resulted in a high degree of price level stability, and was a consideration that originally recommended its adoption in constitutionally responsible states, the gold standard itself could never guarantee a fixed price level.

Other stabilizing monetary policies have appeared in recent years, one of which is the monetarist suggestion for a fixed nominal rate of increase in some aggregate money stock (discussed herein in chapter 23, and also by Mints). Such a policy would be desirable on the grounds that it, too, would minimize discretionary intervention by the central bank and would focus policy on one easily understood variable. While a quantity-of-money policy would not guarantee price level stability either, it would limit price level variation within very small tolerances.[9]

A conceptual weakness of this policy is the current difficulty of defining and measuring the money stocks (except for the monetary base). Before the central bank can increase a given monetary aggregate by a certain annual percentage, it must be able to say that the aggregate chosen is measurable, and that it captures a sufficient share of the monetary properties of the system. In the present financial environment of the United States, and in other countries as well, decontrol of banks and financial institutions has blurred the distinction between items that have clear-cut monetary attributes and those that do not. Monetary measurement therefore has become more difficult. This problem is aggravated for dollar measurement by the fact that so many unaccounted dollars are held and used in foreign countries.

The Current Initiative for Price Level Stability

The overriding advantage of a stable price level policy at this time (1991) is its official Federal Reserve acceptance at the operational level, and its respectability among a sizable group of economists. Indeed, Federal Reserve policymakers do not just accept the idea; a large majority outspokenly favors the policy, and almost to the exclusion of all the other "good things" that Fed managers were concerned with in the past. Interestingly enough, present-day Fed officials, now in agreement with Fisher and Mints, make just the opposite arguments from what their counterparts made in the past. Chairman Greenspan and the Fed bank presidents (cited in chapter 26) claim that stabilizing the price level is the optimal goal the Fed can pursue in order to provide the best environment for maximizing real output. All economists also acknowledge, as did Fisher and Mints, that the maximization of output depends on many other variables in the real economy, and especialy on the abatement of government policies that stifle enterprise, such as high levels of federal taxing, spending, and regulation.

Representative Stephen Neal and his staff, who are trying to muster the needed congressional support to formalize Congress's endorsement of the stable price level policy, polled a representative cross section of professional economists to determine their sentiment for the proposal.[10] Of the 770 who answered the inquiry, approximately 55 percent favored the Neal resolution, while 45 percent preferred that the Fed concentrate on some other target. The number of other choices was about five.

The result of 55 percent favoring price level stabilization might seem on the surface less than enough to constitute a consensus. However, it had several times the support of any other single policy. Furthermore, the written comments to the questionnaire implied that with a few minor changes in details another 20 percent of economists would favor it.[11]

Economists are legendary for not agreeing on anything. Their professional awareness of individual subjective preferences in market behavior seems to rub off on them to the point where they can hardly agree on the time of day. Many have "ideal" monetary policies they would like to see put in place. (See below for this writer's utopian monetary framework.) But in the existing institutional real-life present, the situation is that for the first time in its history a large number of Federal Reserve policymakers are willing to eliminate the problem of an unpredictable purchasing power of money from the economic calculations that households, business firms, and the various levels of government have to make. Not only is Fed rhetoric positive, but FOMC policies over the last four years have made both practical and intellectual headway toward long-term price level stability. In view of the variable goals and targets that the Fed has adopted in the past, or has been coerced politically to adopt, it would seem sensible for everyone to forgo a first-choice "ideal" policy in order to get the best "second-best" policy. A stable price level is one of only a few good policies, and the only one politically and popularly acceptable because it is understandable.

If Representative Neal's resolution cannot obtain congressional majorities, can the Fed Board and Fed bank presidents adopt and maintain a stable price level on their own? They have, of course, the technical powers and the professional prowess. A large number of this group today, unlike their counterparts in times not long past, are professional economists, so they understand the relationship between the quantity of money and prices. The question for immediate consideration is: Can this present-day Federal Reserve contingent maintain its course in the face of determined opposition from political pragmatists, who constantly cry for "lower interest rates," and especially from Treasury officials, who are continually faced with the necessity of floating new issues of securities to cover escalating federal spending deficits?

In addition, one must ask whether the current sentiment for price level stability *within the Fed* can endure. As Robert Black, president of the Richmond Fed, noted in his testimony before Neal's subcommittee, FOMC members come and go. The President of the United States on average appoints one member to the Board of Governors each year, and he always has at least one opportunity to appoint a chairman.[12] In the face of a "pragmatic" Chief Executive who wanted the Fed to "reduce interest rates," what would happen to the FOMC's well-intentioned stable price level policy? The current disrepair of the Gramm-Rudman-Hollings Act to curb fiscal excesses does not encourage the political probability of success for a similar monetary rule that would curb monetary excesses.[13] The implementation of the stable price level policy is therefore a real test of the independence, competence, and determination of the current group of Federal Reserve executives. If they succeed in this quest, they will have raised central-bank policy in the United States to a professionally respectable level it has not had in the past.

Are Central Banks either Necessary or Desirable?

A central bank is a man-made institution that deliberately creates money by means of some kind of governmental prescription or license. Money, however, evolved from barterable commodities a thousand years before central banks were invented. As ancient economies began to specialize, they first bartered goods and services directly. In time, people learned to barter indirectly, obtaining some intermediary items only for use in making subsequent final exchanges. These intermediate exchange devices had to have some nascent monetary properties.

Commodity money emerged as naturally as the wheel, the screw, the inclined plane, a multitude of different languages, and common law. Its appearance was economic and spontaneous, not political and contrived. Nonetheless, as Milton Friedman and Anna Schwartz observed in a recent paper, "History suggests both that any privately generated unit of account will be linked to a commodity and that government will not long keep aloof." No government, they note, has ever permitted free private competitive enterprise to try to produce a viable money.[14]

This observation concisely summarizes the long-term relationship between monetary institutions and states. It also emphasizes a fundamental paradox. All parties agree with Menger's inference—that money evolved from indirect barter, and was a purely economic event in which the state had no part. *How then can the state, in the guise of its central bank, make the monetary system work better than it would have worked without state intervention?* On the surface, the answer would seem to be: It cannot. Experience with central banks over the last two-hundred years also seems to confirm this answer.

The private production of money in the United States has appeared at numerous times and under diverse circumstances when state-supplied moneys proved exceptionally inadequate. Scrip, token, and ledger credit moneys were prominent in the United States in the nineteenth and early twentieth centuries in spite of proscriptive federal laws.[15] Even quasi-monetary base currency became a predictable issue during the latter half of the nineteenth century, when clearinghouse associations issued clearinghouse loan certificates to member banks in an effort to stem losses of the banks' reserves during liquidity crises.[16] Federal laws that prohibited the production of private coinage and private currency laws were ineffectual in preventing the appearance of these various media when economic conditions for their issue were favorable.

Friedman and Schwartz document thoroughly and convincingly the failures of central-banking institutions in the United States to manage monetary systems creditably.[17] They note that "government intervention was at least as often a source of instability and inefficiency as the reverse, and the major 'reform' during the period, the establishment of the Federal Reserve System, in practice did more harm than good."[18] They conclude, nevertheless, with several "good reasons" why government involvement in the monetary system is difficuilt to deny.

First, they concede that the resource costs of a private money system versus those of a governmental money monopoly are at the moment moot. No one has definitively evaluated the costs of each. Second, they claim that the "difficulty of enforcing contracts involving promises to pay that serve as a medium of exchange and preventing fraud in respect of them" is still a problem that requires the intercession of government. Third, they charge that under a fiat paper-money system the government must set limits on the volume of currency that private competitors can issue. The ability of a private system to self-regulate its quantity to noninflationary amounts, they state, "is the most important challenge posed by elimination of a commodity-based outside money."[19]

Friedman and Schwartz agree with the practical contention of Walter Bagehot and Vera Smith.[20] Both of these prominent scholars came to the conclusion that the status quo establishes a strong preference for existing monetary institutions no matter what desirable characteristics alternative systems may promise—unless, of course, an existing system proves to be too terrible. They also note "the element of paradox" when a competitive money advocate, such as Friederich von Hayek, proposes replacing existing monetary institutions with a deliberately constructed system of currency competition.[21]

Friedman and Schwartz's conclusion, although logical within their framework of sticking with what currently exists, is somewhat unsatisfactory. They realize the difference between advocating what is politically practical and what is optimal, but at times they seem to argue that what is practical precludes optimality. Furthermore, they do not address the question raised above: Since money arose spontaneously in the private sector as a market phenomenon without any master design from a government, what presumption is there that the "inputs" of government can improve the quality of the payments system? The question is sharpened by the disappointing experiences of monetary systems with governments over the centuries, and with the reappearance of private moneys as a last resort when governments have too pervasively scourged existing payments systems with coinage debasements and fiat issues of paper. What can a government do *for* a monetary system, beyond its enforcement of laws of contract and its prevention of force and fraud? The burden of proof is on those who advocate the use of government central banks to regulate monetary systems.

One scholar who has made a case for the "natural" evolution of central banks is Charles Goodhart, who argues that central banks, like money itself, are a spontaneous institutional development. Banks' assets, he notes, are of a fixed nominal character and require a period of time until the banks' debtors redeem them with cash. A large share of bank liabilities, however, is redeemable on demand. This asymmetry implies a fundamental liquidity problem. Furthermore, Goodhart argues, bank depositors have an information-cost problem of verifying the soundness of a bank's assets. Fractional reserve banks, therefore, are potentially unstable institutions that require a lender of last resort in the form of a nonprofit governmental central bank.[22]

Legal Restrictions on Banking Aggravate Monetary Instability

Goodhart's arguments, and also those of Friedman and Schwartz, seem to include as constants the legal restrictions on banking that contemporary political systems have legislated. However, the host of special constraints under which banks currently operate is the reason that banks "naturally" need a nonprofit-oriented central bank. Especially in the United States have the legal restrictions been stifling. They have included: (1) legal and variable reserve requirements that have immobilized reserves in liquidity crises; (2) prohibition of interstate banking and the requirement of unit banking in many states; (3) government bonds as collateral requirement for note issue; and (4) a prohibitory tax on issues of state bank notes.[23] Added to these restrictions were prohibitions of option clauses on bank notes and the issue of post-notes. These two arrangements, the first of which was prominent in Scottish free banking before 1765, allowed banks to forestall liquidity problems by paying interest to note holders as a reward for not insisting on immediate redemption in base money.[24] If these defenses proved to be insufficient, banks in the pre–Federal Reserve period could depend on their clearinghouse associations to supplement their reserves when threatened.[25]

Believers in the necessity of central banks have not given bankers enough credit for being able to arrange their proper defenses. When left on their own, bankers innovated the devices that made their credit intermediary position more flexible and less hazardous—option clauses, full employment of their reserves, issues of clearinghouse currency, diversification through branch banking, and anything else mutually acceptable to them and their customers.

As governments awarded special privileges to favored institutions, primarily institutions that would become central banks, it also prohibited many of these beneficial market arrangments. The "necessity" for the central bank to serve as a public surrogate for what had been private market arrangements then became only too manifest, and the modern central bank emerged as the "necessary" extramarket political institution.

Central banks are ubiquitous in the world today. They are governmentally owned; they return seigniorage revenues to their governments; and they frequently bend to political pressures for "quick fixes." Very few if any of them are constrained by explicit rules that limit their money-creating powers. The Federal Reserve System, as well, clearly violates the plain language of the U.S. Constitution.[26]

The Monetary Clauses in the Constitution and Government Production of Money

The Framers of the U.S. Constitution, in limiting Congress's powers to "coin money and regulate the value thereof," knew both what they were doing and what governments should not do. They severely limited money creation by specifying that only gold and silver would be legal tender. In so doing, they indirectly limited the operational quantity of money to noninflationary amounts. One may wonder how, with such constraints, monetary systems—particularly the American and British—fell back under the control of discretionary political authorities.

The flaw in the Constitution, I submit, is found in the double-function clause, "[1] coin money, [and 2] regulate the value thereof." The next two phrases give further evidence of what the Framers intended: "[3] and of foreign coin, and [4] fix the standard of weights and measures."[27] "Regulate the value thereof" only allowed Congress to specify the unit of account (the dollar) to be equal to some quantity of fine gold and to some quantity of fine silver. The only future role for Congress in its regulatory capacity would be to change *incrementally* the monetary quantity of either gold or silver in coins of a given denomination in order to keep both metals current as media of exchange. Otherwise, changing supply conditions over time would have the metal that was becoming cheaper drive the dearer metal out of circulation (Gresham's Law).[28]

Since the Framers put the "regulate" provision in the same clause that had Congress providing a system of weights and measures, their intention was clear. They certainly did not mean for Congress to assume discretionary authority over the value of money, much less delegate any such authority to what is now labeled a central bank.

Unfortunately, the Framers innocently allowed Congress the power to coin the money that it was supposed to regulate. Apparently, the prevailing sentiment at the time of the Constitutional Convention was an uneasiness that private coin-smiths might not be able to do an effective job, or that the prevalence of Spanish coins, widely used at that time, bemeaned the prestige of the fledgling U.S. government.

Without the coinage power, Congresses would have had no more of an excuse to issue paper money and otherwise debase the coinage than to debase weights and measures by producing bogus "five-pound" weights that actually weighed one pound, and "thirty-six-inch" yardsticks that were only fifteen inches long. Neither the power to regulate money nor the power to regulate weights and measures would have provided any possibility for seigniorage, and Supreme Courts would have had no opportunities to validate Congress's constitutional transgressions. As William Brough, a nineteenth-century scholar, stated the matter: "If governments would confine their legislation to fixing by enactment the fineness of the precious metal and the number of grains that shall constitute each piece of a given name, they may safely leave the maintenance of coinage . . . and the value of the pieces to be regulated [to] individual interest and action."[29] (See chap. 10 above.)

More recently, Robert Greenfield and Leland Yeager have proposed a norm for monetary policy that would simulate the "regulate" provision in the Constitution but would delete the "coin money" power. Greenfield and Yeager distinguish properly between the unit of account—the dollar—and the medium of exchange, which is fundamentally the Federal Reserve note. They observe that only an accident of polity makes the two items synonymous in people's minds. For the practical purpose of returning the government to its original constitutional limit, Greenfield and Yeager propose that Congress specify the unit-of-account dollar to consist of a bundle of staple, conventional, commonly marketed commodities. The government would not itself—neither Congress nor the Federal Reserve System—issue dollar-denominated payment media to keep the dollar value of the bundle constant. It would leave these functions to dealers and arbitrageurs in financial and commodity markets.[30]

Greenfield and Yeager's system is analogous to a gold standard, but without the government coining gold or anything else. Their bundle of commodities would become a surrogate for a quantity of gold under a gold standard, and the specified price of their bundle would be analogous to the mint price of gold. The advantage of their system is that it would fit the value of the dollar to a broad-based composite rather than tie it to one commodity. Their system also has the property of being eminently constitutional and workable. It would restore the monetary system to a rule of law and provide benefits that are at the moment inestimable. Unfortunately, their proposal is unlikely to receive more than intellectual consideration.

Constructing a Constitutional Monetary System from Present-day Institutions

If one is to concentrate on existing institutions in the mode of Walter Bagehot and Vera Smith, the question for the moment is: How can present-day monetary institutions be modified so that the monetary system operates under a rule of law with maximum choices of money available to money holders, and with a minimum of governmental discretion and intervention?

In the beginning (1913) Congress designed the Federal Reserve System to be a system of supercommercial privately owned banks. But the Banking Act of 1935 and the Monetary Control Act of 1980 formally changed the Fed from a system in which the Federal Reserve banks were autonomous and the Federal Reserve Board a refereeing committee, to one in which the Board in Washington is all-powerful and the Federal Reserve banks not much more than administrative units; from an occasional discounter of real bills at the initiative of member banks, to a constant and momentous monetizer of government securities at the initiative of the Federal Reserve Open Market Committee; from an institution specifically subordinated to the gold standard, to one that has a monopoly on the initial creation of money with no vestige of a gold standard remaining; from a lender of last resort for banks, to a perpetual motion machine of money creation; from an institution with an avowed interest in providing liquidity in support of sound banks, to a cloak-and-dagger operation that has often bred uncertainty in financial markets. Unless one can argue that what is good for the government is good for the general public, one cannot defend either the mutation of the Fed as it has occurred, or the Fed's continued existence as an all-powerful central bank. Its seventy-seven-year history as an increasingly powerful bureaucratic institution confirms the inability of Congress to bring it to heel. Whenever its own powers are at stake, the Fed exercises an intellectual ascendancy over Congress that consistently results in an extension of Fed authority. This pattern reflects the dominance of bureaucratic expertise, for which there is no solution as long as the specialized agency continues to exist.

"The" Fed, in fact, is no longer a single homogeneous institution, but has become essentially two institutions—the twelve Federal Reserve banks with branches and the Federal Reserve Board of Governors in Washington. Either could exist in its present form without the other. The Board, through its dominant role on the FOMC, for example, can manipulate the quantity of monetary aggregates in any manner it wishes whether the Fed banks exist or not. The banks only serve as convenient accounting media for Board policies. Likewise, the Reserve banks could continue to carry out all of their payment operations and regulatory practices whether the Board existed or not, or even if Congress reestablished a gold standard. These two institutions are not what

Congress intended in 1913 and, even more important, are not even close to what the U.S. Constitution either anticipated or permitted.

To restore a constitutional monetary and banking structure would require, first, the privatization of the twelve Fed banks. This step would be technically, if not politically, straightforward and simple. The member commercial banks already "own" the twelve Fed banks, but they have no property rights. Member banks receive a statutory 6 percent dividend from their parent Fed banks, but retain no other evidences of ownership. True reform would allow the "member" banks in name to become member banks in fact. The stockholder commercial banks would form private corporate structures that would administer the erstwhile Fed banks in a fashion similar to the operations of the private clearinghouse associations of the 1857–1913 period. The privatized Fed banks would provide clearing services for their members as they do now, and would be free to issue bank-note currency. They would also furnish their client banks with deposit insurance programs, and they would make other financial services available to banks that wanted such assistance and were willing to pay for it. Having a source of income as private cost-recovering enterprises, they would no longer pose a fiscal "burden" to the U.S. Treasury.

Constitutionalizing the Board is a separate matter. Of course, Congress would have to defrock the Board of its powers over the banking and monetary system. This procedure, however, would not dispose of the question of what to do with the stock of government legal tender money that the Board has already created and spent into existence (currently, $360 billion). The simplest and least disturbing way to deal with this quantity, which includes all U.S. paper currency (Federal Reserve notes) and depository institution reserve-deposit accounts at Federal Reserve banks, would be to freeze the total dollar quantity and to restrict its legal tender powers to payments due to and from the government. A bureau in the Treasury Department, probably the comptroller of the currency, could manage the bookkeeping and currency printing operations that would keep the base stock constant. Restricting the currency's legal tender properties to government dues and payments would not in any practical way change the acceptability of the notes. It would, however, change their scope. Private parties could in the future make contracts in any alternative medium they wished. (See chapter 10.)

The FOMC's current policy of attempting to promote long-run price level stability and to write it in stone is an attractive alternative to getting rid of the Board entirely and freezing the monetary base. If the current FOMC effort is successful, it would make the Fed a modern-day surrogate for the constitutional gold standard. True, the Fed would still be "coining money"; and it would still be a money-producing government agency. If it could make the stable price level policy a *tradition,* however, and if it were successful in maintaining zero inflation within very small tolerances—say, plus or minus

2 percent—through political thick and thin, it would effectively reduce the private sector's monetary uncertainty to a trivial concern. *If* . . .

Privatizing the Government's Gold Stock

The federal government, through the initiative of the Congress, could promote one additional institutional change—a true beau geste—that would encourage the private creation of money and promote some further progress toward a constitutional monetary system. It would also transfer to private households a large stock of government-sequestered unused wealth; and the policy could be undertaken currently with no real loss to anyone and independently of any other governmental policy. The action I recommend is privatization of the U.S. Treasury's stockpile of gold, which at the moment amounts to approximately 8,200 *tons!* Commercial member banks deposited this gold in Federal Reserve banks when the Federal Reserve System first started operations, but the gold has become Treasury property over the years by means of questionably constitutional federal laws—especially Franklin D. Roosevelt's confiscation under the Gold Reserve Act of 1934. (See chapter 18.) Currently, the gold has absolutely no monetary connection. It serves as no basis for the creation of money, and has no monetary purpose beyond its alleged "psychological" support for existing Federal Reserve issues of base money. Federal Reserve money, however, is full legal tender and does not need any gold "backing." Its acceptability is forced.

This gold could be systematically sold off at auction as a means of covering current fiscal deficits, or it could be popularly distributed to the citizens of the United States on a per capita basis—approximately one ounce for each man, woman, and child. Such a distribution has precedent in an act of this very kind that took place in 1837. (See chapter 5.) To make the current distribution even sweeter, the titles to the gold, redeemable into gold coins on demand, could be issued per capita by the Internal Revenue Service in acknowledgment of income taxes paid during some given tax year. People could then hold or dispose of the gold as they pleased. Some would convert it into gold ornaments or sell it to industrial users. However, many people who wished to retain ownership without paying the forgone cost of holding a "useless" substance would deposit their gold receipts as gold-based accounts in banks. No law would fix the price of gold; it would not become the *official* standard. Private coin-smiths and gold banks would administer its monetization. It would find its market value in dollars by means of its demand and supply relative to the demand for and supply of conventional Federal Reserve money (now a fixed stock). Once an equilibrium market price of gold appeared, in what would probably be a very short period of time, gold could act as the growth element in the money supply much as it did in the days of the gold standard. Its use as money, however, would not preclude the use of other competing moneys that might arise through innovation in the money "industry," nor would new gold money necessitate disuse and abandonment of conventional Federal Reserve money.

All the ramifications that would follow from such a wide distribution of gold are not immediately inferable. However, nothing suggests that they could be other than beneficial. While gold, which would now be widely distributed, might tend to fall in price because of the great increase in its marketable supply, its probable widespread use as money would tend to raise its price by increasing the demand for it. In any case, households and firms in the private economy would now own the gold, and could use it as another form of money if they chose. Indeed, the private possession and possible monetization of gold would serve as a role model for the price level stabilization policy that the FOMC is trying to initiate. From this point on, the private creation of deposits and currency—not being at all prohibited by the Constitution, and laws to the contrary having been repealed—would provide a means for extending money on a voluntary contractual basis between demanders (holders of money) and suppliers (creators of money) on any terms mutually acceptable.

The vehicle for the private production of money would be the free, private competitive banking system. It would be unregulated and unrestricted except for the conventional prohibitions against force and fraud that apply to all other enterprises. The banking industry would implement its own deposit insurance system. Each bank would determine its own reserve necessities and issue its own currency if it wished to do so. Banks could include option clauses in their demand obligations, and initiate other features that would make their money attractive to potential "consumers," i.e., people who held their notes or deposits. In such a competitive environment, the quality of the product would probably improve in many ways. The value of the money unit would at least be of a stable purchasing power, and it might even increase over time as banks paid nominal rates of interest on demand deposit balances. It is not possible to say without experience just what the competitive "price" for a money unit would be; but almost certainly the consuming public would not tolerate a brand of money that depreciated over time. Other innovations, such as have occurred in communications, electronics, and medicine, would enhance the viability and utility of money. The base for private money production might be some part of the existing stock of Federal Reserve money, or gold, or bundles of commodities, or equities packaged by innovating entrepreneurs operating under the severe constraint of competitive markets to make their moneys good.

Clearly, the institutional changes I have suggested are technically simple and would not unduly disturb the present-day payments system. Indeed, any one or more of these changes could be put in place without a ripple. Yet at the moment they are politically impossible. Popular sentiment has become conditioned to the rule of men and women in monetary policy, no matter the evidence that documents its failure. So the case rests: Until the government's monopoly over money is abolished, good private competitive enterprise money will never have the chance to drive out bad governmental monopoly money.

Notes

Chapter One

1. Fritz Redlich, *The Molding of American Banking, Men and Ideas,* part 1, 1781–1840 (New York: Hafner Publishing Co., 1951), pp. 96–100. Redlich argues, I think correctly, that the First Bank of the United States could not have been created as a central bank because there was no commercial banking system to be controlled. No commercial banking system presupposed no central-banking functions.

2. Economists use primarily two concepts of the stock or quantity of money. The "narrow" stock, or M_1, includes currency (coin and paper money) held outside banks, plus demand deposits of commercial banks, minus interbank and government deposits. The "wide" stock, or M_2, includes everything in the narrow stock, plus time deposits in commercial banks, also adjusted for interbank balances. One can think of an even "wider" stock, M_3, that includes all time and savings deposits whether in commercial banks or not. Although any of the concepts is satisfactory, this study uses the "wide" stock, M_2, if only because accounting procedures during most of the nineteenth century did not distinguish between time and demand deposits. In the nineteenth century, common practice was to label only gold and silver as money.

3. A gold dollar was defined as containing 25.8 grains of gold 0.9 fine, which implies 23.22 grains of pure gold. Since 480 grains equal one ounce, one ounce of gold equaled $20.67 (480 divided by 23.22).

4. For an account of the origins and evolution of gold and silver standards, see Richard H. Timberlake, *Gold, Greenbacks, and the Constitution* (Berryville, Virginia: Durell Foundation, 1991).

5. Murray Rothbard, "The Case for a 100% Gold Dollar," in *In Search of a Monetary Constitution,* ed. Leland Yeager (Cambridge: Harvard University Press, 1962), pp. 94–136.

6. Frederick Soddy, *Wealth, Virtual Wealth, and Debt,* 2d ed. (New York: E. P. Dutton and Co., 1933), p. 179.

7. Arthur R. Burns, *Money and Monetary Policy in Early Times* (New York: Augustus M. Kelley, 1965 [1927]). See also Timberlake, *Gold, Greenbacks, and the Constitution.*

8. Bray Hammond, *Banks and Politics in America* (Princeton, N.J.: Princeton University Press, 1957), p. 139. This work is recommended for its rich detail of monetary and banking development in this period.

9. *Annals of Congress,* 1st Cong., 2d Sess., 14 December 1790, "Report on a National Bank." (*Annals of Congress* hereafter cited as *AC.*)

10. Adam Smith, *The Wealth of Nations,* ed. Edwin Cannan (New York: Random House, Modern Library Edition, 1937), p. 304.

11. Ibid., pp. 651, 682, 883–85.

12. *AC,* "Report," pp. 2082–2111.

13. Smith, *Wealth of Nations,* pp. 304–5; *AC,* "Report," pp. 2082–83.

14. Smith, *Wealth of Nations,* p. 305.

15. *AC,* "Report," p. 2095.

16. Smith, *Wealth of Nations,* p. 308.

17. *AC,* "Report," p. 2095.

18. Ibid., p. 2101. Hamilton was at just the right age to have read and been impressed with Smith's *Wealth of Nations.* Hammond (*Banks and Politics in America,* p. 133) noted that Hamilton "followed an explanation of the utility of banks which Adam Smith had presented in the *Wealth of Nations.*" His "Report" in places reads like a copy of Smith.

19. *AC,* "Report," pp. 2095–2103. The bank's notes were to be limited legal tender—that is, "receivable in all [public] debts of the United States."

20. Ibid., p. 2109.

21. Ibid.

22. The English government issued exchequer bills as interest-bearing temporary debt. Frequently, however, they were payable on demand, and they were always receivable for all public dues. Bank of England notes differed only in that they were more permanent and did not bear interest. One observer has argued that the Bank of England's administration of these currencies "served as a bond between the State and the Bank, which bound the two together in ever closer relations" (Eugen von Philippovich, *History of the Bank of England and Its Financial Services to the State,* National Monetary Commission, 61st Cong., 2d sess., Sen. Doc. No. 591, 1911, p. 107). The general acceptance of both currencies was due to their acceptability for all debts owed to the government.

23. *AC,* 1st Cong., 3d sess., p. 1919.

24. Ibid., pp. 1895–96. Madison cited some other minor factors, such as the consequences of a run on the bank.

25. Ibid., p. 1897. He mentioned a Virginia law that prohibited the circulation of notes payable to bearer.

26. Ibid., p. 1916.

27. Ibid., p. 1898.

28. Ibid., pp. 1904 and 1907. Theodore Sedgwick and Elbridge Gerry, both of Massachusetts, also argued for the bank in terms of the expediency it would provide the government as a borrower (pp. 1913 and 1948–49).

29. See James Willard Hurst, *A Legal History of Money in the United States, 1774–1970* (Lincoln: University of Nebraska Press, 1973), pp. 12–13. Hurst argues that the clause "regulate the value" reflected the desire of Congress to achieve "formal standardization of the monetary system." This view presumes too much ex post facto rationalization of subsequent congressional action. All that the Constitution left to Congress was the discretion to stipulate the metallic contents of gold and silver coins in terms of their legal tender monetary values.

30. *AC,* 1st Cong., 3d sess., p. 1957.

31. Ibid., p. 1906.

32. John Thom Holdsworth, *The First Bank of the United States,* 61st Cong., 2d sess., Sen. Doc. No. 571, National Monetary Commission, 1910, pp. 123–25, 136–37, 116. The balance sheet shown in this source is one of the few that endured. Most of the records were destroyed by fires in 1814 and 1833.

33. Ibid., p. 123.

34. Hammond, *Banks and Politics,* pp. 115–16, 198–200.

35. *AC,* 11th Cong., 3d sess., p. 22, "Petition of President and Directors of the Bank of the United States for Re-charter," 18 December 1810. A "memorial" in this context was a written statement presented to a legislative body in the form of a petition or remonstrance. This statement was signed "David Lenox, President." The stockholders thought of the bank only as an orthodox aid to the Treasury.

36. Ibid., p. 32. This memorial was signed "Condy Raguet and one hundred others."

37. Ibid., pp. 212–13.

38. The Democratic party of this day was the anti-Federalist party of Jefferson, Madison, Gallatin, and Crawford, even though they then called themselves Republicans. I reserve this latter label for the descendants of the Whig-Federalist group.

39. *AC,* 10th Cong., 2d sess., p. 458.

40. *AC,* 11th Cong., 3d sess., pp. 394–95.

41. Ibid., pp. 122–25.

42. Ibid., pp. 142–43.

43. See speeches on these points by Clay and William B. Giles of Virginia (ibid., pp. 175–207 and 215–18). See also Redlich, *Molding of American Banking,* p. 100. Redlich's discussion of the First Bank includes many details on its operations that have been abbreviated here. His conclusions about the growth of the First Bank into an embryonic central bank are substantially in agreement with what I have found using different source material.

Chapter Two

1. This part of the story is certainly true even though neither the Constitution of 1789 nor the debates of the Congress in 1790–91 indicated that the First Bank *ought* to regulate the state banks or financial markets. The regulatory function grew without official sanction.

2. R. C. H. Catterall, *The Second Bank of the United States* (Chicago: University of Chicago Press, 1902), p. 4. Catterall's reference to treasury notes as a medium of exchange should be borne in mind for much of the latter analysis.

3. The references for this account are legion. An incomplete list includes Catterall, *Second Bank;* W. B. Smith, *Economic Aspects of the Second Bank of the United States* (Cambridge, Mass.: Harvard University Press, 1953), chap. 7, esp. pp. 114–15; Hammond, *Banks and Politics,* pp. 200–201 and 227–50; E. R. Taus, *Central Banking Functions of the United States Treasury, 1789–1941* (New York: Columbia University Press, 1943), pp. 24–27; Murray N. Rothbard, *The Panic of 1819* (New York and London: Columbia University Press, 1962), chap. 1, pp. 1–23. This last work, while complete and well done on most aspects of its subject, does not mention the existence

of treasury notes, let alone acknowledge their high-powered monetary influence on the inflation of 1814–1817.

4. John Jay Knox, *United States Notes,* 3d ed. (New York: Charles Scribner's Sons, 1899), p. 22.

5. Knox, *United States Notes,* p. 23.

6. United States Treasury Department, *Reports of the Secretary of the Treasury of the United States,* vol. 1, 1790–1814, p. 529. Campbell's reference to the notes "in circulation" was typical affirmation of their monetary character. (Hereafter an annual report of the secretary of the Treasury is cited simply as *Treasury Report.*)

7. Ibid.

8. *American State Papers: Finance,* vol. 3, p. 18 (hereafter cited as *ASPF*).

9. Given a significant increase in bank reserves, the number of banks could be expected to grow. The creation of bank credit, and the issue of bank notes that the new reserves would induce, would require additional bank administrations. In short, one big bank could expand credit and notes in a theoretical model; but the frictions of printing and signing the notes and negotiating loans required an extension of banking offices.

10. *ASPF* 3, p. 131 (*Treasury Report,* 1816).

11. Ibid. The last issue of treasury notes (act of 24 February 1815) included over $3 million in "small" notes (under $20) that did not bear interest.

12. Ibid., p. 132.

13. Ibid., p. 116. Dallas to House of Representatives, 19 March 1816.

14. *AC,* 14th Cong., 1st sess., appendix, p. 1640 (*Treasury Report,* 1815).

15. Ibid., p. 1643.

16. *ASPF* 3, pp. 316–17. Crawford to William Jones, 29 November 1816.

17. Ibid., p. 60. Dallas to John C. Calhoun, 24 December 1815. The emphasis of the secretary continued to be on bank paper rather than on the treasury notes used as reserves that gave rise to the bank-issued currency. Thus was symptom conveniently transposed into cause.

18. Ibid., pp. 60, 58.

19. Ibid., p. 59.

20. Ibid.

21. David Ricardo, "The High Price of Bullion," in *Economic Essays,* ed. E. C. K. Gonner (London: G. Bell and Sons, 1923), p. 41.

22. *ASPF* 4, p. 764. Jones to Crawford, 9 January 1817.

23. *ASPF* 3, pp. 316–17.

24. *ASPF* 4, pp. 283 and 360–62. Government revenues were supposed to be deposited in the Bank of the United States in accordance with the act creating the bank.

25. Ibid., pp. 499, 536, 577.

26. U.S. Bureau of the Census, *Historical Statistics of the United States, Colonial Times to 1957* (Washington, D.C., 1960), series E-1, p. 115.

27. *ASPF* 4, p. 769. See also Leon Schur, "The Second Bank of the United States and the Inflation after the War of 1812," *Journal of Political Economy* 68 (1960): 120.

28. See *ASPF* 3 for an extended correspondence between Crawford and Jones, and between Jones and the state bank executives, on this issue.

29. Ibid., pp. 539–40. Crawford to Directors of the Bank of the United States, 3 July 1817.

30. Ibid., p. 845. Jones to Crawford, 29 May 1818.

31. Ibid., pp. 853–54. Jones to Crawford, 23 June 1818.

32. Ibid., p. 586. Crawford to Jones, 30 June 1818.

33. *ASPF* 2, p. 275 (*Treasury Report,* 1818).

34. Hammond, *Banks and Politics,* p. 249.

35. *ASPF* 3, pp. 494–98. Crawford to House of Representatives, 24 February 1820.

36. *ASPF* 3, p. 498.

37. Ibid., p. 494.

38. Ibid., pp. 501–4. This same "principle" was also stated by Dallas (see epigraph at beginning of chapter).

39. Ibid., pp. 505–7.

40. Ibid., p. 504.

Chapter Three

1. Hammond, *Banks and Politics,* chap. 11, p. 305.

2. Smith, *Economic Aspects of the Second Bank,* p. 263.

3. Redlich noted that the Second Bank performed certain functions not part of the usual operations of a commercial bank: (1) It acted as a fiscal agent for the federal government. (2) It provided a national paper currency. (3) It held the metallic reserves of the monetary system. (Redlich, *Molding of American Banking,* part 1, p. 98.) While every central bank has these functions, they are only the administrative side of central banking. At least a fourth characteristic is necessary: deliberate and purposeful actions to effect some measure of control over the quantity of money.

4. *AC,* 18th Cong., 1st sess., p. 926.

5. *Register of Debates in Congress* (Washington, D.C.), 18th Cong., 2d sess. (*Treasury Report,* 1824), appendix, pp. 40–41 (hereafter cited as *RDC*).

6. David McCord Wright, "Langdon Cheves and Nicholas Biddle: New Data for a New Interpretation," *Journal of Economic History* 13:2 (1953): 305–19. Also Hammond, *Banks and Politics,* p. 278.

7. Hammond, *Banks and Politics,* pp. 301, 323. Biddle in 1819 expressed only the opinion that the government should not trust its funds in the hands of the state banks. He implied no ideas of control over the banks or the money supply.

8. Ibid., p. 305.

9. *RDC,* 20th Cong., 2d sess. (*Treasury Report,* 1828), appendix, pp. 21–22.

10. Ibid., p. 22.

11. Jacob Meerman, "Nicholas Biddle on Central Banking" (Ph.D. diss., University of Chicago, 1961), pp. 14–15.

12. The performance of the Federal Reserve System's policy-making officials in 1929–1933 is a good example of a central bank–inspired disaster.

13. Hammond, *Banks and Politics,* pp. 324, 307–9. See also Meerman, "Nicholas Biddle," pp. 9 and 26; Redlich, *Molding of American Banking,* part 1, p. 136.

14. Hammond, *Banks and Politics,* p. 305.

15. Ibid., p. 311.

16. Rush himself had run for vice president and had been defeated by John C.

Calhoun. Calhoun was probank and Jackson was antibank, but the bank issue had not crystallized at all. Therefore, the positions of the candidates on the bank's role could not have been substantive factors in their political successes and failures at this time (1828).

17. Hammond correctly underscored the significance of the adverb *well* (p. 374). Use of *well* before *questioned* was hyperbole; and the further declaration that the bank had not furnished a sound and uniform currency, implying that it had done just the opposite, was absurd. This argument cannot claim, however, that the currency necessarily would have been unstable and of low quality without the bank. It only suggested that the privileges granted the bank helped improve the quality of the payments system.

18. U.S. Congress, 22d Cong., 1st sess., *Reports of Committees,* House Report No. 283, 9 February 1832 (hereafter cited as the McDuffie report).

19. Ibid., pp. 10, 11. The first quotation suggests that the circumstances of the times were extending the concept of money beyond gold and silver coin. If other things, such as bank notes, were in fact treated and used as money, the argument was that Congress had the power to regulate their value by means of specific legislation.

20. Ibid., pp. 13, 14. Mill's *Principles* was not published until 1848. The similarity of language between this passage and his chapter 8 is striking.

21. McDuffie report, p. 12.

22. Ibid., p. 18; emphasis in original.

23. Ibid., pp. 29–31; emphasis in original. They affirmed here that the treasury notes of 1812–1816 were an example of government-issued currency.

24. Ibid., pp. 25, 19.

25. Ibid., p. 49.

26. Ibid., p. 55; emphasis in original.

27. Ibid., p. 52. See also chapter 1 herein.

28. Ibid., pp. 52, 57.

29. U.S. Congress, 22d Cong., 1st sess., *Reports of Committees, House Report* no. 460, 14 March 1832, submitted 30 April 1832 (hereafter cited as the Clayton report).

30. Ibid., pp. 15–20.

31. Ibid., p. 299.

32. Ibid., p. 309.

33. Ibid., p. 311.

34. Ibid., pp. 404, 406, 52.

35. Ibid., p. 29.

36. Ibid., p. 319.

37. Ibid., p. 320.

38. Ibid., pp. 334, 336–37.

39. Ibid., p. 362.

40. Ibid., p. 363.

41. U.S. Congress, 22d Cong., 1st sess., *Executive Documents,* Doc. No. 300, "Message from the president of the United States returning the bank bill with his objections to the Senate," 16 July 1832, pp. 5–6.

42. Ibid., pp. 9, 10.

Chapter Four

1. Hammond, *Banks and Politics,* p. 345.

2. Carl B. Swisher, *Roger B. Taney* (New York: Macmillan Company, 1935), p. 214. According to Swisher, McLane was the one who proposed Duane for the secretaryship.

3. William J. Duane, *Narrative and Correspondence Concerning the Removal of the Deposits, and Occurrences Connected Therewith* (Philadelphia, 1838), pp. 42 and 58.

4. For an analysis of Jackson's hostility to the Second Bank and Taney's influence on Jackson's actions, see Redlich, *Molding of American Banking,* part 1, pp. 173–77.

5. *RDC,* 23d Cong., 1st sess., appendix, pp. 60–70.

6. *RDC,* 23d Cong., 1st sess., pp. 206–23.

7. Ibid., p. 147.

8. *Congressional Globe,* 27th Cong., 1st sess., p. 177. Henceforth, this source is cited as *CG.*

9. *RDC,* 23d Cong., 1st sess., pp. 81, 758, 2336. Senator Hill argued that to deny the secretary the power to contract or expand the circulation of bank paper was to claim it for the Second Bank.

10. Ibid., pp. 58–59, 4467–69, 1541. These "memorials" to Congress are scattered throughout the *Register of Debates* for 1833–34.

11. Ibid., appendix, p. 160.

12. Ibid., pp. 60, 74.

13. Ibid., appendix, p. 159; pp. 1076–78, 1713, 1797.

14. Horace Binney in the House was almost the only one who seemed to be aware of the possibility of raising the silver content of the silver dollar. But silver, he said, was the basis of the current metallic currency (since no gold was in circulation), and therefore the value of the gold dollar should be changed (ibid., p. 4663).

15. *Treasury Report,* 1835, p. 24.

16. *RDC,* 23d Cong., 1st sess., appendix, p. 160. Taney's letter to House Committee, 15 April 1834.

17. George Macesich, "Sources of Monetary Disturbances in the United States, 1834–1845," *Journal of Economic History* 20 (1960): 412, 430.

18. *RDC,* 23d Cong., 2d sess., p. 1300.

19. *RDC,* 23d Cong., 1st sess., pp. 92, 183, 3232.

20. *RDC,* 23d Cong., 2d sess., pp. 621–30, 721, 1349.

21. Ibid., p. 1437. Polk noted that such a provision "had never been imposed upon the Bank of the United States or its branches."

22. *RDC,* 24th Cong., 1st sess., p. 1763. Since the "surplus" was in the form of a treasury deposit in the depository banks, it could be provided for in the same bill. Chances are that Jackson had indicated that he would not sign a distribution bill if the "pet bank" system were jeopardized. Since the desire for some sort of distribution was almost unanimous, those who wanted genuine bank restrictions had to yield. Possibly many also felt that distributing the surplus would leave no money in the Treasury for them to be concerned about. No money would require no regulations.

23. Ibid., p. 1599. Wright stated: "We should, as far as may be in our power, so

regulate that use [of banks] as to promote, not to disturb, the great moneyed interests of the country" (p. 1612).

24. Ibid., p. 1808. Benton's dissatisfaction with what occurred here had much to do with his promotion of the Specie Circular.

25. *Treasury Report,* 1835, p. 23. This statement was made before the Deposit Act and thus indicates that Woodbury had some awareness of what was needed.

26. *Treasury Report,* 1836, p. 77.

27. Ibid., pp. 79–80.

28. *Treasury Report,* 1834, pp. 95, 108.

29. *RDC,* 23d Cong., 1st sess., p. 219.

Chapter Five

1. Historians have coined the term *pet banks* for the banks chosen to hold the government's deposits. Such a label implies that these banks were selected on the basis of political favoritism. Political compatibility with the Jackson administration probably was a determinant in selecting some of these banks. Just as important was the location of the banks in places where the volume of government revenues (from tariffs and public lands) was likely to be greatest. In view of the crusading zeal with which the hard-money Jacksonians attacked banks, the chosen banks might well have been skeptical of any favors offered by the government. In any event, the "pet" thesis has no utility in an analysis of the economic situation of the period. All the banks were fractional reserve, and this feature is the one that made the bank panic possible. See, however, Frank Otto Gatell, "Spoils of the Bank War: Political Bias in the Selection of Pet Banks," *American Historical Review* 70 (1964): 35–58. Gattell concludes that political considerations were indeed important in the selection of depository banks.

2. Congress defined "the surplus" as the cash over $5 million in the Treasury as of 1 January 1837. The amount finally determined to be "surplus" was $37.5 million, but only three-fourths of this amount, $28.1 million, was distributed to the states because "the surplus" shrank during the distribution. The money, while a de facto distribution, was called a "deposit." This nomenclature was adopted to avoid a veto from Jackson, who was opposed to any distribution. See E. G. Bourne, *The History of the Surplus Revenue of 1837* (New York, 1885), pp. 20, 21.

3. *RDC,* 24th Cong., 1st sess., p. 1649.

4. Under the Independent Treasury System, which came into existence a few years later, balances of specie did accumulate in the Treasury and subsequently had an effect when expended that corresponded to what Webster implied here.

5. Thomas Hart Benton, *Thirty Years' View,* vol. 2 (New York, 1854–1856), pp. 652–55.

6. Ibid., pp. 685, 677. Benton's report of this action is justifiably authoritative. He indicated that Woodbury and the rest of the cabinet were actually opposed to the Specie Circular. Apparently only Benton and Jackson were in favor of it.

7. A. Barton Hepburn, *A History of Currency in the United States* (New York: MacMillan, 1924), p. 122.

8. The stock of money was between $200 million and $300 million. The Treasury Department in 1840 estimated the total of manufactured products to be $1,006 million. Thus an income estimate of $1,000 million is conservative.

9. I am indebted to Milton Friedman for this observation via a marginal comment on an early draft of this analysis in 1959.

10. *Treasury Report,* 1836, p. 86.

11. Ibid., p. 81.

12. Bourne, *History of the Surplus;* R. C. McGrane, *The Panic of 1837* (Chicago: University of Chicago Press, 1924); and Bray Hammond, *Banks and Politics,* are just a few of the works that have argued this way.

13. *Treasury Report,* 1836, p. 81. Woodbury reported later that $25.13 million had been transferred from bank to bank by his orders between 1 July 1836 and 1 January 1837 in order to make the distribution smooth. If a mere transfer of funds could have caused a crisis, the crisis surely would have occurred in late 1836, not in the middle of 1837.

14. Ibid., pp. 77–78. This statement was made before the actual distribution.

15. Quoted in Benton, *Thirty Years' View,* vol. 2, p. 11.

16. *RDC,* 24th Cong., 1st sess., pp. 3259–61.

17. Ibid., pp. 27, 36, 37.

18. *Treasury Report to Special Session,* 1837, p. 17. This report by the secretary was in addition to his regular report at the end of the year.

19. This amount is the sum of the negative values in the third column of table 5.4. If either Mississippi or Louisiana is included in the South, the southern surplus states would also have covered the amount due the southern deficit states.

20. National Archives and Records Service, Record Group No. 56, *Letters on State Deposits* (27 June 1836 to 11 September 1837) (Washington, D.C.). These data were also published as U.S. Congress, 25th Cong., 1st sess., House Document No. 30. (I am indebted to Peter Temin for calling my attention to this latter document.)

21. *Treasury Report,* 1836, p. 78, and *Treasury Report,* 1837, p. 73. These amounts are losses from all *three* installments of the distribution and from ordinary fiscal expenditures.

22. *Treasury Report,* 1836, p. 14.

23. House Document No. 30, p. 78.

24. *Treasury Report to Special Session,* 1837, p. 17.

25. Specie in banks increased from $30 million in May 1837 to $35 million in May 1838. (See *Treasury Report,* 1838, exhibit F, pp. 41–44.)

26. Evidence of this reaction was seen in the congressional debates, already mentioned, which attempted to prescribe reserve requirements.

27. *Treasury Report to Special Session,* 1837, p. 16.

28. *Treasury Report,* 1835, p. 23.

29. For a contrary opinion see Harry N. Scheiber, "The Pet Banks in Jacksonian Politics and Finance, 1833–41," *Journal of Economic History* 23 (1963): 196–214. For a comprehensive supporting opinion, see Peter Temin, *The Jacksonian Economy* (New York: W. W. Norton, 1969), pp. 120–28.

30. Money in the specie-money ratio is the stock of bank-issued currency and deposits. A change in the specie-money ratio at this time had approximately the same effects that a change in the currency-deposit ratio would have today, because specie was legal tender then as central-bank currency is now.

31. Temin, *The Jacksonian Economy,* pp. 172–73. Gold also played a significant role, especially after the devaluation of 1834. See chap. 4.

32. Ibid., p. 81.
33. Ibid., p. 135.
34. Ibid., p. 146.
35. Temin, *The Jacksonian Economy,* pp. 81 and 194.
36. Ibid., p. 69.

Chapter Six

1. *Treasury Report,* 1838, p. 45, Exhibit G. Woodbury reported that $8.5 million of this amount came between April and July of 1838.

2. Ibid., pp. 1–5.

3. For a fuller discussion of economic conditions, see Temin, *Jacksonian Economy,* pp. 148–71.

4. *RDC,* 23d Cong., 1st sess., p. 4641.

5. See William M. Gouge, *A Short History of Paper Money and Banking in the United States* (Philadelphia, 1833). The hard-money men, unlike Gordon, favored the scheme because they honestly wished the federal government to operate independently of all banks.

6. The Democrats passed an independent treasury act in 1840, the last gesture of a lame-duck administration. The Whigs repealed this act in the summer of 1841. The enduring Independent Treasury Act did not pass until 1846.

7. *Congressional Globe,* 26th Cong., 1st sess., p. 495 (hereafter cited as *CG*).

8. In his message to the special session Tyler had indicated that he would favor some kind of national bank scheme (*CG,* 27th Cong., 1st sess., p. 6).

9. Ibid., appendix, p. 6.

10. "Stability" as an ideal for government policy was not confined to the Whigs. Woodbury frequently used the word, as did almost every other Treasury secretary before the Civil War.

11. Section 16 of the bill provoked a great deal of opposition from the states'-rights group in Congress. The intent of this section was that Congress might establish a branch of the bank in any state, whether that state wanted it or not. The Virginia delegation, of which Tyler had been a part, particularly objected to it.

12. Benton, *Thirty Years' View,* vol. 2, p. 319.

13. Ibid., p. 343. William M. Gouge wrote disgustedly: "The President has signed the bill to repeal the 'Sub-Treasury act' and *vetoed* the bill to incorporate a fiscal bank. The result is THE REVIVAL OF THE PET BANK SYSTEM—the *worst* of all possible systems" (*Journal of Banking* 1:4 [1841]: 59).

14. Benton, *Thirty Years' View,* vol. 2, p. 345. Calhoun, although a South Carolinian, was apparently the ringleader of this group. Benton remarked that Calhoun "had that ascendancy over Mr. Tyler which it is the prerogative of genius to have over inferior minds."

15. Ibid., p. 350.

16. Webster was involved in negotiating what became the Webster-Ashburton Treaty. When this work was finished, he also resigned and Calhoun became secretary of state.

17. Ibid., p. 354.
18. Ibid., p. 343.
19. *Treasury Report,* 1841, p. 18.
20. U.S. Congress, 27th Cong., 2d sess., *Report to Congress on a Board of Exchequer,* Sen. Doc. No. 18, 1841, p. 8.
21. Ibid., pp. 10, 13.
22. Benton, *Thirty Years' View,* vol. 2, p. 395.
23. Ibid., p. 33.
24. *CG,* 26th Cong., 1st sess., appendix, p. 305.
25. An amendment to the treasury note bill was offered in the House that would have prohibited the secretary from engaging in this practice, but it failed to pass, 69 to 90 (*CG,* 26th Cong., 1st sess., p. 293). Congressmen apparently felt that such an inflationary effect at this time (1840) would be helpful.
26. U.S. Congress, 26th Cong., 1st Sess., Sen. Doc. No. 359, vol. 6, 25 March 1840; and Sen. Doc. No. 476, vol. 7, 19 May 1840. Woodbury's reply to the March request was unenlightening and undetailed, so another request was made in May.
27. U.S. Congress, 26th Cong., 1st sess., Sen. Doc. No. 476, vol. 7, p. 4.
28. Ibid., p. 6.
29. Ibid., table A, p. 9.
30. Ibid., pp. 21–22.
31. Ibid., p. 89. "Reflux" was a common expression at the time. It referred to the redemption or clearing of a bank's notes in specie or its equivalent to individuals or other banks.
32. *CG,* 26th Cong., 2d sess., p. 227.
33. *CG,* 25th Cong., 2d sess., p. 386.
34. John J. Knox, *United States Notes,* 2d ed. rev. (New York: Charles Scribner's Sons, 1885), pp. 52–62.
35. *CG,* 29th Cong., 2d sess., p. 30. Many other congressmen observed that the note authorizations encouraged the Treasury to engage in monetary management.
36. *CG,* 29th Cong., 1st sess., p. 1115.
37. *CG,* 35th Cong., 1st sess., pp. 96, 67. At the same time, he piously declared that the issue of treasury notes was not a "monetary measure."
38. Ibid., p. 75. Again, congressmen observed that issues of treasury notes would make the Treasury a quasi-bank. See ibid., p. 100, for the remarks of Senator Preston King of New York.
39. *Treasury Report,* 1857, p. 17.
40. *CG,* 35th Cong., 1st sess., p. 94.
41. Ibid., appendix, p. 533.
42. See James Polk, *The Diary of a President, 1845–1849,* ed. Allen Nevins (New York: Longmans, Green, 1929), pp. xix and 26.
43. *CG,* 29th Cong., 1st sess., appendix, p. 13; 29th Cong., 2d sess., appendix, p. 10.
44. *CG,* 29th Cong., 1st sess., appendix, p. 13. "A just and permanent settlement" referred to the resolution of monetary policy Walker hoped would be forthcoming through the policies that the Independent Treasury would foster.
45. To a real hard-money man, Walker's ideas were unacceptably "soft." See *CG,*

29th Cong., 1st sess., p. 820, for a speech by Thomas Hart Benton, who despised Walker.

46. *Treasury Report,* 1848, pp. 28–29. Also *CG,* 30th Cong., 1st sess., p. 901.

47. *CG,* 30th Cong., 2d sess., p. 355.

48. Ibid.

49. *Treasury Report,* 1848, p. 24.

50. One Whig secretary, George Bibb, suggested in 1844 a top-executive open-market committee composed of the chief justice of the Supreme Court, the secretaries of state and the Treasury, and the attorney general, who would have decided when and at what prices debt should be repurchased. Nothing came of his proposal.

51. *CG,* 32d Cong., 2d sess., appendix, p. 350.

52. *Dictionary of American Biography,* vol. 8, pp. 60–61.

53. *CG,* 33d Cong., 1st sess., appendix, p. 2.

54. Ibid.

55. Margaret G. Myers, *The New York Money Market,* vol. 1 (New York: Columbia University Press, 1931), pp. 140–41.

56. *CG,* 33d Cong., 2d sess., appendix, pp. 6–9.

57. *CG,* 34th Cong., 1st sess., appendix, p. 12.

58. *Treasury Report,* 1854, p. 282.

59. *CG,* 33d Cong., 1st sess., appendix, p. 3.

60. *CG,* 34th Cong., 1st sess., appendix, p. 16.

61. Judge George Bibb to Guthrie, July 1854, Guthrie Papers, Box 17, Filson Club, Louisville, Kentucky.

62. *Treasury Report,* 1856, p. 31.

63. *Treasury Report,* 1857, p. 11.

64. Ibid., pp. 17, 9. Cobb to J. Glancy Jones, chairman of the House Committee on Ways and Means, 8 December 1857.

65. Hammond has shown that this principle was important in the fight against the Second Bank of the United States. See *Banks and Politics,* pp. 371, 381, and passim.

Chapter Seven

1. Hepburn, *History of Currency,* p. 180.

2. Hugh Rockoff, "The Free Banking Era: A Reexamination," *Journal of Money, Credit, and Banking* 6 (1974): 151, 143.

3. David Kinley, *The Independent Treasury of the United States* (New York: Thomas Y. Crowell, 1893), pp. 160–61.

4. These alternatives are very clearly discussed and evaluated in Bray Hammond, "The North's Empty Purse," *American Historical Review* 67 (1961): 1–18.

5. Some of the sources for information on the income tax are George S. Boutwell, *A Manual of the Direct and Excise Tax System of the United States* (Boston, 1863 and 1864) and *The Tax Payer's Manual* (Boston, 1865); C. N. Emerson, *Emerson's Internal Revenue Guide* (Springfield, Mass., 1866); and H. E. Smith, *The United States Federal Internal Tax History from 1861 to 1871* (Boston: Houghton Mifflin, 1914). These sources are given in Anna J. Schwartz, "Gross Dividend and Interest Payments

by Corporations at Selected Dates in the Nineteenth Century," *Trends in the American Economy in the Nineteenth Century,* Studies in Income and Wealth, vol. 24, National Bureau of Economic Research (Princeton, N.J.: Princeton University Press, 1960), p. 407, n. 1.

6. Hepburn, *History of Currency,* pp. 306–12.

7. The total value of notes issued could not be greater than 90 percent of the par or market value of the securities, whichever was lower.

8. James K. Kindahl, "Economic Factors in Specie Resumption: The United States, 1865–79," *Journal of Political Economy* 69 (1961): 30–48.

9. James M. Blaine, *Twenty Years of Congress* (Norwich, Conn.: Henry Bill Publishing Co., 1886), p. 320.

10. Bank notes and deposits increased by $117 million, but government currency declined by $252 million. A large part of government currency was held by banks as reserves. Since the data on government currency are much better than the data on bank deposits, such a large decline in currency indicates a strong presumption that net increases in bank obligations could have occurred only if the banks had held "excess" reserves in 1865 and then let those reserves run down as they issued their own currency (national bank notes and deposits). An excellent treatise on the political-monetary developments of this period is Robert P. Sharkey, *Money, Class, and Party* (Baltimore, Md.: Johns Hopkins University Press, 1959). Sharkey errs when he assays the decrease in the currency at "only $45 million" and fails to note that the decrease in the total money stock was much greater.

11. Blaine, *Twenty Years of Congress,* p. 328.

12. *Congressional Record,* 43d Cong., 1st sess., p. 704 (hereafter cited as *CR*).

13. *Dictionary of American Biography,* vol. 2, pp. 489–90.

14. The complete history of this bizarre episode is contained in U.S. Congress, 41st Cong., 2d sess., *The Gold Panic Investigation,* House Report No. 31, by the Committee on Banking and Currency, James A. Garfield, Chairman. See pp. 1–4. See also L. Wimmer, "The Gold Crisis of 1869," *Explorations in Economic History* 12 (1975): 105–22.

15. *The Gold Panic Investigation,* pp. 19 and 342–53.

16. Ibid., pp. 468–69.

17. Ibid., p. 470.

18. *CG,* 38th Cong., 2d sess., appendix, p. 1358.

19. *Report of the Comptroller of the Currency,* 1868, House Exec. Doc. No. 4, 40th Cong., 3d sess., p. iii.

20. *Treasury Report,* 1865, p. x; *Report of the Comptroller,* 1865, House Exec. Doc. No. 4, 39th Cong., 1st sess., p. 65.

21. Hepburn, *History of Currency,* pp. 174 and 329. See also Hammond, *Banks and Politics,* pp. 539 and 545–46. See also note 32 below.

22. *Treasury Report,* 1865, pp. 52–54.

23. *Report of the Comptroller,* 1866, p. xi. Also, *Treasury Report,* 1868. See also Redlich, *Molding of American Banking,* part 2. Redlich argues that the so-called National Bank Act was really a national currency act, which originally would have promoted a national currency by the existing state banks. The bill that Secretary Chase foresaw would have left the chartering of such banks with the states. This idea gave

way in the final bill to national chartering, but with preference given to existing state institutions (pp. 101–2 and 118).

24. *Report of the Comptroller,* 1867, 40th Cong., 2d sess., House Exec. Doc. No. 4, p. 11. See also *Treasury Report,* 1865, p. 4.

25. See, for example, *CG,* 41st Cong., 2d sess., appendix, pp. 525–28, in which E. C. Ingersoll of Illinois discussed not only currency per capita, but also currency per acre of territory in which it was issued. He also compared per capita currency amounts in the United States with those of France and Germany and found the U.S. quantities relatively deficient.

26. *CG,* 41st Cong., 2d sess., p. 4949. Sentiment in the Senate was to hold the total stock of currency constant. It was said that the Senate would not pass a bill that would increase the currency, and the House would not allow a bill to pass that would contract it (ibid., p. 4950).

27. Ibid., p. 4950.

28. Ibid., p. 543.

29. Ibid., p. 544.

30. Congressmen correctly approximated the average national bank reserve requirement at 20 percent. Therefore, the anticipated increase of $45 million in national bank notes would require $9 million of United States notes as reserves in national banks.

31. Ibid., p. 5303. Also appendix, p. 700.

32. The reason for the paucity of national banks in the South has never been satisfactorily explained. An hypothesis that looks more and more appealing, and one that is suggested by the large volume of publicity it received at the time, stems from the relationship between state usury laws and the payment of interest on deposits. By a provision of the National Bank Act, state regulations governed maximum rates of interest that national banks could pay and receive. State usury laws differed from state to state. Some New England states had no maxima, while in many southern states the maximum rate was only 6 percent. As it was, about two-thirds of the national banks paid interest on deposits. In 1870, 1,064 national banks paid $6.5 million, while 540 paid no interest (*Report of the Comptroller,* 1870, p. 28). To compete for reserve funds many national banks felt compelled to pay interest on deposits. If the maximum rates they could charge were regulated in such a way that the spread between what they could charge for loans and what they paid on deposits was not profitable, they could not continue issuing notes and they had little reason to become or remain national banks. (See *Report of the Comptroller,* 1872, pp. 89–90.)

33. "Country" national bank balances in New York national banks increased from $50 million to $63 million, and other reserve city national bank balances with New York national banks increased from $24 million to $31 million.

34. *Treasury Report,* 1872, pp. xix–xxii. He discussed bank-induced inflation and depression. He recognized the inelasticity of commercial bank-note issues. However, he did not attribute the currency inelasticities to the legal restrictions imposed by the National Bank Act.

35. Ibid., p. xxii.

36. *Treasury Report,* 1874, pp. 26–30. The act of 25 February 1862 pledged re-

purchase of at least 1 percent per year of the outstanding interest-bearing debt to be held as an interest-earning asset by the Treasury Department.

37. U.S. Congress, 42d Cong., 3d sess., *Report to the Committee on Banking and Currency on the Increased Issue of Legal Tender Notes,* House Exec. Doc. No. 42, December 1872.

38. U.S. Congress, 42d Cong., 3d sess., *Senate Report* No. 275, 1872, pp. 1–5.

39. *Report on the Increased Issue of Legal Tender Notes,* pp. 1 and 2. (See also *CR,* 43rd Cong., 1st sess., p. 704.) McCulloch had set the precedent Boutwell referred to by reissuing notes several times between 1866 and 1868. "In answer to remonstrance against this practice," wrote James G. Blaine, "the Secretary maintained that the authority . . . [was] within his discretion. This was unquestionably the law of the case" (Blaine, *Twenty Years of Congress,* p. 329).

40. *Senate Report* No. 275, pp. 8–10. The minority consisted of G. W. Wright of Iowa and T. W. Ferry of Michigan. Ferry, especially, was a Republican greenbacker who treated the idea of a metallic standard cavalierly. Their opinion would have had more substance if applied specifically to those periods when Congress was not in session, especially during the fall.

41. Eugene M. Lerner, "The Monetary and Fiscal Programs of the Confederate Government, 1861–65," *Journal of Political Economy* 62 (1954): 506–22; "Money, Prices, and Wages in the Confederacy, 1861–65," *Journal of Political Economy* 63 (1955): 20–40; "Inflation in the Confederacy, 1861–65," in *Studies in the Quantity Theory of Money,* ed. Milton Friedman (Chicago: University of Chicago Press, 1956), pp. 163–75.

42. John M. Godfrey, *Monetary Expansion in the Confederacy* (New York: New York Times Co., Arno Press, 1978).

43. Ibid., pp. 54–58.

44. Ibid., p. 122.

45. Ibid., pp. 118–19.

46. Ibid., p. 123.

47. Ibid., p. 14.

Chapter Eight

1. *Dictionary of American Biography,* vol. 15, p. 578.

2. *Treasury Report,* 1878, p. xi.

3. *Report of the Comptroller,* 1874, House Exec. Doc. No. 2, p. 159.

4. *Treasury Report,* 1872, p. xx.

5. *Treasury Report,* 1873, pp. xv–xvi. By "inflation," Richardson did not mean rising prices but a price level that was still too high to allow convertibility of greenbacks into gold at the prewar parity.

6. Ibid., pp. xii–xx, xxx.

7. Ibid., pp. 95 and 111. This observation emphasizes that United States notes were reserves of the national banks and served to redeem national bank notes. The inability of some national banks in New York City to pay out United States notes for national bank notes triggered the panic.

8. *CR,* 43d Cong., 1st sess., p. 700.

9. Ibid., appendix, pp. 17–19.

10. Ibid., appendix, pp. 20–22. David Mellish, a Republican congressman from New York, had substantially the same opinion as Boutwell on the morality of changes in the price level. His policy ideal, however, waived resumption in favor of a fixed stock of $800 million in United States notes (ibid., pp. 1097–1103).

11. See ibid., pp. 974–75, for a statement by Thomas Bayard of Delaware.

12. Hepburn, *History of Currency,* p. 313.

13. *CR,* 43d Cong., 1st sess., pp. 13–15. The differences in per capita currency holdings between, say, New England and the South were startling—approximately $30 per person in New England to $3 per person in the South. Either prices in the South were much lower or a sizable amount of real income in the South was exchanged by truck and barter.

14. Ibid., p. 455.

15. Ibid., p. 165.

16. See Irwin Unger, *The Greenback Era* (Princeton, N.J.: Princeton University Press, 1964), pp. 251–54, for a discussion of the political climate in which the Resumption Act was wrought. The abrupt about-face from monetary indulgence to apparent monetary austerity still presents some puzzles.

17. Blaine, *Twenty Years of Congress,* pp. 563–65.

18. See *Report of the Comptroller,* 1874, House Exec. Doc. No. 2, pp. 123–33. Even if the states that were entitled to additional notes did not want their shares, provision still had to be made to redistribute the notes in case these states ultimately called for them. Redistribution of note allocations would also provoke other problems.

19. *CR,* 43d Cong., 2d sess., p. 188.

20. Ibid. This passage is followed by the provision that states the date (1 January 1879) for redemption of United States notes in coin. Since national bank notes were convertible by law into United States notes, the date for resumption also applied to coin redemption of national bank notes.

21. Unger, *Greenback Era,* p. 253.

22. *CR,* 43d Cong., 2d sess., p. 195.

23. Ibid., p. 196. Additional statements by Schurz and others at this point again made clear congressional antipathy to the use of the "reserve" of United States notes issued at the discretion of the secretary of the Treasury.

24. Ibid., p. 204.

25. This result would have been contingent on the ability of the national banks to attract United States notes to be used as reserves—not an impossible task since banks in many states were allowed to pay interest on deposits.

26. By this time deposit banking was so well developed that new bank deposits might have taken up the slack.

27. See Unger, *Greenback Era,* p. 264. Unger notes briefly the significance of the 80 percent clause and correctly assesses its impact.

28. United States notes outstanding are not shown in the table. They were $383 million in early 1875 and were fixed at $346.7 million on 31 May 1878. They were reduced by $36 million during this interval. The working of the formula in the Resumption Act thus resulted in a *decrease* in United States notes and an approximately equal *decrease* in national bank notes.

29. *CR,* 43d Cong., 2d sess., pp. 206–8.

30. Ibid., p. 197.

31. True free banking meant not only abolition of the statutory limitations and other restrictions on national bank-note issue but also the relaxation of all other impediments to banking as a free enterprise. I am indebted to the late Bray Hammond for calling my attention to the two uses of the expression.

32. *Treasury Report,* 1877, pp. xv–xx.

33. U.S. Congress, 44th Cong., 2d sess., *Report and Hearings of the Silver Commission,* Senate Report No. 703, 1877.

34. Ibid., p. 1.

35. Ibid., pp. 127 and 133. The verb *repealed* implied "amended so as to include silver."

36. Ibid., pp. 134–38. Boutwell wanted an international conference that would reestablish silver as a universal legal tender and thereby relieve the United States from the burden of absorbing the world's silver.

37. Ibid., pp. 155–56 (their italics).

38. Ibid., pp. 159–60.

39. Ibid., pp. 129–31. The proposed silver dollar of 412.5 grains was already at a 3 percent discount in gold. The silver revaluation suggested by these three men would have promoted an additional 3 percent discrepancy, even though their ratio of 15.5 to 1 was more realistic in the rest of the world.

40. Ibid., pp. 131–33.

41. Kindahl, "Economic Factors," p. 47. Hepburn, while he specifically mentioned the Silver Commission, neither discussed the recommendations for devaluation nor pointed out the pressure for silver remonetization as a political requirement for resumption.

42. *Treasury Report,* 1877, p. xxxiv.

43. Kindahl estimated that the money stock in the hands of the public declined from $1,703 million to $1,557 million (9 percent) between 1875 and 1878, while the index of wholesale prices fell from 130 in 1874 to 99 in 1878 ("Economic Factors," p. 40).

44. Hepburn, *History of Currency,* p. 238.

45. Hindsight suggests that the gold dollar should have been devalued to accommodate the market price of gold no later than 1869 or 1870, by which time the price level and the nominal price of gold had declined to the point where they were only 12 to 15 percent higher than their 1860 values. Such a move would not have seriously compromised any moral codes of polity.

46. The speech in early 1874 by George Boutwell, who had returned to a seat in the United States Senate after his term as secretary of the Treasury, reflects the norm of constancy in the money stock. "We have a citadel," he said, by which he meant a majority that could successfully resist the contractionists on the one hand and the inflationists on the other, "and we had better keep in it. If we are driven out, we shall then only be in the position which the Senator from Missouri [Carl Schurz] advises us voluntarily to accept" (*CR,* 43d Cong., 1st sess., appendix, p. 27). Schurz had suggested to Boutwell that the true way to prevent inflation was to go for contraction.

47. The three secretaries were Benjamin Bristow, Lot Morrill, and John Sherman, all of whom had been congressmen.

48. Friedman and Schwartz, *Monetary History,* p. 82. Friedman and Schwartz had the company of Senator Allen Thurman of Ohio, who made the same observation in 1874. (See above, p. 112.)

Chapter Nine

1. For example, Adam Smith, *Wealth of Nations,* pp. 307–9. Also Henry Thornton, *The Paper Credit of Great Britain,* ed. F. A. von Hayek (New York: Rinehart, 1939), p. 189.

2. An exception is Redlich, *Molding of American Banking,* part 2, p. 89. He observed without further elaboration or explanation that the prejudices prohibiting small notes were "as old as they were incorrect."

3. Neil Carothers, *Fractional Currency* (New York: Reprints of Economic Classics, Augustus M. Kelley, 1967), p. 76.

4. Charles F. Dunbar, *The Theory and History of Banking* (New York: C. P. Putnam's Sons, 1922), pp. 62–63.

5. Davis R. Dewey, *State Banking before the Civil War,* National Monetary Commission, Sen. Doc. No. 581, 61st Cong., 2d sess. (1910), p. 64.

6. Lloyd W. Mints, *History of Banking Theory* (Chicago: University of Chicago Press, 1945), p. 148.

7. See Dewey, *State Banking,* pp. 65 and passim. See also Hepburn, *History of Currency,* pp. 84, 90, 94, 163, 181, 308.

8. Smith, *Wealth of Nations,* p. 308.

9. Henry Thornton, *Paper Credit,* p. 189.

10. Smith, *Wealth of Nations,* p. 306, note.

11. Jacob Viner, *Studies in the Theory of International Trade* (New York: Harper and Brothers, 1937) p. 179, and Ricardo, *Economic Essays,* p. 213.

12. Viner, *Studies,* p. 182.

13. Knox, *United States Notes,* pp. 37–38.

14. Hepburn, *History of Currency,* p. 89. [My emphasis.]

15. *ASPF* 3. See also chap. 2.

16. Hepburn, *History of Currency,* p. 163. Hepburn's use of the word *barter* is revealing. Silver was undervalued at the mint and therefore limited in its currency uses during this period. Without bank-issued small notes, many transactions undoubtedly were barter.

17. Dewey, *State Banking,* pp. 66–83, and Hepburn, *History of Currency,* pp. 166–67.

18. A few writers recognized this truth. See Richard Hildreth, *Banks, Banking, and Paper Currencies* (1840), reprinted by Greenwood Press (1968).

19. Carothers, *Fractional Currency,* pp. 76–78. A common device was to cut the half dollar into four more-or-less equal pieces (p. 81).

20. Ibid., p. 92.

21. Ibid., pp. 110–11.

22. Ibid., p. 160. This example should have proven beyond all doubt that the paper-money inflation and subsequent disappearance of metallic currency came first, and that private issues of tokens and script were the private sector's solution to the

dearth of fractional money. Knox also reported that premiums of 10 to 12 percent over its commodity value were offered for small amounts of silver coin "by businessmen who desired it for convenience in making change" (Knox, *United States Notes,* p. 100).

23. Hepburn, *History of Currency,* p. 308.

24. *Report of the Comptroller of the Currency,* 1872, House Exec. Doc. No. 1562, pp. 96–97. The Alabama notes were in five denominations which read: "The State of Alabama: Receivable as ________ dollars in payment of all dues to the State. Montgomery, May 1, 1867." They were signed by the governor and the comptroller of public accounts.

25. *Report of the Comptroller,* 1873, House Exec. Doc. No. 1603, p. 109.

26. Ibid.

27. House of Representatives, 43d Cong., 1st sess., *Miscellaneous Document* No. 48, 19 December 1873, pp. 1–2.

28. *Report of the Treasurer,* 1874, House Exec. Doc. No. 1641, p. 353.

29. Charles Moran, *Money, Currencies, and Banking* (New York, 1875), p. 4.

30. Ibid., p. 39. While Moran was correct in his evaluation of denominational factors, he was, as an antibullionist, wrong in his assessment of quantitative factors. His argument demonstrates how the quantity of the total money stock can get mixed up with quantities of specific denominations. The former can be overabundant, while specific denominations can be distressingly short—for example, small denominations in 1862 during the first deluge of greenbacks.

31. Richard Selden, "Monetary Velocity in the United States," in *Studies in the Quantity Theory of Money,* ed. Milton Friedman (Chicago: University of Chicago Press, 1956), p. 189 and passim. Also Clark Warburton, "The Secular Trend in Monetary Velocity," *Quarterly Journal of Economics* 63 (1949): 68–91; reprinted in Clark Warburton, *Depression, Inflation, and Monetary Policy* (Baltimore, Md.: Johns Hopkins University Press, 1966), pp. 199–209. Selden's data sources for his V-39 velocity values are the same as those for his V-27 estimates. These latter were taken from Warburton's study and used income data compiled by Robert F. Martin, *National Income in the United States, 1799–1938,* National Industrial Conference Board (New York, 1939). (Warburton, *Depression, Inflation, and Monetary Policy,* p. 201, n. 3.)

32. Friedman and Schwartz, *Monetary History.* See also Warburton, *Depression, Inflation, and Monetary Policy,* p. 212.

33. Friedman and Schwartz treat at length the phenomenon of secular change in velocity. Their data show a slight downward trend from 1900 to 1914, a rough constancy from 1914 to 1929, a sharp decline in the early thirties followed by a rise to 1941, another sharp decline to 1946, and then a constant rise to 1960 (pp. 136, 197, 494, 641). The post–World War II figures, they note, show a "clear upward trend" (p. 643). Later studies on velocity measurement indicate that the upward trend has continued through the sixties and into the seventies and eighties. Therefore no clear-cut *secular* decline appears in the twentieth century, the short-run effects of the depression and World War II notwithstanding.

34. Let M be the stock of money, P the price index value for goods and services exchanged for money, R the volume of goods and services exchanged for money, r the volume of goods and services bartered or exchanged by means of unaccounted money, V_R' apparent velocity, and V_R real velocity. Then apparent velocity is

$V_R' = (PR + Pr)/M$, while real velocity is $V_R = PR/M$. Obviously, $V_R' > V_R$. But over time, as monetary transactions replace barter, PR will come to include the value of goods and services formerly valued as Pr, and $V_R' \rightarrow V_R$ as $Pr \rightarrow 0$.

35. Warburton, *Depression, Inflation, and Monetary Policy,* pp. 208–10.

36. The reliability of Martin's estimates of income is subject to some serious doubts. Aside from questionable methods and some obviously spurious results, he gives no indication of how much nonmonetary income is included in his estimates. In all fairness, it was not his intention to do so. Therefore his income estimates are for the *value* of that income but do not give any indication of how much of this income was exchanged for money. Selden unaccountably reports that Martin's estimates (not identified by name, but just by reference to Warburton) exclude nonmonetary income ("Monetary Velocity," p. 244), but Martin does not make any such adjustment. His estimates are simply projections of production figures from the census of manufacturers multiplied by price relatives. They say nothing at all about the volume of monetary transactions.

37. Fractional currency is not included here. The fractional paper currency in existence from 1862 to 1876, although explicitly recorded in treasurers' reports, is subject to extraordinary error due to unaccounted losses and destructions, such as the amount destroyed in the great Chicago fire. After 1877 metallic fractional currency replaced the paper currency of the earlier years. The totals of this latter coinage are not readily calculable because of the reimportations after 1876 of millions of United States coins that had been exported in 1861 and 1862. No serious fractional currency problems appeared after resumption. Also, these data include neither the very largest denominations ($100 and over) nor state and national bank deposits. However, the denominations listed in the table contain about 90 percent of the high-powered money stock.

38. The price data are from Warren and Pearson's Wholesale Price Index (1910–1914 = 100). This index is very sensitive, so it may exaggerate somewhat the fluctuations in the general price level.

39. The data for 1879 are counted as the end values for the first period and as the beginning values for the second period.

40. Growth of real output and the behavior of velocity do not lend themselves to accurate measurement before 1890. See Friedman and Schwartz, *Monetary History,* pp. 36–44, 87, and passim.

41. Richard Sylla argues that note and deposit issues by private (unincorporated) banks provided another significant core of unaccountable moneys. This contention is both complementary to and compatible with the analysis that refers to scrip, barter, and trade credit. See Richard Sylla, "Forgotten Men of Money: Private Bankers in Early U.S. History," *Journal of Economic History* 36 (1976): 173–88.

Chapter Ten

1. Wesley C. Mitchell, *A History of the Greenbacks* (Chicago: University of Chicago Press, 1903).

2. Elbridge G. Spaulding, *History of the Legal Tender Paper Money Issued during the Great Rebellion being a Loan without Interest and a National Currency* (Westport,

Conn.: Greenwood Press, 1971, pp. 8–9; first published, Buffalo, N.Y.: Express Printing Co., 1869).

3. Ibid., pp. 8–9.

4. Ibid., pp. 9–10.

5. Ibid., pp. 11–12.

6. Ibid., p. 14.

7. Ibid., pp. 29–31.

8. Mitchell, *History of the Greenbacks,* p. 49.

9. Spaulding, *History,* p. 35.

10. Ibid., p. 107; Mitchell, *History of the Greenbacks,* p. 54.

11. Don C. Barrett, "The Supposed Necessity of Legal Tender Paper," *Quarterly Journal of Economic History,* 16 (May 1902): 326.

12. Spaulding, pp. 45–46.

13. Barrett noted that Chase was one of Lincoln's chief rivals for the presidency, and was appointed to the cabinet in the interests of preserving party unity. Chase was "spurred on by his own notion that the administration in general would fare better in his hands than in the President's." In 1868 he coveted the *Democratic* nomination for president, even though Lincoln had appointed him Chief Justice of the Supreme Court in 1864. All accounts agree that Chase's political ambition had no limit (Barrett, "Supposed Necessity," p. 333).

14. Ibid., p. 347.

15. Spaulding, *History,* p. 175.

16. Barrett, "Supposed Necessity," pp. 330–32.

17. Spaulding, *History,* pp. 59, 65.

18. Simon Newcomb, *Examination of Our Financial Policy during the Southern Rebellion* (New York: Greenwood Press, 1969, p. 161; first published, New York: D. Appleton Co., 1865).

19. Barrett, "Supposed Necessity," pp. 349–53; Mitchell, *History of the Greenbacks,* p. 73.

20. Spaulding, *History,* appendix, pp. 24–25. Letter to Hugh McCulloch, 9 December 1868. Also pp. 103 and 202–3.

21. Irwin Unger, *The Greenback Era* (Princeton: Princeton University Press, 1964), p. 175; Bernard H. Siegan, *The Supreme Court's Constitution* (New Brunswick, N.J.: Transaction Books, 1987), p. 34.

22. Hugh McCulloch, *Men and Measures of Half a Century* (New York: Charles Scribner's Sons, 1900), p. 180. See also Unger, *Greenback Era,* p. 175.

23. Arthur Kemp, *The Legal Qualities of Money* (New York: Pageant Press, 1956), chap. 5. See also Unger, *Greenback Era,* p. 174.

24. S. P. Breckenridge, *Legal Tender* (New York: Greenwood Press, 1969), pp. 128–29 (first published, Chicago: University of Chicago Press, 1903); A. Barton Hepburn, *A History of Currency in the United States,* rev. ed. (New York: Macmillan, 1924), pp. 275–80. Also Siegan, *Supreme Court's Constitution,* pp. 30–32.

25. Unger, *Greenback Era,* p. 175.

26. Unger, *Greenback Era,* pp. 177–78; McCulloch, *Men and Measures,* p. 173.

27. Gerald T. Dunne, *Monetary Decisions of the Supreme Court* (New Brunswick: Rutgers University Press, 1960), pp. 77–81; Breckenridge, *Legal Tender,* pp. 131–32; Siegan, *Supreme Court's Constitution,* pp. 32–34.

28. Unger, *Greenback Era,* p. 175.

29. Ibid., p. 178.

30. George Boutwell, *Why I Am a Republican* (Philadelphia: W. S. Fortescue & Co., 1884), p. 71.

31. Spaulding, *History,* p. 65.

32. Newcomb, *Examination,* pp. 94, 180.

33. McCulloch, *Men and Measures,* p. 178.

34. Boutwell, *Why I Am a Republican,* pp. 70–74.

35. Hepburn, *History of Currency,* p. 266.

36. Ibid., pp. 261–62.

37. *Juilliard* v. *Greenman,* 110 U.S. 421 (1884), my emphasis.

38. Ibid.

39. Alva R. Hunt, *A Treatise on the Law of Tender, and Bringing Money into Court* (St. Paul: Frank P. Dufresne, 1903): 137.

40. Siegan, *Supreme Court's Constitution,* pp. 21–28.

41. McCulloch, *Men and Measures,* pp. 178–79.

42. Kemp, *Legal Qualities of Money,* pp. 25–32.

43. William Brough, *The Natural Law of Money* (New York: Greenwood Press, 1969): 135; first published, New York: G. P. Putnam's Sons, 1896.

44. James Bradley Thayer, "Legal Tender," *Harvard Law Review* 1:73 (1887–88): 73–97.

45. Ibid., pp. 90–97.

46. Hunt, *Treatise,* pp. 61–62.

47. Lawrence H. White, *Competition and Currency* (New York: New York University Press, 1989), p. 178.

48. Hunt, *Treatise,* p. 63.

49. Ibid., p. 105. The case was *Brown* v. *Welch,* 26 Ind. 116.

50. Ibid., p. 114.

51. Adam Smith, *The Wealth of Nations* (New York: Random House, 1937 [1776; 5th ed. 1789]), pp. 651, 682.

52. Ibid., pp. 883, 885.

53. Ibid., pp. 40–46.

54. Breckenridge, *Legal Tender,* pp. 46–48.

55. Roy W. Jastram, *Silver, the Restless Metal* (New York: John Wiley and Sons, 1981), p. 9.

56. Breckenridge, *Legal Tender,* p. 155.

57. Timberlake, *Gold, Greenbacks, and the Constitution,* pp. 6–11.

58. Brough, *Natural Law of Money,* pp. 34–35.

Chapter Eleven

1. In 1882 Congress passed a law implying, but not specifying, that the Treasury should maintain a minimum gold reserve of $100 million against outstanding currency obligations. This responsibility was made explicit and the amount was increased to $150 million by the Gold Coin Act of 14 March 1900.

2. Friedman and Schwartz, *Monetary History,* p. 21.

3. Even though national bank notes were legal tender only for government dues and payments, they were almost always exchangeable for United States notes at par, and were treated for the most part as if they were full legal tender and a high-powered money. Occasionally—for example, during a panic—a small premium might appear between them and the greenbacks.

4. The marketable bullion value of silver in the silver dollar was $0.93 in 1878 and fell constantly until it was only $0.49 in 1894. During all this time, the silver dollar was legal tender for one dollar just as were United States notes, which had no bullion value. Thus the bullion value of the silver in the silver dollar could not have been responsible for any of its monetary value. Silver dollars would have circulated as exchange media worth one dollar each, even if they had had no bullion value, so long as the government invested them with the legal tender quality.

5. The market price of silver was already below its mint price at this time. Therefore $24 million expended on silver purchases bought more than enough silver to produce $24 million worth of coined silver. The difference (or "profit") between the total value of the coined silver and the cost of acquiring it (seigniorage) was a revenue that accrued to the government.

6. F. W. Taussig, *The Silver Situation in the United States* (New York, 1893), p. 8.

7. The desirability of increasing the silver content of the silver dollar was recognized by many secretaries and legislators. (See, for example, Sherman's report for 1880, p. xix.) In fact, the real price of silver did not fall before 1894, but its gold price did because of the appreciation in the real value of gold.

8. *Treasury Report,* 1881, p. x. The ratio, he said, had fluctuated between 36 and 45 percent. At this time almost no silver had been issued, so no gold balance had been required against outstanding silver.

9. *Treasury Report,* 1882, pp. xix–xx.

10. Ibid., p. xxix.

11. Ibid., pp. xxvii–xxviii. The so-called 3 percent debt was callable. It amounted to about $130 million.

12. Sprague, *History of Crises,* pp. 108–13, 353, and passim. See also *Report of the Comptroller,* 1884, pp. 149–54.

13. *Treasury Report,* 1885, p. xiv.

14. Ibid., pp. xlvi, xxxvi (his emphasis).

15. *CR,* 48th Cong., 2d sess., pp. 238–44.

16. Ibid., pp. 245–46.

17. Ibid.

18. Ibid., p. 247.

19. Ibid., p. 248.

20. Horace White, *Money and Banking,* new ed. (Boston: Ginn and Co., 1935), p. 272. The authority to issue silver certificates in these lower denominations appeared in an appropriation act passed 1 July 1886 (*CR,* 49th Cong., 1st sess., p. 6421).

21. *CR,* 49th Cong., 1st sess., pp. 6877–78.

22. Ibid., p. 6879.

23. Ibid., pp. 6923–25.

24. Ibid., pp. 6884, 6887. Warner's speech showed that he was familiar with the writings of Colonel Torrens and Lord Overstone. "The 'honest' dollar," he said further

on in his speech, "is the dollar that has the same value—purchasing power—when one parts with it as when he received it" (ibid.). All through the congressional debates on monetary affairs during the nineteenth century, an amazing number of congressmen displayed a keen understanding of prices, the value of money, and the relationship of these variables to the quantity of money.

25. Ibid., p. 6931.

26. The House had a majority of Democrats, but the Senate was still Republican.

27. Ibid., p. 6935.

28. Ibid., p. 6937.

29. A lot of argument developed over just how much of a surplus there was and what items constituted it. The Senate debate over the resolution dealt more thoroughly with these questions.

30. Ibid., p. 6946.

31. Ibid., p. 7675. The separation of purse and sword as a principle of constrained government was noted frequently in debates throughout the nineteenth century.

32. Ibid., p. 7687.

33. Ibid., appendix, pp. 355–59. Jones included in his speech a statement on the impossibility of general overproduction, à la Jean-Baptiste Say: "Whoever produces anything for sale creates thereby a new demand for something else, and the power of the world to consume depends upon the extent to which it produces" (ibid., p. 361).

34. Ibid., p. 7682. He cited the *London Economist* as authority for his Bank of England data.

35. Ibid., p. 7684. Sherman was surely the most experienced and probably the most sophisticated congressman in financial affairs. He was the only speaker who recognized explicitly the semi-fiat nature of the silver dollar.

36. Ibid., pp. 7738–40. The Coinage Act of 1873 allowed private persons to have silver bullion coined into trade dollars of 420 grains each for use in trade with China. As the price of silver fell after 1875, the trade dollars became a problem in domestic transactions. However, the trade-dollar provisions were inappropriate to the Morrison resolution and were taken out later. The trade dollar was then repealed by means of a separate act in 1887. See Horace White, *Money and Banking,* pp. 41–42.

37. *CR,* 49th Cong., 1st sess., pp. 7736–37, 7742.

38. The senators on the committee were Allison of Iowa, Aldrich of Rhode Island, and Beck of Kentucky. The representatives were Morrison of Illinois, Breckenridge of Kentucky, and Hiscock of New York.

39. Ibid., p. 7939. "Suspension" was adopted rather than the "postponement" in the Senate version of the bill.

40. Ibid., p. 7986. Weaver claimed that a caucus of Senate Republicans, who met at the home of a former secretary of the Treasury (Hugh McCulloch), did the actual amending.

41. Ibid., pp. 7988, 7990, 8002. See statements by Bland of Missouri and Warner of Ohio.

42. Ibid., p. 7998. Statement by Benjamin Butterworth of Ohio. The Treasury reserve of $100 million, Butterworth stated, "is the ballast which keeps our monetary ship steady as she moves through the sea of financial troubles which constantly threaten. [Applause.]"

43. *Treasury Report,* 1887, pp. xxii–xxvii. The 3 percent certificates had been

issued in 1882, and were callable at the pleasure of the government. About $130 million were purchased and retired in the two-year period 1887–1889, even though President Cleveland never signed the resolution.

44. Between October 1885 and October 1887, national bank notes declined by $107 million (*Report of the Comptroller,* 1889, p. 412).

45. Ibid., p. 399.

46. *Treasury Report,* 1887, p. xxviii.

47. Ibid.

48. Ibid., p. xxxiii.

49. *Report of the Treasurer,* 1895, p. 34.

50. *Report of the Comptroller,* 1888, p. 453.

51. *CR,* 50th Cong., 1st sess., index, p. 753.

52. Ibid., pp. 1596, 1597. Thomas Reed of Maine made the same allegation in the House of Representatives (ibid., p. 1600).

53. Ibid., pp. 1597, 1598.

54. Ibid., pp. 1601–2. He noted that Secretary James Guthrie (a fellow Kentuckian) had engaged in similar open-market purchases during the administration of Franklin Pierce some thirty-five years earlier.

55. Ibid., pp. 1606, 2394–98, 2739, 2779.

56. *Treasury Report,* 1888, p. xxvi. He stated that the Treasury had paid out $44 million for the purchase of bonds during October and November 1888. However, he did not mention the fact that this action occurred at election time.

57. *Treasury Report,* 1889, pp. lxxxvii and lxxxix.

58. Ibid.

Chapter Twelve

1. Hepburn, *History of Currency,* pp. 342–66 and passim. Also Charles Hoffman, "The Depression of the Nineties," *Journal of Economic History* 16 (1956): 137–64.

2. White, *Money and Banking,* pp. 88–89.

3. All secretaries without exception bought only the minimum $2 million a year.

4. Harrison had 90,000 fewer popular votes than Cleveland but won the electoral vote 233 to 168.

5. *Treasury Report,* 1889, p. lxxiv.

6. Ibid., pp. lxxiii and lxxiv. Silver dollars weighed 412.5 grains. They were coined .900 fine, which meant that only nine-tenths, or 371.25 grains, of the silver dollar was pure silver.

7. *CR,* 51st Cong., 1st sess., p. 6167.

8. Ibid., p. 6172. At a price of $0.4444 an ounce for silver, the expenditure on 4.5 million ounces would have been just equal to the $2 million a month under the Bland-Allison Act. The price of silver averaged $1.05 an ounce in 1890, which meant a monthly purchase of almost $5 million under the terms of the Silver Purchase Act passed that year. The price dropped rapidly thereafter, reaching $0.78 an ounce in 1893 and $0.60 an ounce in 1897.

9. Ibid., p. 6182.

10. Ibid., p. 6982.

11. Ibid., p. 7018.
12. Ibid., p. 7103.
13. Ibid., pp. 7226 and 7264.
14. Friedman and Schwartz, *Monetary History,* p. 705.
15. Ibid., p. 104.
16. Hepburn, *History of Currency,* p. 304.
17. J. Rogers Hollingsworth, *The Whirligig of Politics* (Chicago: University of Chicago Press, 1963), p. 2.
18. *CR,* 53d Cong., 1st sess., pp. 205–6.
19. Ibid., p. 242.
20. One ounce equals 480 grains.
21. Ibid., p. 320.
22. A market ratio of 28-to-1 implied a divergence from par for the silver dollar of 31 cents per ounce if the mint ratio was 20-to-1. With the mint ratio at the traditional 16-to-1—a mint price of one dollar for 371.25 grains of pure silver—the market divergence from par was 55 cents per ounce.
23. Ibid., pp. 307–9.
24. See statement by John Warner of New York, ibid., p. 325.
25. Ibid., p. 553.
26. Ibid., p. 310.
27. Ibid., pp. 363–64.
28. Ibid., p. 276.
29. For example, William Stewart of Nevada (ibid., p. 294).
30. Ibid., p. 496. Data were furnished by Charles Morgan of Missouri.
31. Ibid., p. 463. Sibley had an interesting description of "intrinsic value." This concept, he said, was meaningless. The intrinsic value of a wooden plank was more than a million dollars to a drowning man.
32. Hollingsworth, *Whirligig,* p. 16.
33. *CR,* 53d Cong., 1st sess., p. 561.
34. Ibid.
35. *Treasury Report,* 1893, p. lxxv.
36. *CR,* 53d Cong., 1st sess., p. 1004.
37. House rules of procedure prevent filibuster. It has always been possible in the Senate, although subject to cloture action by a two-thirds majority.
38. Ibid., p. 1102.
39. See statement by Henry Teller of Colorado, ibid., p. 1350.
40. Ibid., appendix, pp. 606–705.
41. Ibid., p. 618.
42. Ibid., p. 1251. The predicted division was 53 to 32 for repeal. The actual vote two months later was 42 to 32. The silver Republicans included Wolcott and Teller of Colorado, Stewart and Jones of Nevada, Dubois of Idaho, Pettigrew of South Dakota, and Hansbrough of North Dakota. They were joined by several populists: Allen of Nebraska, Kyle of South Dakota, and Peffer and Martin of Kansas.
43. Ibid., p. 1092.
44. Ibid., p. 1309.
45. Ibid., p. 705. This same article was reported in the Senate by Richard Coke of Texas the same day.

46. Hollingsworth, *Whirligig,* p. 17.

47. *CR,* 53d Cong., 1st sess., p. 2910. Cited in the Senate, 28 October 1893, by Arthur Gorman of Maryland.

48. Ibid., p. 2597.

49. Ibid., p. 2917.

50. Ibid., p. 2821.

51. Ibid., pp. 2947 and 2933–36.

52. Ibid., pp. 2886–88. Those who had changed from yea to nay were Faulkner (W. Va.), Hill (N.Y.), Mills (Tex.), Ransom (N.C.), Turpie (Ind.), Voorhees (Ind.), Squire (Wash.), and Gordon (Ga.). Most of these men had been outspoken advocates for free silver until 1893.

53. Ibid., pp. 2917–20.

54. Ibid., p. 2953. Stewart's plea for devaluation of the gold dollar was one of many times in the century that such a change had been seriously proposed. In 1834 the gold content of the dollar was reduced 6 percent; and in 1878 one minority report of the Silver Commission recommended devaluation of the gold dollar by 2.6 percent. (See chaps. 4 and 8.) Stewart's proposed devaluation of 25 percent was too large to be politically feasible even though it was economically reasonable.

55. Ibid., pp. 2930–31.

56. Ibid., p. 2946.

57. Ibid., p. 3066.

58. See Hoffman, "The Depression of the Nineties," and W. Jett Lauck, *The Causes of the Panic of 1893* (Boston: Houghton Mifflin, 1907).

59. Carothers, *Fractional Money,* pp. 98–101. Milton Friedman, "Bimetallism Revisited." *Money Mischief* (New York, San Diego, London: Harcourt Brace Jovanovich, 1992), chap. 6.

60. Alfred Marshall, *Money, Credit, and Commerce* (London: Macmillan, 1929), p. 64.

61. Carothers, *Fractional Money,* p. 137.

62. Milton Friedman, *Money Mischief,* chap. 3, "The Crime of '73." Also Timberlake, *Gold, Greenbacks, and the Constitution,* pp. 6–10, 42–44.

63. Friedman and Schwartz, *Monetary History,* pp. 131–34. See also Rendigs Fels, *American Business Cycles* (Chapel Hill: University of North Carolina Press, 1959), pp. 209–12 and passim.

64. Friedman and Schwartz, *Monetary History,* p. 134, note.

65. Alfred Marshall suggested in 1888 a scheme that he labeled "symmetallism." The mint would fashion ingots of gold and silver. The silver ingot would weigh twenty times as much as the gold ingot if the current market ratio of value was 20-to-1. The government would maintain the mint price of a *pair* of ingots. The price of one metal could then fall if the price of the other rose (*Money, Credit, and Commerce,* pp. 64–67). Marshall's scheme had much to recommend it, but it was never discussed in Congress as a possible alternative to either monometallism or bimetallism. Its principal interest seemed to lie in academic circles.

66. World gold production fell gradually but steadily until about 1885. It then rose gradually until 1893, but more rapidly to the end of the century and for many years thereafter. In the two years 1899–1900 production equaled or exceeded that for almost

any five-year period from 1870 to 1890 (Marshall, *Money, Credit, and Commerce,* p. 70).

Chapter Thirteen

1. See *Historical Statistics of the United Stages,* p. 127. A 10 percent decline in prices does not imply a severe depression. However, the peak of prices in 1892 was already 20 percent below the peak for 1872, while prices by 1897 were down almost to their 1860 level.

2. Hollingsworth, *Whirligig,* pp. 84–107.

3. Ibid., p. 102.

4. *Treasury Report,* 1896, p. lxxiii. No vestige of Carlisle's former free-silver principles can be found in any of his secretarial writings.

5. *Treasury Report,* 1897, p. lxxiv.

6. Ibid., pp. lxxvi–lxxvii.

7. Ibid., p. lxxvii.

8. *Treasury Report,* 1899, pp. lxxxvii–xciv.

9. Indianapolis Monetary Commission, *Report of the Monetary Commission of the Indianapolis Convention* (Indianapolis, Ind.: Hollenbeck Press, 1900), pp. 60–74. The convention was composed of "boards of trade, chambers of commerce, commercial clubs, and other similar bodies of the United States." Some of the better-known members were H. H. Hanna, A. Barton Hepburn, and J. Lawrence Laughlin.

10. *Treasury Report,* 1900, pp. lxxii–lxxiii. The Currency Act of 14 March 1900 permitted the national banks to issue notes to the full amount of the par value of the collateral securities (instead of 90 percent), but not in excess of their market price. It also reduced the minimum capital requirement for a national bank to $25,000, and it reduced the semiannual tax on national bank-note circulation from 0.5 percent to 0.25 percent.

11. Ibid., p. xxviii.

12. Ibid., p. xxiii.

13. *Treasury Report,* 1901, p. 22.

14. Ibid., pp. 74–75 (his italics).

15. Ibid., p. 76. Gage never seemed to associate changes in bank credit and deposits with changes in the gold base. He never included in his analyses any awareness of the price-specie flow mechanism.

16. Ibid., p. 77. Gage cited the appealing analogy between a federated United States of America and a federated central bank. This image would enlist a lot of political support in the future.

17. *Dictionary of American Biography,* vol. 17, pp. 43–44. Shaw was also in favor of high tariffs, in contrast with his chief, President Theodore Roosevelt. See *Nation* 81 (1905): 272; *Nation* 82 (1906): 502–3.

18. This kind of transfer had been carried out recently by two previous secretaries—Fairchild and Gage. Gage had done it in 1898 when cash balances had risen exceptionally due to the lack of synchronization between the sale of securities to finance the war with Spain and actual expenditures on the war effort. Fairchild had done

the same thing for policy purposes during 1887. Congress censured his action and passed legislation that countermanded it. (See chap. 11 herein.)

19. A. Piatt Andrew, "Treasury and Banks under Secretary Shaw," *Quarterly Journal of Economics* 21 (1907): 540–41.

20. L. M. Shaw, *Current Issues* (New York: D. Appleton and Co., 1908), p. 322. Comment on Report of American Bankers Association (30 November 1906). Also *Treasury Report,* 1904, pp. 40–41.

21. *Treasury Report,* 1902, p. 58.

22. *Treasury Report,* 1905, p. 34; and 1906, pp. 37, 19, and 40. Shaw directed most of his attention to the call loan rate of interest. "The sure indication of world-wide money stringency," he stated in 1906, "is the fact that legitimate interest rates on commercial paper everywhere are higher than for many years" (p. 40).

23. *Treasury Report,* 1902, p. 58.

24. Ibid., p. 2.

25. Ibid., pp. 58–60.

26. *Treasury Report,* 1905, p. 34. This idea of special issues of currency subject to a nominal tax was widespread at this time.

27. *Treasury Report,* 1904, p. 8. When the Treasury purchased government securities, its balance in the subtreasuries diminished appreciably, and the private sector had more money. When the Treasury deposited its excess balances directly with the national banks, the banks realized an immediate enhancement of reserves.

28. *Treasury Report,* 1905, pp. 8 and 9.

29. *Treasury Report,* 1906, p. 42.

30. Ibid., p. 113.

31. *Nation* 83 (1906): 216–17.

32. The following analysis refers primarily to the articles by Patton and Andrew and to Kinley's book on the Independent Treasury: Eugene B. Patton, "Secretary Shaw and Precedents as to Treasury Control over the Money Market," *Journal of Political Economy* 15 (1907): 65–87; Andrew, "Treasury under Shaw," pp. 519–68; David Kinley, *The Independent Treasury of the United States and Its Relation to the Banks of the Country,* Sen. Doc. No. 587, 61st Cong., 2d sess., National Monetary Commission, 1910.

33. Patton, "Precedents," p. 86.

34. Andrew, "Treasury under Shaw," pp. 520–23.

35. Ibid., pp. 524 and 538.

36. *The Nation,* amusingly enough, by 1906 allowed that Shaw's policy of depositing the public money in banks was justifiable because it "would have followed precedent." The editor did not seem to remember how strongly this same policy had been criticized a few years before as unprecedented. The article went on to attack Shaw's gold-import policy because "the use of Government money, avowedly to influence a financial market with whose movement the Treasury is not itself concerned, is something new" (*Nation* 82 [1906]: 315).

37. Shaw, *Current Issues,* pp. 352 and 358. Address before Bankers' Association of Washington, D.C., September 1905.

38. Andrew, "Treasury under Shaw," pp. 522–23.

39. Patton, "Precedents," p. 86. Kinley made almost exactly the same criticism. See *Independent Treasury,* p. 271.

40. Andrew, "Treasury under Shaw," pp. 559–66.

41. Shaw, *Current Issues,* p. 370. Address before State Bankers' Association, Louisville, Kentucky, 10 October 1906.

42. Ibid., p. 279. Address before the Ohio Bankers' Association, September 1905. Also *Treasury Report,* 1905, p. 8.

43. Andrew, "Treasury under Shaw," p. 547.

44. *Treasury Report,* 1906, p. 49.

45. *Treasury Report,* 1908, pp. 20–22.

46. Kinley, *Independent Treasury,* p. 280. In 1907, Kinley observed, "the surplus was all deposited in banks. The Treasury could do nothing more." Other factors, such as aggressive gold policies by the Bank of England in the first half of the year, also provoked trouble. See O. M. W. Sprague, *History of Crises under the National Banking System,* Sen. Doc. No. 538, 61st Cong., 2d sess., National Monetary Commission, 1910, pp. 241–43.

47. U.S. Congress, 60th Cong., 1st sess., *Response of the Secretary of the Treasury . . . In Regard to Treasury Operations,* Sen. Doc. No. 208, p. 32.

48. Kinley, *Independent Treasury,* pp. 326–38.

49. *Treasury Report,* 1906, p. 37. In 1903 he noted that a stock market decline had not been an issue in Treasury policy-making. The decline had had no effect on general business due to Treasury support of legitimate trade (*Treasury Report,* 1903, p. 45).

50. Shaw, *Current Issues,* p. 295.

51. Remark made during lecture, University of Chicago, 1952.

52. Friedman and Schwartz, *Monetary History,* p. 150.

53. For a supplemental discussion of Shaw's policies that adds some interesting details and an account of the New York money market at that time, see Charles Goodhart, *The New York Money Market and the Finance of Trade, 1900–1913* (Cambridge, Mass.: Harvard University Press, 1969), pp. 107–21.

Chapter Fourteen

1. For example, consider this statement: "For most economists, the debate regarding the desirability of [governmental] central banking is over. Central banking doctrines have become the conventional wisdom" (Ramzi Frangul, book review, *Journal of Finance* 35 [March 1980]: 212).

2. James Graham Cannon, *Clearing Houses,* Sen. Doc. No. 491, 61st Cong., 2d sess., National Monetary Commission, 1910; A. Barton Hepburn, *History of Coinage and Currency in the United States,* rev. ed. (New York: Macmillan, 1924); Margaret Myers, *The New York Money Market, Origins and Development,* vol. 1 (New York: Columbia University Press, 1931); Fritz Redlich, *The Molding of American Banking, Men and Ideas, Part II, 1840–1910* (New York: Hafner, 1951); Oliver M. W. Sprague, *History of Crises under the National Banking System,* Sen. Doc. No. 538, 61st Cong., 2d sess., National Monetary Commission, 1910; Horace White, *Money and Banking,* rev. and enl. by Charles Tippets and Lewis Froman (New York: Ginn, 1935).

3. Two representatives were required, one to handle the debit items and one to present the credit items to the other banks' representatives.

4. Myers, *New York Money Market,* p. 96; Cannon, *Clearing Houses,* p. 44.

5. Myers, *New York Money Market,* p. 97.

6. Clearinghouse certificates must be distinguished from clearinghouse *loan* certificates. The former were the conventional issues made strictly *in lieu* of specie, legal tender notes, or other legal reserves for settlement of clearinghouse balances. The latter were issued only in emergencies on the basis of loans made by clearinghouse policy committees to member banks.

7. Myers, *New York Money Market,* p. 98, Redlich, *Molding of American Banking,* pp. 158–59.

8. Redlich, *Molding of American Banking,* pp. 159–60.

9. Myers, *New York Money Market,* p. 98.

10. Ibid., p. 100.

11. Ibid.

12. Sprague, *History of Crises,* pp. 120–21. Pooling gave rise to what in today's world is labeled a "moral hazard."

13. New York State usury laws limited the maximum rate of interest that the clearinghouse could charge to 6 percent. Interest rates being what they were in that era of stable prices, 6 percent was an effective constraint. For general policy purposes, of course, market interest rates should not have been limited by any politically inspired ceiling.

14. Sprague, *History of Crises,* p. 54.

15. Ibid., pp. 50–63, 90–97. See also Redlich, *Molding of American Banking,* p. 158.

16. Sprague, *History of Crises,* p. 63.

17. Hepburn, *History of Coinage,* p. 351.

18. Sprague, *History of Crises,* p. 197.

19. Cannon, *Clearing Houses,* pp. 109–12.

20. Hepburn, *History of Coinage,* p. 352 (emphasis added).

21. A. Piatt Andrew, "Substitutes for Cash in the Panic of 1907," *Quarterly Journal of Economics* 22 (August 1908): 496–502. Cannon, *Clearing Houses,* pp. 123–31.

22. Andrew, "Substitutes for Cash," p. 497.

23. Ibid., p. 499.

24. Ibid., p. 506.

25. Ibid., p. 509. Generally, the lower the denomination of the currency issues, the greater the collateral value of the securities supporting them.

26. Cannon, *Clearing Houses,* p. 116.

27. Ibid., p. 96.

28. White, *Money and Banking,* p. 383. White implied here that issues of currency were in violation of any or all of the following: the Constitution, the National Bank Act, and the laws prohibiting private issues of fractional currency.

29. Redlich, *Molding of American Banking,* pp. 167–68.

30. Theodore Gilman, *A Graded Banking System* (Boston and New York: Houghton Mifflin, 1898), pp. 44–45.

31. Ibid., pp. 46–47. The clearinghouse agreements already in force called for sharing any resulting losses from the issues in proportion to the participating banks' capital and surplus, or by the proportional amount of their clearings during the previous year.

32. Ibid., pp. 71 and 124.

33. Ibid., p. 119.
34. Ibid., p. 126.
35. Ibid., p. 157.
36. Leslie M. Shaw, *Current Issues* (New York: Appleton, 1908), p. 279.
37. Ibid., p. 293.
38. Ibid., p. 294.
39. U.S. Comptroller of the Currency, *Annual Report* (Washington, 1893), p. 15.
40. Ibid., p. 16.
41. U.S. Comptroller of the Currency, *Annual Report* (Washington, 1907), p. 64.
42. Ibid., p. 75.
43. Ibid.
44. Sprague, *History of Crises,* pp. 273–77.
45. William G. Dewald, "The National Monetary Commission: A Look Back," *Journal of Money, Credit, and Banking* 4 (November 1972): 939–40.
46. Ibid., pp. 934, 941–42. Sprague also favored the "pooling" of reserves in order to reduce the too-ready tendency of the banks to restrict or suspend. Dewald apparently agreed (Dewald, "National Monetary Commission," p. 941). However, this provision would have vitiated an important market constraint. (See pp. 200–201.) Sprague's principal remedy requiring banks to use their reserves, in conjunction with clearinghouse issues, would have been sufficient to stop any panic. Inexplicably, the thought never seemed to occur to him that banks *would* have used their reserves if the reserve requirement laws were repealed.
47. Myers, *New York Money Market,* p. 143.
48. Friedman and Schwartz, *Monetary History,* pp. 163 and 167.
49. Ibid., pp. 167–68.
50. Sprague, *History of Crises,* p. 280. Penalties besides public opprobrium were: (1) prohibition of any new loans or discounts, and (2) no payment of dividends until reserve ratios were again up to the legal minimum.
51. Ibid., p. 170.
52. Redlich, *Molding of American Banking,* p. 168.
53. Sprague, *History of Crises,* p. 392.
54. *CR* 63d Cong, 1st sess., Appendix, 1913, p. 332.
55. Sprague, *History of Crises,* pp. 260–77.
56. Charles Goodhart, *The Evolution of Central Banks* (Cambridge and London: MIT Press, 1988). See esp. chap. 3.
57. Ibid., pp. 38–44 and passim.
58. Ibid., pp. 45–46. See also chap. 16 herein.
59. One can hardly label modern-day central banks "non-profit-maximizing" in view of the substantial seigniorage they generate for their governmental sponsors.

Chapter Fifteen

1. Friedman and Schwartz, *Monetary History,* pp. 189–96.
2. See Hepburn, *History of Currency,* pp. 397–410.
3. J. Lawrence Laughlin, "Currency Reform," *Journal of Political Economy* 15 (1907): 609.

4. *CR,* 60th Cong., 1st sess., pp. 6323 and 6375.
5. Ibid., pp. 7063–64.
6. Ibid., p. 7069.
7. Ibid., p. 7074.
8. Ibid., p. 7077.
9. Ibid., pp. 7146–7244.
10. Ibid., p. 7250. Gore's idea preceded Einstein's general theory of relativity.
11. Ibid., p. 7252.
12. Ibid., p. 7260.
13. Ibid., p. 6320. Sections 11 and 12 created the commission.
14. Nelson W. Aldrich, *The Work of the National Monetary Commission,* Sen. Doc. No. 406, 61st Cong., 2d sess., 1910, pp. 3–29.
15. *CR,* 62d Cong., 2d sess., p. 587.
16. Ibid., appendix, p. 483.
17. Ibid., pp. 484–87.
18. *CR,* 62d Cong., 3d sess., pp. 1775–79.
19. Ibid., p. 1779.
20. Ibid., pp. 1779–83.
21. *CR,* 63d Cong., 1st sess., pp. 4642, 4644.
22. Ibid., p. 4644.
23. Ibid., p. 4783, remarks by Robert Bulkley of Ohio. See also speech by Gilbert Hitchcock, ibid., p. 6015.
24. Ibid., p. 6021.
25. Ibid. (Glass), p. 4643.
26. Ibid., p. 4644.
27. Ibid., p. 4645.
28. Ibid.
29. Ibid., p. 4768.
30. Ibid., p. 4790.
31. *CR,* 63d Cong., 2d sess., p. 703.
32. *CR,* 63d Cong., 1st sess., p. 4692. Perhaps Mondell understood, but the chronic growth of regulatory government would seem in retrospect to have refuted his faith in the people.
33. *CR,* 63d Cong., 2d sess., p. 1137. The two cabinet officers were the secretaries of the Treasury and agriculture. In a final conference before the bill passed, the secretary of agriculture was dropped. Not until 1935 were the secretary of the Treasury and the comptroller of the currency removed from the board.
34. *CR,* 63d Cong., 1st sess., p. 4646.
35. *CR,* 63d Cong., 2d sess., pp. 1480–81. (Emphasis added.)
36. *CR,* 63d Cong., 1st sess., p. 4865.
37. *CR,* 63d Cong., 2d sess., p. 762.
38. *CR,* 63d Cong., 1st sess., p. 4865.
39. Ibid., p. 4691.
40. Ibid., pp. 4651, 4661. See also statement by Richard Austin of Texas, ibid., p. 5089.
41. Ibid., pp. 4661–63.
42. *CR,* 63d Cong., 2d sess., p. 1072.

43. *CR*, 63d Cong., 1st sess., p. 6016. Knute Nelson of Minnesota expressed a similar view.

44. *CR*, 63d Cong., 2d sess., p. 523. Joseph Bristow of Kansas also made this argument (ibid., p. 530).

45. Ibid., p. 525.

46. *CR*, 63d Cong., 1st sess., p. 6001.

47. Ibid.

48. *CR*, 63d Cong., 2d sess., p. 1440.

49. *CR*, 63d Cong., 1st sess., p. 6016.

50. *CR*, 63d Cong., 2d sess., pp. 667–68.

51. Hepburn, *History of Currency,* pp. 501–4.

52. *CR*, 63d Cong., 1st sess., p. 6018.

53. Ibid., p. 5998.

54. *CR*, 63d Cong., 2d sess., p. 279.

55. *CR*, 63d Cong., 1st sess., p. 4680.

56. See statement by Knute Nelson of Minnesota, for example, in which he denounced Treasury monetary policy as "discretionary" and subject to favoritism (*CR*, 63d Cong., 2d sess., pp. 445–53).

57. *CR*, 63d Cong., 1st sess., p. 5109. See also p. 6024 for statement by John Shafroth of Colorado.

58. *CR*, 63d Cong., 2d sess., p. 279.

59. Ibid., pp. 5100–5106.

60. Ibid., pp. 5507–10.

61. Ibid., p. 6018.

62. Ibid., pp. 1063 and 1081.

63. The freeze on United States notes occurred in 1878, while the statutory reserve provision appeared in the Gold Coin Act of 1900.

64. Ibid., p. 6018.

65. Ibid., p. 880.

66. Ibid., p. 904.

67. Ibid., p. 466.

68. Ibid., p. 905.

69. *CR*, 63d Cong., 1st sess., p. 4661.

70. Ibid., p. 829. The original bill stated that the Federal Reserve banks could allow "such discounts . . . as may be safely and reasonably made with due regard for claims and demands of other member banks" (ibid., p. 1063). This statement implies a quantitative limitation based on the discretion of the managers of the Federal Reserve banks' discount window.

71. Ibid., pp. 966–67.

72. Ibid., p. 1037.

73. Ibid., p. 877.

74. Ibid., p. 979.

75. Ibid., p. 903.

76. Ibid., p. 968.

77. Ibid., p. 1074.

78. Ibid., p. 1116.

79. Ibid., pp. 1358, 1196. Carter Glass cited this same argument in the House.

80. Ibid., p. 1200.

81. Ibid., appendix, p. 564. Glass indicated that the House conferees threw out this provision.

82. Ibid., p. 1226.

83. Ibid., pp. 1294, 1352–56.

84. Ibid., p. 1482.

85. Ibid., appendix, p. 562.

86. Ibid., p. 564.

87. Ibid., pp. 1447–86.

88. Ibid., p. 702. Hitchcock, being a part of the loyal opposition, could say that the Federal Reserve System was a central bank and thereby justify his vote in favor of the institution on final passage. But none of the Democratic sponsors could do so because the Democratic party's platform had spoken out against a central bank.

89. See Mints, *History of Banking Theory,* p. 9.

90. *CR,* 63d Cong., 2d sess., p. 904.

91. *CR,* 63d Cong., 1st sess., p. 4652.

92. *CR,* 63d Cong., 2d sess., pp. 537–38.

93. Ibid., p. 1446.

94. Ibid., p. 1225.

95. Ibid., p. 546.

96. For more on this argument, see chapter 16 herein.

97. Ibid., p. 1447.

Chapter Sixteen

1. For an account of monetary evolution see Horace White, *Money and Banking,* pp. 6–20.

2. R. A. Radford, "The Economic Organization of a P.O.W. Camp," *Economica* 12 (1945): 194–98. Chapter 27 herein treats this issue in more detail.

3. The Constitution of the United States of America, Article I, Section 8.

4. "Regulate" meant only to *specify* the amount of gold in the gold dollar and the amount of silver in the silver dollar. "Regulate" had no implication for any discretionary manipulation of the quantity of money.

5. For an account of monetary events and policies during the restriction see Viner, *Studies,* pp. 122–70, and Frank W. Fetter, *Development of British Monetary Orthodoxy* (Cambridge, Mass.: Harvard University Press, 1965), pp. 26–63.

6. Thornton, *The Paper Credit of Great Britain,* p. 90. For analysis of Thornton's monetary theory see Mints, *A History of Banking Theory,* pp. 52–56 and passim. Many of his contemporaries also contributed arguments on the issues, but Thornton was exemplary in furnishing a sophisticated monetary policy as a distillate of monetary issues and events. (See Fetter, *British Monetary Orthodoxy,* p. 45.)

7. Thornton, *Paper Credit,* pp. 90 and 123.

8. Ibid., pp. 127, 163.

9. Ibid., p. 128.

10. Ibid., pp. 116, 123, 124.

11. Ibid., p. 152.

12. Ibid.

13. Ibid., p. 259.

14. See chap. 2 and Rothbard, *The Panic of 1819,* for a detailed account of this inflation.

15. *ASPF* 3, pp. 494–508.

16. Ibid., p. 498.

17. Hammond, *Banks and Politics,* pp. 199–309.

18. Ibid., p. 307.

19. Ibid., p. 324.

20. Viner, *Studies,* p. 254 (my italics).

21. Hammond, *Banks and Politics,* p. 368.

22. See, for example, *AC,* 1st Cong., 3d sess., pp. 1895–1957.

23. Fetter, *British Monetary Orthodoxy,* pp. 23, 24.

24. Hammond, *Banks and Politics,* p. 324.

25. Fetter, *British Monetary Orthodoxy,* pp. 152–64 and passim.

26. Viner, *Studies,* pp. 255–69, and Fetter, *British Monetary Orthodoxy,* pp. 165–97.

27. *Treasury Report,* 1866, pp. 9 and 10.

28. *Treasury Report,* 1872, pp. xx–xxi.

29. *CR,* 43d Cong., 1st sess., appendix, pp. 17–20.

30. Walter Bagehot, *Lombard Street,* rev. ed. (London: Kegan Paul, Trench, Toubner and Co., 1906).

31. In Bagehot's time commercial bank deposits and private deposits in the Banking Department of the Bank of England were about £18 million, and government deposits £8 million. Note reserves were about £10 million, while gold was only £0.9 million. The Issue Department had £33 million in notes outstanding, against which it had £18 million in gold bullion and £15 million in securities.

32. Bagehot, *Lombard Street,* pp. 162–70.

33. Ibid., p. 168. I am indebted to Frank W. Fetter for calling my attention to Bagehot's editorship of the *Economist* and for other helpful suggestions.

34. Ibid.

35. Ibid., p. 172.

36. Thomson Hankey, *The Principles of Banking* (London, 1867), p. 19.

37. Bagehot, *Lombard Street,* p. 175.

38. Ibid., pp. 200, 201.

39. Fetter, *British Monetary Orthodoxy,* p. 282.

40. *Treasury Report,* 1889, p. lxxxviii.

41. Shaw, *Current Issues,* p. 279.

42. Ibid., pp. 293–95.

43. Hepburn, *History of Currency,* pp. 500–504.

44. *American Heritage Dictionary of the English Language.* (Boston, New York: Houghton Mifflin, 1970).

Chapter Seventeen

1. Board of Governors of the Federal Reserve System, *Annual Report, 1914.* Hereafter, the Board's annual reports are referred to as: B of G, *AR,* [*year*].

2. B of G, *AR, 1914,* p. 10.
3. *Federal Reserve Act,* 1913, Section 13, p. 34.
4. B of G, *AR, 1914,* p. 16.
5. Ibid., p. 17. Emphasis added.
6. Ibid.
7. Ibid., p. 32, and *Federal Reserve Act,* Section 10.
8. B of G, *AR, 1914,* p. 33.
9. Board of Governors, *The Federal Reserve Act,* Section 14, "Open Market Operations," pp. 52–55.
10. B of G, *AR, 1914,* pp. 155–56.
11. B of G, *AR, 1915,* p. 6.
12. B of G, *AR, 1917,* p. 8.
13. B of G, *AR, 1918,* p. 4.
14. Ibid., p. 87, and *AR, 1920,* p. 11.
15. B of G, *AR, 1919,* pp. 1–2.
16. See Friedman and Schwartz, *Monetary History,* pp. 216–21.
17. B of G, *AR, 1919,* p. 65.
18. Ibid., p. 4.
19. B of G, *AR, 1920,* p. 1.
20. B of G, *AR, 1921,* pp. 97–98.
21. E.g., see Lloyd W. Mints, *History of Banking Theory* (Chicago: University of Chicago Press, 1945), pp. 25–41 and passim.
22. Lance Girton and Don Roper, "J. Lawrence Laughlin and the Quantity Theory of Money," *JPE* 86:4 (August 1978): 599–625.
23. Lance Girton, "SDR Creation and the Real Bills Doctrine," *SEJ* 41:1 (July 1974): 57–61. At times, governments have changed (lowered) the mint price of gold in order to generate more money and stimulate business activity. However, this procedure not only violates the gold standard rule, it can only be done infrequently.
24. B of G, *Federal Reserve Act,* p. 34.
25. B of G, *AR, 1922,* p. 2.
26. B of G, *AR, 1923,* pp. 32–33.
27. Ibid., p. 33.
28. Elmus R. Wicker, "Federal Reserve Monetary Policy, 1922–33: A Reinterpretation," *Journal of Political Economy* 78:4 (August 1965): 340.
29. B of G, *AR, 1922,* p. 4, and *AR, 1923,* p. 13.
30. B of G, *AR, 1923,* p. 11.
31. Ibid., p. 13.
32. Wicker, "Federal Reserve Monetary Policy," *JPE,* p. 329.
33. John R. Commons, "Stabilization of Prices and Business," *AER, Papers and Proceedings Supplement* 15:1 (March 1925), p. 52.
34. T. E. Gregory, "What Can Central Banks Really Do?" *AER, Papers and Proceedings Supplenment* 15:1 (March 1925), p. 54.
35. Friedman and Schwartz, "The High Tide of the Reserve System," *Monetary History,* chap. 6, pp. 240–98; and Wicker, "Federal Reserve Policy," *JPE,* pp. 332–37.
36. Friedman and Schwartz, *Monetary History,* pp. 279–87.

37. A. C. Whitaker, "Federal Reserve Position and Policies," *AER, Papers and Proceedings, Supplement* 20:1 (March 1930): 93–97.

38. Harold L. Reed, "The Recent Work of the Federal Reserve Administration," *AER, Papers and Proceedings, Supplement* 16:1 (March 1926): 303–4 and 313.

39. Some members of Congress, Reed noted, had introduced bills that would have fixed the discount rate for all Fed banks at 2 percent.

40. Ibid., p. 315.

41. Friedman and Schwartz, *Monetary History,* pp. 221–39.

42. For a more detailed analysis of this period, see Richard H. Timberlake, Jr., "Patinkin and the Pigou Effect: A Comment," *Review of Economics and Statistics* 39:3 (August 1957): 348.

43. Lauchlin Currie, "The Failure of Monetary Policy to Prevent the Depression of 1929–32," *Journal of Political Economy* 42:2 (April 1934): 148.

44. Clark Warburton, "Monetary Difficulties and the Structure of the Monetary System," *Journal of Finance* 7 (December 1952): 523–45; reprinted in Clark Warburton, *Depression, Inflation, and Monetary Policy* (Baltimore: Johns Hopkins University Press, 1966), pp. 327–49. (Citation is from latter source, pp. 339–40.)

45. Clark Warburton, "Monetary Control under the Federal Reserve Act," *Political Science Quarterly* 61 (December 1946): 505–34; reprinted in Warburton, *Depression, Inflation, and Monetary Policy,* pp. 291–316. See also Friedman and Schwartz, *Monetary History,* pp. 400–406, on "the problem of free gold." On the adequacy of eligible paper, see Henry H. Villard, "Fed Monetary Policy in 1931–32," *JPE* (December 1937): 721–39. Also Horace White, *Money and Banking,* rev. and enl. by Charles Tippets and Lewis Froman (New York: Ginn and Co., 1935), p. 703.

46. B of G of FRS, *Banking and Monetary Statistics,* pp. 544–51. Fed Banks' gold holdings of \$3.5 to \$4.0 billion were about one-fourth of the trading world's monetary gold.

47. Walter Bagehot, *Lombard Street,* pp. 198–201.

48. Friedman and Schwartz, *Monetary History,* p. 327.

49. Warburton, "Monetary Control," *Depression, Inflation, and Monetary Policy,* p. 303.

50. In August 1932 total notes outstanding and reserve accounts of member banks at Fed banks were \$4.92 billion. Add \$2.50 billion to get the total of \$7.42 billion.

51. Sprague, *History of Crises,* pp. 279–80. See also Dewald, "National Monetary Commission," pp. 939–40.

52. Andrew, "Substitutes for Cash," p. 459.

53. Sprague, *History of Crises,* pp. 319–20.

Chapter Eighteen

1. Friedman and Schwartz devote 245 pages and three comprehensive chapters to this period (*Monetary History,* pp. 299–545).

2. Seymour E. Harris, *Twenty Years of Federal Reserve Policy,* vol. 2: *The Monetary Crisis* (Cambridge: Harvard University Press, 1933), pp. 685–87. White, *Money and Banking,* pp. 697–702.

3. *Annual Report,* 1931, p. 34.

4. "The Reconstruction Finance Corporation Program," an address before the Associated Press of New York City, 25 April 1932, *Annual Report,* pp. 327–28.

5. Ibid., p. 329 (Emphasis supplied.)

6. *Annual Report,* 1931, p. 48.

7. Harris, *Twenty Years,* p. 686; White, *Money and Banking,* p. 699.

8. White, *Money and Banking,* p. 705.

9. Ibid., pp. 709–10.

10. Ibid., pp. 712–13.

11. Ibid., pp. 714–20. See also William Shughart II, "A Public Choice Perspective of the Banking Act of 1933," in *The Financial Services Revolution,* ed. Catherine England and Thomas Huertas (Boston: Kluwer Academic Publishers, 1987), pp. 87–105.

12. White, *Money and Banking,* p. 718.

13. Ibid., pp. 720–21.

14. James Daniel Paris, *Monetary Policies of the United States* (New York: Columbia University Press, 1938), p. 18.

15. Friedman and Schwartz, *Monetary History,* pp. 465–70.

16. *Annual Report,* 1932, p. 27. Secretary Mellon, in recommending tax increases in his annual report for 1931, had argued that people would "best serve their own interests by doing whatever is required to maintain the finances *of their Government* on a sound basis" (p. 28; emphasis supplied). In his annual report for 1932, Secretary Woodin stated that the Revenue Act of 1932 was an "impressive achievement." However, he complained, "receipts from the new taxes have been disappointing" (p. 22).

17. *Annual Report,* 1932, p. 70, and *Annual Report,* 1933, p. 14.

18. *The Federal Reserve Act,* appendix, "Gold Reserve Act of 1934," pp. 201–6.

19. *CR* 79 (1935), part 11, p. 11915.

20. Donald F. Kettl, *Leadership at the Fed* (New Haven: Yale University Press, 1986), pp. 48–53.

21. Ibid.

22. Ibid., p. 50. Memo, Currie to Eccles, 1 April 1935.

23. *CR* 79 (1935), part 13, p. 13706.

24. Ibid.

25. Ibid., part 11, p. 11825.

26. Ibid., p. 11778. Glass should have noted that these characteristics had marked the lending policies of the earlier clearinghouse associations.

27. Ibid., pp. 11923–24.

28. Friedman and Schwartz, *Monetary History,* 1963, pp. 411–19.

29. *CR* 79 (1935), part 11, p. 11925.

30. Ibid., p. 11842.

31. Ibid., p. 11908.

32. *CR* 79 (1935), part 11, p. 11776.

33. Quoted by R. B. Westerfield in "The Banking Act of 1933," *Journal of Political Economy* (December 1933): 728.

34. Benjamin M. Anderson, *Economics and the Public Welfare* (New York: Van Nostrand Co., 1949; reprinted by Liberty Press, Indianapolis, 1979). See pages 361–64 (in reprint) for Glass's role in resisting the administration on this bill.

Chapter Nineteen

1. The requirement depended on the size of the community in which the commercial bank was located. The smaller the community, the lower the requirement.

2. B of G, *The Federal Reserve Act as Amended through October 1, 1961,* p. 70.

3. Ibid., appendix, pp. 200–206.

4. Friedman and Schwartz, *Monetary History,* p. 544.

5. Ibid., pp. 521–22. See also their comprehensive discussion of the "technical" factors behind the decision to increase requirements.

6. Benjamin M. Anderson, *Economics and the Public Welfare: A Financial and Economic History of the United States, 1914–1946* (New York: Van Nostrand Co., 1949; 2d ed. Liberty Press, Indianapolis, 1979), p. 405. References are to second edition.

7. Ibid., pp. 432–33. See also, James T. Lindley, *An Analysis of the Federal Advisory Council of the Federal Reserve System, 1914–1938* (New York: Garland Publishing, Inc., 1985). Lindley notes that the Federal Advisory Council opposed the second reserve requirement increase. Lindley argues that the Fed could only do little good but much harm by intervention at this time (pp. 144–45 and passim).

8. Ibid., p. 405, n. 4. Anderson's reasons for the collapse in industrial activity in 1937 were (1) the large increase in union wages, unmatched by changes in productivity, as a result of the Wagner Act, and (2) the stock market crash of 1937. His second reason put the cart before the horse.

9. Marriner Eccles, *Beckoning Frontiers* (New York: Alfred A. Knopf, 1951), p. 287. By the "cost" of money, Eccles meant, of course, interest rates.

10. Ibid., p. 289.

11. Ibid., p. 291.

12. The economy's "full employment" stocks of money for the various dates listed here are computed on a strict and simplistic quantity-theory basis in the following manner. The money stock, labor force, and price level for June 1929 are assumed to be bench marks. To get the full employment money stock M_f for any subsequent date, the actual money stock M_t for that date is multiplied (1) by the ratio of the full employment labor force to the number of workers actually employed, N_f/N_t, and (2) by the ratio of the price level of 1929 to the price level for the date being investigated, P_O/P_t. The increases in money necessary for financing increases in total product—assumed to be proportional to growth in the labor force—and for restoring prices to their 1929 level are obtained by subtracting the actual money stock from each of these computed values. Summing the actual money stock and both increases gives the "Full Employment" values in this column. In mathematical terms,

$$M_f = M_t + \left(\frac{N_f}{N_t} \cdot M_t - M_t\right) + \left(\frac{P_o}{P_t} \cdot M_t - M_t\right).$$

This expression reduces to

$$M_f = M_t\left[1 + \left(\frac{N_f}{N_t} - 1\right) + \left(\frac{P_o}{P_t} - 1\right)\right],$$

and to

$$M_f = M_t\left(\frac{N_f}{N_t} + \frac{P_o}{P_t} - 1\right).$$

13. Eccles, *Beckoning Frontiers,* p. 290.

14. Friedman and Schwartz, *Monetary History,* table A-1, pp. 712–14.

15. Eccles, *Beckoning Frontiers,* p. 270.

16. Eccles noted that the Treasury bill rate, which had been at 1⁄10 percent, rose "only" to 3⁄4 percent. His criterion for a "problem" was what might happen to the government bond market. (*Beckoning Frontiers,* p. 291.)

17. Paris, *Monetary Policies,* p. 37. The authorization for the Treasury's action was derived from the Gold Reserve Act of 30 January 1934, which stated, "Title to all gold coin and gold bullion of the Federal Reserve Board the Federal Reserve banks and Federal Reserve agents is vested in *the United States Government,* for which credits in the United States Treasury in equivalent dollar amounts are established." The act also gave the Treasury complete control over disposition of the gold (*Report, 1934,* pp. 27, 28).

18. U.S. Treasury Press Release No. 9-20, 20 December 1936.

19. U.S. Treasury, *Annual Report,* 1938, p. 21. Morgenthau, to give him credit, was against the second and third increases in reserve requirements. (Eccles, *Beckoning Frontiers,* p. 292.)

20. Gove Griffith Johnson, *The Treasury and Monetary Policies, 1933–1938* (Cambridge: Harvard University Press, 1939), pp. 218 and 223.

21. Eccles, *Beckoning Frontiers,* pp. 317–20.

22. Friedman and Schwartz, *Monetary History,* pp. 518–29.

23. Johnson, *The Treasury and Monetary Policies,* p. 45.

24. Ibid., pp. 205–11.

25. Frederick A. Bradford, "The Banking Act of 1935," *American Economic Review, Proceedings* 25 (1935): 672.

26. John H. Williams, "The Banking Act of 1935,"*American Economic Review, Proceedings* 26 (1936): 96–104.

27. Jacob Viner, "Recent Legislation and the Banking Situation," *American Economic Review, Proceedings* 26 (1936): 106–16.

28. Kenneth D. Roose, "The Recession of 1937–38," *Journal of Political Economy* 56 (June 1948): 241.

29. Ibid., p. 246.

30. Ibid., p. 241.

Chapter Twenty

1. Most of the factual history on the wage-price control program is taken from Hugh Rockoff, *Drastic Measures: A History of Wage and Price Controls in the United States* (Cambridge: Cambridge University Press, 1984). Rockoff's book is a superb presentation of the events and data together with a thought-provoking analysis of the

episode. On some points the following account takes issue with Rockoff's conclusions. Nonetheless, his treatment is exemplary.

2. Board of Governors of the Federal Reserve System, *Supplement to Banking and Monetary Statistics,* Section 9 (Washington, D.C.: Government Printing Office, 1965).

3. Eccles, *Beckoning Frontiers,* p. 350.

4. Ibid., p. 358.

5. Ibid., p. 350.

6. Ibid., pp. 358–60.

7. Friedman and Schwartz, *Monetary History,* p. 567.

8. Eccles, *Beckoning Frontiers,* pp. 360–61.

9. Table 19.2, and Rockoff, *Drastic Measures,* pp. 109–10.

10. Rockoff, *Drastic Measures,* pp. 147, 151, 167–69.

11. Ibid., pp. 147, 160, 173; Friedman and Schwartz, *Monetary History,* p. 557.

12. Rockoff, *Drastic Measures,* pp. 139–74.

13. Ibid., p. 138.

14. Ibid., pp. 146–71.

15. Eccles, *Beckoning Frontiers,* pp. 370–75, 382.

16. Ibid., p. 422.

17. Allan Sproul, "Monetary Management and Credit Control," *AER* 37 (1947): 344–45.

18. See Warburton, "The Volume of Money and the Price Level Between the World Wars." *Journal of Political Economy* 53 (June 1945): 150–63, reprinted in Clark Warburton, *Depression, Inflation, and Monetary Policy,* pp. 125–38.

19. E. C. Simmons, "Treasury Deposits and Excess Reserves," *Journal Of Political Economy* 52 (June 1940): 339–40.

20. J. H. Williams, "The Implications of Fiscal Policy for Monetary Policy and the Reserve System," *AER* 32 (1942): 240, 246.

21. Karl R. Bopp, "Central Banking at the Crossroads," *AER Supp.* 34 (1944): 260–69.

22. Lawrence H. Seltzer, "Discussion," *AER Supp.* 34 (1944): 280–85.

23. Seltzer, "The Changed Environment of Monetary-Banking Policy," *AER Proceedings* 36 (1946): 65–73.

24. Friedman and Schwartz, *Monetary History,* pp. 581–83; Eccles, *Beckoning Frontiers,* p. 425; Sproul, "Monetary Management," p. 349.

25. E. A. Goldenweiser, "Federal Reserve Objectives and Policies: Retrospect and Prospect," *AER* 37 (1947): 320–38; Eccles, *Beckoning Frontiers,* pp. 426–33; Sproul, "Monetary Management," p. 346.

26. Lloyd W. Mints, *Monetary Policy for a Competitive Society* (New York: McGraw-Hill, 1950).

27. *FR Bulletin,* September 1937, April 1939. Also, several annual reports.

28. George L. Bach, "Monetary-Fiscal Policy Reconsidered," *JPE* (October 1949): 388–89.

29. The notable exception among economists of the era was Clark Warburton. See the articles listed in part 4 of his collected essays, *Depression, Inflation, and Monetary Policy.* This section, "Central Banking and Monetary Policy," reflects the scholarship

and erudition of a detached observer unaffected by the current wave of popular economic opinion, and impervious to official pronouncements of "intent."

30. George L. Bach, "The Federal Reserve and Monetary Policy Formation," *AER* 39 (December 1949): 1179–90.

31. Friedman and Schwartz, *Monetary History,* p. 596.

32. Ibid., p. 597.

33. Eccles, *Beckoning Frontiers,* p. 484.

34. Ibid., pp. 434–56.

35. Ibid., pp. 483–98.

36. U.S. Congress, 81st Cong., 2d sess., *Monetary, Credit and Fiscal Policies: Report of the Subcommittee ("Douglas Committee") of the Joint Committee on the Economic Report,* Sen. Doc. No. 129, January 1950 (Washington: Government Printing Office, 1950), pp. 2 and 18.

37. U.S. Congress, 82d Cong., 2d sess. *Monetary Policy and Management of the Public Debt: Report of the Subcommittee on General Credit Control and Debt Management ("Patman Committee") of the Joint Committee on the Economic Report,* Sen. Doc. No. 163, February 1952 (Washington: Government Printing Office, 1952), p. 1.

38. Friedman and Schwartz, *Monetary History,* p. 625.

39. In 1935, when Eccles first became chairman of the Federal Reserve Board, he had believed that fiscal policy would be more effective, and he agreed to adapt monetary policy to the Treasury's initiatives. By the end of World War II, he was for reversing the course of the inflationary fiscal-monetary policy to stave off developing inflation. This appropriate consistency brought him into conflict with the John Snyder Treasury, and he fell from grace. See Sidney Hyman, *Marriner S. Eccles, Private Entrepreneur and Public Servant* (Stanford, Calif.: Stanford University Graduate School of Business, 1976), pp. 322–51.

40. Friedman and Schwartz, *Monetary History,* pp. 625–27.

Chapter Twenty-One

1. Board of Governors of the Federal Reserve System, *The Federal Reserve Act as Amended through October 1, 1961,* Section 10, Article 6, p. 31.

2. Eccles, *Beckoning Frontiers,* p. 394.

3. Ibid., p. 425.

4. Friedman and Schwartz, *Monetary History,* pp. 628–29.

5. Patman Subcommittee Report, p. 50.

6. Ibid., p. 51.

7. Ibid.; emphasis added.

8. Ibid., p. 53; emphasis added.

9. U.S.C. title 15, sec. 1021. Cited in *The Federal Reserve Act as Amended through October 1, 1961,* p. 293.

10. Douglas Subcommittee Report, pp. 2 and 18. Patman Subcommittee Report, p. 3.

11. Douglas Subcommittee Report, p. 42.

12. Ibid.

13. Ibid., p. 43.
14. Ibid., pp. 43–44.
15. Ibid., p. 16.
16. Ibid.
17. Patman Subcommittee Report, p. 67.
18. Walter E. Spahr, "A Reply to Mr. Sproul on the Gold Standard," first printed in the *Commercial and Financial Chronicle,* 10 November 1949; reprinted in *Money and Economic Activity,* 3d ed., ed. Lawrence Ritter (New York: Houghton Mifflin, 1961), p. 46. References are to the latter source.
19. Patman Subcommittee Report, p. 68.
20. Ibid. Sproul cited no evidence of his assertion. People could hardly have "stormed the Federal Reserve Banks" when the Fed banks did not do business with the general public.
21. Spahr, *Money and Economic Activity,* p. 44.
22. Patman Subcommittee Report, p. 66.
23. Ibid., p. 65.
24. Ibid.
25. Ibid., pp. 70–71.
26. Ibid., p. 72.
27. Ibid., p. 73.
28. Ibid.
29. Ibid., p. 74.
30. Ibid.
31. Ibid., p. 76.
32. Ibid., p. 77.
33. Friedman and Schwartz, *Monetary History,* pp. 601–2.

Chapter Twenty-Two

1. Bias in a statistical estimate such as a price index may be defined as a *systematic tendency to err.* It occurs in price indexes because the intrinsic qualities of items priced in the sample do not stay constant. Usually common goods and services improve in quality because suppliers compete on the basis of both price and quality. In addition to quality bias, the importance of priced goods and services in consumer budgets—their weights—also change over time, all of which contributes to making computed index values read higher than they would if statisticians could compensate for such biasing effects when they compute the index. But they cannot do so completely. Given such biases, the "increase" in the price level from 93.2 in 1953 to 109.9 in 1965 (18 percent over thirteen years), noted in table 21.1, was hardly an increase. In fact, it would have been in effect a decrease in "prices" if the 1965 product was more than 18 percent "better" than the 1953 product.
2. *Federal Reserve Bulletin,* September 1965, p. 1237. See also a similar statement in FRB, April 1967, p. 561.
3. *FRB,* February 1965, p. 219.
4. Ibid. Under Regulation Q, the Federal Reserve Board had authority over ceiling rates payable on member banks' time and savings deposits.

5. *FRB,* April 1967, p. 561.

6. Ibid., p. 565.

7. *FRB,* December 1967, p. 2033.

8. *FRB,* August 1971, p. 656. Emphasis supplied.

9. Ibid., p. 659.

10. *FRB,* June 1973, p. 406. Borrowings would have been even higher except for the frequent compromises made in easing policy "to avoid further reserve pressure" (ibid.). See also *FRB,* May 1973, p. 320.

11. *FRB,* December 1973, p. 887, and the Federal Reserve Bank of St. Louis, *U.S. Financial Data,* 2 October 1974. The Fed funds rate was three percentage points above the Federal Reserve discount rate at the time.

12. See, e.g., Hepburn, *History of Coinage and Currency,* pp. 500–504.

13. Jacob Viner, *Studies in the Theory of International Trade* (New York: Harper, 1937), p. 153.

14. *FRB,* August 1968, p. 678. Hickman was the only dissenter. In previous meetings, Darryl Francis had expressed an even firmer opinion in favor of restraint. By this time, however, he had rotated off the committee.

15. *FRB,* October 1968, p. 866.

16. *FRB,* November 1968, p. 911.

17. *FRB,* December 1968, p. 1009.

18. *FRB,* April 1969, p. 352. However, in the November 1968 meeting four members had dissented from the majority and favored tighter policy. (*FRB,* March 1969, p. 265.).

19. *FRB,* March 1969, p. 235.

20. Ibid., p. 237.

21. *FRB,* April 1970, p. 339.

22. The "aggregates" included two measures of the economy's money stock, M_1 and M_2, plus the bank-credit proxy—daily average member bank deposits, and member bank reserves.

23. *FRB,* August 1970, p. 624.

24. This lesson was well taught by Milton Friedman in his presidential address to the American Economic Association in December 1967. See Milton Friedman, "The Role of Monetary Policy," *American Economic Review* (March 1968): 1–17.

25. *FRB,* January 1971, p. 26. Here, the Fed implied an ability to cope with business conditions in a specialized industry (housing). Why not the dry-cleaning industry and drugstores? Since money appears in all markets, a monetary policy that favors a particular market necessarily discriminates against other markets.

26. *FRB,* February 1971, p. 119.

27. *FRB,* April 1971, p. 325.

28. Alan R. Holmes, "Open Market Operations in 1972," *FRB,* June 1973, pp. 405–16. RPDs—reserves available to support private deposits—were adopted in March 1972 as one of the official targets for Fed policy.

29. Besides the Economic Stabilization Act, the NEP also included a loosening of fiscal constraints by adoption of a "full employment budget" policy and the abandonment of the policy of fixed exchange rates.

30. *FRB,* December 1971, p. 994.

31. Ibid.

32. *FRB*, February 1972, p. 125. In 1947, the total budget for the federal government was $40 billion.

33. Ibid., p. 126.

34. One may also add the Penitence Principle as a third phase of Federal Reserve actions: The Fed finally realizes the error of its ways and reduces the growth rate in the money supply to a fraction of its former value. The economy then pays penance.

35. *FRB*, December 1972, p. 1020.

36. *FRB*, February 1974, pp. 112 and 121. The question may be raised again as to the propriety of using monetary policy to control a particular industrial problem.

37. *FRB*, February 1973, p. 102.

38. *FRB*, June 1973, pp. 383–402, and March 1974, pp. 210–11.

39. Milton Friedman, "Letter on Monetary Policy to Senator William Proxmire," *Federal Reserve Bank of St. Louis Review* 56:3 (March 1974): 22–23.

40. Arthur F. Burns, "Money Supply in the Conduct of Monetary Policy," *FRB*, November 1973, p. 792.

41. Ibid., p. 793.

42. Milton Friedman and David Meiselman, "The Relative Stability of Monetary Velocity and the Investment Multiplier in the United States, 1897–1958," *Stabilization Policies* (Englewood Cliffs, N.J.: Prentice Hall, 1963), pp. 165–268.

43. Friedman, "Letter on Monetary Policy," *Federal Reserve Bank of St. Louis Review*, p. 22. Lagged reserve requirements meant that accounted reserves consisting of vault cash held during the week two weeks earlier, plus reserve-deposit accounts at the Federal Reserve banks during the current week, were legal reserves against deposits for the week two weeks earlier. This complex accounting procedure, which the Board of Governors initiated in September 1968, according to George Kaufman, increased the complexity of the money supply multiplier and encouraged banks to search out nondeposit sources of funds. It thereby increased the difficulty of controlling the stock of money. "To the extent the increased difficulty supports the long voiced contention of some Federal Reserve officials that they are unable to control the stock of money even if they so wished, the actions truly represent a self-fulfilling prophecy," Kaufman concluded.

44. Alan R. Holmes, "Monetary Policy in a Changing Financial Environment: Open Market Operations in 1974." *FRB*, April 1975, pp. 197–208.

45. Alan R. Holmes, "The Strategy of Monetary Control." *FRB*, May 1976, p. 421.

46. The rate of increase monetarists recommended depended on which money stock was targeted. If it was M_1, the rate was approximately 1 to 3 percent per year; if M_2, 2 to 5 percent. Later monetarism called for targeting the monetary base on the order of 3.5 percent per year. The most important aspect of the monetarist proposal was not the precise rate of increase, but that the rate of increase be constant—month-in month-out, week-in week-out, day-in day-out—in order to excise the discretionary element in Fed policy.

47. *FRB*, September 1968, p. 1238.

48. Milton Friedman, "Reply," *Federal Reserve Bank of St. Louis Review* 56:3 (March 1974): 23.

49. Arthur F. Burns, "The Importance of an Independent Central Bank." *FRB*, September 1977, pp. 777–81. Commencement address at Jacksonville University, Au-

gust 1977. "The Anguish of Central Banking," *FRB,* September 1987, pp. 687–98. Per Jacobsson Lecture, Belgrade, Yugoslavia, September 1979.

50. Burns, "Anguish." *FRB,* September 1979, p. 689.
51. Ibid., p. 691.
52. Ibid., p. 692.
53. Ibid. Emphasis supplied.
54. Ibid., pp. 695–96. Emphasis supplied.
55. For an analysis of pressures on Fed policy see Thomas Havrilesky, *The Pressures on American Monetary Policy* (Boston: Kluwer Academic Publishers, 1993).

Chapter Twenty-Three

1. *FRB* 64, January 1978, p. 59, and March 1978, p. 249.
2. *FRB* 65, August 1979, pp. 631–32.
3. *FRB* 65, December 1979, pp. 972–78.
4. Ibid., pp. 972–73.
5. Ibid., p. 974. Emphasis added.
6. Ibid., p. 977.
7. Ibid., pp. 977–78.
8. Ibid., pp. 958–59.
9. Ibid., pp. 959–62. His emphasis. See also pp. 888–90.
10. *FRB* 66, June 1980, pp. 484–85.
11. Ibid., p. 487.
12. For an explanation of how the inflation rate becomes incorporated into the interest-rate structure, see William Beranek, Thomas Humphrey, and Richard Timberlake, "Fisher, Thornton, and the Analysis of the Inflation Premium," *Journal of Money, Credit, and Banking* 17:3 (August 1985): 371–77.
13. *FRB* 66, June 1980, p. 488.
14. The net transfer of balances over the month of April 1980 from private owners to the Treasury was approximately $12.5 billion. See *FRB* 66, May 1980, pp. A11 and A21.
15. *FRB* 66, September 1980, pp. 747–53.
16. *FRB* 66, October 1980, p. 838. Emphasis added.
17. *FRB* 66, November 1980, p. 885.
18. Ibid., p. 887.
19. Ibid.
20. *FRB* 66, December 1980, p. 969.
21. Ibid., p. 972.
22. Ibid., p. 973.
23. *FRB* 67, January 1981, pp. 29–30.
24. Ibid., p. 31. The reader should remember that I have used "M_1" as a label for what was termed "M_{1B}" at this time. M_{1A} was a narrower stock of money containing only hand-to-hand currency and bank demand deposits.
25. Ibid., p. 32.
26. Ibid., pp. 32–33.
27. *FRB* 67, February 1981, pp. 153–54.

28. *FRB* 66, December 1980, p. 944.

29. Ibid., p. 946.

30. See, again, "Fisher, Thornton, and an Analysis of the Inflation Premium," pp. 371–77.

31. *FRB* 66, December 1980, pp. 946–52.

32. Ibid., p. 946.

33. See Volcker's discussion of discounting tactics. Ibid., pp. 948–49.

34. Ibid., p. 951.

35. David Meiselman, "The Political Monetary Cycle," *Wall Street Journal,* Tuesday, 10 January 1984, op-ed page. See also *Political Business Cycles,* ed.Thomas D. Willett, Pacific Research Institute for Public Policy (Durham and London: Duke University Press, 1988).

36. *FRB* 67, March 1981, pp. 237–41.

37. The Federal Reserve Board itself introduced lagged reserve accounting (LRA) in 1968. Instead of basing required reserves on deposits as accounted in any given week, LRA required reserves in the accounting week for deposits accounted two weeks earlier. These required reserves could be vault cash (currency) held during the week two weeks earlier, plus reserve-deposit accounts at Federal Reserve banks during the current week. (Whew!) This procedure effectively abdicated the Fed's positive control over bank deposits. If commercial member banks overextended their loans and deposits in the accounting week, and appeared cap-in-hand for Fed accommodation in the current week, Fed banks felt obliged to indulge them in order to prevent the bad publicity and possible panic that would follow public knowledge of a reserve "shortage." After two decades of this ill-conceived attempt to court commercial bank membership, and after many scientific studies both in and outside the Federal Reserve System demonstrated its inefficacies, the Fed abandoned the practice early in 1984. By this time, the Federal Reserve Board had the power to fix reserve requirements for all banks and depository institutions, so membership participation by banking institutions was no longer a "problem."

38. *FRB* 67, March 1981, p. 238. For an interesting account of the Carter credit control program, see Stacey L. Schreft and Raymond E. Owens, "Survey Evidence of Tighter Credit Conditions: What Does It Mean?" *Economic Review,* Federal Reserve Bank of Richmond, 77/2 March/April 1991, pp. 29–34.

39. *FRB* 67, March 1981, p. 240.

40. Milton Friedman, "The Federal Reserve and Monetary Instability," *Wall Street Journal,* op-ed page, 1 February 1982.

41. For examples of this misinterpretation of both monetarism and its results, see the following: Jack Kemp, "Talking Back to the Skeptics," *National Review,* 11 June 1982; "Bring Back Bretton Woods," editorial, *Wall Street Journal,* 22 June 1982; Lindley Clark, "What Reagan Likes about Monetarism," *Wall Street Journal,* 20 July 1982; David M. Smick, "Is the Federal Reserve Causing the Recession?" *Human Events,* 31 July 1982; and Tom Bethell, "Bucks Stopper," *Reason,* February 1983.

42. *FRB* 68, December 1982, p. 764.

43. Ibid., p. 766.

44. *FRB* 69, April 1983, p. 286.

45. Ibid., p. 287.

Chapter Twenty-Four

1. *Congressional Record* (hereafter *CR*), vol. 126, part 6 (27 March 1980), p. 6893.

2. Ibid., p. 7318.

3. G. William Miller, Statement to Committee on Banking, Housing, and Urban Affairs, U.S. House of Representatives (*FRB* 65, March 1979, pp. 229–35). See also *FRB*, September 1970, and *FRB*, September 1978, p. A19.

4. Miller, "Statement," p. 230.

5. Paul Volcker, Statement to Committee on Banking, Housing, and Urban Affairs, U.S. Senate, 26 September 1979 (*FRB* 65, October 1979, p. 823).

6. Ibid., p. 825.

7. *CR* 125 (1979), pt. 15, p. 19689.

8. Miller, "Statement," p. 230.

9. *FRB* 76, November 1990, p. A6.

10. *FRB* 66, June 1980, p. 448.

11. *CR* 125 (1979), pt. 15, p. 19678.

12. Ibid., p. 19679.

13. Ibid., pp. 19679–90.

14. *FRB* 65, October 1979, p. 828.

15. *FRB* 66, February 1980, p. 147.

16. *CR* 126 (1980), pt. 6, p. 6897. Emphasis added.

17. *CR* 125 (1979), pt. 15, p. 19669.

18. Letter from Paul Volcker, chairman of the Board of Governors of the Federal Reserve System, to the Honorable Henry S. Reuss, chairman of the Committee on Banking, Finance, and Urban Affairs, 4 March 1980. (Copy furnished to the author courtesy of John McLaughry, former senior adviser to the White House during the Reagan administration.)

19. *CR* 126 (27 March 1980), pt. 6, pp. 6963–85, 7063–73.

20. *FRB*, 1981–1984, table 1.18, p. A-11.

21. Letter from Paul Volcker, chairman of the Board of Governors of the Federal Reserve System, to Congressman Ronald E. Paul, 10 July 1981. (Copy furnished to the author courtesy of John McLaughry.)

22. Ibid.

23. Ibid.

24. Mark Hulbert, "Bailing Out the Bankers," *Inquiry,* 15 and 29 June 1981, pp. 9–11.

25. *FRB* 65, August 1979, pp. 631–32. Volker is now (1991) chairman of the board of the Council on Foreign Relations.

26. *FRB* 69, March 1983, pp. 194–95.

27. *FRB* 70, February 1984, p. 109.

28. *FRB* 65, October 1979, p. 824.

29. *FRB* 65, March 1979, pp. 234–35.

30. *FRB* 76, March 1990, p. 153.

31. *FRB* 65, March 1979, p. 231.

32. *FRB* 65, October 1979, p. 824. Of course, every Board preferred legislation that would extend its turf.

33. *CR* 126 (27 March 1980), pt. 6, p. 6894.
34. *CR* 125 (20 July 1979), pt. 15, p. 19687.

Chapter Twenty-Five

1. For excellent analyses of the velocity shift, see Courtenay C. Stone and Daniel L. Thornton, "Solving the 1980s' Velocity Puzzle: A Progress Report," *Federal Reserve Bank of St. Louis Review,* 69, August/September 1987, pp. 5–23; same authors, "Financial Innovation: Causes and Consequences." *Current Issues in Monetary Analysis and Policy,* eds. Kevin Dowd and Mervyn Lewis. (London: Macmillan, 1991).
2. *FRB* 69, August 1983, p. 623.
3. Ibid., p. 618.
4. Ibid., p. 619.
5. Ibid., p. 621.
6. Volcker, Statement before the Joint Economic Committee of the U.S. Congress, 5 February 1985 (*FRB* 71, April 1985, pp. 205–6).
7. I label it a "spending deficit" because tax revenues constantly increase over the years even without a legislated tax increase. However, congressional appropriations force spending to increase even faster. Thus, the shortfall each year is not a "fiscal deficit" but a "spending deficit."
8. The correlation of annual first differences of U.S. trade deficits against U.S. fiscal deficits has an r^2 value greater than 0.9. For a Federal Reserve perspective on this issue, see E. Gerald Corrigan, Statement before the Committee on the Budget, U.S. Senate, 6 May 1987 (*FRB* 73, July 1987, pp. 569–70).
9. "Monetary Policy Report to the Congress," 19 February 1986 (*FRB* 72, April 1986, pp. 213–28).
10. Ibid., pp. 233–41.
11. Ibid., pp. 234–35.
12. Ibid., p. 238.
13. Ibid., p. 240.
14. Volcker, Statement before the Committee on Banking, Housing, and Urban Affairs, U.S. Senate, 23 July 1986 (*FRB* 72, September 1986, p. 639).
15. Ibid.
16. Ibid., p. 641.
17. Ibid., p. 642.
18. "Record of Policy Actions," *FRB* 72, October 1986, pp. 707–9.
19. Ibid., p. 652. (Emphasis added.) Board member Henry Wallich was the only person on the FOMC who voted for greater restraint.
20. "Record of Policy Actions," 8–9 July 1986 (*FRB* 72, October 1986, p. 710). Thomas Melzer, president of the St. Louis Fed, was the dissenting voice. Melzer favored continuing "the existing degree of pressure on reserve conditions" (p. 712).
21. "Monetary Policy Report to the Congress," 19 February 1987 (*FRB* 73, April 1987, p. 239).
22. Ibid., p. 240. A later statement indicated that the policies referred to were those "in place since the early part of the decade" (p. 243). However, the effects of the disinflationary policy of 1981–82 were surely dissipated by early 1987.

23. Ibid., p. 240. The growth in M_1 was also "unprecedented." But the report ignored the growth in M_1 since the FOMC was not targeting that variable.

24. Ibid., p. 243.

25. Volcker, Statement before the Joint Economic Committee of the U.S. Congress, 2 February 1987 (*FRB* 73, April 1987, p. 275).

26. Ibid., p. 277. Or maybe the Policy Report echoed *him*. The chairman's influence on FOMC decision-making is far more than his vote as one of the twelve Board members.

27. "Monetary Policy Report to the Congress," 21 July 1987 (*FRB* 73, August 1987, pp. 633–37).

28. Ibid.

29. I would have suggested at this time what might be labeled "Timberlake's Golden Constant"—an annual growth rate in the monetary base of 3.65 percent, except for leap years, when the growth rate would be 3.66 percent.

Chapter Twenty-Six

1. *FRB* 73, July 1987, p. 588.
2. *FRB* 73, September 1987, p. 706.
3. "Record of Policy Actions," *FRB* 74, February 1988, p. 114.
4. Ibid., p. 119.
5. "Monetary Policy Report to the Congress," 23 February 1988 (*FRB* 74, March 1988, pp. 151–52).
6. Ibid., p. 154.
7. Ibid., p. A50.
8. Ibid., p. 161.
9. "Record of Policy Actions of the FOMC," *FRB* 74, August 1988, p. 543. Emphasis supplied.
10. Ibid., p. 518.
11. Alan Greenspan, Statement before the Committee on Banking, Housing, and Urban Affairs of the U.S. Senate, 13 July 1988 (*FRB* 74, September 1988, pp. 609–12).
12. Ibid., p. 613. Clearly this volume of per capita currency is *not* held in the United States. (See chapter 25.)
13. Greenspan appeared before the House Committees on Ways and Means and Banking, Housing, and Urban Affairs and their Senate counterparts, and also before the Senate Committee on the Budget during February 1989. *FRB* 75, April 1989, pp. 270–86.
14. Ibid., p. 274.
15. Ibid., p. 275.
16. Ibid.
17. The staff study appeared in the same issue of the *FRB*. See David H. Small and Richard D. Porter, "Understanding the Behavior of M_2 and V_{M2}" (ibid., pp. 244–54). Also Jeffrey J. Hallman, Richard D. Porter, and David H. Small, "M_2 per Unit of Potential GNP as an Anchor for the Price Level" (ibid., pp. 263–64).
18. Ibid., p. 277.

19. U.S. Congress, *Congressional Record,* 101st Cong., 1st sess., vol. 135, no. 106, 1 August 1989, p. H4845.

20. Ibid.

21. Greenspan, Statement to Subcommittee on Domestic Monetary Policy of the Committee on Banking, Finance, and Urban Affairs, House of Representatives, 25 October 1989 (*FRB* 75, December 1989, p. 797).

22. Ibid.

23. Ibid., p. 798.

24. "Record of Policy Actions of the FOMC," 29 March 1988 (*FRB* 74, July 1988, p. 473). Emphasis supplied. The "Record of Policy Actions" for 9–10 February 1988 still included "reasonable" (*FRB* 74, May 1988, p. 324).

25. Donald L. Kohn, "Policy Targets and Operating Procedures," *FRB* 76, January 1990, pp. 1–7.

26. Corrigan, "Statement," *FRB* 76, March 1990, p. 132.

27. Ibid.

28. Ibid., p. 135.

29. Ibid.

30. Ibid., pp. 136–37.

31. Ibid., p. 137.

32. Ibid., p. 138.

33. Ibid., pp. 140–42.

34. Ibid., p. 143. (His emphasis.)

35. Ibid., p. 144.

36. Ibid., p. 145.

37. Ibid.

38. Ibid., pp. 147–48.

39. Ibid., pp. 148–49.

40. Ibid., p. 150.

41. *Congressional Quarterly Weekly Report,* 10 February 1990, p. 383.

42. John R. Cranford, "Fed Expects Moderate Growth, Signals No Drop in Rates," *CQ,* 24 February 1990, p. 574.

43. Ibid. Some months later the Bush administration signed a record-breaking tax increase bill and an "environmental" bill, both of which were bound to have adverse effects on business conditions and tend to raise interest rates.

Chapter Twenty-Seven

1. Richard E. Wagner, "Central Banking and the Fed: A Public Choice Perspective," *Cato Journal* 6:2 (Fall 1986): 519–38.

2. Irving Fisher, *Stabilizing the Dollar* (New York: Macmillan, 1920). The idea itself is much older. See chap. 11 herein for a statement by Senator John P. Jones of Nevada in 1888, and chap. 12, epigraph, for a statement by Senator William Stewart of Nevada in 1890.

3. Ibid., pp. 205–13.

4. Lloyd Wynn Mints, *Monetary Policy for a Competitive Society* (New York: McGraw-Hill, 1950), pp. 9–10.

5. Ibid., pp. 125–26.

6. Ibid., p. 127. Representative Charles Strong, who sponsored the price level bill, was not related to Benjamin Strong, president of the Federal Reserve Bank of New York, who opposed the measure.

7. Ibid., pp. 127–28. Mints cited *FRB* 23, 1937, pp. 827–28, and *FRB* 25, 1939, p. 255.

8. Ibid., pp. 224–25.

9. See Milton Friedman and David Meiselman, "The Relative Stability of Monetary Policy and the Investment Multiplier in the United States, 1897–1958," in *Stabilization Policies* (Englewood Cliffs, N.J.: Prentice-Hall, 1963), pp. 165–268.

10. Neal's staff economist, Mr. Ben W. Crain, sent out questionnaires to 3,000 economists of the American Economic Association who listed their major specialty as "monetary and fiscal theory and policy."

11. Personal communication to author, 21 March 1991.

12. *FRB,* September 1988, pp. 630–31.

13. Of course, fiscal policy has no Federal Reserve Board or FOMC. Maybe it should have one—say a fiscal stabilization board that Congress would delegate as its "conscience" to put an overall cap on federal spending in any one year. Then all the agencies, bureaus, and special interest lobbies would only be able to squabble over a fixed total of expenditures.

14. Friedman and Schwartz, "Has Government Any Role in Money?" *Journal of Monetary Economics* 11 (January 1986): 19.

15. For a treatment of some of these events, see Richard H. Timberlake, "The Significance of Unaccounted Currencies," *Journal of Economic History* 41 (December 1981): 853–66, and "Private Production of Scrip-Money in the Isolated Community," *Journal of Money, Credit, and Banking* 19 (November 1987): 437–47.

16. See chapter 14 herein for an account of this episode.

17. Milton Friedman and Anna J. Schwartz, *A Monetary History of the United States, 1863–1960* (Princeton: NBER and Princeton University Press, 1963).

18. Friedman and Schwartz, "Has Government Any Role in Money?" p. 6.

19. Ibid., p. 34.

20. Bagehot, *Lombard Street;* Vera Smith, *The Rationale of Central Banking* (Indianapolis: Liberty Press, 1990; first published Westminster, England: P. S. King & Son, Ltd., 1936).

21. Friedman and Schwartz, "Has Government Any Role in Money?" p. 37.

22. Charles Goodhart, *The Evolution of Central Banks* (London, England, and Cambridge, Massachusetts: MIT Press, 1988), pp. 85–104.

23. Huston McCulloch, "Beyond the Historical Gold Standard," in *Alternative Monetary Regimes,* ed. C. D. Campbell and W. R. Dougan (Baltimore: Johns Hopkins University Press, 1986).

24. See the following recent works for substantive documentation on the free banking paradigm—how it worked in the past and how it would work in the present: Kevin Dowd, *The State and the Monetary System* (New York: St. Martin's Press, 1989); George Selgin, *The Theory of Free Banking* (Totowa, N.J.: Rowan and Littlefield, 1988); Lawrence H. White, *Free Banking in Britain* (Cambridge: Cambridge University Press, 1984); David Glasner, *Free Banking and Monetary Reform* (Cambridge: Cambridge University Press, 1989).

25. See chapter 14 for an account of this practice.

26. For substantiation and arguments on this point, see, Richard H. Timberlake, *Gold, Greenbacks, and the Constitution.*

27. U.S. Constitution, Article I, Section 8.

28. Timberlake, *Gold, Greenbacks, and the Constitution,* pp. 6–10.

29. William Brough, *The Natural Law of Money* (New York: Greenwood Press, 1969 [G. P. Putnam's Sons, 1896]).

30. Robert Greenfield and Leland Yeager, "A Laissez-Faire Approach to Monetary Stability," *Journal of Money, Credit, and Banking* 15:3 (August 1983): 302–15.

Bibliography

Aldrich, Nelson W. *The Work of the National Monetary Commission*. Sen. Doc. No. 406. 61st Cong., 2d sess., 1910.

Anderson, Benjamin M. *Economics and the Public Welfare, a Financial and Economic History of the United States, 1914–1946*. Liberty Press, Indianapolis: 1979. (First published, New York: Van Nostrand, 1949.)

Andrew, A. Piatt. *Statistics for the United States,* Sen. Doc. No. 570, National Monetary Commission (Washington, 1910).

———. "Substitutes for Cash in the Panic of 1907." *Quarterly Journal of Economics,* 22 (August 1908).

———. "Treasury and Banks under Secretary Shaw." *Quarterly Journal of Economics* 21 (1907).

Bach, George L. "The Federal Reserve and Monetary Policy Formation." *American Economic Review* 39 (1949).

———. "Monetary-Fiscal Policy Reconsidered." *Journal of Political Economy* 57 (October 1949).

Bagehot, Walter. *Lombard Street,* rev. ed. London: Kegan Paul, Trench, Toubner and Co., 1906.

Barrett, Don C. "The Supposed Necessity of Legal Tender Paper." *Quarterly Journal of Economics* 16 (May 1902).

Bennett, Robert A. "A Banking Puzzle: Mixing Freedom and Protection." *New York Times,* February 19, 1984.

Benton, Thomas Hart. *Thirty Years' View,* vols. 1 and 2. New York, 1854–1865.

Bethel, Tom. "Bucks Stopper." *Reason,* February 1983.

Blaine, James M. *Twenty Years of Congress*. Norwich, Conn.: Henry Bill Publishing Co., 1886.

Board of Governors of the Federal Reserve System. "Monetary Policy Report to Congress," February 19, 1987. *Federal Reserve Bulletin* 73 (April 1987).

———. "Monetary Policy Report to the Congress." *Federal Reserve Bulletin* 74 (February 23, 1988).

———. *Federal Reserve Bulletin*. Selected volumes, 1914–1992.

———. *The Federal Reserve Act as Amended through October 1, 1961*. Washington: Federal Reserve Board, 1962.

———. "Monetary Policy Report to Congress," July 21, 1987. *Federal Reserve Bulletin* 73 (August 1987).

———. *Supplement to Banking and Monetary Statistics,* section 9. Washington: Government Printing Office, 1965.

Bopp, Karl R. "Central Banking at the Crossroads." *American Economic Review Proceedings* 34 (1944).

Bourne, E. G. *The History of the Surplus Revenue of 1837*. New York, 1885.

Boutwell, George. *Why I Am a Republican*. Philadelphia: W. S. Fortescue & Co., 1884.

Bradford, Frederick A., "The Banking Act of 1935." *American Economic Review Proceedings* 25 (1935).

Breckenridge, S. P., *Legal Tender*. New York: Greenwood Press, 1969. (First published, Chicago: University of Chicago Press, 1903.)

"Bring Back Bretton Woods." *Wall Street Journal,* June 22, 1982.

Brough, William. *The Natural Law of Money*. New York: Greenwood Press, 1969. (First published, New York: G. P. Putnam's Sons, 1896.)

Burns, Arthur F. "Money Supply in the Conduct of Monetary Policy." *Federal Reserve Bulletin* 59 (1973).

———. "The Importance of an Independent Central Bank." *Federal Reserve Bulletin* 63 (September 1977).

———. "The Anguish of Central Banking." *Federal Reserve Bulletin* 73 (1987).

Burns, Arthur R. *Money and Monetary Policy in Early Times*. New York: Augustus M. Kelley, 1965. (First published in 1927.)

Cagan, Philip. *Determinants and Effects of Changes in the Stock of Money, 1875–1960*. NBER (New York: Columbia University Press, 1965).

Cannon, James Graham. *Clearing Houses*. Sen. Doc. No. 491. 61st Cong. 2d sess. National Monetary Commission, 1910.

Carothers, Neil. *Fractional Currency*. New York: Wiley and Sons, 1930. (Reprinted, New York: Reprints of Economic Classics, Augustus M. Kelley, 1967.)

Catterall, R. C. H. *The Second Bank of the United States*. Chicago: University of Chicago Press, 1902.

Clark, Lindley. "What Reagan Likes about Monetarism." *Wall Street Journal,* July 20, 1982.

Congressional Quarterly Weekly Report, February 10, 1990.

Corrigan, E. Gerald. Statement before the Committee on the Budget, U.S. Senate, May 6, 1987. *Federal Reserve Bulletin* 73 (1987).

Cranford, John R., "Fed Expects Moderate Growth, Signals No Drop in Rates." *Congressional Quarterly,* February 24, 1990.

Dewald, William G. "The National Monetary Commission: A Look Back." *Journal of Money, Credit, and Banking* 4 (November 1972).

Dewey, Davis R. *State Banking before the Civil War*. Sen. Doc. No. 581. 61st Cong., 2d sess., National Monetary Commission, 1910.

Dictionary of American Biography.

Dowd, Kevin. *The State and the Monetary System*. New York: St. Martin's Press, 1989.

Duane, William J. *Narrative and Correspondence concerning the Removal of the Deposits, and Occurrences Connected Therewith*. Philadelphia, 1838.

Dunbar, Charles F. *The Theory and History of Banking*. New York: C. P. Putnam's Sons, 1922.

Dunne, Gerald T. *Monetary Decisions of the Supreme Court*. New Brunswick: Rutgers University Press, 1960.

Eccles, Marriner. *Beckoning Frontiers*. New York: Alfred Knopf, 1951.

Federal Reserve Bank of St. Louis, *U.S. Financial Data*. Selected issues, 1975–1992.

Fels, Rendigs. *American Business Cycles*. Chapel Hill: University of North Carolina Press, 1959.

Fetter, Frank W. *Development of British Monetary Orthodoxy*. Cambridge: Harvard University Press, 1965.

Fisher, Irving. *Stabilizing the Dollar*. New York: Macmillan, 1920.

Frangul, Ramzi. Book review, *Journal of Finance* 35 (March 1980).

Friedman, Milton. "The Federal Reserve and Monetary Instability." *Wall Street Journal*, February 1, 1982.

———. "Has Monetarism Failed?" *Manhattan Report* 4:3 (1984).

———. "Letter on Monetary Policy to Senator William Proxmire." *Federal Reserve Bank of St. Louis Review* 56 (March 1974).

———. "Reply." *Federal Reserve Bank of St. Louis Review* 56 (March 1974).

———. "The Role of Monetary Policy." Presidential address to the American Economic Association, Washington, D.C., December 29, 1967. *American Economic Review* 58:1 (March 1968).

———. ed. *Studies in the Quantity Theory of Money*. Chicago: University of Chicago Press, 1956.

Friedman, Milton, and David Meiselman. "The Relative Stability of Monetary Velocity and the Investment Multiplier in the United States, 1897–1958." Commission on Money and Credit, *Stabilization Policies*. Englewood Cliffs, N.J.: Prentice Hall, 1963.

Friedman, Milton, and Anna J. Schwartz. "Has Government Any Role in Money?" *Journal of Monetary Economics* 11 (January 1986).

———. *A Monetary History of the United States, 1867–1960*. National Bureau of Economic Research, Princeton: Princeton University Press, 1963.

Gatell, Frank Otto. "Spoils of the Bank War: Political Bias in the Selection of Pet Banks." *American Historical Review* 70 (1964).

Gilman, Theodore. *A Graded Banking System*. Boston and New York: Houghton Mifflin, 1898.

Godfrey, John M. *Monetary Expansion in the Confederacy*. New York: New York Times Co., Arno Press, 1978.

Goldweiser, E. A., "Federal Reserve Objectives and Policies: Retrospect and Prospect." *American Economic Review* 37 (1947).

Goodhart, Charles. *The Evolution of Central Banks*. Cambridge, Mass., and London, England: MIT Press, 1988.

———. *The New York Money Market and the Finance of Trade, 1900–1913*. Cambridge Mass.: Harvard University Press, 1969.

Gouge, William M. *A Short History of Paper Money and Banking in the United States*. Philadelphia, 1833.

Greenfield, Robert, and Leland Yeager. "A Laissez-Faire Approach to Monetary Stability." *Journal of Money, Credit, and Banking* 15 (August 1983).

Greenspan, Alan. Statement before the Committee on Banking, Housing, and Urban Affairs of the U.S. Senate, July 13, 1988. *Federal Reserve Bulletin* 74 (September 1988).

———. Statement to the House Committees on Ways and Means, and Banking, Housing, and Urban Affairs, and the Senate Committee on the Budget. *Federal Reserve Bulletin* 75 (April 1989).

———. Statement to Subcommittee on Domestic Monetary Policy of the Committee on Banking, Finance, and Urban Affairs, House of Representatives, October 25, 1989. *Federal Reserve Bulletin* 75 (December 1989).

Guthrie, James. *Papers*. Filson Club, Louisville, Kentucky.

Hallman, Jeffrey J., Richard D. Porter, and David Small. "M_2 per Unit of Potential GNP as an Anchor for the Price Level." *Federal Reserve Bulletin* 75 (April 1989).

Hammond, Bray. *Banks and Politics in America*. Princeton, N.J.: Princeton University Press, 1957.

———. "The North's Empty Purse." *American Historical Review* 67 (1961).

Hankey, Thomson. *The Principles of Banking*. London, 1867.

Harris, Seymour E. *Twenty Years of Federal Reserve Policy, vol. 2, The Monetary Crisis*. Cambridge: Harvard University Press, 1933.

Hepburn, A. Barton. *A History of Currency in the United States*. New York: MacMillan Company, 1924.

Hildreth, Richard. *Banks, Banking, and Paper Currencies*, 1840. (Reprinted, New York: Greenwood Press, 1968.)

———. *The History of Banks*. New York: Augustus Kelly, 1968. (First published, Boston: Hilliard, Gray & Co., 1837.)

Hoffman, Charles. "The Depression of the Nineties." *Journal of Economic History* 16 (1956).

Holdsworth, John Thom. *The First Bank of the United States*. Sen. Doc. No. 571. 61st Cong., 2d sess., National Monetary Commission, 1910.

Holmes, Alan R. "Monetary Policy in a Changing Financial Environment, Open Market Operations in 1974." *Federal Reserve Bulletin* 62 (May 1976).

———. "Open Market Operations in 1972." *Federal Reserve Bulletin* 59 (1973).

House of Representatives, 43d Cong., 1st sess., *Miscellaneous Document No. 48*. 19 Dec. 1873.

Hulbert, Mark. "Bailing Out the Bankers." *Inquiry*, June 15 & 29, 1981.

Hunt, Alva R. *A Treatise on the Law of Tender, and Bringing Money into Court*. St. Paul: Frank P. Dufresne, 1903.

Hurst, James Willard. *A Legal History of Money in the United States, 1774–1970*. Lincoln: University of Nebraska Press, 1973.

Hyman, Sidney. *Marriner S. Eccles, Private Entrepreneur and Public Servant*. Stanford, Calif.: Stanford University Graduate School of Business, 1976.

Indianapolis Monetary Commission. *Report of the Monetary Commission of the Indianapolis Convention*. Indianapolis, Ind.: Hollenbeck Press, 1900.

Jastram, Roy W. *Silver the Restless Metal*. New York: John Wiley and Sons, 1981.

Johnson, Gove Griffith. *The Treasury and Monetary Policies, 1933–1938*. Cambridge: Harvard University Press, 1939.

Kemp, Arthur. *The Legal Qualities of Money*. New York: Pageant Press, 1956.

Kemp, Jack. "Talking Back to the Skeptics." *National Review*, June 11, 1982.

Kettl, Donald F. *Leadership at the Fed*. New Haven: Yale University Press, 1986.

Kindahl, James K. "Economic Factors in Specie Resumption: The United States, 1865–79." *Journal of Political Economy* 69 (1961).

Kinley, David. *The Independent Treasury of the United States and Its Relation to the Banks of the Country.* Sen. Doc. No. 587. 61st Cong., 2d sess., National Monetary Commission, 1910.

Knox, John J. *United States Notes,* 2d ed. New York: Charles Scribner's Sons, 1985.

Kohn, Donald L. "Policy Targets and Operating Procedures." *Federal Reserve Bulletin* 76 (January 1990).

Laughlin, Lawrence J. "Currency Reform." *Journal of Political Economy* 15 (1907).

Lerner, Eugene M. "The Monetary and Fiscal Programs of the Confederate Government, 1861–1865." *Journal of Political Economy 62* (1954).

———. "Money, Prices, and Wages in the Confederacy, 1861–65." *Journal of Political Economy 63* (1955).

Macesich, George. 'Sources of Monetary Disturbances in the United States, 1834–1845." *Journal of Economic History* 20 (1960).

Marshall, Alfred. *Money, Credit and Commerce.* London: Macmillan, 1929.

Martin, Robert F. *National Income in the United States, 1799–1938.* New York: National Industrial Conference Board, 1939.

McCulloch, Hugh. *Men and Measures of Half a Century.* New York: Charles Scribner's Sons, 1900.

McCulloch, Huston. "Beyond the Historical Gold Standard," in *Alternative Monetary Regimes,* ed. C. D. Campbell and W. R. Dougan. Baltimore: Johns Hopkins University Press, 1986.

McGrane, R. C., *The Panic of 1837.* Chicago: University of Chicago Press, 1924.

Meerman, Jacob. "Nicholas Biddle on Central Banking." Ph.D. diss., University of Chicago, 1961.

Meiselman, David. "The Political Monetary Cycle." *Wall Street Journal,* Tuesday, January 10, 1984.

Miller, G. William. Statement to Committee on Banking, Housing, and Urban Affairs, U.S. House of Representatives. *Federal Reserve Bulletin* 65 (1979).

Mills, Ogden. "The Reconstruction Finance Corporation Program." An address before the Associated Press of New York City, April 25, 1932. U.S. Treasury, *Annual Report,* 1932.

Mints, Lloyd W. *History of Banking Theory.* University of Chicago Press, 1945.

———. *Monetary Policy for a Competitive Society.* New York: McGraw-Hill, 1950.

Mitchell, Wesley C. *A History of the Greenbacks.* Chicago: University of Chicago Press, 1903.

———. "The Role of Money in Economic History," in *Enterprise and Secular Change,* ed. Frederic C. Lane and Jelle C. Riemersma. Homewood, Ill.: Richard D. Irwin, 1953.

Moran, Charles. *Money, Currencies, and Banking.* New York, 1875.

Myers, Margaret G. *The New York Money Market,* vol. 1. New York: Columbia University Press, 1931.

Nation 82 (1906).

National Archives and Records Service, Record Group No. 56, *Letters on State Deposits,* 27 June 1836 to 11 September 1837. Washington, D.C.

Newcomb, Simon. *Examination of Our Financial Policy during the Southern Rebellion.* New York: Greenwood Press, 1969. (First published, New York: D. Appleton Co., 1865.)

Pacific Research Institute for Public Policy. *Political Business Cycles,* ed. Thomas E. Willett. Durham and London: Duke University Press, 1988.

Paris, James Daniel. *Monetary Policies of the United States.* New York: Columbia University Press, 1938.

Patton, Eugene B. "Secretary Shaw and Precedents as to Treasury Control over the Money Market." *Journal of Political Economy* 15 (1907).

Polk, James. *The Diary of a President, 1845–1849,* ed. Allen Nevins. New York: Longmans, Green and Co., 1929.

Radford, R. A. "The Economic Organization of a P.O.W. Camp." *Economica* 12 (1945).

Redlich, Fritz. *The Molding of American Banking, Men and Ideas, part 1, 1781–1840.* New York: Hafner Publishing Co., 1951.

Ricardo, David. "The High Price of Bullion." *Economic Essays,* ed. E. C. K. Gonner. London: G. Bell and Sons, 1923.

Rockoff, Hugh. *Drastic Measures, A History of Wage and Price Controls in the United States.* Cambridge: Cambridge University Press, 1984.

———. "The Free Banking Era: A Reexamination." *Journal of Money, Credit, and Banking* 6 (1974).

Rothbard, Murray. "The Case for a 100% Gold Dollar," in *In Search of a Monetary Constitution,* ed. Leland Yeager. Cambridge, Mass.: Harvard University Press, 1962.

———. *The Panic of 1819.* New York and London: Columbia University Press, 1962.

Scheiber, Harry. "The Pet Banks in Jacksonian Politics and Finance, 1833–41." *Journal of Economic History* 23 (1963).

Schreft, Stacey L., and Raymond E. Owens. "Survey Evidence of Tighter Credit Conditions: What Does It Mean?" Federal Reserve Bank of Richmond, *Economic Review* 77 (1991).

Schur, Leon. "The Second Bank of the United States and the Inflation after the War of 1812." *Journal of Political Economy 68 (1960).*

Schwartz, Anna J., "Gross Dividend and Interest Payments by Corporations at Selected Dates in the Century," in *Trends in the American Economy in the Nineteenth Century, Studies in Income and Wealth,* vol. 24. National Bureau of Economic Research, Princeton, N.J.: Princeton University Press, 1960.

Selden, Richard. "Monetary Velocity in the United States," in *Studies in the Quantity Theory of Money,* ed. Milton Friedman. Chicago: University of Chicago Press, 1956.

Selgin, George. *The Theory of Free Banking.* Totowa, N.J.: Rowan and Littlefield, 1988.

Seltzer, Lawrence H. "The Changed Environment of Monetary–Banking Policy." *American Economic Review Proceedings 36* (1946).

———. "Discussion." *American Economic Review Supplement* 34 (1944).

Sharkey, Robert P. *Money, Class, and Party.* Baltimore, Md.: Johns Hopkins University Press, 1959.

Shaw, L. M. *Current Issues.* New York: D. Appleton and Co., 1908.

Shugart, William. "A Public Choice Perspective of the Banking Act of 1933," in *The*

Financial Services Revolution, ed. Catherine England and Thomas Huertas. Boston: Kluwer Academic Publishers, 1987.

Siegan, Bernard H. *The Supreme Court's Constitution.* New Brunswick, N.J.: Transaction Books, 1987.

Simmons, E. C. "Treasury Deposits and Excess Reserves." *Journal of Political Economy* 48 (1940).

Small, David H., and Richard D. Porter. "Understanding the Behavior of M_2 and V_{M2}." *Federal Reserve Bulletin* 75 (April 1989).

Smick, David M. "Is the Federal Reserve Causing the Recession?" *Human Events,* July 31, 1982.

Smith, Adam. *The Wealth of Nations,* ed. Edwin Cannan. New York: Random House, Modern Library Edition, 1937.

Smith, Vera. *The Rationale of Central Banking.* Indianapolis: Liberty Press, 1990. (First published in Westminster, England: P. S. King & Son, Ltd., 1936.)

Smith, W. B. *Economic Aspects of the Second Bank of the United States.* Cambridge, Mass.: Harvard University Press, 1953.

Smith, W. B., and Arthur Cole. *Fluctuations in American Business, 1790–1860* (Cambridge, Mass.: Harvard University Press, 1935).

Soddy, Frederick. *Wealth, Virtual Wealth, and Debt,* 2d ed. New York: E. P. Dutton and Co., 1933.

Solomon, Anthony. "Reassessing the Role of the Central Bank." Remarks to New York State Bankers Association, January 26, 1984. *Occasional Paper,* Federal Reserve Bank of New York, 1984, p. 11.

Spahr, Walter E. "A Reply to Mr. Sproul on the Gold Standard." *Commercial and Financial Chronicle,* November 10, 1949. (Reprinted in *Money and Economic Activity,* 3d ed., ed. Lawrence Ritter. New York: Houghton Mifflin, 1961.)

Spaulding, Elbridge G. *History of the Legal Tender Paper Money Issued during the Great Rebellion Being a Loan without Interest and a National Currency.* Westport, Conn.: Greenwood Press, 1971. (First published, Buffalo, N.Y.: Express Printing Co., 1869.)

Sprague, O. M. W. *History of Crises under the National Banking System.* Sen. Doc. No. 538. 61st Cong., 2d sess., National Monetary Commission, 1910.

Sproul, Allan. "Monetary Management and Credit Control." *American Economic Review* 37, (1947).

Stewart, Donald. Speech in *Congressional Record,* 96th Cong., 1st sess., vol. 126, part 6, March 27, 1980.

Swisher, Carl B. *Roger B. Taney.* New York: MacMillan Company, 1935.

Sylla, Richard. "Forgotten Men of Money: Private Bankers in Early U.S. History." *Journal of Economic History* 36 (1976).

Taus, E. R. *Central Banking Functions of the United States Treasury, 1789–1941.* New York: Columbia University Press, 1943.

Taussig, F. W. *The Silver Situation in the United States.* New York, 1893.

Temin, Peter. *The Jacksonian Economy.* New York: W. W. Norton and Co., 1969.

Thayer, James Bradley. "Legal Tender." *Harvard Law Review* 1:73 (1887–1888).

Thornton, Daniel L. "Solving the 1980s' Velocity Puzzle: A Progress Report." *Federal Reserve Bank of St. Louis Review* 69 (August/September 1987).

Thornton, Daniel L., and Courtney C. Stone. "Financial Innovation: Causes and Consequences." *Current Issues in Monetary Analysis and Policy,* ed. Kevin Dowd and Merwyn Lewis. London: Macmillan, 1991.

Thornton, Henry. *The Paper Credit of Great Britain,* ed. F. A. von Hayek. New York: Rinehart, 1939.

Timberlake, Richard H. *Gold, Greenbacks, and the Constitution.* Berryville, Virginia: Durrell Foundation, 1991.

———. "Private Production of Scrip-Money in the Isolated Community." *Journal of Money, Credit, and Banking* 19 (November 1987).

———. "The Significance of Unaccounted Currencies." *Journal of Economic History* 41 (December 1981).

Timberlake, Richard, Thomas Humphrey, and William Beranek. "Fisher, Thornton, and the Analysis of the Inflation Premium." *Journal of Money, Credit, and Banking* 17 (1985).

U.S. Bureau of the Census. *Historical Statistics of the United States, Colonial Times to 1957.* Washington, D.C. 1960.

U.S. Congress. *Annals of Congress.* Selected volumes.

———. *Congressional Globe.* Selected volumes.

———. *Congressional Record.* Selected volumes.

———. *Register of Debates in Congress.* Selected volumes.

———. *Executive Documents,* Doc. No. 300. "Message from the President of the United States Returning the Bank Bill with His Objections to the Senate." 22d Cong., 1st sess., July 16, 1832.

———. *Reports of Committees, House Report No. 460* (the "Clayton Report"). 22d Cong., 1st sess., 14 March 1832.

———. *Reports of Committees,* House Report No. 283 (the "McDuffie Report"). 22d Cong., 1st sess., 9 February 1832.

———. House Document No. 30. 25th Cong., 1st sess., 1837.

———. Senate Document No. 85. 25th Cong., 2d sess., 1838.

———. Senate Report No. 275. 42d Cong., 3d sess., 1872.

———. Report to the Committee on Banking and Currency on the Increased Issue of Legal Tender Notes. House Exec. Doc. No. 42. 42d Cong., 3d sess., December 1872.

———. *Report and Hearings of the Silver Commission,* Senate Report No. 703. 44th Cong., 2d sess., 1877.

———. *Monetary Credit and Fiscal Policies.* 81st Cong., 2d sess. Report of the Subcommittee ("Douglas Committee") of the Joint Committee on the Economic Report, Sen. Doc. No. 129, January 1950. Washington: Government Printing Office, 1950.

———. *Annals of Congress.* "Report on a National Bank." 1st Cong., 2d sess., 14 December 1790.

———. *Response of the Secretary of the Treasury . . . In Regard to Treasury Operations,* Sen. Doc. No. 208. 60th Cong., 1st sess., 1908.

———. *The Gold Panic Investigation.* 1872. House Report No. 31. 41st Cong., 2d sess, Committee on Banking and Currency, James A. Garfield, chairman.

U.S. Treasury. *American State Papers-Finance,* 3. 1815.

———. *Annual Report of the Secretary of the Treasury.* U.S. Treasury Press Release No. 9–20, Dec. 21, 1936.
———. *Annual Reports,* 1815–1990. Selected Years.
———. *Report to Congress on a Board of Exchequer.* Senate Doc. No. 18. 27th Cong., 2d sess., 1841.
———. *Report of the Comptroller of the Currency, 1868.* House Exec. Doc. No. 4, 40th Cong., 3d sess.
———. *Report of the Comptroller of the Currency, 1865.* House Exec. Doc. No. 4, 39th Cong., 1st sess.
Unger, Irwin. *The Greenback Era.* Princeton: Princeton University Press, 1964.
United States Treasury Department. *Reports of the Secretary of the Treasury of the United States,* vol. 1, 1790–1814.
Viner, Jacob. "Recent Legislation and the Banking Situation." *American Economic Review Proceedings* 26 (1936).
———. *Studies in the Theory of International Trade.* New York: Harper and Brothers, 1937.
Volcker, Paul. Statement to Committee on Banking, Housing, and Urban Affairs. *Federal Reserve Bulletin 65* (October 1979).
———. Letter to the Honorable Henry S. Reuss, Chairman of the Committee on Banking, Finance, and Urban Affairs, March 4, 1980.
———. Letter to Congressman Ronald E. Paul, July 10, 1981.
———. Statement before the Joint Economic Committee of the U.S. Congress, *Federal Reserve Bulletin* 71 (April 1985).
———. "Monetary Policy Report to the Congress." *Federal Reserve Bulletin* 72 (April 1986).
———. Statement before the Committee on Banking, Housing, and Urban Affairs, U.S. Senate, July 23, 1986. *Federal Reserve Bulletin* 72 (September 1986).
———. Statement before Joint Economic Committee of the U.S. Congress, February 2, 1987. *Federal Reserve Bulletin* 73 (April 1987).
Von Philippovich, Eugen. *History of the Bank of England and Its Financial Services to the State.* Sen. Doc. No. 591. 61st Cong., 2d sess., National Monetary Commission, 1911.
Wagner, Richard E., "Central Banking and the Fed: A Public Choice Perspective." *CATO Journal* 6:2 (Fall 1986).
Warburton, Clark. *Depression, Inflation, and Monetary Policy.* Baltimore, Md.: Johns Hopkins University Press, 1966.
———. "The Secular Trend in Monetary Velocity." *Quarterly Journal of Economics* 63 (1949).
———. "The Volume of Money and the Price Level between the World Wars." *Journal of Political Economy* 53 (1945).
Westerfield, R. B. "The Banking Act of 1933." *Journal of Political Economy* 41 (December 1933).
White, Horace. *Money and Banking,* rev. and enl. by Charles Tippets and Lewis Froman. New York: Ginn & Co., 1935.
White, Lawrence H. *Competition and Currency.* New York: New York University Press, 1989.

———. *Free Banking in Britain*. Cambridge, England: Cambridge University Press, 1984.

Williams, John H. "The Implications of Fiscal Policy for Monetary Policy and the Reserve System." *American Economic Review* 32 (1942).

———. "The Banking Act of 1935." *American Economic Review Proceedings* 26 (1936).

Willis, H. Parker. "The Banking Act of 1933—An Appraisal." *American Economic Review Proceedings* 24 (1934).

Wimmer, L. "The Gold Crisis of 1869." *Explorations in Economic History 12* (1975).

Wright, David McCord. "Langdon Cheves and Nicolas Biddle: New Data for a New Interpretation." *Journal of Economic History* 13:2 (1953).

Name Index

Subject Index